First Nights at the Opera

THOMAS FORREST KELLY

First Nights at the
Opera

Yale University Press   New Haven and London

Published with assistance from the Louis Stern Memorial Fund.

Designed by Sonia Shannon.
Set in Linotype Sabon by Duke & Company, Devon, Pennsylvania.
Printed in the United States of America by Sheridan Books,
Ann Arbor, Michigan.

Library of Congress Cataloging-in-Publication Data
Kelly, Thomas Forrest.
First nights at the opera / Thomas Forrest Kelly.
p. cm.
Includes bibliographical references (p.   ), discography (p.   ), and index.
ISBN 0-300-10044-2 (cloth : alk. paper) 978-0-300-11526-0 (paperback)
1. Operas—First performances—Europe. I. Title.
ML1720.K45 2004
782.1'09—dc22   2004006932

A catalogue record for this book is available from the British Library.

The paper in this book meets the guidelines for permanence and durability
of the Committee on Production Guidelines for Book Longevity of the
Council on Library Resources.

10 9 8 7 6 5 4 3 2 1

To Adam Christian French

Contents

Preface

This book is about five moments in operatic history: the first performances of five famous operas. Each chapter focuses on one piece, narrating the preparation and execution of a single performance on a single day. And each chapter includes a variety of other materials: a selection of pictures to situate the look of the times, the people, the place, and the performance; a variety of original texts that allow us to hear words written or spoken at the time. And each chapter carries a section of original documents related to the performance: reviews, letters, memoirs, newspaper articles. These collections of texts, all translated into English and gathered in one place, will, I hope, be of interest to those who like to envision what was going on at the time and what it was like to be present at the performance.

There is a brief bibliographical note for each chapter, and a series of notes identify the sources of quotations and of other information. A discography, by Robert Dennis, guides readers to interesting recordings.

I am grateful to many friends and colleagues who have collaborated in the making of this book. Aaron Allen, Michael Cuthbert, Petra Gelbart, Richard Giarusso, Zoë Lang, and Christina Linklater have been ingenious and thorough in helping with research; Mari-Hélène Coudroy-Saghaï and François-Xavier Adam have been generous and tireless in providing documents on Meyerbeer; Dexter Edge and Michael Lorenz generously helped with difficult German. A number of friends read portions of this book in its early stages and made comments and suggestions and provided advice that made the result a much better book: Peggy Badenhausen, Reinhold Brinkmann, Dexter Edge, Ellen Harris, Robert W. Kent, Lewis Lockwood, David Rosen, and Harriet Rubin. Harry Haskell's imagination, patience, and persistence planted the seed of this book and tended it with care; his successors at Yale University Press, Lara Heimert, Keith Condon, and Heidi Downey, have generously pruned and shaped it. May the reader's harvest be worth all their efforts.

As for operas, they are essentially too absurd and extravagant
to mention; I look upon them as a magic scene, contrived to please
the eyes and ears at the expense of the understanding; and I consider
singing, rhyming and chiming heroines, and princesses and
philosophers, as I do the hills, the trees, the birds, and the beasts,
who amicably joined in one common country dance to the irresistible
tune of Orpheus' lyre. Whenever I go to an Opera, I leave my sense
and reason at the door with my half-guinea, and deliver myself
up to my eyes and my ears.

—*Lord Chesterfield to his son, 1752*

INTRODUCTION

hat is it about opera that fascinates? For some it is being in the presence of great singing voices; for others it is the beauty of the music; still others feel a heightened sense of drama when music makes its contribution to theater. It may be the sheer spectacle of so grand an entertainment, or even the purely social aspects of gathering with the élite.

For the twenty-first century—at least at its beginning—opera is a ritual in which predictable actions can be expected to take place in the presence of audience members who know how everything should go and will know immediately when things are not done properly. We mostly seek to hear operas we already know: we know the play, we know the tunes, we have heard many other singers in these roles and we want to compare them with the singers in tonight's performance.

Until recently opera was considered the summit of high art, combining theater and music, sight and sound, for the most discriminating audiences. It is still considered so by many. But opera is not, in our time, the grandest possible entertainment; there are rock concerts and sports events that cost more and entertain more people at once. Yet the many ways that the word opera is used to add glamour to entertainments and places make clear that the word itself adds luster. "Opera houses" that never housed an opera exist far and wide. "Light opera," "semi-opera," and "comic opera" describe musical entertainments of various sorts. And what of such terms as "soap opera," "horse-opera," "space-opera," and "Grand Ole Opry"?

An opera is a visual and dramatic experience, no matter how often we listen to one on a compact disc with our eyes closed. It is theatrical: it has characters, costumes, scenery, plot, movement, spectacle. But it is a form of drama in which the music dominates, and everything flows from this premise. Composers of opera, some of whom have made the greatest music ever composed, nevertheless intend their music to exist in this multimedia form. A recording is only the auditory portion of a much wider sensory experience.

The operas discussed in this book are among the greatest works by composers known in their own times primarily for their operas. Mozart and Handel perhaps are now known more for some of their other music, but they probably would have preferred to be remembered for their operas. Verdi, Wagner, and Puccini knew full well how to compose concert music, but they found their fullest expression in the theater. Making opera requires special insights, exceptional dramatic skill, a knack for balancing music and drama, and a knowledge of one's own audience. Not every composer has these talents: Schubert was a notorious failure at opera.

But composers of opera composed for people: for singers who would sing; for managers with a public to entertain; for, most of all, the people who would attend the performance.

A performance of an opera, like any performance, engages the active participation of many people—ushers, firemen, seamstresses, chorus members, orchestra members, music-copyists, scene-painters, machinists, singers, audience members. All are part of what makes the performance happen, and in some sense the performance is an expression of the society that comes together to produce it.

The five operas in this book are among the favorites of their day. They have such a long history that any performance before an audience of experienced opera-goers brings with it a lot of baggage involving other performances, other conductors, other singers, other theaters. Modern audiences have heard many operas in many styles, from Hasse to Harbison, Monteverdi to Messiaen. In this context we tend to situate one of these great operas in a historical continuum, which our own culture allows and encourages. We are blessed with being able to hear almost any music, from any time and place, and from any culture, virtually any time we wish. We can have a breadth of stylistic and historical experience that is unparalleled in human history.

But the blessing may also be a curse: because we have everything it is difficult to attach value to anything in particular. When we can cause the Festspielhaus at Bayreuth to perform the *Ring* for us whenever we want—and to pause when we tire—we may lose the excitement of being present at the magical moment when all those people came together on one occasion to give one performance.

Mozart's listeners knew exactly what a late-eighteenth-century opera was like, what to expect, where the novelties were, which arias profited from the voice of a singer whom they had heard in many other roles. They knew the music around them, the theater around them, the people around them. For them this performance was the only performance, it was familiar and at the same time it was new. And it was happening now.

Of course, those attending the first performances of these operas came to the program fresh, without knowledge of the variety of operatic styles from many countries and centuries. But they had what we may lack: an intimate knowledge of the stylistic idiom of their own time and place.

There is something about performance that is exciting to everyone concerned. When the performance begins, we pay close attention. We don't want to miss anything— if we don't listen now we may never have another chance. Then there is the exhilaration of so many musicians making every effort to provide a good performance. Still, we can't be sure that nothing will go wrong. A singer may forget a line; another may not be in good voice; the orchestra may or may not be able to play the music in time and in tune. On a modern recording we can be pretty sure that the music will be of excellent quality and that there will be no musical disaster—otherwise the recording would not exist. So we can relax in a way, but we miss the adventures of uncertainty, of savoring every moment of an event happening in real time.

Opera is one of the easiest things in the world to mock. It has been ridiculed almost from its beginnings with portly women in horned helmets, Bugs Bunny cartoons, the cult of Florence Foster Jenkins, Anna Russell's summary of the *Ring,* "The opera ain't over till the fat lady sings." Most of the jokes are related to the two basic aspects of opera that provide its energy but also create its problems.

The first of these is the duality of music and words. We do not go to the opera to see a great play; we go to hear the music. But the music does not move us nearly so much as when it also encompasses emotion, when it is the heartfelt expression of a character in a particular situation. Music can heighten drama in ways that any playwright would envy. But at the same time it can distract, slow the pace, even ruin the drama.

Music works differently from the spoken word. An actor speaking a part needs to go forward, to say more. But music often needs to pause, to repeat phrases, to give emphasis by lingering or to build up a mood or an effect over time. This is why words are so often repeated in music. Leporello makes his point, as well as a musical cadence, when he says in his first song:

Voglio far il gentiluomo,
e non voglio più servir,
e non voglio più servir,
no, no, no, no, no, no
non voglio più servir.

Opera involves a tension between esthetic forces: the drama wants to move forward while the music wants to pause and reflect. The balance between these forces has shifted enormously over time. Whereas the earliest operas sought to provide simple melodies in speech-rhythms for a play of classical form, some later operas have been almost purely strings of beautiful songs connected by the thinnest of plots. Opera's continual "reform" is just a reshifting of that balance.

Second, opera is conventional. Nobody sings all the time in the real world. Nobody has an orchestra that begins to play whenever he feels emotional. Conventions are of course necessary in the theater, and even more so in opera. We like conventions, provided that we understand, accept, and desire them. Conventions are simply the result of participants' agreeing on the rules, of simplifying a complex world so that we can concentrate on what interests us. We are accustomed, for example, to detective novels, television situation comedies, and western movies. We understand how each genre works, and we know that not every murder has six suspects who can be gathered in one room in the last chapter by a brilliant detective. Yet we gladly accept the unreality of the situation because of the pleasure it provides us.

The theater is by its nature conventional. In the operas we consider here, the theater allows us to look into a box in which people carry on their lives, oblivious to the hundreds of people watching them. What we perceive as an opening in that box they must see as another part of their world, a fourth wall transparent only to us. And yet they do not turn their backs to that fourth wall; they do not stand in a circle to have a conversation; they sometimes appear to freeze; their words are in verse; and an orchestra happens to be playing. We understand these conventions—they are characters in a play being presented for our pleasure: that is not really Julius Caesar but a famous castrato. We can ridicule the conventions if we like, or we can stay and enjoy the performance.

And these characters *sing*. In our world we communicate by speaking; but in theirs, all discourse is sung. This is perfectly acceptable and desirable, so long as we accept and desire it. And at the opera, of course, we do. Indeed, that is why we are there. But the convention itself raises challenges. For if singing on the stage represents speaking in nature, how can we represent singing on the stage? Suppose a singing character invites another to sing a song? Composers have devised many ways to deal with this challenge: sometimes the speaking is done in recitative and the singing in arias, so that when the orchestra begins to play, we know that we will hear lyrical song. (More often, though, the aria represents not singing but an interior emotional reflection.) Sometimes the distinction is made in the lyrical nature of the melody, the clear musical references to song (a lullaby, for instance, or a serenade). Elsewhere a middle ground between speech and song is maintained in such a way as to make speech itself into song. And in some genres, including Singspiel (Mozart's *Magic Flute,* Beethoven's *Fidelio*), French comic opera *(Carmen),* and Broadway musicals, the dialogue is spoken.

Sometimes the characters who sing are not speaking at all—they are thinking. That is, in opera it is possible for time to stop and for a character to express in song what is known only in the heart. These are moments we remember for their beauty or their passion, but they do not contribute to the real-time advancement of the drama. They can be a sort of freeze-frame, stopping the action and allowing us to be a part of the exterior drama on the stage and the interior drama of the heart. If we understand and appreciate this the opera can be a rich source of emotional and esthetic pleasure.

Opera houses, at least in the eighteenth and nineteenth centuries, were, like churches, imposing buildings in which all of society might gather together to view the grandest and most expensive entertainments available. Every small city in Europe has an opera house, and each tried to provide the most dazzling possible venue for opera. The velvet, gilt, mirrors, assembly rooms, and grand staircases made the opera house a palace for the public and a fitting temple for the ritual acts that the society would enact inside.

Those ritual acts, however, have evolved . . . . . . t was usual in eighteenth-century London to hold a bo . . . . . . e opera repeatedly but to come to the front of the box . . . . . . e singer and then to retire to cards or other diversions. T . . . . . . acred silence and rapt attention that we now think of as . . . . . . ght it fashionable to come to the opera house partway th . . . . . . ists and first-timers came at the beginning. At La Scala in . . . . . . e private property of their owners—an extension of their . . .

But the first night of a . . . . . . rdi's audience for *Otello* sought tickets by any means, an . . . . . . re more interested in the opera itself than in the singers; \ . . . . . . ost tuneful places in his operas to be rehearsed only at th . . . . . . d not be whistled in the streets before the premiere. This . . . . . . we greet a new work at the beginning of the twenty-first . . . . . . re familiar with the operas discussed here. But there was . . . . . . s new, and the audience was eager to know whether this new entertainment would measure up. We now know the judgment of history, of how these operas and others have been revered and repeatedly performed. But there was a time when each was a cutting-edge contemporary music-drama, and it is those moments that we seek to recapture here.

Five operas are discussed in this book out of a vast number that might have been chosen. I selected these because I like them. But they are also among the great operas of all time, and they are representative, in a way, of major themes and trends in the period —roughly the eighteenth and nineteenth centuries—when opera was the undisputed acme of the performing arts. There is, alas, no Monteverdi here, or any of the other great operas of the seventeenth century; nor is there anything from the important repertories of the twentieth and twenty-first centuries. I focus on the period when opera was preeminent, on composers whose chief activity was in opera, and on places that have influenced the formation of opera traditions.

Nothing in this book is meant to suggest that we must reproduce opera in the style in which it was originally presented, or that first performances are the best or most authoritative. But something about premieres is exciting for everybody involved. The composer is on edge, hoping that the public will like what is being offered, and the impresario's fortunes may be made or ruined by whether viewers are pleased. The singers have studied and rehearsed, but they have not yet mastered these roles. Everybody is nervous, everybody is excited about being present for a significant event, everybody hopes for the best, everybody is waiting for the orchestra to play and the curtain to rise.

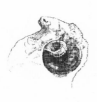

There are no men or women dancers at the opera, neither is there any machinery, but the scenes and decorations are often changed, some of them being of rare beauty; and it is a delight to the eyes to see the King, the Queen, and the Royal Family, the peers and peeresses, always beautifully dressed. One cannot understand much about the intrigue of the piece; it is sung in Italian, and the words that suit the music are sung over and over again. The opera is expensive, for you must pay half a guinea for the best places.

— *César de Saussure, 1728*

CHAPTER ONE

George Frideric Handel, *Giulio Cesare in Egitto*

London, February 20, 1724, 6:00 P.M.

*H*igh-Baroque serious opera (or *dramma per musica,* as it was called in the eighteenth century) is not much in vogue nowadays, even though Baroque music in general has never been more in fashion. Perhaps listeners do not want music sung in another language; perhaps they tire of long successions of arias; perhaps they don't want to follow complex plots. Even the perennially popular Handel does not attract as many listeners to his operas as to his instrumental music and oratorios. And yet Handel would have considered himself chiefly a composer of operas, I believe, even late in his life, after devoting much effort to his newer hybrid oratorios. Certainly in 1724 his job was in the opera house, and opera was all the rage.

Opera was an odd entertainment: a complex story told in a series of recitatives and arias sung entirely in Italian. Opera grew up in Italy and was sung in Italian throughout Europe (only the French avoided it) even where nobody could understand the language. The vogue for Italian opera among London aristocrats was linked with their desire for continental pictures, classical sculpture, and the culture of the Grand Tour. It was a style from Italy, the source of much highbrow culture, and its subjects were from classical antiquity, which appealed to those who had been taught to read Latin.

What attracted the audience to the opera house? Part of the appeal was social standing: everybody who was anybody was there—the whole town, all the world. The main attractions were the singers: the most famous stars of the day performing feats of virtuosity or touching the heart with their expressive singing. Plot, acting, costume, and scenery were important but secondary. It was a brilliant and exclusive entertainment.

George Frideric Handel, a German composer writing Italian opera in England, was one of three staff composers at the Royal Academy of Music, whose season in the King's Theatre was the musical entertainment of choice for the nobility and the wealthy classes. Handel's only new contribution to the 1723–24 opera season was *Giulio Cesare in Egitto;* it had a moderately successful run, it was well liked, and it was part of a series of seasons that made up the high point of Italian opera in England. Of all of Handel's Italian operas, *Giulio Cesare* is the one most often revived in modern times. It may be that Julius Caesar is better known to modern audiences than are many of Handel's other historical subjects (we are not brought up on the classics these days), or perhaps the role of Cleopatra, and the love interest that her presence provides, continue to fascinate, or maybe Handel's beautiful music is the reason for so many revivals. But there are treasures in his other operas, too.

Italian opera was sung all over Europe, and there were dozens of competent composers to supply the international need for works in the Italian style (Vivaldi, Scarlatti, Giovanni and Antonio Bononcini, Gasparini, Lotti, Porpora, and so on), and there were thousands of operas produced in the eighteenth century. Usually the production was new (even if the libretto was old) and arranged on the spot by librettist and composer. Revivals were relatively rare, in part because operas were written with specific singers in mind. A new production of an older opera could require so much rewriting for the cast that a new composition might be more appropriate. And operas were generally supervised by their composers, so a revival would require the composer's presence. Why not produce something new? This novelty was what an audience sought, but novelty in the context of a well-understood convention.

Even though Handel's music resembles that of his contemporaries, it is uniquely his own. The eighteenth-century music historian Charles Burney wrote of Handel's *Ottone* (1723): "The passages in this and the other operas which Handel composed about this time, became the musical language of the nation, and in a manner proverbial, like the *bons mots* of a man of wit in society. So that long after this period all the musicians in the kingdom, whenever they attempted to compose what they called Music of their own, seem to have had no other stock of ideas, than these passages."

Background
LONDON IN THE 1720S

Geographically, London was not central to Europe, although it certainly seemed the center of society, culture, and commerce to those who frequented the opera. A work by a German composer set to an Italian libretto beginning with a French overture and played to an English audience was certainly cosmopolitan. The city was about the size of Paris, or of modern Toledo, Ohio. Its seven hundred thousand inhabitants made up about 20 percent of England's population. London Bridge was the only way to cross the Thames without a boat. The river was clogged with sewage, and the streets were littered with mud, night soil, and dead animals between cleansings by the frequent rains. But in the streets were also sedan chairs, carriages, street vendors crying their wares, hawkers of printed ballads, chimney sweeps, knife-grinders, old clothes men, and postmen ringing bells. In the absence of house numbers, street names combined with major intersections and shop signs to form addresses.

A French visitor described London's streets in 1725:

A number of them are dirty, narrow, and badly built; others again are wide and straight, bordered with fine houses. Most of the streets are wonderfully well lighted, for in front of each house hangs a lantern or a large globe of glass, inside of which is placed a lamp which burns all night. Large houses have two of these lamps suspended outside their doors by iron supports, and some have even four. The streets of London are unpleasantly full either of dust or of mud. This arises from the quantity of houses that are continually being built, and also from the large number of coaches and chariots rolling in the streets day and night. Carts are used for removing mud, and in the summer time the streets are wa-

tered by carts carrying barrels, or casks, pierced with holes, through
which water flows.

Places of public assembly included taverns where gin and beer were cheap and
plentiful; coffeehouses were places for talking, reading the newspapers, and finding out
about the current opera at the King's Theatre. There were 550 coffeehouses by 1739 (including one called Lloyd's where insurance was brokered). There was one main meal each
day, a dinner eaten in the afternoon; breakfast and supper were very light by comparison.

The difference between the upper classes and everybody else was enormous.
Grand houses with grand rooms, excess and ostentation in dress, and enormously expensive

---

César de Saussure on the Dress of the English

I daresay it would interest you to hear of the style and the way Englishmen usually dress. They do not trouble themselves about dress, but leave that to their
womenfolk. When the people see a well-dressed person in the streets, especially
if he is wearing a braided coat, a plume in his hat, or his hair tied in a bow,
he will, without doubt, be called "French dog" twenty times perhaps before he
reaches his destination. . . . Englishmen are usually very plainly dressed, they
scarcely ever wear gold on their clothes; they wear little coats called "frocks,"
without facings and without pleats, with a short cape above. Almost all wear
small, round wigs, plain hats, and carry canes in their hands, but no swords.
Their cloth and linen are of the best and finest. You will see rich merchants and
gentlemen thus dressed, and sometimes even noblemen of high rank, especially
in the morning, walking through the filthy and muddy streets. . . .

Most English women are fair and have pink and white complexions,
soft though not expressive eyes, and slim, pretty figures, of which they are very
proud and take great care, for in the morning as soon as they rise they don a
sort of bodice which encircles their waists tightly. Their shoulders and throats
are generally fine. They are fond of ornaments, and old and young alike wear
four or five patches, and always two large ones on the forehead. Few women
curl or powder their hair, and they seldom wear ribbons, feathers, or flowers,
but little headdresses of cambric or of magnificent lace on their pretty, well-kept
hair. They pride themselves on their neatly shod feet, on their fine linen, and
on their gowns. . . . Gowns have enormous hoops, short and very wide sleeves,
and it is the fashion to wear little mantles of scarlet or of black velvet, and
small hats of straw that are vastly becoming.

This detail from a 1720 map of London shows the location of the
King's Theatre, at the bottom of the Haymarket where it meets
Pall Mall and Charing Cross Road.

opera tickets distinguished those few who had "breeding" and resources. In 1723 and 1724 the speculation in land (houses were being built at a furious rate) and stocks (despite recent difficulties with the South Sea Company) made the shareholders of the opera feel that they could only win. The anti-Catholic furor of 1722 under Prime Minister Robert Walpole had made life difficult for the many "papist" singers, instrumentalists, composers, and librettists who populated the Italian opera. Even so, opera continued to hold the attention of those who could afford it.

Operas competed with plays and other entertainments. The rage for ballad operas —plays with songs, mostly to familiar tunes, sparked by *The Beggar's Opera* in 1728— had not begun to challenge opera's dominance. The theaters of Drury Lane and Lincoln's Inn Fields had long had a competitive relationship, and they often produced musical plays —full of songs but with spoken text. The New Haymarket Theatre was featuring a company that called itself the New Company of English Comedians. All of these theaters had a complement of dancers and singers, and presumably a company of instrumentalists.

And there were concerts, pantomimes, and other entertainments as well. Lighter entertainment included harlequinades, which were whole plays or shorter afterpieces starring Harlequin and his commedia dell'arte companions. John Rich's elaborate pantomime harlequinades at Lincoln's Inn Fields were justly famous. Tony Aston's Medleys appeared in various inns throughout London, featuring song, dance, and often low comedy (a performance on November 6, 1723, featured the flatulent fluting of "A fine forced Wind-Instrument performed by an Anonymous Person").

There was much to choose from in the way of entertainment. Cockfights, skittles, cricket, and barely dressed women wrestling for money may not have distracted many operagoers, but there were exhibitions of a curious and educational nature: dwarves, giants, learned horses, North American "Savages" and elk, Bengal tigers and rhinoceros. A favorite entertainment, especially when Lent closed the theaters to opera, was masquerade balls. There were also occasional fireworks displays, hangings, and duels. There was little way of knowing more than a day or two in advance what was being performed in any of the theaters. Audiences had to rely on notices in the newspaper and on handbills.

The 1723–24 theatrical season included Shakespeare in many forms; Dryden and Lee's *Oedipus;* Ben Jonson's *Alchemist;* works by Congreve, Addison, Beaumont and Fletcher. Plays usually included dancing and singing between the acts, and often a comic afterpiece.

On February 20, those seeking an evening's theatrical entertainment might have chosen the opening of *Giulio Cesare* at the King's Theatre; but they might also have chosen from the following:

> *The Scornful Lady,* by Beaumont and Fletcher, at Drury Lane, with dancing.
> *The Pilgrim,* with singing and dancing; followed by *The Necromancer, or Harlequin Doctor Faustus* ("A New Dramatick Entertainment in Grotesque Characters") at Lincoln's Inn Fields.
> *The Royal Convert,* with *The Adventures of Half an Hour,* followed

by *The Plots of Harlequin,* a benefit for four performers at the New Haymarket.

THE OPERA

Opera was the entertainment of the nobility and the higher ranks of bourgeois society. Ever since the Hanoverian monarchs and their families had begun attending the opera, beginning with George I in 1714, its social cachet had been considerable. The German royal family was familiar with Italian opera from the continent and probably could not have understood stage plays in English anyway. Opera, in the sense of a play sung throughout, had been introduced to London by 1705, and Italian opera had been performed there since 1710. By 1724 the genre was all the rage, as a Mr. Lecoq wrote to a correspondent in Dresden in 1724: "The passion for the opera here is getting beyond all belief. It is true that the music is beautiful and varied. There are three composers, including the famous Handel, each of whom writes two operas every winter. The orchestra, by and large, is of high quality and good care is taken to procure new voices at the theatre from time to time."

The Royal Academy of Music, producer of *Giulio Cesare,* had been in operation since 1719 as a plan for bringing top-quality opera to London. The academy, a joint stock company guaranteed by a group of wealthy noblemen, had produced many new works by its staff composers, and it boasted the finest singers of the age. Handel was now the leading house composer. He had engaged in a sort of composing contest in 1721, in which he and the other two composers, Giovanni Bononcini and Attilio Ariosti, had each composed one act of a new opera called *Muzio Scevola;* Handel's music was generally judged the best. By 1724, Handel's chief rival was Bononcini, and this often-cited doggerel by John Byrom was published in 1725:

> Some say, compar'd to Bononcini
> That Mynheer Handel's but a Ninny:
> Others aver, that he to Handel
> Is scarcely fit to hold a Candle:
> Strange all this Difference should be
> 'Twixt Tweedle-dum and Tweedle-dee.

These were great years for Italian opera in London, and in 1719 many imagined that speculative investments like opera houses were no more risky than stock in the South Sea Company, which had done so well that it offered to take over the whole national debt. Ultimately investors in both lost their shirts, and the Royal Academy of Music was out of business by 1728, but the original enthusiastic "Proposall for carrying on Operas by a Company of Joynt Stock" seemed more concerned with civic improvement than with profit:

> Operas are the most harmless of all Publick Diversions. They are an Encouragement and Support to an Art that has been cherished by all Polite Nations. They carry along with them some Marks of Publick Magnificence

and are the great Entertainment which Strangers share in. Therefore it seems very strange that this great and opulent City hath not been able to support Publick Spectacles of this sort for any considerable time. The reason of which seems to be cheifly that they have been hitherto carryed on upon a narrow Bottom of temporary Contributions Extreamly Burthensome to the People of Quality and entirely unproportioned to the Beauty Regularity and Duration of any great Designe. . . . As the Operas themselves will be in greater Perfection that [sic] what have hitherto appeared (Joyning what is excellent both in the French and Italian Theatre) so they will undoubtedly procure Audiences And by the Constancy and Regularity of the Performance the Taste rendred more universall.

The opera season began in late autumn and continued, with a break during Holy Week, until mid-June. Operas were performed twice a week, on Saturday and either on Tuesday (in 1724) or Wednesday (in 1723). On Tuesday or Wednesday there was no competition from other theaters, but on Saturdays all the theaters were seeking to attract patrons.

The King's Theatre, 1723–24 Season

November 27–December 7	*Pharnaces* [Bononcini's *Farnace*: premiere]
December 11–January 1	*Otho, King of Germany* [Handel's *Otto, re di Germania*: revival]
January 4–January 11	*Pharnaces*
January 14–February 15	*Vespasian* [Ariosti's *Vespasiano*: premiere]
February 20–April 14	*Julius Caesar* [Handel's *Giulio Cesare in Egitto*: premiere]
During the run of *Julius Caesar*:	
March 17	*Coriolanus* [Ariosti's *Caio Marzio Coriolani*: revival] and English cantata; benefit for Durastanti
March 30–April 4	Holy Week
April 16	*Coriolanus* [a benefit?]
April 18–May 16	*Calphurnia* [Bononcini's *Calfurnia*: premiere]
May 21–June 3	*Aquilius* [Ariosti's *Aquilio consolo*: premiere]
June 6–June 13	*Calphurnia*

Johann Jakob Heidegger managed the operatic performances of the Royal Academy of Music, and he organized lucrative balls in the theater. This mezzotint, dated 1749, shows a much older Heidegger, but he was thought to be ugly even in his earlier years.

Generally a new opera played until the audience tired of it or until the next opera was ready. But runs were generally short, probably because the audience able to pay the high ticket prices was relatively limited. The three composers of the Royal Academy—Handel, Bononcini, and Ariosti—each contributed new works. In this season Handel had only one new opera and a revival, while each of his colleagues presented two new works (though Ariosti's *Calfurnia* lasted only four performances). Handel, though, had a preeminent position as Master of the Orchestra, and it was he who recruited the singers.

The opera was run by its manager, Johann Jakob Heidegger, the ugliest man in the city. (Heidegger won a bet with Lord Chesterfield that Chesterfield could not produce an uglier man in all of London.) The Swiss-born Heidegger had been in control, personally or jointly, for five years, and would continue to manage opera for another twenty. He was a skilled businessman who knew that the public wants spectacle and singing. He was regularly praised for the theater's sets and costumes, and he competed to recruit the finest singers in England and on the continent for his company. He also kept the opera afloat by using the house for masked balls. The Bishop of London, no friend of the opera or, especially, of masked balls, had been strongly opposing such infamous entertainments, which of course simply encouraged that segment of the public inclined to such festivities. The *Plain Dealer* of March 27, 1724, says that such masquerades are "always the Confusion, and very commonly, the Ruin of Ladies of the First Quality, and of all young Women whatsoever of good Condition and Fortune in the World."

Running an opera company has seldom worked well without the help of a great deal of private patronage. Despite the large sums pledged by the nobility, the Royal Academy continued to have money troubles. The house was relatively small, and despite the extremely high prices for opera tickets, even completely full houses—which seldom materialized—would scarcely meet the running expenses, which included the stupendous salaries commanded by the star singers. This formula for gradual—or swift—ruin is familiar to opera managers today.

HANDEL

George Frideric Handel was a cosmopolitan composer operating in a relatively insular city. Born in Germany in 1685, he had produced operas in Hamburg and in Italy and now was bringing the tradition of Italian opera to England. Although he was a German he wrote in an international Italian style for Italian singers—which, at least for the moment, was just what the London audience for opera wanted.

Rinaldo, Handel's first opera for London, was one of his most spectacular, and in 1711 it made his name instantly. He continued to compose operas from time to time and was engaged as well in many related enterprises, including travels to Europe to recruit the finest singers. He had not yet embarked on the series of oratorio performances that would produce the pieces for which he is best known today.

By 1724, Handel was established in London. The summer after *Giulio Cesare* opened he moved to a house in Brook Street (now no. 25), prompted by the speculative development that was engaging the British economy. His parish church (Handel was a Protestant, and his allegiance to the Church of England helped assure his citizenship) would be the nearby St. George's, Hanover Square (not yet built). He ultimately owned a few good pictures (a Rembrandt, a portrait of himself by Denner), but he never furnished the house elegantly.

Handel was a handsome man when he arrived in England at twenty-five, but his girth increased with age. Those who knew him remarked on his authority, his humor, and his size. William Coxe described his as follows:

> He was large in person, and his natural corpulency, which increased as he advanced in life, rendered his whole appearance of that bulky proportion, as to give rise to Quin's inelegant, but forcible expression; that his hands were feet, and his fingers toes. From a sedentary life, he had contracted a stiffness in his joints, which in addition to his great weight and weakness of body, rendered his gait awkward; still his countenance was open, manly, and animated; expressive of all that grandeur and benevolence, which were the prominent features of his character. . . . In temper he was irascible, impatient of contradiction, but not vindictive; jealous of his musical pre-eminence, and tenacious in all points, which regarded his professional honour.

As a staff composer to the Royal Academy, Handel was presumably paid a substantial sum, not only for the composition of operas but for his regular services conducting his works, for trips abroad to recruit singers, for rehearsing, and so on. Unfortunately, we do not know what his salary was, though it may have been around £800—enough to live comfortably but far less than the star singers earned.

George Frideric Handel cut a large figure and was known to be an amusing conversationalist—with his German accent and generosity he could please almost anybody. A large white wig seems to have been a part of his public attire. Anonymous eighteenth-century portrait.

Preparations

The job of procuring, adapting, or composing libretti for the opera fell to the secretary of the Royal Academy of Music. In 1723 the secretary was the remarkably versatile Nicola Haym, cellist, dealer in books and artworks, composer, antiquarian, and author. (In addition to his surviving antiquarian and bibliographical works, he wrote a history of music, apparently lost.)

Haym had been a member of Cardinal Ottoboni's orchestra in Rome before coming to London as chamber musician to the Duke of Bedford in 1700. He had played a large part in establishing Italian opera in London, producing Bononcini's *Camilla* (first performed in 1706), the most popular Italian opera of eighteenth-century London. In 1707 all of London's theater-musicians had been required to form a single orchestra at the Queen's Theatre, and Haym arranged that he would "never be made second to any other Person of the Musick." Haym was engaged also in publishing: his two sets of trio sonatas were published in 1703 and 1704, and he had got himself into some trouble by selling his edition of Arcangelo Corelli's trio sonatas to two publishers.

Haym had spent many years playing *basso continuo* accompaniments with Handel, starting with *Rinaldo*, Handel's magnificent first opera for London in the 1710–11 season. Haym served also as manager for "The Baroness," a skilled Italian singer who for several years coached Anastasia Robinson—Cornelia in *Giulio Cesare*. The Baroness, who died in 1724, was probably the mother of Haym's child.

A major part of Haym's job as secretary of the Royal Academy of Music from 1722 to 1728 was adapting librettos for the company's use. He was, in fact, very skillful at this. He also composed overtures, additional songs and recitatives, and whatever new music was required to fit an older opera into new circumstances. As was usual with librettists, he undoubtedly served as stage director.

Haym had collaborated regularly with Handel, and his libretto for *Giulio Cesare in Egitto* is very well made, but it is not altogether new. Elderly patrons of the opera might have seen an earlier version, by Giacomo Francesco Bussani, in any number of Italian cities, by any number of composers, from 1677 to 1722, or any number of other operas on the subject of Caesar and Cleopatra.

The subject of Julius Caesar was well known on the London stage. Colley Cibber had produced the play *Caesar in Egypt* at Drury Lane on December 9: it had been only moderately successful. And a version of Shakespeare's *Julius Caesar,* with music by John Ernest Galliard (and "an intire new Sett of Scenes representing Ancient Rome, Painted by Monsieur Devoto") played in London in 1723; it might have been seen by the theater-loving Handel, by his librettist, and by much of his audience. But Handel's Caesar is not the great ruler or the terrible tyrant but a young hero. Following classical story, Caesar arrives in Egypt to find rival claimants to the throne, the siblings Ptolemy and Cleopatra. Ptolemy offers Caesar the head of his rival Pompey while the wily Cleopatra, in an attempt to seduce Caesar, steps into her own trap and falls in love with him. (Subplots with Pompey's widow, Cornelia, and her son Sesto are not part of the classical tradition.)

Bussani's older libretto needed to be adapted to the modern conventions of serious opera, pruned of all its comic eunuchs and other characters, most of its travesties and disguises (although Cleopatra still disguises herself here as Lidia), and at least some of its romantic intrigues. Haym adjusted Bussani's libretto for Handel's purposes, keeping much of the dialogue and some of the best lyrics ("Alma del gran Pompeo," "V'adoro, pupille," etc.); he apparently contributed many of the aria texts, and he strengthened the plot by getting rid of a number of secondary characters and subplots. He also adjusted the number of arias to reflect the relative importance of the singers. It was important for the chief singers to have the largest number of arias, and for each of them to have a variety of songs in different moods. This permits each singer to display a range of skills, and it also allows for the development of character, one song at a time.

Handel's composition of *Giulio Cesare* involved a great deal of revision and what appears to be a close collaboration with Haym. The surviving score, bound years after Handel's death, has a variety of materials that became part of the opera as it appeared on the stage; it also contains material that ultimately found its way into other operas. Handel began composing the opera in 1723, evidently having a somewhat different cast in mind, and he later made adjustments for the 1724 singers. Texts were borrowed from Bussani and from a Milanese adaptation of Bussani's libretto and arias were moved from character to character and scene to scene to provide a clear and balanced libretto. Some characters were eliminated: Cleopatra's cousin—the descendant of the seventeenth-century comic

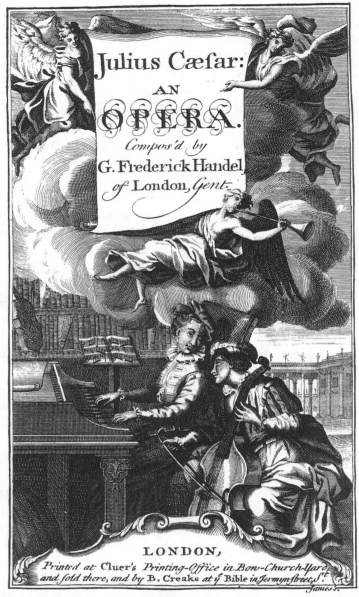

Title page of the score of *Giulio Cesare*. The publication by Cluer and Creake was announced in May 1725, and in June it was advertised as being "Curiously engrav'd on Copper Plates Corrected and Figur'd by Mr Handel's own Hands; there fore beware of incorrect pirated Editions done on large Pewter Plates."

nurse—eventually disappeared, giving up her best arias: "Tutto può donna vezzosa" to Cleopatra herself, and "Va tacito e nascosto" to Caesar.

Handel's writing for the voice is so tailored to particular singers that scholars feel quite confident in recognizing the intended singer from the music. For example, Senesino, the famous castrato who plays Caesar, had a limited range, and most of his highly impressive and difficult passagework is limited to a constellation of six notes right where he liked them. There is telling emphasis in his music on breath control, on the *messa di voce* (the technique of making large crescendos and diminuendos on a single note), and on the expression of the words.

For natural men's voices Handel tended to feature large ranges, big leaps, and arpeggios. The typical "rage" or "vengeance" aria of a bass is a characteristic topos. Generally, though, tenors and basses are subsidiary characters—old men, servants, tyrants. The leading men are always sopranos or altos. Castrati, famous for their power and clarity, were favored for the heroic roles. But sometimes, as in the role of Sesto, a woman's voice was used for a heroic male part, either when no suitable castrato was available or when the role was a specialty of the woman involved (in this case Margherita Durastanti).

Not everybody was willing to suspend disbelief in order to be ravished by a castrato voice. William Popple wrote in *The Prompter:* "The introduction of eunuchs upon public theatres is only fit for nations of corrupt and dissolute morals, and that if operas cannot be performed without presenting such striking Figures to the eyes of my fair country-women, we had much better lose the pleasure we receive from that species of harmony, than have the eyes, ears, and thoughts of our ladies conversant with Figures they cannot well see, hear, nor think of, without a blush." Other ladies, however, were so fond of Senesino that they presented him with gold snuffboxes, a tweezer-case set with diamonds, or deprived their children of sustenance in order to give presents to him.

Handel concerned himself with all aspects of the production. Because operas had no formally appointed stage director, Handel took on as much as he could of these duties. He was particularly interested in staging, and he was careful to include many stage directions in his score; the libretto is full of such details, and that is how we know as much as we do about the sets and the movement in *Giulio Cesare*. The traditions and customs of stage movement for individual actors were so well understood that staging was essentially a matter of coordinating entrances and exits and letting the singers rely on their own skill in the matter of addressing each other.

The actual stage direction generally fell to the librettist, or to the local poet. Somebody had to coordinate the shifting of scenery, the arrangement of the many supernumeraries who accompany the leading characters, and the presence, when needed, of the offstage chorus.

Rehearsal was apparently not a matter of strict coordination: Handel was sometimes able to mount a new opera with a week's rehearsal. Most rehearsals were held informally in a room rented for the purpose, probably with very limited accompaniment, usually harpsichord and cello. Handel was known to have conducted rehearsals at his house with the singers, and his insistence on having his music performed as written (with the addition, of course, of the traditional ornaments) was famous. At least one final rehearsal was held "in form" (that is, a dress rehearsal), with the public admitted for a fee.

A scandal of the sort that fashionable society loves to keep alive through gossip was still in the air at the time of *Giulio Cesare*'s premiere. Back in January, Anastasia Robinson (the noble Cornelia in Handel's opera) had been offended by what she considered liberties taken by Senesino in a rehearsal of Handel's *Vespasiano*. On January 18 the *Weekly Journal* reported: "We hear there have been strange Commotions in the State of Musick in the Opera-House in the Hay-Market, and that a civil Broil arose among the Subscribers at the Practice of the new Opera of *Vespasian*, which turn'd all the Harmony into Discord." Lady Mary Wortley Montagu, who described Robinson as both a prude and a kept mistress, said that Robinson took offense at the "too near approach of Senesino in the Opera." And for that approach, Burney was told by Horace Walpole, "Lord Peterborough publicly and violently caned him behind the scenes."

There were two scurrilous pamphlets in circulation, and the disputes in the press over the relative merits of Handel and Bononcini continued after the opening of *Giulio Cesare*. On March 7 an anonymous poem in support of Handel ("An Epistel to Mr. Handel, upon his Operas of Flavius and Julius Caesar") mocked his opponents as

> a spurious Breed,
> Who suck bad Air, and on thin Diet feed . . .
> Supine in downy Indolence they doze . . .
> And soothing whispers lull 'em to repose.

Friedrich Ernst von Fabrice wrote on March 10 that "the squabbles between the

Directors and the sides that everyone is taking between the singers and the composers, often provide the public with the most diverting scenes." Much of the fun of going to the opera had to do with keeping up with the scandals.

Performance
GOING TO THE THEATER

The King's Theatre in the Haymarket, particularly on opening nights, was populated by lovers of opera who had strong opinions, especially about singers. Those without private carriages arrived in hired hackney coaches and sedan chairs. Footmen waited in the top gallery. Performances generally began at six in the evening, and the house opened an hour before (sometimes, on days of premieres, it opened two or three hours early). Arriving at the theater in plenty of time, spectators would find a crowd gathered around the door to the pit. Seats were not reserved, so many patrons sent servants to occupy their places. Sometimes a couple of grenadiers were engaged to keep order. There was barely enough light to see who was who. In the pit were gentlemen, intellectuals, critics. In the boxes were the nobility, many of whom were season subscribers. The middle gallery held tradesmen and their wives, and the upper gallery had spaces for servants and anyone who could afford a ticket.

The Earl of Mount-Edgcumbe described the scene in the theater nostalgically in his reminiscences:

> Both of these [pit and boxes] were filled exclusively with the highest classes of Society, all, without exception, in the full dress then universally worn. The audiences thus assembled were considered as indisputably presenting a finer spectacle than any other theatre in Europe, and absolutely astonished the foreign performers to whom such a sight was entirely new. At the end of the performance the company of the pit and boxes repared to the coffee room, which was then the best assembly in London, private ones being rarely given on opera nights and all the first society was regularly to be seen there. Over the front box was the five shilling gallery, then resorted to by respectable persons not in full dress: and above that an upper gallery to which the admission was three shillings. Subsequently the house was encircled by private boxes, yet still the prices remained the same, and the pit preserved its respectability and even grandeur till the old house was burnt down in 1789.

The upper gallery was sometimes the site of irregular behavior. The *London Daily Post and General Advertiser* reported on February 11, 1735, that "a Disturbance happen'd at the opera House . . . occasion'd by the Footmen's coming into the Passages with their lighted Flambeaux, which gave Offence to the Ladies, &c. in the House; whereupon the Footmen were order'd out, but they refus'd to go, and attack'd the Centinels, but a stronger

Guard coming to their Assistance, with their Bayonets fix'd, drove them out; in the Fray one of the Footmen was stabbed in the Groin, and in the Body, and its thought will die of the Wounds."

The stage boxes, reserved for the royal family, were occupied for the premiere of *Giulio Cesare,* as the newspaper reported: "Last Night His Majesty, the Prince and Princess, with great Numbers of the Nobility, went to see the new Opera."

The theater was magnificent to look at, with its semicircular seating and its superimposed columns. Designed as a playhouse by the playwright and amateur architect John Vanbrugh, the theater opened in 1705. It had acoustical problems from the beginning, being too resonant for some tastes. Various improvements were made over the years, and in 1714 it was renamed the King's Theatre in honor of George I. It remained the principal opera house until the conversion of the theater in Covent Garden in 1847.

Colley Cibber, the actor and playwright, described acoustics that, while disadvantageous for plays, must have given an admirable resonance to music:

> For what could their vast columns, their gilded cornices, their immoderate high roofs avail, when scarce one word in ten could be distinctly heard in it? Nor had it then, the form, it now stands in, which necessity, two or three years after, reduced it to. At the first opening it, the flat ceiling, that is now over the orchestre, was then a semi-oval arch, that sprung fifteen feet higher from above the cornice; the ceiling over the pit too, was still more raised, being one level line from the highest back part of the upper gallery, to the front of the stage; the front-boxes were a continued semicircle, to the bare walls of the house on each side. This extraordinary and superfluous space occasion'd such an undulation, from the voice of every actor, that generally what they said sounded like the gabbling of so many people, in the lofty isles in a cathedral.—The tone of a trumpet, or the swell of an Eunuch's holding note, 'tis true, might be sweeten'd by it; but the articulate sounds of a speaking voice were drown'd by the hollow reverberations of one word upon another. To this inconvenience, why may we not add that of its situation; for at that time it had not the advantage of almost a large city, which has since been built, in its neighbourhood.

The theater had been redecorated the previous autumn "by some of the best Masters," and it was looking splendid. The 413 seats "below stairs" included those in the pit and those in the boxes. There were some 350 seats available in the galleries, though they were seldom all occupied. The rare full house might bring some £150 in revenue, but expenses far outstripped income. The success and continuing popularity of the opera depended on superstar performers and lavish productions. The prices were very high—about twice the cost of a theater ticket—but not high enough. For the two opening nights of a new production in 1719, seats in the pit and boxes cost 10s 6d, seats in the gallery 5s; these were reduced for later performances. Subscribers paid 20 guineas, which allowed

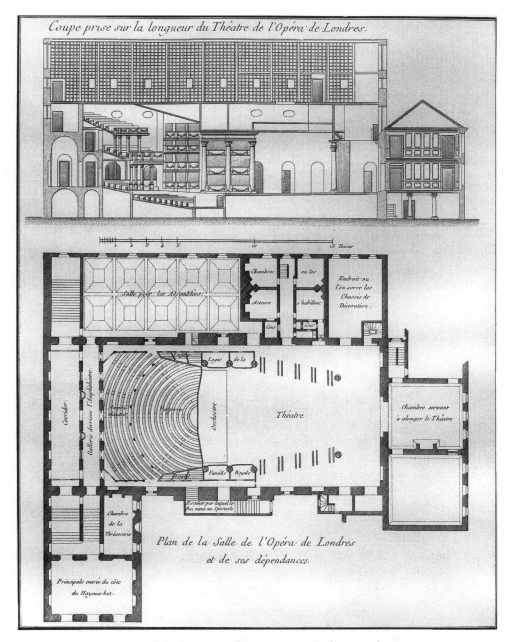

Coupe prise sur la longueur du Théatre de l'Opéra de Londres.

Salle pour les Assemblées.

Chambres ou les Acteurs s'habillent.

Endroit ou l'on serre les Chassis de Décoration.

Cour   Cour

Corridor.

Galerie derriere l'Amphithéatre.

Amphithéatre.

Parterre.

Orchestre.

Loge de la

Loge

Famille Royale.

Théatre.

Chambre servant à alonger le Théatre.

Chambre de la Thrésorerie.

Escalier par lequel le Roi vient au Spectacle.

Plan de la Salle de l'Opéra de Londres
et de ses dépendances.

Principale entrée du côté du Haymarket.

The plan of the Haymarket Theatre shows the five sets of wings,
which could be expanded by an opening into an adjacent room. Along
one side of the theater were a public assembly room, dressing rooms,
and storage for sets. On the other side were the entrance and
the king's private staircase.

Richard Steele Complains of Stage Seats in the *Spectator,*
March 16, 1711

Tho' the Gentlemen on the Stage had very much contributed to the Beauty of
the Grove by walking up and down between the Trees, I must own I was not
a little astonish'd to see a well-dress'd young Fellow in a full-bottom'd Wigg,
appear in the Midst of the Sea, and without any visible Concern, taking Snuff.

entry to fifty performances. But for benefits—an important source of income for singers
—tickets were sold at prices that varied with the fame of the performer. The *London Journal* reported in March 1723, "The new Opera Tickets are very high, and like to continue
so as long as Mrs. Cotzani [Cuzzoni] is so much admired. They are traded in at the other
End of the Town, as much as Lottery Tickets are in Exchange-Alley."

Gallery seats were sold at the door on the day of the performance, all other seats
in advance. Previously it was possible to enter without paying and to leave after the first
act, but this was corrected in 1714. In the first season of the Royal Academy, seats on the
stage itself could be had for one guinea. This practice was later abandoned, and there were
probably no dandies among the scenery at *Giulio Cesare,* as there had been at many other
operas. A 1715 announcement in the *Daily Courant* read: "And whereas there is a great
many Scenes and Machines to be mov'd in this Opera, which cannot be done if Persons
should stand upon the Stage (where they could not be without Danger), it is therefore
hop'd No Body, even the Subscribers, will take it Ill that they must be Deny'd Entrance
on the Stage."

A certain Monsieur Fougeroux described the hall as he saw it in 1728:

> The room is small and in very mediocre taste, the theatre is fairly large
> but with bad decorations (in scene-changes they use a little bell instead
> of a whistle). There is no amphitheatre, only a parterre, where there are
> large benches all the way to the orchestra where men and women are
> seated pell-mell. The loges are rented by the year. In the rear of the hall
> is raised a gallery held up by pillars which opens into the parterre and
> raised like our second loges. This is for the middle classes (la petite bour-
> geoisie), they nevertheless pay five shillings, which make five French
> francs. Places in the parterre are worth a half guinea, or 11 francs 10.
> The King has two boxes next to the stage, he comes there twice with
> the Queen. The princesses are facing him in another box. Everyone claps
> hands when the King arrives, and they are saluted when leaving; he only

had two halberdiers as a guard. The sides of the theatre are decorated with columns, along which are attached mirrors with sconces of several candles, which are also attached to the pilasters which support the rear gallery. Instead of chandeliers are ugly wooden candleholders, held up by ropes like those used by tight-rope dancers. Nothing could be uglier, but still there are candles everywhere.

Before the opera the stage is swept of orange peels, bottles, and debris of various kinds that accumulates during and after a performance. The house is lit with candles and oil lamps; they will necessarily remain lit throughout the performance. The curtain is down, dividing the forestage, on which almost all the acting and singing will take place, from the rear stage, where the sets and their illuminations are being prepared. The famous Haymarket orchestra is in the pit. It is not a sunken pit as in modern theaters but is on the floor of the opera house, with a low barrier dividing the players from the spectators at the same level. The orchestra is a large one for its day, and it is full of famous performers and accomplished composers. Johann Joachim Quantz, on hearing the orchestra in 1727, wrote, "The orchestra consisted for the greater part of Germans, several Italians, and a few Englishmen. *Castrucci,* an Italian violinist, was the leader. Altogether, under Händel's conducting, made an extremely good effect."

Handel himself, seated at one of the two harpsichords, begins the overture, and we are pleased to hear that it begins as an overture should: with the full orchestra of strings, oboes, bassoons, and harpsichords in stately dotted rhythms. There can be no doubt that this will be followed by a lively fugue, as almost always happens in a French-style "ouverture," and the curtain will rise on the first scene.

ORCHESTRA

The opera orchestra was large: though we cannot say exactly how many played in 1724, we know that an initial plan for the Royal Academy drawn up in February 1720 called for seventeen violins (in groups of eight, five, and four), two violas, four cellos, two double-basses, four oboes, three bassoons, a theorbo (or arch-lute), and a trumpet. Nothing is said about instruments that are usually present: harpsichords, an additional trumpet, kettledrums, pairs of horns, flutes. Sir John Clerk of Penicuik, after attending a performance of Handel's *Orlando* in May 1733, listed a very similar orchestra in his diary: "above 24 violins, four cello, 2 large basse violins each about 7 foot in length at least with strings proportionable that co'd not be less than ¼ of an inch diameter," two oboes, four bassoons, a theorbo, and two harpsichords. (There is no mention of horns.) He notes that the violins "made a terrible noise & often drown'd the voices" but notes the Castrucci brothers, Pietro and Prospero, "who play'd with great dexterity."

Sir John was not the only observer to remark on the volume of sound in the orchestra. Fougeroux also described the orchestra, its size, the skill of the Castrucci brothers, and the loudness (though he didn't notice the violas and says nothing of horns):

The orchestra was composed of twenty-four violins, led by the two Castrucci brothers, two harpsichords, of which Indel [Handel] the German, a great player and composer played one, an archlute, three cellos, two contrebasses, three bassoons and sometimes flutes and clairons. *Cet orchestre fait un grand fracas.* As there are no middle parts, the twenty-four violins normally play only the first and second treble parts, which is extremely brilliant and performed well. The two harpsichords and the archlute play the chords and the middle parts. There are only one cello [who reads from a harpsichordist's part], the two harpsichords and the archlute for the recitative.

It was a distinguished orchestra full of expert players, many of whom are still well known for their skill as performers or composers. The composer Pietro Castrucci led the orchestra from the first violinist's chair. He was an expert performer, if somewhat unpredictable in behavior. Charles Burney said, "This violinist, who was more than half mad, is represented in one of Hogarth's prints as the enraged musician."

Despite the noise, the *fracas,* noted by some observers, the players did not always play all together, as they do in the overture. There was a variety of tonal combinations available from the band of strings and double reeds. For the full band, the violins play two parts (the first and second violins on the first part, the third violins on the second) with violas and cellos. All the oboes join in on the top line, and all the bassoons and double-basses on the bass.

But there are many other configurations. Sometimes Handel calls for five-part strings (three violin parts plus viola and bass), sometimes four (two violin parts), sometimes three (two violins plus bass, or violin-viola-bass), sometimes two (all the violins together, plus bass); sometimes, especially in arias for the bass voice, the orchestra consists only of bass instruments playing a single line. When accompanying arias, especially while the singer is singing, a smaller group of the better players—a "concertino"—performed, the full band joining in on the ritornellos.

To the basic sound is added a variety of instrumental colors for special effect. There are horns for military moments (the opening chorus, the march at the end) and to refer to hunting (the wonderful solo horn in Caesar's "Va tacito e nascosto," likening the stealthy hunter to Ptolemy's treachery). In this opera Handel uses two pairs of horns in two different keys to give more tonal flexibility to an instrument limited to the notes of the harmonic series; it is a very early example of what became a commonplace in symphonic music. There is a violin solo for Castrucci as Caesar is captivated by Cleopatra, as well as solos for a variety of other instruments (oboes often double the violins, and have occasional solos). There are recorders in pairs for Cornelia and transverse flute for plaintive moments, including Cleopatra's famous "Piangerò." (The recorders and flutes were doubtless played by the oboists.)

THE ENRAGED MUSICIAN.

The Enraged Musician, by Hogarth. According to Charles Burney,
this engraving represents Pietro Castrucci, the "more than half mad"
leader of the Haymarket orchestra.

SETS

The curtain goes up during wonderful music in minuet time; Handel's audience is used to overtures that conclude with a minuet, but in this one the minuet becomes the opening chorus of Egyptians and provides an elegant transition from the opera house to the Nile.

We recognize the setting for the first scene because it is described in the word-book sold in the theater; the book includes the Italian text to be sung, along with an English translation, and indications of which texts are sung as arias and which as recitatives. It also contains copious stage directions, which assist the spectators in knowing what, exactly, and who are being represented on stage. The libretto, printed by "Tomaso Wood," opens with Haym's flowery dedication to the Princess of Wales, and it contains an "argument," a background and summary of the plot, in both English and Italian. The first scene is described as "A plain in Egypt with an ancient bridge across a branch of the Nile." This

GIULIO CESARE
In Egitto.

DRAMA.
Da Rapprefentarfi

Nel REGIO TEATRO
di HAY-MARKET,
PER

La Reale Accademia di Mufica.

IN LONDRA:
Per *Tomafo Wood* nella Piccola Bretagna.
M·DCC·XXIV·

A printed libretto of *Guilio Cesare*, in Italian and English, was available for sale and undoubtedly was useful in the theater for those whose Italian was less than perfect.

is a splendid perspective: in the middle ground is a bridge over which Caesar and Curio and their followers walk while the Egyptians sing a chorus of praise. It is a splendid view, using most of the resources of the theater.

Sets were made not to provide realism but to delight the eyes. They were constructed, as were all sets in this period (and for a very long time before and after), of a series of painted wings on each side of the stage and a (usually) flat painted backcloth. The result for the audience was a continuous painted scene, each wing overlapping our view of the next, and each illuminated not only from above but by the candles attached to the back of the next downstage flat. The raked stage and the receding wings permitted scene-painters to create an exaggerated perspective, allowing the viewer to imagine a scene of boundless depth.

The Haymarket Theatre had five sets of grooves on each side for sliding wings, which could be moved manually or by machine. The scene could be closed with a backcloth or with a "shutter," a pair of flats meeting in the center; or the vista could be lengthened to some sixty feet by using the space made available by an opening into an adjoining house. There was not enough fly space to allow scenes to be raised from sight, but there was room enough above the stage for cloud machines. There were evidently also trap doors in the stage.

Changing settings is simple in such a theater. At a signal (here, a bell was rung) all the wings are withdrawn at once and others are moved forward while the painted backcloth is removed to reveal another—all in the twinkling of an eye. It is a wonderful thing to see, and it is done in full view of the spectators; the front curtain does not come down until the end of the opera. (This is one reason that acts need to end by removing the last remaining character from the stage.)

This drawing is from a series of set designs by Filippo Juvarra
for *Giulio Cesare nell'Egitto,* an opera by Antonio Ottoboni given
in Rome in 1713. It appears to show a practicable bridge from a ship
on the left, with figures standing along the shore into the distance.
As this would be a difficult effect to achieve in a typical theater,
this is perhaps an imaginative rendering of a set.

Several scene painters working at the opera at about this time are known: Roberto Clerici was scenic artist and machinist to the Royal Academy from about 1716; Giovanni Niccolò Servandoni was scene-painter at the Haymarket from 1721 to 1723 (perhaps some of his settings were recycled in *Giulio Cesare*); the artists Joseph Goupy and Peter Tillemans were known to have decorated scenes about 1724–25, so perhaps they are responsible for the Nile, the bridge, and much else.

Sometimes, though, older scenery was reused; there are so many scenes set in a garden, or a "rural prospect," or a room in the palace, and so on, that many settings were useful for more than one production. Handel's operas had more new sets than anybody else's, but this is not one of those that advertised new scenery.

Spectacular scenery and effects were not featured in this theater—most of the money was spent on expensive Italian singers. But Handel's magic opera *Rinaldo* (1711) had used all the trapdoors and flying machines, as well as live birds and fireworks. Even in *Giulio Cesare* there are magical effects, like the view of Parnassus that begins act 2, where the mountain opens and "Virtue appears setting on a throne, attended by the nine muses"; after some beautiful music, the mountain shuts again. This may have been a moment to use the room at the back of the stage to lengthen the perspective. Another piece of mime occurs for the battle in act 3, when Ptolemy's forces overpower those of Cleopatra to the sound of a martial Sinfonia; here back-flats surely opened to show the battle waged by supernumeraries and closed as the captive Cleopatra is led onstage by Ptolemy.

Sometimes a shallower scene masks a larger one. Especially when a scene in an act requires the use of a set piece (what the French would call a *praticable*), like the bridge in the opening scene, it needs to be preceded or followed by scenes using only a few of the wings so that the object can first be revealed, and then, in a successive scene, removed. Shallower scenes are needed, too, when, as in this opera, characters die on stage—a relatively rare occurrence in serious opera. Here the traitorous Achilla expires in the sight of all; and near the end of act 3, Sesto kills Tolomeo on stage. The actors can leave the stage only after a subsequent short set has masked them. Both deceased singers will be needed for the final chorus; presumably they sing offstage. The final scene, showing the port of Alexandria, is revealed by opening shallower sets to reveal the full depth of the stage. Joseph Addison, though he mocks some of the excesses and fripperies of sets and costumes, remarks that "Scenes affect ordinary Minds as much as Speeches; and our Actors are very sensible, that a well-dress'd Play has sometimes brought them as full Audiences, as a well-written one."

In act 1 there are ten scenes, according to the libretto, but four sets. A scene, of course, is the dramatist's way of marking a change of characters on stage: whenever somebody leaves or enters, a new scene begins. Since such an exit (usually after an aria) or arrival usually marks a change in the drama, this labeling makes dramatic sense. But several such scenes may take place in the same location.

The four sets in act 1 are labeled thus in the libretto:

A *plain in Egypt with an old Bridge across a Branch of the Nile,* scenes
   1–4;
Cabinet (presumably in Cleopatra's palace), scenes 5–6;
Caesar's Camp, with an Urn in the middle, wherein the Ashes of Pom-
   pey's Head are inclos'd upon an eminent Pile of Trophies, scene 7–8;
A Court in Ptolomey's palace, scenes 9–10.

As experienced theatergoers we might have glanced ahead at the English translation and determined how the set changes would be accomplished. The first scene is a long set, using the full depth of the theater. (It may, indeed, use the real water effects for which the theater was famous.) The second set (a Cabinet) will be a short set, enabling the stage hands to remove the bridge and get Pompey's urn ready so that the third set,

Caesar's Camp, can be revealed. And then comes another short set, allowing for the removal of the urn and the preparation of the grandest set piece of all (the view of the mechanical mountain) at the beginning of act 2.

It is no wonder that Haym arranged for all the characters to have left the stage by the end of each of these groups. It would be odd to have the location change around one of the characters, though as spectators we enjoy watching these marvelous things happen before our eyes and being transported instantly to another place.

Lighting is done with candles and oil lamps. Chandeliers over the apron provide most of the light for the singers, along with the many lights in the hall that burn throughout the performance so that the audience members can read librettos and see one another. The set is lit by candles and lamps affixed to the backs of wings and flats. These "scene-ladders" were provided with hoods that could be raised or lowered for effect. (We cannot be certain that such a mechanism existed in the King's Theatre, but it was quite common.) Footlights were provided on a ramp that could be moved for greater or lesser amounts of light. Between acts candles were replaced and lamps trimmed, and the spectators sometimes applauded a particularly deft lamplighter.

COSTUMES

The opening song of praise is sung by an offstage chorus that the libretto assures us is made up of Egyptians but we know is those characters who are not now onstage.

Onto the stage during the chorus strides our hero, Julius Caesar, accompanied by the tribune Curio; he moves downstage to sing, and we are in the presence of one of the brightest stars of the age: the great Senesino. He is dressed in a version of classical military garb: breastplate, short tunic, helmet. He wears a wig—as does everybody—and his helmet is adorned with plumes to increase his stature. Caesar's dress sets him apart from the other military men: a touch of gold, a higher plume.

Except for some military equipment, costumes are essentially street clothes; actresses wore hooped gowns like those in the ballroom—or rather, in the opera house, as ballroom dress was often drawn from the opera house. The singers were expected to provide their own clothes. This was universally so in the theater and must have been true to some extent in the opera. Men's costumes were more stylized, borrowing from military and classical elements. We have no pictures of *Giulio Cesare* from 1724, but there are pictures of Senesino in military costume (see pages 43 and 48), and from these we can imagine the look. Such a costume would be useful in many an opera on classical subjects.

BAROQUE OPERA

Most operagoers went to hear the singers. They wanted to hear the stars: Senesino as Julius Caesar and Cuzzoni as Cleopatra—or perhaps just Senesino and Cuzzoni, regardless of what roles they were playing. The stars were castrati or women, high voices; the few natural-voice men played secondary roles. The opera was in Italian, of course, but the word-book was available, which gave a translation on facing pages for those who were

This mezzotint after a Thomas Hudson portrait shows Senesino (Francesco Bernardi) in his full glory. The open book is the score of *Giulio Cesare,* perhaps Senesino's finest role.

interested. But many spectators paid little attention to the recitative or the plot—often very complicated—and waited for the best songs.

The formal design of an Italian opera was entirely predictable, to the entire satisfaction of the audience. The plot, generally based on a well-known mythological or historical subject, was arranged in a series of acts, with the characters all singing in rhyming verse. The interest was not so much in what happens as in how this telling of a familiar story will provide us with insights into character and emotion, and will provide moments in which a character's spirit can take flight in beautiful song.

The clear distinction between recitative and aria was well understood. In recitative, the characters recite—that is, they seem to speak. Although they are in fact singing, they proceed generally in the rhythms and at the speed of speech, with the simplest of chordal accompaniments from the harpsichord or theorbo. This style of musical recitation had worked well from the time of Monteverdi, and it still worked, only now the flexible arioso style of the seventeenth century had given way to a system in which a clear differentiation is made between speech and song, between real-time speaking out loud and the lyrical freeze-frame for the expression of emotional states in song.

In Italy the opera was essentially a recitation of poetry, the verse being well understood and closely heard; in fact, it was the chief form of drama at the time. In England, however, audiences were well served with dramatic poetry on the various stages and did not see in the opera a particularly dramatic or poetic event—they paid much less attention to the words than did their Italian contemporaries. Despite their libretti, the English audiences did not much like long recitatives. They wanted songs, and Handel gave them songs, and indeed used the songs themselves to move the drama forward.

The song—or *aria* in Italian—is the place where the musical interest is concentrated, and the plot and the language of the opera are constructed to provide a splendid series of such moments. The song is the place where an individual expresses what is in the heart at the moment.

Joseph Addison Mocks Heroic Costume in the *Spectator*

The ordinary Method of making an Heroe, is to clap a huge plume of Feathers upon his Head, which rises so very high, that there is often a greater Length from his Chin to the Top of his Head, than to the Sole of his Foot. One would believe, that we thought a great Man and a tall Man the same thing. This very much embarrasses the Actor, who is forced to hold his Neck extremely stiff and steady all the whole he speaks; and notwithstanding any Anxieties which he pretends for his Mistress, his Country, or his Friends, one may see by his Action, that his greatest Care and Concern is to keep the Plume of Feathers from falling off his Head. For my own Part, when I see a Man uttering his Complaints under such a Mountain of Feathers, I am apt to look upon him rather as an unfortunate Lunatick, than a distress'd Heroe. As these super-fluous Ornaments upon the Head make a great Man, a Princess generally receives her Grandeur from those additional Incumbrances that fall into her Tail: I mean the broad sweeping Train that follows her in all her Motions, and finds constant Employment for a Boy who stands behind her to open and spread it to Advantage. I do not know how others are affected at this Sight, but, I must confess, my Eyes are wholly taken up with the Page's Part; and as for the Queen, I am not so attentive to any thing she speaks, as to the right adjusting of her Train, lest it should chance to trip up her Heels, or incom-mode her, as she walks to and fro upon the Stage. It is, in my Opinion, a very odd Spectacle, to see a Queen venting her Passion in a disordered Motion, and a little Boy taking Care all the while that they do not ruffle the Tail of her Gown. The Parts that the two Persons act on the Stage at the same Time, are very different: The Princess is afraid lest she should incur the Displeasure of the King her Father, or lose the Heroe her Lover, whilst her Attendant is only concern'd lest she should entangle her Feet in her Petticoat.

As an example, Caesar's first song after his opening entrance expresses his rage. Achilla, sent by Ptolemy, has obsequiously presented Caesar with the head of his enemy Pompey, hoping to gain Caesar's favor. But the lordly conqueror instead is enraged by the misdeed. Just before he sings he makes clear in his recitative whom he is addressing and how the plot will proceed. "Go!" he says to Achilla. "I will come to the palace [Ptolemy's] before sundown." And then he turns his rage on Achilla and Ptolemy, who thought to please him. The orchestra plays its introduction, Caesar strikes an appropriate pose, and sings:

HANDEL, *GIULIO CESARE*

This engraving shows a stage setting from the 1725 Hamburg
production of *Giulio Cesare*—act 5, "A harbour near the city of
Alexandria." Successive wings show, first, towers and gates,
and then rows of ships; the backcloth depicts the sea.

Empio dirò, tu sei;
Togliti agli occhi miei;
sei tutto crudeltà!

(I will call you a villain.
Quit my sight!
You are all cruelty.)

Having expressed this sentiment to Achilla in suitably outraged music, Caesar
explains the nature of his anger at Ptolemy:

Non è di re quel cor,
che donasi al rigor,
che in sen non ha pietà.

(That heart is not royal
that gives itself to cruelty,
that has no pity in its breast.)

For this the music changes; the expressions of cruelty and pity are made clear.
And the reasons for Caesar's anger are thus outlined. This makes the repetition of Caesar's

opening music and words ("Empio dirò") logical and interesting; when we hear the opening section again, we hear it anew, not only because it is now familiar musically but because the second, contrasting musical section has given further depth and clarity to the sentiment expressed at the beginning, so that we also feel it in a new way.

And that shape—exposition, explanation, reexposition—is the standard form for a song in this opera, and indeed it is the norm for every song in every opera in the earlier eighteenth century. It is amazing that poets could think of so many ways to make language and emotions correspond to this musical form, and that composers could devise so many brilliant or plaintive compositions within this framework without boring anybody.

The librettist most often provides a short text—usually three lines—for the opening portion and a corresponding amount for the contrasting section. The composer's challenge is to make a beautiful, expressive, and extended composition using these words.

Nowadays we call this a da capo aria, since after the contrasting section the opening music is repeated from the beginning, "da capo" in Italian. This three-part form, ABA, can be put to many uses. The contrasting section may explain, embellish, emphasize, or contrast with the sentiment expressed on the opening music. When Sesto thinks to avenge the murder of his father, Pompey, he sings a classical "revenge" aria, full of martial sentiments:

> Svegliatevi nel core
> furie d'un alma offesa,
> a far d'un traditor
> aspra vendetta!

> (Awake in my heart,
> ye furies of an offended soul,
> to take upon a traitor
> bitter revenge!)

And in the second section he explains what it is that motivates him and why he must gather his courage (which he does when he sings the opening section again).

> L'ombra del genitore
> accore a mia difesa,
> e dice: a te il rigor
> figlio, aspetta!

> (The shade of my father
> hastens to my defense
> and says: it is expected of you,
> my son, to be merciless!)

The same arrangement works equally well for passionate, tender, lamenting, and rejoicing songs. It is a convention that admirably suits the chief objective of eighteenth-century opera, which was to express feelings in music.

There are other aspects of the conventional aria that Handel's audience would have understood and expected. One is that the repetition of the opening section, the da capo, gives the singer a perfect opportunity to augment the original music with ornaments suited to the singer's voice and to the emotional state being portrayed. Everybody waited for these moments, and informed listeners, who remembered the unadorned opening section, could appreciate the artistry and virtuosity of the singer in embellishing the da capo. When the singer was brilliant, the listeners applauded, and this applause was milked for all it was worth by having the libretto arranged in such a way that the singer exits after the aria. In the examples above, Caesar rages at Achilla and then leaves (amid tumultuous applause) for the palace. Later Sesto vows revenge ("Svegliatevi!"), and exits to take that revenge. And so on. If the applause is loud, the singer may return to acknowledge the public; and if it is long, the singer might even return to sing the aria a second time (regardless of the effect this may have on the plot) and make a second exit. This is, after all, why we came to the opera: not to learn about Julius Caesar but to hear our favorite singers in arias of exquisite beauty or dazzling virtuosity.

Occasionally an aria is not of the da capo type. Usually such an aria (often called a cavatina) is used at the entrance of a character who will remain on stage, as for Caesar's entrance at the beginning of act 1. Two further cavatinas are given to Cornelia, and in neither case does she exit.

Although the aria is the musical center of the opera, it is not the only thing that happens. There are, however, very few ensembles—duets, choruses, and the like. If there is a chorus, it is generally performed by members of the cast, not by a separate choral ensemble. In *Giulio Cesare* there are two choruses: the opening chorus of Egyptians acknowledging Caesar's victory (here surely sung offstage, since some of the singers, named in Handel's score, will very shortly need to appear as Cornelia, Sesto, and others) and a closing chorus of general rejoicing, this one sung by the principal characters. (Crowd scenes of this kind can really happen only at the very beginning of the opera, where they are revealed by the rising of the curtain, or at its end, when the curtain falls—the curtain remains up throughout the piece.) Choruses, when they are sung at all, are generally not very complicated and are far from being the great compositions that are the cornerstones of Handel's oratorios.

Occasionally there are duets. There are two in *Giulio Cesare,* beautifully placed to contrast with each other in emotion and to give each of the four principal characters a chance to participate. The first is a da capo duet of sorrow sung by Cornelia and her son Sesto to close the first act before they are led away to their separate punishments. And the third act is closed by a splendid love duet between Caesar and Cleopatra, just before the final chorus. The duets differ from arias only in that they show two characters simultaneously feeling the same emotions.

Only occasionally does anything interrupt the succession of recitatives followed by arias. These are generally moments of considerable intensity in which a single character may display more than one emotion. These moments occupy a middle ground between recitative and aria—they are more musical than recitative but not so structured and repeti-

This is one of several versions of a caricature painting, *Rehearsal of an Opera,* thought to be by Marco Ricci, a Venetian painter and set designer invited to London in 1708. Cello, double-bass, archlute, and harpsichord seem to be the instruments used for accompaniment. The scene may represent the practice room at the Haymarket Theatre shortly before Handel's arrival in England.

tive as an aria. Depending on their place on that middle ground, they may be labeled recitativo accompagnato (or simply accompagnato) when they are accompanied by the orchestra rather than the harpsichord, or arioso when they are more melodious. One such moment is Caesar's meditation on Pompey's urn. Opening a new scene in act 1, the wavering orchestral introduction, in the remote key of G-sharp minor, introduces a recitative, accompanied by strings, in which Caesar meditates on the changeability of human fortune (and goes as far afield musically as E-flat minor). It is one of the most remarkable moments of harmonic boldness in Handel. Charles Burney called this the "finest piece of accompanied Recitative, without intervening symphonies, with which I am acquainted. The modulation is learned, and so uncommon, that there is hardly a chord which the ear expects." Caesar has another such scene in the third act, when he has swum the harbor and saved himself but not, he thinks, his army and his love. And Cleopatra, too, has her scene of accompagnato followed by aria when she hears of the conspiracy against Caesar and expresses horror, anger, sadness, and love.

Generally, though, we expect arias and lots of them, and we expect each to bring a scene to a close with the exit of its singer.

ACTING

Senesino comes downstage center, and so we know that he is about to sing. This is where the singer stands in almost all cases, even when an aria is addressed to another character. Where else should he stand? He is, after all, singing to the audience at least as much as to Curio, and we want to be able to see and hear him clearly.

The acting here is no more naturalistic than it is in most theatrical traditions, where actors always need to be seen and heard. But in the eighteenth century there was a highly stylized code of acting, clearly understood by the audience, that was part of a tradition stretching back at least to the sixteenth century and continuing well into the nineteenth.

Posture, gesture, and the relationship of actors to the audience and to each other told audience members everything they needed to know. Stage position relates the characters to each other; because the stage is raked, a position upstage places the character physically above the others—this is the place for kings and emperors; stage right is nobler than stage left. We can tell a great deal about relationships from the physical arrangements of actors, and knowing these conventions makes it easy for actors to know where to go and what to do.

The postures of the body were those of the dance. From the feet to the top of the head the body was held always in an appropriate posture. Feet were never parallel: one was always forward of the other; hips were not in line with the feet, nor shoulders with the hips; the head was not in line with the shoulders. Arranging feet, hips, shoulders, and head, provided for an enormous variety of curves, contrapposto, reverse curves, and other expressive positions. The arms, held at the sides when not speaking, were never at the same level; the hands were held with the middle and ring fingers together, the others somewhat spread; alternative positions for the hands included having each separated finger, starting with the extended thumb, progressively more curved; or—in the manner of preachers and lawyers and others making a point—the thumb and index finger making a circle, with the other fingers extended.

The head was turned toward the interlocutor but never more than a quarter turn away from the audience; a speaker was not to be seen in profile. The eyes looked toward the person addressed so that a curve from shoulders to head to eyes created a strong sense of direction, though the actor still faced the audience.

There was a repertory of conventional gestures that accompanied what was being said; gesture was especially used in recitative, whereas in an aria the singer generally struck a single expressive posture that could be altered for the singing of the second section of the aria or for the singer to address a second person.

Father Franciscus Lang's 1727 treatise on acting, *Dissertatio de actione scenica,* gives all sorts of specific advice, in Latin. In this illustration from the book we see an actor, in classical armor, obeying many rules: feet apart, one forward; weight on one leg; feet, hips, shoulders, and head never aligned but in some sort of curve; arms at different levels; hand held properly with thumb out and fingers progressively curved; face forward, never turned more than a quarter turn.

Gestures were delivered to emphasize and underscore important words and concepts as they were spoken (actually, an instant before they were spoken to give punctuation to the word as it arrived); they ranged from gestures relating to the self (heart, resolve, sadness, and so on) to those involving others to gestures involving third persons, objects, and concepts.

This was a heroic style of acting, befitting the noble characters in this and other operas. If it seems stiff and overstylized, it is perhaps because we are not fully aware of all its expressiveness (and because we seldom see it done well).

It was a style well known to Handel's contemporaries. Colley Cibber described the superb acting of the castrato Nicolo Grimaldi, known as Nicolini, who sang in London from 1708 to 1717, performing in Bononcini's *Camilla,* Handel's *Rinaldo* and *Amadigi,* and Mancini's *Idaspe fedele:* "Nicolini sets off the Character he bears in an Opera, by his Action, as much as he does the Words of it by his Voice; every limb and finger contributes to the part he acts, insomuch that a deaf Man might go along with him in the Sense of it. There is scarce a beautiful Posture, in an old Statue, which he does not plant himself in, as the different Circumstances of the story give occasion for it.—He performs the most ordinary Action, in a manner suitable to the Greatness of his Character, and shews the Prince, even in the giving of a Letter, or dispatching a Message, etc."

Caesar has entered, along with Curio and "Attendants." There are plenty of super-numeraries in this opera and others: soldiers, "one of the guard," child attendants for noblewomen. They add grandeur, scope, and importance, though they sometimes are mocked; Joseph Addison commented in the *Spectator,* "Another mechanical method of making great Men, and adding Dignity to Kings and Queens, is to accompany them with Halberts and Battle-Axes. Two or three Shifters of Scenes, with the two Candle-Snuffers, make up a compleat Body of Guards upon the *English* Stage; and by the Addition of a few Porters dress'd in red Coats, can represent above a dozen legions."

Caesar is the great Senesino, a superb singer and one of the reigning stars of the opera. In fact, he is the star of every opera produced by the Royal Academy: he earns his very high salary. Born Francesco Bernardi in Siena (Senesino means "the little Sienese"), he is one of the great Italian castrati. He had been hired by Handel in Dresden for the 1720 season at the enormous salary of 3,000 guineas.

Senesino's vocal range was relatively narrow, and Handel accommodated this, along with his virtuosity in florid passages, in the seventeen roles that he wrote for him. Senesino was described in the newspaper as "beyond all criticism" for his performance in *Giulio Cesare.* The eighteenth-century music historian John Hawkins wrote that "in the pronunciation of recitative he had not his fellow in Europe." And Charles Burney reported that he was unsurpassed in the accompanied recitatives in *Giulio Cesare,* especially "Alma del gran Pompeo," which Burney said "had an effect, when recited on the stage by Senesino, which no Recitative, or even Air, had before, in this country." Johann Joachim Quantz, who heard Sensino at Dresden in 1719, described his voice:

> Senesino had a well-carrying, clear, even, and pleasantly low soprano voice (mezzo soprano), a pure intonation and a beautiful trillo. He rarely sang above the fifth line "f." His way of singing was masterful, and his execution perfect. He did not overload the slow movements with arbitrary ornamentation, but brought out the essential ornaments with the greatest finesse. He sang an allegro with fire, and he knew how to thrust out the running passages with his chest with some speed. His figure was quite favorable for the theatre, and his acting was quite natural. The role of a hero suited him better than that of a lover.

Senesino was a star, and he took a star's prerogative to disagree with Handel. In 1733 he joined with a rival company, the Opera of the Nobility, making a decisive break with Handel after many years of collaboration. Horace Walpole in 1740 met the aging and wealthy Senesino in his chaise: "We thought it a fat old woman; but it spoke in a shrill little pipe, and proved itself to be Senesino."

But Senesino is now at the height of his power, and he comes downstage and sings "Presto omai," requiring Egypt to recognize its conqueror. The power is there in the

JULIUS CÆSAR.
ACT I.

SCENE I. A Plain in *Egypt*, with an old Bridge over a Branch of the *Nile*.

C ÆS A R *and* C U R I U S *paſſing over the Bridge with Attendants.*

C H O R U S of *Egyptians.*

L I V E Great Alcides, let Nile rejoice
(this happy Day :
Each Shore appears to ſmile,
Our Troubles vaniſh,
And our Joys return.
Cæſ. Let Egypt's Laurels wreath the Con-
(queror's Brows.

*Curius : Cæſar no ſooner came, but ſaw and conquer'd :
Pompey now ſubdu'd, in vain endeavours to ſupport him-
ſelf, by joining with the King of Egypt.*
*Cur. You timely interpos'd to croſs his Purpoſe ; but who
comes toward us ?*

SCENE

GIULIO CESARE.
ATTO I.

SCENA I. *Campagna d' Egitto con an-
tico Ponte ſopra un Ramo del Nilo.*

C E S A R E *e* C U R I O, *che paſſano il Ponte con ſeguito.*

C O R O *di Egizzi.*

V I V A viva il noſtro Alcide,
Goda il Nilo in queſto dì.
Ogni ſpiaggia per Lui ride,
Ogni affanno già ſparì.
Ceſ. Preſti omai l'Egizzia Terra
Le ſue palme al Vincitor.

Curio Ceſare venne, e vide, e vinſe :
Già ſconfitto Pompeo, invan ricorre
Per rinforzar de' ſuoi Guerrier lo ſtuolo
D' Egitto al Re.
Cur. Tu quì Signor giungeſti
A tempo appunto a prevenir le trame :
Ma ! Chi ver noi ſen' viene ?

B 3   SCENA

The libretto of *Giulio Cesare* offers English and Italian versions of the text. Generous stage directions help set the scene, and typography distinguishes recitatives from songs and choruses.

music, and in the voice. This song, unusually, is not a da capo aria but a staccato pronouncement of Caesar's order that Egypt should bow down. It provides Senesino with a trumpetlike opening; with elaborate ornaments in his relatively narrow range; with a very long note on which he can display his fabulous *messa di voce* (a swelling and lessening of volume on a single note); and with a moment for a cadenza. Handel's music is perfectly tailored to his skill.

From here on the standard Baroque theatrical arrangement leads us further into the plot. The opera is essentially a series of arias preceded by recitatives, but from a dramatic point of view it is a series of short scenes, each provoked by the arrival or departure of somebody, until at last the stage is empty, the scene shifts, and we begin again. When Caesar is finished with his triumphant song, there's not much to do. He turns to Curio and says his famous "veni, vidi, vici" ("Curio, Cesare venne e vide e vinse"). Curio points out that Caesar can foil the defeated Pompey's plan to appeal to King Ptolemy for help (information that helps us set the scene), and then, just in time to move the plot, he says, "But who is this I see coming?" and Caesar helpfully says, "It is Cornelia." Cornelia, widow of Pompey, arrives with her son Sesto, and a new scene takes place. This will give rise to arias by both the newcomers, and everybody will have occasion to leave the stage.

One of the most tiresome things in writing and reading about opera is the summaries of the plot that seem always necessary—especially for Baroque opera—but are wearisome to the reader because the plot by itself, without the adjuncts of music, scenery, movement, very often seems hopelessly confused and silly. In this case we might dispense with the plot summary by considering the general shape of the first act in order to see that the plot is a beautifully crafted mechanism for providing entrances and exits, an alternation of settings, and a series of emotional crises that provoke beautiful arias. Each musical moment is a reaction to what has just happened; it is a sort of freeze-frame in the course of a movie. The emotion that an aria expresses usually provokes its character to leave on some mission or other. The characters who remain continue (sometimes with the arrival of fresh news) until a further emotion is discharged in an aria. And so on until nobody is left on stage.

Table 2 summarizes the sets, action, music, and entrances and exits in act 1. Sets alternate full-depth scenes with shallow ones behind which the next set can be prepared. The table allows us to see how carefully made each scene is; entrances are marked with arrows at the left, exits with arrows at the right. Counting arrows makes clear that each of the four settings provides occasion for various entrances, and that before the set-change everybody who entered has left, usually after singing an aria.

Note, too, that the characters are given music and placement in order of their importance—that is, the great singers have the great roles and the most arias. It's a matter of some complexity to produce a plot that gives the stars absolutely equal billing, exactly the same number of arias, and that gives the subsidiary characters enough so that they sing in each act and we remember who they are. The distribution of arias works as well to show off this star system within each act as it does in the opera as a whole.

Requirements for Librettists, from a Letter of September 7, 1724, by Giuseppe Riva

For this year and for the next two, there must be in operas two equal parts for Cuzzoni and Faustina. Senesino is the leading male character, and his part must be heroic. The other three male parts must go gradually one by one, one aria in each act. The duet should be at the end of the second act, between the two women. If the subject should have three women, it can be done, for there is a third.

Table 1. Arias in *Giulio Cesare*

	Act 1	Act 2	Act 3	Total
Caesar	4	2+duet	2+duet	8+duets
Cleopatra	3	3+duet	2+duet	8+duets
Cornelia	1+cav. +duet	1+cav.	1	3+2cav. +duet
Sesto	1+duet	1	1	3+duet
Achilla	1	1	1	3
Tolomeo	1	1	1	3

The distribution of arias among the characters, and among the acts, is shown in Table 1. Note that Caesar and Cleopatra have the same number of arias and duets. Each also has a special moment: in act 2, Cleopatra as Lidia is revealed in a mountain, and, in act 3, Caesar has his spectacular combination of recitative and aria ("Dall ondoso periglio") when he recounts his escape by swimming the harbor. Everybody else sings one song in each act, with the role of Cornelia enriched with two cavatinas and a duet with Sesto.

The first act has provided all the characters and the main themes of the story. Cleopatra will seduce Caesar and will fall in love with him. This provides the occasion for a splendid series of songs on the subject of love. Cornelia and Sesto provide a subplot: various characters try to seduce the noble Cornelia, and Sesto is committed to avenging the death of his father. This provides occasions for noble lament and virile vengeance on the part of the young boy. Both plots come together neatly at the end.

THE PLAYERS

Senesino is the male lead and the highest-paid member of the company. But we may have come to hear La Cuzzoni as Cleopatra.

Francesca Cuzzoni was twenty-six years old in 1724, married to the composer and harpsichordist Pietro Giuseppe Sandoni. She began singing in London the previous year, and her début in Handel's *Ottone* was a sensation. The *British Journal,* anticipating her arrival, reported that "as 'tis said, she far excells Seigniora Durastante, already with us, and all those she leaves in Italy behind her, much Satisfaction may be expected by those who of later Years have contributed largely to Performances of this Kind, for the great Advantage of the Publick, and softening the Manners of a rude British people." Cuzzoni is the soprano whom Handel threatened to throw out the window if she refused to sing his arias his way. She was paid 2,000 pounds a season—not at Senesino's level, but still a star.

Cuzzoni had a large following among the audience; at first her supporters compared her favorably with Senesino. After 1726 a great rivalry grew up between Cuzzoni and Faustina Bordoni, which by 1727 culminated in a catfight on stage. "But who," wrote John Arbuthnot,

Table 2. Entrances, Arias, and Exits in Act 1 of *Giulio Cesare*

Set 1: The Bridge (long set)
→   Caesar
→   Curio
        Aria (Caesar): "Presto omai"
           Caesar has triumphed; Cornelia is identified: Curio once loved her.
→   Cornelia
→   Sesto
        They sue for peace
→   Achilla
        He brings gifts and invites Caesar to Ptolemy's palace. Pompey's head is shown. Caesar reacts:
        Aria (Caesar): "Empio dirò"   →
                (Achilla)   →
        Cornelia, who has fainted, tries to kill herself; Curio restrains her, and leaves when his declaration of love is spurned.
                (Curio)
        Cornelia laments   →
        Aria (Cornelia) "Priva son"   →
        Sesto vows revenge
        Aria (Sesto) "Svegliatevi"   →

Set 2: Gabinetto (short set)
→   Cleopatra
        She extols her greatness.
→   Nireno
        He reports that Ptolemy has sent Pompey's head to Caesar; she resolves to charm Caesar and gain the throne.
→   Tolomeo
        He scorns her; she retorts with an aria.
        Aria (Cleopatra) "Non disperar"   →
                (Nireno)   →
→   Achilla
        He reports Caesar's displeasure; he promises to deliver Caesar in return for the beautiful Cornelia. Ptolemy rages against Caesar.
        Aria (Tolomeo) "L'empio, sleale"   →
                (Achilla)   →

Set 3: Caesar's camp (long set)
→   Caesar
        He reflects on Pompey's head.

Accomp. ("Alma")

→ Curio

> He reports the arrival of Cleopatra (disguised as Lidia).

→ Cleopatra (disguised)
→ Nireno

> Both Caesar and Curio are charmed by "Lidia," servant of Cleopatra.
> Caesar sings her praises.

Aria (Caesar) "Non è si vago" →

(Curio) →

> She exults in her deceit of Caesar.

Aria (Cleopatra) "Tutto può" →(but "held back" by Nireno)

→ Cornelia

> She laments over her husband's head, and vows vengeance:

Arioso (Cornelia) "Nel tuo seno"

→ Sesto

> He stops her: vengeance if for him to accomplish. "Lidia" offers to take
> them to Caesar. Before they leave Sesto expresses his hope of prompt
> revenge.

Aria (Sesto) "Caro speme" →

(Cornelia) →

(Nireno) →

> Cleopatra, alone, sings of her own hope of the kingdom.

Aria (Cleopatra) "Tu la mia stella" →

Set 4: Court in Ptolemy's palace (short set)

→ Caesar
→ Ptolemey
→ Achilla

> Ptolemy welcomes a suspicious Caesar, who recognizes deceit and sings
> of it.

Aria (Caesar) "Va tacito" →

→ Cornelia
→ Sesto

> Cornelia and Sesto challenge Ptolemy; charmed with Cornelia, he sends
> Sesto to prison, her to the seraglio (where Achilla can admire her).

(Ptolemy) →

> Achilla offers liberty in exchange for marriage; Cornelia chooses prison.
> Achilla sings his love.

Aria (Achilla) "Tu sei il cor" →

> They sing their sadness before being led away.

Duet (Cornelia, Sesto) "Son nato" →
→

FRANCESCA CUZZONI SANDONI,

DA PARMA.

Francesca Cuzzoni, who played Cleopatra in *Giulio Cesare,* was the reigning female opera star until the arrival of Faustina Bordoni in 1726. She was renowned more for her singing than for her appearance or acting, but to succeed as Cleopatra, as she did, required voice, looks, and acting.

"would have thought the Infection should reach the Haymarket, and inspire two Singing Ladies to pull each other's coiffs? . . . It is certainly an apparent Shame that two such well bred Ladies should call Bitch and Whore, should scold and fight like Billingates."

But in 1724, Cuzzoni was peerless. She was especially admired for her expression and cantabile singing; she had good high notes, to judge from the part that Handel wrote for her, and there are plenty of opportunities to use her famous trill. The role of Cleopatra provides a great variety of expressions, from the sly, scheming politician to the seductive role of Lidia to the triumphant queen. It certainly provides an enormous range of emotional attitudes, and it must have contributed much to Cuzzoni's reputation.

Johann Joachim Quantz, the flutist, composer, and author, heard Cuzzoni in 1727: "Her style of singing was innocent and affecting; her graces did not seem artificial, from the easy and neat manner in which she executed them: however, they took possession of the soul of every auditor, by her tender and touching expression. She had no great rapidity of execution, in allegros; but there was a roundness and smoothness, which were neat and pleasing. Yet with all these advantages, it must be owned that she was rather cold in her action, and her figure was not advantageous for the stage."

Burney was at particular pains to describe Cuzzoni's technical mastery:

It was difficult for the hearer to determine whether she most excelled in slow or rapid airs. A native warble enabled her to execute divisions with such facility as to conceal every appearance of difficulty; and so grateful and touching was the natural tone of her voice, that she rendered pathetic whatever she sung, in which she had leisure to unfold its whole volume. The art of conducting, sustaining, increasing, and diminishing her tones by minute degrees, acquired her, among professors, the title of complete mistress of her art. In a cantabile air, though the notes she

Three of the singers of *Giulio Cesare* appear in this caricature
in Handel's *Flavio* (1723), possibly by John Vanderbank. The towering
Gaetano Berenstadt (Tolomeo in *Giulio Cesare*) and the imposing
Senesino (Caesar) flank Francesca Cuzzoni (Cleopatra), who was
described as "short and squat." This illustration gives a good idea
of suitable costume for operas on classical Roman subjects.

added were few, she never lost a favourable opportunity of enriching
the cantilena with all the refinements and embellishments of the time.
Her shake was perfect, she had a creative fancy, and the power of occasionally accelerating and retarding the measure in the most artificial and
able manner, by what the Italians call *tempo rubato*. Her high notes were
unrivalled in clearness and sweetness; and her intonations were so just
and fixed, that it seemed as if it was not in her power to sing out of tune.

Walpole described Cuzzoni in Handel's *Rodelinda,* making it clear that her appeal
must have been in her music and not her acting: "She was short and squat, with a doughy
cross face, but fine complexion; was not a good actress; dressed ill; and was silly and fantastical. And yet on her appearing in this opera, in a brown silk gown, trimmed with silver, with the vulgarity and indecorum of which all the old ladies were much scandalised,
the young adopted it as a fashion, so universally, that it seemed a national uniform for
youth and beauty." Gaetano Berenstadt, appearing here as Tolomeo, respected her singing

but not her character, according to his letter to a friend in Italy: "If Cuzzoni's behavior were as good as her singing, she would be a divine thing; but, unluckily for her and ruinous for any who associate with her, she is mad, unpredictable, and—what is worse—always without a halfpenny, even with a salery of 1,500 guineas a year."

The other roles in the opera are played by singers of professional competence but not of the star level of Senesino and Cuzzoni.

Cornelia, the noble and plaintive Roman matron, was played by the thirty-two-year-old Anastasia Robinson. She was the daughter of a painter and not originally a professional musician: she had sung in her father's house in Golden Square and elsewhere, turning professional when he lost his sight. She began as a soprano but by the 1720s was a contralto, perhaps as the result of an illness. Her salary is thought to have been about 1,000 pounds a year. Shortly after *Giulio Cesare* she retired from the stage, having secretly married the aged Earl of Peterborough two years earlier (she had long been his mistress). The arrival of Cuzzoni may have hastened her departure from the stage. Her range was not very wide, and she was not burdened with much coloratura. Her part here, as often elsewhere, is highly emotional, requiring a nobility of carriage and a pathos of expression.

Sesto, he of the many vengeance arias, was sung by the Italian soprano Margherita Durastanti. Now about thirty-five, she had worked with Handel for a long time; she had met him in Rome years earlier, where she had sung in Handel's early oratorio *La resurrezione* (until the pope objected and she was replaced with a male singer). Handel had hired her for the company in 1720; her salary in 1721 was 1,100 pounds (in the same year King George I stood godfather to her daughter). This was to be Durastanti's last season (although she did return briefly to the stage in 1733–34). In 1724 she was described as a "woman already old, whose voice is both mediocre and worn out." Burney said her "person was coarse and masculine"; the librettist Paolo Antonio Rolli described her as being an elephant. Her roles were usually dramatic, and sometimes, as here, those of men. She must have been a good actress, for she made a distinct impression on the stage.

Tolomeo was played by the alto castrato Gaetano Berenstadt, born in Italy of German parents. Berenstadt was titanically tall ("an evirato of a huge unwieldy figure," said Burney), and he is easily recognized in pictures. He had a substantial German and Italian career before singing two seasons with the Royal Academy as a second man to Senesino. By 1724, at the age of about twenty-five, his voice might already have been fading. Like most castrati, his range was not very wide, but his voice was flexible.

Achilla was the baritone Giuseppe Maria Boschi, about thirty years old. He had first sung in London in 1710–11. Handel had engaged him for the Royal Academy, and he sang in almost every opera produced there. He was evidently a very useful second-rank singer. Boschi seems to have specialized in agitated and warlike arias (as seems typical of bass roles)—he seldom sings tender or slow songs. A poet's line from the time reads: "and Boschi-like be always in a rage." Handel wrote arias for Achilla that feature big leaps, particularly suitable for agitation (but used too in his awkward courting of Cornelia) and also, apparently, for Boschi's voice.

Nireno, who gets no aria at all, was sung by the alto castrato Giuseppe Bigonzi,

Anastasia Robinson, who played Cornelia in *Giulio Cesare,* was secretly married to the Earl of Peterborough, who is said to have caned Senesino for coming a little too close to Robinson in a rehearsal.

who had been engaged for this season to replace the tenor Gordon. Nireno moves the plot along, but there is little evidence that Bigonzi impressed the world much with his musical talent.

Curio, a Roman tribune who is present mostly to give Caesar somebody to address, was sung by the bass Lagarde. He never gets to sing an aria, though he stirs the plot with his love for the beautiful Cornelia. The son of the painter and baritone Laguerre, the young Lagarde (probably about twenty-one) sang a few small roles in Italian opera; mostly he performed in lighter ballad operas, pantomimes, and afterpieces. In his later years he worked as a scene painter and published engravings on theatrical subjects.

Secondary roles were carefully kept secondary. As Burney put it, "There must be, in every drama, inferior characters, voices, and abilities; and to make a hero of every attendant, would be as injudicious as to degrade the real great personages of the piece to a level with their domestics. If all the airs of an opera were equally laboured and excellent, the Music would be monotonous, and all abilities confounded."

IN THE THEATER: HANDEL, SINGING, AND THE MUSIC

Handel, presiding at one of two harpsichords, was so lively in his playing and conducting that he attracted attention himself. At a premiere the audience was sure to be attentive during most of the evening, and to applaud at the end of every aria. The singer's exit provided the invitation, and the rivalries that existed between the supporters of one singer and another were enough to generate applause even when the performance itself might not have been Senesino's or Cuzzoni's best. Sometimes long and loud applause would stop the show, and the aria would be repeated. Management tried to suppress this practice: beginning in 1714 this appeared on opera bills: "Whereas by the frequent calling for

"A full & true Account of the proceedings
of the Royal Academy of Music anno 1723"

The matter thus happily brought to Conclusion,
Up Burlington started, & made new Confusion;
For in he brought Berenst—head, shoulders and all.
And swore he could sing well, because he was tall.

With submission, says Bruce, his height I admit,
And will have him sing, for his learning and wit:
At which the Lord Stair was provoked to Ire,
And said high notes did not high persons require.

As witness Cuzzoni, cry'd Peterbro's Earl,
Who sings high & sweet, tho' a very low Girl.
Now least the debate should grow languid & scanty,
Some nam'd Senesino, & some Durastanti.

But for what, I ha'nt heard. Then Pult'ney arose,
And he told us nothing, but sure Pult'ney knows.
And so they went on, about this debate,
Till they found they knew nothing, but that it grew late.

the songs again, the operas have been too tedious; therefore, the singers are forbidden to sing any song above once; and it is hoped nobody will call for 'em, or take it ill, when not obeyed."

In later runs of an opera, subscribers and boxholders paid attention only part of the time; some attention was given to eating, talking, card playing, and other amusements. A nobleman might come to the front of his box to attend to a favorite aria or singer and then retire for other amusement. Generally the applause was for the aria; there was not applause for the work as a whole.

There was a great deal to notice in this opera, even for those who had ears only for Senesino or who were so familiar with the rituals of Italian serious opera that nothing could surprise them. For one thing, Handel's music stands out in its strength and passion. There is an energy and aptness in his music that outstrips that of his rivals. It is not that his music is overcomposed, that it has (perhaps like that of his contemporary Johann Sebastian Bach) more in it that the listener can possibly comprehend at a single hearing. Rather, it provides forward motion, a variety of accompanimental figuration, a wealth of melody that none of Handel's contemporaries could match. But it is, at the same time, music for the theater. There is nothing that the listener can't hear and appreciate. Handel's listeners were used to the opera, and they knew a "rage" aria or a "simile" aria when they heard one. The listener, then, wanted to see how Handel could give yet another bass an opportunity to express raging passion for revenge with lively figuration and agitated melody in a way that was new but comparable with other examples of the genre. Likewise, when a singer says that she is like a river or a bird or a pilot in a storm, we listen to see how well Handel can give in music a picture of this simile. And we enjoy Caesar's aria in the third act, when he resolves to return to Ptolemy's palace and like an alpine torrent crush the conspiracy that almost cost him his life:

> Quel torrente che cade dal monte
> tutta atterra che incontro gli sta.
> Tale anch'io, a chi oppone la fronte:
> dal mio brando atterrato sarà.

> (The torrent that falls from the mountain
> sweeps away everything in its path;
> So shall I, to whoever opposes me:
> by my sword he shall fall to the ground.)

An aria typically begins with the orchestra (while the singer comes downstage), and a listener might well try to guess what the subject, the passion, of the song is to be. (It is always possible to cheat by looking ahead in the word-book.) How will this inventive music be related to the singing? Will the singer sing this tune? Or will this be an accompaniment to something yet to be announced by the singer? Sometimes the orchestra gives a picture of the image: the rushing torrent, the clangor of arms, the hidden bird. Often the orchestra begins with a tune that will be sung to the opening text of the song, and then it will return many, many times, in wonderful combinations of voice with instruments. And always it will set the mood, the emotional stance, of the song.

The orchestra itself, despite its "fracas," is one of the most varied and splendid ever used by Handel. It has grand instrumental movements (representing battles and triumphant fanfares) and arias with instrumental solos for horn (very rare in Handel), oboe, and violin. (The bird-song violin aria, Caesar's "Se in fiorito ameno prato," took on a life of its own, as did many others.) Three months after the premiere, on May 8, 1724, at the New Haymarket Theatre, the oboist Mr. Kitch, who liked to play the vocal parts of arias as instrumental solos, included "a solo Song out of the Opera of Julius Caesar, the Song Part by Mr Kitch, the Violin by the Youth [John Clegg, the beneficiary of the concert], as done by Sig. Castrucci in the Opera."

And there are other novelties. The opening chorus, which sings during the minuet of the overture, and the chorus of conspirators who begin before the close of Caesar's "Al lampo dell'armi" are elements of surprise. Most striking is the miraculous scene in act 2, in which Caesar hears an unearthly music made by an orchestra backstage including such

Ti caro caro Si — *Ti Stringo* — *al fin così* — *Nel Seno amato*

Senesino and Cuzzoni in the last scene of Handel's *Admeto* (1727).
This anonymous engraving caricatures Cuzzoni's embrace of Senesino
as she sings, "Yes, beloved, yes, finally I embrace you thus, on the
beloved breast." The engraving is on the title page of a printed letter
claiming to be from Senesino to Cuzzoni.

remarkable (and archaic) instruments as harp, theorbo, and viola da gamba. He takes it for the harmony of the spheres; as the pit orchestra joins in, the mountain is opened to reveal Cuzzoni as Cleopatra disguised as Lidia dressed as Virtue, surrounded by the nine muses (supernumeraries miming the music) as she sings "V'adoro, pupille," a song that was instantly famous. This is an attempt to seduce Caesar (and it works), but it is also a pretext for some unearthly and beautiful music. It is also a rare instance of singing upstage of the proscenium arch.

If we care anything about the plot and the drama we are surely pleased to have a story about historical characters we already know: Caesar and Cleopatra. There is much less confusion and intrigue in this libretto than in many others, and we are able to trace the growth of the love affair, as well as the complexities of character that Handel depicts. Cleopatra in particular becomes more and more human as we learn, aria by aria, about her character. The modern Handel scholar Winton Dean (who knows Handelian opera probably better than anyone did in Handel's day) describes the characterizations in *Giulio Cesare* like this:

Cleopatra has eight arias, besides two magnificent accompanied recitatives and a duet. They show her in an infinite variety of moods, teasing her brother Tolomeo about his love affairs, confident in the compelling power of her beauty, setting out to seduce Caesar with a tableau of the Muses on Mount Parnassus, praying to Venus to aid her amorous designs, uttering a more urgent prayer when Caesar is attacked by conspirators, lamenting her fate and threatening to haunt Tolomeo when he has captured her and she thinks Caesar is dead, and finally rejoicing in her conquest of the conqueror of the world. Unlike Cornelia she cannot be described as tragic or heroic, but she is one of the great characters of opera, an immortal sex-kitten whose emotions, if ephemeral, are obsessive while they last.

The other characters, too, emerge in the course of the opera. Sesto develops from a youth into a warrior who avenges his father's murder. The grieving widow Cornelia achieves tranquil resignation through the exploits of her son. And Caesar does survive his trials, military and amorous, to be reunited with a delighted Cleopatra. The final scene, preceded by a splendid sinfonia with grand horn solos, concludes with a beautiful jig of a duet for Caesar and Cleopatra, a grand chorus in dance tempo, and a further duet for the principals accompanied by oboes. The curtain closes on Senesino and Cuzzoni and the others, and the applause.

Reactions

Giulio Cesare was a success, to judge from the thirteen performances—more than any other opera of the season—and successive revivals; there were ten performances the next season and further revivals in 1730 and 1732. It was reported in the *Mercure de France* that even the Italians considered the opera a masterpiece. The poet John Byrom, who wrote the Bononcini jingle, saw *Giulio Cesare* on February 29 and was not so impressed: "I was engaged to dine at Mrs. de Vlieger's on Saturday, whence they all went to the opera of Julius Caesar, and I for one. Mr. Leycester sat by me in the front row of the gallery, for we both were there to get good places betimes; it was the first entertainment of this nature that I ever saw, and will I hope be the last, for of all the diversions of the town I least of all enter into this." A Monsieur de Fabrice reported in a letter of March 10 on the opera's success: "The opera is in full swing also, since Handell's new one, called *Jules César*—in which Cenesino and Cozzuna shine beyond all criticism—has been put on. The house was just as full at the seventh performance as at the first."

Those who liked opera seemed to think more about the singing than about the story, and they certainly spent little time considering whether opera itself was an art form different from and somehow greater than the combination of poetry, narrative, and music. Burney, who gives detailed discussions of all Handel's London operas, barely mentions story or plot; he refers to the singers by their names, not their characters; and describes what he thinks to be the best songs in each opera. His view is probably typical of most of Handel's audience.

While the opera was still running, music from *Giulio Cesare* began to appear in concerts and drawing rooms. On March 27 a concert at the Haymarket Theatre, for a Mr. Johnson, included "Three songs out of Julius Caesar, performed [on oboe] by Kytch." And a concert on May 8, mentioned above, included a song from the opera "as done by Sig. Castrucci in the Opera."

The music was printed almost immediately, in competing editions. A publication by Cluer and Creake was announced in May 1725, and in June it was advertised as being "Curiously engrav'd on Copper Plates Corrected and Figur'd by Mr Handel's own Hands; there fore beware of incorrect pirated Editions done on large Pewter Plates." The edition we are being warned of is the pirated edition by the prolific publisher John Walsh. Handel's operas were generally published, but usually only as collections of songs containing the arias only, without orchestrations and without the recitatives. They would not be useful for someone wishing to produce the opera, but they could have good sales to persons

---

From *Faustina: or the Roman Songstress, A Satyr, on the Luxury and Effeminacy of the Age* (1726)

BRITONS! for shame, give all these Follies o'er,
The ancient British Nobleness restore: . . .
They talk not of our Army, or our Fleet,
But of the Warble of CUZZONI sweet,
Of the delicious Pipe of SENESINO,
And of the squalling Trill of HARLEQUINO,
Who, were they English, with united Rage,
Themselves would justly hiss from off the Stage:
With better Voice, and fifty times Her Skill,
Poor R[OBINSON] is always treated ill:
But, such is the good Nature of the Town,
'Tis now the Mode to cry the English down. . . .
I hate this Singing in an unknown Tongue,
It does our Reason and our Senses wrong;
When Words instruct, and Music chears the Mind:
Then is the Art of Service to Mankind;
But when a Foreign Ox, of monstrous Size!
Squeaks out at Treble, Shrill as Infants cries,
I curse the unintelligible Ass,
Who may, for aught I know, be singing Mass.

This drawing by Marco Ricci shows the plumed Senesino
on stage with Faustina Bordoni, the soprano who rivaled
Francesca Cuzzoni and set off enormous factional diatribes.

wishing to use them in concert or parlor performances of the songs. A flute arrangement
of *Giulio Cesare* was published by Cluer in the summer of 1724, evidently for the use of
amateurs; the second volume of Cluer's *Pocket Companion* (1725) included ten songs from
the opera.

The musical world was finely attuned to what was going on in the international
world of Italian opera. *Giulio Cesare* was immediately popular in Germany, being produced as early as 1725 in Braunschweig. It had later productions in Paris and Hamburg.
But pamphleteers, favoring one singer or another, or objecting to opera or to Handel or
to all these things, kept the popular press warm with operatic opinion. This would burst
into flame a year later with the arrival of Faustina Bordoni and the warfare over leading
parts. But that is another—and a very good—story.

At the revival of 1732, Senesino had just uttered the boast "Cesare non seppe
mai, che sia timore" ("Caesar does not know what fear is") when "a Piece of the Machinery tumbled down from the Roof of the Theatre upon the Stage just as Senesino had
chanted forth these words. . . . The poor Hero was so frightened, that he trembled, lost
his Voice, and fell a-crying."

HANDEL, *GIULIO CESARE*

Documents: *Giulio Cesare*

I have often heard travellers and scholars declare that London is undoubtedly the largest and most populous city in the whole of Europe. The city is ten miles long from Millbank to Blackwall, and its width is about three miles from Southwark to Moorfields; it contains more than one million inhabitants. The streets are long, wide, and straight, some of them being more than a mile in length. On either side of the street the ground is raised and paved with flat stones, so that you can walk in the streets without danger of being knocked down by coaches and horses. The City of London itself is not very large, being only three miles in circumference. It is inclosed by stone walls and has gates; but so many houses have been built around, especially on the western side, that London has been joined to Westminster, which latter place was formerly two miles distant. The space between consisted of fields and pastures, but now is part of the town. That which is surrounded by walls is called the City, and is almost entirely inhabited by merchants; the other part of London is called the liberty of Westminster, and here you will find the Court, and the residences of the peers and noblemen and of other persons of distinction. . . . (pp. 22–23)

Do not expect me to describe to you all the streets of London. I should have too much to do, and we should get tired of one another. A number of them are dirty, narrow, and badly built; others again are wide and straight, bordered with fine houses. Most of the streets are wonderfully well lighted, for in front of each house hangs a lantern or a large globe of glass, inside of which is placed a lamp which burns all night. Large houses have two of these lamps suspended outside their doors by iron supports, and some have even four. The streets of London are unpleasantly full either of dust or of mud. This arises from the quantity of houses that are continually being built, and also from the large number of coaches and chariots rolling in the streets day and night. Carts are used for removing mud, and in the summer time the streets are watered by carts carrying barrels, or casks, pierced with holes, through which water flows. . . . (p. 42)

The houses are of bricks; the walls are thin, most of them having only one foot and a half thickness. The finest houses sometimes have cornices and borders to divide the floors, and round the doors and windows you occasionally see a sort of polished marble. In all the newly-built quarters the houses have one floor made in the earth, containing the kitchens, offices, and servants' rooms. This floor is well lighted, and has as much air as the others have. In order to accomplish this a sort of moat, five or six feet in width and eight or nine deep, is dug in front of all the houses, and is called the "area." This moat is edged on the side next the street with an iron railing. The cellars and vaults where coal is stored are very strongly built beneath the streets, and to reach them you cross the area. Hangings are little used in London houses on account of the coal smoke, which would ruin them, besides which woodwork is considered to be cleaner and prevents damp on the walls. Almost all the houses have little gardens or courtyards at the back. . . . (p. 43)

The four streets—the Strand, Fleet Street, Cheapside, and Cornhill—are, I imagine, the finest in Europe. What help to make them interesting and attractive are the shops and the signs. Every house, or rather every shop, has a sign of copper, pewter, or wood painted and gilt. Some of these signs are really magnificent, and have cost as much as one hundred pounds sterling; they hang on big iron branches, and sometimes on gilt ones. The signs belonging to taverns and pothouses are generally finer than the others. Every house possesses one or two shops where the choicest merchandise from the four quarters of the globe is exposed to the sight of the passers-by. A stranger might spend whole days, without ever feeling bored, examining these wonderful goods. . . . (p. 50)

I daresay it would interest you to hear of the style and the way Englishmen usually dress. They do not trouble themselves about dress, but leave that to their womenfolk. When the people see a well-dressed person in the streets, especially if he is wearing a braided coat, a plume in his hat, or his hair tied in a bow, he will, without doubt, be called "French dog" twenty times perhaps before he reaches his destination. . . . Englishmen are usually very plainly dressed, they scarcely ever wear gold on their clothes; they wear little coats called "frocks," without facings and without pleats, with a short cape above. Almost all wear small, round wigs, plain hats, and carry canes in their hands, but no swords. Their cloth and linen are of the best and finest. You will see rich merchants and gentlemen thus dressed, and sometimes even noblemen of high rank, especially in the morning, walking through the filthy and muddy streets. . . . (p. 70)

In London there are a great number of coffee-houses, most of which, to tell the truth, are not over clean or well furnished, owing to the quantity of people who resort to these places and because of the smoke, which would quickly destroy good furniture. . . . What attracts enormously in these coffee-houses are the gazettes and other public papers. All Englishmen are great newsmongers (p. 101). Some coffee-houses are a resort for learned scholars and for wits; others are the resort of dandies or of politicians, or again of professional newsmongers; and many others are temples of Venus. . . . (p. 102)

Most English women are fair and have pink and white complexions, soft though not expressive eyes, and slim, pretty figures, of which they are very proud and take great care, for in the morning as soon as they rise they don a sort of bodice which encircles their waists tightly. Their shoulders and throats are generally fine. They are fond of ornaments, and old and young alike wear four or five patches, and always two large ones on the forehead. Few women curl or powder their hair, and they seldom wear ribbons, feathers, or flowers, but little headdresses of cambric or of magnificent lace on their pretty, well-kept hair. They pride themselves on their neatly shod feet, on their fine linen, and on their gowns. . . . Gowns have enormous hoops, short and very wide sleeves, and it is the fashion to wear little mantles of scarlet or of black velvet, and small hats of straw that are vastly becoming (pp. 126–27).

César de Saussure, *A Foreign View of England in 1725–1729: The Letters of Monsieur César de Saussure to His Family,* trans. and ed. Madame Van Muyden (London: Caliban, 1995).

2. A CONTEMPORARY OPINION ON THE OPERA

From James Ralph, The Taste of the Town, *1731, a reissue of* The Touch-Stone, *1728.*

It is impossible to have a perfect musical Dramma, without Recitative: No Ear can support the Whole being all Air; therefore if you take away the Recitative, it is not Opera: And the best Judges value a Master as much upon the Merit of one as the other: The Recitative is but a tuneable Method of speaking; and in the Article of Musick, but refines upon Speech, as far as polite Comedy excels common Conversation, or Tragedy in Heroicks, the ordinary Stil of the Great. . . . (p. 18)

Nothing is ridiculous that executes a regular Design: That of an Opera, is to represent to us, in the Drammatick Way, some instructive Fable, where the Words are all to be deliver'd in Musick, therefore a King must rule, a General fight, a Lover sigh, in Harmony: nor is there wanting in this Art a Variety to touch the different Passions, as justly as any Kind of Poetry: Nor can I observe any thing in singing a Conversation-Piece, more absurd or ridiculous than a familiar Dialogue in Heroick Rhime. . . . (p. 19)

The Dispute will not then be, who is the justest, or brightest Composer, or which the finest Operas; those of our own Growth, or those imported from Italy? Every Man would be set to Work, and strive to excel in his own Way. H[ande]l would furnish us with Airs expressive of the Rage of Tyrants, the passions of Heroes, and the Distresses of Lovers in the Heroick Stile. B[ononcin]i sooth us with sighing Shepherds, bleating Flocks, chirping Birds, and purling Streams in the Pastoral: And A[riost]o give us good Dungeon Scenes, Marches for a Battel, or Minuets for a Ball, in the Miserere. H[ande]l would warm us in Frost or Snow, by rousing every passion with notes proper to the Subject: Whilst B[ononcin]i would fan us, in the Dog-Days, with an Italian Breeze, and lull us asleep with gentle Whispers; Nay, the pretty Operas from t'other Side of the Water, might serve to tickle us in the Time of Christmas-Gambols, or mortify us in the Time of Lent; so make us very merry, or very sad (pp. 30–31).

3. CARLO GOLDONI DESCRIBES HOW A LIBRETTO OUGHT TO BE COMPOSED

Early in his career, Goldoni is given advice by a certain Count Prata.

The three principal personages of the drama ought to sing five airs each; two in the first act, two in the second, and one in the third. The second actress and the second soprano can only have three, and the inferior characters must be satisfied with a single air each, or two at the most. The author of the words must furnish the musician with the different shades which form the chiaroscuro of music, and take care that two pathetic airs do not succeed one another. He must distribute with the same precaution the bravura airs, the airs of action, the inferior airs, and the minuets and rondeaus.

He must, above all things, avoid giving impassioned airs, bravura airs, or rondeaus to inferior characters; those poor devils must be satisfied with what they get, and every opportunity of distinguishing themselves is denied them.

Memoirs of Carlo Goldoni, Written by Himself, trans. John Black (New York: Alfred A. Knopf, 1926), p. 124.

4. MONSIEUR FOUGEROUX ON THE OPERA IN LONDON IN 1728

The opera, which was formerly nothing, has in the last three years become a considerable spectacle. They have brought from Italy the best voices and the ablest instrumentalists and added the best of what Germany has to offer. It costs so much that as I left London they were speaking of the bankruptcy of the opera. There were only six voices, of which three were excellent. The famous Faustina from Venice, la Cuzzoni and Senesino the famous Castratte—two other Castrattes, Balbi and Palmerini, and Boschi for the bass, as good as Italians generally are for this part, which is quite rare there. I had already heard the three beautiful voices at Venice, and since it was twelve years ago they were even better than today. La Faustina has a charming voice and a fairly large one, though a bit rude, and her figure and her beauty are quite mediocre. La Cuzzoni though she has a weaker voice has a sweetness which enchants, with divine passage-work, after the famous Santini of Venice who no longer performs. Recently Italy has not had such beautiful voices as these two women: the Senesino is the best they have, a good musician, good voice, and a fairly good actor. Senesino got 1600 pounds (worth 35000 in French money) and 1600 for each of the two actresses, though the opera is played only twice a week, on Tuesdays and Saturdays, and stops during Lent. It is an exorbitant price, and is the means they use to abduct the best that Italy has to offer.

The orchestra was composed of twenty-four violins, led by the two Castrucci brothers, two harpsichords, of which Indel the German, a great player and composer played one, an archlute, three cellos, two contrebasses, three bassoons and sometimes flutes and clairons. Cet orchestre fait un grand fracas. As there are no middle parts, the twenty-four violins normally play only the first and second treble parts, which is extremely brilliant and performed well. The two harpsichords and the archlute play the chords and the middle parts. There are only one cello, the two harpsichords and the archlute for the recitative. The music is good, and completely in the Italian taste, except for a few tender pieces in the French taste. It is Indel who composed the three operas I saw. The first was Ptolemé Roy d'Égypte, the second Siroé Roy de Perse, and the third Admette Roy de Tessalie. They were old Italian operas for the words, which had been translated into English verse alongside the Italian for the benefit of the ladies. As there is no spectacle in dance, in decorations, in machines, and since the theatre is not provided with Choirs (there is only a trio or quartet and two duos in a whole opera), or with that multitude of actors which decorate the stage, one can say that the name of opera is badly applied to this spectacle, which is rather a handsome concert given on a stage.

The room is small and in very mediocre taste, the theatre is fairly large but with bad decorations (in scene-changes they use a little bell instead of a whistle). There is no amphitheatre, only a parterre, where there are large benches all the way to the orchestra where men and women are seated pell-mell. The loges are rented by the year. In the rear of the hall is raised a gallery held up by pillars which opens into the parterre and raised like our second loges. This is for the middle classes (la petite bourgeoisie), they nevertheless pay five shillings, which make five French francs. Places in the parterre are worth a half guinea, or 11 francs 10. The King has two boxes next to the stage, he comes there twice with the Queen. The princesses are facing him in another box. Everyone claps hands when the King arrives, and they are saluted when leaving; he only had two halberdiers as a guard. The sides of the theatre are decorated with columns, along which are attached mirrors with sconces of several candles, which are also attached to the pilasters which support the rear gallery. Instead of chandeliers are ugly wooden candleholders, held up by ropes like those used by tight-rope dancers. Nothing could be uglier, but still there are candles everywhere.

As you are not a partisan of Italian music, I do not dare tell you, Sir, that apart from the recitative and the bad habit of accompanying by cutting off the sound of each chord, there are arias that are magnificent for the harmony, with an accompaniment of violins that leave nothing to be desired. The overtures of these operas are a sort of sonata in fugue that is very beautiful. I heard a piece imitating sleep like those that you know in our operas.

In one of these overtures they had added hunting horns, and in the final Chorus as well (the Chorus is made up of only four voices), which made marvelous effect.

Excerpted from Winton Dean, "A French Traveller's View of Handel's Operas," *Music & Letters* 55 (1974): 172–78.

5. LADY MARY WORTLEY MONTAGU DESCRIBES THE FEUD BETWEEN ANASTASIA ROBINSON AND SENESINO

The second heroine [Robinson] has engaged half the Town in Arms, from the Nicety of her virtue, which was not able to bear the too near approach of Senesino in the Opera; and her Condescention in acception of Lord Peterborough for her Champion, who has signalized both his love and Courage upon this occasion in as many instances as ever Don Quixote did for Dulcinea. Poor Senesino, like a vanquished Giant, was forced to confess upon his knees that Anastasia was a non pareil of virtue and of Beauty. Lord Stanhope, as dwarf to the said giant, joked of his size, and was challenged for his pains. Lord Delawar was Lord Peterborough's second, my Lady miscarry'd—the Whole Town divided into partys on this important point.

Cited Elizabeth Gibson, *The Royal Academy of Music, 1719–1728: The Institution and Its Directors* (New York: Garland, 1989), 203.

6. COLLEY CIBBER COMMENTS ON RECITATIVE, ON ITALIAN SINGERS, AND ON THE MANAGEMENT OF THEATERS

No Criticism upon our Operas has prevail'd more universally, nor more unjustly, than that upon the *Recitative;* yet so it happens, that the Generality of our Audiences have a secret distaste to it; and many, even of our Patrons of Musick, are shock'd with it: How to remedy this Want of Taste, or how to sacrifice our Recitative to Caprice, I know not: We must therefore find out some moderating Expedient to humour the first; for giving in to the latter, would demolish the Design and Nature of an Opera quite. . . . (p. 31)

There is, too, in the very species of an Italian singer, such an innate fantastical pride and caprice, that the government of them (here at least) is almost impracticable. This distemper, as we were not sufficiently warn'd or apprised of, threw our musical affairs into perplexities we knew not easily how to get out of. There is scarce a sensible auditor in the kingdom that has not, since that time, had occasion to laugh at the several instances of it. But what is still more ridiculous, these costly canary-birds have sometimes ingested the whole body of our dignified lovers of musick, with the same childish animosities; ladies have been known to decline their visits, upon account of their being of a different musical party. . . . (p. 214)

Sir, by our books it is apparent that the managers have under their care no less than one hundred and forty persons, in constant daily pay; and among such numbers, it will be no wonder if a great many of them are unskillful, idle, and sometimes untractable; all which tempers are to be led, or driven, watch'd and restrain'd by the continuall skill, care, and patience of the managers. Every manager is oblig'd in his turn, to attend two or three hours every morning, at the rehearsal of plays, and other entertainments for the stage, or else every rehearsal would be but a rude meeting of mirth and jollity. The same attendance is as necessary at every play, during the time of its publick action, in which one, or more of us, have constantly been punctual, whether we have had any part in the play, then acted, or not. A manager ought to be at the reading of every new play, when it is first offer'd to the stage, though there are seldom one of those plays in twenty, which upon hearing, proves to be fit for it; and upon such occasion the attendance must be allow'd to be as painfully tedious, as the getting rid of the authors of such plays must be disagreeable and difficult. Besides this, sir, a manager is to order all new cloaths, to assist in the fancy, and propriety of them, to limit their expence, and to withstand the unreasonable importunities of some, who are apt to think themselves injur'd, if they are not finer than their fellows. A manager, is to direct and oversee the painters, machinists, musicians, singers, and dancers; and to have an eye upon the door-keepers, under-servants, and officers, that without such care, are too often apt to defraud us, or neglect their duty (p. 274).

John Maurice Evans, ed., *A Critical Edition of "An apology for the life of Mr. Colley Cibber, Comedian"* (New York: Garland, 1987).

7. SIR JOHN VANBRUGH TO THE EARL OF CARLISLE, FEBRUARY 18, 1724

The Masquerade flourishes more than ever. Some of the Bishops (from the true spirit of the clergy to meddle in everything) had a mind to attack the King about them, which I believe he did not like, for he took occasion to declare aloud in the Drawing-room that whilst there were Masquerades he would go to them. This, with what the Bishops understood from some Ministers they applied to, made them think it might be as well to be quiet. The Bishop of London however, during this [Lent] preached one very spiritless sermon on the subject, which I believe has not lost Heydegger one single ticket.

Cited in Gibson, *Royal Academy,* p. 205.

8. PETITION BY THE GRAND JURY FOR THE COUNTY OF MIDDLESEX TO THE HOUSE OF COMMONS, 12 FEBRUARY 1723

Whereas there has been lately publish'd a Proposal for Six Ridotto's, or Balls, to be managed by Subscription at the King's Theatre in the Hay-Market, &c. We the Grand Jury of the County of Middlesex, sworn to enquire for our Sovereign Lord the King, and the Body of this County, conceiving the same to be a Wicked and unlawfull Design, for carrying out Gaming, Chances by Way of Lottery, and other Impious and Illegal Practices, and which (if not timely suppressed) may promote Debauchery, Lewdness, and ill Conversation: From a just Abhorrence, therefore, of such Sort of Assemblies, which we apprehend are contrary to law and good Manners, and give great offence to his Majesty's good and virtuous Subjects, We do present the same and recommend them to be prosecuted and suppressed as common Nuisances to the Publick, as Nurseries of Lewdness, Extravagance, and Immorality, and also a Reproach and Scandal to Civil Government.

Otto Erich Deutsch, *Handel: A Documentary Biography* (New York: W. W. Norton, 1955), p. 159.

You would have seen all your hopes for opera fulfilled

to the highest degree in the recent "Don Juan";

but this piece stands alone, and all hope for something similar

in the future has been cut off by Mozart's death.

— *Johann Wolfgang Goethe to Friedrich Schiller, December 20, 1797*

CHAPTER TWO

Wolfgang Amadé Mozart, *Il dissoluto punito, ossia Il Don Giovanni*

Prague, October 29, 1787, 7:00 P.M.

on Giovanni is the happy conjunction of the international network of Italian opera with the musical public of Prague, where Mozart's genius sparked the success of what would come to be called by E. T. A. Hoffmann the Opera of Operas. It is an opera in the tradition of Italian comic opera, in a very real way the successor to Mozart's *Marriage of Figaro*. It was the charm and the success of *Figaro* that got Mozart the commission to produce a new opera for Prague, and it was *Figaro* that some would say he transcended.

Comic opera has the great advantage of allowing music to advance the drama. Handel's characters pause for musical reflection on a single emotion, but in the tradition of opera buffa wonderfully transfigured by Mozart much music happens in real time, and the action on the stage can be complemented, enhanced, or explained by the music.

Don Giovanni is called *dramma giocoso* in the printed libretto; this is an eighteenth-century term, used especially by Carlo Goldoni, for plots that mix the traditional comic roles with characters from serious drama—usually involving upper and lower classes and comically overdone observations of normal life combined with the fascination for distant aristocracy. Mozart's score, however, simply calls it an opera buffa, a comic opera, but it has tones of evil and seriousness that make it a "semi-serious opera," an "opera semiseria." This doesn't mean that we should take it in the modern sense only half seriously; it is a serious opera with a serious admixture of comedy. It is the way life is. It's a joke, but the joke is on us.

Don Giovanni is really a comic opera of a very dark sort; Don Juan, who is in a sense the wicked side of all males, has his way with the world and the women who inhabit it ("Ma in Ispagna son già mille e tre"); makes his swashbuckling way through morals, ethics, and class structures; has no concern for the rights or feelings of others; and gets his punishment only at the very end from a statue (a replica of a person who even in life didn't have much fun). He is like the amusing child who, after entertaining us at length, gets the spanking that morality requires only in the last frame of a long comic strip.

Mozart expected audiences for *Don Giovanni* to be attuned to the traditions of the theater and to the class structure of the modern world. This is an opera like many others in that it has characters in couples who can provide parallel amorous intrigues and can be happily paired up at the end. In *Figaro*, everybody is satisfactorily matched up after many entertaining adventures: the Count and Countess, Figaro and Susanna, Bartolo and Marcellina, Cherubino and Barbarina. This is perfectly normal in comic opera, and it is what we expect.

And in *Don Giovanni* there are those same happy pairs at the end: Donna Anna and Don Ottavio, Masetto and Zerlina. But there are also characters who do not fit the comic pattern. Don Giovanni himself is condemned to infernal flames; the tragic and unbalanced Donna Elvira, far from being paired up with the man she so haplessly pursues, retires to a convent; Leporello, a sort of eighteenth-century Falstaff, clever on the surface and profoundly stupid at the core, simply wanders off to find another master (will he ever find one like the Don?). The noble Commendatore, the representative of all that is good and traditional, dies in the first act and causes the ultimate dénouement. His animated statue at the end is a reminder of morality (Don Giovanni's punishment) and of the consequences of evil (a good man's death).

And there are issues of class, so central to the structure of eighteenth-century society on the eve of the French Revolution. It is amusing but somewhat risky to the stability of the social structure for servants to outwit their masters, as is the chief amusement of *Figaro*. It is less amusing to us—but perhaps not to the élite audiences for opera at the time—for masters to take advantage of servants. This is one of the plot-driving aspects of *Figaro*, when the Count's desire to exercise his *droit de seigneur,* despite his having recently abolished the lord's right to bed the prospective bride, is repeatedly thwarted. The same theme is present in *Don Giovanni*, when the Don's desire to seduce Zerlina leads to one of the most thrilling moments in opera. But here Don Giovanni is not class-conscious: he chases anything in a skirt. And the servants are not cleverer than their masters: Leporello, an amusing fellow, is no Figaro, and he repeatedly fails to understand what is going on. His courage fails him where a "noble" heart would not be deterred; he is a reversion to the traditional depiction of the comic servant.

Indeed, the classes are pretty well identified and stratified in *Don Giovanni*. Donna Anna and Don Ottavio sing noble music, and we recognize their virtue by the virtuosity of their singing, and their nobility by their high voices (in earlier operas even Don Ottavio would have been a soprano) and the exalted character of their music. Zerlina and Masetto sing charming, lilting, simple tunes appropriate for villagers. Only Don Giovanni can sing anything: he can make himself appealing to a villager ("La ci darem la mano") or to a lady ("Elvira idolo mio").

Don Giovanni has held the stage since 1787, and of course its principal attraction is the richness of Mozart's music. Almost every number is a musical treasure, but each is also attractive in its astounding relation to the drama. There are ensembles in which everybody speaks his mind at the same time but in different rhythms; charming love songs; virtuoso arias; and ensemble finales of unequaled complexity. The whole thing moves along swiftly; the songs are relatively short; there are no long orchestral introductions; the pacing, musically and dramatically, leaves us almost breathless. Prague was not perhaps where Mozart would have chosen to produce his next opera, but it was a city that knew the value of what it was getting.

Background
PRAGUE IN 1787

The Bohemian capital was second in importance to Vienna in the Austro-Hungarian Empire, but the rich and powerful Bohemian nobility had made it something of an artistic center. Bohemia had rebelled against Austria in the early seventeenth century and had been under careful control ever since. High taxes, military conscription, religious intolerance,

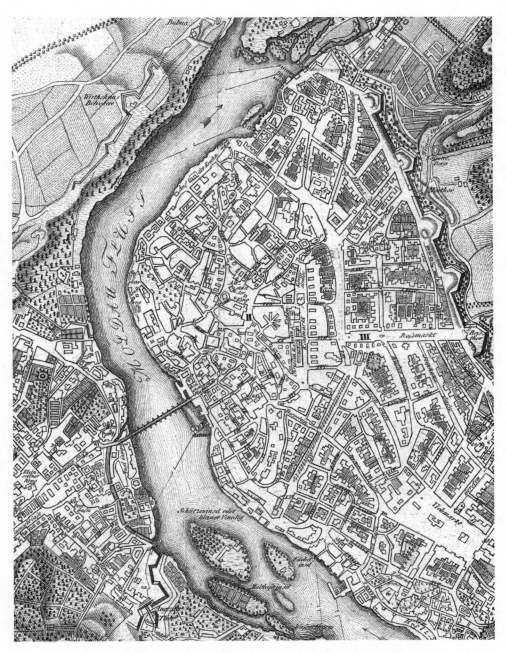

This 1823 map of Prague *(Grundriss des k.k. haupstadt Prag)* shows
the Karlsbrücke (Charles Bridge), crossing the Moldau
from the Kleinseite on the left to the Altstadt on the right;
almost in the center of the Altstadt stands
(at no. 15) the Nostitz Theater.

and the creation of a local nobility of German extraction all contributed to making Prague and its lands an integrated portion of the Austrian empire. The local language was not used in schools, in newspapers, on the stage, or in official communication. Previous Habsburg emperors had been crowned as kings of Bohemia, but Joseph II, the reforming and centralizing emperor, had not bothered to be crowned. Some of those in Prague may have feared that Bohemia would disappear into a homogenized and centralized empire. The "new" nobility was mostly foreign, and they wanted to clear the bad name of Bohemia, if only for their own advancement. Though the nobles built grand palaces and supported the arts in Prague, they tended to spend most of their time in Vienna.

Prague had been a famous Gothic city, but in the seventeenth and eighteenth centuries it was remade as a grand Baroque center, based on the international influence of Italian architecture. We know few of Prague's Baroque architects, but one of them was Anton Hafenecker, who was chosen by Count Nostitz to build the theater in which *Don Giovanni* would have its first performance.

The city, whose population in 1787 was slightly less than 100,000, lies on both sides of the Moldau, which was (and is) spanned by the splendid fourteenth-century Charles

---

A Description of Prague, from an English Translation of a German Geography of 1762

The metropolis of the kingdom, which lies almost in the middle thereof on both sides of the Moldau or Molda which is here about eight hundred paces broad, but likewise shallow and not navigable. The bridge of stone, which Charles IV. in the year 1357, caused to be erected over this river, exceeds in length those of Ratisbon and Dresden, being seven hundred and forty-two common paces long. Its breadth amounts to fourteen common paces, and three carriages may pass upon it abreast. It stands on sixteen piers, being ornamented on the sides with twenty-eight statues of saints. . . .

The fortifications of Prague are not very important, the town may be flanked or raked on all sides. The houses are wholly built of stone, and for the most part consist of three stories. It has broader streets, but fewer stately palaces than Vienna. In it are computed ninety-two churches and chapels, with about forty cloisters. The town, considered with respect to its extent, is not sufficiently populous, as containing only about 70000 Christian, and between 12 and 13000 Jewish inhabitants. Neither is the commerce, which is carried on here considerable, but exclusive of the arts and handicraft-trades, its principal means of subsistence is drawn from the brewing of beer.

The Charles Bridge in Prague, pictured here in 1781, remains
one of Prague's most impressive sights. A 1762 geography manual
describes the bridge: "The bridge of stone, which Charles IV.
in the year 1357, caused to be erected over this river, exceeds in length
those of Ratisbon and Dresden, being seven hundred and forty-two
common paces long. Its breadth amounts to fourteen common paces,
and three carriages may pass upon it abreast."

Bridge, built by Charles IV, founder of Prague's university. On the west side of the river was the ancient Kleinseite, surmounted by the citadel of the Hradschin, with its palaces and the Cathedral of St. Vitus, the large Strahov monastery occupying the highest ground. Here was the palace of Count Nostitz. On the east side of the river is the Altstadt, or Old Town, once encircled by walls and by 1787 surrounded by the Neustadt, or New Town. The Old Town, the center of activity in Prague, also included the substantial Jewish quarter. (The Jewish population numbered about 12,000.) Standing by itself, in an irregular configuration of streets and blocking off the Fruit Market, was the Nostitz Theatre.

The city has many broad streets and a great many churches and monasteries, but fewer grand palaces than Vienna. Charles Burney had this impression on his visit around 1700: "The houses are all of white stone, or stucco, in imitation of it, and all uniform in size and colour. . . . A great part of the town is new, as scarce a single building escaped the Prussian batteries, and bombardment during the blockade, in the last war. A few churches and palaces only, that were strongly built, and of less combustible materials than the rest, were proof against their fury; and in the walls of these, are still sticking innumerable cannon balls, and bombs, particularly in the superb palace of count Czernin, and in the Capuchin's church."

Bohemia, and Prague in particular, was known for its rich musical life and its remarkable number of musicians. Almost all children received music training, and the Bohemian nobility engaged many musicians for their households, some of them retaining entire orchestras. A German observer, in a book on Prague, was impressed with the city's love of music:

> Whether the general talent for music among the Bohemians lies in the temperament of the nation, or whether the former glorious epoch of the country contributed to this cannot be determined exactly, at least I cannot do it. That it exists, however, can very easily be seen. Nowhere does one find so many children going about with instruments, especially the harp, and although very young, nevertheless earn their living. The mechanical practice that they receive in youth renders them all the more skillful when grown, provided that their talent corresponds to their choice. For the greater portion that is the case. However, because the Bohemians themselves do not need this crowd of musicians, especially with so much private amateur music-making, many travel abroad and seek to earn a living. It was precisely this youthful training, advancement, and learned skill that always gave the wandering musicians of Prague preference in Germany over the native ones. . . . In general, though, one finds better music in taverns here in Prague than at balls and redoutes in many cities. Whoever is a friend [of music] and whose ear is pleased by charming music, finds himself occasionally obliged to stop in the street to satisfy his inclination under the window of a beer hall; and this happens not rarely, but often. And thus at larger occasions one also finds increasingly compounded art. All public festivities here employ very good musicians, and many among them could hold the stage with virtuosi.

The presence of a regular opera company, and the existence of many concerts and musical parties in private houses, may explain the relative scarceness of public concerts in Prague. There were occasional performances, or "academies," by visiting virtuosi and sometimes by local musicians. Among the leading lights of Prague musicians were Mozart's friends Josepha Dussek, a "beloved singer who has much strength of voice and a pleasing tone, especially in the low range, and who is also very musical," and her husband, Franz Xaver Dussek, the well-known composer and keyboard virtuoso. Although the nobility had maintained private musical establishments, or Kapellen, these were fewer than formerly, and many Bohemian musicians sought their living by emigrating to Vienna or elsewhere.

Dancing, at public balls or *Redouten* in theaters and elsewhere, or at private entertainments, was a favorite musical pastime in Prague. A German observer was particularly impressed with the deutscher Tanz:

> The general inclination for music has become so typical of the local inhabitants, that they cannot be fully happy without it. . . . Dancing is the

favorite passion especially of the female sex. The German dance, the so-called waltz [Walzen], is the most fashionable. The lowliest maiden waltzes well, and the dance is danced here with a restraint that is unknown in other German regions, where we believe that this type of dance consists of the craziest and most foolish twirling. It is pleasant to see when so many couples one after the other turn without disturbing each other. . . . Here I must also add that music is indeed a free art for amateurs, but that anyone who wishes to earn money at public or private balls and other entertainments where there is dancing must pay a tax of 30 kreuzer per person, the so-called "music duty." As soon as I have music in my house for this purpose and do not pay for a permit ahead of time, then I have committed a criminal offense.

Prague had had a considerable history of theater. Private theatricals sponsored by the nobility had long been a feature of social life, and there had been occasional large operatic productions. Johann Joseph Fux's *Costanza et fortezza,* performed in 1723 for the coronation of Charles VI as King of Bohemia, was a brilliant event in the collective memory.

There had been an Italian opera company in Prague earlier in the century; this was Count Sporck's opera, run by the Italian Antonio Denzio, whose close collaborator

Count Johann Thun was a patron of Mozart's, and the composer stayed in his palace during his visit to Prague in 1787. The Thun Palace incorporates a small theater, where the Bondini opera company often performed for a small paying public. Bondini had also operated a casino in the palace.

Antonio Vivaldi provided several operas that premiered in Prague. Denzio's was an autonomous company, not dependent on players or repertory from Vienna. It was known not only for serious opera but also for its comic presentations, especially at carnival time. Denzio staged Prague's first opera on the Don Juan theme, in 1730 (as a Lenten oratorio!), although the story was already well known from presentations on the stage. Later Don Juan productions in Prague, by puppeteers (1777) and opera companies, included Vincenzo Righini's *Il convitato di pietra* in 1776, which may well have been in the minds of the older of *Don Giovanni*'s performers and listeners. "He composes very charmingly," wrote Mozart of Righini in 1781, "but he is a monstrous thief."

The Kotce Theater was established in the Old Town's covered market in 1737, and many Italian opera impresarios leased the theater and played seasons in Prague. The city was attractive to Italian companies, who must have preferred to be dependent on ticket sales rather than on the wishes of a court. Such companies, though they toured other cities, tended to be based in Prague. This may have had to do with the city's rich musical life—not only its love of opera, but also its many private entertainments for which members of the company might be hired. Although Prague was politically dependent on Vienna, its theatrical life was its own. There was no particular opposition to Italian things—as there had been from Joseph II in Vienna—and there was plenty of opportunity for members of a company to engage in further professional musical activities. Impresarios of Italian companies in Prague could choose a repertoire based entirely on the public's taste and the strengths of the company, without being limited by the taste of the emperor. Few Italian works that played in Prague came there from Vienna; productions in Prague were generally mounted there for the Prague audience. By the later years of the century there was sometimes more than one company playing in the city.

The opera season was divided into three periods in Prague, and each was expected to produce at least two new works. They ran from September or October to the beginning of Advent; the carnival season from the last days of the year until the beginning of Lent; and the spring season, after Easter.

The Kotce Theatre had been taken over by Count Franz Anton Nostitz, Supreme Burgrave and Governor-General of the Bohemian lands. Nostitz decided to build a new theater, and the National Theatre, or Nostitz Theatre, which opened in 1783, was Prague's first permanent theater open to the public and built for that purpose. Since 1784 it had been leased to Pasquale Bondini, impresario of the Italian opera company and commissioner of *Don Giovanni*. It was sold to the state after Nostitz's death in 1798 and is still standing, considerably altered, in Prague. Massive flooding in 2002 caused serious damage to musical scores, costumes, and so forth in the theater's basement.

THE BONDINI COMPANY
AND THE COMMISSION FOR *DON GIOVANNI*

Pasquale Bondini was an experienced actor and singer (a buffo bass). An earlier company of his had performed plays by Shakespeare, Lessing, and Schiller. As the popularity

Domenico Guardasoni was the partner of Pasquale Bondini and stage manager of the Bondini opera company. Guardasoni later took over the company and spread the "Bondini style." *Don Giovanni*'s librettist Lorenzo Da Ponte reports that Guardasoni wrote to him as follows: "Long live Da Ponte! Long live Mozart! All impresarios, all virtuosi should bless their names. So long as they live we shall never know what theatrical poverty means!"

of the company grew, the National Theatre, previously "unavailable" to the company, became more available, and Bondini's company played there from 1783 until the theater closed, in 1807.

During this time Bondini was principally concerned with opera. His company, which in Prague alternated performances between the National Theatre and Count Thun's theater in the Kleinseite, consisted of three female and four male principals, all Italians. This company performed in Prague in the winter and in Leipzig in the summer. Bondini also performed seasons of German theater and Singspiel in Dresden with another company, which in turn performed in Prague in the summer. German theater in the winter in Prague was performed by companies of lesser rank that were engaged by Bondini, who managed the theater. He thus organized two simultaneous companies and directed theatrical activities in two cities, in addition to performing in Dresden. He also conducted masked balls in the Prague theater in the 1785 and 1786 seasons.

Bondini was an impresario: he was not the manager of a court theater with a substantial subsidy and the obligation to respond to a patron's wishes. He succeeded if he pleased the public, and this made his theater very different from those in Vienna and elsewhere.

Bondini's stage manager and partner was Domenico Guardasoni, a talented and resourceful associate who was second in importance to Bondini himself. Guardasoni was régisseur from 1783 to 1788 and afterward took over the company, spreading the "Bondini style" with a winter season in Prague and summer in Leipzig. From 1789–91 he was in Warsaw. Returning to Prague in 1791 he leased the National Theatre and played there with his company until his death in 1806.

Friedrich Ernest Arnold, in his 1787 travel book on Prague, had much to say about Bondini:

This impresario offers good salaries, and pays promptly, a reputation he has built up over many years. He is an Italian, he has an honest character, and one can trust his word. He was formerly a good comic actor. . . .

He is likewise the impresario of the local Italian opera buffa. We have already said that Prague has an extraordinary taste for music and it is very happy with this opera, and this is a sign that it must be good. Herr Bondini furthermore spares no expense in acquiring the best and newest scores, in paying good men and women singers so that they are happy to work with him. This opera plays throughout the entire winter, and last winter alternated with the spoken theater. Connoisseurs by and large prefer it to the Dresden court opera, which is supported at the electoral court's expense. The costumes and settings are excellent.

Two years ago, Herr Bondini also put on a ball in the theatre, and like last year held it in the large playhouse here. Especially in the first year it was particularly lively and magnificent. The parterre was placed on the same level as the stage, thus making an excellent hall that, for the part of the public that prefers this entertainment, compensated for the problems at theatrical performances. This great hall is then always richly lit with chandeliers, and Herr Bondini occasionally spends something on special charming decorations. The actual redoutes or masked balls are held in the Wusinisch Hall, where the ball mentioned above was also held.

Three years ago he also organized a casino for the nobility in the palace of Count Thun, which he had rented entirely. However, just as everyone in Prague eagerly investigates everything new, and finds everything tasteless as soon as it becomes older (an obvious consequence of idleness), so this arrangement too has paled, and the impresario thus suspended it very phlegmatically, because he knows his public.

He deserved to be the *maître des plaisirs* at one of the great courts. He has all the requisite knowledge of how to harmonize his own gifts with those of many others, and a certain dryness of character restrains the presumptuous ones with whom he must often surround himself.

Novelty was needed to please the audience, and the city surely did not wish to be seen as a provincial consumer of Viennese culture. There had been many premieres in Prague; most frequently premiered up until the 1760s were operas of Baldassare Galuppi.

Like Italian companies presenting opera in other cities, the Bondini company was made up of Italians singers who were part of the international network of Italian opera. They had all been trained in Italy and had sung in a variety of Italian houses and operas. The communication of the international style of Italian opera was largely accomplished through this informal but dense association of Italian impresarios, composers, and singers. As Johann Adam Hiller said in his 1780 treatise on singing, "It is very encouraging for an

Italian singer to have so many opportunities in and outside his homeland to show his talent and to be handsomely rewarded for it. . . . It is well known to what extent Italian singing is appreciated outside of Italy, at the various German courts, in England, in Russia, and in almost all the European realms."

As we know from Handel's experience, singers were regularly recruited from Italian opera houses or from other companies, and a great many singers, operas, and managers moved from one opera house, or company, to another. Most self-respecting courts, even of moderate size, had some sort of opera, even if the season was presented by a company that performed in more than one city. This fluid situation led to a sort of homogenization of the style, the sound, and the look of Italian opera, created by an ever-shifting international network whose communication crossed political, cultural, and geographical boundaries and was conducted mostly in Italian. Bondini's company, in this context, was a relatively stable one, as many of his singers had performed with the company for several years. This was a decided advantage for Mozart, for even though the company was small he had come to know its members from their performances of *Figaro* and so was able to compose his new opera with specific voices and talents in mind.

The sound and the style of Italian opera were everywhere—the naive and tender music of Niccolò Piccini's comic operas; the melodies of Domenico Cimarosa, known for his ensemble finales; and the facile and elegant works of Baldassare Galuppi. More locally, the music of Salieri and Martín y Soler often held the stage. But no familiarity with the works of these and other composers could prepare listeners for the depth and complexity of Mozart's best operas.

MOZART AND PRAGUE AND BONDINI

Prague enjoyed Mozart's music, and he was more successful there than in Vienna. His Singspiel *Die Entführung aus dem Serail* found success with the public in 1783, and Mozart's first biographer, Franz Xaver Niemetschek, marks this as the beginning of Prague's love of Mozart: "Now the Bohemians proceeded to seek out his works, and in this same year, Mozart's symphonies and piano music were to be heard at all the best concerts. From now onwards preference for his works was shown by the Bohemians."

Mozart's real concern, though, was with Vienna, where he operated as a free-lance musician. Among other things, this meant that he was engaged in many pursuits—teaching, performing, composing—but all of his activity put together was not quite enough to support his growing family. What he really wanted was a fixed, salaried position at court. His recent plan to take a trip to England was probably as much related to his lack of official advancement in Vienna as it was to his real desire to travel or emigrate. He would have liked to have been commissioned by the emperor to compose an opera; and he would have liked to have been appointed one of the court composers. Although he had written three full-length stage pieces for Vienna, none was commissioned by the court theaters.

In January 1787, Mozart had traveled to Prague following on the great success of *Le nozze di Figaro* there and after receiving an invitation from members of the opera

This portrait of Mozart was made for the Philharmonic Academy of Bologna, to which Mozart was elected in 1770. In that same year Pope Clement XIV created him a Knight of the Golden Spur, and Mozart wears his knightly insignia in this picture.

orchestra and other musicians. He stayed a month and conducted *Figaro* ("At once the news of his presence spread in the stalls, and as soon as the overture had ended everyone broke into welcoming applause"). Mozart, according to standard practice in the region, probably sat at the keyboard and acted as co-director with the leader of the first violins (who probably in fact led the orchestrally accompanied numbers). He also composed some German dances, gave a concert in which he improvised at the piano, and premiered his "Prague" symphony. One of his improvisations was on "Non più andrai" from *Figaro*—a favorite tune in Prague, which returns in the banquet scene of *Don Giovanni*. He was welcomed by his old friend and patron Count Thun, for whom he had written the "Linz" Symphony in 1783, and by the Dusseks, who were leading musicians of Prague and old friends.

Mozart enjoyed being lionized in Prague. As he wrote to his friend Gottfried von Jacquin:

> Immediately after our arrival at noon on Thursday, the 11th, we had a dreadful rush to get ready for lunch at one o'clock. After the meal old Count Thun entertained us with some music, performed by his own people, which lasted about an hour and a half. This kind of real entertainment I could enjoy every day. At six o'clock I drove with Count Canal to the so-called Bretfeld ball, where the cream of the beauties of Prague is wont to gather. Why—you ought to have been there, my friend. I fancy I see you running, or rather, limping after all those pretty women, married and unmarried! I neither danced nor flirted with any of them, the former, because I was too tired, and the latter owing to my natural bashfulness. I looked on, however, with the greatest pleasure, while all these people flew about in sheer delight to the music of my "Figaro" arranged for quadrilles and waltzes. For here they talk about nothing but "Figaro."

Nothing is played, sung or whistled but "Figaro." Nothing, nothing but "Figaro." Certainly a great honor for me! . . . My concert is to take place in the theatre on Friday, the 19th, and I shall probably have to give a second one, which unfortunately will prolong my stay here.

He visited the opera and was commissioned by Bondini, presumably for the customary 100 ducats, to provide a new opera for the winter season. Niemetschek described the commission: "The opera director Bondini commissioned Mozart to compose a new opera for the Prague stage for the following winter, which the latter gladly undertook to do, as he had experienced how much the Bohemians appreciated his music and how well they executed it. This he often mentioned to his acquaintances in Prague, where a hero-worshipping responsive public and real friends carried him, so to speak, on their hands. He warmly thanked the opera orchestra in a letter to Herr Strobach, who was director at the time, and attributed the greater part of the ovation which his music had received in Prague to their excellent rendering." (Niemetschek claims to have seen and read the letter, but apparently it does not survive.)

It may have been partly the importance of Vienna, rather than of Mozart and Da Ponte, that led to Bondini's commission. Vienna was the capital, the cultural center, the imperial city. Despite the independence of Prague's Italian opera company, whatever was the rage in Vienna should set the standard for the Bohemian capital. With *Figaro* the company was reviving an opera first given in Vienna, but at the end of the year the tables would be turned, and it was Prague that would have the first performance of an opera that subsequently would be presented in the capital.

Wolfgang Amadé Mozart was at the top of his form and reputation. (Mozart did not know this, of course, and was striving for higher things still.) It was an eventful year for Mozart, but not one in which he had many musical obligations (the seventeen-year-old Beethoven visited Mozart in Vienna that spring—"Keep your eye on him," Mozart said). He wrote some concert arias and the beautiful C major quintet. His wife, Constanze, was expecting another child, and Mozart moved his growing family to a cheaper apartment in the suburbs of Vienna, Hauptstrasse 224 (where now Landstrasser Haptstrasse 75 stands), where he remained until the end of the year. His father, Leopold, died on May 28; Leopold had been Mozart's teacher, manager, and correspondent for many years, and his absence inevitably made a substantial difference in Mozart's life. The younger Mozart completed other music that spring, not at all mournful: songs, his "Musical Joke" serenade, and the immortal *Eine kleine Nachtmusik*.

The commission from Bondini for a new opera was met with pleasure. Though it was not the assignment Mozart most wanted (it was not for Vienna, and it was not for the emperor), he returned to Vienna and set about producing an opera for a company that he knew and an audience that liked his work. He was evidently offered Bertati's libretto *Don Giovanni Tenorio*, but he chose an adaptation by Lorenzo Da Ponte, his librettist for *Figaro*. Da Ponte, in an 1819 brochure, indicated that Bondini had sent Mozart a one-act libretto —perhaps Bertati's?—but that Mozart had insisted on setting a libretto by Da Ponte.

The new opera was to be performed for the visit of the Archduchess Maria Theresia, recently wed to Prince Anton Clemens of Saxony. Prague wanted more of the latest and the best, and *Figaro* had been a great success, musically and dramatically. Prague now wanted to welcome the royal couple with a work worthy of the empire, and of Prague's place in it.

LORENZO DA PONTE

Da Ponte was desperately busy at the time of the commission for *Don Giovanni*, but he was eagerly sought for the opera, and he undertook the job. He received 50 sequins for *Don Giovanni* from Domenico Guardasoni, the director at Prague, as he says in his memoirs.

Da Ponte is one of the most remarkable figures in operatic history. Having been trained in seminaries and taken religious orders (despite his Jewish background), Da Ponte at one time taught in Venice. He lost his job at Treviso on account of his liberal views, and he was banned from Venice for adultery. For some years he resided in Vienna, where he enjoyed the patronage of the emperor, and where he had already adapted Beaumarchais as *Le nozze di Figaro*.

He later taught at Columbia University in New York; ran a grocery store on Staten Island; was a friend of Giuseppe Garibaldi; and wrote a remarkable set of memoirs, in which he gives his side of the *Don Giovanni* collaboration. (Remember that Da Ponte's memoirs were written many years later, when the Enlightenment had turned to Romanticism and when the long-dead Mozart had been sanctified.)

Da Ponte does not mention that his libretto is an adaptation of *Don Giovanni Tenorio, o sia Il convitato di pietra* by Giovanni Bertati (his critic and rival: Da Ponte called him a "bag of wind"), which had been performed in Venice in February with music by Giuseppe Gazzaniga. Antonio Baglioni, who would sing the role of Don Ottavio in Prague, had performed in it first in Vienna.

Not only does Da Ponte not mention Bertati, but his description of the creation of *Don Giovanni*'s libretto is a charming piece of braggadocio in which the brilliant abbé, a Don Juan himself, composes three operas at once while satisfying all his physical wants and desires:

> The three subjects fixed on, I went to the Emperor, laid my idea before him, and explained that my intention was to write the three operas contemporaneously.
>
> "You will not succeed," he replied.
>
> "Perhaps not," said I, "but I am going to try. I shall write evenings for Mozart, imagining I am reading the Inferno; mornings I shall work for Martini and pretend I am studying Petrarch; my afternoons will be for Salieri. He is my Tasso!"
>
> He found my parallels very apt.
>
> I returned home and went to work. I sat down at my table and did not leave it for twelve hours continuous—a bottle of Tokay to my right,

Lorenzo Da Ponte, Mozart's brilliant librettist, was a priest and a high-liver. The story of his subsequent career, in New York and elsewhere, is itself worth the price of his memoirs.

a box of Seville to my left, in the middle an inkwell. A beautiful girl of sixteen—I should have preferred to love her only as a daughter, but alas . . . ! —was living in the house with her mother, who took care of the family, and came to my room at the sound of the bell. To tell the truth the bell rang rather frequently, especially at moments when I felt my inspiration waning. She would bring me now a little cake, now a cup of coffee, now nothing but her pretty face, a face always gay, always smiling, just the thing to inspire poetical emotion and witty thoughts. I worked twelve hours a day every day, with a few interruptions, for two months on end; and through all that time she sat in an adjoining room, now with a book in hand, now with needle or embroidery, but ever ready to come to my aid at the first touch of the bell. Sometimes she would sit at my side without stirring, without opening her lips, or batting an eyelash, gazing at me fixedly, or blandly smiling, or now it would be a sigh, or a menace of tears. In a word, this girl was my Calliope for those three operas, as she was afterwards for all the verse I wrote during the next six years. At first I permitted such visits very often; later I had to make them less frequent, in order not to lose too much time in amorous nonsense, of which she was perfect mistress. The first day, between the Tokay, the snuff, the coffee, the bell, and my young muse, I wrote the two first scenes of *Don Giovanni,* two more for the *Arbore di Diana,* and more than half of the first act of *Tarar,* a title I changed to *Assur.* I presented those scenes to the three composers the next morning. They could scarcely be brought to believe that what they were reading with their own eyes was possible. In sixty-three days the first two operas were entirely finished and about two thirds of the last.

MOZART, *DON GIOVANNI*

There are many, many tellings of the Don Juan story, reaching back through Goldoni (*Don Giovanni Tenorio,* 1736) and Molière (*Dom Juan ou Le festin de pierre,* 1666) to Tirso de Molina's *El burlador de Sevilla, y convidada de pietra* of 1630. The basic story is shared by many versions: the libertine, the Commendatore, often a rustic wedding, the statue, the banquet at which the statue appears. There had been puppet plays, parodies, operas, and ballets on the subject all over Europe.

Bertati's libretto had been pure comedy in which everybody takes part. But at the hands of Da Ponte (and Mozart) there is only one purely comic role—that of Leporello —and all the personages are defined by their relationship not so much with each other as with Don Giovanni (an exception is Don Ottavio, who is really defined by his devotion to Donna Anna).

As is normal in a dramma giocoso, there are purely comic characters, purely serious characters, and those of *mezzo carattere:* this last category includes not only Donna Elvira but Don Giovanni himself. Like the count in *Figaro,* Don Giovanni is a nobleman who consorts with peasants, dresses himself as a servant, and seduces women from all ranks of society: he is surely not a noble serious character.

Mozart must have had a hand in the shaping of the drama. Although we cannot be sure exactly what his role was, it was he who knew the Prague company and how the drama might be made to fit the seven individuals who would perform it. We know from his close involvement with the libretti of *Idomeneo* and *Die Entführung aus dem Serail* that he worked closely, and demandingly, with his librettists. He also had earlier expressed a strong opinion as to the distribution of female roles in a projected opera (in a letter to his father of May 7, 1783); he wanted two roles of equal importance, one serious and the other mezzo carattere, with a third role of lesser importance and entirely buffa. This matches so well the distribution in *Don Giovanni* (the serious Anna, the mezzo carattere Elvira, the buffa Zerlina) that it is difficult not to see Mozart's influence reflected in Da Ponte's libretto. One adjustment needed to be made in his plan of 1783: in Prague the buffa role was to be played by the company's prima donna (who was also the wife of the director), so she would have to have her fair share of arias. As it happens, each female role gets two arias; those of Donna Anna are grand, serious, and virtuosic, as befits a noble lady; Elvira's —both in act 1—are not so grand, since she is not so noble, and so distraught that perhaps she cannot be properly reflective. Those of Zerlina, played by the prima donna, are much more extensive than one might expect, though they are in a simple tuneful style that befits a peasant girl, and that surely pleased the audience.

There are two surviving printed librettos for Don Giovanni. Both give the title as *Il dissoluto punito, o sia il D. Giovanni,* and both call it a dramma giocoso. One libretto, printed in Vienna, announces that the opera is for the arrival of the noble couple. But it is incomplete and has puzzled scholars for some time. Why was it printed? For approval by the censors? Because Bondini used it as advertising, hoping for performances in Vienna, Dresden, or elsewhere? And why is it incomplete? Because Mozart and Da Ponte had not yet finished? Or because they did not want the imperial censors to know everything that would actually take place on the stage?

The National Theater in Prague was built by Count Nostitz and opened in 1783. The performances of *Le nozze di Figaro* held at the National made Mozart famous in Prague. The theater also housed the premieres of *Don Giovanni* and, in 1791, *La Clemenza di Tito*. Despite flood damage in August 2002, the theater is still standing.

The Vienna libretto lacks a substantial portion of the end of act 1, closing about where Bertati's original libretto ends. It is impossible that act 1 could be thought of as complete in this version (Don Ottavio and Don Giovanni have just said that they must remain and see what develops); and it is unlikely that Da Ponte had got only this far. But the portion omitted does happen to omit "Viva la libertà," a sentiment unlikely to appeal to the censors.

All plays and operas that had not been already approved for performance in Vienna had to be submitted to the central imperial censors. Libretti could be submitted in printed form; perhaps the Vienna libretto is designed to fool the Viennese censors. The Prague libretto is the one intended for use by spectators.

Preparations

Mozart himself arrived in Prague by October 4, 1787, to rehearse with the company and conduct the first few performances. His wife, then seven months pregnant, accompanied him (their son Carl had been placed in a boarding establishment). Mozart's arrival was noted in the *Prager Oberpostamtszeiting* of October 6: "Our celebrated Herr Mozart has again arrived in Prague, and the news has spread here since that the opera newly written by him, *Das steinerne Gastmahl,* will be given for the first time at the National Theatre."

It took about three days to travel from Vienna, and Mozart put up at the Three Lions inn in the Kohlmarkt. Occasionally he stayed also with the Dusseks at their handsome Villa Bertramka at Smichov, just outside the city.

Mozart's letter to Gottfried von Jacquin suggests that preparations were not as advanced as he had hoped, and that the singers were lazy and poor learners: "The stage personnel here are not as smart as those in Vienna, when it comes to mastering an opera of this kind in a very short time. Secondly, I found on my arrival that so few preparations and arrangements had been made that it would have been absolutely impossible to produce it on the 14th, that is, yesterday."

Da Ponte's arrival three days later was noted in the newspaper; he stayed at the inn Zum Platteis, across from Mozart's lodging. They are said to have shouted at each other from their respective windows.

It was the normal task of the librettist to arrange the staging of an opera. This was partly because he best knew what was meant by the various speeches, but also because he could, if necessary, actually change the text, especially in recitatives, to suit the needs of specific singers, stages, and situations. In serious opera, staging almost takes care of itself. Traditional gestures of emotion, standard placement on stage (kings in the center, good characters on the right, bad on the left), and the limited nature of the action make it relatively straightforward. For comic opera—or, in this case, dramma giocoso—matters are more complex. There is a lot of comic business—disguises, blows, double-takes—that requires carefully timed and well-rehearsed actions on stage.

Da Ponte, however, stayed only a few days (he had operas under way elsewhere), and though he surely helped to make adjustments, he was not able to see the rehearsals through to the end. Giacomo Casanova (best known now for his memoirs) arrived in Prague after Da Ponte's departure and may well have helped Mozart with last-minute changes in the words. But Mozart must himself have been closely involved in getting his opera on the stage.

Mozart had ten days to get the opera ready. But the company also had to perform three days a week and was unwilling to rehearse on those days, so there were really only five working days between Mozart's arrival and the scheduled premiere. He arrived on Thursday, so he had Saturday and Sunday (if the singers agreed), and Tuesday, Thursday, and Saturday of the following week. The premiere was planned for Sunday, October 14, to celebrate the marriage of Archduchess Maria Theresia to Prince Anton Clemens of Saxony when the archduchess passed through Prague.

But it rapidly became clear that Don Giovanni would not be ready by the archduchess' visit; *Figaro,* well known to the company, was performed instead, with Mozart conducting. Mozart was amused by the politicking in Prague:

> In this connexion I have a good joke to tell you. A few of the leading
> ladies here, and in particular one very high and mighty one, were kind
> enough to find it very ridiculous, unsuitable, and Heaven knows what
> else that the Princess should be entertained with a performance of "Fi-

garo," the "Crazy Day," as the management were pleased to call it. It never occurred to them that no opera in the world, unless it is written specially for it, can be exactly suitable for such an occasion and that therefore it was of absolutely no consequence whether this or that opera were given, provided that it was a good opera and one which the Princess did not know; and "Figaro" at least fulfilled this last condition. In short by her persuasive tongue the ringleader brought things to such a pitch that the government forbade the impresario to produce this opera on that night. So she was triumphant! "Ho vinto" [I have conquered], she called out one evening from her box. No doubt she never suspected that the *ho* [have] might be changed to a *sono* [am]. But the following day Le Noble appeared, bearing a command from His Majesty to the effect that if the new opera could not be given, "Figaro" was to be performed! My friend, if only you had seen the handsome, magnificent nose of this lady! Oh, it would have amused you as much as it did me!

The occasion was a splendid one, and efforts were made to please the visiting royalty. But they were too tired to stay until the end of the performance. The occasion was reported in the newspaper of October 16:

> At half-past six o'clock they [the archduchess and the prince] betook themselves to Nostitz's National Theatre, which for this occasion was embellished and illuminated in a very distinguished manner. The auditorium was so much glorified by the finery of the numerous guests that one has to admit never having beheld such a magnificent scene. At the entry of Their Highnesses they were greeted with the most evident marks of joy by the whole public, which they acknowledged with gracious gratitude. At their request the well-known opera *Die Hochzeit des Figaro*, generally admitted to be so well performed here, was given. The zeal of the musicians and the presence of Mozart, the Master, awakened a general approbation and satisfaction in Their Highnesses. After the first act a sonnet, ordered by several Bohemian patriots for this festivity, was publicly distributed. By reason of their early departure, Their Highnesses returned to the royal castle before the conclusion of the opera.

So the premiere of *Don Giovanni* was delayed until Wednesday the 24th, allowing five extra rehearsals. On Sunday the 21st, four days before the premiere, a further delay was decided, because a singer was ill. Mozart expressed his frustration to Jacquin: "It was fixed for the 24th, but a further postponement has been caused by the illness of one of the singers. As the company is so small, the impresario is in a perpetual state of anxiety and has to spare his people as much as possible, lest some unexpected indisposition should plunge him into the most awkward of all situations, that of not being able to produce any show whatsoever! So everything dawdles along here because the singers, who are lazy, refuse

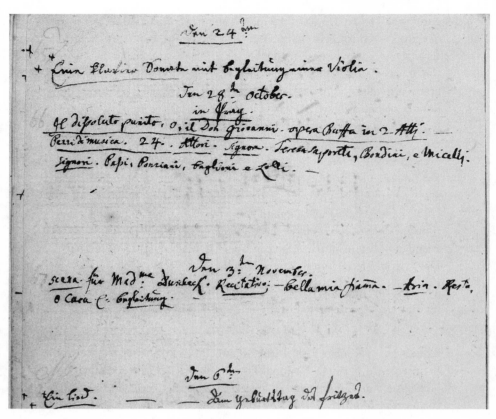

Mozart's entry for *Don Giovanni* in his handwritten "Catalogue
of all my works." Note that Mozart calls this an "opera buffa"
(the libretto has "dramma giocoso") and indicates that there are
twenty-four "pieces of music." This document is the only existing
indication of the casting (see p. 87).

to rehearse on opera days and the manager, who is anxious and timid, will not force them."

The planned rehearsal time was so short that Mozart had surely sent some of the
music for *Don Giovanni* ahead (despite the risks in the absence of copyright protection);
he had certainly done so with other operas, and would again. But much remained to be
done. When he arrived, his score still lacked much of the music. Several of the musical
numbers in his manuscript were clearly composed after his arrival. They include the overture, the entrance of Zerlina and Masetto with the chorus and Masetto's following aria
("Ho capito"), and, in the second act, the first duet between Don Giovanni and Leporello,
Don Giovanni's serenade, the graveyard scene, and the finale.

A number of changes and adjustments were made in the course of rehearsals.
This was natural; indeed, it was much easier to develop an opera in rehearsal with the
composer present than it was to proceed, as this one had, with most of the music arriving

before the composer himself. It had meant that singers needed to learn their music without the coaching of the composer; that they could not ask for changes, substitutions, or transpositions that would make a role particular to a given singer; and that they had had to begin rehearsing without guidance in those matters of staging that can be worked out only in the space in question and with particular actors in mind.

Mozart may have delayed some of the pieces on purpose. The duet for Masetto and Zerlina with chorus was composed in Prague, perhaps when Mozart found that there was an adequate chorus. Or there may have been pressure from the impresario to include more music for his wife (Zerlina).

The aria for Masetto ("Ho capito") is on a text that is part of the original libretto, but the typography in the first text-book suggests that it was intended as a recitative. Mozart may have wanted the singer, who also played the Commendatore, to be spared for the finale; we know so little about the Masetto, Giuseppe Lolli, that we can't be sure that he sang in the earlier *Figaro,* so perhaps Mozart was reluctant to compose music in advance for a singer whose voice he didn't know.

The duet that opens the second act was added, but not because Mozart waited to meet the singers; the autograph manuscript actually begins the act with the following recitative. The addition was made in Prague and so was not a hole waiting to be filled. Don Giovanni's serenade, though, was foreseen from the beginning; only the music was added in Prague. It is often reported that Luigi Bassi, playing Don Giovanni, was unsatisfied because he had no real aria in the opera, but this anecdote is difficult to verify.

It must have happened that Mozart received a flurry of requests and pent-up complaints at the moment of his arrival. These needed to be dealt with, along with the music that certainly needed to be composed—the second finale and the overture.

Franz Niemetschek, a patriotic Bohemian and Mozart's first biographer, reports a conversation during rehearsals:

> One day—(after the first rehearsals of his Don Juan)—Mozart went for a walk with the orchestra director and Kapellmeister Mr. Kuchař. In their private conversation they came to talk about Don Juan. Mozart said: "What do you think of the music for Don Juan? Will people like it as much as Figaro? It is so different!"
>
> Kuchař: "How can you doubt it? The music is beautiful, original and has depth (tief gedacht). The Bohemians will certainly like everything that comes from Mozart's hand."
>
> Mozart: "Your words reassure me, coming as they do from a connoisseur. I for my part have worked hard and spared no effort to give Prague something special."

After various delays and what must have been frantic work, the dress rehearsal finally took place on Sunday the 28th, and the first performance was the next day.

There is no surviving poster or ticket or program for the performance (although a fake poster has often been reprinted). There is, however, an announcement of the performance

1787.

Nro. 87.

von Schönfeldsche.

k. k. Prager Oberpostamtszeitung.

Dienstags den 30. Oktober.

Politische inländische Neuigkeiten.

Prag den 29. Oktober.

Der Direkteur der hiesigen italienischen Gesellschaft gab gestern Nachricht von der für die Anwesenheit der hohen toskan. Gäste bestimmt gewesene Oper, Don Jouan, oder die bestrafte Ausschweifung. Sie hat den Herrn Hoftheaterdichter Abbe da Ponte zum Verfasser, und wird heute den 29ten zum erstenmale aufgeführt. Alles freuet sich auf die vortreffliche Komposizion des großen Meisters Mozart. Nächstens mehr hievon.

Die berühmte uralte Uhr am altstäd- ter Rathhause ist itzt ganz hergestellt, und blos von ihrem Alterthume belebt. Jede Kleinigkeit ist durch die Erfrischung der Far- ben dabey ausgedrückt. Im Ganzen macht sie ein prächtiges Ansehen, und wird all-

gemein bewundert. Sie zeigt nebst dem Sonn- und Mondlauf die beweglichen Fest- täge, die Jahrszeiten, Monate, Wochen, Tage, Gestirne und alle Veränderungen des Horizonts. Ehe die Stunde schlägt, tritt ein künstliches Skelet hervor, und zieht die Glocke. Gegenüber steht ein Greis, der den Kopf bewegt. Es scheint bey allem dem, daß die Angeber dieser Uhrreformen wirkli- che Freunde des Alterthums seyn müssen, weil man nebst dieser auch noch verschiedene Ple- cen daselbst antrift, z. B. die alte Rathhaus- stube, bey der die ganze Decke von schwerem gothischen Gehölze in eisernen Ketten hängt. Neben diesen sind die Füllungen im her- kulanischen Alter, humsgeschmäcke in lebende Farben gesetzt, was sehr auffallend her- sieht, weil das eben itzt der herrschende Ge- schmak beym ganzen Ameublement ist. Das Ganze verräth einen ehrwürdigen Anblick,

S s ss   und

A Prague newspaper article for October 30 announces the premiere of *Don Giovanni*. The opening paragraph reads: "The director of the Italian opera company here yesterday issued news of the opera *Don Jouan, or Dissolution Punished,* appointed for performance during the sojourn of the exalted Tuscan guests. It has the Court Theatre Poet, the Abbé Da Ponte, for its author, and is to be performed for the first time to-day, the 29th. All look forward with pleasure to the excellent composition of our great master, Mozart. More of this anon."

of November 30, which may reproduce the language of the original. The German text reads, in translation:

Il dissoluto punito osia Il D. Giovanni: Der gestrafte Ausschweifende, oder: Don Jean.

A grand singspiel in two acts. The poetry is by the Imperial Royal theater poet Herr Abbé Da Ponte, written expressly for the purpose. And the completely new, excellent music is by the famous Kapellmeister Herr Mozart, also especially composed for the occasion. . . . N.B. The libretto, in Italian only, is to be had at the box-office, bound in gold paper, price 40 kr. a copy, and ordinary, price 20 kr. The arias and other pieces of the music in score are to be had of the Impresario Herr Guardasoni, domiciled opposite the national Theatre in Bergmand's house, No. 285, on the first floor. . . . The curtain rises at 7 o'clock and falls at 9:30 o'clock.

The Performance

The premiere, several times delayed and much anticipated, began at 7:00 P.M. on a mostly cloudy day. By 6:30, according to Niemetschek, the overwhelmed box-office had been shut down, and many of the audience members could not get to their reserved seats. Alfred Meissner's imaginative picture of the premiere sets the scene:

> The carriages began to arrive by five-thirty, and traffic soon came to a standstill. Impeccable ladies left their carriages and despite their careful toilettes had to find their way to the entrance through a sea of mud. In the hall they found the parterre and galleries already full. The appearance of the galleries was almost terrifying, spectators packed cheek by jowl to the last row, who held on to the iron rods that connected one roof-beam to another and seemed as if they would fall down on the rows below them. In the buzz of the excited crowd could scarcely be heard the servants circulating with the cry of "Beer and fresh Wurst" to serve the insatiable appetites of the gallery, while in the spaces below the cry of "Lemonade! Almond milk" rang out.

The National Theater, placed in the center of the city, was intended to show that Prague was as cultured as other capitals. The building was a symbol of the arts, of society, and of national pride. The shield on the outside read "Patriae et musis" ("To the fatherland and to the muses"). The theater was meant to give Bohemia a theater second to none. (Bohemian patriotism at this time was not Czech but German—or rather Austrian.)

The narrow side of the box-shaped building, facing the square, had a covered entrance on the ground floor (for carriages of distinguished theatergoers). There were modest rooms for refreshment on each of the three upper floors, and staircases on each side leading to the boxes (other staircases were at the stage end of the auditorium). There were three levels of boxes and a gallery.

The auditorium seated about eight hundred. It was decorated inside with gold; a central box with plumes was provided for royalty. Boxes were decorated with festoons and garlands, and the ceiling above the gallery was supported by caryatids.

The 1783 Gotha theater calendar describes the building as follows: "The new theater will be finished next Easter. It is a beautiful, noble and comfortable building, and gives the greatest credit to its builder in every respect, for he spared no cost to provide Prague with a theater that would compete with any theater in Germany. It contains 52 boxes, two very spacious parterres and a comfortable gallery. The decorations are painted by Herr Platzer, a young and talented painter. The front curtain has been executed by Herr Jahn, the local historical painter. On the front of the building can be read the inscription: Patriae et Musis 1781. Over the portal is a bust of Shakespeare and the remaining decorations will depict the most famous poets."

The proscenium arch was made of white pilasters topped with giant gold volutes supporting a decorated lintel faced with a medallion of Gotthold Ephraim Lessing, whose high standards for the German theater were thus set as a mark on the stage. (Lessing's

---

The Bondini Company, and Their Roles in *Don Giovanni* and *Figaro*

Don Giovanni	Luigi Bassi (Almaviva)
Donna Anna	Teresa Saporiti (Countess)
Don Ottavio	Antonio Baglioni (not in the *Figaro* cast)
Commendatore	Giuseppe Lolli (Bartolo and Antonio?)
Donna Elvira	Caterina Micelli (Cherubino?)
Leporello	Felice Ponziani (Figaro)
Masetto	Giuseppe Lolli
Zerlina	Caterina Bondini (Susanna)

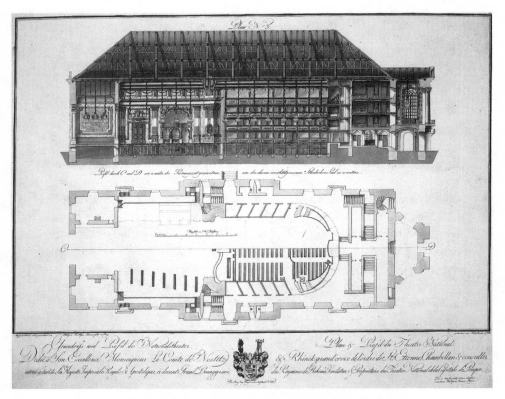

This engraving by Philip and Franz Heger gives a view of the
National Theater. There are seven sets of wings and,
as in the Haymarket Theatre, the perspective can be extended
by the use of a further room beyond the wings.

Emilia Galotti was the opening performance in the new theater.) The theater followed
Lessing's priorities, so opera came third, after German theater and Singspiel.

The theater was noted in Mozart's time for acoustics that must have been too resonant. As one traveler put it, "The city of Prague will have to make do with an Italian opera
where one hears the singing and sees the grimaces, but can understand nothing of the text.
In fact, given the current state of things, this is best for the city."

The unusually large audience cheered Mozart three times as he entered the pit to
conduct. The overture, beginning with the portentous harmonies that return with the Commendatore's statue at the end, was composed at the last minute, as was customary with
operas. There are many probably apocryphal stories recounting how Mozart had to be
cajoled, begged, and tricked into composing the overture, and how the ink was still wet
on the orchestral parts at the performance. ("At seven in the evening, as the opera was to
begin, the copyists were still working on the parts, so one had to wait, and only at a quarter

to eight were the orchestra parts brought into the pit, still strewn with sand, when Mozart
also arrived to direct this first production.")

The orchestra in the theater was small but competent. Three first violins, three
seconds, two each of violas, cellos, and double-basses, plus the extraordinarily able wind
players for which the orchestra was renowned. The local paper had said of *Figaro* in 1786:
"Connoisseurs who have seen this opera in Vienna are anxious to declare that it was done
much better here; and this is very likely, since the wind instruments, of which the Bohemians
are well known to be decided masters, have a great deal to do in the whole piece." The
winds have beautiful solos here and there in the opera, and Mozart had no hesitation in
writing virtuoso music for them, but their parts are not extraordinarily featured in *Don
Giovanni.* Additional personnel were needed for this production—players for the stage
bands in the finales of act 1 (the three dance bands) and act 2 (the wind-band selections
of opera tunes), and singers for the chorus.

Johann Joseph Strobach, the leader of the orchestra, had led the performances
of *Figaro* and was well known to Mozart, who sent Strobach a letter of thanks after *Figaro*
in which he attributed much of its success to the quality of the orchestra. Playing in the
orchestra was not a full-time occupation, and all the members were engaged in other sorts
of activities, as teachers, copyists, and performers. They were in a sense the most stable
element of the opera, since the orchestra consisted of local musicians while the various

opera companies came and went and their singers changed. Niemetschek describes the orchestra at the time of *Figaro:* "There was the incomparable orchestra of our opera, which understood how to execute Mozart's ideas so accurately and diligently. For on these worthy men, who were mostly not professional concert players, but nevertheless very knowledgeable and capable, the new harmony and fire and eloquence of the songs made an immediate and lasting impression."

Mozart undoubtedly directed from the keyboard and accompanied the recitatives himself. The overture, with its unearthly beginning (the opera is not totally comic), anticipates the statue's appearance at the end but saves the trombones for later. It soon turns sunny and leads directly into the first scene, and the curtain opens on a garden outside Donna Anna's house, with Leporello complaining about his sorry lot ("Notte e giorno faticar").

SETS

The first set is a long one, which will later be covered by a street scene probably only as deep as the second of the six wings of the theater. This alternation of long and short sets, just as in Handel's day, allowed for continuous changes of scene without the need for lowering the curtain.

The stage is thirty-three feet wide, sixty-five feet deep, and the proscenium opening is twenty-eight feet high. There are two trapdoors, left and right, between the first and second wings (they can be seen in a drawing and will be needed at the end of the opera). Of the seven coulisses, or wings, six are for the side panels, and the seventh is for the backcloth, though of course the stage can be closed at shallower points also. There is also a room beyond the stage that can be opened for long perspective effects.

Pasquale Bondini had a large number of stock settings. Many had been brought from the older Kotce Theater, and Count Nostitz had hired the gifted young painter Josef Platzer to paint a series of twelve new decorations, and soon appointed him scene-painter. When Bondini hired the theater he took over Platzer's decors. In doing so he probably acquired most of what he needed for *Don Giovanni* (and for many other operas), as we can tell from the inventory of the sets he bought, including street scenes, a garden, a drawing room, a ballroom; possibly all he needed for *Don Giovanni* that was not already on hand was the cemetery scene. Or he may have used the older cemetery scene taken over from the Kotce Theater, described in the inventory as a "sepulcher with eight flats and one backdrop. Newly painted on new canvas." What is usually called a cemetery, however, is evidently an indoor space *(loco chiuso)* like a mausoleum *(in forma di sepolcreto)*. It is a large one, since it can contain equestrian statues (painted?), but it is indoors, because Don Giovanni says "vien dentro" ("come inside").

The High-Baroque influence of Galli-Bibiena and others is clearly felt in the sets of Prague and other theaters of the time. Double perspectives, curious angles, and elaborate decoration were the norm in late eighteenth-century stage design. By now, however, there was a tendency toward simplicity, naturalness, and unity in a sort of neoclassical spirit

A series of engravings by Norbert Bittner of Joseph Platzer's set designs give us some idea of Platzer's style, even though we do not have specific images for *Don Giovanni*. This ballroom, with an angled perspective that gives the impression of a small portion of a very large room, might be too big for *Don Giovanni*'s ballroom, and it does not have obvious spaces for three dance bands.

that may have been apparent in the settings for *Don Giovanni*. Platzer, who went on to become scene painter to the court at Vienna, was a skilled young artist in the neoclassical style; he was described in 1784 as a "young but highly skilled artist, whose decors make the noblest effect." Unfortunately none of this work survives, but it was of real quality, as can be seen in Bittner's prints after Platzer's sketches.

It is unlikely that Bondini used Platzer's older scenery without making substantial improvements, since his company is often cited for its new scenery and fine costumes. Domenico Guardasoni must have been responsible for cobbling together whatever was needed and for ordering extra pieces—a window for a serenade, the cemetery vault, and so forth.

The settings for *Don Giovanni,* alternating longer and shorter sets, allow for the continuity of the opera. Christof Bitter's plausible suggested arrangement appears in the table (descriptions are combined from the libretto and the score).

Table 3. Settings for *Don Giovanni*

ACT 1

1. (long stage)

   *[Giardino.] Notte. Leporello (con ferrajuolo che passeggia davanti la casa di
   Donna Anna).*

   [Garden.] Night. Leporello (wrapped in a cloak, who walks in front of Donna
   Anna's house).

2. (short stage)

   Strada. Notte. (Street. Night.)

3. (medium stage)

   Giardino con due porte chiuse a chiave per di fuori. Due nicchie. (later: *Leporello
   apre la finestra*).

   Garden with two doors locked from without. Two niches. (Later: Leporello opens
   the window).

4. (long stage)

   Sala illuminata e preparata per una gran festa di ballo.

   A salon lit and prepared for a grand ball.

ACT 2

5. (short stage)

   Strada. (Street.)

   Si fa notte poco a poco.

   Gradually it becomes night.

6. (medium stage)

   Atrio [terreno] oscuro con tre porte [in casa di Donna Anna].

   A dark [ground-floor] courtyard with three doors [in Donna Anna's house].

7. (long stage)

   *Loco chiuso [in forma di sepolcreto. Diverse statue equestre; statua del
   Commendatore].*

   An enclosed space [in the form of a cemetery. Various equestrian statues;
   statue of the Commendatore].

8. (short stage)

   Camera tetra. (Gloomy chamber.)

9. (long stage)

   Sala; una mensa preparata per mangiare.

   Salon; a table prepared for eating.

The first wing of the stage has working doors at each side, which are used throughout the performance in various ways. In the first setting, one door (at the right?) provides entry to the Commendatore's house, through which he comes for his ill-starred moonlight duel. In the second set, the left-hand door serves as an entry to the inn. And in the third set they are the niches in the garden (and *not* the doors specified in the libretto, which being locked will not need to open). And they certainly are used in the ballroom scene, where Zerlina and Don Giovanni exit left for sinister business and Leporello and Don Giovanni enter right.

The street scene of act 2 is surely the same as that of act 1; the gradual darkening in act 2 brings it back to the level of light seen in act 1; it must be dark so that Leporello's disguise can work. Darkening the set is a matter of extinguishing lights: candles, oil lamps, and lanterns attached behind the wings. Many theaters had a mechanism for lowering tin covers over lights so as to change their intensity. Since the auditorium is illuminated, persons singing downstage are lit from the front, but those upstage may not be seen on a relatively dark set. This is a practical reason for the many servants with torches who accompany members of the cast. They are not just signs of rank but serve also as human spotlights. Goethe, in his handwritten notes to a later production of *Don Giovanni*, included the following: "In the first act Donna Anna and Don Giovanni must not remain in the dark when the Commendatore is taken away; a third supernumerary must be added to light them."

Bondini's company was as up to date in its costumes as in its sets. We have little to go by except general praise, but the modern trend toward costumes that are related to the time and place in which the action takes place—rather than the generalized theatrical costume of Handel's day—suggests something Spanish, or at least a bit foreign. And we can expect a servant to dress like a servant and a peasant and a noble lady to be distinguishable, not only by their deportment and their musical style but by their reasonably realistic dress.

THE SINGERS

Felice Ponziani is the first member of the cast to appear on stage. As Leporello he paces back and forth; his aria is one of the rare ones in *Don Giovanni* that is not addressed to anybody. Leporello is thinking aloud, complaining of the unfairness of his position as a servant. The scene is laid carefully: I the servant; he the gentleman; the lady is inside with him. Something will happen. . . . Rather like the maid in the drawing-room comedy ("The master will be down in a moment . . ."), Leporello introduces us to a situation. But he is not the maid: he will be with us throughout the drama, providing a comic foil to Don Giovanni's evil sexual exploits.

Ponziani permits himself more breadth in his acting that is usual for more noble characters. He was praised for his skill in comedy, which was "inexhaustible and true to nature." Inexhaustible in that it was wide-ranging and full of variety, and true to nature not in the sense that the audience recognized a "real" person, one who behaves on stage rather like people behave on the street, but rather that idealized Naturalism that was characteristic of stage deportment at the time.

TERESA SAPORITI
Hic effigies: ubique fama

Teresa Saporiti, the singer of the role of Donna Anna, is here presented with the legend "Her image here, her fame everywhere."

As the company's leading bass, Ponziani had made himself known to Mozart in the role of Figaro, and he had previously sung at Venice and Parma. His voice was even and large but not blustery. He was praised for his enunciation and was good at patter (good for a catalogue aria or a chattering fear at the sight of the Commendatore's statue). Rather a stiff actor, he was a great success at buffo roles. In 1782 (September 21) the *Berliner Theatre-und Literaturzeitung* called him "a bass who has few equals, since he combines strength with smoothness of his voice, and has furthermore the merit that one can understand every word he says, even in the fastest singing. Prominent though he is as a singer, he is equally praiseworthy as an actor. He always enters into the spirit of the character and puts him truly before us. As a lover he is perhaps somewhat stiff, but he always is master of his role, and in comic roles on the other hand his playing is inexhaustible and true to nature; he has roles that few can play as well; and he is also one of the best singers." The Prague *Oberpostamtszeitung* of January 9, 1787, described him as a "man who here, and wherever he has appeared, has been the favourite of connoisseurs and of all who have heard him."

Teresa Saporiti appears next, as Donna Anna, rushing on stage in pursuit of Don Giovanni after what we later learn was an attempted rape. Saporiti, now twenty-four years old, was the impresario's sister-in-law, and she was a beauty; there are rumors of Mozart's flirtations with her. She was perhaps a still unfinished singer; a 1782 report from Leipzig indicated that she "is a complete beginner as an actress, and halfway so as a singer; not so gifted, however, in her figure." Though she is not named, she must have sung the role of the Countess in Figaro; at any rate Mozart must have known her voice, since he seems to have written her part in Vienna before he came to Prague. Saporiti evidently continued to improve as a singer and actress; she was very histrionic, and her fury in the opening scene must have been impressive. She had a long career in Venice, Parma, Bologna, and St. Petersburg, dying in Milan at the age of 104 (three weeks after Verdi's revised *La forza*

Luigi Bassi portrays Don Giovanni in an engraving by Medardus Thoenert. This is the only view we have of the original production, but it is unlikely to be an accurate representation. Even though Don Giovanni does sing two serenades to the same lighted window, he is wearing Leporello's costume both times. Here he wears a feathered hat, a French-style coat, and short boots (rather than buckle shoes). This is a fine costume for a gallant, but not for a servant.

del destino opened at La Scala). She published two arias of her own composition in 1796.

Don Giovanni, played by the twenty-one-year-old baritone Luigi Bassi, is trying to escape Donna Anna's fury. Mozart had met Bassi during the composer's first visit to Prague, and Bassi's performance as the wayward Count Almaviva in *Figaro* had prepared him for the role of the wayward Don. Born in Pesaro, Bassi had sung in various Italian houses, and he joined the Bondini company as an eighteen-year-old. He was known for his good voice, but even more for his acting. He was an excellent mimic, and his act 2 impersonation of Leporello must have been fine. "Very handsome," said one observer, "and very stupid." His voice was in decline by the time he was twenty-nine; he remained in Prague until 1806 and continued to sing the role of *Don Giovanni* until 1814. From 1815 he was a singer and opera producer in Dresden. A libretto of *Don Giovanni* supposedly prepared by him in 1814 served as the basis for Carl Maria von Weber's productions in Prague and Dresden. (It lacks the final scene, and all the additions that Mozart made in Vienna.) Beethoven in 1824 called the sixty-year-old Bassi a "fiery Italian."

"This meritorious singer," reported the 1793 *Gothaer Taschenkalender,* "has been the ornament of society, and he is so still. There are few singers or actors for whom nature has so richly provided as for this darling son. His voice is as well-sounding as his acting is masterly. Wherever he plays, he meets with equal approval in tragic and comic roles, and he pleases wherever he plays. In Italy, his homeland, as well as in Warsaw, Leipzig, and

Prague, he was the darling of the public. As soon as he appeared, joy and cheerfulness broke out throughout the house, and he never left the stage without unqualified loud applause."

Looking back on Bassi's better years, Niemetschek reported in the *Allgemeine musikalischer Zeitung* of April 1800:

> Before his voice was lost Bassi was a splendid singer, and he still uses what remains very well. It lies between Tenor and Bass, and though it sounds somewhat hollow, it is still flexible, full, and pleasing. Herr Bassi is furthermore a fine actor, without becoming too histrionic in tragedy, nor too low and tasteless in comedy. In his fine and comic moods he parodies for example many of the errors of the other singers so well that the audience notices but the singers don't. His best roles are *Axur, Don Giovanni, Theodore,* the notary in *Molinara,* the Count in *Figaro,* and several others. He never spoiled a role, and is the only actor in the current Italian company.

Niemetschek, who heard Bassi often in Prague, liked him better as an actor than a singer; perhaps Niemetschek's memory was of the older Bassi after his voice was gone: "Herr Bassi is a very able actor, but no singer, for he lacks the first requisite: a voice! I wish he could add this to his other qualities, for then we would wish for no better Don Giovanni, Almaviva, and Axur, roles that he acts in unmatched fashion. He has the best taste of all his colleagues, and understands the preferences of German artists. He enjoyed the favor of the Prague public for all the years he was there."

As Donna Anna returns to the house, her father comes out to protect her and to challenge Don Giovanni. The Commendatore is played by Giuseppe Lolli, the second bass of the company—who also sings the role of Masetto. Nowadays we would call him a comprimario. He might have performed Bartolo and Antonio in *Figaro,* though we cannot be sure. He was known as a good singer, but we know little else except that he had sung in Rome, Florence, and Parma. He was living in Vienna in 1825.

A challenge is issued, a duel fought, the Commendatore murdered by the libertine, and the plot set in action. Don Giovanni and Leporello make their escape, and Donna Anna returns with her fiancé, the noble Don Ottavio, but too late to capture Don Giovanni; in a passionate duet they swear vengeance. The duet is preceded by a recitativo accompagnato, something that Mozart reserves here for his noble characters (though he did later add an accompagnato for Elvira in Vienna). Such recitatives, as in Handel's operas, are reserved for moments of high intensity and ones in which a variety of emotions may be present, where action advances. This is true here: Donna Anna has returned with Ottavio (she had retired before the swordfight) to help her father, and instead discovers his body and faints; Ottavio attempts to console her. Mozart's recitative is far from perfunctory, describing the changing emotions with amazing effect.

Don Ottavio is Antonio Baglioni, the newest member of the company, and a prize recruit. Having recently arrived from Venice he had not been present for *Figaro* (he was in Venice performing Gazzaniga's version of the Don Juan story) and was thus the only member of the company that Mozart would not have known. Mozart did know his sister Clementine, for whom he may have composed the role of Rosina in *La finta semplice*. Baglioni was admired for his purity and good taste, which must have suited him well in his role as Don Ottavio. (Mozart certainly wrote him some challenging florid music: when *Don Giovanni* was later done in Vienna, the tenor could not manage "Il mio tesoro," so Mozart wrote him the more lyrical "Dalla sua pace.") Da Ponte said he was "a man of perfect taste and great knowledge in music and had trained the most celebrated singers in Italy. I had known him as a man of great worth at Prague, at the time my *Don Giovanni* was performed there." The 1793 *Gothaer Taschenkalender* reported of Baglioni, "Certainly he deserves his loud applause; his voice has developed, it is well-sounding, clear and full of expression, such that few theatres can boast of having such a tenor. We have not heard his equal for a long time. His chief role is Colloardo in 'La molinara.' Here he blends acting and singing in the most masterful way." Niemetschek was less enthusiastic—as were most of his comments on Italians: "This singer left the company a year ago [1795] and remained some time in Italy; here he industriously collected all the bad habits of Italian artists and non-artists, and thus equipped, he came back to Herr Guardasoni. He sings no note the way its composer intended and wished, he drowns the most beautiful thoughts in his alien leaps and trills, and expects us to take his unformed wavings of the hands for action, so that one has difficulty understanding an aria when he sings it. Admittedly, he needs such flourishes to cover his faulty voice, which is more a mezzo basso." Baglioni later sang the title role in Mozart's 1791 *La clemenza di Tito* and worked in Venice (1793–94) and Vienna (1796), where he also functioned as a respected teacher of singing.

As Donna Anna and Don Ottavio retire, Don Giovanni smells his prey ("odor di femmina"), and he and Leporello retire to see who it is. Donna Elvira, in her traveling costume, sings of her rage at being abandoned by her promised husband. She displays her desperation with a jagged melody in what sounds like a solo aria; we might sympathize with her plight, but Mozart makes the aria into an ensemble, and we watch as she is overheard and mocked by Don Giovanni and Leporello ("Let's console her"; "He has already consoled a thousand and eight"). Only when they approach from their concealment does Don Giovanni realize who she is and that it was he who had done the abandoning.

Caterina Micelli, the third woman of the company, sang the role of Elvira. Not much is known about her, but her voice was considered agile if not beautiful. She must have sung Cherubino in *Figaro*, which she was still performing in 1792; at any rate, Mozart felt confident enough to write her music before he came. A 1793 report is that "her chief accomplishment is acting in soubrette roles, but her voice is not pleasing, though she has much accomplishment."

Don Giovanni makes his escape, using Leporello as a foil, and Leporello is left to explain the situation to Elvira (and to us) in his famous catalogue aria. This is actually the first solo aria in the opera, and it fits Ponziani perfectly—opportunities for acting, mockery, for quick and witty language, changes of voice. Mozart liked arias to fit a singer "as perfectly as a well-made suit of clothes."

Elvira departs, and a chorus of peasants arrives accompanying a bride and bridegroom to their wedding. The chorus has beautiful but relatively simple music. These super-numeraries who work in the theater when called for will also serve as servants bearing torches, the infernal chorus at the end, and the other groups of mute actors who are needed from time to time. Mozart was not sure about the chorus in Prague, and perhaps this accounts for his delaying the composition of this scene until he could see whether the extras could sing. Fortunately for us, they could at least manage this charming music. The nuptial pair who arrive with them are Masetto (Giuseppe Lolli has changed out of his Commendatore's costume) and Zerlina, the last actor to appear on stage, and the prima donna of the company.

Caterina Bondini was the wife of the company's director, the sister of one of the singers, and a favorite with audiences. She sang the role of Zerlina though she was well along in pregnancy (she was already the mother of four children). She had been Susanna in *Figaro* and perhaps was best suited not to noble carriage but to a lively acting style. Poems were written about her extraordinary singing and acting abilities ("Bondini sings / And the saddest heart is filled with joy"), and she was much admired in Prague. A Berlin report of 1782 says that she "worked formerly as a concert singer in Leipzig. She sings the most difficult passagework with ease; it is a pity that her voice is somewhat slender, and that she neglects the expression in recitative." Her daughter Marianne (a younger sibling of the child carried onstage in *Don Giovanni*) also became a singer; she performed in the first Italian-language *Figaro* in Paris (1807).

ACTING

Actors in *Don Giovanni* played to the audience even though they were almost always addressing another character; a quarter turn toward that person was enough. Arias were generally sung downstage, as is traditional, even though most of them are addressed to another character. Ensembles were played in a semicircular group or in a line.

In *Don Giovanni,* as in Handel's work, the distinction between aria and recitative is not only a musical one, for in arias time generally slows or stops. An aria is generally an explanation ("Notte e giorno faticar"), an exclamation ("Quel barbaro dov'è?"), an acknowledgment of an emotion that reveals a character but does not advance the action very much. Recitative is where the plot unfolds in Mozart, as in Handel, but Mozart's great dramatic contribution is in the ensembles, in which musical complexity is combined with action. Zerlina feels very differently at the end of "Là ci darem la mano."

The stylized schematization of stage deportment and gesture, codified in French manuals, was widely observed, as we saw in Handel's London. The trend toward a more "natural" style can be seen in the praise of the acting in Bondini's company. But even the natural style employs the widely understood language of gesture and posture. Lessing, whose principles were admired and understood in the theater, acknowledged the continuing relevance of the classical style of acting, though he disliked the artificial conventions of French tragedy. For Lessing, "every movement made by the hand in such passages [those of special moral importance] should be significant. It is possible often to be picturesque if only the pantomime be avoided." Feeling, he writes in his *Hamburg Dramaturgy* (1769), "is something internal of which we can only judge by its external signs."

Goethe's rules for his Weimar theater, designed to provide a modern and natural acting style, are still largely based on the old rules. They are rules, evidently, because they work. They help audience members to understand the action, hear the words, and know how a character feels. There are not many possibilities for idiosyncratic "natural" expression, but comic characters are the most likely to bend those rules in the interest of comedy. Such characters are usually peasants or servants, occasionally pompous doctors or notaries in the tradition of the commedia dell'arte. Leporello is allowed to stutter, to imitate the statue, to shiver, to sing with his mouth full—all elements of comedy. Donna Anna and Don Ottavio, members of the nobility, would not behave like this. Indeed, they would surely act, despite all demands for "naturalism," much like the characters in a Handel opera half a century earlier and half a continent away.

From Goethe's Rules for Actors

35. First the actor must consider that he should not only imitate nature but present it in idealized form, and thus unite the true with the beautiful in his presentation.
39. Actors should also avoid playing to one another, out of a sense of misunderstood naturalness, as if no third person were present; they should never act in profile nor turn their backs to the audience. If this is done for the sake of characterization or out of necessity, then let it be done with care and grace.
60. Whoever stands on the right side should act with the left arm, and contrariwise, whoever stands on the left side should act with the right, so that the chest is covered by the arm as little as possible.
88. Anyone who enters for a monologue from the upstage wings does well to move diagonally down to the proscenium on the opposite side, since in general diagonal movements are very pleasing.
91. It should be evident, by the way, that these rules should be particularly observed when one is portraying noble, dignified characters. On the other hand, there are characters for whom this dignity is totally unsuitable, for example, peasants, boors, and so on. Yet one will portray these characters much better if one carries out with artistry and calculation the reverse of what decorum suggests, while always remembering that this should be an imitative appearance and not dull reality.

ACT I

Now everybody is present and the characters have been introduced; the death of the Commendatore in the first scene has created a problem that will hang over the plot until the end. And the proximate complications—Donna Anna's vengeance, Elvira's rage, Masetto's jealousy—are converging on Don Giovanni's house and the finale of act 1.

Donna Elvira complicates matters: she arrives in time to warn Zerlina of Don Giovanni's nature ("Ah fuggi il traditor") and to spirit her away. And when Donna Anna and Don Ottavio arrive and seek Don Giovanni's help in their revenge (not recognizing him as the villain), he has to feign enthusiasm. When Donna Elvira returns to chastise him again, the ensuing quartet is a marvelous opportunity for one of those magical ensembles in which everyone speaks in a different voice: the noble couple, the enraged Elvira, the fast-talking Don who tries to assert that Elvira is mad. He makes his escape claiming that he needs to protect the unfortunate Elvira and invites the nobles to his house.

Don Giovanni sends everybody away so that he can woo Zerlina. Masetto is not pleased, and he sings his aria ("Ho capito"—composed in Prague) before being led away with the others by Leporello. Don Giovanni seduces Zerlina in the infallible "Là ci darem la mano" and leads her toward his house. Now follow three scenes, each with two characters and one aria: the nobles, the master and servant, and the peasant couple. Donna Anna, alone with Don Ottavio, announces in a passionate accompanied recitative that she has recognized Don Giovanni as her attacker, and she recounts to him the attempted rape. In an even more impassioned aria ("Or sai chi l'onore") she demands that he avenge her. Don Ottavio cannot believe that a gentleman could do such a deed, and he determines to resolve the situation. (This is the place where, in Vienna, Mozart inserted the aria "Dalla sua pace" for Francesco Morella, who could not manage the more difficult aria in the second act.)

Leporello and Don Giovanni appear, and Leporello reports that the party is under way and that he has managed to lock Elvira out of the house. Don Giovanni looks forward to his evening ("Fin ch'han del vino"), and they depart as the scene changes to a garden. The backdrop is removed to reveal Zerlina, Masetto, and the chorus of peasants. Masetto rebukes Zerlina, provoking her charming aria ("Batti, batti, o bel Masetto") with gavotte-rhythm and its virtuoso cello.

Now, according to the score, begins the finale. This means that the orchestral music is continuous to the end of the act: no more recitatives accompanied by keyboard. It also means that the action will converge, bringing everybody on stage, and that there will be all kinds of music. As Da Ponte put it, "Everybody sings; and every form of singing must be available—the *adagio,* the *allegro,* the *andante,* the intimate, the harmonious, and then—noise, noise, noise; for the *finale* almost always closes in an uproar."

Don Giovanni arrives, Masetto hides in a niche (to find out the truth about what happened with his fiancée), and the Don sends the peasants off to his party. Zerlina fails to escape, and Don Giovanni, in another seductive duet, makes the mistake of luring Zerlina to the niche where he discovers Masetto, and has to cover his tracks hastily. A dance band sounds from the palace, and Don Giovanni leads them in.

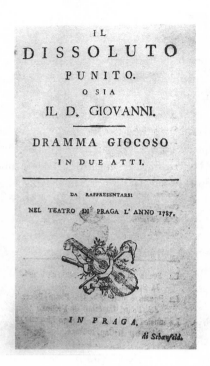

The printed libretto for the Prague performances is titled "The Dissolute Punished, or, The Don Giovanni." Whereas the librettist, Da Ponte, is listed as "Poet of the Imperial Theaters of Vienna," the composer, "Wolfgango Mozzart," is called a "German chapel-master."

Donna Anna, Don Ottavio, and Donna Elvira come masked, planning to infiltrate the party. They hear the minuet through the window and respond to the invitation of Don Giovanni. Before going in they invoke heaven's protection in a beautiful solemn and virtuosic trio, accompanied by Prague's splendid wind players.

The scene changes to the brilliant ballroom. Masetto and Zerlina are already there, expressing different opinions about the advisability of being in such a place. The masked nobles appear to the noble music of trumpets. They are invited in by Don Giovanni: "It is open to all: viva la libertà!" The cry of liberty is taken up by the maskers as a great fanfare.

This became a famous passage, and it seems clear that Don Giovanni's exclamation is ironical in a way. He is a libertine and so might be expected to make this toast. But he is saying it to persons, like Masetto, who must remain silent and know their place, while his bride is carried off in the name of liberty. The phrase is repeated so often, and with such resounding fanfare, that it might well cross the footlights and be taken up as a political cry. Bohemians might hear it in one way, Viennese censors another. No wonder it did not appear in the early Vienna libretto. And what an effect it must have had when

Mozart conducted it in Prague just before the premiere of his *La clemenza di Tito* in 1791, on the occasion of the coronation of the emperor as king of Bohemia. By then the French Revolution, with its own ideas of liberty—including the revocation of titles of nobility—must have made the cry of liberty sound very different to the assembled grandees.

The ballroom, scene of the most spine-chilling scream in opera, is the place where three little dance bands play three simultaneous tunes, starting with the famous minuet that makes everything so formal and threatening at once. That set may have had the sort of double perspective much favored at the time and seen in Platzer's "Gothic Hall." This gives the impression of three spaces, one near and two receding, but they are not really three spaces (the two distant ones are the result of careful scene-painting), and so the stage bands will need to have been placed probably near each other and not too distant from the proscenium.

The increasing complexity of the action—Donna Anna and Don Ottavio's noble minuet, Don Giovanni's middlebrow contradanse with Zerlina, and the comic Deutscher with which Leporello distracts Masetto—are matched with Mozart's miraculous three stage bands playing three dances in different meters at the same time. Mozart does what he can to make his momentary miracle audible. The first two dances have already been heard separately floating out the windows, and each new orchestra calls attention to itself by a tuning-up process with open strings and plinks and plunks. While the formal, organized social element plays itself out in dance, the private and antisocial abduction goes by in an instant, and just as everything is happening, Zerlina's scream dissolves the revels.

Mozart apparently did care about that scream. Joseph Svoboda, the concertmaster, is reported many years later as recollecting its rehearsal:

> At the final rehearsal of the opera Mozart was not at all satisfied with the efforts of a young and very pretty girl, the possessor of a voice of greater purity than power, to whom the part of Zerlina had been allotted. The reader will remember that Zerlina, frightened at Don Giovanni's too pronounced love-making, cries for assistance behind the scenes. In

---

Mixed Music in the Ballroom

If you should leave the room in which the Deutsche is danced and walk into the gallery that divides the rooms, you will be startled by the mixture of different music which sounds from the two spaces . . . in a new and unpleasing way; as you go further, the sound of the whirling dance fades, and you soon hear clearly the minuet-music in the other room.

spite of continued repetitions, Mozart was unable to infuse sufficient force into the poor girl's screams, until at last, losing all patience, he clambered from the conductor's desk on to the boards. At that period neither gas nor electric light lent facility to stage mechanism. A few tallow candles dimly glimmered among the desks of the musicians, but over the stage and the rest of the house almost utter darkness reigned. Mozart's sudden appearance on the stage was therefore not noticed, much less suspected, by poor Zerlina, who at the moment when she ought to have uttered the cry received from the composer a sharp pinch on the arm, emitting, in consequence, a shriek which caused him to exclaim: "Admirable! Mind you scream like that tonight!"

Don Giovanni is in trouble: he is caught in the act of abducting Zerlina, and the maskers reveal themselves. But Don Giovanni's courage, at least, does not fail him. He pretends to have caught Leporello in the act and, in the confusion of the animated stretto, master and servant make their escape.

ACT 2

Some modern critics have seen the second act of *Don Giovanni* as badly planned, repetitive, and illogical, an act in which Da Ponte brings out old stage tricks—disguises and beatings—to make the opera longer than it needs to be. It certainly is an act full of jokes, and of splendid music.

It begins with a duet in which Leporello threatens to leave Don Giovanni's service. This duet was not in the original conception; the act originally opened with the following recitative, as the title in the autograph manuscript shows. Why the duet was added in Prague is not clear. Perhaps the contrast with the staggering finale of act 1 was too great, or perhaps the singers or the public just wanted more music. In any event, the duet underscores the fact that Leporello cannot break his ties to Don Giovanni.

There follows a double seduction in which Don Giovanni twice disguises himself and twice serenades the same window using similar tunes.

The light dims as night falls; Leporello and Don Giovanni change costumes so that the master can seduce Elvira's servant. But the lady herself pines at the window and Don Giovanni sings to her while Leporello mimes his master's serenade.

Leporello's job, once this beautiful trio is over, is to lure Elvira out of the way. His comic dialogue with Donna Elvira, in which he courts her in his master's clothes, was extended in Prague (it is written on a separate page in Mozart's score). This may be a late contribution by Da Ponte (it is in the Prague libretto) and must have increased Micelli's and Ponziani's scope as actors.

Don Giovanni wants to seduce Elvira's maid. His beautiful canzonetta in act 2 ("Deh vieni alla finestra") was provided for from the beginning in the libretto; it is surprising, then, that it was not composed in Vienna. But its music, and the recitative that precedes it, are on Prague paper. There are many reports that Bassi exacted five changes from Mozart for "Là ci darem la mano," but it is more likely, as Christof Bitter suggests, that this song was adjusted in rehearsal to Bassi's voice. It certainly lies higher than most of his other music, and it gives him his most lyrical moment: Don Giovanni, of course, is disguising his voice and trying to be as seductive as possible. He sings a melody similar to the one he just sang to Elvira, but in a higher key and with his mandolin accompaniment.

Bassi's skill at imitation was put to good use in these scenes. The libretto has been fleshed out considerably, and Don Giovanni's imitation of Leporello's voice is brought to the fore. In the following exchange between Masetto and Don Giovanni, the fake Leporello sends the others away in an aria, disarms and beats Masetto, then flees without being recognized; this will have tested Bassi's skill (and the audience's credulity). As Niemetschek remembered, "The worth of this artist is known; he is a splendid comic, and in his gestures an excellent actor, a complete connoisseur of mime, and—he doesn't exaggerate." The acting must have been altered in the course of rehearsal. The early Vienna libretto calls for Masetto to try to grab Don Giovanni by the hand and for Don Giovanni to beat Masetto with pistol and musket, but the scene was altered so that the characters are more distant (no hands touching), and Don Giovanni in Prague uses his nobleman's sword for the beating.

Masetto's bruises provide another occasion for a splendid aria by the prima donna: Zerlina has the medicine to cure him ("Vedrai, carino").

The scene changes to a dark room in Donna Anna's house; this must be a short set in which one of the three required doors is painted on the backdrop, making something of a joke when Leporello tries to escape from Elvira. One of Mozart's great ensemble numbers, a sextet ultimately involving everybody in the cast except Don Giovanni himself, moves this great imbroglio forward. Arriving with Elvira, Leporello (still disguised as his master) is in deeper trouble. He tries to flee, gets the wrong door, hides. Donna Anna and Don Ottavio enter, armed for vengeance, unaware that Elvira and Leporello/Don Giovanni are also there. Leporello tries again and comes face to face with Masetto and Zerlina. Elvira now begs pity from the others (she thinks she is reconciled with Don Giovanni). To save himself, Leporello reveals his disguise, and all are astonished in a grand ensemble. The revelation does not help: Ottavio, Zerlina, and Masetto all blame him for what his master has done. In his aria ("Ah, pietà") Leporello tries to explain, shows how he mistakenly got the wrong door earlier, and finally makes his escape through a door that works.

Those remaining are urged by Don Ottavio, who is now convinced of the villain's identity, to remain while he seeks help to avenge the Commendatore and to satisfy his betrothed. Now comes his big song, so long delayed but worth waiting for: "Il mio tesoro," a florid aria in the da capo tradition of serious opera, reminding us of his noble character.

In the Vienna production, Mozart inserted a new recitative and comic duet for Leporello and Zerlina ("Restate qua"; "Per queste tue manine") in the place occupied by "Il mio tesoro." And for Elvira (Caterina Cavalieri, his original Constanze) he added a spectacular recitative and the aria "Mi tradì quell'alma ingrate," a real summation. This would have given too much music to the Elvira of the Bondini company and would not have been practical with the mediocre voice of Micelli, the company's third female singer.

The scene changes to a graveyard—a "closed space in the form of a cemetery."

Joseph Platzer's design for a cemetery in *Don Giovanni* would
do very nicely. All that is needed is the equestrian statue of
the Commendatore and a lower outer wall so that Don Giovanni
and Leporello can enter by leaping over it.

It is not so closed, though, that Don Giovanni cannot jump over the wall and recount his adventures while Leporello arrives in the same way.

Mozart's original cemetery scene received improvements in Prague. The opening recitative, in which the statue speaks, was added to the score after Mozart's arrival. It must have been worked out with Da Ponte and the actors.

An unconfirmed story describes Mozart's difficulty with one of the trombonists in rehearsal for this scene.

While Mozart held the first rehearsals of his opera Don Juan in 1787, he had to stop at the Commendatore's lines "Di rider finirsi," etc. and "Ribalto audace," etc., which were accompanied only by three trombones, because one of the trombonists did not perform his part correctly. When it did not go better a second time, Mozart went to his desk and explained to him how he wished the passage to go, whereupon the player answered very dryly, "It cannot be played thus, and I will not learn how from you." Mozart answered smiling, "God forbid that I should want to teach you the trombone; give me the parts: I will change them." This he did, and added to the passage pairs of oboes, clarinets, and bassoons.

Neither libretto mentions the statue following the action with its eyes; this must have been worked out in rehearsal. Also lacking is the direction "Leporello imita la statua," found in Mozart's score. Ponziani, with his gift for comedy, must have invented this piece of business in rehearsal. Originally it must have been Don Giovanni who first sees the statue move.

Don and servant leave for home, and the scene changes to a dark room presumably in Donna Anna's house (the final set is being prepared behind it). Don Ottavio woos Donna Anna, but she can think of nothing but her father. She has a grand accompanied recitative and aria ("Crudele . . . Non mi dir, bel idol mio") in which, through the use of trills, scales, and arpeggios, she convinces him to wait. She leaves, he follows, and the set disappears to reveal the hall prepared for the final scene.

The famous finale of act 2, with its stage band playing dinner music from other operas for Don Giovanni, was evidently worked out in rehearsal, and perhaps indeed in the course of performances. First comes a melody from the first-act finale of Martín y Soler's *Una cosa rara*, probably not yet known in Prague, though in Vienna it overshadowed *Figaro*. It may have been an inside joke by Mozart, perhaps appreciated by the members of the orchestra. Or it may refer back to its opera, in which two peasant couples have escaped the designs of another Don Giovanni. The other two selections seem to have been made in the course of rehearsals. One quotes the aria "Come un agnello" from Giuseppe Sarti's *Fra i due litiganti,* known from recent performances in Prague. Mozart had composed variations on the same tune in 1784. Perhaps Mozart intended it as a tribute to Count Thun, his friend and host in Prague, in whose palace theater the opera had been performed. Or maybe its text ("Like a lamb going to the slaughter, you will go bleating through the city") is a warning of Don Giovanni's fate. The third tune will have delighted the audience: the aria "Non più andrai" from *Le nozze di Figaro,* known everywhere in Prague (remember Mozart's letter cited above: "Nothing is played, sung or whistled but 'Figaro'"). And of course its original text tells a butterfly that his nectar-sipping days are over.

In the surrounding dialogue the characters on stage take full advantage of the joke. As each tune is heard, Leporello praises it and identifies it ("Bravo! 'Cosa rara!'" "Evvivano 'I litiganti'"). When Don Giovanni asks him what he thinks of the first tune ("Che ti par del bel concerto?") Leporello manages to insult both Martín and his master: "It matches your merit" ("È conforme al vostro merto"). Other jokes are worked in also: Don Giovanni's "Ah che piatto saporito" may well be a reference to the attractive Teresa Saporiti; and when Leporello, caught in the act of eating his master's food, excuses himself by noting the quality of the cook ("si eccellente è il vostro cuoco"), he may have winked at Herr Johann Baptist Kuchartz ("cook"), the well-known keyboardist, arranger,

Dividere i martiri;
Saran meco men gravi i suoi sospiri.
                              (*parte*)

S C E N A. XII.
Sala.
F i n a l e

D. Gio. *Leporello alcuni suonatori, una mensa pre-*
parata per mangiare.

D. Gio. Già la mensa è preperata,
    Voi suonate, amici cari,
    Già che spendo i miei danari
    Io mi voglio divertir.
    Leporello presto in tavola;

Lep.   Son prontissimo a ubbidir.   (*i servi*
    portano in tavola mentre
    Lep. vuol us cire.)

D. Gio. Che ti par del bel concorto?
    (*I suonatori cominciano a*
    suonare e D. Gio. mangia)

Lep.   E' conforme al vostro merto.

D. Gio. Ah che piato saporito!

Lep.   Ah che barbaro appetito   (*a parte*)
    (Che bocconi da gigante,
    (Mi par proprio di svenir.

D. Gio. (Nel veder i miei bocconi

a 2 (Gli par proprio di svenir.   D.

D. Gio. Piato.

Lep.   Servo.

D. Gio. Verſa il vino.   (*Lep. versa il vino*
    nel bicchiero)
    Eccellente marzimino!   (*Lep. can-*
    gia il piato q D. Gio. e mangia
    in fretta etc.)

Lep.   (Questo pezzo di fagiano

a 2 (Piano piano vo inghiottir.

D. Gio. (Sta mangiando quel marrano;
    (Fingerò di non capir.

D. Gio. Leporello.   (*Lo chiama senza guardarlo*)

Lep.   Padron mio... (*risponde colla bocca piena*)

D. Gio. Parla schietto mascalzone:

Lep.   Non mi lascia una flussione
    Le parole proferir.

D. Gio. Mentre io mangio fischia un poco.

Lep.   Non so far:

D. Gio. Cos' è?   (*Lo guarda, e s'accorge*
    che sta mangiando.)

Lep.   Scusate:
    (Si eccellente è' il vostro cuoco

a 2 (Che lo volli anch' io provar.

D. Gio (Sì eccellente è' il cuoco mio
    (Che lo volle anch' ei provar.
            SCE.

These pages from the original Prague libretto show the act 2 finale;
Don Giovanni is at table while his musicians play. Not present
in the libretto are the references to the operatic selections ("Bravo, *Cosa
rara*"; "Evvivano *I litiganti*"), including Leporello's reference to the
favorite tune in *Figaro* (the singer of Leporello had been the original
Figaro), "I know this one all too well." Probably the tunes were
selected, and the dialogue added, during rehearsals.

and composer, in the orchestra pit. Kuchartz (Jan Křtitel Kuchař), among other things, sold keyboard versions of Mozart's operas, including this very song.

When the band plays "Non più andrai," Leporello says, "I know this one all too well!" Ponziani (Leporello) had himself sung that aria as Figaro in Prague, so his remark ("Questa poi la conosco pur troppo") has a double sense that must have delighted the audience—though the remark is not in the Prague libretto.

The stage band was intended from the first, but much of the finale must have been arranged in Prague; it may have arisen in part from improvisations during rehearsals, as much of the dialogue related to the band's tunes does not appear in the printed libretto. In his later years in Dresden, Luigi Bassi is reported as saying: "This is all nothing, it lacks the liveliness, the freedom, that the great Master wanted in this scene. In Guardasoni's company we never sang the scene the same from one performance to the next, we did not keep the beat exactly, and instead used our wit, always new things and paying attention only to the orchestra; everything parlando and almost improvised—that is how Mozart wanted it."

The persistent Elvira enters to reconcile with Don Giovanni once more, but in a trio with Leporello she is rejected by the Don in favor of his dinner. She leaves but returns screaming as she crosses the stage. Elvira's scream was originally intended to be heard from offstage, to judge from the Vienna libretto; it must have been arranged in Prague that she would reenter screaming ("D. Elv. sorte poi rientra mettendo un grido orribile, e fugge dal'altra parte"). The statue enters, trombones accompany his words, and there is plenty of comic business from Leporello. When Don Giovanni accepts the Commendatore's invitation and gives his hand on it, a deathly chill seizes him: he is given his last chance. Don Giovanni, who has never reflected for a moment in his life—this is why he has no real aria—refuses to repent, the statue departs (just in time to make a very quick change to Masetto), and Don Giovanni is swallowed up in flames as an infernal chorus sings.

Everything has taken place over a twenty-four-hour period, from one midnight to the next. Since Leporello paced the midnight stage when the curtain went up two and a half hours ago, much has happened. The Commendatore, returning as a statue at the second midnight, makes repeated references to time: "piu tempo non ho; è l'ultimo momento; Ah, tempo più non v'è."

The trapdoor in the stage (between the first and second wings), which opens to receive Don Giovanni, is evidently left open when the others break in with the authorities. Leporello stops them ("Fermate il passo") so that they don't fall in, and he points to where his master has disappeared. Once they understand, the finale is standard; each character recounts his future intentions: two weddings, a convent, and a better master, and a final chorus, led off by the prima donna ("this is the reward of evildoers"), closes the Opera of Operas.

Reactions

Mozart was cheered at the end. Evidently the applause was for the opera and its composer, not just for the performers, the usual reason for eighteenth-century applause. The local newspaper, echoed in Vienna by the *Wiener Zeitung*, gives us our only review:

> Monday, the 29th, the Italian Opera Company presented Maestro Mozart's eagerly awaited opera *Don Giovanni or The Stony Banquet (Das steinerne Gastmahl)*. Connoisseurs and musicians say that nothing like it has ever been performed in Prague. Herr Mozart conducted himself, and when he entered the pit, he received a triple ovation, repeated when he left. Incidentally, the opera's execution is very difficult, and everyone admires the good performance, despite the limited time of

study. Stage and orchestra did everything to reward Mozart with a good execution. Much expenditure was required by choruses and scenery, all provided splendidly by Herr Guardasoni. An unusually large crowd guaranteed the applause, which was shared by all.

The anonymous reviewer seems to think that "connoisseurs and musicians" are best suited to appreciate the qualities of the work. Niemetschek, looking back ten years, seems to agree:

It is now ten years since it [Don Giovanni] was first performed—and it is still being heard with pleasure and still attracts a large audience. In short, Don Giovanni is the favorite opera of the élite of Prague. When Mozart appeared at the piano in the orchestra at the first performance, everybody in the crowded theatre applauded by clapping enthusiastically. ...The masterpieces of Rome and Greece are appreciated the more often they are read and the maturer our taste becomes. This applies equally to knowledgeable as well as ignorant people when listening to Mozart's music, particularly to his dramatic works. Those were our feelings at the first performance of Don Giovanni.

The Bondini company performed the piece again in Leipzig and Warsaw, without much effect. Critics of performances elsewhere, in 1789 (Hamburg) and 1790 (Berlin), generally say that Mozart's music is good but too difficult and that the subject is tasteless and base.

The work was certainly difficult (it still is), but the performers, especially the orchestra, seem to have acquitted themselves well. Wilhelm Kuhe reported Wenzel Svoboda's view of the performance (we are a long way from Mozart here): "At the end of that memorable first night Mozart declared that such a performance at sight was an extraordinary feat, 'obschon manche Noten unter die Pulte gefallen sind' (although several notes fell under the desks)."

Mozart himself appeared pleased with the reception. As he wrote to Jacquin, "My opera 'Don Giovanni' had its first performance on October 29th and was received with the greatest applause." And he had anticipated success: "I would be inconsolable," he had said to friends in Prague before the performance, "if this opera were not a *universal* success at the first performance."

As was customary, Mozart led three performances, and a fourth for his own benefit. He remained in Prague another three weeks, staying with Josefa Dussek, for whom he wrote the aria "Bella mia fiamma." He declined another commission and returned to Vienna on November 13. As he wrote to Jacquin, "It [Don Giovanni] was performed yesterday for the fourth time, for my benefit. I am thinking of leaving here on the 12th or 13th. . . . But perhaps my opera will be performed in Vienna after all! I hope so. People here are doing their best to persuade me to remain on for a couple of months and write another one. But I cannot accept this proposal, however flattering it may be." *Don Giovanni* continued its success in Prague and enriched the company. Da Ponte reports that Guarda-soni wrote to him as follows: "Long live Da Ponte! Long live Mozart! All impresarios, all virtuosi should bless their names. So long as they live we shall never know what theatrical poverty means!"

But Mozart hastened back to Vienna despite Prague's desire to keep him. The court composer, Christoph Willibald Gluck, was on his deathbed, and Mozart hoped for an appointment. He got one: he was appointed chamber musician, though for his remaining four years he seems to have been asked only for minuets and German dances.

Da Ponte reported that the emperor himself was eager to hear *Don Giovanni*: "The Emperor sent for me," wrote Da Ponte, "and overloading me with gracious felicitations, presented me with another hundred sequins, and told me that he was longing to see *Don Giovanni*." Indeed, Mozart did hear his *Don Giovanni* in Vienna. He made a number of alterations in the score to suit his new cast (the Vienna version is a story in itself). He switched tenor arias, composed a new scene in act 2 and a new aria for Elvira, and may have considered—and may have put into effect—an ending that eliminates the final ensemble scene. Remarkable, perhaps, is how little he did change for Vienna given that none of the singers was the same. Mozart directed three performances in Vienna; fifteen were given in all. The last Viennese performance in Mozart's lifetime was on December 15, 1788. Mozart did not enjoy the success he had had in that most musical city of Prague. As Da Ponte reports,

> The opera went on the stage and . . . need I recall it? . . . *Don Giovanni* did not please! Everyone, except Mozart, thought that there was something missing. Additions were made; some of the arias were changed; it was offered for a second performance. *Don Giovanni* did not please! And what did the Emperor say? He said:
> "That opera is divine; I should even venture that it is more beautiful than *Figaro*. But such music is not meat for the teeth of my Viennese."
> I reported the remark to Mozart, who replied quietly:
> "Give them time to chew on it!"

Mozart returned twice to Prague. In 1791, when he was there to produce his opera *La clemenza di Tito*, he directed a performance of *Don Giovanni* on September 2, with the original company. Presumably it was his original version, and presumably Prague again showed how much it loved Mozart's music.

Documents: *Don Giovanni*

1. FROM ANTON FRIEDRICH BUSCHING, *A NEW SYSTEM OF GEOGRAPHY* (LONDON: A MILLAR, 1762), P. 69.
Prague

The metropolis of the kingdom, which lies almost in the middle thereof on both sides of the Moldau or Molda which is here about eight hundred paces broad, but likewise shallow and not navigable. The bridge of stone, which Charles IV. in the year 1357, caused to be erected over this river, exceeds in length those of Ratisbon and Dresden, being seven hundred and forty-two common paces long. Its breadth amounts to fourteen common paces, and three carriages may pass upon it abreast. It stands on sixteen piers, being ornamented on the sides with twenty-eight statues of saints. . . .

The fortifications of Prague are not very important, the town may be flanked or raked on all sides. The houses are wholly built of stone, and for the most part consist of three stories. It has broader streets, but fewer stately palaces than Vienna. In it are computed ninety-two churches and chapels, with about forty cloisters. The town, considered with respect to its extent, is not sufficiently populous, as containing only about 70000 Christian, and between 12 and 13000 Jewish inhabitants. Neither is the commerce, which is carried on here considerable, but exclusive of the arts and handicraft-trades, its principal means of subsistence is drawn from the brewing of beer.

Prague consists properly of three towns . . . as namely, of the old and new towns, which lie on the east-side of the Mulda, and of the Small Side, which is on the west-side of that river. The Old Town is less ancient than that which is called the Small Side, but older than the New Town, and was also, from its ancient citadel, formerly called Wischerad, and the Greater Town, by way of distinction from the Lesser Side or Town.

2. CHARLES BURNEY ON BOHEMIA AND PRAGUE

The country is flat, naked, and disagreeable to the eye, for the most part, all the way through Austria, Moravia, and Bohemia, as far as Prague, the situation and environs of which are very beautiful (p. 131).

The city is extremely beautiful, when seen at a distance. It is situated on two or three hills, and has the river Mulda running through the middle of it. It is divided into three different quarters, or districts, which are distinguished by the names of Alt Stadt, Neue Stadt, and Kleine Stadt or Old Town, New Town, and Little Town; the Kleine Stadt is the most modern, and the best built of the three. The houses are all of white stone, or stucco, in imitation of it, and all uniform in size and colour. . . . A great part of the town is new, as scarce a single building escaped the Prussian batteries, and bombardment during the blockade, in the last war. A few churches and palaces only, that were strongly built, and of less combustible materials than the rest, were proof against their fury; and in the walls of these, are still sticking innumerable cannon balls, and bombs, particularly in the superb palace of count Czernin, and in the Capuchin's church (pp. 132–33).

Charles Burney, *An Eighteenth Century Musical Tour in Central Europe and the Nether-lands,* ed. Percy A. Scholes (New York: Oxford University Press, 1959).

3. FROM FRIEDRICH ERNEST ARNOLD, *BEOBACHTUNGEN IN UND ÜBER PRAG, VON EINEM REISENDEN AUSLÄNDER.* 2 VOLS. (PRAGUE: W. GERLE, 1787).

[On the opera house:] It seems, he says [a building expert whom the author has consulted], that the builder of this house had all the necessary expertise in construction, but not that of the theater, because here above all, the science of sound must be taken into account.

If, as I am assured, a complete renovation could be done with 10 to 12,000 gulden, then it is to be hoped, that the amount would be used for this purpose. The overtaxed ears of the public, its frustration at hearing nothing, not to mention the lungs of all the actors and actresses, who now consequently must nevertheless continue to play there as long as an accident does not render the house unusable—all this cries out for such an alteration.

Otherwise the city of Prague will have to make do with an Italian opera where one hears the singing and see the grimaces, but can understand nothing of the text. In fact, given the current state of things, this is best for the city. In order to defend this statement, I must say that Prague's theater-going public is divided into two groups, a division which of course differs considerably from that of box, noble parterre, parterre, and the gallery. The first group goes to the theater to kill time, the other to be entertained. The first group is by far the larger. This teaches us something quite important about the racket that constantly reigns in the theater. All those who make it cannot possibly intend to watch and listen to the play with attention, and they also lack the discretion to consider that others may want to do so; this justified reproach applies mainly to the noble parterre. The greater part of the boxes belong also under this rubric. The chatting of some could, to be sure, be excused by the fact that not much can be heard in most of the boxes, and that they must therefore entertain themselves; and it is all the same to them whether those beneath them, who must carefully prick up their ears, hear their often interesting conversation or that of the actors. However, it is impossible for me to understand why connoisseurs and ama-teurs of the theater should not at least take notice of situations and groups, and if they have not understood everything, even in places that are spoken loudly and with strong feeling, they do not turn around in order to see what circumstance has brought this about. But in most boxes this does not happen, backs remained turned to the stage, and con-versation is uninterrupted.

In Italy it is thought not proper for ladies to pay attention to the play and be af-fected by it. Perhaps this taste has been passed on to the ladies of Prague.

However, fair is fair. I admire certain lady amateurs of the theater, who combine passion and enthusiasm for it with a good judgment; but I beg their forgiveness when I say that not all think as they do. I do hate it when persons of position, taste, and educa-tion, who should have good and correct taste, laugh at the most moving moments; when I see that nothing comes across to them of the sensitivity of the actors and actresses, who perform with heartfelt warmth, I can only assume that they have made every effort to suppress their natural feelings—when I see half a row of boxes where nobody gives any evidence in their face that any change is taking place within.

Is it not generally ill-bred to leave the parterre with an unrestrained noise during an act, and to disturb the concentration of all one's neighbors? Is the interval between acts not time enough? I have seen one and the same person repeat this ill-mannered action two or three times during a single act. People have paid their money to see the play, not to go promenading in the parterre. If the other more attentive spectators were bold enough to ask the strolling gentlemen—emphatically if necessary—to be quiet, then this would all soon change. But this characteristic is lacking in Prague, as we shall report later.

This summer the impresario of the local Italian opera is Herr Bondini of the German company, which in the winter is engaged at the electoral court in Saxony, and plays at Leipzig during the fair season, from which, however, as already a few times previously, it took a hiatus because the Italian opera played at the past Jubilate fair. This company is already too well known for me to need to describe it in detail. It has long had the reputation that its members aim for natural acting that approaches reality. All the visitors who saw them at the Leipzig fair came to the same conclusion. In addition, it is considered important that the conduct of the members be, in so far as possible, moral. I say in so far as possible, because situations that are now nearly universal in everyday life cannot be avoided here, and are all the more notable because everyone feels justified in speaking about them.

The secluded way of life of the actresses does not of course suit many of the gentlemen here who seek conquests, and from time to time it is said that the former could act rather more badly if only they were more beautiful and more accommodating. However, this arises merely from the spite of this riff-raff. In general, the fine acting of this company is valued by the judgment of connoisseurs, something that is not so entirely rare here, but is shot through with too many weeds.

They play three times a week in the large theater in the Old City, where the greater part of those who attend have subscribed cheaply, and once a week they play with suspended subscription in the theater in Count Thun's palace in the Kleinseite, where connoisseurs would have the pleasure of being able to enjoy the play in its entirety, were there not nearly as much noise here in the greater houses as there is in the large one, which in this crowded district causes all the more racket.

This is the place where one can actually observe the effect on the audience; here it is unforgivable that the boxes talk so loudly that the entire audience hears it—unforgivable that the actors themselves are disturbed by it. Here one sees every expression of feeling and sees how many remain as unmoved as blocks of wood. Here one notices who has taste and who is bored to death.

I cannot forgo this opportunity to mention what I take for a widespread abuse, not only here, but also in many other places: that when a piece does not last exactly to the end of the time allotted for a play, the actors are compelled to give another one. This can well be said to reduce art to the status of a trade. And the second piece often spoils the feeling of the first. That is, of course, a matter of indifference to those who feel nothing, and in retrospect I shall say not a word more about it, for in fact I do not want to be at fault should someone be half dead of ennui by supper because a play ended too early.

However it may be, by chance or by art (the latter I doubt), Prague always does a lot in the summer, and supports the theatre with a considerable subscription.

Herr Bondini last winter established his own German company here. Since it did not pay he let the company go, taking only a few members into the other company. It must naturally be difficult to find good actors, for there is not a company in Germany that is uniformly well staffed. This impresario offers good salaries, and pays promptly, a reputation he has built up over many years. He is an Italian, he has an honest character, and one can trust his word. He was formerly a good comic actor.

Concerning the company itself I must refer my readers to the theatrical journals.

He is likewise the impresario of the local Italian opera buffa. We have already said that Prague has an extraordinary taste for music and it is very happy with this opera, and this is a sign that it must be good. Herr Bondini furthermore spares no expense in acquiring the best and newest scores, in paying good men and women singers so that they are happy to work with him. This opera plays throughout the entire winter, and last winter alternated with the spoken theater. Connoisseurs by and large prefer it to the Dresden court opera, which is supported at the electoral court's expense. The costumes and settings are excellent.

Two years ago, Herr Bondini also put on a ball in the theatre, and like last year held it in the large playhouse here. Especially in the first year it was particularly lively and magnificent. The parterre was placed on the same level as the stage, thus making an excellent hall that, for the part of the public that prefers this entertainment, compensated for the problems at theatrical performances. This great hall is then always richly lit with chandeliers, and Herr Bondini occasionally spends something on special charming decorations. The actual redoutes or masked balls are held in the Wusinisch Hall, where the ball mentioned above was also held.

Three years ago he also organized a casino for the nobility in the palace of Count Thun, which he had rented entirely. However, just as everyone in Prague eagerly investigates everything new, and finds everything tasteless as soon as it becomes older (an obvious consequence of idleness), so this arrangement too has paled, and the impresario thus suspended it very phlegmatically, because he knows his public.

He deserved to be the *maître des plaisirs* at one of the great courts. He has all the requisite knowledge of how to harmonize his own gifts with those of many others, and a certain dryness of character restrains the presumptuous ones with whom he must often surround himself.

The small stage, which he had built in a special hall in the very same Thun palace, is very prettily laid out. The sets are painted with such beautiful perspective that it appears to be quite deep. It seats many people, and a full house with low prices brings in about 400 gulden. It offers thirty-three boxes and a gallery. From this one can calculate the size of the hall, and from this the size of the palace. Pity that it sits in a corner.

The company, which played here last winter, occasionally gave plays in the na-

tional language, and I am surprised that reflection about this has not been greater. . . .
(vol. 1, pp. 130–39)

Particularly in view of the finery among the great houses, things have become so bespangled that one can no longer speak of a national costume. One thing goes this way, the other that, striking the eye because of the spangles, but not real. One needs only to compare a Saxon dance floor for common people with one here. Here one finds charm at first glance, superficial goodness, but overloaded with frippery. There one finds charming simplicity, purity, and although lacking charm for the sensualist, yet there is satisfaction for the patriot.

I have said above that the love of musical art is almost universal in Prague, and I must say a bit more on the subject. Whether the general talent for music among the Bohemians lies in the temperament of the nation, or whether the former glorious epoch of the country contributed to this cannot be determined exactly, at least I cannot do it. That it exists, however, can very easily be seen. Nowhere does one find so many children going about with instruments, especially the harp, and although very young, nevertheless earn their living. The mechanical practice that they receive in youth renders them all the more skillful when grown, provided that their talent corresponds to their choice. For the greater portion that is the case. However, because the Bohemians themselves do not need this crowd of musicians, especially with so much private amateur music-making, many travel abroad and seek to earn a living. It was precisely this youthful training, advancement, and learned skill that always gave the wandering musicians of Prague preference in Germany over the native ones—from which, however, I except the Thuringians, who also have many musicians among the country folk who are equal to their metier.

In general, though, one finds better music in taverns here in Prague than at balls and redoutes in many cities. Whoever is a friend [of music] and whose ear is pleased by charming music, finds himself occasionally obliged to stop in the street to satisfy his inclination under the window of a beer hall; and this happens not rarely, but often. And thus at larger occasions one also finds increasingly compounded art. All public festivities here employ very good musicians, and many among them could hold the stage with virtuosi.

One thing that the Bohemians lack in comparison to the Italians is a certain delicacy in performance and taste. But one cannot thereby give the latter the advantage. The Bohemians in comparison have a much deeper knowledge and skill in music, and are, as they say, more solid in their art.

Everybody in Prague loves music, and everybody takes part in it. This is why Prague is for the most part in a position to support an Italian opera by itself, or one should rather say that it could completely, if it did not please the nobility to alternate it with German plays, for which the taste has become ever more universal and refined.

The presence of this opera, and the wide amateur music-making among private persons, with the many private concerts that result, are probably the reason why there are no public concerts. For it would be difficult to staff one as well as one could here. There are men on every instrument who could compete with virtuosi, and the ample income that they make from teaching suffices to show the undivided enthusiasm for this art.

Public academies are given only occasionally in the large National Theater, and these exceptionally, by traveling foreign virtuosi who put them on themselves. The house is usually quite full, and the generosity of the nobility reaps a good reward for many, especially foreigners who come recommended or who recommend themselves.

This goes for the locals as well as foreigners. This summer Madame Duschek, a beloved singer who has much strength of voice and a pleasing tone, especially in the low range, and who is also very musical, gave an academy for the benefit of the poor. The receipts produced a surplus for the Institute of 225 gulden. A noble gesture by Madame Duschek, who, because she has a rich inheritance, no longer requires the support of the public and now employs her talent for the unfortunate. Herr Duschek is a great keyboard player and gives very profitable instruction in it. Herr Maschek, also a virtuoso on this instrument, plays with much delicacy. If space did not forbid it, I would mention several other worthy men whose names deserve to be listed here.

Formerly the local nobility maintained various splendid private *Kapellen*. Circumstances or ruin have reduced this luxury. Because of the dissolution of these *Kapellen*, many very good musicians have been dispersed in Germany, and I ran across one such *Kapelle* reunited in Frankfurt am Main, where they had been engaged by the theatrical enterprise of Herr Tabor because they did not want to separate. I found a virtuoso on the violin and an excellent horn player among them. They were very well received, which must have been all the more flattering to them, since music is understood and valued there.

The general inclination for music has become so typical of the local inhabitants, that they cannot be fully happy without it. When one goes to open houses on days when music is forbidden, one finds everyone hanging their heads, everyone looking morose. Conversation is not a concern of the common man. He must make do merely with food, and stuffing his body with it is the reason for the actual as well as apparent sluggishness that one notices in everyone. For this music is the most effective charm. Scarcely has he heard it, and he jumps up and begins to dance around. Every fibre of his body is in motion. Dancing is the favorite passion especially of the female sex. The German dance, the so-called waltz [Walzen], is the most fashionable. The lowliest maiden waltzes well, and the dance is danced here with a restraint that is unknown in other German regions, where we believe that this type of dance consists of the craziest and most foolish twirling. It is pleasant to see when so many couples one after the other turn without disturbing each other. Among the better ones there is even greater precision, and I have seen 50 couples waltzing without one disturbing another; indeed, only few dance at anything other than a regular distance from the other couples. Even at distinguished gatherings, those who are not up to it do not easily take part in the dancing (vol. 2, pp. 68–74).

Here I must also add that music is indeed a free art for amateurs, but that anyone who wishes to earn money at public or private balls and other entertainments where there is dancing must pay a tax of 30 kreuzer per person, the so-called "music duty." As soon as I have music in my house for this purpose and do not pay for a permit ahead of time, then I have committed a criminal offense.

This musical toll is leased to an entrepreneur for all four cities of Prague, and if

I am not mistaken, brings in several thousand gulden per year. The theaters are not exempt from this, and must pay 2 gulden for every evening.

It is very pleasant to listen to the excellent wind instruments on the Moldau, either from the bank or on the vessels themselves that are returning to the city from Podol. These water-cruises with music are one of the most exquisite entertainments of Prague, only it is a pity that it is not undertaken by those affluent enough to have suitable gondolas built. In the cliffs of Vysehrad there is such a magnificent echo that one can imagine nothing more pleasant and could happily listen to it for hours (vol. 2, pp. 75–76).

4. MOZART TO GOTTFRIED VON JACQUIN IN VIENNA, BEGUN OCTOBER 15, 1787

Dearest Friend!

You probably think that my opera is over by now. If so, you are a little mistaken. In the first place, the stage personnel here are not as smart as those in Vienna, when it comes to mastering an opera of this kind in a very short time. Secondly, I found on my arrival that so few preparations and arrangements had been made that it would have been absolutely impossible to produce it on the 14th, that is, yesterday. So yesterday my "Figaro" was performed in a fully lighted theatre and I myself conducted.

In this connexion I have a good joke to tell you. A few of the leading ladies here, and in particular one very high and mighty one, were kind enough to find it very ridiculous, unsuitable, and Heaven knows what else that the Princess should be entertained with a performance of "Figaro," the "Crazy Day," as the management were pleased to call it. It never occurred to them that no opera in the world, unless it is written specially for it, can be exactly suitable for such an occasion and that therefore it was of absolutely no consequence whether this or that opera were given, provided that it was a good opera and one which the Princess did not know; and "Figaro" at least fulfilled this last condition. In short by her persuasive tongue the ringleader brought things to such a pitch that the government forbade the impresario to produce this opera on that night. So she was triumphant! "Ho vinto," she called out one evening from her box. No doubt she never suspected that the "ho" might be changed to a "sono." But the following day Le Noble appeared, bearing a command from His Majesty to the effect that if the new opera could not be given, "Figaro" was to be performed! My friend, if only you had seen the handsome, magnificent nose of this lady! Oh, it would have amused you as much as it did me! "Don Giovanni" has now been fixed for the 24th.

October 21st. It was fixed for the 24th, but a further postponement has been caused by the illness of one of the singers. As the company is so small, the impresario is in a perpetual state of anxiety and has to spare his people as much as possible, lest some unexpected indisposition should plunge him into the most awkward of all situations, that of not being able to produce any show whatsoever!

So everything dawdles along here because of the singers, who are lazy, refuse to rehearse on opera days and the manager, who is anxious and timid, will not force them. . . .

October 25th. . . . My opera is to be performed for the first time next Monday, October 29th. You shall have an account of it from me a day or two later. . . .

Emily Anderson, ed., *Letters of Mozart and His Family,* 4th ed. (New York: Norton, 1989), no. 550, pp. 911–12.

5. MOZART TO GOTTFRIED VON JACQUIN IN VIENNA, NOVEMBER 4, 1787

Dearest, most beloved Friend!

I hope you received my letter. My opera "Don Giovanni" had its first performance on October 29th and was received with the greatest applause. It was performed yesterday for the fourth time, for my benefit. I am thinking of leaving here on the 12th or 13th. . . . But perhaps my opera will be performed in Vienna after all! I hope so. People here are doing their best to persuade me to remain on for a couple of months and write another one. But I cannot accept this proposal, however flattering it may be. . . .

Anderson, *Letters of Mozart,* no. 551, pp. 912–13.

6. FROM THE *PRAGER OBERPOSTAMTSZEITUNG*

From Otto Erich Deutsch, Mozart: A Documentary Biography, *ed. Eric Blom, Peter Branscombe, and Jeremy Noble (Stanford: Stanford University Press, 1965).*

October 6, 1787: Our celebrated Herr Mozart has again arrived in Prague, and the news has spread here since that the opera newly written by him, Das steinerne Gastmahl, will be given for the first time at the National Theatre (p. 299).

October 9, 1787: The I[mperial] & R[oyal] poet, Herr Abbee Laurenz Da Ponte, a Venetian by birth, has arrived here from Vienna and will remain here for a few days (p. 299).

October 16, 1787: At half-past six o'clock they [Archduchess Maria Theresia and Prince Anton Clemens of Saxony] betook themselves to Nostitz's National Theatre, which for this occasion was embellished and illuminated in a very distinguished manner. The auditorium was so much glorified by the finery of the numerous guests that one has to admit never having beheld such a magnificent scene. At the entry of Their Highnesses they were greeted with the most evident marks of joy by the whole public, which they acknowledged with gracious gratitude. At their request the well-known opera Die Hochzeit des Figaro, generally admitted to be so well performed here, was given. The zeal of the musicians and the presence of Mozart, the Master, awakened a general approbation and satisfaction in Their Highnesses. After the first act a sonnet, ordered by several Bohemian patriots for this festivity, was publicly distributed. By reason of their early departure, Their Highnesses returned to the royal castle before the conclusion of the opera (p. 300).

October 30, 1787: Prague, 29 October. The director of the Italian opera company here yesterday issued news of the opera Don Jouan, oder die bestrafte Ausschweifung, ap-

...ance during the sojourn of the exalted Tuscan guests. It has the Court ...bé Da Ponte, for its author, and is to be performed for the first time ...look forward with pleasure to the excellent composition of our great ...re of this anon (p. 302).

..., 1787: Prague, 1 November. On Monday the 29th the Italian opera ...dently awaited opera by Maestro Mozard, Don Giovanni, or das stein- ...noisseurs and musicians say that Prague has never heard the like. Herr ...i person; when he entered the orchestra he was received with threefold ...happened when he left it. The opera is, moreover, extremely difficult ...y one admired the good performance given in spite of this after such ...dy. Everybody, on the stage and in the orchestra, strained every nerve ...rewarding him with a good performance. There were also heavy addi- ...y several choruses and changes of scenery, all of which Herr Guardasoni ...ed to. The unusually large attendance testifies to a unanimous approba- ...ame notice appeared in the *Wiener Zeitung*, November 14).

FRANZ NIEMETSCHEK'S BIOGRAPHY OF MOZART

...etschek was Mozart's first biographer. Citations from Franz Nieme- ...rt (1798), trans. Helen Mautner (London: Leonard Hyman, 1956).

...med almost without a break throughout the winter and . . . it greatly alleviated the straitened circumstances of the manager. The enthusiasm shown by the public was without precedent; they could not hear it often enough. A piano version was made by one of our best masters, Herr Kuchartz; it was arranged for wind parts, as a quintet and for German dances; in short, Figaro's tunes echoed through the streets and the parks; even the harpist on the alehouse bench had to play "Non piu andrai" if he wanted to at- tract any attention at all. This manifestation was admittedly mostly due to the excellence of the work; but only a public which had so much feeling for the beautiful in music and which included so many real connoisseurs could have immediately recognized merit; in addition, there was the incomparable orchestra of our opera, which understood how to execute Mozart's ideas so accurately and diligently. For on these worthy men, who were mostly not professional concert players, but nevertheless very knowledgeable and capable, the new harmony and fire and eloquence of the songs made an immediate and lasting im- pression. The well-known Orchestra Director Strobach, since deceased, declared that at each performance he and his colleagues were so excited that they would gladly have started from the beginning again in spite of the hard work it entailed. Admiration for the com- poser of this music went so far that Count Johann Thun, one of our principal noblemen and a lover of music, who himself retained a first-class orchestra, invited Mozart to Prague and offered him accommodation, expenses, and every comfort in his own home. Mozart was too thrilled at the impression which his music had made on the Bohemians, too eager to become acquainted with such a music-loving nation, for him not to seize the opportunity with pleasure. He came to Prague in 1787; on the day of his arrival Figaro was performed and Mozart appeared in it. At once the news of his presence spread in the stalls, and as soon as the overture had ended everyone broke into welcoming applause. . . . (pp. 35–36)

The opera director Bondini commissioned Mozart to compose a new opera for the Prague stage for the following winter, which the latter gladly undertook to do, as he had experienced how much the Bohemians appreciated his music and how well they executed it. This he often mentioned to his acquaintances in Prague, where a hero-worshipping responsive public and real friends carried him, so to speak, on their hands. He warmly thanked the opera orchestra in a letter to Herr Strobach, who was director at the time, and attributed the greater part of the ovation which his music had received in Prague to their excellent rendering (p. 37).

It is now ten years since it [*Don Giovanni*] was first performed—and it is still being heard with pleasure and still attracts a large audience. In short, Don Giovanni is the favorite opera of the élite of Prague. When Mozart appeared at the keyboard in the orchestra at the first performance, everybody in the crowded theatre applauded by clapping enthusiastically (p. 38).

The masterpieces of Rome and Greece are appreciated the more often they are read and the maturer our taste becomes. This applies equally to knowledgeable as well as ignorant people when listening to Mozart's music, particularly to his dramatic works. Those were our feelings at the first performance of Don Giovanni (p. 55).

8. WILHELM KUHE'S RECOLLECTIONS

I remember a tall, gaunt, elderly man by name Wenzel Swoboda, a performer on the double bass at the Opera House. He had been a member of the orchestra on the occasion of the production (October 29, 1787) of Don Giovanni, which was specially written for the Prague Opera House, the master coming from Vienna to finish his work and conduct its first performance. . . .

The conceit (as I may term it) of the good people of my native city was increased a hundredfold when Mozart, in a speech delivered at a banquet in his honour, declared (so Swoboda told me) that the citizens of Prague were the only people in the world who understood his music. Had he lived longer he might have modified his opinion. Speaking of Mozart, I am reminded that my friend Swoboda used also to refer to the pleasure evinced daily by the great master in the game of billiards. He would also from time to time recall Mozart's habit of laying aside mere speech in favour of musical recitative, which even in public he would use as a means of making remarks and conveying requests to his circle of friends. From the same authority I learned the positive truth of the story (often told and as frequently denied) that on the night before its production the overture to Don Giovanni had not even been sketched. . . .

At the end of that memorable first night Mozart declared that such a performance at sight was an extraordinary feat, "obschon manche Noten unter die Pulte gefallen sind" (although several notes fell under the desks).

And now another of Swoboda's reminiscences: At the final rehearsal of the opera Mozart was not at all satisfied with the efforts of a young and very pretty girl, the possessor of a voice of greater purity than power, to whom the part of Zerlina had been allotted. The reader will remember that Zerlina, frightened at Don Giovanni's too pronounced love-making, cries for assistance behind the scenes. In spite of continued repetitions, Mozart was unable to infuse sufficient force into the poor girl's screams, until at last, losing all patience, he clambered from the conductor's desk on to the boards. At that period neither gas nor electric light lent facility to stage mechanism. A few tallow candles dimly glimmered among the desks of the musicians, but over the stage and the rest of the house almost utter darkness reigned. Mozart's sudden appearance on the stage was therefore not noticed, much less suspected, by poor Zerlina, who at the moment when she ought to have uttered the cry received from the composer a sharp pinch on the arm, emitting, in consequence, a shriek which caused him to exclaim: "Admirable! Mind you scream like that tonight!"

Wilhelm Kuhe, *My Musical Recollections* (London: Richard Bentley and Son, 1896), pp. 6–10.

9. FROM THE MEMOIRS OF LORENZO DA PONTE

From Memoirs of Lorenzo Da Ponte, *ed. Arthur Livingston, trans. Elisabeth Abbott (Philadelphia: Lippincott, 1929; repr., New York: Da Capo, 1988).*

I thought however it was time to refresh my poetical vein, which had seemed to me utterly dried out when I was writing for Reghini and Piticchio. The opportunity was offered me by maestri Martini, Mozart, and Salieri who came all three at the same time to ask me for books. I loved and esteemed all three of them, and hoped to find in each compensation for past failures and some increment to my glory in opera. I wondered whether it might not be possible to satisfy them all, and write three operas at one spurt. Salieri was not asking me for an original theme. . . . What he wanted, therefore, was a free adaptation. Mozart and Martini were leaving everything to me.

For Mozart I chose the Don Giovanni, a subject that pleased him mightily; and for Martini the Arbore di Diana. . . .

The three subjects fixed on, I went to the Emperor, laid my idea before him, and explained that my intention was to write the three operas contemporaneously.

"You will not succeed," he replied.

"Perhaps not," said I, "but I am going to try. I shall write evenings for Mozart, imagining I am reading the Inferno; mornings I shall work for Martini and pretend I am studying Petrarch; my afternoons will be for Salieri. He is my Tasso!"

He found my parallels very apt.

I returned home and went to work. I sat down at my table and did not leave it for twelve hours continuous—a bottle of Tokay to my right, a box of Seville to my left, in the middle an inkwell. A beautiful girl of sixteen—I should have preferred to love her only as a daughter, but alas . . . !—was living in the house with her mother, who took care of the family, and came to my room at the sound of the bell. To tell the truth the bell rang rather frequently, especially at moments when I felt my inspiration waning. She would bring me now a little cake, now a cup of coffee, now nothing but her pretty face, a face always gay, always smiling, just the thing to inspire poetical emotion and witty thoughts. I worked twelve hours a day every day, with a few interruptions, for two months on end; and through all that time she sat in an adjoining room, now with a book in hand, now with needle or embroidery, but ever ready to come to my aid at the first touch of the bell. Sometimes she would sit at my side without stirring, without opening her lips, or batting an eyelash, gazing at me fixedly, or blandly smiling, or now it would be a sigh, or a menace of tears. In a word, this girl was my Calliope for those three operas, as she was afterwards for all the verse I wrote during the next six years. At first I permitted such visits very often; later I had to make them less frequent, in order not to lose too much time in amorous nonsense, of which she was perfect mistress. The first day, between the Tokay, the snuff, the coffee, the bell, and my young muse, I wrote the two first scenes of Don Giovanni, two more for the Arbore di Diana, and more than half of the first act of Tarar, a title I changed to Assur. I presented those scenes to the three composers the next morning. They could scarcely be brought to believe that what they were reading with their own eyes was possible. In sixty-three days the first two operas were entirely finished and about two thirds of the last (pp. 174–76).

Only the first performance of this [Martini's] opera had been given, when I was obliged to leave for Prague for the opening of Mozart's Don Giovanni on the occasion of the arrival of the Princess of Tuscany in that city. I spent eight days there training the actors who were to create it; but before it appeared on the stage, I had to hurry back to Vienna, because of the fiery letter I received from Salieri, wherein he informed me, truly or not, that Assur had to be ready at once for the nuptials of Prince Francis, and that the Emperor had ordered him to call me home (p. 178).

I had not seen the première of Don Giovanni at Prague, but Mozart wrote me at once of its marvelous reception, and Gardassino, for his part, these words:

"Long live Da Ponte! Long live Mozart! All impresarios, all virtuosi should bless their names. So long as they live we shall never know what theatrical poverty means!"

The Emperor sent for me, and overloading me with gracious felicitations, presented me with another hundred sequins, and told me that he was longing to see Don Giovanni. Mozart returned, and since Joseph was shortly to depart for the field, hurried the score to the copyist, to take out the parts. The opera went on the stage and . . . need I recall it? . . . Don Giovanni did not please! Everyone, except Mozart, thought that there was something missing. Additions were made; some of the arias were changed; it was offered for a second performance. Don Giovanni did not please! And what did the Emperor say? He said:

"That opera is divine; I should even venture that it is more beautiful than *Figaro*. But such music is not meat for the teeth of my Viennese."

I reported the remark to Mozart, who replied quietly:
"Give them time to chew on it!" (pp. 179–80)

10. DA PONTE'S REFLECTIONS ON OPERA MANAGEMENT

When he left the emperor's service in 1791, Da Ponte left behind a handwritten set of
riflessioni *on theater management (now in the Austrian State Archive) from which the
items below are excerpted.*

New operas are always more useful than old ones, despite their high cost; the reasons can be
seen in a flash. Suffice it to say that if there are six new operas, one that succeeds will pay
the expenses of all the others, and will carry the whole year. . . . With old operas it is always
best to economize, and better to choose wisely those one knows and which have succeeded,
than those coming from Italy, which are always uncertain, and almost always failures.

No one should be allowed onto the stage; too many problems arise from lax supervision, which are fatal for the illusion of the spectacle, and harmful to the box office.

In each singer's contract should be unequivocally described the duties of each,
not omitting the clause about costumes.

A tuner should be paid for the whole year, not allowing him the choice of writing down each time he tunes the harpsichords according to his judgment, which can lead
to problems.

The issue of tailors requires careful reflection. I have seen inexcusable things, and
damages that can only depend on their dishonesty.

From the facsimile and transcription in Ulrich Müller and Oswald Panagl, *Don Giovanni
in New York: Lorenzo da Pontes italienisch-englisches Libretto für die US-Erstaufführung
von Mozarts Oper (1826): mit dem Libretto der Oper "Mozart in New York" von Herbert
Rosendorfer/Helmut Eder (1991)* (Anif/Salzburg: U. Müller-Speiser, 1991, pp. 56–60).

11. GOETHE ON ACTING

*Director of the court theater in Weimar for many years, Johann Wolfgang von Goethe
wrote up a series of rules for actors in 1803, summarizing many years of experience in
German theater. Many of these rules apply equally well to the opera.*

35. First the actor must consider that he should not only imitate nature but present it in
    idealized form, and thus unite the true with the beautiful in his presentation.
37. The body should be held thus: the chest up, the upper half of the arms to the elbows
    somewhat close to the torso, the head turned somewhat toward the person with whom
    one is speaking—only a bit, however, so that three-quarters of the face is always turned
    toward the spectators.
38. For the actor must always remember that he is there for the sake of the public.

39. For the same reason, actors should also avoid playing to one another, out of a sense of misunderstood naturalness, as if no third person were present; they should never act in profile nor turn their backs to the audience. If this is done for the sake of characterization or out of necessity, then let it be done with care and grace.

40. One should also be careful never to speak upstage in the theatre but always toward the audience. For the actor must always divide his attention between two objects: the person to whom he is speaking and the spectators. Instead of turning the head entirely, make greater use of the eyes.

41. It is very important, however, that when two are acting together, the one speaking should move upstage and the one who has ceased speaking should move a bit downstage. If the actors skillfully use this advantage and learn through practice to do it with ease, then their declamation will have its best effect for both the ear and the eye. An actor who masters this strategy will, with others of similar training, produce a very beautiful effect, and will have a great advantage over those who do not follow this practice.

42. When two persons are speaking together, the one on the left should be careful not to approach too closely the one on the right. The more honored person always stands on the right—women, elders, nobility. Even in everyday life one keeps a certain distance from those he respects; contrary practice suggests a lack of breeding. The actor should show himself well bred and therefore adhere strictly to this rule. Whoever stands on the right should insist upon his privilege and not allow himself to be pressed toward the wings, but should stand fast and with his left hand give a sign to the person pressing him to move back.

47. The hand itself must never form a fist, or be placed flat against the thigh, as soldiers do; rather some of the fingers must be half bent, others straight, but never held entirely stiff.

48. The two middle fingers should always remain together, the thumb, index finger, and little finger remain somewhat bent. In this way the hand is in its proper position and ready to execute any movement correctly.

49. The upper half of the arm should remain rather close to the torso and should move much less freely than the lower half, which should have the greatest flexibility. For if I raise my arm only a little when everyday matters are being discussed, then a much greater effect is achieved when I raise it high. If I do not suit my gestures to the weaker expressions in my speech, then I have nothing strong enough for the more powerful ones, and thus all gradation of effect is lost.

50. Nor should the hands ever retire from action to their position of rest until the speech is concluded, and then only gradually, as the speech draws to a close.

51. The movement of the arms should always proceed in order. First the hand moves or rises, then the elbow, then the entire arm. Never should it be lifted all at once without this sequence, because such a movement would appear ugly and stiff.

55. Descriptive gestures must be made, but they should be made as if they were spontaneous. There are certain exceptions to this rule also, but in general it can and should be followed.

57. When gesturing, one should avoid as much as possible bringing the hand in front of the face or covering the body.

59. The actor should consider on which side of the stage he is standing and adjust his gestures accordingly.

60. Whoever stands on the right side should act with the left arm, and contrariwise, whoever stands on the left side should act with the right, so that the chest is covered by the arm as little as possible.

61. In emotional scenes when one is acting with both hands, these observations should still form the basis of movement.

62. For this very reason and so that the chest will not be turned toward the spectator, it is advisable for the actor who stands on the right side to place his left foot forward, and the actor on the left his right one.

63. . . . One should stand before a mirror and speak what one is to declaim softly or preferably not at all, but only think the words. In this way one will not be distracted by the declamation but rather easily observe every false movement that does not express one's thought or softly spoken words. Thus one can select the most beautiful and most suitable gestures and can express through the entire pantomime a movement analogous with the sense of the words, with the features of the art.

65. In order to acquire skill in pantomime and to make the arms agile and supple, it is of great advantage for the beginner to attempt to make his role understandable to another through pantomime alone, without giving his lines, for he will be forced to choose the most suitable gestures.

74. The actor should never allow his handkerchief to be seen on the stage, still less should he blow his nose, still less spit. It is terrible to be reminded of these physical necessities within a work of art. One can carry a small handkerchief, which is in fashion now anyway, to use in case of need.

82. The stage and the auditorium, the actor and the spectator form a whole.

83. The stage should be considered as a figureless tableau for which the actors supply the figures.

84. Therefore one should never perform too close to the wings.

85. Nor should one step under the proscenium arch. This is the greatest error, for the figure thereby leaves the space in which it makes a whole with the painted scenery and the other actors.

86. He who stands alone on stage should consider that it is his responsibility to fill the stage with his presence, all the more so since attention remains focused on him alone.

88. Anyone who enters for a monologue from the upstage wings does well to move diagonally down to the proscenium on the opposite side, since in general diagonal movements are very pleasing.

89. Anyone who enters from an upstage wing to join someone already onstage should not come downstage parallel with the wings, but should move slightly toward the prompter.

91. It should be evident, by the way, that these rules should be particularly observed when one is portraying noble, dignified characters. On the other hand, there are characters

for whom this dignity is totally unsuitable, for example, peasants, boors, and so on. Yet one will portray these characters much better if one carries out with artistry and calculation the reverse of what decorum suggests, while always remembering that this should be an imitative appearance and not dull reality.

Translated in Marvin A. Carlson, *Goethe and the Weimar Theatre* (Ithaca, N.Y.: Cornell University Press, 1978), pp. 309–18.

Is there any thing in the world so perfectly French as this?

Something like their pretty *opéra comique* may exist elsewhere;

we have our comic opera, and Italy has her buffa; the *opéra italien*,

too, may be rather more than rivalled at the Haymarket;

but where out of Paris are we to look for any thing like the

Académie Royale de Musique? . . . le grand opéra? . . .

l'opéra par excellence?—I may safely answer, nowhere."

— *Frances Trollope*

CHAPTER THREE

Giacomo Meyerbeer, *Les Huguenots*

Paris, February 29, 1836, 7:00 P.M.

*P*eople who speak of opera—especially those who do not like it—often call it grand opera. They seem to mean something pretentious, hifalutin, something that goes beyond the necessary and the appropriate. They seldom speak of any other, less grand, category of opera: grand opera is the general term for any kind of musical theater with loud continuous singing. In fact, these people are using a specific term in a more general sense, in the same way that we sometimes say "classical music" to refer to all of the art music of high culture in the West. But the term grand opera has a more particular sense that refers to the remarkable combination of spectacle, stagecraft, and music at the opera house of Paris in the 1830s: a style that is indeed grand, that intends to dazzle a large paying public with ballet, scenery, costume, historical information and social commentary, and beautiful music. This style of *grand opéra* is the flowing together of a number of traditions: Italian opera, Parisian boulevard theater, recent technological marvels, and the Romanticism of nineteenth-century literature and visual art. Although it is easy to make fun of the overblown qualities of some of the operas that held the Parisian stage in this period, it is also true that this was a central and influential moment in the development and history of opera. It involved a widening of audiences, it had a social and political relevance, and it required what was essentially a national organization to produce entertainments on such a scale. The style of grand opera as practiced in Paris was enormously influential on opera houses everywhere at the time, and on many generations of composers. Verdi and Wagner both wrote music for the Paris opera in the hope of pleasing the most important audience in the operatic world. If both of them, and many other composers, chose to react against this style, it only shows that the style of grand opera itself was a benchmark against which anything else would be measured.

Not all the grand operas of Paris continue to hold the stage. Meyerbeer's *Robert le diable,* enormously influential in its time, is scarcely performed today (Chopin's music for cello and piano on themes from *Robert le diable* is probably heard more often). We do not now hear much music by Hérold, Auber, Rodolphe Kreutzer, Schneitzhoeffer, or Sacchini. But Giacomo Meyerbeer's name, and his music, have continued to be admired, and his major works for the Paris opera are milestones, chefs d'oeuvre, of the style of grand opera. Beginning with *Robert le diable* (1829), Meyerbeer continued with the enormously successful *Les Huguenots,* later contributing to the repertory *Le prophète* (1849) and *L'africaine* (1865), his final masterpiece.

Meyerbeer's *Les Huguenots* is one of a small number of Parisian grand operas that continues to hold the stage, despite the enormous effort required of the singers and the production. In its time this opera was the result of the remarkable collaboration of a variety of artists and managers in a single central institution. These creators included, in addition to Meyerbeer, Louis Véron, manager of the Opéra in the early 1830s; Eugène Scribe, the amazingly prolific playwright whose works were seen in almost every theater; and the *peintres-décorateurs* Pierre Cicéri and Edmond Duponchel. It was a Romantic fusion of the arts in response to the desires of the bourgeois audience. It resounded to a Gothic trend in the arts; it reflected the current interest in history; and it sought an exactitude of historical detail that we now recognize in period movies or in the early-music movement.

Les Huguenots, like other grand operas of its time, explored social problems: the political aspects of religious intolerance between Catholics and Protestants are interwoven with individual love stories. Such religious themes are not nowadays considered suitable for operas, but it was not uncommon then: Halévy's *La Juive* has similar themes. The presence of religious music in the opera—a *Te Deum,* a Protestant chorale that recurs, a hymn to the Virgin—is a phenomenon in operatic history, though later religious music is more often overheard than performed on stage (for example, the *Regina coeli* in *Cavalleria rusticana,* or the *Te Deum* of *Tosca*). The centrality of religion to the story caused repeated difficulties. The opera was actually called *La Saint-Barthélémy* for the day on which the climactic massacre of Protestants took place, but its name was changed at the last minute (the performance parts in the library of the Opéra still bear the original title). And the opera was given a wide variety of other names when it played in Protestant countries: *The Anglicans and the Puritans* (Munich), *Marguerite of Navarre* (Cologne), *The Ghibellines in Pisa* (Vienna).

It is a colorful opera; in a technical sense, the current Romantic trends demanded "local color." Even though that local color here is that of Paris, it is the Paris of 1572, and the costumes and scenery were expected to be historically correct. The music, too—or at least aspects of it—evoked the color of the past. The Lutheran chorale known in English as "A Mighty Fortress Is Our God" serves to introduce the opera and to represent the Protestant religion; it plays an important role throughout the opera. There are minuets, Baroque-sounding rhythms, antique harmonies at the riverbank, Catholic hymns.

There are contrasts of all kinds. Protestant music (Marcel's song, the chorale that permeates the score) contrasts with Catholic (the splendid scene of the blessing of the swords by the monks, the processional "Vierge Marie," wonderfully combined with the Protestant "rataplan"). The first act is sung by men (except for one trouser role), and the second, until the entry of Raoul, by women. Enormous ensemble scenes are contrasted with intimate duets.

And it is a great ensemble opera: not many houses would be able to provide so many singers for so many roles. Meyerbeer, says the English critic Henry Chorley, is "restrained by no pity for his executants, by no tradesmanlike wish to conciliate minor theaters, where three respectable singers at most are the amount of vocal force available." The splendor of the costumes and the settings, and the enormous numbers of people on stage, are reflected in the musical demands. There are huge choruses, many changes of tempo. The plot unfolds primarily through grand choral and ensemble numbers, not through solos.

Romanticism was the vogue in the arts. By this was meant a great many things, but mainly it meant discarding the rules and conventions of literature, painting, and music. The classic literary example is the uproar at the premiere of Victor Hugo's *Hernani* at the Théâtre Français on February 25, 1830, the noise starting at the forbidden enjambement of the first line. The search for a wider subject matter, particularly the exotic and colorful, led to an interest in history, especially in the Middle Ages; it was at this time that the long rehabilitation and restoration of medieval monuments began, and the monastery of Solesmes, founded in 1833, dedicated itself to the restoration and performance of Gregorian chant. The word "romantic" is used nowadays for amorous love, a usage that preserves an important aspect of Romanticism: the conception of a single overpowering love, and an interest in the interior life of the individual. Berlioz's *Symphonie fantastique* of 1830 demonstrates this Romantic passion in musical terms. Romantic love is not necessarily reciprocal, it is not maudlin, and it is so powerful as to result in irrational behavior or in great works of art.

Meyerbeer is not generally reckoned a great Romantic, but *Les Huguenots* responds to many artistic currents of its time. It is historical, describing Gothic castles and events in French history; it features exoticism, not only by the insertion of Gypsies, peasants, and such requirements of the operatic ballet, but also in the detailed reconstruction of the life and times of other places—even if they are the Paris or Anjou of the sixteenth century. And it features the doomed Romantic love of Raoul and Valentine, separated in life by religious faith but united in death by their love.

There is a considerable extension of range and detail in this opera: the orchestra provides elements that will be important to the future of opera—even Wagner, who detested Meyerbeer, could not help being influenced. *Les Huguenots* was a piece for its time and its audience, a fully mature collaboration of high art and boulevard theater, a fusion of musical styles that combined the Italian style of Rossini and others with the French operatic tradition.

Background
PARIS IN THE 1830S

Paris was a great metropolis and an international center for the arts. And at the center of the arts, many would say, was opera and the Opéra. Paris had attracted Rossini, Meyerbeer, and many others, and it would one day attract Wagner and Verdi. Everybody of consequence in music visited, at least for a time: Paganini, Liszt, Chopin, Mendelssohn.

In this second largest city of Europe, three-quarters of a million people lived in an area considerably smaller than the twenty arrondissement that became official after 1845. Paris was enclosed by walls and entered through a series of toll houses.

Much of what the modern visitor expects was already there: the Louvre on the right bank (it then included the palace of the Tuileries, burned in 1871), the university on the left bank, and the cathedral of Notre Dame on its island, then being "restored" by Viollet-le-Duc, a symptom of the Romantic revaluation of the Middle Ages.

But much was not there. There were no Eiffel Tower, no stone embankments, no Sacré-Coeur on the hill of Montmartre, no great railway stations linking the city with the world in all directions (the first rail line, toward Saint-Germain-en-Laye, opened in 1837 —it still operates, incorporated into a line of the RER). The Arch of Triumph (then called the Arc d'Angoulême) was a set of monumental stumps at the top of the Champs-Élysées. There were some wide boulevards but a great many narrow, unpaved streets with foul-

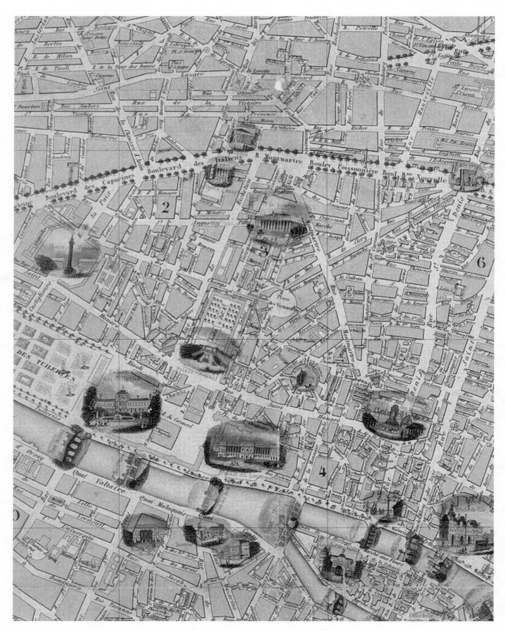

Map of Paris, 1840. The opera house is in the rue Lepelletier,
just north of the Boulevard des Italiens, a short distance
north of the Opéra-Comique.

smelling gutters in the middle. The city was not well lit, though gas was beginning to be used in street lamps.

Most Parisians, then as now, lived in apartment buildings, which were themselves a cross section of society, with shops on the ground floor and the better classes of society on the two floors above. The higher floors decreased in cost and social scale, and servants and laborers lived under the mansard roofs. There were new systems for delivering water to individual buildings and for removing waste; although the wealthy began to install bathrooms with hot water, only one building in five was connected to the water supply. A system of public baths was available to those wishing to bathe for a price. (In 1850, 2 million baths were taken in public baths for a population of 2 million.) Generally unsanitary conditions, along with the medical treatments available at the time, led to widespread disease. There was an outbreak of cholera in 1832. Cathérine Labouré, a twenty-four-year-old novice of the Sisters of Charity, had a vision of the Virgin Mary warning of the epidemic and instructing her to have a commemorative medal struck: by 1836 8 million were in circulation. Persons who survived childhood lived an average of thirty-nine years. No wonder an unmarried twenty-five-year-old woman was considered an old maid.

There was not much industry; most Parisians worked in commerce, administration, or government, or were artisans or servants. A growing bourgeois class, accumulating capital and trading shares on the new stock exchange (the Bourse), was vying with the aristocracy for places in society. Frances Trollope noted that "it is evident that the wealth of the *bourgeoisie* is rapidly increasing, and their consequence with it; so rapidly, indeed, that the republicans are taking fright at it—they see before them a new enemy, and begin to talk of the abominations of an aristocratic *bourgeoisie*." The enormous underclass engaged in occasional hunger riots.

Dress had been much simplified since the ancien régime. Rather than jewelry and lace, men tended to wear "business suits"; fashion required high collars, trousers pulled tight by a strap underfoot, high hats, and a display of whiskers. Women's dress was becoming fussy with messages about standing and wealth, but it always involved narrow bodices and flounced skirts. Like men, women wore their hair high and their waists small. New department stores, *magasins de nouveautés,* made it possible to buy ready-to-wear clothing in the latest style along with a wide range of consumer goods. The bourgeoisie and the workers could imitate and assimilate the fashions of those higher up on the social scale.

There was a huge output of the printed word—newspapers, plays, handbills, pamphlets, popular music, and pictures. Men might join a *cabinet de lecture,* and there were many clubs, political organizations, and local councils contributing to a sense of citizenship based on fairness and efficiency. The annual salon of the fine arts opened at the Louvre on the day after the premiere of *Les Huguenots,* and it attracted many viewers and much notice in the press (Delacroix exhibited a Saint Sebastian).

Women came to have positions of considerable influence and power, though they continued to be disenfranchised and removed from politics. Feminist newspapers of the 1830s (including *La Femme libre,* founded in 1832, and *Le tribun des femmes,* 1833) provided a sense of solidarity. Women were prominent as leaders of salons and as authors. In the 1830s George Sand was an important journalist; Daniel Stern was likewise a significant author. Stern was the countess d'Agoult (who bore Franz Liszt three children, one of whom, Cosima, married Richard Wagner). The most famous women, though, were actresses, dancers, and opera singers. There was always something tainted about a woman's exhibiting herself in public, that curious double standard whereby the stars attract the admiration of everybody and yet are held in contempt for inappropriately exhibiting themselves in public. There is a hint of prostitution attached to women who were performers. About four thousand licensed workers were employed in about two hundred brothels in Paris, graded by luxury and cost.

There was a strong sense of French national identity, a collective feeling of having traversed a revolutionary period; more than a million French had died in the revolutionary and imperial period, and the survivors had seen the restoration of the Bourbon monarchy. The recent revolution of 1830, the "three glorious days" of fighting in the streets of Paris, had placed the former Duke of Orléans, Louis-Philippe, on the throne as King of the French, and this "bourgeois" king reigned over a country in which the ancien régime, the revolution, and the triumphs and defeats of Napoleonic times gave way to a period of prosperity and relative calm. Institutions were strengthened, money was to be made, culture could thrive, and the people of Paris could enjoy unparalleled access to theater, music, and opera.

THE THEATERS OF PARIS

There was entertainment everywhere, and Giacomo Meyerbeer was one of many who went to everything. There was a variety of genres and styles for all tastes: classical tragedy, Romantic drama, Italian opera, and the comic opera and its cousins on the boulevards, melodrama and vaudeville.

The dramatic theaters included the Théâtre-Français, then as now the guardian of the classics and of the classical style. The plays of the seventeenth-century golden age were performed in the traditional manner, the actors standing essentially in a semicircle under the chandelier, emphasizing by placement and gesture the Alexandrines of Corneille, Racine, and the more modern Voltaire. This is the acting style known to Handel's and Mozart's audiences, and it continues unchanged, though its luster may have faded. There was also comedy by Molière, and Beaumarchais' *Le barbier de Séville* and *La folle journée* (the source of *Le nozze di Figaro*).

At the Odéon, by the Luxembourg Gardens, the fare was more modern, though sprinkled with the classics. Plays were billed as *tragédies, comédies,* or *drames* (a modern mixture of both the others). The Odéon was also used for touring companies, having notably presented an English company in the late 1820s and early 1830s, whose leading actress, Harriet Smithson, is the heroine of Berlioz's *Symphonie fantastique*. There had been an enormous vogue for Shakespeare's histories and "Romantic" tragedies, and his effect was to be felt among the modern playwrights in French. He even penetrated the Théâtre-Français, where Alfred de Vigny's translation *Le more de Venise* was presented in the 1829–30 season.

The Theaters of Paris, 1830–31

1. Principal theaters:
    dramatic:
        Comédie-Française
        Odéon
    lyric:
        Opéra
        Opéra-Comique
        Théâtre-Italien
2. Secondary theaters authorized under the First Empire:
    Ambigu
    Gaité
    Variétés
    Vaudeville
    Cirque-Olympique
3. Theaters opened since 1814:
    Comte
    Folies-Dramatiques
    Gymnase
    Luxembourg
    Molière
    Nouveautés
    Palais-Royal
    Porte Saint-Martin
4. Rope and acrobatic shows:
    Funambules
    Mme de Saqui
5. Marionette theaters:
    Joly

The principal lyric theater was the Opéra—and we will return to it—but there was much opera and musical theater to be heard elsewhere, particularly at the Opéra-Comique, the Théâtre-Italien, and in the boulevard theaters.

The Opéra-Comique was in principle the second lyric theater of Paris (though actually the Italian opera was thought to give better performances). The Opéra-Comique was in one sense a building, the new 1,290-seat Salle Ventadour in the Place de la Bourse. The chandelier with its hundred gas jets, the proscenium opening larger than the Opéra's, the decoration of gold on white with boxes lined in green, and the Herculaneum-style ceiling painting made this a very grand house. But opéra-comique was also a genre of musical theater in French in which spoken dialogue alternated with singing. The language requirement excluded the opéra-comique from the recent Rossini fever, and the admission of spoken dialogue made it sometimes difficult for the opéra-comique to be distinguished from some of the more ambitious musical entertainments on the boulevards. In 1828–29 the leading composers were Adrien Boieldieu and Daniel-François-Esprit Auber (eight works each); other composers were Ferdinand Hérold (six works), Henri-Montan Berton (five), Nicolo Caraffa, and Nicolas-Marie Dalayrac (four each), André-Ernest-Modeste Grétry and Nicolas Charles Bochsa (two each), and a number of others, including those better known (Fromental Halévy, Étienne-Nicolas Méhul, Rodolphe Kreutzer, Ferdinano Paer) and others unremembered (Charles-Simon Catel, Charles-Frédéric Kreubé, Stanislas Champein, Pierre-Antoine-Dominique Dellamaria). But nobody was as present on the stage as Eugène Scribe, the librettist of nine different shows. This was a theater of intense activity; unlike the Opéra and the Théâtre-Italien, shows were performed every night, sometimes several pieces in an evening.

The Théâtre-Italien in the rue Favart was the highly respected venue for Italian operas, in Italian, especially those of Rossini. Rossini himself had been director of the house in the 1820s, and it was he who brought Meyerbeer to Paris in 1825. It was Rossini, too, who influenced the subsequent directors of the house to produce works by modern Italian composers, and who commissioned new works from Italian composers including Bellini (*I Puritani*, 1835), Donizetti (*Marino Faliero*, 1835), and Mercadante (*I Briganti*, 1836). Bellini had been in Paris for two years, a favorite in salons but a lonely man. He died in 1836, and his funeral on October 2 at the Invalides was to be a splendid occasion of musical tribute.

The Théâtre-Italien boasted a group of superb singers, especially in the 1830s (including Luigi Lablache, Maria Malibran, Giuditta Pasta, and Henriette Sontag). Its orchestra, though smaller than that of the Opéra and less experienced (players would move to the Opéra if offered a place), was known for its superb solo instrumentalists and its skill in the Italian style, and in the accompaniment of singers. The repertory in 1828–29, though it did include one work by Halévy *(Clari)* and one by Mozart *(Don Giovanni),* was devoted to nine works by Rossini. A season of German opera was given in the spring at the Salle Favart on Tuesday, Thursday, and Saturday. A visiting company organized by Anton Haitzinger (who had sung *Fidelio* for Beethoven) and including Mme Schroeder-Devrient, performed *Fidelio, Don Giovanni* (in German), works of Weber *(Der Freischütz, Oberon, Euryanthe),* and works of Spohr, Pixis, and others. The hall itself, coveted by the Opéra-Comique, was about the same size, seating only 1,282 spectators. The Théâtre-Italien performed on non-Opéra days.

BOULEVARD THEATER

Though the major theaters and opera houses provided a range of high art, there was an enormous variety of theatrical and musical entertainment to be found in the theaters strung along the boulevards extending from the Place de la Madeleine to the Place de la Bastille. These were the chief attractions of the larger portion of the population, and their productions and styles were to lend dazzle to the grand opera. They combined circus with pathos, attractive music with the latest technological production values.

Boulevard theater can mostly be understood in the genres of pantomime, vaudeville, and melodrama. Each has its offshoots and varieties, but they account for most popular boulevard entertainments. And everything is designed to appeal, guided by the taste of the public.

Pantomime, as derived from the old Italian commedia dell'arte, was an entertainment that featured stock characters in a great deal of mime, elaborate conventional gestures, and farcical imbroglio. Some shows were silent and sometimes placards were used (as in early silent film), but dialogue was often present. There were "harlequinades," often involving a fairy story, enchantment, and a transformation. There were "Faits historiques," comic interpretations of sensational recent episodes. Pantomime increasingly emphasized display —dungeons, castles, cathedrals, wild landscapes—and spectacle—storms, assaults of fortresses, battles, magical effects, even fireworks. Plots were designed specifically to use such scenes and effects. Often descriptive music was played. At the Luxembourg theater, on the corner of the rue Madame and the rue de Fleurus (600 seats), the standard fare was *pantomimes dialoguées* and *scènes comiques mêlées de couplets*. The house had a permit for four speaking actors per piece, provided that only three of these were on the stage at one time.

The *comédie-vaudeville* had entertained the public for years, especially at the Théâtre Madame, the Vaudeville, the Variétés, and the Nouveautés. Scribe had produced dozens of popular works at the Gymnase theater before taking his talents into the lyric theater. The style of the vaudeville of the 1830s is that of a well-made play interspersed with songs, either traditional tunes (rather like those in *The Beggar's Opera*) or newly composed "ariettes." The result is something like a Broadway musical comedy in which the play is much more than a vehicle for the songs. Sometimes additional elements were added—satire, variety acts, spectacle. (By the late nineteenth century, the variety show with music, but without much plot, became the American vaudeville show.)

Melodrama is characterized by sincerity, sentimentality, and morality in its subjects; there is usually a theme of persecution of a pure heroine by a pure villain (who is either punished or reformed). Melodramas were played in the Théâtre de L'Ambigu-Comique, the Théâtre de la Gaité, and the Théâtre de la Porte Saint-Martin. Guilbert de Pixérécourt, director of the Gaité, had developed a formula that never failed to please and made him the undisputed master of the genre.

In a Pixérécourt melodrama the audience could count on impressive settings, local color, and a spectacular tableau at the end of each act; the play had predictable intrigue, passion, thrills. The settings combined the everyday with the exotic in a plot of headlong speed, piling episode on episode, misunderstanding on misunderstanding, with letters, disguises, and birthmarks all contributing to the revelation that untangles various complexities of the plot. There is a final tableau with everybody on stage, and each play has at least one spectacular scenic effect: a military festival, an assault, a forest fire, an explosion, full-rigged ships *(Christophe Colomb),* a flood with the heroine carried across the stage on a floating log (Pixérécourt's invention). Pixérécourt directed everything with great care: he was something of a martinet behind the scenes.

Dance was expected, and each play provided village weddings, processions, or exotic festivals as occasions for a series of characteristic and contrasting dances. Alexandre Piccinni, composer at the Gaîté, provided a vast number of such scores, and many other boulevard composers generated music for the melodrama.

There was plenty of music: an overture, entr'actes, songs on familiar or borrowed melodies; there were ballets and divertissements, and descriptive orchestral passages during mimed portions. A few bars of music (a proto-Leitmotiv?) identified characters at their entrances and often their exits—a rumble in the basses for the villain, a fanfare for the hero, flute trills for the heroine, bassoons for the comic character. And, as the identifying element of melodrama, orchestral music accompanied dialogue to heighten various effects (a tradition that continued through the silent cinema to modern film scores).

The tradition of melodrama is close in many ways to opera. Mozart's *Zaïde* and Beethoven's *Fidelio* have many of the elements of melodrama. *Fidelio,* in particular (in its original form as *Leonore*), owes much also to the French "rescue opera" of the type of Cherubini's *Les deux journées:* it has the three-act form, with a persecuted innocent (Florestan), a pure heroine (Leonore), an evil villain (Pizarro), last-minute revelation, recognition, and rescue; and it uses spoken dialogue with music.

There were many other sorts of entertainment along the boulevards and elsewhere in Paris. The Cirque-Olympique was famous for its "mimodrames" including music, spectacle, and horses. The Acrobates and the Funambules entertained with ropewalking, acrobatics, pantomime, and harlequinade. There were two marionette theaters and a children's theater. Eleven *bals publics* provided halls where the latest in dance music could be enjoyed.

Of some importance for the look of grand opera were the *spectacles d'optique,* spaces in which an audience could view historical, natural, or imaginary scenes created by lighting effects on gauzes and painted scenery. One of the earliest such spectacles had been introduced in Paris by Robert Fulton in the late eighteenth century, but the most famous was the Diorama of Louis Daguerre (known to us for his photographic process). The Diorama was a circular room seating about 350. The floor revolved to reveal different views created with partly opaque and partly transparent scenery and using ingenious lighting. A number of Daguerre's scenes had their influence in the opera house: the eruption of Vesuvius (borrowed first by Pixérécourt, and then for Auber's *La muette de Portici*), the view of Holyrood Chapel by Moonlight (borrowed for the famous ballet of nuns in Meyerbeer's *Robert le diable*). The Diorama had many imitators (the Néorama, Géorama,

Cosmorama, Peristréphorama), and Daguerre himself—who seems to have invented the curved cyclorama—was to lend his talents to the opera.

The boulevard audiences had at their command everything that one might have at the opera: song, dance, spectacle—and the management of the opera was not slow in borrowing the dancers, the stage designers, and the technicians of the Boulevard to enhance the grand opera.

THE PARIS OPÉRA

The Paris Opéra, officially the Académie Royale de Musique, in its theater on the rue Lepelletier, was the summit of the French musical and theatrical world. Every composer wanted to have his work performed there, every singer wanted to be heard there, every instrumentalist sought a place in its orchestra, and almost every theatergoer thought of the Opéra as the acme of the musical and social world. The Opéra was a house, but it was also a bureaucracy and a business. It had a monopoly on the performance of operas in French (defined as plays in the French language with continuous musical accompaniment).

The company performed operas on Mondays, Wednesdays, and Fridays. Friday

The Paris Opéra—officially the Académie Royale de Musique—
was in a building never intended to be permanent, though it lasted
half a century before burning in 1871. The rue Lepelletier side
is shown here; passageways on the other side connected
the theater with the Boulevard des Italiens.

MEYERBEER, *LES HUGUENOTS*

was the chief day for society, the day to be seen. Performances alternated operas and ballets in repertory; new operas or ballets opened with a dense series of performances, and if they were a success they remained in the repertory. Many patrons had boxes by subscription and came several times a week, though they may not always have stayed the whole evening or paid close attention to what was happening on stage. The house was generally well lit during the performance so that audience members could see each other, as well as the drama on stage. There was no season as such, and the opera continued essentially all year, sometimes adding performances on Saturday or Sunday during the winter.

The Opéra had a cumbersome hierarchy in that it depended ultimately on the government for its support and management. Until 1831 all the lesser theaters and other entertainments had been taxed to support the Opéra; government supervision had been the price of the huge government subsidy. But this favored status ceased under Louis-Philippe, and in 1831 the remarkable Louis Véron signed a six-year contract to manage the Opéra at his own risk in exchange for a bond of 250,000 francs.

As a businessman, Véron gave the public what it wanted—spectacle and stars. After 1831, Véron had cut the salaries of orchestra, chorus, and lesser employees so as to pay very high prices to a few star singers and dancers. Laure Cinti-Damoreau, for example, had a salary of 16,000 francs, as compared to 3,000 for the great violinist Pierre Marie Baillot and 600 for the bass drummer.

The opera had long been mismanaged, in Véron's view, and had lost much money, so he organized it as a profit-making business. Véron resigned in 1835, in the season before *Les Huguenots,* but not before he had instituted many changes that would persist long after him.

Depending on whom you asked, Véron might be described as a quack physician with no taste and no knowledge of music, or as a brilliant manager and businessman who himself created grand opera. Véron had made a fortune from Regnault's Chest Ointment, and in 1829 he had founded *La Revue de Paris.* He made a show of whatever he did, and he was famous for his carriage, his cravat, his table at the Café de Paris. He was an expert at publicity and cultivating the press. He was "ruddy, with a pock-marked face, barely any nose, scrofulous, his neck enfolded in cloth that protected and hid his affliction, pot-bellied; his eye round and brilliant, scintillating and avid; mouth smiling, lips thick, hair rare, eyebrows absent, dressed like a little lackey aping his master and with the affectations and the mincing airs of the salon."

He made the opera into a bourgeois entertainment, competing with the boulevard theaters for the discretionary income of the better classes. Véron changed many boxes from six to four seats. He cultivated his subscribers, allowing them backstage; this privilege was particularly appreciated on ballet days. What had once been the province of the nobility now became more accessible and attractive to a wide audience. Many of the former, snobbish patrons of the opera, began to patronize the Théâtre-Italien as the only remaining serious musical theater. The German poet Heinrich Heine described Véron's attitude to the public:

The businessman and publisher Louis Véron managed the Opéra for several years after 1831, and he ran it as a business: he provided spectacle for the public and paid high salaries to a few star singers. A skin disease was hidden by his characteristic high collar.

[Véron] himself has remarked that Franconi's circus gave him more pleasure than the best opera; he convinced himself that the majority of the public shared his feelings, that most people go to the grand opera out of convenience, and only then do they take delight if beautiful settings, costumes, and dances capture their attention so that they completely disregard the unpleasant music. The great Véron got where he is by the ingenious idea of satisfying the public's desire for show to such a degree that the music could no longer annoy them, so that they would take as much pleasure in opera as in Franconi's circus. The great Véron and the great public understand each other: the former wanted to make the music harmless, and gave under the name of "opera" nothing but magnificent spectacle; the latter—the public—could take their daughters and their wives to the grand opera, as befitted their social rank, without dying of boredom. America was discovered, the egg stood on its end; the opera house was full every day, Franconi was outbid and went bankrupt, and Véron is now a rich man.

The Opéra audience who attended the premiere of *Les Huguenots* in 1836 were for the most part aware of the traditions that had been established in Parisian opera in the last decade, and that would affect the course of the art in Paris, and elsewhere, for a long time to come.

The year 1828 had seen the premiere of *La muette de Portici,* that collaboration of Auber, Scribe, and the decorator Cicéri that revolves around the figure of a deaf-mute girl in the center of a Neapolitan revolution. That the central role in an opera should be taken by a character who never sings was an interesting gimmick (it was tried again, in a ballet and elsewhere, but without the same success); the role of Fenella was taken by the star dancer Marie Taglioni, whose movements, mime-gesture (borrowed from the melo-drama), and beauty served the piece well. The opera ends with a spectacular eruption of Vesuvius (Cicéri borrowed the idea from Daguerre's Diorama) and is the only opera to have caused a revolution. At its performance in Brussels in 1830, Scribe's plot of a popular uprising, and Auber's patriotic music, led to an uprising of their own that ultimately led to the end of Spanish domination and the establishment of modern Belgium.

Rossini's *Guillaume Tell* (1829) was the first full-scale work by the enormously popular Italian composer given at the Opéra. With this production the modern Italian style infiltrated the Opéra, and it allowed the house to cash in on the Rossini fever that had enriched the Théâtre-Italien. *Tell,* like *La muette,* had a patriotic plot of popular up-rising, and it had spectacular singing such as only Rossini could produce.

The premiere of *Robert le diable* in 1829 is marked by many as the beginning of the tradition of grand opera. It had a supernatural plot (by Scribe), spectacular scenery (by Cicéri, whose setting for the famous third-act ballet of nuns was also pilfered from Daguerre), and music by the young Giacomo Meyerbeer.

Almost exactly a year before *Les Huguenots,* on February 23, 1835, Halévy's *La Juive* was premiered at the Opéra. Its plot (again by Scribe) centered on the Council of Constance in 1414, and it used the conflicting religious beliefs of Jews and Catholics to drive the central plot. There was much attention to period detail in the settings, and the procession in act 1, culminating in the appearance of the Holy Roman Emperor amid a host of dignitaries, cardinals, clerics, and soldiers, is just the stuff of which grand opera is made. The staging was said to have cost 150,000 francs, and the twelve horses and countless costumes sometimes gave it the nickname Opéra Franconi, after the equestrian circus.

The artistic personnel of the Opéra consisted of singers, dancers, and players. Of these, the singers were of course preeminent. The singing personnel in 1830–31 were presided over by two composers who themselves made substantial contributions to opera: Hérold, *premier chef du chant,* and Halévy, *deuxième chef du chant.* They supervised the solo singers and the chorus. Hérold's *Le pré aux clercs* was one of the most popular opéras-comiques of the day; Halévy, composer of *La Juive* and professor of harmony at the Conser-vatoire, had worked at the Théâtre-Italien before coming to the Opéra in 1830.

Solo singers were divided into *premier sujets, remplacements,* and *doubles.* Of these only the *premier sujets* were the stars, playing leading roles in important performances. There were six male *remplacements,* and three women; the four *doubles* were all male. The choirs were divided into five voice parts, essentially basses, tenors, and sopranos, each with its leader, or *coryphée: premières basses-tailles* (seven singers), *deuxièmes basses-tailles* (seven), *tailles* (seven), *premiers dessus* (nine), *seconds dessus* (thirteen).

The ballet was under the direction of a *premier maître des ballets,* and two assis-tants. The solo dancers, like the singers, held positions as premier sujets, remplacements, or doubles. Members of the ballet numbered twenty-seven men and twenty-nine women. There were two ballet teachers for the regular classes for the men and women. The ballet had an indispensable place in the opera, and it provided ballet evenings. The maîtres des ballets were artists of the first rank: Jean Aumer; Ferdinand Albert; Filippo Taglioni; Jean Coralli. And the star in the 1830s was Marie Taglioni, who appeared in *La sylphide* in 1832 and essentially invented the new style of female-oriented ballet. Taglioni's worldwide preeminence was rivaled after 1834 by Fanny Elssler.

The orchestra consisted of eighty-five players, including some of the finest instrumentalists in the world. At their head was the fifty-five-year-old François-Antoine Habeneck, who was conductor of the Opéra orchestra and of the Concerts du Conservatoire; he was one of two professors of violin at the Conservatoire, and his influence was as far-reaching in his time as that of Lully or Boulez in theirs. He was the most important musician in Paris; he could even get his pupils into the opera orchestra without going through the stringent audition process. It was Habeneck who introduced the symphonies of Beethoven to the Parisian public and who, as a champion of the music of younger composers, conducted the premiere of Berlioz's *Symphonie fantastique*. At twenty-three Habeneck had entered the Opéra orchestra as a rank-and-file violinist; he had served as concertmaster and first assistant conductor, and indeed had served as general director of the Opéra from 1821 to 1824. From 1824 until 1844 he returned to the pit as chief conductor. It was Habeneck who, in the opera pit on August 28, 1828, at the première of Rossini's *Le Comte Ory,* conducted for the first time facing the musicians of the orchestra and using a violin bow rather than the large baton of the time-beater. Before then the orchestra had faced the stage, with the time-beater closest of all and also facing the stage (see p. 175). Communication with the players is obviously accomplished not with eye-contact but with the impulse of the baton struck on the floor of the pit. Such pounding, however discreet, had always been a part of operatic performance in France (it was just such pounding that gave Lully his mortal blow). At the Opéra, however, Habeneck continued for years to rely on audible beats when necessary, striking on the prompter's box with his bow. Charles de Boigne, in his 1857 *Petits mémoires de l'Opéra*, says that "Habeneck had the bad habit of letting the audience in on the secret of the clams (couacs) that occurred in his orchestra. At every wrong note, he turned around and pointed out the culprit to the vindictive public with his violin-bow."

There were twenty-four violins in the orchestra, and eight violas, nine cellos, and eight double-basses. Woodwinds were in threes, with the exception of the fourth bassoon, which was characteristic of this orchestra. Among the famous instrumentalists were Pierre Marie Baillot, first violin, professor at the Conservatoire and organizer of a respected chamber music series. Gustav Vogt played first oboe, Jean-Louis Tulou first flute, Louis Pierre Norblin cello—it was a superb ensemble that played together for years.

The opera orchestra was mostly recruited from the graduates of the Paris Conservatoire, an institution of great importance in the musical life of the city and the country. For every position in the orchestra there was a competition, and players often joined the orchestra first as *aspirants,* supernumeraries who took regular positions as they became available. Most of the players performed also in the famous Concerts du Conservatoire, a cooperative musical society founded and conducted by Habeneck, whose Sunday afternoon concerts were the artistic high point for musical Paris. The orchestra shared a similar training, it rehearsed regularly and played concert music at a high level, and it paid the highest salaries and recruited the finest players. No wonder it was so highly regarded.

The musicians of the orchestra were paid according to a hierarchical scale that went from 600 francs annually for the bass drum to 3,000 francs for Pierre Marie Baillot. The average violinist was paid about 1,200 francs. The leading wind players, Tulou, the flutist who had moved up from the Théâtre-Italien, and the first oboist Vogt, made 3,000 francs a year. Other wind players had salaries similar to those of the strings, though horn players were paid something above the average.

The job had its drawbacks. Players had regular contracts, but these could be broken by management; a player who resigned could not leave until a year after giving notice. There were three or four performances of opera and ballet every week, plus rehearsals and concerts; a total of more than 180 performances in a year. Discipline was strict, and repeated absences were forbidden. Members of the orchestra, even if they had the time, could not play elsewhere for an opera or as soloists without prior permission; they could play for other concerts—but not as soloists—provided that it did not interfere with work at the Opéra.

The opera had a great deal of management, but it had no stage director. Matters of staging were generally worked out among the management, the composer, the singers, the peintre-décorateur, and others involved in the production. The scene painter, Pierre Cicéri, was one of the influential people in the formulation of grand opera. He served at the Théâtre-Français, as well as the Opéra, from 1810 onward, and he also worked for many other theaters. His first major production for the Opéra was *La muette de Portici* in 1828; it was in a way the first major example of nineteenth-century sets and staging. There was careful attention to detail, to accurate Neapolitan costume; there was a splendid palace of the Spanish viceroy with a flying staircase; and there was the eruption of Vesuvius! Other Cicéri productions included the major works of the time: *La belle au bois dormant; Guillaume Tell;* the spectacular *Robert le diable; La Juive,* with its medieval city and its spectacular costumes in procession. Cicéri had the sole right to design for the Opéra, but after 1830 he shared duties with his students, and most of his productions were collaborations.

An opera house requires a lot of personnel: not only singers, dancers, and decorators but administrative and service personnel. At the Opéra there were five répétiteurs, a *sous-inspecteur du chant et de la danse,* a *garçon de classe* for the ballet school, an assistant conductor, a librarian, a *préposée* (evidently in charge of the house), various controllers and supervisors for the house staff, a doctor, many ushers and *ouvreuses* (including a staff member especially in charge of the *porte du roi*), many workmen for the maintenance of the house (locksmiths, felt-makers, lamp-lighters, furnace-stokers, instrument repairmen). There were three concierges, four persons in charge of costumes (including Hippolyte Lecomte, designer, and Duponchel, second designer); the machines and lighting were operated by machinists and lampists. Cicéri is listed in the *Almanach des spectacles* for 1830 as a salaried painter *(peintre à l'année).* There was an enormous list of official suppliers of every thing from musical instruments to firewood, brooms, rope, statuary busts, printing, papers, candles, shoes, and metalwork.

There were some forty or fifty seamstresses and tailors who worked to build the costumes and served at performances as dressers; those who saw to the properties, stored in two enormous rooms; those who distributed shoes (they came in puce, white, and flesh, and for lead singers they were discarded after two or three performances). There were persons who made purchases every day; those who went to singers' houses to announce rehearsals and performances. And of course there was an army of cleaners. It was an enormous operation.

Nowhere on the books of the Opéra appears one of the most important, if informal, groups of workers: the claque. Such a group of professional applauders was considered a necessity in almost all Parisian theaters, and the Opéra was no exception. The claque was run by Auguste Levasseur, known to everybody simply as Auguste. He collected payments from artists, composers, and librettists, and in exchange he arranged for a group of hired hands to generate enthusiastic applause at the right time: for a splendid aria; for the first appearance of a singer on stage; for the sets.

Débuts and premieres were especially lucrative. Auguste received tickets from the management that he distributed to his cohort. Every artist also received two to four complimentary tickets, which were often put at Auguste's disposal. Before premieres Auguste was known to have long meetings with Véron to plan the placement and amount of applause, depending on the management's wishes and on Auguste's clients. Auguste is said to have made about fifty thousand francs a year.

Charles de Boigne described Auguste's plans for *Les Huguenots*:

The premiere of a grand opera was for him what a battle is for a general. He prepared for it long in advance; he made his preparations, his notes; he attended rehearsals, he studied the poem, the music, the settings. On the day before, he conferred with the director, telling him of his plan and receiving his last orders. One day—if I am not mistaken, it was *Les Huguenots*—the director had not had the time to work with Auguste; a report written by the distinguished claqueur replaced the conference. The report began as follows:

"Monsieur le directeur,

I am very pleased with the new opera. It is a pleasure to work for such pieces. We can do all the arias and almost all the duets. I can undertake to crown the one in the fourth act with three salvos. For the trio of the fifth act I expect to shout.

As to what to do for the artists and the authors, I await the orders of the administration."

Spectacle was what was expected. If, as Mrs. Trollope said, "we go to this magnificent theater for the purpose of seeing the most superb and the best fancied decorations in the world, we shall at least not be disappointed, though before the end of the entertainment

The claque, a group of professional applauders, was an important part
of any production. This humorous volume, *Mémoires d'un Claqueur,*
claims to contain "the theory and practice of the art of success"; the
illustration, of a claqueur about to use his hands, is labeled with a line
from Voltaire, "I have seen the destinies of the world within my hands."
This volume is distributed by "Levasseur, successeur de Ponthieu," who
was the leader of the claque at the time of *Les Huguenots.*

we may probably become weary of gazing at and admiring the dazzling pageant." Much
of what attracts audiences to the opera is visual, in the auditorium and on the stage. And
the stage of the Paris Opéra was the site of technological and visual innovations, many of
them adapted from boulevard entertainments.

At the time of *Les Huguenots,* the Opéra was directed by a stage designer, Edmond
Duponchel, who had been appointed in 1827 by a committee to improve the scenic effects
at the Opéra; he succeeded Véron as director of the Opéra in August 1835. Heinrich Heine
described him as a "lean, yellowish, pale man, . . . who looked as if he were in perpetual
mourning." Assisted by Cicéri and others, he made the spectacle a chief ingredient of the
opera.

In recent operas there had been a trend toward the Gothic *(La Juive),* toward the
fantastic and supernatural *(Robert le diable),* and toward an exactitude of detail in historical

re-creation *(La muette)*. Settings were praised not only for their lavishness but also for their realism. Several technological improvements helped with this illusion. Lowering the curtain between the acts (first done in 1831 for Auber's *Le philtre*) deprived the audience of the sight of marvelous machinery but gave each set a sense of solidity and realism. The backdrop was no longer the traditional painted cloth but a curved cyclorama allowing the set to recede in depth and give a further illusion of space and distance.

"There are, I am very sure, more things at present above, about, and underneath the opera stage, than are dreamed of in any philosophy, excepting that of a Parisian carpenter," said Mrs. Trollope, and she was right. This was the opera house that all the others emulated. Its capacity for spectacle was admired everywhere, and although the Opéra was made like almost any other opera house, it is worth pausing to consider how the mechanism of the spectacle was arranged.

The stage of the Opéra, like that of almost any theater, has a curtain in front, this one painted with Louis XIV handing the keys of the Académie Royale de Musique to Perrin and Cambert (founders of the Opéra, 1669). When the curtain is raised the *manteau d'arlequin,* movable side and top panels just behind the curtain, can reduce the size of the proscenium opening from its maximum height of forty-five feet and width of forty-one feet. (Note that the height exceeds the width. This is true of most traditional theaters, where the audience is brought near and stacked up in boxes, but is not true of most modern theaters.) The stage consists of the *rampe,* the apron projecting nine feet into the auditorium, and eighty-eight feet of stage, raked at the angle of one inch in two feet, extending to the back wall. The stage is one hundred eight feet wide, including the sides.

The stage itself was divided into twelve *plans,* numbered from the apron: each plan corresponded to one set of wings, left and right (what the French have always called in any theater *côté jardin* and *côté cour,* garden and courtyard sides, from the old Tuileries theater). Each plan consists of a *rue* with two sets of *trapillons* and *costières.* The rue is a row of large traps extending across the stage, each three feet wide by four feet long; end to end, with all the traps removed, one rue makes a three-foot chasm running across the stage. The traps are only removed, however, when something is raised from below; the traps can be replaced by *trappes à tampon,* piston traps used for raising scenery to the stage or lowering it. There were also *trappes anglaises* introduced for *Robert le diable,* quick self-covering traps for quick disappearances from the stage.

Behind the rue is a trapillon, a foot-deep section of stage, behind which is a costière, a slit about 1.5 inches wide running across the stage. The costières were normally left open for moving scenery, but they could be closed with lengths of wood called *baguettes.* Each of the twelve plans, then, was about five and a half feet deep and consisted of rue-trapillon-costière-trapillon-costière; the twelve plans occupied about sixty-six feet of the total depth of eighty-eight feet.

Through the slits of the costières poles could be extended from the substage; on these were attached the flats *(châssis)* of the scenery. Two poles joined by braces were called *faux châssis* and were used to support larger flats. These poles, eighteen to twenty-four feet high, had attachments, each carrying three to ten lights. The poles *(mâts)* and faux

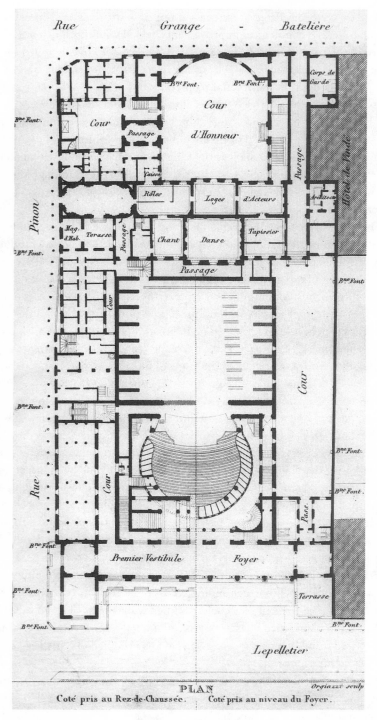

The Paris opera house had an enormous stage (compare it to the seating space for the public). The plan shows two floors of the building, giving an idea of the spaces required for rehearsals, public gatherings, storage, and all the other requisites of the grandest opera in the world.

châssis were attached to *chariots,* monorail trolleys in the first basement about five inches wide and about eight feet high and eight to twelve feet long, which slid along a rail under the costière, allowing scenery to be moved sideways. For larger pieces, the chariots could be connected in a series, like a train.

The substage extended below the stage for thirty-three feet, arranged in several floors, each with lattice planking. The floors had the same rake as the stage, and the system of rues and costières extended downward from the stage through all the levels of the substage, so that a rue or costière could be opened all the way to the bottom for moving or removing scenery. The many openings in the framework made the *dessous* a dangerous place to work.

Above the stage, extending upward for 102 feet, was the *cintre,* the flies; these had four levels and two floors of machine storage above the gridiron, which was surrounded on three sides by a catwalk. Here, in addition to backdrops and side panels that were lowered onto the stage, were the flying machines. They did not always work.

The settings were among the glories of the Opéra. In the 1830s the *machiniste,* who had previously been in charge of all aspects of the set, was gradually replaced by the *décorateur* as the chief designer of sets. Authors, composers, and décorateurs would have long discussions—and arguments—over a series of models before the final sets were executed.

Scenery was composed of borders, drops, *fermes,* and *praticables.* The borders and drops were painted to match the side wings, which are carried on chariots. Borders were not allowed to touch the stage, since they might wrinkle and spoil the effect of a wall, or a rock; a flap sewed to the bottom closed the gap. Drops usually provided the back horizon and might contain wooden structures to make openings. Fermes were any pieces of painted scenery too heavy to be raised to the flies. They usually included the doors and windows of the set. Flats, if unusually wide, had folding panels, ten feet wide, that could be extended on the stage. These were attached by poles to chariots so that they could be moved aside or lowered into the substage when not in use.

A praticable was any piece of scenery on which an actor could stand: a rock, a balcony, a bridge, the deck of a ship. Levels could be added to the stage by the use of a series of praticables at angles. Their frail framing, and the failure to use all the hooks provided, sometimes made for instability, jammed scenery, and crashing praticables.

An impressive level of depth could be achieved by using many backdrops in close succession, with mesh in parts of those in front. Sometimes a raked ceiling was placed on the top of a *salon fermé* for small indoor scenes. Sets could give the impression of enormous size by having the stage show only part of a much larger room or building or square.

The idea was to make the traditional look of wing-and-drop theater disappear: and this had its effect, at least on Mrs. Trollope, who wrote of *La Juive:* "The arrangement and management of the scenery were to me perfectly new. The coulisses have vanished, side scenes are no more."

Before 1833 there had been individual oil lamps attached to each set, trimmed during set changes. Until the act curtain came into use in 1831 the audience saw this trimming. Trimmers sometimes were applauded for their dexterity. This originated, of course, in the era of candles, when all candles were extinguished before each intermission. Improvements in lighting, however, made many new effects possible. The older (and dangerous) Argand house lights were replaced by gas; gas lamps were first used in the theater for, appropriately enough, *Aladin ou la lampe merveilleuse* in 1822. On stage they were introduced for *Robert* in 1832; the effect of lowering the lights for the third-act moonlight ballet of nuns was marvelous.

The rampe itself was surrounded by a ring of footlights of open gas lamps. These could be raised or lowered to provide varying amounts of light, but they were risky: they generated heat and smoke, and if a dancer lost her footing and slid into them she could be badly burned. Before the ballet a dancer always dampened the floor of the rampe, and during performances a fireman with a wet blanket stood between the proscenium arch and the manteau d'arlequin.

Rows of gas lamps were also overhead and attached to the backs of fermes. Though lighting could be lowered in the house and on the stage, the light could not be directed, in the manner of modern spotlights, to cast impressive shadows. Any shadows wanted on the set had to be put there by the painters.

Careful painting gives the effect of varied lighting, as do lighter and darker costumes. The German poet Franz Grillparzer admired the Opéra's style of scene-painting:

> The French school of scene painting differs from that of all other nations in that the others paint truthful imitations and leave it then to chance whether poor lighting, bad grouping and costuming of characters heighten the truthfulness or disturb or even annihilate it. Here the scene painter paints everything into his set; the gradations of light, intensified here and toned down there, the essential and the trivial aspects alike are painted in so that nothing is left to chance. In order to compensate for the unfortunate uniformity of the illumination of the stage lighting, lighter or darker stage areas are created by costuming people in lighter or darker fabrics. In this manner veritable pictures of an incomparable effectiveness are created.

La Juive, designed by Séchan, was particularly famous for these effects of light. Frances Trollope, for one, was deceived: "These admirable mechanists have found the way of throwing across the stage those accidental masses of shadow by aid of which Nature produces her most brilliant effects; so that, instead of aching eyes having to gaze upon a blaze of reflected light, relieved only by an occasional dip of the footlights and a sudden paling of gas in order to enact night, they are now enchanted and beguiled by exactly such a mixture of light and shade as an able painter would give to a picture."

A change of scene at the Opéra generally required about sixty machinistes to operate the winches and drums, and forty or fifty crewmen. Things needed to be timed carefully in order to effect changes between acts, and enormous numbers of people were moving about in the flies and on the substage. On performance nights four beds were reserved at the Beaujon hospital for injured machinistes.

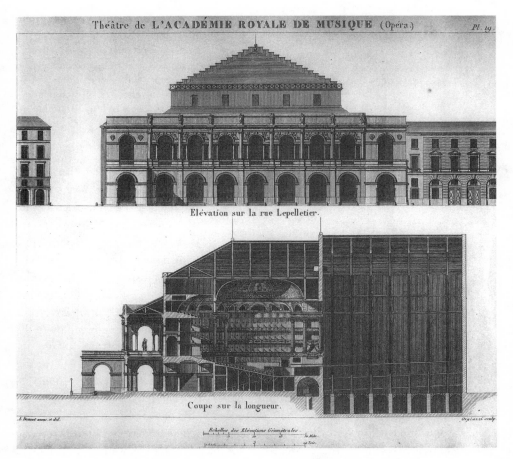

Elévation sur la rue Lepelletier.

Coupe sur la longueur.

In this elevation and cross-section of the Opéra, note the rake
of the stage, and the three levels of substage. There is room enough
below and above the stage to sink or fly a set of full height.

Preparations

Giacomo Meyerbeer may not be at the top of most modern lists of great composers of opera, but his creations held the stage all over Europe in his day and afterward.
They are the epitome of the style called grand opera. The majority view may be that of
Franz Stoepel, writing about *Les Huguenots* in June 1836: "The opera is one of the most
admirable creations of the human spirit. It depicts the fine arts of poetry, of music and of
painting in enchanting effects with the rich life of scenic presentation, enhanced by the
fairy play of the dance and the dazzling finery of the costumes, all in the powerful process
of seductive illusion."

But there are some, and great musicians among them, who had little use for
Meyerbeer: Wagner ("Effect without cause"), Schumann ("I place him with Franconi's

The young Jacob Liebmann Meyer Beer, the son of Jacob Herz Beer of Berlin, soon became known as Giacomo Meyerbeer. He combined his parents' names and adopted the Italian version of his first name during his visits to Italy beginning in 1816.

circus people"), Mendelssohn, the poet Heinrich Heine. Wagner's anti-Semitic diatribes concealed a more personal resentment against a composer who had once supported him financially and to whom he owed a large musical debt. Schumann's review of *Les Huguenots* is puzzlingly negative ("But what is all this in contrast to the commonness, the distortion, the artificiality, immorality, and the non-music of the whole?"). Heine's close relationship with Meyerbeer was essentially one of a leech: his repeated appeals for money were often heeded, but not often enough for the poet. Mendelssohn perhaps recognized a composer who succeeded in the one area of music that eluded Mendelssohn, and a fellow Jew who had maintained his religious identity. But in 1836 these relationships, which were to trouble Meyerbeer for the rest of his life, were only beginning.

Meyerbeer was forty-four at the premiere of *Les Huguenots*. His distinctive nose and dark complexion made him an easy target for anti-Semites, and he was particularly sensitive to any sort of criticism. He was now famous, after the success of his *Robert le diable* (1831); he was a Chevalier of the Legion of Honor and was appointed Kapellmeister at the Prussian Court in 1832. He was named a foreign associate of the Académie des Beaux-Arts early in 1835. And yet he was always terribly nervous, insisting on many rehearsals, cultivating the press, and generally showing uncertainty about everything. Heine—who knew him well, if not always amicably—described his impossible temperament: "On days when his opera is given, even the dear God can do nothing right: if it is cold and wet, he fears that Mademoiselle Falcon will get a cold; but if the evening is warm and bright, he worries that the good weather will entice people outdoors and that the theater will be empty."

Meyerbeer was born into a wealthy Jewish family in Berlin. He was a formidable pianist but never wanted a soloist's career. He spent nine years in Italy, where he composed operas with considerable success. A performance of his *Il Crociato in Egitto* at the Théâtre-Italien in 1826 made him famous in Paris (though he had hoped to have it presented at the Opéra); equally important events of that year are that he met Eugène Scribe and began working on *Robert le diable*. His *Marguerite d'Anjou* (the French version by Pixérécourt) played at the Odéon in 1826.

Meyerbeer spent much of his time listening to concerts. He knew the virtuosi of his day, including Paganini and Liszt, and made a point of knowing as much music by his contemporaries as possible—even those contemporaries whom he didn't understand (Berlioz) or who didn't like his music (Schumann). He was an admirer of the music of the past, and his knowledge of Bach and Handel can be heard in *Les Huguenots* (he studied Bach cantatas and chorales in preparation for the opera).

Meyerbeer never had a house in Paris: he was always a visitor, usually residing at the Hôtel des Princes in the rue Richelieu. Meyerbeer was devoted to his wife, Minna (who was also his first cousin), and his three surviving daughters. Minna was not much interested in Paris, preferring to remain in Berlin. One fortunate result is that we have his detailed personal letters to her. When in Paris Meyerbeer gave many dinners; he is accused, perhaps falsely, of having worried too much about critics and of trying to buy their favors. His diary of March 21, 1831, reads: "I hosted a dinner for Paganini. The guests were Boieldieu, Auber, Rossini, Bertin [owner of the *Journal des débats*], Cherubini, Casimir and Germain Delavigne, Habeneck, and Count Moretti."

Meyerbeer's later career consisted of traveling to the great operatic centers of Europe to supervise productions of his operas and the composition of two more grand operas (among other works): *Le prophète*, produced after considerable delay in Paris in 1849, and *L'africaine*, left unfinished and performed posthumously in 1865.

Meyerbeer had two specters haunting him at the time of *Les Huguenots:* the premiere, on February 23, 1835, of Halévy's *La Juive,* whose splendor and success was a thing to be topped (Halévy's most popular comic opera, *L'Éclair,* premiered at the Opéra-Comique on December 16, 1835); and his own *Robert le diable,* against which any of his future work was certain to be measured—and, Meyerbeer feared, found wanting.

NEGOTIATIONS

After the success of *Robert le diable,* Véron, director of the Opéra, had undertaken negotiations with Meyerbeer in 1832 for a new opera, fearing the repeated rumors in the press that Meyerbeer had composed a piece for the Opéra-Comique. When personal and family events prevented Meyerbeer from delivering his score, Véron enraged Meyerbeer by collecting the contractual penalty of 30,000 francs.

Negotiations in the fall of 1834, through Scribe and Meyerbeer's lawyer Isaac-Adolphe Crémieux, finally resulted in a revised contract with Véron, signed on September 29, 1834, according to which Meyerbeer had to deliver the score, entitled *Léonore ou la Saint Barthélemy,* by April 1835 (Meyerbeer did deliver the score to Crémieux on April 5). The score was not required to have an overture or any ballet music (these of course had to be arranged with the ballet master). On delivery of the score Véron was to pay Meyerbeer 30,000 francs, independent of royalties. (At the time of the contract, Véron paid Meyerbeer the 30,000 francs he had collected in September 1833.)

Remarkable at the time was the extent to which Meyerbeer—and not the libretto —was the driving force. Previous operas had been commissioned by the house on the basis of a libretto already chosen, composers being engaged to set a specific text. Meyerbeer was himself a valuable property, but it also seems that composers were now considered the chief creators of opera.

The following terms were included in the contract:

Véron promises to put the opera into rehearsal a month after delivery of the score, and to produce or rehearse no new work until Meyerbeer's opera is produced. (An exception is made for any ballet already in rehearsal, and in fact Nourrit's *L'Île des Pirates* was produced.)

Meyerbeer agrees to three and a half months of rehearsal as sufficient.

Ballets will be by one of the two principal ballet masters and will provide all the principal dancers (except for Taglioni, whose appearance will be decided by Véron).

The cast is named, and a list appended. Provision is made for the fact that Damoreau and Levasseur might need to be replaced. (In the event, Damoreau was replaced.)

Véron agrees to as many as twenty extra stage musicians.

Meyerbeer agrees to present no new works at the Opéra-Comique.

The opera will be presented by September 1, 1835, at the latest.

The cast was part of the agreement (see the box); subsequent changes in the cast included the transfer of Serda to the role of Saint-Bris, Dérivis taking that of Nevers. Dabadie had evidently left the Opéra.

There were later revisions to this contract:

June 1835: It is agreed that [Julie Aimée] Dorus Gras is taking a month off; rehearsals will be extended to four months. Dorus Gras will sing Marguerite de Valois, Flécheux will sing the page (Damoreau's departure is being provided for, so everybody moves up one; but if she stays, Meyerbeer can insist on her). Flécheux will have her debut at the Opéra at least a month before this opera opens.

July 9, 1835: Meyerbeer consents to the ballet *L'Île des Pirates*. Only act 1 and the first half of act 3 can be rehearsed during Meyerbeer's absence of a month. Rehearsals should finish by November 16–20. Véron agrees to four additional harps, making a total of six.

September 22, 1835: Duponchel and Meyerbeer agree to cancel the provision that rehearsals should be finished, and the opera produced, by November 16–20.

This was serious business, and it was treated seriously on both sides. There were several further postponements owing to various factors, including the change of director at the Opéra. In December it was thought that the opera could go on by the end of January; then by early February (the 5th or the 8th, said Meyerbeer on January 22); then it was set for February 15 ("but nobody believes it but Duponchel," wrote Meyerbeer, "for neither decoration nor *mise en scène* are ready"); then for the 24th. It finally did open, on Rossini's birthday, February 29. No wonder there was enormous anticipation in the press and among the public.

Meyerbeer stood to profit considerably from the opera, and its success would be his success. In addition to the fee negotiated with Véron, he would receive 250 francs for each of the first forty performances and 100 francs for each performance thereafter; and he could expect fees from publishers (in fact he received 24,000 francs from the publishing house of Schlesinger).

THE LIBRETTO

The story of *Les Huguenots*, in its libretto by Eugène Scribe, describes events of August 1572 culminating in the St. Bartholomew's Day Massacre, in which Catholics murdered Protestants. It involves historical, political, and religious events, and it was thus an opera easy to censor both at home and in other countries. But the great political events are seen through subplots of passion, devotion, heroism, and amorous love. It is a perfect combination for the talents of Scribe (1791–1861) and his workshop.

At the famous Gymnase theater Scribe had produced dozens of vaudevilles before taking his talents into the lyric theater, where he produced a hundred opéras-comiques. In collaboration with Auber in *La muette de Portici* he created a new style in the opera house, and he continued to be a central figure of French grand opera. He provided libretti for Cherubini, Auber, Halévy, Donizetti, Gounod, Verdi, Boieldieu, Adam, and Offenbach. He was the best, and he made himself deservedly very rich (though Meyerbeer ultimately made himself richer still).

Shows by Scribe were played in almost every theater. On the boulevard, it was the Age of Scribe. Mrs. Trollope admired these "pretty, lively trifles" and called Scribe a "national museum of invention"; she said that she had seen many of "these little comedies and vaudevilles, which are not only free from every imputation of mischief, but absolutely perfect in their kind." Scribe's enormous output—at least 425 dramas—can be attributed in part to his libretto factory. Scribe (and many other writers) worked with collaborators and often had many plays going at once in his workshop. Such collaborations were not at all unusual: many theater pieces were the work of two or more authors; Alexandre Dumas *père* produced his feuilleton-novels in a workshop, and the collaboration at the Opéra of composer, librettist, scene painter, and régisseur was nothing unusual.

Everybody knew how a Scribe libretto worked, and nobody was much interested in the text itself. As one critic wrote, "M. Scribe's words are there to give value to everything else, without having any value themselves, just like the zeroes we place after a number to represent absent decimal qualities."

A typical Scribe plot is concerned with Romantic passions, exotic subject matter, or historical events of recent importance. It involves a series of delayed-action events culminating in a final dénouement or *scène a faire* (in the case of *Les Huguenots,* the final union of the lovers Raoul and Valentine at the moment of their death, her identity devastatingly revealed to her father only at the last moment). The heroic struggle to overcome obstacles, present in every Scribe plot, is here seen in the Protestant Raoul's love for Valentine, thwarted by her Catholic faith and his own duty to his fellows.

This plot, like others, is based on misunderstandings that allow the audience to know things that the characters do not; this provides tension and allows the spectator to anticipate certain key events and discoveries. Thus, for example, in the first act, all the nobles realize that Raoul has been summoned to Queen Marguerite of Valois while he departs ignorant and blindfolded to end the act—but not before he has seen Valentine, the beautiful unknown girl whose praises he has just sung and mistakenly thinks is the mistress of the Count of Nevers.

So when Raoul agrees in act 2 to make a political marriage at the command of Marguerite, he is shocked to find that his bride is to be Valentine, and he refuses. Only in act 3 does he find out the truth, and by then she is married to Nevers and he is back in love with her. Disguises, veils, blindfolds, and secret letters are the stock in trade of Scribe's delayed-action plots, and they keep us in suspense.

There are, of course, many complexities—including the delicate question of who is married to whom. Raoul and Valentine are "married" by Marcel just after the death of Nevers is announced and just before the final curtain. And there are splendid interruptions for music and dance: a troupe of gypsies interrupts the bridal festivities with dancing; a splendid barque sails onstage with a band playing; there is a charming choreographic bathing scene, and a ball where the Huguenot nobility dance just before the slaughter.

Such a gigantic production required many alterations of the libretto—and of the music—right up to the last minute. The poet Emile Deschamps worked for a time on adjustments to the libretto; he was littérateur, a sort of go-between between Scribe and Meyerbeer. Meyerbeer had some additional verses made in Milan, which he then had to translate for Deschamps and Scribe, to his annoyance.

The role of Catherine de Medici, who originally was to appear in act 4, was still in the opera as late as December 1835; her role was to have been sung by Laure Cinti-Damoreau. Owing to Damoreau's departure, and to pressure from the censors (the queen should not appear on stage in the midst of religious and political violence), the part was changed to the expanded bass role of Saint-Bris, sung by Serda.

REHEARSALS

The rehearsals took some nine months (ten times what it took to get Handel or Mozart on the stage), during which anticipation in the press and in the public forum aroused much interest and box-office. Meyerbeer had been in contact with Habeneck from the early stages, playing him part of the score in June 1835 with apparently mixed results: "I wanted to play him all five acts, but at the end of the third I was so exhausted that I had to send him away. Decidedly my opera so far has pleased nobody who has heard it."

Rehearsals with singers began long before anything else. In early June, Meyerbeer was eager to start rehearsals, but the singers had not yet learned their parts. The first singers' rehearsal took place on June 20 at noon in the Foyer des Rôles. Very early on (July 23) there was a rehearsal of soloists and choir together of act 1; this was at Véron's request, and Meyerbeer very much wanted to make a good impression. But the singers did not rise to the occasion. "Everybody knew that the destiny of the opera is in his [Véron's] hands," Meyerbeer said, "and that it was important to make an impression on him. And yet nobody sang with full voice." Meyerbeer insisted to Véron that nobody should attend rehearsals during his two weeks' holiday in Dieppe at the beginning of August.

Meyerbeer's relations with the singers seem not to have been especially warm. Early in the rehearsal process (July 28) he wrote, "Until now there has been no trace of enthusiasm in the rehearsals, and though I care nothing about such enthusiasm in rehearsal, this continuing coldness is beginning to worry me. And I am so far not happy with any of my singers, though admittedly we have rehearsed only acts 1 and 2."

The cast of *Les Huguenots* was the regular roster of the Opéra, entirely familiar to the public, who had seen them in *Robert, La Juive,* and many other productions.

Adolphe Nourrit was the reigning star among the tenors of the Opéra, and as

Raoul he was the leading man in *Les Huguenots*. A student of the famous Manuel Garcia, he had made his debut at the Opéra in 1821. He studied further with Rossini and went on to create many starring roles, including Masaniello in *La muette* (1828), Arnold in *Guillaume Tell* (1829), Robert in *Robert le diable* (1831), Eléazar in *La Juive* (1835). He also performed as a tenor Don Giovanni.

Nourrit had a handsome figure and was admired also for his acting ability. He had sung "La Marseillaise" from the top of the barricades during the revolution of 1830 and was often called to repeat it in theaters. He introduced Schubert songs to Paris, and he also sang with Liszt (Liszt's Petrarch songs may have been composed for him).

He sang a high tenor and was known for the lightness of the top notes sung in falsetto. Perfect for him is the high C-flat (on "aimes"), sung lightly, in the great act 4 love duet ("Tu l'as dit que tu m'aimes"). Nourrit sang his last in Paris at a benefit concert on

---

Véron Describes the Contretemps Among Adolph Nourrit, Nicolas Levasseur, and Julie Dorus-Gras at the Premiere of *Robert le diable*

An even more disturbing accident happened in the fifth act; after the admirable trio that serves as the work's dénouement, Bertram [Levasseur] alone was to throw himself into a trap to return to the realm of death; Nourrit, converted by the voice of the Gods, by Alice's prayers, was to remain on earth in order finally to marry Princess Isabelle; but this passionate artist, carried away by the situation, threw himself without thinking into the trap after the god of the underworld. There was only one cry on the stage: "Nourrit is dead!" Mademoiselle Dorus [Alice], who could not but be moved by the personal danger she had experienced, left the stage sobbing; there took place on the stage, in the *dessous*, and in the hall, three very different scenes. The audience, surprised, thought that Robert had given himself to the devil and followed him to the somber realm. On stage there were only groans and despair. At the moment of Nourrit's fall, they had fortunately not yet taken away the sort of bed and mattress on which M. Levasseur had fallen. Nourrit came away from the fall safe and sound. In the dessous of the theatre, M. Levasseur, calm, was going to his dressing room: "What the devil are you doing here," he said on seeing Nourrit; "have they changed the ending?" Nourrit was too rushed to reassure the audience by his presence to engage in a conversation with his colleague Bertram; he finally was able to appear, bringing with him Mademoiselle Dorus, now weeping with joy. Unanimous applause broke out in the hall, and the curtain fell.

The handsome Adolphe Nourrit (here portraying Raoul) was a fine actor and the reigning tenor of the Opéra. A student of the famous Manuel Garcia, he had made his debut at the Opéra in 1821. He studied further with Rossini and went on to create many starring roles, including Masaniello in *La muette* (1828), Arnold in *Guillaume Tell* (1829), Robert in *Robert le diable* (1831), and Eléazar in *La Juive* (1835). He also performed as a tenor *Don Giovanni.*

April 1, 1837. The role of Raoul was taken over, with Meyerbeer's coaching, by the new first tenor of the Opéra, Gilbert-Louis Duprez. Duprez (1806–1896) put Nourrit and his style out of business. The delicacy of Nourrit's singing was replaced by Duprez' famous "do a voce piena" and by a style that featured forceful high notes. Nourrit, after touring in Europe and studying with Donizetti, committed suicide in Naples in 1839.

His biographer cannot perhaps be blamed for holding Nourrit in high esteem: "One never missed a note of his role: it is true that he never omitted any, as tenors often do who are husbanding their resources. He dominated massed ensembles by the energy and accent of his voice, just as he fixed attention on himself by the expressivity of his acting." Chorley, who heard Nourrit about this time, wrote about him later in less than flattering terms:

> The very elegance so highly prized and loudly regretted in poor Adolphe Nourrit by a portion of the Parisian cognoscenti, bordered so closely upon a mannered over-grace and over-sweetness, that I never heard that fine singer, and never saw that elegant and careful actor, without feeling that neither his clear and metallic voice—nasal in its falsetto—nor his

graceful postures, belonged to the greatest school of art. There was a smile when he threw his head back to launch a *mot* at some one behind him—a mincing elongation of his "Oui"-s and "Patrie"-s and the other sounds, which sung in French are intrinsically offensive, that annoyed my insular eyes and ears, as imparting to grace and sentiment and emphasis a touch of make-believe, destructive of their effect. He appears on recollection to have been more conscious of his handsome person, and high voice, and artistic accomplishments, than any one I have ever seen on the French stage—to have attitudinized more premeditatedly—to have declaimed with more of that conventional exactness, which, as English ears unhappily know, can become so utterly intolerable—than the generality of his brethren.

Nourrit was much interested in questions of mise-en-scène. He wrote the scenario for the ballet *La Sylphide,* Taglioni's triumph. He suggested ending the fourth act of *La Juive* with an air instead of a chorus and is said to have contributed to, if not written, a revised version of act 4 of *Les Huguenots.*

Marie Cornélie Falcon (Valentine) had a short but brilliant career at the Opéra, making her debut at eighteen in 1832 in *Robert le diable.* Having studied with Nourrit, she became his equal in fame. She created the roles of Alice in *Robert le diable* and Rachel in *La Juive,* and she would sing the title role in the ill-starred *Esmeralda* of Louise Bertin (November 1836). In 1837 she had serious vocal problems,

Marie Cornélie Falcon (portraying Valentine) had a short but brilliant career at the Opéra, making her debut at eighteen in 1832 in *Robert le diable.* She studied with Nourrit and became equally famous. She had created the roles of Alice in *Robert le Diable* and Rachel in *La Juive.*

and by 1840, after a disastrous benefit performance, was forced to retire from the stage; she lived to be eighty-three.

Like Nourrit, Falcon combined an exceptional voice with good looks and a real talent for acting. Meyerbeer had this opinion of her during the run of *Robert:* "It can only be said that she has a strong and beautiful voice, and not without agility, and that she is also a lively and expressive (but somewhat overcharged) actress. Unfortunately her intonation is not always clean, and I fear she will never overcome these weaknesses. In sum, I think that she could be an outstanding star, and I will certainly in any case write her a leading role in my new opera." She was for a time the young rival of the reigning Damoreau, until the latter left for the Théâtre-Italien.

Falcon was noted for her long, lyrical lines, for the clarity of her voice, with its narrow vibrato, which could be heard clearly above the orchestra. Her wide range extended from a low B to a high D. She was certainly the leading soprano of the opera at the time. Chorley remembered her—using anti-Semitic doubletalk—as follows: "She, indeed, was a person to haunt even a passing stranger. Though the seal of her race was upon her beauty, and it wore the expression of a Deborah or a Judith, rather than of a Melpomene, I have never seen any actress, who in look and gesture so well deserved the style and title of the Muse of Modern Tragedy. Large, dark, melancholy eyes,—finely-cut features,—a form, though slight, not meagre,—and, above all, an expressiveness of tone rarely to be found in voices of her register, which was a legitimate soprano,—the power of engaging interest by mere glance and step when first she presented herself, and of exciting the strongest emotions of pity, or terror, or suspense, by the passion she could develop in action—such were her gifts."

Nicolas Prosper Levasseur, six months younger than Meyerbeer, was the leading bass; Levasseur had been around a long time, having made his debut at the Opéra in 1813. He had been known to Meyerbeer since his performance in the premiere of the composer's *Margherite d'Anjou* at La Scala in 1820. He had recently come from several years of Rossini at the Théâtre-Italien. At the Opéra he was famous for his roles in Rossini's *Le Comte Ory* (1829) and *Guillaume Tell* (1829), and in *Robert le diable* (1831); he sang Brogni in *La Juive* and later returned at Meyerbeer's request to sing in the premiere of *Le prohète* in 1853. Shortly before the premiere of *Les Huguenots,* Meyerbeer dedicated two of his songs to Levasseur. The role of Marcel gives Levasseur plenty of occasion to show off his superb low notes, and to engage in the strenuous acting at which he was expert.

Julie Aimée Dorus-Gras was known as one of the best coloratura singers at the Opéra, where she had been engaged in 1830 at the age of twenty-five. She was perhaps expected to produce virtuoso singing and little more. Her role of Marguerite, with its elaborate coloratura, is brilliant but not dramatic. Meyerbeer later called it "ein schlectes hors d'oeuvre." Meyerbeer did like her voice. He reported, of a performance of *Robert* in 1834, that "the little Dorus exceeded my expectations. Almost better than Falcon!" One happy result of the premiere of *Les Huguenots* for Dorus-Gras was that her contract, which expired immediately after the premiere, was renewed with a raise to 40,000 francs.

The first choral rehearsal took place on June 2. The singers sat on benches and

Julie Aimée Dorus-Gras as Queen Marguerite de Valois. The bravura coloratura required of this role suited Dorus perfectly even though the role had been originally intended for the former prima donna Damoreau. Her virtuoso aria "O beau pays de la Touraine" that opens the second act was evidently a triumph.

were accompanied by piano or a small group of instruments. The chorus, which plays an important role in this and every other grand opera, was under the leadership of two well-known composers. Its director was Fromenthal Halévy, whose nomination to the Institut de France had been rejected at the end of May 1835 (despite the success of *La Juive*). At least one newspaper suspected anti-Semitism. Halévy was assisted by Jean Madelaine Schneitzhoeffer, professor at the Paris Conservatoire and the composer of the ballet *La Sylphide*.

Dance rehearsals took place in the dancers' green-room, where sometimes, especially under the directorship of Véron, holders of season tickets and other influential persons were allowed to ogle the dancers. The Opéra's ballet master, Filippo Taglioni, prepared the choreography. It included the bathers' chorus and the blindfold scenes in act 2, along with gypsy dancers in act 3 and the ball that begins act 5.

Taglioni, whose children Marie and Paul were among the great dancers of the age, was the originator of a new style of ballet and was already renowned for his choreography of *Robert le diable* and of the ballet *La Sylphide* (1832, with Marie Taglioni in the title role). He also had a great deal to say about the music; Meyerbeer's original contract noted that his score would not at first contain ballet music, since of course that would be worked out with the ballet master. And in August, Meyerbeer began in earnest on the ballet music, when Taglioni could be present. "Taglioni has returned," wrote Meyerbeer, "and

I now have daily conferences with him about the ballet music I must make." Meyerbeer was particularly concerned that Marie Taglioni should be featured in the ballet scenes.

The first staging rehearsal was held on the evening of October 6. Stage direction was not an important part of preparing an opera. The stage director essentially indicated entrances and exits and suggested movement and placement of characters in tableaux. The singers themselves generally decided on their postures and gestures. Meyerbeer was more than usually active in rehearsal, and his zeal—or what the singers may have thought was meddling—surely contributed to the friction that is everywhere documented in his diaries and letters. Charles de Boigne, in his *Petits mémoires de l'Opéra*, sympathized: "Never will we know the true cost of rehearsals to Meyerbeer in terms of insomnia, anxiety, fear, work, and despair. He saw everything, he thought of everything, he supervised everything: libretto, music, staging, scenery, costumes, songs, and dancing."

Véron in his memoirs described the rehearsal process at the Opéra:

> The *foyer du chant*, reached by going down a staircase behind the theater, is very spacious; the ceiling and the panels of this former salon of the hôtel de Choiseul are white and gold. In the middle of the room is a piano, and beyond the piano are many benches. There is where artists and choristers come to audition in the hope of being hired. It is also in this *foyer du chant* that soloists and chorus begin and end the musical study of opera scores. At the first rehearsals, the composer presides at the piano, and indicates to the *maîtres de chant* and to the soloists the various tempos of the ensemble numbers. The principal singers study the various arias, duos, trios, whatever they have to sing, separately with the maestro. When an act has been read through, rehearsals with string quartet begin, under the direction of the conductor; all the string players, violins, violas, cellos and double basses, come one by one to play these quartet accompaniments. As soon as the work is learned by the choir and the soloists, full orchestral rehearsals begin. All the singers rehearse seated. During these two or three rehearsals for the orchestra copying errors are corrected. The study rehearsals conclude with more quartet rehearsals, to which a piano is added to accompany the recitatives, with action and staging; then at last with the full orchestra, with sets, with lighting, with costumes. All these tiring and painful rehearsals demand a great firmness on the part of the conductor and the *maîtres de chant*. Of all the composers, M. Meyerbeer is the one that brings the most inflexible severity to rehearsals, but to the benefit of the performance and of the talent of the artists themselves.

Meanwhile orchestra rehearsals began. A rehearsal of the woodwinds is noted in Meyerbeer's diary for October 28. The first rehearsal of the full strings was on November 3, though the individual players had each played in the small ensembles that accompanied singing rehearsals. Meyerbeer was in constant contact with Habeneck about details of orchestration and rehearsal. He consulted him on September 13 about cellos: the chords that accompany Marcel's recitatives, and the accompaniment (later changed to viola d'amore) of Raoul's romance.

Rehearsal time was limited to some extent by other productions; *Le Siège de Corinthe* opened on November 27, and Meyerbeer complained of nine rehearsals missed. He also complained of the Opera Balls, which occupied space and time that could otherwise be given to rehearsal.

November saw the first rehearsals of full acts: on November 12, acts 1 (at 12:30) and 2 (1:30) were rehearsed. By late December there were, when possible, two rehearsals a day of three or four hours each. Some rehearsals with singers and staging, such as that of February 11, featured Meyerbeer presiding from a piano in the orchestra.

There was an enormous amount of revision in the course of rehearsals. Meyerbeer's diaries are full of lists of changes being made; and in November 1835, in the midst of rehearsals, the composer wrote a long list of projected abridgements and adjustments, including several numbers in each act. These revisions were mostly to shorten the work, to judge from an addition he makes to this list: "In the greatest necessity also the following cuts: the whole of Falcon's romance; the second couplet of Nourrit's romance; the Quarrel chorus [act 3] by half." As it happens, these last changes were not necessary; but Valentine (Falcon) suffered considerably: a romance in act 1, and another in act 4, disappeared before the performance, and the heroine ended up with no solo number at all.

Only in early February did Meyerbeer finally give in to pressures from the censors and alter the role of Catherine de Medici (censors forbade her appearance on stage), creating instead the role of Saint-Bris, to be sung by Jacques-Émile Serda. "The one piece which up until now has had the greatest effect," he wrote to Minna on February 6, "is the big ensemble number of Catherine de Medici ('pour cette cause sainte'), and this has unfortunately been ruined for me by the censors."

And there were the famous revisions of act 4. Berlioz seems to have been the first to say that Nourrit was the originator of the love duet, in *Soirées dans l'orchestre*; Véron says the same in his memoirs. There has been much discussion and supposition, and even the most recent literature says that Nourrit suggested the duet. But it appears from the documents that the duet was planned from the beginning. A letter from Meyerbeer to Scribe of September 9, 1835, asks for the "new scene of delirious love for Raoul and modest reticence for Leonore in the final duet of the fourth act." Meyerbeer's diary entry of November 20 indicates that Nourrit contributed only some prose suggestions. But Nourrit does seem to have induced Meyerbeer to make a new musical version.

One thing is clear: Nourrit did not get on with Meyerbeer. Whether this was a sort of egotism for which certain singers are well known or really a matter of artistic difference is not easy to determine, as we have only Meyerbeer's side of the story. At any rate, the composer ultimately felt compelled to replace his original act 4 duet with one more to Nourrit's (and Falcon's) liking. He wrote in August, "Nourrit, who has exerted the greatest possible influence on Falcon, has turned her so much against the great duet in the fourth act (which takes up half the act) that nothing more will be left to me except to throw this whole major number out and make a new one." And later in August he laments the "fatal history with Nourrit over the fourth act, who flatly refuses to sing the grand duet, and now has suggested that I must change not only the duet, but the preceding pieces in the fourth act. Scribe, who should sort it out, is out of town." The controversy continued; on October 22, Meyerbeer wrote, "Finally Nourrit's dissatisfaction has grown so much, and our relationship has grown so bitter, that I'm afraid it may come to a formal break. Unfortunately he has also involved Falcon in this dissatisfaction." And a few days later: "Nourrit is tormenting me in such a way, and forces me to make so many alterations, that I am driven almost mad. Today we quarreled so much that I left the rehearsal" (November 4). "We no longer speak to each other; you can imagine how that hampers learning the role" (November 8). Nourrit did suggest alterations in the language, and Meyerbeer finally relented and gave Nourrit his (and our) duet: "Tired with war, I had agreed to make that *cabotin* [ham-actor] tenor his new duet in the fourth act. . . . [This duet], I think, has turned out very well" (December 18).

Meyerbeer was unhappy when he saw the sets: "Decorations and costumes are so poor and bad as never has been seen in the opera, and you know how important these things are to an opera." August had brought Meyerbeer a setback: "The painters . . . have done the exact opposite on the third and fifths acts from what I prescribed *pour les exigences musicales.*"

The sets were executed by the firm of Séchan, Feuchère and Company, who were regularly engaged for major productions. The six sets cost 44,000 francs, far more than any sets in the decade except for the same company's sets for *La Juive* the year before (46,540 francs). Although we have paintings of the sets that disappointed Meyerbeer so much, the originals do not survive. When the Opéra burned in 1873 the twelve most popular sets of the nineteenth century were destroyed, including *La Juive, Robert le diable,* and *Les Huguenots.* (Most other sets had been destroyed in a warehouse fire in 1861.)

The composer had a great deal to do with painting, staging, and machinery. He was constantly in contact with personnel regarding the wedding barque, the torches, the litter with horses, the shooting machines (made by the mechanic Brodt—after interminable fiddling a new machine was made just in time for the opening).

Though the Opéra was famous for its lavish productions, Véron was trying to cut costs. Meyerbeer was unhappy to learn in May 1835 that the sets for the upcoming ballet *L'Orgie* were being designed so that they could be used also for the third and fourth acts of his opera. He thus hoped that the change of director at the Opéra would benefit him with respect to the sets; Duponchel was, after all, a set designer. As Meyerbeer wrote in anticipation, "Although I would not claim to have had a warm friend in him, at least he was not an obvious fiend as the miserable Véron was, and furthermore I have gotten from him an increase of 24 voices in the chorus, which especially for this opera were of great importance. Also with respect to decors and costumes I would do much better, since Véron would put me on stage very meagerly." And after Duponchel's official appointment, he wrote: "Duponchel has been named director; he will want this opera to succeed as it's

Charles Edmond Duponchel, Louis Véron's successor as director of the Opéra, was a scene designer by trade. Meyerbeer, who had hoped for grander scenes and costumes for *Les Huguenots* after the change of management, was disappointed. The German poet Heinrich Heine described Duponchel as a "lean, yellowish, pale man . . . who looked as if he were in perpetual mourning."

the first under his direction. And I get 20 more in the chorus according to his new *Cahier de charges,* and maybe a brilliant mise en scene." But a month later he is not so sure: "I now truly think what I did not want until now to believe, namely that Véron has just withdrawn from the public eye, and that Duponchel is not really the director, but just a scoundrel. With respect to my opera he now does everything for which he previously reproached Véron. We had such an argument yesterday that I was ill all night. Among other things, he wants to premiere the opera with an old set."

In late January and early February there began to be rehearsals with dress, scenery, and lighting; an important part of these was the calculation of the time needed between acts for changes. Meyerbeer needed to cut a half-hour of music from the first three acts while adding fifteen minutes to the entr'actes: "So I must now offer to the ineptitude of the machinists another quarter hour of music, and my assignment since this morning is to remove three quarters of an hour of music from three acts."

On February 6, Meyerbeer wrote to his wife that Duponchel had put the performance off by two weeks, to February 22, since the set painting could not be done in time. An announcement to this effect appeared the next day in the *Revue et Gazette musicale.* There followed the Opera Balls and other festivities associated with the days before Lent, which added to technical delays by occupying the Opéra. Baron Rothschild planned his ball for the 29th and was horrified when further delays made it clear that most of his guests would be at the Opéra. In the last days, Meyerbeer had several meetings with Auguste (leader of the claque), which concerned not only the opening but also the dress rehearsal.

Final preparations included rehearsals with lighting on the 24th and 26th, and the *répétition générale* at 1 P.M. on the 28th. Meyerbeer was not happy: "Our next-to-last rehearsal, with more than 100 persons present, was atrocious. Nourrit, completely hoarse, could not sing; the choruses, for whose guests we had provided tickets, was evil, and purposely sang out of tune and badly; the hall, through that stupid Duprez's organization, was neither lit nor heated; in short, those present found it all disgraceful, and I fear that this rehearsal will have done the opera great damage. The day before yesterday [actually yesterday] was the last rehearsal without listeners present, and that one went much better. The fourth act made a great effect, but the trio in the fifth will still not go together, which naturally destroys much of the effect."

The Performance

There were posters everywhere. Hundreds of locations in Paris displayed the offerings in the theaters, so that the various delays of the premiere were easily communicated to the interested public. There were many little press notices—and some not so little —reporting tidbits of gossip about the upcoming opera: troubles with the sets of act 3; the suppression of the role of Catherine de Medici; Nourrit's indispositions; the suppression of the act 2 ballet. There was much anticipation, and much was known about the opera before it opened. The last performances of *Robert le diable* had been given on January 15 and February 1 and 14. Much hinged, for the audience, and for Meyerbeer, on how his new opera would compare with the stunningly successful *Robert*. The house had been sold out for two or three months, the box-office was closed on the day of the performance,

Véron Describes the Effects of Premieres

When there is rehearsal with choir, with soloists, with the whole orchestra, without sets, costumes, or lighting, the musical performance gains much and always produces a great effect in the darkness and silence of the empty and more resonant hall. Without any distraction for the other senses, one is so to say all ears; none of the fine nuances of singing is lost, or of the most detailed filigree in the orchestra; but at the first performance, the disappointment is great, in this immense hall, splendidly lit, full of a curious and distracted audience; all the elegance and rich detail of the score are smothered in the cloth of the splendidly dressed women and in this hall made less resonant by a crowded audience in the orchestra, the parterre, and in the boxes. Nothing is left to move them but the grand musical ideas, the grand effects of the score.

and those going to the opera had to pass through a press of people wanting tickets. Scalpers made fortunes.

The audience of the Opéra was anticipating this new event, but there had been plenty of entertainment to keep them amused. Some other recent events, at the Opéra and elsewhere, include:

> January 25, 1835, the premiere of Bellini's *I puritani di Scozia* at the Théâtre-Italien;
>
> March 23, 1835, the premiere of the Auber-Scribe *Le cheval de bronze* at the Opéra-Comique;
>
> August 12, 1835, the premiere of the ballet *L'Île des pirates* at the Opéra. Fanny Elssler danced as Matilde;
>
> January 23, 1836: the premier of *Actéon,* by Auber and Scribe, at the Opéra-Comique; Damoureau, who had left the Opéra, starred. Meyerbeer said that it has exactly the same plot as act 2 of *Les Huguenots.*

Although the Opéra, in the rue Lepelletier, had always been intended as a temporary house, it continued to operate until it burned in 1871, making way for the grand Garnier building. Turned longways to the street, it had a porch that allowed patrons to arrive by carriage and alight under cover. The building was not sumptuous, and its architecture had never been loved. The interior was relatively plain: a wooden staircase with iron railings led to the auditorium, which was decorated with gold and white, with blue and gold on the balconies. Material from the earlier opera house had been reused, and the framing of the proscenium and many other details were the same as in the earlier house. The backstage area, however, had been considerably improved in the new house, permitting the technological marvels that are the glory of grand opera.

The audience for the Opéra was not quite so exclusive as that for the Théâtre-Italien, where the nobility thought that the most refined singing took place before the most refined audience. Véron and Duponchel had converted the Opéra into a money machine, a bourgeois attraction. Nevertheless, all of society was there for the premiere. The queen, princes, and princesses came half an hour late, as was fashionable for many.

There were almost two thousand seats available in the house, ranging from the men-only seats on the floor—divided into orchestra (front) and amphitheater (rear), with an area of standing room, the *parterre,* between them—to the seats in the topmost boxes in the fourth range. Cheap seats, at the back of the orchestra and in the highest gallery, were not so cheap, but they were available.

The well-to-do could reserve orchestra seats in advance, and the rich could have boxes for the season, or for an evening. Boxes, seating six to ten, had an open section in front (this was an improvement of Véron's) and a rear section that could be curtained off. There were also *baignoires* ("bathtubs") of five or six seats; these were like the boxes but had no private area.

Subscribers were members of the nobility, military officers, and rich bankers and

The interior of the Opéra during the finale of Auber's *La muette de Portici* (1828), which ends with the eruption of Vesuvius. The interior of the Opéra was decorated with gold and white, with blue and gold on the balconies. Material from the earlier opera house had been reused, and the framing of the proscenium and many other details were the same as in the earlier house.

merchants. Single subscription seats were available on the floor, but boxes had to be taken whole (they could then be decorated to the subscriber's taste and become a place for entertaining). Season subscriptions had a waiting list among the fashionable, and there was a brisk business in ticket scalping.

Henry Chorley, present in 1836, described the hall, and its new front curtain:

> There is a certain pleasure in seeing a place filled by its assembly—in watching vacant benches and gloomy corners, one after the other, painted with forms and colours, which turn out to be human beings. . . . If there be any who share this with me, I would invite them to take stalle or box at L'Académie a quarter of an hour before M. Habeneck makes his appearance; not, however, to watch the bright-looking exquisitely-dressed ladies gliding into the balcony—not to catch snatches of the odd, blithe, vehement dialogue which goes on in the parterre—nor yet to give themselves up to the perusal of the entr'acte of the evening. That interesting publication I would fain supersede for one night by offering a brief study of the drop-curtain of the grand opera.

This is not one of those venerable veils of dingy green baize, the sight of which has awakened such an undefined and thrilling curiosity within many a young playgoer on his first night; nor yet a splendid piece of mock upholstery, like that which has so long swayed to and fro to conceal the Grisis and Rubini, the machinists and the loungers of our own opera stage. Neither is it the old most irrational design of eight mounted cavaliers, preparing from a central pillar to ride down eight flights of steps, which used to give me an impression of insecurity and discomfort whenever I entered L'Académie, sufficient to distract me from all speculations on the three tiny fingers, or the one bright eye, which are never wanting to both of the two peepholes of the toile. The new curtain in the Rue Lepelletier is a grand historical composition, representing none other than Louis Quatorze signing the charter which he granted to Lulli for the establishment of a national opera.

Expectation was high, for spectacle as well as for music. As Véron put it, "When one has the largest theater, with fourteen sets of wings, an orchestra of more than eighty musicians, almost eighty choristers, men and women, eighty extras not counting children, a team of sixty technicians to maneuver the sets, the audience demands and insists on grand things. You fail in your mission if you only use these resources to play comic operas or vaudevilles."

ACT I

Les Huguenots begins with an introduction, not a full-fledged overture. (Meyerbeer's grand overture, still present in the surviving orchestra parts, was never played in performance.) From the beginning, the Lutheran chorale "Ein' feste Burg," played by the winds so that they sound like an organ, is taught us so well that we will certainly not fail to hear its many recurrences in the course of the opera—essentially, whenever a Huguenot thinks or expresses a matter of faith.

The opera orchestra, famous all over the world, had certain features that might not be familiar to us and others that were unusual then but have since become standard. The strings were strung with gut, and the double-basses were the traditional three-string instruments that never made enough sound. The orchestra included pairs of piston and natural trumpets, and of valved and natural horns (Meyerbeer prepared his score, however, to accommodate provincial orchestras that had only natural horns). Trombones, bass trombones, and ophicleides rounded out the brasses.

Characteristic of the Parisian orchestra were the four bassoons and the English horn heard right at the beginning in the second phrase of the chorale. The bass clarinet, employed for the first time in act 5 of *Les Huguenots,* was a novelty of the opera, as was the archaic *viole d'amour* in act 1. Meyerbeer insisted on, and received, permission to use six harps. There also was to be music on the stage: a band of winds and brass in the wedding barque, and a brass fanfare in the final scene; for these, extra players needed to be hired.

Charles de Forster Describes the Excitement of a Premiere at the Opéra

A *first performance* at the Opéra is always an event in the annals of the dilettante. People flow in from everywhere, one notes even foreigners from distant countries who come to be present at this musical solemnity. First of all, the roof of the hall is astounding: it seems a vast enameled basket of the most beautiful flowers. Rich *toilettes* in the best taste display their sparkling luxury; charming heads, adorable faces, expressive and animated, wreathe the hall and the front of the boxes; behind them stands a somber wall made by the black dress of men of all ages and positions. The connoisseurs and the journalists take their places in the orchestra seats; the floor, ardent and impatient, buzzes like a working beehive; an army of performers, eyes fixed on their able leader, M. Habaneck, awaits the signal, and prepares to attack the notes which will soon stop all the intrigues, the chattering, the buzzing; the chandeliers throw off showers of flames, and the shimmering gas is reflected in a thousand cascades from the diamonds of the ladies. The impatience is great! Suddenly the three blows are struck, a prolonged *ssshh!* runs through the hall, a magical silence ensues; M. Habeneck raises his arm, and at this movement a flow of harmony is born, and overflows into the vast space, where thousands of eager ears are attentive to its accents.—The basses snore, the brasses resound, the flutes warble, the violins rustle, the oboes weep, all the instruments mix together, and a loud *tutti* attacks the *stretta* with energy.—One feels electrified, the beauty of the music absorbs you, transports you and, with the last measure of the overture, a thunder of applause suggests to the maestro that his work is understood, and he can allow himself to breathe a bit more easily.—Finally the curtain rises majestically, and reveals a compact mass of people, knights, soldiers, princes, potentates; then all that the magic of the paintbrush can produce is revealed to your view.

The chorale builds to a frenzied climax with plenty of brass, and the curtain opens on a party of reveling Catholic nobles—the religious conflict is present from the beginning.

The set is revealed. In the score it is described as follows: "The stage represents a room in the chateau of the Count of Nevers; at the back, large open casement windows show gardens and lawns on which several young lords play ball [the ball-playing was eliminated before the premiere]; to the right [stage left] a door leading to interior apartments;

The opening page of the score of *Les Huguenots* gives an idea of
Meyerbeer's orchestra, though not all the instruments are listed on
this page. Note how the opera begins with an ominous, distant threat
from the kettledrums ("Timballes") followed by the Protestant hymn
"A Mighty Fortress." The hymn is played by clarinets and bassoons,
perhaps intended to sound like an organ; in the second phrase the
English horn ("Cor anglais"), a rare and typically Parisian instrument,
joins in. Note the ophicleide as the bass instrument of the brass section,
and the presence of both piston trumpets and natural trumpets.

to the left, a large casement closed by a curtain which is understood to give onto an oratory; downstage other lords play dice, bilboquet, etc.: the Count of Nevers, Tavannes, de Cossé, de Retz, de Thoré, Méru and other Catholic nobles watch them and talk among themselves."

Franz Grillparzer saw the production in April and was not overly impressed: "The overture began, really just an introduction. I was so tense that it could not have pleased me. The curtain is raised. A sort of festival of Catholic gentlemen. The arrangement nothing special."

Nevers sets the musical scene with a rollicking song ("Des beaux jours de la jeunesse"), joined by the other lords and the chorus. "In these days of our youth, let's forget everything except pleasure." No plot yet, only gaiety. The tables are set, but one guest is missing: the new young gentleman, sent by the admiral. "Heaven!" they cry. "So he is a Huguenot?" They are to treat him with respect. Grumbles all around. Raoul enters, and his politeness is charming. This is the great Nourrit, soon to lose his voice and his job but for the moment the reigning tenor. And he is a careful, detailed, and persuasive actor. A French journalist remembered that "he carried his activity and care into the minutest details of his part, and, from his first entrance to his final exit, never ceased to be the person he represented." Chorley was equally impressed: "Costume, attitude, by-play, nothing was neglected by Nourrit. Hence he might be the darling of a people to whom mere musical emotions will not be compensated for want of interest in the drama, want of tact in the actors, want of taste in the mise en scene."

A table is brought in, everybody sits down, and the "orgy" follows, a song of the pleasures of the table (this *is* a French opera) and of wine. It is a grand number, by the end of which all the actors are down at the edge of the apron with their glasses. Applause is sure to follow. And some plot.

It is agreed that everybody must tell a tale of love, starting with Raoul. He consents, and he will compromise nothing in telling of the beautiful woman he has seen and fallen in love with—since he knows nothing about her. He tells of rescuing the unknown beauty, and he sings his splendid romance, "Plus blanche que la belle ermine," whose two verses are accompanied by the solo viole d'amour of Chrétien Urhan.

Raoul's romance, whose accompaniment was originally written for Norblin to play on the cello, was altered, probably in January, for the new viola d'amore played by the remarkable Urhan. A first violinist and the original viola soloist for Berlioz's *Harold en Italie,* Urhan was an unusual character and a devoutly religious man. He was the organist at the church of St. Vincent de Paul, where Liszt often heard him. Urhan's reluctance to look up at the stage for fear of seeing the dancers' legs made him the butt of jokes in the orchestra. Charles de Boigne:

> One evening he was distracted, tempted; he saw the toe of mademoi-
> selle Fanny Elssler, only the toe, and for a month he put himself on bread
> and water; a little higher and he would have considered himself damned!
> One day there was an accident with Madame D.'s costume . . . it was
> like an electric spark. Affected, struck by the spark, M. Urhan lifted his

eyes and . . . it is a miracle that he did not die on the spot. He had to be carried out. He never fully recovered; he languished; it is even said that he wears a hair-shirt which he never takes off day or night. These ladies of the ballet and these gentlemen of the orchestra play a thousand jokes on him, which he appears not to notice; the former write him impassioned letters, and the latter draw pictures on his music, scenes of more than Anacreontic gatherings.

The romance is a lovely lyrical piece, which, as Joseph Mainzer noted, "will be sung everywhere; but it is completely foreign to the action." It is a virtuoso demonstration of Nourrit's agility, his expressiveness, and his high notes, including a couple of cadenzas that show off his beautiful high C. "Nourrit delivered it with a ravishing suavity," wrote his biographer Louis Quicherat. "He had in his accents something intimate, vaporous, which touched you deeply." It is an intimate song, contrasting completely with the boisterous chorus that preceded it. The audience applauds at length.

Raoul's devout and faithful servant Marcel appears (accompanied here as elsewhere by low strings) and is shocked to find his master in such company. He delivers himself of an ecstatic prayer—set to a full verse of "A Mighty Fortress"—which gives Levasseur an opportunity to show off his low E. Applause. Cossé recognizes Marcel as the soldier who wounded him at La Rochelle. He offers to make it up with Marcel by having a drink together. Marcel declines—he does not drink, he says—and is required to sing instead. He agrees, challenging them by singing the Huguenot battle song from La Rochelle, with its "piff paff" sound of musket fire. This is Marcel's big set-piece, with its military accompaniment of piccolo, cymbals, and snare and bass drum. Anybody who could understand the words would see that it is a nasty insult to Catholics ("Let them weep; let them die; show no mercy.") Marcel may be a servant, but he is no Leporello: he continues to be steadfast, undeviatingly faithful to his religion first and his master second. His singing in this piece was admired by Quicherat: "One remembers the clarity of his diction, the contained sonority of his voice in low pieces. Since he was a first-class singer, the composer had no fears in giving him fast numbers which along with vigor required lightness and verve, like the Huguenot song *Pif, paf*."

A mysterious veiled woman crosses upstage, led by a valet who then comes down to announce her arrival. We are at table, says Nevers, and I will see nobody (he did not see her—the audience did). But when he learns that she is beautiful, and not one of his usual mistresses, he agrees to see what he hopes will be a new conquest. While Marcel and Raoul stand apart where they can't hear, the others take turns looking at the beauty through the window that gives on the oratory. In this choral ensemble, Raoul is finally convinced to peek also, and, "Grand dieu!," it is she whom he had rescued and recently hymned. Raoul is furious, and the others laugh. As Nevers returns they conceal themselves. Nevers, to himself, tells how the Queen of Navarre has asked him to call off his intended wedding —the bride herself has come to inform him; as a gentleman, he will do so, though not happily. The others return, not knowing the situation, and sing of his latest triumph in

Maria Flécheux in the coloratura trouser role of the page Urbain. A critic wrote: "A young girl, Maria Flécheux, given the role of the page Urbin, demonstrated a magnificent voice and Quasimodo legs."

a rousing chorus ("Honor to the conqueror!").

The page Urbain appears upstage; he (sung by Mademoiselle Flécheux, except for Nevers' page the first female voice heard) salutes the company with an enormous vocal flourish, and in a gracious cavatina full of cadenzas announces that he has a message for one of the company—a message that anybody would wish to receive. From this song onward, critics—and surely others—noticed in some of Meyerbeer's melodies reminiscences of old French popular melodies, designed to contribute to local color and historical accuracy. Other reminiscences were noticed in act 2, in Marguerite's cavatina and in the final chorus.

The page's cavatina provokes two salvos of applause, and the message turns out, of course, to be for Raoul. Raoul reads the letter (Scribe's plots are full of letters): he is to come blindfolded to a secret rendezvous, if he dares. Raoul agrees. He carelessly shows the letter to the others, who instantly recognize the seal of Marguerite de Valois, and they crowd around Raoul trying to ingratiate themselves. In a grand chorus they send Raoul away to his glory while Marcel sings a *Te Deum*. The curtain falls.

Much has happened in this first act, and much of it was expected. The standard lines of a "well-made" play by Scribe have been drawn. We have been introduced to two of the three principal characters (the third, who crossed mysteriously upstage, will appear in the next act, giving us something to anticipate); conflicts have been set in motion, larger (religious conflict) and smaller (Raoul's adoration of the mysterious and distant lady), which will result in the final dénouement. We have been given to know certain things that others do not: we know the source of Raoul's letter; we know something about the mysterious lady that he does not. We are aware of misunderstandings and tensions that will need to be resolved.

And we have heard some splendid music, both grand and intimate. Much of it has been overt, sociable, and loud: the nobles' party, the "orgy," the great chorus of congratulation (with Marcel's counterpoint *Te Deum*) at the end. But there have also been splendid solos: Raoul's romance, Marcel's character-song "Piff paff," and even a hint of coloratura to come in the valet's cavatina.

Meyerbeer creates the act in a series of specific numbers, each of which essentially begins with action (usually in recitative) and concludes with a musical piece intended to close the scene and win applause. The structure is as follows:

> no. 1 Overture and introduction
> > Overture
> > Chorus (Nevers' song and chorus, "Des beaux jours de la jeunesse")
> > Morceau d'ensemble and Raoul's entrance
> > Orgy
> no. 2 Scene and romance (Raoul's "Plus blanche que la blanche ermine")
> no. 3 Recitative and chorale (Marcel's entrance and chorale)
> no. 4 Scene and Huguenot song (Marcel is induced to sing "Piff paff")
> > Recitative (The valet enters and announces the lady)
> no. 5 Morceau d'ensemble (the men try to see her)
> > Recitative (Nevers, alone, discloses that he is commanded to break
> > > his engagement)
> no. 6 Finale
> > Chorus (the nobles congratulate Nevers on his conquest: "Honneur
> > > au conquérant")
> > The page's cavatina
> > Finale, continued (the letter for Raoul; the nobles seek his favor)
> > Stretta (grand sendoff chorus, Marcel's *Te Deum*)

Meyerbeer's recitatives are often like Handel's or Mozart's accompanied recitatives. Text is delivered at a speaking rate, with interjections or accompaniments from the orchestra (not unlike boulevard melodrama). In the case of Marcel, the accompaniment is given by chords on a single cello (with a double-bass doubling the lowest notes); these accompaniments even have old-fashioned figures attached to them in the score.

Meyerbeer's solo and ensemble numbers are grand self-contained pieces of music. That is what we come for. The choruses have good tunes, splendid toe-tapping accompaniments from the orchestra. The solo numbers are occasions for great virtuosity from the singers, involving one or more elaborate cadenzas (Meyerbeer was always rewriting cadenzas for singers), usually with some characteristic instrumental color: the viola d'amore for Raoul; Marcel's bassoons; strings and winds for the page (the harps and flutes that often go along with soprano coloratura are saved for Marguerite's big aria in act 2).

This is a great deal to accomplish in one act, and we have discussed it at length in order to show the combination of text and music that operates in each of the acts in a similar way.

Not all observers found the first act perfect. Grillparzer said that he could not follow it, and that the obligation of setting up the plot left too little room for music (despite all those tunes): "The fault of the first act is in the book. The complicated love-game and the excess of text make it impossible for the music to follow." Gustave Planche thought that the first act was timidly and indecisively performed—inexcusable after so many months of rehearsal.

Meyerbeer felt that his songs had succeeded: "In the first act, the Orgy, Nourrit's romance, the chorale and the chanson, and Flécheux's little aria, all pleased. The whole act made a very charming effect."

ACT 2

The curtain is lowered between the acts, and the entr'acte music features a splendid flute solo by Tulou. Meanwhile the stagehands effect the scene change. Véron in his memoirs described the stage during an entr'acte:

> Imagine that you are setting foot on a war-machine; ropes, pulleys, men climbing to the tops of the masts; incessant maneuvers, curtains descending from the flies, *fermes* rising from below the stage, traps opening or closing, flats being pushed or pulled, counterweights descending from the grid, *praticables* being moved, sometimes being stacked one on another; props being placed, lamps lit, gas lights, borders of gas lamps which make explosions of light; words of command pronounced audibly and clearly by the chief of the machinists, or by the head machinist himself: all that under the watchful eye of the firemen, their petty officers, their lieutenant or their captain; a workman who, in the midst of all this movement, waters and sweeps the front wings of the stage; two inspectors who shout and agitate to make room on the stage, and to warn actors and spectators of danger; here and there singers or dancers in costume, singers preluding and vocalizing, dancers leaping on the stage; in the midst of all this hurly-burly, the director, smiling if the house is full, frowning if empty. Such is the animated picturesque tableau of the Opéra during an intermission, until the moment when the inspectors, with Stentorian voices, cry "Places, gentlemen, places on stage, the curtain is going up."

The second act is set in contrast to the first. Here the ladies rather than the gentlemen take their pleasure; the setting is outdoors; and Raoul is introduced yet again into a company that he disturbs.

The scene is laid, according to the score, in "the chateau and the gardens of Chenonceaux, near Amboise. The Chateau of Chenonceaux is built on a bridge (it is painted in perspective on the backdrop): the river winds in curved lines down to the middle of the stage, disappearing from time to time behind clumps of green trees. To the right a large stone staircase leading from the chateau to the gardens."

The act begins with a splendid scene. Queen Marguerite, seated at the water's edge to the audience's left, has just finished her toilette; the page Urbain, kneeling, holds her mirror. Marguerite delivers a great coloratura set-piece, "O beau pays de la Touraine," whose virtuosity puts the page of the first act into the shade. Accompanied by harps, with solos for flute and cello, she is joined by her page and a chorus of ladies in praise of love.

Madame Dorus-Gras as Marguerite de Valois was loved and hated. She had the job of being the prima donna in the wake of the great Damoreau, who had recently left the Opéra. The best she can do, it would seem, is not to call attention to herself by falling too far short. In fact, she could certainly sing the very difficult part, beginning with the virtuoso pastoral "O beau pays de la Touraine" that opens the act. She then must go on to be imperious, coquettish, and many other things. The always-negative drama critic Gustave Planche reports her as being "what she always is, correct, careful, monotonous, which does not correspond to a character which should be animated, mocking, and slightly racy. Brought to its legitimate and true nature, [the second act] would have stood out from its background, and would have contrasted in a happy and poetic way with the first and third acts, that is, with the orgy and the duel; but sung by Mme Dorus, it slows the action instead of varying it." But she certainly sang it, according to the critic François-Joseph Fétis (who surely was more interested in the music): "This role was the occasion of a complete triumph for her. Her pieces in the second act demand enormous agility, bristling with vocal difficulties originally intended for Madame Damoreau; Madame Dorus-Gras triumphs over these difficulties with a talent which does her the greatest honor, and which places her much higher than before in public opinion. The public shows its pleasure at hearing her by lively applause." Quicherat, in his biography of Nourrit, agrees: "The second act opens with a grand air for Queen Marguerite: 'O beau pays de la Touraine.' It was a triumph for Madame Dorus-Gras; a pleasing and natural sound, correctness in phrasing, security and delicacy of technique, the lightness of her vocalization, gained her well-deserved applause."

In a brief recitative, Valentine, descending the grand staircase, reports that Nevers has agreed to call off their marriage and is told in turn that she is to marry Raoul. (A side intrigue is that Urbain is not so secretly in love with Marguerite.)

Then comes the bathing scene. A ballet with chorus, in which young ladies (of the ballet) appear in gauze bathing-costumes and, as the score indicates, "before entering the water dance, play, and run after each other forming different groups. A divertissement that the Queen, while she makes her toilette, watches with a smile, calmly stretched out on a green bank. Other young girls have disappeared behind clumps of trees at the back, and are seen just afterwards bathing in the Cher, which makes various curves on the stage." They bathe in the river, the chorus sings, and the ballet dances, all to the accompaniment of lovely music, in which the bassoons, accompanied by muted cellos, make the sound of the rolling waters. Urbain is chased away. Finally the stage is empty (the chorus continues offstage) except for the bathers in the river, and all ends pianissimo, leaving the queen alone.

MEYERBEER, *LES HUGUENOTS*

A design for act 2 of *Les Huguenots*. Local color, nature, and historical accuracy in the depiction of the Château de Chenonceaux make this a characteristic set for Romantic grand opera. The river will be the scene of a bathing ballet, and the grand staircase (a *praticable*) will be used for a grand entry of the nobles.

Meyerbeer had expected this bathing scene to be a hit. But for some reason nothing seemed to work. The spectacle of bathing on stage was hampered by the scene painters; Meyerbeer later wrote "By a false calculation of the painters in Paris, the water in the set of the second act was made so deep that nobody could be seen while bathing in it; and it remained in this state." And there was noise from the pit: one observer complained about the noise of the "foot, or we don't know what, with which M. Habeneck beats his Teutonic time, and which destroys the musical and scenic illusion."

There is more action: Urbain returns, along with the women of the ballet, to announce the arrival of Raoul, and there is a charming "Scène du bandeau" in which the chorus and ballet comment on the blindfolded Raoul and dance around him.

In a recitative and duet, Raoul removes his blindfold and swears his love and devotion to the beautiful woman he sees (the first male voice in the act; he *still* does not know that she is Marguerite); Marguerite, charmed by his looks and actions, considers what she might do if she were not queen . . . A splendid composition, increasing in tempo and excitement, and drawing considerable applause for the virtuosity of the singers.

Raoul finally understands who Marguerite is when she commands him to marry

Valentine in order to join Protestants and Catholics; and there is a grand entrance of the nobles (finally the grand staircase is used to advantage). Led by Saint-Bris and Nevers, they are required to swear their loyalty to this union—but not before Marcel arrives and reproaches Raoul for agreeing to marry a Catholic.

The finale begins as the nobles swear eternal friendship in a grand chorus (with a virtuoso male quartet for the principals). Only now does Raoul see his intended bride, whom he recognizes (incorrectly) as Nevers' mistress and refuses to marry. General confusion, in a great final ensemble and chorus; Valentine's innocent voice soars over the chorus (it is the first time we have really heard her), the outraged nobles swear revenge, and Marguerite reproaches everybody, sending them off to Paris at the king's orders. Marcel interjects the usual chorale of thanksgiving.

It is an act full of music, but the plot has advanced by continuing Raoul's confusion as to Valentine's identity, and his refusal has inflamed factional passions that his marriage was intended to soothe. The oath of friendship sworn here will be echoed by an oath of revenge in act 4.

The musical layout is clear (these indications are from the score), and centered around a series of musical numbers:

> no. 7 Entr'acte and air
>   Recitative
> no. 8 Choruses of bathers (danced)
>   Recitative
> no. 9 Scene of the blindfold
>   Recitative
> no. 10 Duo
> no. 11 Recitative and entrance of the court
>   Recitative
> no. 12 Finale
>   Oath
>   Scene
>   Stretta

The second act somehow did not work. As Meyerbeer wrote to his wife, "The second [act], though I had counted on it, and though it was applauded, finally left the audience cold." Grillparzer felt that the act had too much plot and not enough music: "In the second [act] some good music could have been made—but it was not. The beginning at least provides the opportunity, but then comes another piece of theatre, as in the first act."

ACT 3

The scene shifts to the *Pré aux clercs* in Paris, along the left bank of the Seine. (The mise-en-scène indicates that the set from act 5 of Hérold's comic opera *Le pré aux clercs* will do here: "On the backdrop is painted the Old Louvre and a part of Paris in the

Nicolas Prosper Levasseur, famous for the strength of his low notes, sang the role of Marcel. He was the leading bass of the Opéra, having sung there for more than twenty years.

distance, in the foreground the Seine; several sections of water are visible, on which boats are painted. A handsome sunset").

The essential plot features of this act are Valentine's wedding to Nevers; a duel between Raoul and Saint-Bris, intended as an ambush for Raoul but averted by Valentine, who in disguise warns Marcel, who in turn summons aid from the nearby Protestant soldiers and creates a grand interfaith mêlée. Marguerite de Valois intervenes, and the arrival of a splendid illuminated barge (Nevers coming with his guests to collect Valentine, who had remained to meditate in church) and a group of gypsy dancers provides the occasion for dancing, a large stage band, and spectacular display.

The opening scene is a great choral number. The inhabitants of Paris stroll about, enjoying their Sunday ("C'est le jour du dimanche, c'est le jour du repos"); from the inn on the right, Huguenot soldiers sing an unaccompanied soldiers' chorus, with verses sung by Wartel ("Rataplan"; this was applauded and repeated in the performance). A procession of young women appears (accompanying the bridal procession of Valentine and Nevers) and sing an archaic-sounding litany ("Vierge Marie, soyez bénie"); and then the two songs are heard together (a trick employed by many a later composer), joined by the Catholic group at another tavern on the other side of the stage, while Marcel refuses to reverence the passing sacrament. This is all interrupted by the ballet: Bohemian dancers with tambourines entertain—for quite a while.

In a recitative, Nevers reports that Valentine will remain in the chapel to pray; Marcel delivers a challenge from Raoul (another of Scribe's letters); and Saint-Bris and Maurevert arrange an ambush for Raoul later that evening. But Valentine overhears it all (she knows, and we know, but Raoul does not). An archaic curfew is sung, bells ring, night falls, and the stage is cleared.

In a long duet, the veiled Valentine warns Marcel of the plot, and he resolves to save Raoul but does not learn Valentine's identity. There is splendid solo singing from Falcon and Levasseur, contrasting with the enormous choral scene that preceded.

Saint-Bris and the witnesses arrive, and there follows a rousing septet of preparation for the duel. Nourrit is placed at the center of the ensemble, the focus of the audience's attention and that of those on stage. Just as they begin to fight, Maurevert arrives to ambush Raoul; he is challenged by Marcel, who calls for help. The Protestant students arrive ("Rataplan"), Marcel sings his chorale, the Catholics come pouring out of the other tavern, and there is a choral quarrel interrupted by the arrival of Marguerite de Valois with her train and torchbearers. (Dorus-Gras has to sing on horseback while managing her steed.)

As the finale begins, the mysterious woman who revealed the plot to Marcel is herself revealed as Valentine, and Raoul learns what we already know: she is innocent, she has saved him, and she is now another's wife. When she was available he misunderstood, and now that he understands, she is not available.

Now arrives the splendid barque (at the fourth *plan* of the stage) with its own band, and Nevers descends to conduct Valentine away. Meyerbeer described the barque in a letter to potential producers:

> In Paris it [the barque] has a good scenic effect. There it is very large, and contains, by the way, 30 persons. The risers provided in it should be arranged in an amphitheater facing the audience. The Barque itself is in a fantastic bizarre shape, and the whole architecture of it is covered with many colored paper lanterns. The stage is dark, and Nevers' many followers carry each two burning torches, and the queen's followers are likewise given torches, and there are also many so-called pitch-baskets brought on stage, so that the whole theater seem to be lit only by torches and pitch-baskets, which for the ballet and the final number gives a very unusual and effective impression.

The Bohemians dance, everybody sings, the bands play, Marguerite remounts and departs, the barque sails away, and the curtain falls. It is the grandest moment of this grand opera.

Meyerbeer was relatively pleased with the effect of this act: "The third [act], where I was worried, on the contrary, pleased very much; especially Rataplan, which had to be repeated, the septet of the Duel, and the quarrelling chorus, which was truly excellently performed. Less, although applauded, the duet of Falcon and Levasseur. On the whole, a success was not fully assured." But the first three acts, in Meyerbeer's judgment, did not make as much effect at the first performance as they did later. Reporting on the later performances, Meyerbeer noted that the first three acts, though applauded at the premiere, seemed to be better received at the second, and even more at the third.

Franz Grillparzer, too, in his grumpy way, felt that the opera really gets going in this act. On April 22 he reported: "The music of the opera begins with a duet in the middle

Madame Montessu as a Bohemienne.
Local color, and a welcome ballet
interlude, are provided by the band
of gypsies who dance in the finale
of act 3.

of the third act, and is quite artful, often extraordinary, all the way to the end." But a week later he was not so impressed: "The third act begins with a very good chorus, then subsides a bit, but raises itself in the duet between Valentine and Marcel. Near the end I was overcome by my usual theater boredom. I remember, though, that it pleased me the first time."

ACT 4

The fourth act is the one that gave Meyerbeer such trouble; Nourrit had worried him almost to death with requests for changes. It is an act, like others, that contrasts grand scenes with intimate ones; and it is the one with the great love-duet.

The scene, according to the score, is an apartment in the hotel of Nevers. (In the mise-en-scène it is described as a "Grand Gothic salon, severe and rich.") This is one setting where Duponchel may have economized by using a standard interior. It requires a great Gothic window and door at the back; a door at the left, which leads to Valentine's bedroom; a fireplace at the right, near which is a closet closed by a curtain (where Raoul will hide). Downstage right is a window onto the street.

Valentine is alone, and she expresses her sadness in a recitative. Raoul arrives through the upstage door ("I wanted to see you before dying"). But steps approach, and she hides Raoul behind the curtain.

Then follows the grand scene in which plans are laid for the murder of the Protestants (at the second tolling of the bell of Saint-Germain l'Auxerrois); the Catholic lords are joined by many others; monks arrive to bless the swords. In the fiery chorus "Dieu le veut, Dieu l'ordonne," Berlioz at least was fascinated by the means Meyerbeer uses to produce his menacing effect, by the use of two kettledrummers on two drums. At the end of the scene, the nobles kneel at the footlights brandishing their swords and repeating their oath in unison (with roaring trombones):

Pour cette cause sainte
j'obéirai sans crainte
à mon dieu et mon Roi!

This scene was intended to stir the hearts of everybody, and it still does, at least for those who like swaggering grandeur. It is a piece worthy to stand beside the great patriotic choruses of *Guillaume Tell* and of *La muette de Portici*. Originally the lines were intended for the queen, Catherine de Medici, and had to be changed to Saint-Bris. Nevers alone refuses to swear.

As the nobles steal away during the applause, Raoul comes from behind the curtain, Valentine returns from her room, and the "Grand duo" follows. Raoul needs to warn his fellow Protestants but love bids him stay: the plot in miniature. She pleads with him and finally says the words "Je t'aime." This transports Raoul to a high and light C-flat ("Tu l'as dit que tu m'aimes"), in a beautiful melody echoed by the cellos with shimmering string accompaniment. It is a beautiful scene, better to hear than to describe. It has served, with its slow triple rhythm and its far-out key of G-flat major, as the model for many, many later love duets. Nourrit acted it with almost no gestures, Falcon with many. Just as Raoul is thinking of escaping with Valentine, the bell recalls him to his duty. To the same beautiful melody they now sing opposite sentiments: she laments the end of their time together ("C'est la mort, voici l'heure!") while he continues his words of love ("Nuit d'amour!"). Valentine faints and Raoul escapes through the downstage window into the street. Curtain.

This act—or the duet that closes it—brought the house down. There was enormous applause, and Nourrit and Falcon appeared before the curtain. On the act 4 duo, over which Meyerbeer (and Nourrit) had labored so much, the critic for L'Artiste wrote: "Never before has music had so moving a power; this duet is worth all the most beautiful music that Beethoven wrote."

ACT 5

The final act brings the dénouement, the final revelations, and the deaths of the lovers—but not before a grand ballroom scene. An entr'acte begins with a theme from the earlier lovers' duet, and in a grand crescendo the curtain is raised to reveal a great ballroom in which the Protestants are celebrating the marriage of Marguerite to Henri of Navarre. This is a short set, described in the mise-en-scène as "Superb palace, limited to 2 and a half plans, lit at the 2d plan by two chandeliers painted on the backdrop." Marguerite and Henri appear upstage as the rest dance a majestic minuet and a faster dance, interrupted twice by the tolling of bells. That second bell was the arranged signal, and Raoul bursts in, and in an agitated recitative he reports the slaughter of Protestants. A chorus of revenge ("Courons aux armes!") leads all offstage.

The scene changes—in sight of the audience—by shortening the set: "When the nobles run for vengeance, a backdrop is lowered between the 1st and 2d chassis, which cover the palace. This is a peristyle interior of the Protestant church, lit as by night. This is for the scene of the great trio, which begins the denouement and facilitates the set of the finale."

The score gives a more complex description: "A cemetery. At the back a protestant church falling to ruins. Through broken windows can be seen the upper galleries of the church. On the left, a door into the church. On the right, a grill giving onto an intersection."

Marcel is wounded, and Raoul arrives (and a group of Protestant women take refuge in the church). Valentine arrives to save Raoul; he has only to convert (Valentine reports that she is free: Nevers has died trying to protect Marcel). Raoul refuses. Valentine, unwilling to be parted from Raoul, decides to adopt his faith. The women in the church are heard singing the well-known chorale.

Marcel unites Raoul and Valentine in marriage to the remarkable accompaniment of a bass clarinet. This unusual instrument was heard to good effect by Fétis, who wrote about it on March 5: "The accent of the instrument completes and reinforces the feelings expressed by the characters. The religious inspiration of Marcel and the resignation of Raoul and Valentine are admirably expressed in this piece, which the addition of the bass clarinet so admirably completes."

The chorale is interrupted by a "chorus of murderers"; they fire on the Protestant women (this is where the new shooting machine is put to work). There are offstage fanfares, more shooting (flashes are seen through the broken windows), and finally the chorale is silenced. The musical truncation of the chorale, of which we hear shorter and shorter fragments, and the increasing speed and higher pitch of each iteration, allows us to feel the tension of the invisible massacre.

Marcel has a celestial vision, with six harps, which inspires Raoul and Valentine to similar transports. They bid a farewell to this life with the melody of the chorale. They link arms and present their chests to the murderers. They are dragged into the street through the grill, and shots are heard.

For the final moment, a full-depth scene is revealed of Paris in 1572 seen by starlight; the stage is dark. Soldiers with torches pursue fleeing Protestants. Raoul, mortally wounded, enters from the right with Marcel and Valentine. Saint-Bris and soldiers come from the left. Raoul, with his dying breath, identifies himself and his companions as Protestants. They are fired on, and Saint-Bris recognizes that he has killed his own daughter. She says that she will pray for him, and dies. Queen Marguerite's litter and her train—red velvet, sparkling with gold, bright with lanterns—lights up the stage as the queen returns from the ball. (This litter had been the subject of endless negotiations with the censors.) Marguerite, horrified, stops the soldiers with a gesture (since this could be mimed, Dorus-Gras at later performances had often already left the theater); the remaining Protestant women and children crowd around her, and the chorus of soldiers deliver their final words: "Dieu veut le sang!" (God wants blood!).

This last act is designed by Meyerbeer to be played continuously; though it has three large sections (with three sets), and although the compositions are carefully made, there are none of the grand endings designed to provoke applause. Instead, transitions are arranged to make the action continuous.

The trio of the vision, on which Meyerbeer had counted so much, had had trouble in rehearsal. Meyerbeer wrote on February 22: "yesterday's general rehearsal of acts 4 and 5 produced the distressing phenomenon that the trio of the fifth act, on which all my hopes were built, and whose effect in the rehearsal was immense, in the theater not only left everyone cold, but the murder-chorus behind the scenes produced such an unpleasant effect, that now they insist on more changes, which I have not yet found possible, and which in any case will interfere with the deepest heart of the trio." And after the rehearsal that preceded the dress rehearsal he wrote: "The fourth act made a great effect, but the trio in the fifth will still not go together, which naturally destroys much of the effect." But it did succeed in performance: "In the fifth [act], the trio—which amounted to little in rehearsal—took its brilliant revenge."

The opera was greeted with enormous applause. The principal singers were called for, and if Meyerbeer and Scribe did not appear, there may have been practical reasons, as a German reporter related: "Nourrit, Levasseur, and Falcon were called for at the end; Meyerbeer and Scribe were no longer in the house, and perhaps they did not appear because it was necessary to empty the theater, which otherwise would not have happened until half past twelve, even though the police-ordinance prescribes midnight and must be observed."

The opera had lasted five full hours, and the temperature was a reported 24 Réaumur (30 degrees Celsius, 86 Fahrenheit).

Reactions

The audience members had much to listen to and much to think about. They were eager to hear new music sung by great singers, and to see a spectacle as only the Opéra can present it. But for this audience there were comparisons to make. Is this work a fitting successor to *Robert*, and how does it compare with other operas? Is this opera as spectacular as the recent *La Juive*? The audience members were familiar with the singers and with the house, and they were in a position to be keen judges of the singers, the roles, and the performances.

There were many published reviews of such an important event; these were the early years of what we now call musical criticism. The chief musical journals included Fétis' *La revue musicale* (founded 1827); *La gazette musicale,* from the music publisher Schlesinger (1834); and *Le Ménestrel,* from the publisher Heugel (1835). Most reports of the performance are from newspapers; chief critics included Fétis, Castil-Blaze, Blaze de Bury, and Berlioz; there are reports from Jules Janin, Gustave Planche, and Joseph D'Ortigue. (Some of their reports are in the documents.) Many journalists, then as now, report more on the music than on the performance, and it is sometimes difficult to distinguish details of the performance itself within a report that seems to be based on a study of the score. We also have private opinions, including those of Meyerbeer himself and of the poet Franz Grillparzer.

It had long been customary for gentlemen to be allowed backstage
to the Opéra's Green Room to consort with performers—
especially dancers in the ballet. Louis Véron made this privilege
into a source of considerable income for the house.

Meyerbeer's music was justly praised. Hector Berlioz called it a "musical encyclopedia"—is this praise? And he had sympathy for Meyerbeer:

> The author of the music needed a great deal of courage in order to en-
> dure the complaints, the expressions of discontent of all kinds, which
> were raised around him on account of the length of preparations re-
> quired by the style of his work, and the detailed exactitude with which
> he supervised them. It is unperformable! is has no common sense! said
> many ill-tempered persons, their fairness taxed by endless rehearsals.
> And the composer, at each such event, resignedly lowering his head, let
> the wave pass, and drawing new breath, continued on his way, mur-
> muring to himself: "If it is unperformable today, we will see tomorrow;
> if my music has no 'common sense,' it may have another sense." Experi-
> ence has proved how right he was.

Berlioz acknowledged that most listeners would need more time to appreciate
the musical treasures of the opera: "Several attentive listenings are absolutely necessary
in order to understand such a score completely." The same view is expressed by the reviewer

"J. L." in *Le Ménestrel:* "As the public listens to *Les Huguenots,* the magnificent details of the score will become more clearly delineated, the public ear will become accustomed to it, the motifs will be understood, and from then on its popularity will be assured forever." What most people noticed was the tunes, of which there are plenty, and the successful execution of difficult vocal parts.

Though we may not usually think of Meyerbeer in the same breath as Stravinsky, at least one critic described the novelty and the surprising harshness, as he heard it, in terms that could serve as well for the reception of *Le sacre du printemps* in 1913: "Weber and Beethoven supplied the model of these harsh sonorities, these covered sounds, these savage dissonances, the breaks in rhythm, this bizarre pacing, the brusque transitions, the unexpected modulations, these sudden caprices, in a word, of all those somber, explosive prodigious colors which are the only things that their masterworks can teach. Meyerbeer's merit is to have brought together in a short span all that was spread here and there in the scores of all the great masters." The writer has noticed Meyerbeer's willingness to be dramatic at the expense of beauty in his music.

The press was almost unanimous in describing the music as accomplished rather than inspired. The music, wrote "J. T." in *La Quotidienne,* "is not remarkable as a work of verve and inspiration, it is a work of learning and labor." There are references to the Teutonic style of the music ("the author's name ends in *-er,* therefore it is learned music"), as compared to the Italian lyricism that privileges melody over everything; perhaps there is a touch of partially submerged anti-Semitism.

Nobody seems to have much to say about the story—except to note the relatively static quality of the first three acts. If the protagonists, Raoul and Valentine, are both victims of circumstance, reacting stoically to events far beyond their control; if the story is one of individuals caught up in the tide of history, of passive heroes and obedient heroines, this seems to be entirely natural and not noteworthy. The libretto was dismissed as worse than usual by some ("M. Scribe has made every effort to make the flattest, most insignificant, the worst-dialogued poem in the world"); others note ridiculous incongruities—what is the cream of society doing at the Pré aux Clercs in act 2 in the midst of all these soldiers, Bohemians, and prostitutes? What indeed is the queen doing there at the end of act 3? Scribe was acknowledged for his usual competence and blamed for the static quality of the opening acts. Joseph Mainzer in *Le monde dramatique* wrote, "All of Meyerbeer's talent, with his immense resources of harmony and instrumentation, was not enough to fill the void left by the poet, nor to give movement to a machine without springs. Where there is no drama, how can we demand dramatic music? . . . No doubt *Les Huguenots,* in three acts, would be one of the most beautiful operas."

Scribe's libretto was criticized also for its failure to provide local color and historical authenticity. The lack of local color was also attributed to Meyerbeer, at least by Mainzer: "Every number is a beautiful and interesting piece, but which lacks local color and could be placed anywhere else." As for the authenticity, "It is not allowed," wrote Nourrit's biographer Quicherat, "to announce a tableau of a great era, and then reproduce neither any of its details or any of its historical figures. The author substituted a vulgar novel for the truth, he multiplies vague suppositions, awkwardness in the language and the action; in a word, the libretto of *Les Huguenots* is the very ordinary work of a writer who is too fertile."

It was generally agreed that the first three acts were not as successful as the last two. "The first three acts encountered that alternation and that mixture of applause and hesitant silence that is neither a defect nor a success," said *Le Constitutionnel*. The fourth and fifth acts were especially applauded, according to *L'Artiste*.

Grillparzer thought there were too many words, too many situations, too much business: "The libretto has the failing of being three quarters too long. The music always has to run along behind the words, and never escapes, so that the music, especially at the beginning, cannot concentrate on itself. It makes a rather scattered effect. There are too many complicated situations, so that even with the libretto in hand it's hard to find one's way."

Of the singers, Nourrit, the great tenor, was not as pleasing to everybody as Raoul. In his scathing review, Planche said that Nourrit "sang more as a careful professional than a passionate lover," that he forgot the Opéra for the Conservatoire, that "do what he might to animate and rejuvenate himself, we could willingly see in him the Huguenot warrior, but not the lamented lover . . . that he moderated the head voice which he indulges far too much and which gives his voice the imprint of the third sex."

Levasseur as Marcel was thought, at least by Fétis, not to have measured up to his performance as Bertram in *Robert,* "either because this role has certain things that do not favor his voice, or because he does not yet have the degree of certainty that he will no doubt achieve after several performances." Others found him a "cold actor, without excitement, who freezes the stage: with him we are never in the drama, we are attending a concert, though he does have a powerful, sure, extensive instrument, remarkable in the lowest notes." "Levasseur is an excellent performer," wrote Grillparzer, "but it always sounds as though a violin piece were being played on a viola. Raw, unpleasant, without resonance."

"The crown of all," for Grillparzer, "is Mlle Falcon, whom I place as the best, with the exception of the great Italians, that I have ever heard in this category. Her singing advances the play, and her acting takes nothing away from her singing. And with a diligence, a zeal, not to use the word effort." But most thought that Falcon overacted, especially in contrast to Nourrit's reserved style. One observer thought that her second performance had "a bit less pretence in her acting equipment; but of real soul, facial expression, eloquence in the eyes, personal charm: nothing! And see how, in the duet, where she repeats what Nourrit says to her, she has no effect with all her movements, while this talented singer is so captivating with an almost complete immobility."

Dorus-Gras as Marguerite de Valois has been discussed above, along with Flécheux as Urbain, with respect to their virtuoso coloratura. What for Fétis was Dorus-Gras' triumph was less so for Grillparzer, who heard her in April: "I liked Dorus less today. By all rights, by all opinion, she is the coming star, especially for the delivery and speed of her passage-work. She and Mlle Flécheux, the page, cold voices with a hard A-sound." She was what she always is, thought Planche: correct, vigilant, monotonous.

The young Flécheux pleased more for her voice than her appearance, at least according to Charles de Boigne: "A young girl, Maria Flécheux, given the role of the page Urbin [*sic*], demonstrated a magnificent voice and Quasimodo legs. Jarry would not have said of her what he said of mademoiselle A., that her legs saved her. Poor Maria Flécheux! she did not live long; she died quite young; not from grief, not a victim of Meyerbeer's music, as has been seriously reported: she died of lung ailments, of that terrible disease that needs no one to accomplish its work of destruction."

"Serda [Saint-Bris] alone is musical," wrote Grillparzer, "with his voice which, though it is not pleasant at least cuts through. The other singers are actors. Dérivis, who plays the Count of Nevers, bleats but is much applauded. 'Bleats' is not the expression. One seems to hear in the place of every vowel an impure E, shouted with a repulsive vehemence." Perhaps Grillparzer was not very attentive to the French language: the *Journal des Débats* cited Dérivis as the only singer besides Nourrit who has the advantage of perfect articulation.

Grillparzer, who liked the women, did not like the men: "The men, who are called dramatic singers; that means: bad. They are highly expert in making the wretched doggerel of a libretto understood, but they are not capable of bringing to life the musical intentions of a good composition. To scream from within a chorus, or to shine a light from within a dark background of violins—they are men for that; let anyone else who wishes deal with lyrical singing. Mostly they are like new soldiers when they first come under fire, when the cannons, that is the basses, roar."

Clearly there are two things to evaluate in a singer, and the first is vocal skill; those who have it may well be criticized for a lack of dramatic ability; those who lack it may possibly redeem it through passionate acting. But seldom does a singer get praised for both.

Grillparzer's criticism of the singing, which seems to deprecate the shouting that takes place on stage, is echoed by Charles de Forster, writing a few years later on the singing tradition of the Opéra:

> If the settings are faultless, the performances often leave much to be desired. Talent is rare and expensive, tenors are beyond price, and pirouettes are worth their weight in gold. A few exceptional throats, richly gifted by youth, have introduced a frightful manner of singing, by forcing all the power of the lungs; and in shouting, rather than singing, they have borrowed against time, and traded away both their future and that of the *Académie royale*. They call that "having energy"; they praised with the word "sublime" that perilous struggle between the tired voice and the notes of the score they have demanded from the composer in order to make themselves stand out. We should say, furthermore, that the audience, who never enjoyed anything more, astonished and dumbfounded, finally accepted this style; and like those drinkers for whom there is no longer, so to speak, a strong enough liquor, any man who does not shout,

who does not behave as though possessed, is nothing but a poor fellow, without talent and without means. Who knows how long this will last, but I fear that this way of hearing music and singing will tend to ruin them completely; and we may not be far from the moment when all will succumb to exhaustion, and when it will be necessary, like it or not, to return to singing pure and simple.

Adolphe Nourrit, near the end of his career, already introduced this vicious style on the stage; but the arrival of Duprez finally implanted it completely. And what happened? Nourrit, worn out by that fatal struggle, succumbed to the pain, gave up his place to his rival, and went off to Italy to die under the weight of his regret and his despair.

The grandeur of the spectacle was a matter of interest to everybody. They had seen the stupendous procession in *La Juive,* and they expected stunning effects. The effects were there: the bathing scene, the splendid torchlit barge, the final scene of Paris by night. The grandeur is grand, but Mainzer at least felt that the musical grandeur was spent at the beginning: "The grand choruses placed at the beginning, in addition to the fact that they also delay the action, have a further and more serious disadvantage: that of deploying all the luxury at the beginning of the piece. The pomp disappears little by little, and the effect instead of increasing diminishes. That is why the fifth act seems almost nothing." And more than one critic complained that there was not as much dancing as usual in an opera.

Authenticity and local color were matters of close scrutiny; the costumes were appropriate to the period, as were the swords and daggers, and the sets. Meyerbeer's historical references in the music, from the chorale to the romance to the curfew, were part of the much-appreciated historical accuracy.

The concern for the display of religious issues on stage could be a screen for anti-Semitism: H. de Bonald wrote in *La France* on March 2:

> Poetry has its licenses, no doubt. But those licenses must have their obligations, independent of those imposed by taste; but, for the love of fashion, for the attraction of music, for the delights of the stage, to sacrifice constantly to the appetite of vulgar sensation the sacred traditions on which the morals and the religion of the country are based; to make now a Jewish apotheosis to the detriment of the dogma of our faith, simply to serve the inspiration of a composer of the Jewish faith [he means Halévy's *La Juive*]; and now a sacrifice of the Catholic faith in favor of Luther's and Calvin's schisms, simply in order to tune the poem to a protestant lyre—that is what seems to us to go too far in the art of exploiting scenes in the theater.

Many thought the opera was too long. Five hours of exhilaration, thought one critic, would not be less exhilarating if an admirable hour were removed; another thought it should be divided into two evenings. And yet many wanted more ballet and even more splendid sets. For a long time to come, wrote Planche, "France will be more eager to see than to hear; she prefers spectacle to the most beautiful verse or music."

Despite his initial success, Meyerbeer continued to be nervous. Owing to the director's careful choice of the audience at the first performance and its management by the claque, and perhaps owing also to Meyerbeer's well-known fear of the press, he felt that success could not be assured until the third performance. Writing to his wife after the second performance, he noted that the first three acts seemed to be better received at the second performance (though they had been duly applauded at the premiere), that "Rataplan" was encored, and that Nourrit and Falcon had been called for after act 4, and Nourrit, Levasseur, and Falcon after the act 5. Only after the third performance did Meyerbeer feel he could breathe the air of success. To Minna he reported increased enthusiasm for the first three acts, and the same encores and curtain calls. All Paris is talking of this opera, he says, and two sentries are needed to protect the ticket office. "Do not think, however," he says, "despite the huge unanimous applause in the theater, that there is not opposition and criticism in the foyer and the salons. Many people disapprove the aesthetic standpoint of my compositional art, either entirely or in certain parts, especially Levasseur's role; they find only skill in the first three acts, genius only in the last two, and put the whole thing second to *Robert*. But the opera has won many, countless many enthusiasts, who not only put it above *Robert*, but place it on such a high plane that I blush to repeat their expressions. What pleases me most is that even those who oppose the opera speak of it as one of the most significant events of recent times, even when they are not in agreement with my tendencies."

The theater journal *Le monde dramatique* summarized the reason for success of an opera of this kind, and attributed to *Les Huguenots* the quality that make grand opera grand: "It is above all at the Opéra that we recognize the great role that performance plays in the success of a piece, and that sometimes secondary matters take precedence over more important ones. The richness and the variety of the settings, the luxury of the *mise-en-scène*, the elegance and exactitude of the costumes, the talents of the actors, the precision of the dancers, all comes together to make an admirable ensemble which affects taste. . . . Thus the *Huguenots* is the work of everyone: author, composer, actors, painters, costumiers, all can claim a part, for all contributed, even if not with equal talent, at least with equal success."

Documents: *Les Huguenots*

1. A DESCRIPTION OF THE OPERA HOUSE FROM A CONTEMPORARY GUIDEBOOK

The ACADÉMIE ROYALE DE MUSIQUE, or FRENCH OPERA-HOUSE, which was intended only for a temporary building, was erected in the space of a year, by M. Debret, architect, and was thus hastily constructed in order to replace, as speedily as possible, the opera-house that stood in the rue de Richelieu. At the door of the latter, it will be remembered, the Duke de Berry was assassinated, in 1820 . . . and the demolition of that theater was immediately ordered by the government. The present building has, however, stood so long that it may be questioned whether any alterations in it will take place for many years to come. It communicates with three streets, that of Lepelletier for carriages, of Pinon for fiacres, and of Grange Batelière for persons on foot. Two elegant passages, skirted with shops, also form a communication between the Boulevard des Italiens and the Opera House. The front consists of a series of arcades on the ground floor, forming a double vestibule. At each end a wing projects, and between these wings, from the top of the arcades, proceeds a light awning supported by cast-iron pillars, beneath which carriages set down. At the first floor is a range of nine arcades, which form the windows of the saloon. From the lobby two other staircases lead to the pit, the *baignoires,* and the orchestra. Between the latter and the lobbies of the stage-boxes are two staircases, which lead to the top of the building, and so numerous are the outlets that the house may be entirely cleared in the space of ten minutes. The interior will accommodate 1937 persons, and its dimensions are 66 feet from side to side, while the stage is 42 feet in width by 82 in depth. Beneath the latter is a space for the play of machinery 32 feet deep; the wall between the house and the stage rises above the roof, and in case of fire the communication between the two can be entirely cut off by a sheet of iron tissue, while ventilators can be opened to carry the flames in any direction. Reservoirs of water are constructed under the roofs. The saloon is 186 feet in length, extending throughout the entire width of the front of the building, and is one of the finest rooms for balls in Paris. . . . The representations at this establishment are always got up in the most admirable and unrivalled style; the scenery is splendid, and the attention paid to the costumes of the actors, and to the general dramatic effect, is too well known to need any but a slight allusion. No foreigner should quit Paris without visiting this theater. Performances take place here on Mondays, Wednesdays, and Fridays, and sometimes on Sundays.

Galignani's New Paris Guide (Paris, 1839), pp. 458–59.

2. MEYERBEER'S CONTRACT WITH VÉRON
A. *The Original Contract, September 29, 1834*

Between the undersigned, Monsieur Louis Désiré Véron, Director and impresario of Theater of the Royal Academy of Music, domiciled in Paris, rue Pinon, no. 8, on one hand;

    And Monsieur Giacomo Meyerbeer, composer of music, living in Berlin, presently at Paris, rue Rivoli, hôtel de Wagramm, on the other hand; the following agreement has been reached:

Article 1.

Monsieur Meyerbeer agrees to deliver to Monsieur Véron, on the 15th of April 1835, the score of the opera on the words of M. Scribe, entitled: Léonore ou La Saint Barthélémy, the authors either retaining this current title or changing or modifying it. The opera is in five acts.

Article 2.

Since Monsieur Véron is in possession of a manuscript of this piece, it is expressly agreed that the changes that Monsieur Meyerbeer shall see fit to make in the various Scenes of the Work shall be considered as having been part of the work since its origin; the piece shall be received as Monsieur Meyerbeer shall choose to modify it in the interest of his music.

Article 3.

It is clearly understood that the score will not contain the ballet music, which can only be made, according to usual practice, with the collaboration of the ballet master; the score will also not contain an overture, since this will depend on the development that the ballet master will give to the introductory divertissement if it should be convenient to have one.

Article 4.

At the moment Monsieur Meyerbeer delivers his score to Monsieur Véron, Monsieur Véron will deliver either to Monsieur Meyerbeer or to the person charged with delivering the score, the sum of thirty thousand francs, as an advance, independent of royalties, this sum serving to reimburse Monsieur Meyerbeer for the penalty of thirty thousand francs he paid on September 30, 1833 for the same work.

Article 5.

Monsieur Véron may not, for any reason whatever, refuse the immediate payment of this sum. Any delay will consist of a refusal to pay. If after such delay Monsieur Véron shall not, by April 20, 1835 at the latest, paid the said sum of thirty thousand francs, the contract will be broken, Monsieur Meyerbeer shall have the right to withdraw his score, and to dispose of it as he sees fit to any theater whatsoever, and Monsieur Véron will nevertheless owe thirty thousand francs, for payment whereof Monsieur Meyerbeer will have the right to seek a judgment against Monsieur Véron, without a tribunal's having the right to modify this sum, whose payment is stipulated in this case, as a penalty clause between the parties.

Article 5 bis.

Articles 4 and 5 above form a correlative obligation: that is, if on April 15, 1835, and at the latest, after a delay, on April 20, 1835, Monsieur Meyerbeer does not deliver to Monsieur Véron the score described in articles 1, 2, and 3, he shall in turn be obligated, according to Articles 4 and 5, to pay to Monsieur Véron thirty thousand francs as a penalty. The contract shall be voided and Monsieur Véron shall have the right to seek payment of the said thirty thousand francs as described in Article 5.

Article 6.

Monsieur Véron engages to put the opera in question into rehearsal without fail on May 15, 1835, and to continue from that day the rehearsals of singers and chorus without any sort of interruption. From that same May 15 no [in the margin: new] work, neither opera, nor ballet, nor translation of foreign opera may be presented nor rehearsed at the Opera, until the work of Monsieur Meyerbeer shall have been performed. Nevertheless, if on May 15th there shall be a ballet in rehearsal, and far enough advanced that its premiere can be given before June 15, Monsieur Meyerbeer agrees that the ballet may be rehearsed concurrently with the rehearsals for his opera until June 15. After that date, if the ballet has not been performed, it can be neither rehearsed or performed until after the premiere of the work of Monsieur Meyerbeer. For his part, Monsieur Meyerbeer will be satisfied with three and a half months of musical rehearsal, saving illness of singers or other obstacles not of his making.

Article 7.

The distribution of roles is definitively fixed according to the list attached here, signed by Messieurs Véron and Meyerbeer. This distribution can be changed only by mutual agreement. Nevertheless, if Madame Damoreau and Monsieur Levasseur, or either of them, should not be members of Monsieur Véron's troupe at the time of the staging of the work, they will be replaced by those artists who will have been engaged to replace them in their employment.

Article 8.

Monsieur Véron undertakes to cause the ballets and dances of the said opera to be designed and staged by one of the two chief ballet masters attached to the Royal Academy of Music, and to have all the first dancers perform [Meyerbeer's marginal addition: at Monsieur Meyerbeer's choice], except for Mademoiselle Taglioni, whose appearance as a dancer in this work will depend solely on Monsieur Véron.

Article 9.

Monsieur Véron grants to Monsieur Meyerbeer for this work an extraordinary supplement of stage musicians who should not exceed the number of twenty, and the means of obtaining the effect prescribed in the number in the score.

Article 10.

The work will be performed on September 1, 1835, at the latest. [Meyerbeer's marginal addition: except for cases of force majeure independent of the will of MMs Meyerbeer & Véron.]

Article 11.

Monsieur Meyerbeer agrees not to present any new work composed by him at the Theatre of the Opéra-Comique before September 2, 1835.

Article 12.

Monsieur Véron declares that in his capacity as Director and Impresario of the opera he has the right to conclude the present contract and to cause it to be executed under his personal responsibility without requiring the approval of anyone, that in the event that the Commission of supervision of the Opera, or another superior authority, or the author of the poem, should raise any difficulty as to the validity or the execution of this contract in whole or in part, he takes on himself the responsibility of resolving these difficulties, which in any event will not prevent him from discharging in their entirety the obligations he takes on with the present contract.

Article 13.

The violation of articles 6, 7, 8, 9, 10, 11, and 12 will give rise to the payment of a sum of twenty to thirty thousand francs as shall be established by the following arbiters: this sum shall be paid by whichever party shall contravene one or more of the said articles within the space of twenty days, and, in such case, the present contract shall be void and considered as never having been made, and each party free to proceed as he shall think fit.

In consequence, in the event of dispute over the execution of the said articles, 6, 7, 8, 9, 10, 11, and 12, it is agreed that the difficulties shall be submitted to two judge-arbiters, chosen by each of the parties, which arbiters shall name a third to form a majority. . . .

Article 15. [there is no article 14]

The present contract will bind Monsieur Véron's successor, whomever he is, and under the personal responsibility of Monsieur Véron; each article of this contract shall be [in the margin: equally] applicable to the successor, whether it relates to the indemnity and of the immediate execution of the first six articles, or to the arbitrage for the following articles.

Article 16.

In the event of any dispute whatever, the cost of registering the present act shall be at the expense of the party who shall initiate it.

Made double at Paris, the 29th of September 1834.

[Meyerbeer signs:] Approved the writing above and facing: Giacomo Meyerbeer

B. Distribution of Roles [appendix to the contract]

Distribution of the roles as definitively established by the two contracting parties:

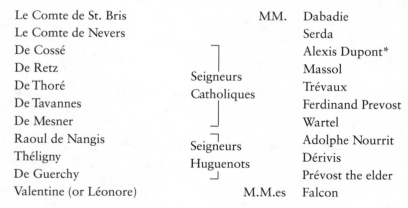

Le Comte de St. Bris	MM.	Dabadie
Le Comte de Nevers		Serda
De Cossé		Alexis Dupont*
De Retz		Massol
De Thoré	Seigneurs	Trévaux
De Tavannes	Catholiques	Ferdinand Prevost
De Mesner		Wartel
Raoul de Nangis	Seigneurs	Adolphe Nourrit
Théligny	Huguenots	Dérivis
De Guerchy		Prévost the elder
Valentine (or Léonore)	M.M.es	Falcon

Marguerite de Valois	Dorus-Gras
Cathérine de Médicis	Mori Gosselin
Marcel, servant of Count Raoul	M. Levasseur
Le Capitain Boisrosé	Roles to be
A Bohemian woman	assigned
A lady-in-waiting	later

*If he has left the Opéra by then, M. Lafont will fill his role.

Giacomo Meyerbeer. *Briefwechsel und Tagebücher,* ed. Heinz Becker, vol. 2 (1826–36) (Berlin: Walter de Gruyter, 1970), 2: 664–67.

C. Additions of November 26

And after the signature, the parties have agreed the various dates in question in articles 5, 5 bis, 6, 10, and 11, shall be deferred 20 days later. Thus article 1 will have a delay from April 15 to May 5, and so on for the other articles named above; without any further alteration whatever to the terms of the contract.

Made double at Paris, the 26th of November 1834.

[Meyerbeer signs:] Approved the writing above and facing: Giacomo Meyerbeer

Briefwechsel, 2: 667.

D. Additions of June 23

Mr Véron wishing to grant a month's holiday to Madame Dorus Gras during the month of July, Mr Meyerbeer has given his consent; but since Madame Dorus Gras will not be able to be present at rehearsals during her absence, it is agreed by the parties:

1. Instead of 3 ½ months, Mr Meyerbeer has the right to four months of rehearsals.
2. Since the copying of parts for act 1 was only finished on June 20, rehearsals could begin only on that day. As a consequence the four months of rehearsal began on June 20 and will finish next October 20, without this delay affecting other clauses of Article 6 and the additional article.
3. The roles of act 2 will be copied by July 10, and the choruses of that act by July 20, in order to put act 3 into rehearsal during Madame Dorus Gras' absence, which has caused the suspension of act 2.

Furthermore, the casting has been modified as follows:

1. The role of Marguerite of Valois intended for Madame Damoreau will be given to Madame Dorus Gras.

2. The role of the page, intended for Madame Dorus Gras, will be given to Mademoiselle Flécheux.

3. This new casting is only for the eventuality that Madame Damoreau leaves the Opéra, either of her own will or that of Mr Véron.

4. In consequence, if Mme Damoreau remains attached to the Opéra M. Meyerbeer will have the right to insist that Mme Damoreau take the role of Marguerite.

5. In this case Mr Véron will make it his personal responsibility to see to it that Madame Dorus Gras relinquishes the role of Marguerite to Madame Damoreau.

6. Mademoiselle Flécheux shall make her début at the Opéra, in a role other than that of the page, at least a month before the premiere of *La Saint Barthélémy*.

All without affecting any other arrangements of the contract.

Made double at Paris, the 23d of June 1835.

[Véron signs:] Approved the writing above and facing: L Véron

Briefwechsel, 2: 673–74.

E. *Additions of July 9*

It is agreed by the parties signed below:

Article 1. By exception to Article 6 of the contract of last September 29, to the article added after the signature, and to the additional article of 23 June 1835, M. Meyerbeer agrees that M. Véron may give the first performance of the ballet *L'Île des Pirates* as late as next August 5. In consequence, up until that day M. Véron may rehearse this ballet, without affecting the rehearsals of *La Saint Barthélémy*.

Article 2. If M. Meyerbeer thinks it best to absent himself for a month, beginning on July 24th, in his absence the singers may rehearse only the entire first act and the first half of the third, whose rehearsals have already begun under his direction. No other piece from the opera may be rehearsed until his return.

The musical rehearsals must nevertheless be finished between the 16th and the 20th of November, instead of the 20th of October, except for impediments beyond the control of M. Meyerbeer.

The remainder of the contract will be scrupulously observed without other exceptions.

Article 3. M. Véron agrees to put at M. Meyerbeer's disposal for the performance of his opera a supplement of four harps, that is, to employ six in the orchestra or on the stage, instead of the two currently employed.

Made double at Paris, this 9th of July 1835.

[Véron signs:] Approved the writing above: L Véron

Briefwechsel, 2: 674–75.

F. Additions of September 22

Between the undersigned agreed as follows:

By exception to the last paragraph of Article 6 and Article 10 of the agreement of September 29, 1835, of the first and second additional articles of June 23, 1835, and the second additional article of July 9, 1835, Monsieur Duponchel, currently Director of the Opéra, and Monsieur Meyerbeer are agreed to cancel the clause that obligated Mr Meyerbeer to have finished the musical rehearsals of the opera *La Saint Barthélémy* between November 16th and 20th, 1835, and to cancel likewise the clause that obliged Monsieur Duponchel to give at the same time the first performance of this work.

Made double at Paris, the 22d of September 1835.

[Duponchel signs:] Approved the writing above: Duponchel

Briefwechsel, 2: 675.

3. EXCERPTS FROM MEYERBEER'S LETTERS TO HIS WIFE, MINNA

May 5: [Meyerbeer will deliver the score to Crémieux to give it to Véron; also a power of attorney.] "Furthermore, the swine [Hundsvott; he means Véron] intends to present my operas as shabbily as possible. At the moment they are arranging the decor of the 'Orgie' (you already know this ballet) so that it can serve for the third and fourth acts of my opera. Duponchel said to me: '[in French] Unfortunately Véron is in a bad humor for your work, he wants no expenses at all.' He said that to me in his repulsively honeyed way. '[French] This time I leave it to the music alone to create a success.' Imagine, he is now beginning to make difficulties even about the instruments that play solos, for example the English horn, the contrabassoon, etc. '[French] I am not obliged to give you all that, your opera is already costing me 20,000 francs.' In Halévy's opera there is a children's choir which makes a very good effect. When I told him how pleased I was with it, he said '[French] Ah, I engaged them only for M. Halévy's opera'" (p. 455).

June 5: "He [Habeneck] is one of those who must really know the opera before the rehearsals begin; I wanted to play him all five acts, but at the end of the third I was so exhausted that I had to send him away. Decidedly my opera so far has pleased nobody who has heard it" (p. 461).

July 24: "Yesterday for the first time we had the singers and chorus together to rehearse act 1. It was Véron who wanted this, and everybody knows that the destiny of the opera is in his hands, and that it was important to make an impression on him. And yet nobody sang with full voice. My friends fear for me that I will not have a success like Robert" (p. 472).

July 28: "Duponchel is still not the director of the opera, and great difficulties are arising from it. Although I would not claim to have had a warm friend in him, at least he was not an obvious fiend as the miserable Véron was, and furthermore I have gotten from him an increase of 24 voices in the chorus, which especially for this opera were of great importance. Also with respect to decors and costumes I would do much better, since Véron would put me on stage very meagerly. . . . Until now there has been no trace of enthusiasm in the rehearsals, and though I care nothing about such enthusiasm in rehearsal, this continuing coldness is beginning to worry me. And I am so far not happy with any of my singers, though admittedly we have rehearsed only acts 1 and 2; we have not begun the second, fourth, and fifth acts" (pp. 473–74).

August 16: "Duponchel has been named director; he will want this opera to succeed as it's the first under his direction. And I get 20 more chorus according to his new Cahier de charges, and maybe a brilliant mise en scene" (p. 476).

August 26: "Nourrit, who has exerted the greatest possible influence on Falcon, has turned her so much against the great duet in the fourth act (which takes up half the act) that nothing more will be left to me except to throw this whole major number out and make a new one" (p. 477).

August 31: "Taglioni has returned, and I now have daily conferences with him about the ballet music I must make; the same daily with the painters, who have done the exact opposite on the third and fifths acts from what I prescribed *pour les exigences musicales* [for musical necessity]. So there are difficulties and conferences without end. And also rehearsals, where little alterations are required daily; the fatal history with Nourrit over the fourth act, who flatly refuses to sing the grand duet, and now has suggested that I must change not only the duet, but the preceding pieces in the fourth act. Scribe, who should sort it out, is out of town" (p. 478).

September 15: "I now truly think what I did not want until now to believe, namely that Véron has just withdrawn from the public eye, and that Duponchel is not really the director, but just a Canaille. With respect to my opera he now does everything for which he previously reproached Véron. We had such an argument yesterday that I was ill all night. Among other things, he wants to premiere the opera with an old set; and what is more important, he refuses me the singer which he definitely intended to engage for the role of Catherine de Medici, so that I do not know where to turn [wo aus noch ein]." [He goes on to worry that this opera will fall short of *Robert,* and the press makes this more difficult (p. 480).]

c. September 20: "And so, a dreary outlook for the near future of my work, a life and death struggle lies ahead for me, not only with my demons but with Duponchel's, who surely know that if my opera fails Duponchel cannot continue, and consequently everything conspires to make me fail. Including Halévy, Duponchel's adviser and confidante, who on account of his *Juive* naturally cannot wish my opera any success and Nourrit, who is the librettist of the opera that is supposed to follow mine immediately." [Nourrit was the librettist of "Le diable boîteux," a ballet-pantomime by Burat de Gurgy and Nourrit, music by Casimir Gide, which opened on June 1, 1836.] (p. 481)

October 16: "The papers are not on my side this time. There have already been several malicious articles against my opera. The ass Duponchel certainly does not have the press on his side, and Véron cabals often against him. The overture is done, but not orchestrated. I will do that later. I don't know whether to use it. It is difficult, and lasts a quarter hour" (pp. 483–84).

October 22: "Finally Nourrit's dissatisfaction has grown so much, and our relationship has grown so bitter, that I'm afraid it may come to a formal break. Unfortunately he has also involved Falcon in this dissatisfaction. Finally, the press is not nearly so friendly to Duponchel as to Véron, and there have already been strongly negative articles against my opera in many papers which are completely false" (pp. 484–85).

November 4: "From some unknown hand (it can only be Véron, trying to interfere with Duponchel's direction) the most ridiculous fabrications against the opera. Yesterday, among others, one journal wrote: '[in French] We will have a symphony of cannon, a scale of musketry, and firing squads instead of singers.' Something different every day. . . . All this writing to discredit the work. What's more, Nourrit is tormenting me in such a way, and forces me to make so many alterations, that I am driven almost mad. Today we quarreled so much that I left the rehearsal" (pp. 488–89).

November 8: "My quarrel with Nourrit has not only the most unfortunate results for my opera (we no longer speak to each other; you can imagine how that hampers learning the role), but also for my body. . . . The attacks of the newspapers against me do not stop. Recently the Journal de Commerce reported that it is being said in public that I wish to put off my opera as long as possible, so that the existing repertory will be wearisome to the public [um damit vorher das bestehende Repertoire dem Publikum zum Ekel würde]. They say also that for this reason I oppose the reprise of [Rossini's] 'Le siège de Corinthe.' Note that nobody from the Opéra has asked me about it. (This article was surely suggested by Rossini's friends, to force me to allow the reprise.) A few days later in fact Duponchel came to ask my agreement to allow them to get on with preparations for the reprise of 'Le siège de Corinthe.' Naturally after this newspaper article I could do nothing but say yes; through that alone I have lost 12 to 14 rehearsals. Arnold Bertin, who was there (Rossini was also present) said to me when we were alone '[in French] It is an enormous mistake of Duponchel's to give this work before yours and to hinder you, but in the presence of Rossini you could not say anything but "yes"'" (pp. 489–90).

December 18: "My composition-work is still not finished, new alterations are continually being forced on me, indeed diabolically forced. What's more, tired with war, I had agreed to make that *cabotin* [ham-actor] tenor his new duet in the fourth act, when Scribe at yesterday's rehearsal wheedled still more important changes in the third act, which I must make. The new duet in the fourth act, I think, has turned out very well. So we have two daily rehearsals of three or four hours each, which seems right to me, since it is in my interest that the opera should definitely open in the last days of January" (pp. 491–92).

December 24: "You should know that the management has forbidden the person of Catherine de Medici, the end, and the scene with the monks. With a few important changes that will cost me new work, the first two points might be possible. But the last, if I have to compose again half of the fourth act, is impossible. You can imagine how many endless and countless petitions this means, to the Minister and the Commission. So far nothing is decided except that Catherine definitely must go, also the ending, and the title. ... If the monks' scene must be altered, I will be forced to withdraw my opera if it doesn't go otherwise. Scribe is interceding for this last point" (pp. 493–94).

December 29: "The difficulties with the censor for my opera continue as before, but the rehearsals are going forward. I still hope that, according to how things go, and if no singer is ill, and if there are no big changes imposed by the censors, we can open at the end of January or the beginning of February. We rehearse mornings and evenings, only the work is difficult beyond all measure" (p. 495).

January 10: "Yesterday we rehearsed the three first acts in order. I purposely waited so long with the cuts so as to determine where it would be the least harmful. I had estimated their timing (with the two ballets that are in the second and third acts) at three-quarters of an hour, and I was prepared to cut ¼ hour of music, only I had erred in my calculations by a good quarter hour, and had then to cut a half hour of music. I alone must bear not only my sins but those of others. That miserable Duponchel has for months gaily had the nerve to say that the four entr'actes would not last longer than an hour. Instead, the two entr'actes of the first three acts alone lasted more than three quarters of an hour, and Duponchel said today that the machinists cannot manage it in less. So I must now offer to the ineptitude of the machinists another quarter hour of music, and my assignment since this morning is to remove three quarters of an hour of music from three acts" (pp. 501–2).

January 22: "Despite the fact that we have two long rehearsals every day I have finished the cuts in the third act, and they are already being studied. I have laid aside my grand overture, that was thought too long and too difficult, and made a new one, and this evening the last sheets of it, God willing, go to the copyist. I have also written the last of my 3 ballet pieces, and tomorrow I hope it will be orchestrated. I could now begin to breathe, except that yesterday's general rehearsal of acts 4 and 5 produced the distressing phenomenon that the trio of the fifth act, on which all my hopes were built, and whose effect in the Zimmerprobe was immense, in the theater not only left everyone cold, but the murder-chorus behind the scenes produced such an unpleasant effect, that now they insist on more changes, which I have not yet found possible, and which in any case will interfere with the deepest heart of the trio. What is more, Scribe insists that in the grand number in act 4, 'pour cette cause sainte,' which because the role of Catherine is forbidden had to be given to one of her confidantes, [Gosselin] Mori does not please him, and I should alter this role for a man! ... The opera will open on the 5th or the 8th" (pp. 502–3).

January 30: "My cuts are done, the new overture is ready, as is the complete ballet music, all orchestrated and copied, and was supposed to have been rehearsed two days ago; but Duponchel and Halévy had it put off in order to have mise en scène rehearsals; for music is the last thing for Duponchel, and it only suits Halévy very well not to protect it [my music] with all his might. Now they have put off this rehearsal to this evening, when there is an opera ball, the whole orchestra is turned into a ballroom, and I must place the orchestra in some corner of the theater. ... A week from the day after tomorrow [February 15] is set for the premiere, but nobody believes it but Duponchel, for neither decoration nor mise en scène are ready" (pp. 503–4).

February 17: "We have just had a dress rehearsal with costumes and sets. I have been had by that miserable Duponchel. Decorations and costumes are so poor and bad as never has been seen in the opera, and you know how important these things are to an opera. . . . The opera has been put off until a week from today [the 24th], and if there is no illness it can go on the stage then" (p. 506).

February 29: "Idol of my soul!

"A few hours before the fateful moment on which my musical future will be decided with terrible severity, pained with a thousand doubts and anguishes I take my refuge in you, my only one. [expressions of tenderness]. . .

"Our next-to-last rehearsal, with more than 100 persons present, was atrocious. Nourrit, completely hoarse, could not sing; the choruses, for whose guests we had provided tickets, was evil, and purposely sang out of tune and badly; the hall, through that stupid Duprez's organization, was neither lit nor heated; in short, those present found it all disgraceful, and I fear that this rehearsal will have done the opera great damage. The day before yesterday [actually yesterday] was the last rehearsal without listeners present, and that one went much better. The fourth act made a great effect, but the trio in the fifth will still not go together, which naturally destroys much of the effect.

"Adieu, Idol of my soul. God keep you and the child healthy and happy, and send us an extraordinary success.

"Your ever loving Moor" (pp. 508–9).

March 1: "Idol of my soul!

"I have mentioned to you in these last moments my doubt and anguish, and now I will speak to you, my dear, after the happy outcome has quieted my worries. Our 'Huguenots' opened yesterday with what appears to be a brilliant success. I say 'appears' because how the Administrations in Paris arrange the first performance, so that only later can one get the scent of the true opinion of the public. This is less true of the Opéra than of other theaters.

"In the first act, the Orgy, Nourrit's romance, the chorale and the chanson, and Flécheux's little aria, all pleased. The whole act made a very charming effect. The second, though I had counted on it, and though it was applauded, finally left the audience cold. The third, where I was worried, on the contrary, pleased very much; especially Rataplan, which had to be repeated, the septet of the Duel, and the quarrelling chorus, which was truly excellently performed. Less, although applauded, the duet of Falcon and Levasseur. On the whole, a success was not fully assured. The fourth act excited real enthusiasm, and in the fifth, the trio—which amounted to little in rehearsal—took its brilliant revenge. After the fourth act Nourrit and Falcon were called for; after the fifth, I myself (I then excused myself), and then all. The little notices in today's newspapers all seem favorable. How it will seem over the long run, God knows. I am still not at ease, but much easier than yesterday.

"Adieu idol of my soul, and the child,

"Your ever loving Moor" (pp. 509–10).

March 4: [Writing to Minna after the second performance, he noted that the first three acts seemed to be better received at the second performance (though they had been duly applauded at the premiere), that "Rataplan" was encored, and that Nourrit and Falcon had been called for after act 4, and Nourrit, Levasseur, and Falcon after the fifth; the musical performance was excellent (pp. 510–11)].

March 6: [Meyerbeer reported increased enthusiasm for the first three acts, and the same encores and curtain calls. All Paris is talking of this opera, he says, and two sentries are needed to protect the ticket office.] "Do not think, however, despite the huge unanimous applause in the theater, that there is not opposition and criticism in the foyer and the salons. Many people disapprove the aesthetic standpoint of my compositional art, either entirely or in certain parts, especially Levasseur's role; they find only skill in the first three acts, genius only in the last two, and put the whole thing second to Robert. But the opera has won many, countless many enthusiasts, who not only put it above Robert, but place it on such a high plane that I blush to repeat their expressions. What pleases me most is that even those who oppose the opera speak of it as one of the most significant events of recent times, even when they are not in agreement with my tendencies" (pp. 511–12).

Briefwechsel, vol. 2.

4. JOSEPH MAINZER IN *LE MONDE DRAMATIQUE*

This theatrical review published several articles on Les Huguenots. *The first was essentially a plot summary; what follows is excerpted from the second.*

In the analysis which we have given of M. Scribe's poem, without commenting on either the choice of subject nor on the scenes and the details they contain, one thing has escaped no one: there is a complete lack of action in the first two acts. The music naturally suffers the consequences of this fault; a series of handsome choruses and gracious airs is indeed notable, but all of Meyerbeer's talent, with his immense resources of harmony and instrumentation, was not enough to fill the void left by the poet, nor to give movement to a machine without springs. Where there is no drama, how can we demand dramatic music? Without M. Meyerbeer's skill the first two acts would have compromised the success of the work.

With the filler material Meyerbeer begins the moments for connoisseurs to study. How else can one retain the attention of the audience for five acts when there is barely enough action for two acts and music enough for a dozen? An opera in five acts is a monstrosity. . . . No doubt *Les Huguenots,* in three acts, would be one of the most beautiful operas; we find it supremely surprising that the will of an administrator can have the power to impose an absurd law on a man who by his position and his talent has earned the right to command.

The first two acts of *Les Huguenots* have no interest and no dramatic life. M. Scribe, not knowing how to fill five acts, gives two of them over to exposition. The poem's voice must be reflected in the music, whose every number is a beautiful and interesting piece, but which lacks local color and could be placed anywhere else. Raoul's romance, *Plus belle que la blanche ermine* is pretty, gracious, it will be sung everywhere; but it is completely foreign to the action. Marguerite's air, in the introduction to the second act, has pretty figures, but again it stops the drama in a desperate way. We are waiting for action, and Marguerite sings us streams and feasts, nightingales and warblers, whose strains of love are echoed by the mountains.

The grand choruses placed at the beginning, in addition to the fact that they also delay the action, have a further and more serious disadvantage: that of deploying all the luxury at the beginning of the piece. The pomp disappears little by little, and the effect instead of increasing diminishes. That is why the fifth act seems almost nothing.

The singers, by contrast, were worthy seconds to Meyerbeer. Mesdames Falcon and Dorus-Gras, MM. Nourrit, Levasseur and Serda understood their tasks well, and the audience rewarded them with applause approaching frenzy.

Le monde dramatique, vol. 2 (1825), pp. 249–53.

5. FROM *LE MONDE DRAMATIQUE*'S REVIEW OF THE 1836 SEASON

The great success of the Opéra last year was *Les Huguenots,* a work judged variously at its premiere, and which has not failed to be properly appreciated by all lovers of the musical art. This composition, so cleverly varied, this score, so brilliantly and energetically written, which abounds in gracious situations and dramatic effects, saw its success consolidated and increased day by day. This triumph is surely due in great measure to the immense talent of Meyerbeer. But the play, too, was well conceived and ingeniously cast. At the Opéra, as everywhere else, the choice of the subject is important, and in this connection M. Scribe's skill cannot be contested. His designs, expertly combined, almost always contain a great number of scenes well arranged for the musician. His verse is flowing, harmonious, accented; his lyrical expression is elevated or lowered according to the situation, but there is never in his poetry anything strange, clashing, *misunderstood.* This author well understands that clarity must be the dominant quality of operatic intrigue, and he makes every effort not to torture the imagination of the audience.

But it is above all at the Opéra that we recognize the great role that performance plays in the success of a piece, and that sometimes secondary matters take precedence over more important ones. The richness and the variety of the settings, the luxury of the *mise-en-scène,* the elegance and exactitude of the costumes, the talents of the actors, the precision of the dancers, all comes together to make an admirable ensemble which affects taste. If the performance suffered in any one of these parts, despite the perfection of the others, if the music were weak when the poem was spiritual and interesting, if there were skimping in the *mise-en-scène* even when there was considerable talent among the actors, if neglect of the costumes were opposed to the splendor of the settings, then no success is possible. Thus the *Huguenots* is the work of everyone: author, composer, actors, painters, costumiers, all can claim a part, for all contributed, even if not with equal talent, at least with equal success.

From "The plays and the authors in 1836," *Le monde dramatique* 3 (1836), 21–22.

6. FROM THE REVIEW BY "J. L." IN *LE MÉNESTREL,* MARCH 6, 1876

We are far from wishing to make a definitive and inalterable pronouncement on such a colossal work; we can only report our first impressions to our readers. Since the melodic parts of a score are those that penetrate most clearly into the souls of the listener, we can declare from today that what struck us most is the richness of the cantabile in Meyerbeer's new production.

Some persons praise only the two last acts to the detriment of the first three. This too is an impression that we do not fully share. What is more suave than Nourrit's aria accompanied by viole d'amour, so superbly performed by M. Urhan! what is more vigorous than the finale of act 2! what is more original than the Huguenots' song, *Vive la guerre!* and that beautiful duet of Levasseur and Mlle Falcon, one of the score's most remarkable pieces! And that women's chorus! and that trio, and that septet, and a host of musical beauties with new effects, that critics persist in sacrificing to the last two acts!

If we admit to a sort of relative inferiority in the beginning of the score, we think it grows out of an absence of dramatic interest. As the action moves towards its crisis, you see the composer's inspirations progress, until they become sublime at the dénouement. Thus the scene of the three monks, the duet of Nourrit and Mlle Falcon, and that grand final trio in energy and allure.

We do not dare to state that the score of the *Huguenots* is superior to its elder sibling *Robert-le-Diable;* but we hesitate also to affirm the contrary. These sorts of parallels are inadmissible in the presence of two masterpieces of such different elements. For, as the public listens to *Les Huguenots,* the magnificent details of the score will become more clearly delineated, the public ear will become accustomed to it, the motifs will be understood, and from then on its popularity will be assured forever.

We will return more than once to this great and beautiful work; but we cannot end this article without paying our tribute of praise to the ensemble of performers, to the dramatic acting, the expressive singing of Nourrit, Levasseur, and Mlle Falcon, to the conscientious zeal of the orchestra and to the brilliant mise-en-scène, done with care by the new administration. The costumes and sets are of a matchless magnificence and fidelity. The final tableau representing our old Paris seen by moonlight has a ravishing effect. *De ce mois malheureux l'inégale courrière* [a poetic reference to the moon] is not present in person; but her place is taken this time by thousands of stars which twinkle in the firmament. The moon has been so overworked in our dramas and melodramas that it is truly a proof of good taste not to show her to the elegant audience of the Opéra.

Paris. Meyerbeer's new opera was finally produced on February 29th, and indeed under the name *Les Huguenots,* after the provisional titles of *La Saint-Barthélémy, Leonore,* and *Valentine* were abandoned. It is barely possible to describe the effect of this opera, whose appearance the Paris public and indeed the whole musical world had awaited so eagerly. No musical work, either by Meyerbeer himself nor by any other contemporary composer of opera, has been received with such enormous applause! The very crowd at the opera house was stupendous; tickets were only to be had at enormous prices; I am told that a seat in a box sold for 200 francs. By special lucky circumstances I got a seat, and I hasten to report something of the opera.

The overture, or better the Introduction (Meyerbeer has not written a real overture) begins with the well-known Lutheran chorale "Eine feste Burg ist unser Gott" which, played by a strong choir of trombones, prepares us for something grand and religious. Then the violins enter, and as they play the curtain rises without any noise. The first act has three lovely moments and a splendid finale; the second offers much to the eyes, it has two very lovely arias for soprano, an excellent, grandiose men's quartet, and a finale which exceeds that of the first act. In the third act the interest of the action increases; the Huguenots' chorus at the beginning made a furor such as I have never before experienced. A repetition was requested, and granted without any objection. This chorus, in my opinion, decided the fate of the opera, since it refreshed the audience, a thing sorely needed in an opera that lasts five full hours in a house heated to 24 degrees Réaumur by the crowd. In this act a brilliant aria sung by Falcon stood out; then comes a noble septet and a finale with double orchestra, where two choirs of trumpets, one in C, the other in F, call to each other. A similar effect was in the Introduction to the *Crociato.*

The highlight of all is the fourth act, in which the composer demonstrates all his greatness. In my opinion it exceeds anything that the world of opera has yet seen in terms of grandeur and drama. The choruses (p. 34) and the duet (p. 35 of the text-book) leave the listeners beside themselves. *Robert le diable* recedes to the background, and one cannot grasp all the imagination and the beauties. Everyone was beside himself, and I am still not quite able to recover from my musical intoxication.

The fifth act moves swiftly to the end; but the effect of awaiting the murder scenes in a rich ballroom, where one has previously heard a sarabande in the orchestra without knowing its purpose, is priceless. Now, however, the chorale, the cornerstone laid for the whole opera, comes forth in all its power and beauty. Six harps accompany Marcel's vision, but although the fifth act is full of power, it naturally has fewer individual moments. Perhaps I was so exhausted from the music of the fourth act that I cannot summon up particular individual details. In a word the opera received, as it should have, a brilliant performance. Nourrit, Levasseur, and Falcon were called for at the end; Meyerbeer and Scribe were no longer in the house, and perhaps they did not appear because it was necessary to empty the theater, which otherwise would not have happened until half past twelve, even though the police-ordinance prescribes midnight and must be observed (cols. 158–60).

8. HECTOR BERLIOZ ON THE FIRST PERFORMANCE

Les Huguenots, (first performance). Opera in five acts, Music by M. Meyerbeer, words by M. Scribe, divertissements by M. Taglioni, decors by MM. Sechan, Feuchères, Dieterle and Despléchin.

It was last Monday that there finally took place, before an immense audience, the first performance of this musical encyclopedia, on which the friends of art had based such high hopes. The success was colossal, just as was expected by all those who attended the rehearsals. From the first act onwards, two pieces were encored, and the author himself could escape the enthusiasm, increasing to the end, only by fleeing the cries of the whole hall which called him to the stage. Several attentive listenings are absolutely necessary in order to understand such a score completely; thus, for today, we will limit ourselves to the analysis of the piece, to a few general ideas on the score as a whole, and the clearly superior fashion in which it was given by the performers.

The author of the music needed a great deal of courage in order to endure the complaints, the expressions of discontent of all kinds, which were raised around him on account of the length of preparations required by the style of his work, and the detailed exactitude with which he supervised them. It is unperformable! is has no common sense! said many ill-tempered persons, their fairness taxed by endless rehearsals. And the composer, at each such event, resignedly lowering his head, let the wave pass, and drawing new breath, continued on his way, murmuring to himself: "If it is unperformable today, we will see tomorrow; if my music has no 'common sense,' it may have another sense." Experience has proved how right he was. Already at the last dress rehearsal, the same artists who a few days earlier had been cursing the composer and his work could not resist the force of this music, whose forms were finally being made clear for the first time, and saluted the composer several times with lively acclamations. Today these family quarrels have been completely forgotten on both sides; the performers have only a deep admiration, and a satisfaction felt by the composer for the intelligence and the eminent talent of his interpreters.

Since it is the invariable custom in France to make comparisons, everyone today is asking whether or not the new score is superior to that of *Robert le Diable;* we will avoid questions on this subject by saying frankly our preference for *Les Huguenots.*

We are far from having a deep enough understanding of this work to be able to appreciate it properly, as we have said, but taken together, it seems to us to have a more elevated style, more severe, more noble, and above all more grandiose than its predecessor.

The actors, the choir and the orchestra were rivals in zeal and talent. The performance was among the most remarkable, under the double heading of intelligence and precision. Levasseur showed himself to be what he always is: a singer of the first rank and an actor of much merit; everyone noticed the progress of Dérivis, in the way he spoke several scenes of the first act (which are the best of his role), and above all his perfect pronunciation which let not a single word be lost. Serda and Wartel, too, performed their tasks equally well. Mesdames Gras and Flecheux, in two roles full of vocalises and gracious details, both demonstrated much taste and a rare ability to surmount the often great difficulties of this music. For Nourrit and Mademoiselle Falcon, they were both admirable; one must see them, and hear them, in the famous act-4 duet, in order to understand the perfection with which this beautiful scene is rendered. They are indeed expressing passion, love, despair, terror, anxiety, but without ceasing to be noble in their attitudes, natural in their gestures, and without letting even the most vehement expression take anything away from the perfection of their singing. Each of them stopped just short of the point beyond which there is only the caricature of passion. Called for by the audience as the curtain fell, they returned with Levasseur to receive the bravos of the whole hall, which they so much deserved.

The ballets are short, very fortunately: the scenery and the costumes do the greatest honor to the wise taste of M. Duponchel, and several sets have a magnificent effect. An immense success!

From Berlioz's article in the *Revue et gazette musicale de Paris,* March 6, 1836, pp. 73–77.

9. GEORGE SAND ON *LES HUGUENOTS*

In her Lettres d'un voyageur, *the novelist writes an imaginary letter to Meyerbeer on the subject of* Les Huguenots.

It was natural that these imaginary strains should take, in my mind's ear, the form of the beautiful psalm in the opera of *"Les Huguenots,"* and while I fancied, too, that I heard, without, the furious cries and the close firing of the Catholics, a tall figure passed before mine eyes—one of the noblest figures of Drama—one of the finest personifications of the religious idea which the arts have produced in our time—the Marcel of Meyerbeer. And I saw, face to face, that statue of iron, in its strong buff suit, animated by the breath from above which the composer had bade descend and give it life.

Save in the last two acts the character of Raoul, with all your skill, is unable to rise from the weight of commonplace insipidity with which M. Scribe has laden it. Even Nourrit's true sensibility and rare intelligence contended in vain against the sentimental and silly nonentity of the hero, who is "a thorough victim of circumstances," as the romance writers phrase it. But how the part rises in the fourth act—how it tells in the great scene, which (prudery and objection put aside) I find so pathetic, so intensely mournful, so fearful! ...What a duet! What a dialogue! How has the musician wept, implored, raved, and conquered, where the author should have done it!

George Sand, *Lettres d'un voyageur,* in Henry Chorley, trans., *Music and Manners in France and Germany,* 3 vols. (London: Longman, Brown, Green, and Longmans, 1844), 1: 179–80, 185.

The first work presented by M. Duponchel was the opera *Les Huguenots* (February 29, 1836). Before arriving at their destination on stage, the *Huguenots* suffered certain accidents and delays en route.

Wanting to achieve a second *Robert le Diable,* his California, but aware of the wise and modest slowness of Meyerbeer, M. Véron made a contract with him. By this contract, the maestro undertook to deliver his opera of the *Huguenots* on a certain day; if, on that day, he did not deliver his work, he would pay a penalty of 30,000 francs.

On his side, the director undertook to perform the piece within a fixed time from the date of its arrival.

On the day appointed, *Les Huguenots* was not ready, but the penalty was ready; Meyerbeer complied, paid the 30,000 francs which it would certainly have been more generous and clever not to accept. . . .

Meyerbeer, we have already said, was the most disinterested of men. But the process had wounded him. As long as M. Véron remained at the Opéra, *Les Huguenots* would not be performed there. Meyerbeer would never pardon M. Véron. Although he was innocent, and Meyerbeer's friend, M. Duponchel did not triumph without suffering from Meyerbeer's legitimate grudge; finally the maestro bent; he gave the *Huguenots* to M. Duponchel, and he found ways of making it known that in all these debates, the thing that concerned him least of all was the question of money.

The forfeit paid by Meyerbeer had been 30,000 francs. M. Duponchel wanted to give it back, but Meyerbeer only accepted 20,000. M. Véron having actually cashed only 20,000, M. Duponchel owed only that which had been taken by M. Véron.

But what had become of the other 10,000 francs? The other 10,000 had been given to M. Scribe, the author of the words, and one of the signers of the contract, and his position was not too bad. M. Scribe could not lose, he could only win. If Meyerbeer failed in his promise, M. Scribe gets 10,000 francs! if M. Véron fails in his, M. Scribe gets another 10,000 francs. And it is good to hold on to what one has: M. Scribe did not give back the 10,000 francs of his collaborator Meyerbeer, who had the delicacy not to ask for it, which however did not prevent M. Scribe from claiming from M. Duponchel the usual fee of 1,000 francs per act: here, five acts, so 5,000 francs; with the result that even before the premiere M. Scribe had already received 15,000 francs. Not too shabby.

Les Huguenots was destined to demonstrate the generosity of Meyerbeer. The scene in the fourth act between *Raoul* and *Valentine* had been written by M. Scribe in that poetic style typified by this couplet:

Un vieux soldat sait souffrir et se taire
Sans murmurer.

[An old soldier knows how to suffer in silence
without complaining.]

Meyerbeer was worried by this somewhat ludicrous poetry; he asked for some changes. M. Scribe declined, proud of his wares, and finally refused any sort of alteration. Too good a judge to change his opinion, but too polite to insist, Meyerbeer begged a poet, a true poet, to come to the aid of Raoul and Valentine, condemned as they were to M. Scribe's verses. Emile Deschamps had pity on their sad fate, and he rewrote the grand scene of the fourth act.

Meyerbeer wished to recognize this act of kindness, but did not know how. He had the delicate idea to give to Emile Deschamps, from his own royalties, an author's portion, a portion which Deschamps still receives today.

Les Huguenots proved to be worthy brothers of *Robert le Diable*. Enthusiasm was divided between Nourrit-*Raoul* and mademoiselle Falcon-*Valentine*. A young girl, Maria Flécheux, given the role of the page Urbin [*sic*], demonstrated a magnificent voice and Quasimodo legs. Jarry would not have said of her what he said of mademoiselle A., that her legs saved her. Poor Maria Flécheux! she did not live long; she died quite young; not from grief, not a victim of Meyerbeer's music, as has been seriously reported: she died of lung ailments, of that terrible disease that needs no one to accomplish its work of destruction.

That year 1836 was a good one for M. Duponchel. February 29, *Les Huguenots*; June 1, *Le Diable boîteux* [a ballet]; August 10, *the return of Taglioni* after a nine months' absence; September 20, *La Fille du Danube*. What magnificent box-office receipts! . . . what regrets, what remorse for M. Véron!

Charles de Boigne, *Petits mémoires de l'opéra* (Paris, Librairie nouvelle, 1857), pp. 120–23.

11. HENRY CHORLEY ON THE OPÉRA AND *LES HUGUENOTS* IN LATE 1836
On the Orchestra

The impression made on me by the orchestra that evening [a performance of Louise Bertin's *Esmeralda* at the Opéra in late November 1836], and deepened by every subsequent visit, will never fade away. . . . What a brilliancy is there in its violins, when their strength is put forth in such sparkling passages as accompany the Fishermen's Chorus in "La Muette" or wind up the overture to "Guillaume Tell"! What a clearness and body of support, and pertinence of answer, and sensitiveness of expression in the violoncellos! Nor are the wind instruments inferior, though perhaps less dazzling in their regularity: if their tone be not of the highest quality, and partake somewhat of that thin shrillness which seems generic to all wind-tones (the human voice included) in France, they are still admirable for their certainty, for their freedom from grossness, and for the subdued but not subordinate part they take in the dialogue of the score. When matters are pushed to an extremity, they can speak loudly enough, and still not too loudly. Indeed, the double drums allowed for,— and these, of late, have seemed to my ear less wooden and overweening than formerly,— I think that the charge of noise brought against the French orchestra is a popular fallacy. Powerful it is, but the foundation of stringed instruments is so substantially clear and firm, that the tissue (to speak fancifully) never loses it coherence by the ornaments and embroideries assuming an undue prominence. Then there is an uniform but well-proportioned care in finish, and consent of execution—an understanding with the chorus—and understanding with the singers—a sensitiveness to every nicest gradation of time, slackened or hastened, never displayed by our most sensitive English orchestras,—which carry on the enchantment; it is a machine, in short, in perfect order, and under the guidance of experience and intellect;—for these, as regards French music, are thoroughly personified in M. Habeneck.

Nothing can exceed his perfect sway over his forces. Though he directs with his violin bow, I have never seen him use it; and by the exquisite neatness and precision of the least important or most unmanageable instruments (the piccoli, for example), as they enter, not scramble, into their parts when the composition demands them, it may be seen that his presence is every where—that his method and meaning have pervaded the whole hundred he commands ere they are paraded before the public (16–20).

On the House

There is a certain pleasure in seeing a place filled by its assembly—in watching vacant benches and gloomy corners, one after the other, painted with forms and colours, which turn out to be human beings. . . . If there be any who share this with me, I would invite them to take stalle or box at L'Académie a quarter of an hour before M. Habeneck makes his appearance; not, however, to watch the bright-looking exquisitely-dressed ladies gliding into the balcony—not to catch snatches of the odd, blithe, vehement dialogue which goes on in the parterre—nor yet to give themselves up to the perusal of the entr'acte of the evening. That interesting publication I would fain supersede for one night by offering a brief study of the drop-curtain of the grand opera.

This is not one of those venerable veils of dingy green baize, the sight of which has awakened such an undefined and thrilling curiosity within many a young playgoer on his first night; nor yet a splendid piece of mock upholstery, like that which has so long swayed to and fro to conceal the Grisis and Rubini, the machinists and the loungers of our own opera stage. Neither is it the old most irrational design of eight mounted cavaliers, preparing from a central pillar to ride down eight flights of steps, which used to give me an impression of insecurity and discomfort whenever I entered L'Académie, sufficient to distract me from all speculations on the three tiny fingers, or the one bright eye, which are never wanting to both of the two peepholes of the toile. The new curtain in the Rue Lepelletier is a grand historical composition, representing none other than Louis Quatorze signing the charter which he granted to Lulli for the establishment of a national opera (pp. 23–25).

I must see Meyerbeer's operas as well as hear them, and at L'Académie Royale; and all arrangements and transcripts of them have but a value, in proportion as Fancy is pliant, and willing to call up all the pride, pomp, and circumstances which belong to their representation in Paris. . . . To those who are not familiar with these works in their birthplace there is danger of seeming extravagant, perhaps even unintelligible; in offering some account of them; while those familiar with the music of Paris have already either accepted them as chefs d'oeuvre, or rejected them as confused and elaborate masses of noise and pageantry (pp. 45–46).

On Nourrit

The very elegance so highly prized and loudly regretted in poor Adolphe Nourrit by a portion of the Parisian cognoscenti, bordered so closely upon a mannered over-grace and over-sweetness, that I never heard that fine singer, and never saw that elegant and careful actor, without feeling that neither his clear and metallic voice—nasal in its falsetto—nor his graceful postures, belonged to the greatest school of art. There was a smile when he threw his head back to launch a mot at some one behind him—a mincing elongation of his "Oui"-s and "Patrie"-s and the other sounds, which sung in French are intrinsically offensive, that annoyed my insular eyes and ears, as imparting to grace and sentiment and emphasis a touch of make-believe, destructive of their effect. He appears on recollection to have been more conscious of his handsome person, and high voice, and artistic accomplishments, than any one I have ever seen on the French stage—to have attitudinized more premeditatedly—to have declaimed with more of that conventional exactness, which, as English ears unhappily know, can become so utterly intolerable—than the generality of his brethren (p. 63).

. . . When I heard Nourrit, too, his best days had long passed: it was a very few months before his departure—the fame of his rival [Duprez] cast its shadow before; he looked feverish and anxious, and as it was he favoured the plaudits with a jealous ear, which could detect whether one hand less was raised than had acknowledged his triumphs the night before. But while the public was listening to him, it was already busily talking of Duprez (pp. 63–64)!

On Les Huguenots

The morning scene of the cavaliers in the first act, with its crowd of young nobles in courtly dresses, not forgetting the pair playing at chess in the left hand corner, with all the gentlemanly abstraction of real life, who may be there seen even unto this day;—the rich terrace under the walls and above the moat of Chenonceau, with its imposing flight of steps, down which the court of Marguerite is to sweep in all the number and gorgeousness of a real court procession;—the third act in the Pré aux Clercs, with its apparently countless multitude of people;—the gay bridal procession of the ill-starred Valentine;—the arm waving a wild torch out of the upper window of the cabaret, when the fray between Catholics and protestants breaks out;—Queen Margaret, on her white palfrey (not forgetting that property of Queen Elizabeth, on which M. Puff laid so much stress, to wit, her side-saddle);—the throng of Bohemian dancers in their little scarlet caps and black plumes de coq;—and the illuminated gondola which glides in "with harp, and pipe, and symphony," to bear the bride to the arms of her unloved lord and master:—I find all these things, I say, journalized in precedence of the grand septuor, or the magnificent fourth act (pp. 171–72).

Meyerbeer's master work, to be enjoyed as it deserves, demands not only the execution, but also the pomp of the Parisian stage (p. 173).

"*Les Huguenots*" . . . unites in itself the most striking features of the chef's d'oeuvre of French Opera. . . . A local colour has been given to some of its scenes—witness the opening to the third act, with the revelry of the Clercs de la Basoche, and the Catholic litanies to the Virgin, the song of Coligni's soldiers, and the simple but impressive "couvre feu," in the Prè aux Clercs (p. 176).

On Marcel

The old servitor becomes not so much an embodied thought as a melody on two legs! In most cases his coming is indicated by the same psalm tune; which, as we know it be one of Luther's, must of course denote him to be a Lutheran (p. 187).

Chorley, *Music and Manners,* vol. 1.

12. THE MISE-EN-SCÈNE

Following is a translation of the introductory description and the first act of the manuscript mise-en-scène.

Les Huguenots
Grand Opéra en cinq Actes
Paroles de Mr Scribe
Musique de Mr Meyerbeer
Mise en scène
par Mr Duverger père, 1836

Decorations

ACT 1

Gothic palace painted on the backdrop, gardens in front. Rich salon with three Doors open at the back, well-lit; interior window, in the foreground the room where Valentine is, to the left of the public.

Seat	Chair
Seat	Table
Table	Chair

Note: Where the grand opera Gustave has been performed, the salon of the first act can usefully be used by opening the three rear doors opening onto the garden.

ACT 2

Superb Gothic castle painted on the backdrop, with high walls surrounded by moats full of pure water where there are trees, a sort of palace of Armide [an enchantress]. By going down one of the slopes of the garden, to the left of the public, one arrives at the water's edge, but on the right of the garden is a vast and long staircase of marble, which leads to the upper part of the garden, from where Valentine, Raoul, and his entourage, arrive. This beautiful place must be carefully lit.

To the public's left, the Queen's seat.   Staircase side.

Cushions

ACT 3

Decoration of the 5th act of *Le pré aux clercs*

On the backdrop is painted the Old Louvre and a part of Paris in the distance, in the foreground the Seine; several sections of water are visible, on which boats are painted.

A handsome sunset.

A huge tree

3d plan: A church	Table. A cabaret.
entranceway	Gothic windows
Stools. Chairs	Table
	Seat

At the end of the act a rich and grand launch in the form of a gondola gilded and decorated and garnished with lit and domed lanterns, arrives on the 4th level in the water, bringing the wedding party, lords and a good number of musicians. {Use the decor of the 5th act of Le pré aux clercs with a few slight changes.}

ACT 4

Grand Gothic salon, severe and rich.

Door at the rear

Window and large curtain   Embrasure
behind which Raoul hides   Drapery

Valentine's chamber   Table on which
Sofa   are two torches

                    Seat   Window through
                    Seat   which Raoul escapes,
                    Seat   1st plan
                    Seat (for Valentine)

ACT 5

Superb palace, limited to 2 and a half plans, lit at the 2d plan by two chandeliers painted on the backdrop. When the nobles run for vengeance, a backdrop is lowered between the

1st and 2d chassis, which cover the palace. This is a peristyle interior of the Protestant church, lit as by night. This is for the scene of the great trio, which begins the denouement and facilitates the set of the finale. At the entry of the murderers, of Raoul, Valentine, and Marcel, this curtain disappears and reveals old Paris by night, lit by moonlight and a starry sky.

Marguerite arrives at the death of Valentine, of Raoul, and of Marcel, she is in the great litter richly adorned carried by eight domestics and lit by torches. Margaret can be played by a woman in a dress of black velours, with a toque of white satin, to spare the actress playing the role, who finishes in the 2d act, from having to stay.

It is a small pantomime action at night, for this disastrous night is lit only by the stars and by torches.

Accessories

Act 1: Tablecloths, napkins, place settings, vases, seats, two balls for playing, checker- or chessboard, letter for the valet, glasses, plates, etc. [blindfold]

Act 2: Screen. Gothic fans, seats, cushions.

Act 3: Glasses, bottles or jugs of wine, pitchers, stools, halberds, bells, torches, candlesticks, candelabra for the tables.

Act 4: Seats, sofa, large bell, for the distant alarm, little bell, instruments at the right pitch for the stage band, swords for the Catholics, daggers.

Act 5: Lighted torches for the murderers, 1 white handkerchief, 1 small white scarf for Valentine, muskets, loaded arquebuses, for the murderers, lit flambeaux.

ACT I

SCENE 1

In a vast salon, rich, having two great casement windows open and the door at the back also open, giving a view of gardens, with a chateau at the back, a number of young Catholic noblemen are conversing as the curtain rises, others play chess or checkers, others, outside, play ball (eliminated); the tables, right and left, have been set, they are covered with vases, flowers, plates.

De Tavannes, de Nevers, de Cossé, and other nobles dressed à la Henri II, are waiting for a new [illegible]. Soon the ball-players outside are seen to greet Raoul who enters from the back and receives the salutations of the company; he takes the center of the stage.

SCENE 2

Lords   De Cossé   De Tavannes   Raoul   De Nevers   Thorré(?)
Prompter

Servants bring a table into the middle of the stage, covered with china, pastries, meat, and fruit. It seats 7 or 8 persons. The principal diners sit at this table, the others at the tables to right and left, according to the number of persons.

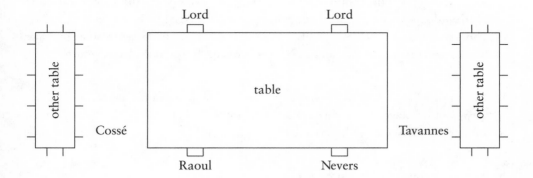

Raoul is seated when he begins the speech which precedes the Romance, and he rises to finish it. The nobles are near him, then follows the romance, after which everyone sits down again. The servants serve drink, the wine sparkles in the glasses, when Marcel enters at the rear, after the Romance, comes down to the public's right, seeking his master Raoul.

SCENE 3

Diners seated. Marcel—Raoul—de Nevers—Nobles.

Raoul has risen to speak with Marcel, the others remain at the table. After Marcel's first Lutheran chant, four nobles get up, the servants remove the center table without any noise, which they take away upstage.

Then follows Marcel's air *Pif paf*. De Nevers sits down again.

Valentine, covered by her black mask, crosses upstage outside, followed by a page; she moves from the right to the public's left.

SCENE 4

The valet enters and addresses de Nevers. Then de Nevers leaves upstage to greet the woman who has been announced. The announcement can be made by one of the nobles, in which case the valet will whisper to him.

SCENE 5

When de Nevers leaves, the nobles begin to chatter, they come and go, Raoul strolls upstage. After the musical piece, they look at the left window, where a little green curtain floats, and they go to see out of curiosity, a few step up on stools, one on the table, and they say "Ah! Je la vois! Attraits divins!" ("I see her: what divine features!"). Raoul, who was pensive, seated, goes to see also, and cries "Oh! Grand dieu!" and comes down to the apron. Then:

Nobles
1   2   3
Nobles   Raoul   Marcel

At the end of the choral passage, one sees de Nevers giving his hand to Valentine upstage, outdoors, they cross slowly from the public's left to right. The nobles watch when the choir sings "Silence! Je les entends." Everyone moves all the way left, so as to make visible the passage of Valentine and de Nevers at the back. Soon de Nevers returns.

SCENE 6

De Nevers says his récit "Il faut rompre l'hymen" ("I must break my engagement"), etc. all the way downstage. Meanwhile the nobles have moved all the way back, and return to compliment de Nevers on his good luck.

SCENE 7

In the distance one sees Urbain, page of Queen Marguerite.
Position:

		2		4		
		Tavannes	3	The Page		
Nobles			de Nevers	5		6
1				Cossé		Raoul
Nobles					seated	7
						Marcel

When the page addresses Raoul to give him the letter, Raoul rises, takes it, comes to the center, reads with surprise and smiles and then passes the letter to de Nevers, at these words: "Lisez vous-même" ("Read it for yourself").
Position:

		3			
		de Nevers			
Noble	2		5		
1	Tavannes				
			4	The Page	
Nobles		Raoul		6	
			Marcel		

The finale continues, and before the end, we see at the back of the salon, outdoors, three men in black, with black masks, one of them with a white headband and a white handkerchief. The nobles are a bit restless. The Page and Raoul leave just as the curtain falls. The public sees Raoul being blindfolded. The nobles laugh and watch with surprise. Marcel hopes that this adventure will finish well for Raoul.

End of the First Act

Bibliothèque Historique de la Ville de Paris, Association Régisseurs Theatrales MES 53 (1); facsimile in H. Robert Cohen, *The Original Staging Manuals for Ten Operatic Premieres, 1824–1843*, (Musical Life in Nineteenth-Century France, vol. 6) (Stuyvesant, N.Y.: Pendragon, 1998), pp. 133–71.

One thing is certain, that something has happened
at Bayreuth, something which our grandchildren
and great-grandchildren will remember.

—*Tchaikovsky*

CHAPTER FOUR

Richard Wagner, *Das Rheingold*

Bayreuth, August 13, 1876, 7:00 P.M.

*F*or some reason there are opera lovers who do not love Wagner, and there are others for whom Wagner is the only composer worth listening to. It is certainly true that Wagner is the most discussed opera composer who has ever lived. Much of his influence began during his own lifetime, but the later effects of Wagner's music on that of others, and perhaps more importantly the use and misuse of his music by the National Socialist Party in Germany, have made his operas, and to some extent his world-view, a matter of continuing controversy. Wagner as a man was a hero to the Nazis, owing mostly to his virulent anti-Semitic writings and to the ideology he built up around himself. But in his time he was seen as a genius, and as a musician he is nothing short of a genius.

What is there not to like in the music? Perhaps the fact that there are not many songs in the later operas: there are few set-piece arias (with the exception of the pieces specifically composed as songs in *Die Meistersinger*); there are no thrilling ensembles (duets in *Tristan* excepted); there is not much that is easily excerpted. It does not seem to be music to which one goes for the tunes. And yet the Wagnerian singer is often the most admired, the rarest to find: the "Wagnerian soprano," the "Heldentenor," the voices that have the power and stamina to perform a full evening's role as Siegfried or Wotan or Brünnhilde.

Wagner, never modest, thought of himself as a successor to Beethoven, especially the Beethoven of the Ninth Symphony. And in a way he was right, because as he saw it, Beethoven was trying in that symphony to give voice to the orchestra, and that is also what Wagner means to do. The action of the opera is really in the pit. The symphonic development of the orchestral music, the many moments when characters advance the plot by things that are not said but are thought or felt, and that are heard by the audience, are among the many marvels of his music.

Wagner would have been reluctant to admit it, but he was also the successor of the grand opera of Paris. He worked in Paris, composed his early operas *(Rienzi, Der fliegende Holländer, Tannhaüser, Lohengrin)* under its influence, and learned a great deal about the French style that he put to good use in his later works. Like Meyerbeer, whom he came to despise (though he had once written a favorable review of *Les Huguenots*), Wagner is a Romantic composer, but he carried certain of the Romantic tendencies, especially the expansion of traditional harmony by delayed and unexpected resolutions, to a culminating extreme. He was a consummation of German Romanticism, and he created operatic and musical forms that have affected every composer since his time.

Wagner was an egotist and a pleasure-seeker; he disproves the often-held opinion that the personality of the musician can be heard in the music. And yet he inspired the finest musicians of his day; his music had an indelible effect on later composers; he revolutionized theatrical practice; and his literary influence extended to the psychological interior stream of consciousness. He was idolized in his own time, and by the end of the nineteenth century the pilgrimage to his Festspielhaus at Bayreuth was essential to anyone serious about the musical world. There were guidebooks to Bayreuth, explaining in detail all the little recurring themes that one needed to know in order to "understand" a Wagner opera. Albert Lavignac's *Le voyage artistique à Bayreuth* also includes the names of everybody who went there—names like Debussy (who was haunted by Wagner while composing *Pelléas et Mélisande*).

At the center of Wagner's idea of opera is a fusion of poetry, music, and drama into what he called a *Gesamtkunstwerk*, a Total Work of Art. As to the poetry, Wagner created his own librettos, fashioning most of them from the timeless tales of Norse mythology, with their gods and mortals, their fundamental mythic values, and their whopping good stories that make excellent theater. The poetry is based on the ancient alliterative verse of Teutonic poetry (it is found also in "Beowulf"), where the repeated alliterations of beginning consonants gives a connection within the line, and from one line to the next:

> Sorglose Schmiede
> Schufen wir sonst

The music, too, is based on the oneness of music and drama. The music is in some ways more like a symphony than an opera. There are no arias, no long melismas and ornamented songs: singers are expected to declaim their words in a sort of heightened speech-rhythm, in association with the orchestra. The singer's challenges are those of power and stamina. There are no ensembles in his *Ring* cycle, no choruses (until the very end); the drama is in the words, and in the orchestra.

Wagner does like to use ancient Teutonic musical forms (including the bar-form, the song—like those in *Die Meistersinger*—that has a repeated opening section and a closing section not repeated: anybody who can remember the tune of the Lutheran chorale "A Mighty Fortress" or "Sleepers, wake" knows at least one bar-form), but his music is mostly known for having both an outer and an inner aspect. The outer aspect is the spoken word, the action on stage, what gets sung. The inner aspect is what adds so much richness to Wagner's music dramas: the emotions and thoughts of the characters, which take place in the music of the orchestra, not only by the general mood of the music, but by an intricate pattern of recurring themes that are more or less closely connected with persons, events, moods, and actions, and whose appearance can tell us what a character is thinking about.

Such a recurring theme is usually called a *Leitmotiv;* these themes are found especially in the operas of *Der Ring des Nibelungen* and in his other later operas *(Tristan, Die Meistersinger, Parsifal)*. There is nothing original, of course, in the use of recurring themes. Plenty of composers had used them before Wagner. The chorale ("A Mighty Fortress") that recurs throughout *Les Huguenots* is just one example. Berlioz used them in the *Symphonie fantastique,* Schumann in his symphonies and elsewhere, Debussy in *Pelléas,* and on and on. But they are used to particular psychological and musical effect in Wagner, and often long stretches of music are entirely made up of versions of a small number of these themes.

A Leitmotiv is characterized by its memorable shortness—a chord, a characteristic rhythm. Some are basically fixed, recurring in the same form, and usually standing for objects: Valhalla, the sword, Hunding. Some are highly malleable, sometimes so indistinct that we can't quite be sure that we are hearing them. These tend to be those of emotions, such as pity and love. There are about twenty such themes that recur in all four of the *Ring* operas, and about thirty others. Though Wagner himself did not define them, and although he did not call them by any name (he did refer to a "web of themes" is his last essays), there can be no doubt that they are central to his music. They inform everything that we hear, and we are taught everything we need to know as we go along, so that the theme of Valhalla is introduced to us as we *see* what the music is about. It becomes so clear and fixed in our memories that when somebody later refers to Valhalla, and we hear the same music, it reinforces what we already know. And still later, if somebody thinks about Valhalla without mentioning it, we will be inside his mind. So the orchestra in one sense is the primary factor in the drama—the heart, the unspoken center—of which the words are only a part.

Wagner uses both harmony and melody in ways that contribute to the detailed excitement of the moment and to the overall unity of his conception. Recurring themes are used to express action, and to advance it by their manipulation and development; but they also contribute to an overall sense of unity by their continual presence throughout a work. Likewise, harmony can contribute to action when it is used to characterize and develop individual motives, but harmony also serves Wagner in the creation of very large musical forms. He is able to keep a musical event up in the air for a very long time by suspending the eventual and longed-for cadence, often with the use of pedal points and by deceptive harmonic motions. These larger shapes, which may be as long as an entire act, contribute to our sense of motion, our idea that everything is of a piece—though I'm not sure that the average operagoer can—or should—perceive them consciously. They are there, they work, and we go away satisfied that this is not a moment-to-moment patchwork of often-repeated incomplete tunes.

Das Rheingold is not, in fact, an opera. It is the evening-long prelude to a three-evening music drama. Thus it is part of a much larger work, and it was conceived with that in mind. This is not to say that it is not a good and complete evening's entertainment —it has everything that an opera needs—but that it was conceived as a drama, not an opera. After his Romantic *Lohengrin* (1848), Wagner insisted that his later works would not be operas, but dramas. He might regret that his later works are, in fact, usually considered operas—they are played in opera houses and are discussed in books about opera. And of course operas are dramas, but these particular operas are a special sort of drama, and a special sort of opera.

Background

Richard Wagner, who always spoke with a strong Leipzig accent, was sixty-three years old in the summer of 1876, and he had worked long and hard to get where he was. Some would say that he had trampled and used and misled people in his climb, others

This 1877 photograph of Wagner may give some idea of his fierce dedication to his ideals, and perhaps also of his ability to mesmerize those around him.

that he was singleminded, with a burning artistic flame that could not be quenched. In any event, he managed, after many years of effort, to attain what no composer ever had: a theater specially built for the single purpose of performing his work.

He had always been a man of the theater, and a man of strong opinion. Working as chorus-master, répétiteur, and conductor in the opera houses of Würzburg, Magdeburg, Königsberg, and Riga, Wagner had broad experience of the opera of his time. He knew, and conducted, works of Mozart and Beethoven, Auber and Meyerbeer, Rossini and Bellini. He composed his early operas in traditional German *(Die Feen)* or French *(Das Liebesverbot, Rienzi)* style, and was impressed by the Riga opera house, which was wooden and relatively unornamented, with a raked auditorium and a deep orchestra pit—and where the house lights were lowered during the performance.

He had done his apprenticeship, paid his dues, and made his mistakes. He had had dismal years in Paris (1839–42), where he failed to make an impression, despite Meyerbeer's recommendations. He survived by making musical arrangements and writing journalistic prose.

As assistant conductor in Dresden from 1842, Wagner had two of his works performed: the French-style *Rienzi*, and his newer *Der fliegende Holländer* (The flying Dutchman) which attempted something innovative in terms of musical continuity and the avoidance of self-contained musical numbers. *Rienzi* was a success, but it was *The Flying Dutchman* that set the pace for the future. Wagner's literary concern for Norse and German mythology, which was to be at the root of all his subsequent operas, led first to *Tannhäuser* (Dresden, 1845) and *Lohengrin,* produced by Franz Liszt in Weimar in 1848.

Wagner began to produce the series of polemical articles and essays that continued throughout his life, that got him into trouble, and that give us a remarkable view of his thinking (and posing). He was a man of the theater all his life. He cared deeply about singing, acting, gesture, settings, and all aspects of the theater that, in his view, worked together to make the supreme artwork that is opera. It was not until the *Ring,* though, that he had the opportunity to put all his theories into practice in what should have been ideal circumstances. Even then he was disappointed.

A combination of inappropriate complaining in print and active participation in an 1849 uprising in Dresden got Wagner exiled, and he spent a number of years in Switzerland (he returned to Germany only in 1860). In his banishment he read widely, and he befriended the philologist and philosopher Friedrich Nietzsche, who for a time was among his strongest supporters. He also wrote some of the literary pieces that are a sort of position paper for his later operatic works: "The Artwork of the Future" and "Opera and Drama," in which he envisioned a drama arising from the German people, based on myth, and re-unifying the arts. (The trend in these years toward German unification gave his writings a special resonance.) And he conceived the *Ring.*

Wagner imagined a work called *Siegfrieds Tod* in 1848, and he envisioned a temporary wooden theater for its production as a music festival, at the end of which the theater would be pulled down. The original work gradually expanded to three evenings with a prelude, and by 1852 the text was complete (though none of the music was written). By early 1854, Wagner had printed a version of the text of the whole *Ring* and had drafted all the music of *Das Rheingold.* And the original conception of the theater for its performance ultimately resulted in the Bayreuth Festspielhaus.

The disastrous premiere of *Tannhäuser* in Paris (1861) did little to encourage Wagner to seek traditional operatic venues. Although opera was essentially a social and urban phenomenon, Wagner conceived the idea of a rural festival, with admission free to all. He had come to regret the imperfections in the staging of his own and other operas and was theorizing about ideal—but probably not realistic—circumstances. He thought of his festival, and his later music dramas, as opposing the destructive forces in modern society.

By 1862, when Wagner published the poem *Der Ring des Nibelungen,* he expressed his desire for a theater in a small town, and although it was all a pipe dream at the time, his vision corresponds closely to what ultimately happened.

> Here a provisional theatre would be erected, as simple as possible, perhaps only of wood, and with the interior designed only for artistic purposes. I should confer with an experienced and intelligent architect as to a plan for such a house, with amphitheatrical arrangement of the seats, and the decided advantage of an invisible orchestra. Here then, in the early spring months, the leading dramatic singers, chosen from the ensemble of German opera houses, would be assembled, in order to study the various parts of my stage work, entirely uninterrupted by any other claims upon their artistic abilities.
>
> On the days appointed for performance—of which I have in mind

three in all—the German public would be invited to be present, as these performances, like those of our large music festivals, are to be made accessible, not only to the partial public of any one city, but to all friends of art, far and near.

A complete performance of the dramatic poem in question would take place in midsummer—on a fore-evening *Das Rheingold* and on the three following evenings the chief dramas *Die Walküre, Siegfried* and *Götterdämmerung.*

To complete the impression of such a performance, I should lay great stress upon an invisible orchestra, which it would be possible to effect by the architectural illusion of an amphitheatrical arrangement of the auditorium.

Such an undertaking could only be done, wrote Wagner, with the support of a great prince. "But where will such a prince be found?" The patron appeared in the person of King Ludwig II of Bavaria. Two months after his accession, at the age of nineteen, the Wagner-mad king summoned his fifty-year-old idol. Wagner's relationship to Ludwig in the succeeding years was fruitful for him, but difficult. Ludwig wanted an enormous grand theater in Munich, but Wagner's experience with the premiere of *Tristan und Isolde* in 1865 in Munich, where the orchestra nearly overwhelmed the singers, confirmed his resolve for a temporary structure in the country. Ludwig wanted to produce *Meistersinger* and the *Ring* in Munich; Wagner had other ideas.

Matters grew worse between Wagner and Ludwig; the king insisted on performances in Munich of *Rheingold* and *Walküre,* against Wagner's wishes and which he did not attend. He actually delayed composing the last parts of the *Ring* so as to deprive Ludwig of the possibility of performing them in other circumstances than those Wagner had in mind.

And there were other problems: Wagner was in political trouble with officials who disapproved of the king's Wagnerian building plans; Wagner himself aroused disapproval by his affair with Cosima von Bülow, the daughter of Franz Liszt and the wife of the court Kapellmeister Hans von Bülow. (She gave birth to their daughter Isolde during rehearsals for *Tristan.*) And in 1865, Wagner went again into exile in Switzerland.

Cosima came to live with Wagner in Tribschen, where she gave birth to their son Siegfried. In 1869, after her divorce (Wagner's wife, Minna, had died), she married him and became a powerful force in his life and after it; it was she who saw to it that the Bayreuth tradition continued essentially unchanged until 1910 (when Siegfried Wagner took over the running of the festival; Cosima died in 1930). Wagner's descendants are still dealing with his legacy.

Preparations

BAYREUTH

Wagner's Festspielhaus at Bayreuth, about 125 miles north of Munich, is perhaps the greatest monument to any individual composer. It is the realization of what might be thought of as one of the three inseparable elements in Wagner's works: poetry, music, and representation. The actual effect on the audience created by the staging, settings, acting, and costumes, not to mention the sound of the music and the poetry, could only be accomplished, in Wagner's view, by a purpose-built theater. And he built it. It was decidedly and intentionally simple—Garnier's opera house in Paris, which opened in 1875, cost seventy times more.

The theater as seen by visitors in 1876 was about a half-mile outside the town, on a gentle hill with a higher wooded hill behind it, on which stood a round tower. A road ran through fields to the theater, from whose terrace there was a good view of the town.

A view of Bayreuth from the Festspielhaus, 1876. Joseph Bennett wrote in the *Daily Telegraph*: "The site has been well chosen, some half-a-mile beyond the skirt of the town, and on the top of a gentle eminence which itself is backed by a wooded hill, crowned with a round tower. Rather a pretty way runs thither, the tree-shaded road being flanked by corn-fields and gardens, while the little terrace in front of the building commands an interesting view of the quaint old town and the hills beyond—a view none the less German because the most prominent object in the foreground, next to a lunatic asylum, is a big brewery."

WAGNER, *DAS RHEINGOLD*

Wagner himself had moved to Bayreuth in 1872 and lived there until he died. His house, Wahnfried, was paid for by King Ludwig, and Wagner lived there from 1874. It was the only house he ever owned. Partially destroyed in 1945, the house is now a Wagner museum, and Wagner himself is buried on the grounds.

"Of all the dull towns I imagine Bayreuth, in its normal state, to be the dullest," wrote Joseph Bennett for the *London Daily Telegraph* in 1876. Bayreuth had about 18,000 inhabitants, mostly Protestant. The town boasted a splendid eighteenth-century theater (the former Margrave's Theater of the so-called New Palace); the home of the Romantic Jean-Paul Richter; a substantial insane asylum; and a large brewery. It also quartered a large garrison of soldiers.

Wagner had visited Bayreuth in 1871 (the year of German unification) with a view to using the Margrave's Theater for his dramas; he liked the town for its small size and its isolation, but not the older theater, despite its large stage. The town authorities, alarmed at losing Wagner's festival, made serious efforts to keep him there. They allocated a piece of land for a new theater and helped to organize, under the local banker Friedrich Feustel, a committee to oversee finances and help raise money. It was easy to see the advantages of hosting such a famous composer, whose festival would attract many performers and visitors who would need housing, meals, and souvenirs.

The estimate—like most estimates, woefully inadequate—was that it would take 300,000 thaler (900,000 marks) to build a new theater and present three cycles of the *Ring*. What that amounts to today is difficult to estimate, but it is on the order of several million dollars.

Where was the money to come from? Initial fund-raising was by patron's certificates, a scheme devised and run by the pianist (and Liszt pupil) Carl Tausig and the ardent Wagnerian Countess Marie von Schleinitz. The certificates were expensive (300 thaler), and many people could not afford them. German princes could, but not many of them subscribed—though the sultan of Turkey and the khedive of Egypt did. Another admirer, the music dealer Emil Heckel, founded a Wagner Society in Mannheim, whose members would be part owners of a patron's certificate, and who by lottery might draw a seat for a *Ring* cycle. The idea was quickly taken up, and Wagner Societies were formed in cities from New York to St. Petersburg. Nietzsche wrote an *Exhortation to Germans* encouraging their participation. Alas, all these efforts did not raise enough money. Wagner contributed his own funds (including the 20,000-thaler commission for the 1876 American *Centennial March*) and undertook a number of concert tours to raise money, but it was still not enough. Cosima considered pawning her property. Theater construction stopped; King Ludwig refused to contribute because he had not been consulted. At the last minute—in 1874—the king relented and helped with a loan. An unfortunate result of the financial difficulties was that Wagner's ideal of free tickets could not be realized. His audience, despite its democratic seating, would be drawn from the economic and social élite.

Wagner had collaborated with the distinguished architect Gottfried Semper on the plans for King Ludwig's enormous theater in Munich, and many of the ideas they had worked out then were incorporated into the Festspielhaus. For this theater Wagner worked first with the Berlin architect Wilhelm Neumann, switching, after many delays, to the architect Otto Brückwald, from Leipzig. He chose Brückwald on the advice of Karl Brandt, with whom Wagner had consulted at length on the details of the stage machinery. The construction was supervised by Carl Runkwitz, from Altenburg.

The foundation stone of the Festspielhaus was laid on May 22, 1872, Wagner's fifty-ninth birthday, a nasty rainy day. There was a grand ceremony, after which all retreated to the Margrave's opera house, where Wagner conducted Beethoven's Ninth Symphony, performed by artists he had recruited from many different places: it was a test, in a way, of his plan for recruiting artists for his music dramas.

A further milestone, on August 2, 1873, in the middle of rehearsals, was a roof-raising ceremony when the framework was complete. At the same time Wagner was building Wahnfried, where many of the rehearsals and other events surrounding the *Ring* were to take place.

Wagner's original plan had been to give the first performances of the *Ring* in 1873; but this was put off to 1874, owing to lack of funds. The score of *Das Rheingold* was published in 1873, and there was great celebration in Bayreuth. But Wagner did not finish composing the *Ring* until November 1874. The performances were postponed again, to 1875 and finally to 1876.

The Theater

Wagner considered his Festspielhaus, the largest free-standing timber-framed building ever built, a temporary structure. It is made of the simplest possible materials, with no ornamentation but with great attention to the details of machinery and sets and all the latest techniques of stagecraft. The Festspielhaus was entirely remarkable in its time, and if it is less so now, the reason is that many modern theaters are built along the same lines.

The theater is made of timber filled in with red and yellow brick, resting on a stone foundation. The stage house is very large: high enough (108 feet from floor to ceiling) to fly all the sets, and deep enough (40 feet below the stage) to lower them (the basement regularly had problems of water in the foundations). In the bottom are two long wooden drums for the machinery and a steam pump to drive them. The wings, not especially wide, contain five galleries for machines; but the depth and height are impressive, making the theater from the outside look like what it is: two buildings joined together at the proscenium.

In the auditorium there are no bad seats (well, hardly any). The audience is not separated by boxes and tiers into social and economic classes as in traditional houses. Seating consists of thirty curved rows of chairs, each row higher than the one in front; there are two galleries in the back, the "princes' gallery" and a smaller one above it. Total seating is 1,345 in the auditorium, 200 in the artists' gallery, and up to 100 in the princes' gallery. The seats themselves were squeaky cane-bottomed chairs, replaced only in 1968. "It only required seats which were adapted to acts which lasted for two hours," wrote Sir Charles Villiers Stanford, "to make the bodies of the listeners as comfortable as their eyes and ears." Below the fairly low roof is a large ceiling of painted canvas produced by the

The Festspielhaus (1876) is the largest timber-framed building ever
built. The theater is made of timber filled in with red and yellow brick,
resting on a stone foundation. Wagner thought of it as a temporary
building that would eventually be replaced.

Brückner brothers, installed at the last minute. Joseph Bennett described the theater as "a college lecture-hall on a large scale."

The orchestra is placed below the floor of the stage, so that it is not seen by the audience. This has the effect of bringing the audience closer to the drama, but a separation was still necessary: Wagner envisioned what he called a "mystical gulf" between the audience and the stage—far different from the boxes that overhung the stage in Italianate theaters —and he created this by the double proscenium, extended into the hall by a further series of frames.

Since the seats fan out from the stage, the back row being nearly twice as wide as the front, the spaces between the rows nearer the stage and the side walls are occupied by entablatures supported by Corinthian columns; the effect is of a series of boxes within boxes, or proscenia within proscenia, or of being inside the bellows of a camera of which the proscenium is the lens. And the divided curtain, made of green gauze, opens like a lens, drawn aside left and right. Everything is focused on the performance.

Over and around the pillars are the gas lamps, not very many, which light the hall, and which are extinguished for the performance. Wagner caused the house lights to be totally darkened during the performance. It was usual practice in other theaters to make a libretto available, but it would be impossible to read one during the performance at Bayreuth. There is little ventilation: the theater gets very hot.

The stage, raked at an angle of three degrees, has seven sets of wings, each with openings in the floor for the raising and lowering of flats. The proscenium opening is 42½ feet wide and 39 feet high. The stage extends 75 feet deep and is 91½ feet wide. For each wing there are three narrow transverse slots and a *Kassette,* a wider transverse slot, for the raising and lowering of flat scenery (in Paris these would be called costières and rues). The bottom of the Rhine, for example, behind which the swimming trolleys operate, is raised from a slot in the first opening. There is also a *Versenkung,* a trap, at each wing except the first.

The sides are a maze of wooden galleries for machinery and machinists, and above the stage are three work galleries with machine space above. There are some fifty flies for drops, six for panoramas, and fourteen apparatus for raising and lowering overhead lighting borders. It is an entirely modern theater.

Three levels of mechanism below the stage allow for the simultaneous operation of machinery in all the wings. Behind the main stage is the Hinterbühne, a space allowing the perspective to be lengthened another 37 feet.

Most of the settings depended for their effect on painted scenery, which could be quickly changed behind a curtain of steam. Sets of borders and wings making a single frame, one seen inside another, provided the depth, the color, and the atmosphere. These could be quickly withdrawn and others put in their place. The *Ring* had, obviously, new settings for each scene of each evening—a luxury not common in opera houses, where sets were most often assembled from stock materials.

Gas lighting was installed in 1876, at the last minute. There were 3,246 gaslights on stage, and a special gas plant to provide for them. (On the day of the premiere laborers were still installing and regulating the gas illumination, which still did not work perfectly.) Gas lighting was provided for footlights, sides and tops of wings, flats, and borders, and gas flames could be attached to movable settings. Light in different colors was available by regulating separate gas systems. There were also a few electric arc lamps used for such special effects as spotlights and magic lantern projections (as for the ride of the Valkyries). The variability of the light, and the possibility of changing colors, brightness, and intensity during the course of a scene, was important to Wagner and was a relatively new aspect of stagecraft: consider the need, at the opera in Paris, to provide all shadows by painting them on the set.

One set of gas lamps was installed around the interior of the second proscenium, so that the stage could be lit from the front and the sides as well as from above.

John R. G. Hassard describes the lighting effects for the *New York Tribune:*

> The stage is not lighted in the usual way from the wings, borders and foot-lights, but by some contrivance which I do not understand a light seems to be diffused over the whole scene. Sometimes it comes from the back. Moreover, the light is continually changing. Night and day, sunshine and storm, follow each other by nice gradations, and even when all the action takes place by day there are shifting lights and shadows as there are in nature. The cloud effects are beautiful, and Wagner employs them

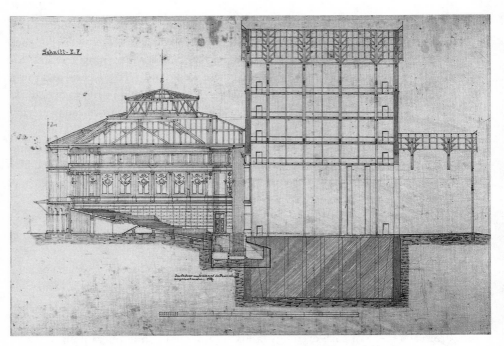

This architect's drawing makes clear what is not clear to the audience
at the Festspielhaus: the enormous size of the ultramodern stage house,
with its large substage, several floors of flies, and potential for
extending the perspective. Note too the orchestra pit below the stage.

freely. Transparent vapors float over the heavens with incessant motion
or hover around the rocky steeps. For this purpose very thin painted
gauzes are used. For heavier exhalations an illusion is produced by clouds
of steam. . . . It is by means of steam, reddened by reflected light, and
shot here and there with small flames, that the effects of fire are produced.

All this machinery and the carefully designed settings and lighting are designed
to create an absolute illusion; Wagner wants the spectator to feel as though he is on the
stage, in the action. Nothing stylized, nothing conventional, nothing unreal. It may be,
however, that his style, his idea of convention, and his reality are not ours. What is more,
his subject is unreal: swimming Rhinemaidens, flying Valkyries, underworld workshops,
rainbow bridges: this is the stuff of fantasy, not of nature. And yet Wagner wanted all his
illusions to be natural. Difficulties were inevitable.

PERFORMERS

Wagner had laid out his plan for the festival in a letter of October 1, 1874, to
King Ludwig, and he carried it out almost to the letter. There would be a first year in which

singers would gather in July and August for a month of piano rehearsals and then a month of rehearsals on stage with basic scenery and props. In the following year, after a long series of rehearsals with orchestra and machinery, there would be a series of general and dress rehearsals, followed by three performances of the *Ring* in August. He detailed the times of performances. Performances begin at 4 (*Rheingold* at 5), with an hour's intermission between acts so that the audience can refresh itself with walks, food, and drink. Each act is to be announced by a brass fanfare from the top of the theater.

Wagner began planning early. In the summer of 1874 he invited Richard Fricke, ballet-master at Dessau, to serve as a sort of stage director; Carl Emil Doepler (professor and lecturer on costume at Weimar and Berlin) was invited in December to produce the costumes; Josef Hoffmann, a Viennese landscape painter, agreed to design the settings, which were to be executed by the Brückner brothers from Coburg; Karl Brandt from the theater in Darmstadt was in charge of technical stage furnishings.

Wagner had a group of musical assistants, often called his Nibelung Chancellery, who copied parts, corrected scores, worked with singers, and generally assisted Wagner with musical work. They included Hans Richter, who would conduct the *Ring*, Felix Mottl of the Vienna opera, the Hungarian Anton Seidl, Franz Fischer, the Russian Joseph Rubinstein, and Hermann Zumpe.

In his tour of opera houses in 1872, Wagner had admired the productions at Dessau (where he borrowed the admirable Fricke) and had determined that the Bayreuth opera house was unsuitable for his purposes; but on that tour he was mostly looking for singers for his festival. By the summer of 1874, Wagner had recruited the best singers of Germany for the two following summers; they were a superb group of performers, most of whom came for expenses only and who were granted leaves by the managements of their various opera houses as a courtesy to Wagner. Most of them were delighted to be asked. A notable exception was Emil Scaria from Vienna, originally recruited for Hunding, who demanded too high a fee.

This ability to gather singers from a variety of opera companies was unparalleled. Opera houses generally had a roster of regular singers, and any opera sung there was necessarily sung by the house singers. To assemble a specific group of the finest singers from a variety of houses, each selected uniquely for her or his fitness for a single role, may be normal in today's top jet-set opera houses, but it was close to revolutionary in 1874.

Wagner was looking for a specific kind of singer who could act and who could project words clearly. There was little of Italian virtuosity required, but for some major roles an enormous amount of stamina. He also wanted actors to look their parts ("I desired none but tall and imposing figures for my Gods, Giants, and Heroes"), but it seems that he allowed musical considerations to take precedence over a good figure.

Wagner worked the singers very hard, and he cast the *Ring* in such a way that most singers sang several roles, often on successive nights (see page 244). Few singers today would take on the role of Wotan for a four-night *Ring*.

Of these singers, Lilli Lehmann is the only one to have made recordings. Wagner never heard her as Brünnhilde, though he admired her as a Rhinemaiden.

Singers in the First *Ring* at Bayreuth

GODS

Wotan: Franz Betz (Vienna); he had premiered Hans Sachs in Munich;
also appears in *Walküre, Siegfried*

Donner: Eugen Gura (Leipzig); also Günther *(Siegfried)*

Froh: Georg Unger (Bayreuth); also Siegfried

Loge: Heinrich Vogl (Munich)

Hagen: Gustav Siehr (Wiesbaden); also Hunding in *Walküre* (Siehr replaced
Kögel at the last minute on July 15)

GIANTS

Fasolt: Albert Eilers (Coburg)

Fafner: Franz von Reichenberg (Stettin); also appears in *Siegfried*

NIBELUNGS

Alberich: Karl Hill (Schwerin); also appears in *Siegfried, Götterdämmerung*

Mime: Karl Schlosser (Munich); also appears in *Siegfried*

GODDESSES

Fricka: Friedericke Grün (Coburg); also appears in *Walküre* and as a
Norn in *Götterdämmerung*

Freia: Marie Haupt (Kassel); also a Valkyrie

Erda: Louise Jaïde (Darmstadt); also appears in *Siegfried;* Waltraute in
Siegfried and *Götterdämmerung*

RHINEMAIDENS

Woglinde: Lilli Lehmann (Berlin); also appears in *Götterdämmerung;*
also a Valkyrie, forest bird in *Siegfried*

Wellgunde: Marie Lehmann (Berlin); also appears in *Götterdämmerung;*
also a Valkyrie

Flosshilde: Minna Lammert (Berlin); also appears in *Götterdämmerung;*
also a Valkyrie

OTHER PRINCIPAL SINGERS OF THE *RING* WHO DO NOT APPEAR IN
DAS RHEINGOLD

Siegmund: Albert Niemann (Berlin)

Sieglinde: Josephine Scheffzky (Munich); also a Norn in *Götterdämmerung*

Brünnhilde: Amalie Materna (Vienna)

Gutrune: Matilde Weckerlin (Munich)

Valkyries: Haupt, Jaïde, the three Rhine-maidens, with the addition of
Johanna Jackmann-Wagner (who also appeared as a Norn in *Götterdämmerung*) and Hedwig Reicher-Kindermann.

There is a chorus, of twenty-eight men and ten women, who appear
only in *Götterdämmerung*.

The very large orchestra, which included some unusual instruments, was recruited from the best players in several orchestras, including those of Berlin (twenty-six players), Meiningen (twenty-three), Dessau (eleven), Vienna (nine), Munich (seven), and Weimar (seven). They rehearsed in the summer of 1875 and returned for 1876. The orchestra, even though it was composed of superb musicians, had its work cut out for it: it had to play fifteen hours of music in four days.

The complement of strings was sixteen each of first and second violins, twelve each of violas and cellos, and eight double-basses. A newly designed large viola was used. Strings were of gut or wound gut throughout, and instruments were mostly played with chin-rest or end-pin. The double-bass was now standardized at four strings and played underhand.

The winds for *Rheingold* consisted of three flutes plus piccolo, three oboes and alto oboe (Wagner disliked the traditional English horn and had a special alto oboe built; it is especially important for *Siegfried* and *Götterdämmerung*), three clarinets plus bass clarinet, three bassoons (one of which must be able to reach a low A). The bass clarinet, formerly an unusual instrument (as in *Les Huguenots*), is regularly used.

The brass section is enormous. There are eight French horns, four tenor and bass tubas (played by four of the horn players), three trumpets and a bass trumpet, three trombones (one of whom also plays the double-bass trombone), and a double-bass tuba. Wagner now accepted the idea of valved horns as usual, though he continually specified stopped notes in the score. A specially made set of "Wagner tubas" used for the 1876 *Ring* performances remained in use at Bayreuth until 1896.

Percussion includes two pairs of kettledrums and the usual battery of other instruments (triangle, cymbals, bass drum, gong). Additional instruments include the eighteen backstage anvils of Nibelheim, the six harps of Valhalla, and the organ that contributes so much to the opening sound of *Rheingold*. The organ was a little instrument of seven deep bass notes, used to support the contrabass tuba in the introduction to *Rheingold* and in a few other places where there are sustained bass notes.

The orchestra played at a pitch about half a tone lower than that of today, adding to the effect of mellowness.

This is not the average opera orchestra. It is much larger than most and has a great deal more to do. There is much symphonic music, descriptive music, and complex accompaniment, whose varied coloration requires the constant attention of a variety of combinations of instruments, as well as the full force of the orchestra at key moments. Wagner's orchestration is a miracle of inventiveness, balance, and imagination. The scoring for *Rheingold* was undertaken before Wagner determined to have a theater of his own, but it is difficult to see how it falls short, in terms of its success in Wagner's theater, of the orchestration from the third act of *Siegfried* onward (which is the only part of the *Ring* composed for this theater).

The orchestra was led by the violin virtuoso August Wilhelmj (who in 1885 had the distinction of playing for the ladies of the Turkish sultan's harem). The conductor, Hans Richter ("then a yellow-haired Viking of some thirty years," according to Stanford), was

Orchester-Probe.

This 1876 drawing by Ludwig Bechstein shows Wagner on stage
speaking to the conductor in the pit; Hans Richter is not wearing
shirtsleeves and standing against a black cloth as Lilli Lehmann
said was the practice.

a brilliant musician and an experienced Wagnerian. He played almost every instrument—
flute, violin, trombone—and he had even sung the role of Kothner in *Die Meistersinger*
in Munich as an emergency replacement. Lavignac described him some years later at
Bayreuth as "Hans Richter, who, with his sandy beard, large-brimmed hat, and short velvet coat, would be recognized among a thousand." Richter was obliged to follow Wagner's
instructions, and various reports suggest that Richter's tempos in *Rheingold* were sometimes
faulty or unsteady.

The particular situation of the orchestra pit at Bayreuth has much to do with the
sound. The pit is under the stage, sloping downward in several steps. When Wagner discovered that the original pit was too small, it was enlarged and projected slightly into the
auditorium, but at a lower level and with a hood facing toward the stage.

Wagner sought to solve two problems with his unusual orchestra pit. In the first place, he saw the physical motions of conductor and players as a distraction, competing for attention with the drama. And second, normal placement of his enormous orchestra would overpower the singers. And so he created what he called an invisible orchestra.

The sound of the orchestra is a very round and blended one, providing at once a warmth of sound and a sort of damper to keep it from overpowering the singers. The pit reduces the sound of the orchestra, and blends it. The effect is superb, but the orchestra has a difficult time in the pit. There is an oil lamp on each music stand, but the players can see and hear nothing of the singers, and their arrangement in nine rows descending further and further under the stage is crowded and makes it difficult to hear what is happening elsewhere in the orchestra. There are two rows of violins just in front of the conductor (first violins on the right, seconds on the left); two rows of violas, one of cellos with double-basses on the sides; then the woodwinds, with outlying harps; and the brass and percussion at the bottom. There is a sort of hood over the front of the pit, designed to keep light out of the audience's eyes, which serves to mix the sound of the orchestra and direct much of it toward the stage.

Emil Naumann described the sound of the orchestra in the *Neue Zeitung:*

> One must realize the significance of the effect made by the orchestra, covered according to Wagner's orders. I cannot deny that the first impression, received at the beginning of the prelude to *Rheingold,* was most pleasing. The tone of individual instruments and groups, as well as that of the whole orchestra came forth stripped of its material side, that is, of everything to do with the mechanical and inessential aspects of its production, such as the frequent taking in or expulsion of the breath, the too obvious friction of the bow and the string; or again, of what give the brasses their blare, certain woodwinds their dry sharpness, and lastly the violin and its relatives the sound of the attack and of the bow-stroke. The tone has only those qualities that one might count as ideal. Here I may add that in general the lower and middle instruments, that is, the basses, celli, violas, horns, trombones, bassoons and low clarinets have a rounder and fuller tonal sound than the higher winds and especially the violins, which on the E-string suffer a loss of some brilliance and clarity of detail in quick figures and scales. One must consider further that the present Wagner orchestra counts more than a hundred persons, and its strength and power has no relationship to the number of players, so the question remains, whether such an arrangement is desirable, especially in smaller theaters.

Among the discoveries made in rehearsal was that the orchestra, if it played at the level indicated in the score, was too loud. Heinrich Porges wrote: "The stage rehearsals of the *Ring* brought home the imperative need to moderate dynamic expression-marks, convert fortissimos into fortes, fortes into mezzo fortes, etc., in order to ensure that the singers' words and inflections make their proper impact." Porges, in an often quoted statement, noted that "Wagner declared that the orchestra should support the singer as the sea does a boat, rocking but never upsetting." Indeed, Wagner's last written instructions to the orchestra before the premiere (which remained in the pit for decades), said, "No preluding! Piano pianissimo—then all will be well."

One effect of the sunken orchestra is that its sound is directed at the stage and therefore heard by the audience mostly as reflected, if beautifully blended, sound. The result is that it seems much louder to the singers than to the audience, so the singers tend to overcompensate, imagining that they cannot be heard over the orchestra.

Everybody acknowledged that this was a superb orchestra, well rehearsed and of a technical level not available anywhere in Germany. Hermann Kretzschmar expressed his admiration this way: "Anyone who knows the challenges, and sees the joyful smoothness with which they are dispatched, must be full of admiration. There is for every time and place a fund of enthusiasm and commitment of skill to orchestra-playing, and the dear God makes these relationships improve with time; but here the demands are of such difficulty that I cannot hold back my admiration for the artists of the orchestra, and indeed must award them the first place among the performers. How these three-voiced chromatic scales flow in such a precise ensemble, as though they required no rehearsal! what a quantity of virtuosity and lively quickness of nuance!"

Evidently the orchestra rehearsed, and performed, in comfortable clothes: nobody could see them. "Allow me today," wrote the journalist Wilhelm Marr, "to have a look into the sunken orchestra pit, which extends partly under the stage. There stands Capellmeister Richter and conducts in simple shirtsleeves; the same for the renowned violinist Wilhelmj, and all the members of the orchestra have made themselves comfortable in the same way. A droll sight, to see artists working thus! From the lofty to the comical is just a step. But what does it mean? They sigh and groan under the exertion, and persevere."

REHEARSALS

Wagner wanted his Bayreuth productions to serve as models for productions elsewhere, and he was careful to document as much of the rehearsal process, and the final result, as possible. We are fortunate to be so well informed.

Preparations began in earnest in the summer of 1875. Several singers had been working at Bayreuth since mid-year. Wagner's plan was to begin piano rehearsals—which would also be a sort of audition—on July 1, at the rate of a work every week, and to conduct reading rehearsals from August 1 to 16 with orchestra and singers, followed by a week of staging rehearsals to work out the most difficult movements, among which he included the scenes with the Rhinemaidens. He kept to this schedule fairly closely.

Some of these early rehearsals are described by Julius Hey, whom Wagner had brought as a singing coach—especially for Georg Unger, who was to sing the role of Siegfried. His intention in this preliminary summer was to sing through all the music, without detailed correction, in order to judge the singers and the effects they made to-

In the rehearsals of the summer of 1875, Wagner sat with his score at a table with an oil lamp downstage.

gether. From the beginning Wagner was tirelessly concerned with diction and dramatic expression, and he himself sang, acted, and gestured for the singers. But vocal quality was of prime importance: Albert Eilers, who was to sing Fasolt, was accustomed to sotto voce whispering and hissing; and perhaps he imagined that Wagner's style would require a more spoken delivery. But Wagner lost no time in getting him to adapt to his own style.

On June 24 a huge assembly of singers, technicians, and musicians gathered to see the theater, the machinery, the scenery. In July there were sessions of reading through, and then learning, individual roles (all with piano, mostly played by Joseph Rubinstein and other assistants); these took place in the Hotel Sonne and at Wahnfried.

Three weeks into the rehearsals the sets for *Rheingold* arrived. Wagner approved the sets and, since the cast was present, asked for some music for the Rhinemaidens; joined by Alberich, they gave out the opening scene of the opera, for the first time in the house. The effect was a delight.

Orchestra rehearsals began in August. When Wagner entered the house, the orchestra played the Valhalla motive, and Franz Betz sang Wotan's words "Vollendet das ewige Werke" ("The everlasting work is ended"). The sound was "just what I wanted," said Wagner. "Now the brass instruments no longer sound so harsh." The players seemed to like the "mystical abyss" despite the crowded conditions in the pit. For two weeks the orchestra rehearsed alone for two hours in the morning and two in the evening with the singers, an act a day; there were no sectional rehearsals but simply a playing through to familiarize the orchestra with the enormous score. Wagner's assistants stood here and there to prompt the singers, who arranged themselves in a semicircle and stood to sing their parts. Orchestra rehearsals ended on August 13, when Wagner gave a garden party for the singers and orchestra, at which Franz Liszt played.

The theater was found to have a resonant acoustic. In order to see what the sound would be like with an audience, Wagner arranged for a group of soldiers stationed at

Bayreuth to be present for a rehearsal; they sat on the floor since there were no seats yet. The result was very satisfactory, and Wagner thought they were the ideal audience: they were in place before the music began, they did not talk during the performance, and they made no claim afterward of having understood anything.

Generally there was a very good atmosphere, rather like a summer camp; the Nibelungs, as they called themselves, gathered in the evenings at the Hotel Sonne, or at Angermann's beer hall on the Kanzlei-Strasse. Lilli Lehmann described the spirited antics of the singers:

> Suddenly an unusual degree of life began to animate the dead little town. Bayreuth was taken over by the artists in 1875, they had it to themselves and they turned it upside down; they used it as their playground and the narrow-minded Bayreuthers knew not what to make of it. After our work was over, in the evenings, it became very lively at the "Sonne"— Scaria [a singer who ultimately left the cast] had a little monkey which constantly was scampering about the window-sills. Also, when his wife, who was tiny, annoyed him, he used to pick her up and sit her on top of the high stove from where she could not get down. Gura and some other fellows dressed up in linen sheets and did wild dances outside the front of the inn. Amalie Materna [Brünnhilde] would sit in the empty hotel carriage that stood at the door, without its horses, and my sister and I would perch up on the box, whip in hand, while Friedric and Scaria dragged it through the streets—all in broad daylight! We used to serenade each other every evening too. Every morning all the boots and shoes outside the doors were mixed up. And so it went on . . .

It was a summer of camaraderie, of dedication, and of commitment to the performances next year. The cast and orchestra dispersed for their winter seasons elsewhere.

The summer of 1876 gathered all the performers at Bayreuth again for preparation of the performances. After many personal communications, Wagner had sent out a printed request to all the participants on April 9 asking for their commitment; he proposed to distribute the proceeds from the festivals of 1877 and 1878 among the performers.

In May, Wagner began working with a number of the singers (especially Siegfried, since Unger was based at Bayreuth) before the rest of the performers arrived. Unger was Wagner's discovery, but his heroic appearance was not matched by his vocal ability: he had a lot to learn.

At the same time Wagner was at work on technical matters in the theater; there were many problems to be resolved: scaffolding was still in place inside, the gas lighting was inoperative; much equipment was still missing. Some singers had not yet been hired, or were having troubles with releases.

On May 30 there began a series of daily rehearsals (at 7 P.M.) for the orchestra and machinists. At one of these, a June 8 rehearsal of the second and third scenes of *Rheingold*, Nibelheim steam came through the wall of the pit, and the harps could not stay in tune. Fricke reports that the orchestra members "complain of the almost unbearable drafts. Wagner ordered someone to see to it, went along, and then came back, shouting to the orchestra, 'I have composed the opera, now you want me even to close the windows!'"

In June and early July there were afternoon run-throughs with blocking and interpretive direction, taking two or three days for each act (*Rheingold* was rehearsed July 3–11). These were generally accompanied by piano (the orchestra rehearsed in the morning). Then followed a series of more intense rehearsals (July 14–26), usually with singers and orchestra, one act per day, starting with *Rheingold*. One of these, on July 24 (the first act of *Götterdämmerung,* at which Nietzsche was present), was a public rehearsal to which tickets had been sold. Wagner, who had expected an invited audience, was furious to learn that the tickets had been sold to raise money.

Then came rehearsals with orchestra, costumes, and some scenery, one whole work every other day, beginning with *Rheingold* on July 29. The first four rows of seats had been set aside for guests; the others, as yet numbered only with chalk, were roped off. Wagner shouted at those seated in the upper rows to move down and not erase the chalk; he then addressed the orchestra, asking them to play through without stopping, whatever happened. Nevertheless, it was necessary to repeat the transition to the fourth tableau, since the Nibelung anvils were missing the first time. "R. very sad afterward," wrote Cosima in her diary, "because Herr Brandt himself is in error."

A plaque with the names of the singers was unveiled in early August, enraging the orchestra members, who thought that their names should also appear on it. Wagner answered them courteously and managed to restore confidence.

August 6–9 saw the final dress rehearsals, one drama a day. Three days of rest were followed by the first of three cycles of performances of the complete *Ring*.

It was an enormous task: there are thirty-six scenes to stage and thirty-four roles to direct, and Wagner took them all on, on a daily basis. No wonder his health suffered. Wagner had headaches, hangovers, abdominal complaints, and at one point an abscess on his gum; he was bled with leeches and was in considerable discomfort, but he carried on after an interruption of several days.

"During rehearsals," Lehmann remembered, "Wagner sat on the stage, his legs crossed and the score on his lap. He conducted away to himself while Richter led the orchestra in the pit. They started off together but Wagner became so absorbed in the score that he did not keep up with the orchestra and they went on ahead of him. Then, when he chanced to look up, he perceived for the first time that it was playing something quite different from what he was inwardly hearing."

A temporary bridge (naturally nicknamed the Rainbow Bridge) was erected from the stage, where Wagner's table with its oil lamp stood downstage, toward the auditorium. Once during an orchestral rehearsal, as Emil Doepler reports, "it happened that after the orchestra had just completed playing a brilliant piece of music, the Master stepped onto the bridge and looking into the orchestra pit called out to the musicians 'Not badly played Gentlemen! What!' Following this exclamation by the Master the whole orchestra which was composed of exceptional virtuosos, stood up spontaneously and overwhelmed him with enthusiasm and acclamation, showing their agreement with such frenzied excitement as I have never witnessed on similar occasions."

There was no prompter's box, and as the singers learned their roles, according to Lehmann, "an army of prompters arose behind every bit of scenery and in every corner of the wings. I myself prompted Siegmund from behind Hunding's fireplace!"

"The singers on the stage saw almost nothing of the conductor," recalled Lehmann. "A black sheet was nailed up behind him against the sounding-board, so that Richter in his shirt-sleeves could be made out."

Tensions were bound to arise. Joseph Rubinstein, who had increasing difficulties getting on with others, left on July 13; Cosima's diary displayed her anti-Semitism: "The piano rehearsals ended with the wholesale dismissal of Herr Rubinstein, who here once more displayed all the dismal characteristics of his race." Doepler's journal for July 19 reports, "It is absolutely impossible to work with Herr Brandt, who rules the stage. Everything has to take second place to his machinery and one cannot have one of his workers for a moment." Wagner put it this way: "I am the rager, Doepler the irritated and Brandt the melancholic."

Wagner was brilliant but difficult in rehearsal. He had strong and traditional likes in singing; for many years he claimed an early admiration for the great Wilhelmine Schroeder-Devrient, and he believed that the standard of singing in Germany was low. He thought singers took on roles too taxing and too early, without enough preparation; and he felt that singers paid too little attention to the words. Indeed, he once planned a music school that would train singers.

Although the vocal writing in the *Ring* does not involve elaborate coloratura, there are many traditional ornaments—mordents, turns, and so on. Generally, though, the vocal line is tied quite closely

Friederike von Sadler-Grün as Fricka. An observer described her costume in the second tableau as a white tunic with red mantle with red trim. In the role of Wotan's consort, Grün used her powerful midrange voice and was said to sing with *grandezza*.

to the declamation of the words. Wagner is nevertheless usually viewed as making unreasonable and new demands on singers.

To learn a role in one of his dramas, in Wagner's view, a singer should first learn the play, the role, the character, without music; only then should the music be added, giving first place to pronunciation and enunciation. Every word is sung: there is no distinction between recitative (or sotto voce or parlando) and song. And the music must be sung as written: no alterations, no ornaments, no cadenzas, no coloratura.

Wagner himself sang a great deal in rehearsal, often repeating a passage many times for a singer to imitate. There was not much room for individual expression or display.

Richard Fricke, evidently a gifted and tactful man, with much experience in the theater, wrote, "They are discouraged, because today he wants it done this way, tomorrow a different way. It is impossible to firmly establish the various scenes. He interrupts continuously, he demands outrageous things, which downright confuse these professionals who after all are not appearing on the stage for the first time. . . . I am beginning to worry about Wagner's health. He jumps in among the singers, he stands close to them, showing them how he wants them to move. His lively temperament makes him forget everything he told them and arranged yesterday, how he wanted the scenes, the poses, the changes in position done. . . . (If that should happen to me, as an actor or singer, ordered around like that by a stage director, I would . . . I don't know what.)"

There was as yet no profession of stage director. In the past, stage managers had usually dealt with group matters but did not interfere with what concerned only individual singers: Wagner wanted to get into those details also. Stage directing as a separate element may have been Wagner's unwitting invention. In the past a mise-en-scène had usually been negotiated by a combination of composer, ballet-master, stage manager, and librettist (much as had been done for Meyerbeer in Paris). Though Wagner himself was the generator of much of the action and gesture, he relied heavily on Fricke, the ballet-master from Dessau, whose staging Wagner had deeply admired in 1872. "I have no stage director, no senior or deputy superintendent, no—God knows what. You will have to do everything for me!" wrote Wagner to Fricke on April 10, 1876. Fricke took charge of group movements, and he invented many moves and gestures and solved many difficult problems (how Alberich is to slide down the rock and so forth). He was an agreeable and compromising figure, and he contributed a great deal to the effective working of the ensemble, smoothing over many of Wagner's habitual tirades and new ideas.

Wagner had signed up thirty local athletes (hiring dancers would have been too expensive) to serve as Nibelungs. He called them his "warthogs." These were local workers, amateur athletes, whom Fricke had to train in group movement on the stage. Fricke was proud of them, and he worked them very hard, mostly in the Margrave's Theater in the town; and they seem to have done a good job, though they complicated rehearsals because they could come only outside of working hours. One of them, Herr Schnappauf, was also Wagner's barber.

It should be no surprise that Wagner had strong views about "natural" acting. A singer knowing, indeed being, the character will act naturally. It will not be acting but a spontaneous and accurate portrayal of the character. He was highly critical of what he saw as hidebound, traditional, and conventional ways of acting and blocking; these may have been convenient because they were quick and easy, but they were no substitute for doing things Wagner's way.

Heinrich Porges, recruited to take careful notes of how Wagner staged the *Ring,* gives us the official view of the Bayreuth manner. Wagner opposed any sort of "coldly objective, elegant, formal" acting (as Porges reports), and rejected any sort of "false pathos or mannerism." By this he seems to have meant traditional—that is, French—acting. And yet his use of expressive gesture may not have varied enormously from what was customary in his time. Fricka, in her dialogue with Wotan, is described by Porges, who recorded the rehearsals: "Although her movements and gestures should be passionately animated, she should always convey an impression of dignity and resolution." She "should have a heroic character, made still more impressive by the earnestness of her facial expression and her significantly upraised arm." Wagner later asked her to turn away ashamed, and he insisted that her gestures reinforce the meaning of the words. When the giants are heard, she should point to the back of the stage and so on. "Fricka's cries for help were accompanied by eloquent gestures." When Donner threatens to strike down the giants he keeps his hammer raised high; the singer of Loge "should make a point of accompanying his speeches with gestures and movements suggestive of the restlessness of his nature as a fire-god." When Loge describes the theft of the Rhinegold, "all the gods must make involuntary movements and exchange glances as though under a spell." "Those not actually participating in the dialogue should indicate their involvement by characteristic gestures and motions. His [Wagner's] underlying principle was that stage action ("mimische Aktion") should have the quality of living sculpture." It sounds like a sort of acting no longer in style.

One thing on which Wagner was insistent was that singers never address or look at the audience. In his "last request," posted before the premiere, he wrote: "Never say anything to the public, but always look at each other in the monologues; look either up or down, but never directly in front of you." Wagner's training was not lost on the spectators; the *New York Tribune* reported, "The actors, though differing in degrees of merit, are all imbued with the spirit of the drama and the music. Not one of them thinks of such a thing as singing to the audience, or coming down to the front." Wagner must have been a very good mimic, acting all the roles. "He constantly instructed the singers," wrote Doepler. "Very often it happened that he not only explained the situation to the performers but also demonstrated himself with sublime devotion and enthusiasm what they had to do and how they should do it." John Hassard overheard the following: "'Ah,' exclaimed one of the artists the other day, 'if we could only do these things like him!'"

Dramatic considerations took precedence over purely musical ones (this is unusual coming from a composer). The orchestra was often reduced in volume in the course of rehearsals, and Richter was required to follow the singers carefully, and indeed to match the speed of the orchestra to actions and set-changes (which sometimes resulted in awkward tempi).

Wagner did not seem to care as much about costumes as he did about singing,

Franz Betz as Wotan. A series of studio photographs gives a view of the ideal look of Emil Doepler's costumes for the *Ring*. For the chief of the gods this involves jewelry, armor, helmet, and, as for all the men, leggings wound with straps. The costumes were based, said Doepler, on "the latest discoveries of pre-historic times."

acting, and sets. Costumes are not much described in the poem or score. He was concerned, though, that the costumes not be what usually passes for mythological, namely Classical dress with some characteristic modifications, nor the current Romantic versions of Nordic dress. He wanted appropriate medieval costumes based on what the ancient Romans had to say about northerners. Carl Doepler, the somewhat stuffy costume designer, replied that he would use imagination and also the "latest discoveries of pre-historic times." He based his designs, as he said in March 1874, on Nordic remains of the Stone and Bronze Ages. Doepler made an enormous number of sketches, as well as a set of figurines shown at royal request to Ludwig II; designs had been essentially completed by late December 1875. The costumes arrived on time, and they set the pattern for Wagnerian costume for a long time to come.

There was also an enormous amount of armor, swords, winged and horned helmets, and so forth, which Doepler arranged to have made in Berlin where he could oversee them. When not in use these were kept in a special weapons room next to the stage. (The duke of Meiningen had the benevolence to admire the swords and armor even though they had not been made in Meiningen.)

During rehearsals Doepler was criticized by "experts" for using blue in the costumes, since some thought that the color was not used in prehistoric Nordic times. Cosima Wagner got involved, and a little tempest arose from the suggestions and criticisms made by her and her various emissaries. Blue was retained. Cosima also thought that the sword Nothung was too short—even though Doepler had reproduced it from the Hallstädter sword, the longest Germanic sword in existence. During the costume rehearsals she insisted that certain costumes were too bright ("I should like everything to be simpler, more primitive. As it is, it is all mere pretense"). Doepler threatened to quit, and Wagner had to soothe him.

During the course of rehearsals and performances Cosima was creating a court at Wahnfried (although she did not usually smoke her cigarettes in company). She managed to get Fricke to give dancing lessons to her children. Wagner's nephew Clemens Brockhaus remarked on seeing Cosima at Bayreuth in 1876: "I saw Cosima, she has become really ugly and faded. She goes around in white silk with a Mozartzopf [a hairdo]." Cosima's weekly invitations were commands. The great and good were gathered; there was an endless stream of visitors: journalists, artists, aristocrats, supporters. Franz Liszt, Cosima's father and a great champion of Wagner's, arrived on August 1; he often played at Wahnfried, and Wagner sometimes illustrated points at the piano. Wilhelmj occasionally played his violin. On one occasion a gentleman from Berlin said to Wagner: "God in Heaven, what could you have achieved, honored Sir, together with the late Meyerbeer, had he still been alive." Wagner was not pleased.

When not required to appear at Wahnfried, the performers seemed to be having a good time in their free hours. As Fricke put it, "There was the free 'union' at Angermanns where one tried to recover in the most pleasant way after the theater or the obligations of the evening levée at Wahnfried. Angermanns was only a simple beer tavern." On May 29, Fricke's journal reads, "My lunches at Schierbaum's are getting better every day. For eighty-six pfennigs we get a delicious meal, with a light Pfalz wine, and afterwards we play écarté. Mottl is homesick for Vienna, and this feeling makes him grumble about northern Germany, sometimes comically. We often tease him about this, humming in a duet manner tunes from different operas, Auber, Meyerbeer, or Mendelssohn, but not Wagner. Sometimes there is also something from Italian composers, Bellini, Donizetti, or Verdi. How long will this last? Tomorrow we really get started in earnest."

On other evenings many liked to gather after rehearsal at the restaurant to the right in the forecourt of the theater. Wagner and Cosima often came too, and held court. Doepler reports on such an evening (Wagner was not present): "Mottl delights us in an extremely amusing way with variously made piano flourishes in which, for example, Wagner's motives are mixed up with those of Offenbach."

On July 9 there was a party at Wahnfried for Amalie Materna's birthday. Everybody brought a rose. There was a procession with torches, illuminations, fireworks. The next day, July 10, was her actual birthday, and there was a party in the garden of the Hotel Sonne. It started late because of a rehearsal of *Götterdämmerung*. There were speeches and popular songs. "Combined with these," Doepler recalled, "was a pas de deux danced by Lilli [Lehmann] and Balletmaster Fricke the like of which you will never see or hear again. The whole orchestra consisted of one piano, a pair of cymbals and a bass drum." Lehmann: "I danced with the ballet-master Fricke from Dessau, a 'Pas de bouquet' which caused a sensation despite my becoming inhibited by the presence of the audience."

The dress rehearsal for *Rheingold,* on August 9, had a single spectator: Ludwig II, who had arrived in the night. His agoraphobia made a grand entrance distasteful; he was received at the railway station by Wagner and driven in a carriage to the "Eremitage," the pleasure palace of the Margrafin of Bayreuth. He inspected the drawings for the costumes

The Bayreuth Festival, 1876. This somewhat fanciful drawing
does show the difference in structure between the auditorium
and the enormously tall stage house.

and attended the dress rehearsals. In fact there were a few other spectators unseen by the king, who managed to find places in the orchestra pit and in the gallery above the royal gallery. Among those in the orchestra were Franz Liszt and Edvard Grieg. It was found that the empty house did not sound good, and Ludwig generously allowed an invited audience to attend the other three dress rehearsals. The king left Bayreuth before the performances began, and before the kaiser's arrival.

At the dress rehearsal of *Rheingold*, Grieg was impressed with the orchestra: "There are about one hundred and twenty-five in the orchestra and what tremendous artists they all are! All of the very first rank. And with their magnificent fullness of tone each one sounds like two—so this orchestra could be taken for one of two hundred ordinary players! As they gather in the pit it comes to resemble a huge ant-hill of players and instruments."

After the rehearsal, the whole city was illuminated in Ludwig's honor, but he stole away in a simple carriage. There were, of course, three further dress rehearsals, of the other operas, before the first performance of *Rheingold* on August 13.

The Performance

"Bayreuth is uncommonly alert," wrote Joseph Bennett in the *Daily Telegraph,* "having actually two things on its mind at once—making money in abundance out of the strangers within its gates, and spending a little economically in decoration. . . . The result is that Bayreuth has a fir eruption out all over it." And "souvenirs were everywhere," according to the *Manchester Guardian:* "Portraits of the composer and the singers who are to take part in the approaching festival adorn every shop. From each window frame his characteristic features stare one in the face. The cigar shops are selling but one form of pipe, meerschaum carved with the heroic features of Bayreuth's present idol; wine, cigars, hats, collars, cravats, etc., are all of the Wagner brand; and from the windows float snatches of Nibelungen music."

People coming for the performance had the serious problem, once they found a place to stay (which could cost 14 or 15 marks a day during the festival), of getting anything to eat. "The little town offers," wrote Tchaikovsky, "it is true, sufficient shelter to the strangers, but it is not able to feed all its guests. So it happened on the very day of my arrival, I learnt the meaning of the words 'struggle for existence.' . . . One can only obtain a piece of bread or a glass of beer, with immense difficulty, by dire struggle, or cunning stratagem or iron endurance. . . . Throughout the whole duration of the Festival, food forms the chief interest of the public; the artistic representations take a secondary place. Cutlets, baked potatoes, omelettes—all are discussed much more eagerly than Wagner's music."

And the famine was not limited to the audience. Clemens Brockhaus caught sight of the Rhinemaidens in an off moment: "The most elegant of ladies are having to force themselves into low pubs and even sit on the doorsteps in the alleyways—and still get nothing. The three Rhinemaidens have just managed to make their midday meal in this fashion, one of them getting sausages, another bread, and the third beer." An elegant lady was heard to say, "We are the Nibelungs and Wagner is our Alberich. Where did he get this *Ring,* whose power binds us to be obedient against our will, to gather in this miserable hole and endure hunger and thirst for his sake?" The same lady was moved to tears by the performances.

THE AUDIENCE

The event was talked about all over Europe. Somehow Wagner's dramas, produced in Bavaria and unsupported by any government aid, had become symbolic of the recently unified new Germany. Karl Marx, passing through Nuremberg, complained to Engels that he could not get a hotel room anywhere because of the Wagnerians ("People from all over the world came for the Bayreuth Fools' Festival of the State Musician, Wagner"). To his daughter he lamented that wherever he went he was asked, "What do you think of Wagner?" This was an event that excited almost everybody in the musical and artistic worlds, and in Germany it was seen by some as an event of national importance. Wagner was creating, said some, a German music, redeeming the national culture, reviving the national legends, and raising the symphonic tradition to the realm of high art. There were opponents, too, and the polemics in the press before the festival were almost more extensive than reports on the festival itself.

Unlike Marx, much of the audience was prepared to worship the Master—as Wagner was often called—and to consider him a high priest, even a messiah, who would bring deliverance to the bondage of German art. Musicians and critics were already well informed about Wagner's work. The poem of the *Ring* had been published many years before, the scores of the operas were available, and much writing had discussed, explained, supported, and opposed the Wagnerian methods. The idea of Wagner's leading motives was understood, and the basic ideas of his dramaturgy were the subject of much polemic —by Wagner and by his supporters and detractors. Indeed, *Rheingold* and *Walküre* had already had performances. Surely no audience had ever been so well prepared before the performance; music criticism was leading the music. Martin Plüddemann wrote in 1877, "I met many people in Bayreuth [he was at the third cycle of performances] who assured me that they had an enormous interest in the thing, that they had read all the German critics, and also devoured those in French and English; I ventured to ask whether, since they had read so much about the work, they had learned anything at all about its poetry; and there was always the same answer: 'The text was the first thing I bought.'"

Kaiser Wilhelm of Prussia, who had not responded to appeals for help, arrived on Saturday, the day before *Rheingold,* and Wagner was at the station to meet him (he felt more obliged than desirous). All the performers, wearing formal dress, lined the road, and there was great cheering as the kaiser and his retinue proceeded in carriages to the Eremitage. Wagner later reported to Ludwig II that the kaiser said it was a great moment for Germany. Wagner had replied, "What has Germany to do with my work and its realization?"

There were many German and foreign princes and nobility: the king of Württemberg; Prince Liechtenstein; Prince William of Hessen; the grand dukes of Weimar, Schwerin, and Mecklenberg; the grand duchess of Baden; the duke of Anhalt; Grand Duke Vladimir of Russia; and many others. Dom Pedro II, emperor of Brazil, at the hotel gave his name as "Pedro," and his occupation as "emperor." (Of Wagner's other supporters, the khedive of Egypt was absent, and the sultan of Turkey had just been deposed.)

This was an important musical event, and many composers took the trouble to be present: Tchaikovsky (as a journalist), Liszt (as a father-in-law: Stanford reported that Liszt slept through much of the music), Saint-Saëns, Grieg, Bruckner, César Cui. Some musicians were conspicuous by their absence: Brahms, Joachim, Verdi, Gounod, Ambroise Thomas, Anton Rubinstein, Hans von Bülow.

And there were journalists from everywhere. The *New York Tribune* was careful to list some fifteen New Yorkers (including Mrs. Schirmer, Dr. Damrosch, and Theodore Steinway).

"To judge from their clothes," wrote Grieg, "there are people here from all social classes, the gentry in their grand attire and jewels, young fanatical intellectuals and hundreds of artists and musicians of all kinds, all united by the excitement of the unique occasion."

Nietzsche, who had been present for most of the rehearsals, wondered, "Why, then, is it that faith in the 'Art-Work of the Future' goes in company with spectacles, long hair, and funny head-gear?"

Gustav Engel in the *Vossische Zeitung* noted the elevated level of the audience:

> For a distinguished prince, who wished to entertain his guests with a theatrical performance, the Wagner theater would answer all requirements; it is an aristocratic, not a democratic, theater. The same character is shared by the audience that has gathered to experience the long planned and long awaited "art-work of the future." Our German music festivals —not to speak of the Greek festivals of antiquity—are often folk-like; but Germany has never experienced such a distinguished gathering for cultural purposes. There is the German emperor, and at his side a number of other German and foreign princes, along with members of the highest aristocracy and the financial world; above all, however, the musical, literary, and theatrical worlds of Germany, indeed of other countries, have appeared in comprehensive numbers. From all sides stream in the capellmeister, the composers, the virtuosi, the critics; and one could say that the distinguished performers whom Wagner has gathered for the performance of this work must appear before a house filled with capellmeister and musicians.

Wagner had wanted an audience of the German People, prepared to participate in an almost religious theatrical festival. But the financial needs of the festival, and the resultant sale of patronage-shares, had negative results, Wagner later complained. "The evil consequences were only too evident: the seats for our festival were publicly hawked, and vended just like those for a metropolitan operatic performance. For a very large part we again had to do with a mere Opera-public, with reporters and all the other ingredients."

Backstage Wagner posted a note to his singers:

> Last requests
> to my faithful artists
>
> ¡Distinctness!
> The big notes will take care of themselves;
> the little notes and their text are the chief thing.
>
> Never say anything to the public, but always look at each other in the monologues; look either up or down, but never directly in front of you.
>
> Last wish:
> Be good to me, you dear children.

And in the orchestra pit: "No preluding! Piano pianissimo—then all will be well."

Wagner had made clear in a letter to King Ludwig precisely how performances were to proceed, and they proceed even now just as he dictated: "Every performance is to begin at 4 o'clock in the afternoon [7 for *Rheingold*], the second act follows at around 6 o'clock and the third at around 8 o'clock, so that between each act there is an appreciable time for relaxation, which the audience should use to stroll in the park area around the theatre, to take refreshments outdoors in the charming neighbourhood, so that, thoroughly refreshed, they gather again—following the sound of the brass from the heights of the theatre—with the same receptivity they had for the first act."

There was a general sense of excitement, but there also was puzzlement at the unfinished and unusual quality of the venue. There was no running water, no lighting along the road. Everybody was kept outdoors beforehand and during intermissions, as there were no lobbies or other spaces for the audience except for the hall itself, though there were restaurants at the sides. As Heinrich Ehrlich noted, "Had it rained hard even once during the performances, the audience would have had to remain from four until ten in their chairs."

The performance began at 7, the audience summoned indoors by a brass ensemble playing the motive with which Donner summons the mist. But the audience, and those who gathered to watch the audience arrive, began their activity much earlier. Tchaikovsky described going to the performance:

> At three o'clock we make our way to the Theatre, which stands on a little hill rather distant from the town. That is the most trying part of the day, even for those who have managed to fortify themselves with a good meal. The road lies uphill, with absolutely no shade, so that one is exposed to the scorching rays of the sun. While waiting for the performance to begin, the motley troop encamps in the grass near the Theatre. Some sit over a glass of beer in the restaurant. Here acquaintances are made and renewed. From all sides one hears complaints of hunger and thirst, mingled with comments on present or past performances. At four o'clock [actually at 7 for *Rheingold*] to the minute the fanfare sounds and the crowd streams into the Theatre. Five minutes later all the seats are occupied. The fanfare sounds again and the buzz of conversation is stilled, the lights are turned down and darkness reigns in the auditorium. From the depths—invisible to the audience—in which the orchestra is sunk float the strains of the beautiful prelude; the curtain parts in the middle, and the performance begins.

The darkness of the auditorium noted by most observers—a darkness that is typical in modern theaters—was the result of last-minute arrangements in the gas lighting, which had not yet been adjusted to allow the low light that Wagner intended; complete darkness was the only choice that day.

WAGNER, *DAS RHEINGOLD*

The interior of the Festspielhaus during a performance of
Das Rheingold, 1876. The excitement of the performance is evident,
but some details would not please Wagner. Wotan stands
downstage singing and looking directly at the audience,
against Wagner's express wishes. And in the orchestra pit we see
tubas and the scrolls of the double basses, which in reality
were placed in the lower depths, under the stage.

John Hassard looked around the hall and described the scene for the *New York Tribune:*

> The long *Fürstenloge,* or Box of the Princes, extending entirely across
> the theatre at the back of the auditorium, was filled with noble person-
> ages, the old Emperor in the middle, grand dukes, duchesses, court offi-
> cials and titled ladies all about him. Most of the audience were in full
> evening dress, and the scene reminded me much more of a fashionable
> metropolitan opera season than of a hot Summer in this remote little
> Bavarian city. There were tremendous cheers at the entrance of the Em-
> peror, the whole multitude rising to welcome him, and his majesty stood
> bowing for some time before quiet was restored. At length the trumpet
> blast was heard which serves here as the signal; the lights were immedi-
> ately turned down, and the poem of "The Ring of the Nibelungs" began.

WAGNER, *DAS RHEINGOLD*

Backstage there was a flurry because the soloists' hairdresser was alarmingly late; he had been required to do every single lady of what Doepler called Cosima's "Headquarters."

FIRST TABLEAU: THE RHINE

The opening sound is almost inaudible, a deep E-flat that grows in harmony and rhythm over a very long span. It was then surely the longest unchanging harmony ever written, and yet it is fascinating for its swell of volume, its waves of rhythms. That sound is the Rhine, the representative German river, in the Middle Ages called simply "der Fluß"; and the endurance of the sound is nature, good and pure, the music of the world in order. Only after the curtain opens, with Alberich and Wotan, comes the conflict that disturbs this cosmic order.

"Now the celebrated prelude to *Rheingold*," wrote Grieg, "sets out on its one hundred and thirty-six bars of E-flat major, beginning on a pedal note of thirty-two foot organ pedal, plus the contrabass tuba and string basses specially tuned down. It is impossible to imagine the depths of the waters of the Rhine portrayed to better effect than in this veritable sea of tone—the greenest of green one could call it. And then when the curtain parts the song of the Rhine-maidens adds to the effects of nature."

The scene opens, as Anna Russell says, "in the river Rhine. In it." At the front a flat shows the bottom of the Rhine, and its transparent top allows us to see through the water. In the foreground and at the third wing are "Wasserbewegungen," gauzy representations of water that are moved slowly, left to right. Three Rhinemaidens swim beautifully through the water, singing just as beautifully. A spectator, Wilhelm Mohr, described the scene from the audience: "The curtain parted to the sides and blue haze rose and sank before the open stage, darker below, lighter above. As the orchestra's music rises in the oboes and violins, the light brightens. Reefs stare from the dark bottom with undulating outlines, and around their rugged tops we see first a blur, and then with increasing light something like women's arms, blue garments, flowers and strings of pearls. A charming sight: three water-maidens circle above in delicate motions around the central rock and sing the praise of the Rhine-gold."

All the settings for the *Ring* had been designed by the Viennese landscape painter Josef Hoffmann based on a reading of the text; they were executed by the Brückner scenic studio in Coburg, but only after a heated dispute as to whether Hoffmann's sketches could be made into scenery and the dismissal of Hoffmann. Nothing survives of the original sets: there are no photographs, and Hoffmann's sketches may not give a clear idea of the final sets (especially given the Brückners' complaints). Angelo Neumann's later touring production of the *Ring* as performed at Bayreuth may give some idea. The settings were impressive at least to John Hassard of the *New York Tribune*: "The flat picture let down at the back and made to do duty as a house, or a field, or a river, as the case may be, is unknown here. Every scene is built up with the most minute attention to details. There are no wings, but the realistic construction of the scene is continued along the sides and down to the front. There are no flapping borders overhead, but tree, sky, or roof goes up as high as the eye can

Josef Hoffmann's design for the first tableau of *Das Rheingold*.
Hoffmann was engaged by Wagner to design the sets, which were
to be executed by the Brückner brothers of Coburg. There were
heated disputes, and Hoffmann was dismissed. We cannot be sure
how closely the final settings—which do not survive—resembled
Hoffmann's designs. Compare the illustration on p. 266.

reach. . . . The scene-painting is magnificent. Every picture shows the sentiment and hand of an artist in idea and treatment. There is none of the false brilliancy and glaring color of the conventional stage decorator; the painting is not theatrical at all, but it is truthful."

The opening scene had been a nightmare to prepare. The swimming apparatus, designed by Brandt, had been ready for trials by May 30. ("Swimming machine dubious," Cosima wrote in her diary of May 18.) The machines were a sort of corset or frame attached to a long iron pole (which the Rhinemaidens' long costumes would cover), which in turn was attached to a cart on the floor of the stage. The apparatus could be tilted, the poles raised and lowered, and the cart driven around on the stage: all motions through the air were possible—provided only that the singers were willing and able to perform while belted into these contraptions, and that suitable motions could be devised and executed.

Wagner began, on May 21, trying to develop a choreography for the scene by working with Fricke and making colored marks in a copy of the vocal score. These signs

—red, blue, orange, for left and right, up and down, and lying down or getting up—would be interpreted by three music directors with scores (Seidl for Woglinde, Fischer for Well-gunde, Mottl for Flosshilde), sitting in the wagons pushed around by stagehands under their direction; on each wagon is a stagehand with a sort of steering wheel, and another stagehand who moves the swimmer up and down. "These music directors," wrote Fricke, "are the three dancers who have to perform the pas de trois." It was to be executed in the same way as a ballet, which would be practiced and learned before the Rhinemaidens themselves ever tried out the apparatus. The addition of Alberich makes it a pas de quatre, all of which must be carefully choreographed. Ultimately Wagner gave up the idea of choreo-graphing in advance and relied on Fricke to devise a suitable series of movements during rehearsals. This was done, beginning on May 30, with three of Fricke's gymnasts filling in for the Rhinemaidens.

On June 3 came the day when the Rhinemaidens were to try out the machines. Fricke reported on the trial:

> "No," said Lilli. "Nobody can expect me to do that. I will not do that under any circumstances. I have just arisen from my sick-bed, and I am also continuously dizzy." The other two were quiet. I said, "Fräulein Marie, have courage. Try it just once, and I'll wager the fear will disappear, and a feeling of pleasure in swimming will prevail." They brought the ladder; Brandt and I helped her get in. Amid her "OOH" and "EEE" and screechings and squeaks we strapped her in firmly, and the voyage began, very slowly. She started to lose her terrified expression, began to laugh, and said, it was going very nicely. Now Lilli has agreed, and voilà! in a few minutes she has become the bravest one. Fräulein Lammert now follows, and all three are swimming, amid happy laughter.

Wagner placed flowers in their machines the next day. At one point Wagner himself got into one of the machines to show how safe they were. Three fourteen- or fifteen-year-old girls were added to the scene in mid-July to double the Rhinemaidens, giving perspective as they swim away. Lehmann's recollection of the scene was not that of a spectator:

> For the first scene in *Rheingold* we were pushed about on a high plat-form that stood on wooden supports which wobbled back and forth. . . . As soon as our scene was over we were pushed into the wings and Fricka and Wotan were already well into their duet before anybody gave a thought to releasing us poor creatures. At the very last rehearsals some-one had the dreadful idea of fastening a tail to our supporting cradles. This set up a constant quivering motion in the machine which was trans-mitted back to us. I can hear, even now, the voice of Flosshilde calling out "Mottl, if you don't hold me still, I'll spit on your head!"

Hassard was impressed: "We looked into the obscure depths of the Rhine. The stage to its whole height seemed to be filled with water. At the bottom were rugged rocks

The Rhinemaidens in their swimming machines. The three machines,
each steered by a conductor and pushed by stagehands, propel the
Rhinemaidens in the first tableau. In the center is the rock on which
the gold reposes, illuminated by an electric "Rheingold-Regulator."
Note the rows of gas lamps overhead and on the side.

and dark caverns. Toward the top the waters were a little clearer, and a faint quivering light struggled through them from above. . . . At first, in the dim and watery light, it was impossible to distinguish one shape from another. Little by little we became aware of graceful forms in flowing blue robes rising and sinking in the upper waters, gliding among the rocks with waving white arms, and calling to one another in a gentle and joyous melody. . . . The illusion was perfect." Not everybody was as carried away as Hassard. Brockhaus wrote: "The lighting of the water was so dim the nixies were almost invisible and it was obvious they were in a machine—their swimming movements were just like a roundabout. . . . The Rhine gold was a feeble glimmer on the rock and had no real glow." These three singers had been well prepared even before they began rehearsals, and Wagner had never been less than satisfied with them. Lehmann was the strongest voice, physically and artistically, her younger sister, Marie, being not so concentrated: Hey compared them to an oil painting and a watercolor, Minna Lammert, with her rounded sonorous voice being like a bronze relief.

WAGNER, *DAS RHEINGOLD*

The absolute correspondence of movement to music, so important to Wagner for this scene and so difficult to achieve, serves in a way as a model for the stagecraft in general: no movement or gesture unrelated to the music, and no music without a relationship to the action.

The gold glows (the work of a "Rheingold-Regulator" built by the electrician Hugo Bähr), and Alberich appears; he not only has to sing but to clamber over rocks and plunge into the depths of the Rhine. Karl Hill had been quite nervous about whether he would be adequately supported by the machinery. Fricke had volunteered in the early stages to act the part of Alberich while Hill sang offstage. Wagner himself had forcefully demonstrated Alberich's leap in rehearsal, and ultimately Hill himself took the plunge. His part in all this was difficult to stage. Fricke wrote on June 8: "The movements and disappearance of Alberich through steam and trap doors leave much to be desired. Our good Hill suffers much."

Hill sang superbly and acted his part to universal praise. He gave his opening words ("He, He! Ihr Nicker . . .") with what Porges calls a "certain rough dryness of tone, the voice growing warmer as he is swept by lust compounded by hatred and fury." Hermann Kretzschmar admired him, too: "Herr Hill performs his Alberich with a superhuman power; one hardly knows where this artist finds the gifts for such exertions, how he softens the tyrannical traits of this passionate tyrant: the tones of soft longing he directs at Woglinde:

In this studio photograph the Rhinemaidens—Marie Lehmann, Lilli Lehmann, and Minna Lammert—appear behind a transparent scrim.

WAGNER, *DAS RHEINGOLD*

'Komm doch wieder' ['Come back!'], the heartfelt sorrow when he laments Flosshilde's flight: 'Die Dritte so traut' ['The third one so dear']." When Woglinde describes the renunciation of love required of those who have the gold, here as elsewhere, "the individual feeling of the performer must be restrained," wrote Porges. "She is the instrument of a higher power; the vitally important melody she is singing must have the chiselled effect of a piece of sculpture."

Alberich pronounces a curse on love and strains to reach the summit and seize the gold. (Hill received a burst of applause, according to Kretzschmar.) The light fades, and the audience can just see Alberich throw himself headlong from the rock into the river, while the dismayed Rhinemaidens sink from sight. Here the waters are supposed to disappear, almost imperceptibly, as a slowly moving double-height prospect is raised, covered by a cloud of steam; but at the performance a stagehand prematurely raised the backdrop during the first scene change, revealing workers in shirtsleeves. Brockhaus noted that "a few curtains rose and fell at the wrong time and the effect of the transformation from the bottom of the Rhine to the upper ground was lost. . . . The steam curtain came at the wrong time and failed to conceal what was behind it."

The clouds of steam blown in from below the stage were provided by a railway engine installed by an engineer from the Royal Bavarian Railway and situated some distance away in a "machine-house." Colored lights were added for effects of clouds, fire, and so on. "It was the first theatre to use steam upon the stage," wrote Sir Charles Villiers Stanford, "causing a noise so great as to drown the music." In principle the effect is stunning, as Hassard noted: "A scene is never raised or lowered in sight of the audience; when a change becomes necessary during the progress of an act, clouds settle gradually over the picture, dropping gently from above, while steam rises from a crevice in the stage; and when the atmosphere clears the change has been made."

SECOND TABLEAU: THE GODS

At any event, the scene did change and revealed the second tableau, which to Hassard appeared thus: "The foreground was a flowery field, supposed to represent a high table-land. A barrier of rock, overlooking the valley of the Rhine, bounded it in the rear, and in the distant background the gates and towers of Walhalla loomed indistinctly through the clouds. . . . The splendor of the morning came forth as the orchestra played the magnificent passage which symbolizes the stately castle of the gods." This Valhalla theme introduces the majestic "Wagner tubas" to Bayreuth and continues to be important throughout the cycle. The passage brought this remark from Porges: "When the motive is depicting an actual event it should be delivered in grand style, slowly and broadly, but when serving as a reminiscence—as for example in Sieglinde's narration [in *Die Walküre*]—it should be slightly faster with accents less pointed." Valhalla, built by the giants for Wotan, appears in the background. "The Wagnerian experts," wrote Wilhelm Mohr, "explain that the building is historically true and stylistically correct, like the Rhinemaidens' costumes."

Wotan and Fricka are discovered sleeping. She wears a white tunic with a red mantle with red trim, he an archaic stylized beard of flax and a severe blue Catalonian covering over his short skirt, leggings wound with cord (like all the gods, giants, dwarves, and humans). Fricka (Friedericke Grün), with her idiosyncratic and powerful middle-range voice, awakens Wotan (Betz), and they discuss the agreement with the giants Fasolt and Fafner to pay them for the construction of Valhalla. Fricka's sister, the beautiful Freia (Haupt, a bright, high soprano), whose golden apples keep the gods young, has been promised to the giants; Fricka gestures as Fasolt and Fafner arrive, their heavy tread heard in the orchestra, to claim their reward from Wotan. Three bass voices with three different timbres: the dignified Wotan (though Betz was not in voice), Fasolt with his tendency to speech-qualities, and Fafner's strong, bright bass.

Fricka and Freia are alarmed; the brother gods Donner and Froh are enraged, but the giants are unmoved. Wotan's appeal brings Loge, the crafty god of fire, who reports Alberich's theft and declares that there is nothing the gods could offer the giants in exchange for Freia, except for the gold, including the ring that Alberich has forged. "This Loge is a singular fellow," declared Wilhelm Mohr. "He appears on stage as an already somewhat decrepit gentleman, in a red skirt and yellow mantle with fox-red hair and beard, speaks like a professor and behaves like a bibulous eccentric. He is a sort of unlucky Mephistopheles (of the Gluck sort, not the Goethe). . . . At any rate this Fire-Loge has the job of giving us our first musical warmth." Heinrich Vogl's singing elicited a burst of applause from the audience. Indeed, one critic suggested that the applause was not just for Vogl, but for a kind of good old-fashioned real melody that was rare in Wagner's work.

The giants agree to a delay, but they take Freia with them, and "at once," wrote Hassard, "a gray mist settled upon the heights. The light faded. Everything began to wear an appearance of hoary age." Porges described how this effect is acted: "The gods immediately begin to lose their glowing youthful splendor [through lighting]. As the music expresses the feeling of mortality, so the positioning and gestures of the actors must convey their feeling of being in the grip of a magical spell threatening their lives. They group themselves around Wotan who stands brooding, eyes downcast, his spear lowered, its tip pointing downwards."

Wotan agrees to go with Loge to the abode of the dwarves and take the gold to ransom Freia. Hassard again: "A thick vapor issued from the opening and gradually overspread the whole scene. The vapor changed to dense clouds. The music of the orchestra became more animated; the fire-motive recurred; a deep red glow began to suffuse the clouds, and as they slowly dissolved we heard the hammering of anvils, and then there lay before us the subterranean caverns of the Nibelungs, with a long vista of rock, at the extremity of which shone the gleam of forges."

This is one point where Wagner let the orchestra play loud. Nobody is singing, and the effect of the Valhalla music changing to the clanging anvils of Nibelheim, in a substantial orchestral interlude for the change of set, is one of the places where the orchestra can show its mettle.

Josef Hoffmann's design for the third tableau of *Das Rheingold*.
Alberich is captured when he turns himself into a toad and
Wotan traps him underfoot.

THIRD TABLEAU: NIBELHEIM

The underworld of Nibelheim, with its fires, forges, and anvils, is wonderfully depicted in the orchestra, and also on the stage. This is a very complex set, full of rocks and chasms lit with red light; the *Bühnenwagen* that Brandt had built in the rear of the theater must have been used here to bring a substantial portion of the set forward onto the stage quickly.

The original thirty Nibelung gymnasts were too many for the stage, and on June 11 Fricke had decided to reduce the number to fifteen. They are enormously active and effective as oppressed workers at the forges, and Fricke was proud of them (and of his own work).

Karl Schlosser as Mime acted so comically and effectively that he was actually applauded after his "numbers"; this enraged Wagner, who had a poster printed for the following performances warning the audience not to interrupt the performance with applause. Wagner had worked to establish a strong difference in character and sound between

Alberich and the oppressed but megalomaniacal Mime, in addition to the obvious musical differences between this underworld scene and those of the gods that surround it.

There are many theatrical effects here, not all of them successful at the performance. The Tarnhelm, forged by Mime, makes its wearer invisible; Alberich tries it on and vanishes in a cloud. He later shows off by turning into a serpent, and then into a toad (which Wotan steps on as Loge grabs the Tarnhelm). Nobody seems to have liked either effect very much: "puppet-theater," "commonplace theatrical devices," and so on. Fricke felt that these two transformations (along with the rainbow bridge) were the worst disasters in the *Ring*. Wagner had probably not thought about these practical problems when writing his mythic poem a quarter-century earlier.

The gods leave with the captive Alberich and the Tarnhelm. "Cloud and mist covered the stage once more" (Hassard again) "as the orchestra, in an interlude so vivid that it might be called a musical panorama, led us back to the assemblage of the divinities. We passed again through the noise of the smithy, and we heard the heavy tread of climbing feet which had ushered in the giants in the second scene. At last we were shown the table land."

FOURTH TABLEAU: THE GODS AND THE HOARD

Alberich forces the Nibelungs to bring all their treasures for his ransom, which will be used by the gods to pay the giants. He lays a curse on the ring; whoever has it must renounce love. (At this point in the performance Wotan dropped the ring, twice, and it rolled into the wings, where he had to go, twice, to fetch it.) Alberich's rapid disappearance is the occasion for another substantial and unrestrained orchestral interlude.

The giants arrive, bringing Freia, and perpetual youth returns. The giants agree to be paid whatever amount of treasure will cover Freia when it is heaped up between their staves. That treasure had cost Fricke some trouble in the rehearsals: "Wagner commissioned me," he wrote, "to drive to town with Frau Cosima to try to borrow from a coppersmith or plumber the props needed for the Nibelung hoard, for today's rehearsal. At the shop of Vogel, the plumber, we found the hoard, in the form of forty-four items: oil cans, boxes, funnels, cake pans, buckets, water cans, kettles, etc., and managed to lug these treasures to the Theatre."

Porges describes the stage picture at this point: "in the foreground Wotan struggling to control his feelings; Loge and Froh piling up the treasure between the two staves; Fricka bewailing Freia's plight and reproaching Wotan. Soon a quarrel breaks out between Fafner, who roughly demands more and more gold, and Donner who can scarcely restrain himself. Raising his hammer he is about to attack Fafner."

Everything is needed, even the Tarnhelm, but Wotan refuses to surrender the ring, even though it is needed to fill a chink; the giants are enraged.

Erda appears: "The scene grew dark again," writes Porges, "when from a cleft in the rocks on the right a bluish light appeared, and the figure of Erda . . . rose from the earth, and warns Wotan to avoid the gold. The last words of her speech ('Meide den Ring!')

Karl Hill (Alberich) had to plunge into the depths of the Rhine, which he did magnificently. He was applauded at his curse on the owner of the ring.

were sung in the most piercing and horrifying tones." Here is one place, noted Kretzschmar, where Wotan had a moment of passion: "Herr Betz . . . knows how to represent the unshakeable dignity of the chief of the gods. His task in 'Rheingold' deserves to be thought exceptional, for it gives him little opportunity to stir the audience. At only one place all evening, in that elevated religious scene where Erda appears, and the all-wise one approaches with the whispered words 'Wer bist du, mahnend Weib' ['Who are you, threatening woman?'], was he permitted to abandon his tone of unchangeable calm." Some felt that Betz was perhaps not in top voice, and that the role was a challenge. Naumann described Betz and his role in the *Neue Zeitung:*

> If the excellent Betz from Berlin was somewhat weak and not in his usual voice, it seemed not to be the singer's fault, but the result of an indisposition. One should also remember that the part of Wotan is the most tiring in the whole *Ring* of the Nibelungs, and that it continues for three uninterrupted evenings. Even the voice of a singing hero might ultimately give out. Furthermore Wotan, at least in *Rheingold,* has the same unfortunate role to play that the ruler has in all of Wagner's operas be they dukes, kings, or, as here, Kings of the Gods. They all never escape a certain passivity, as well as a reflective and didactic quality, so that where his dramas, as here in Bayreuth, are given to us in their unshortened form, they achieve a certain horrible length in the Master's usual speech-song, and they easily communicate to the singers a certain fatigue.

Wotan gives up the ring, and its curse works immediately: Fafner kills Fasolt and makes off with all the treasure. In later performances it became customary for Wotan to

Louise Jaïde as Erda. Her enunciation was perhaps less than perfect, possibly hampered by her appearance from below stage in a bluish light—which may have made a full view of this costume difficult.

brandish a sword left behind by Fafner—the same sword which, repaired by Siegfried, will be used to kill him three nights later (actually four nights, since the first *Siegfried* was delayed for a day because Betz was hoarse). But this piece of business was not part of the original production.

In a sort of finale, the gods take possession of their castle. Donner gathers the clouds, strikes the rock, electric lightning flashes, the thunder machine roars (steel balls cascading in a chute from the top of the theater into the understage), and Valhalla is revealed, to which the gods pass crossing over on a rainbow. The Rhinemaidens are heard lamenting. The curtain closes.

The rainbow bridge was, according to Grieg, on the wrong side of the stage, and Valhalla looked more like a royal castle than the abode of the gods. The rainbow, made as it was of a solid element (so that gods can walk on it) and the feeble projected lighting effects passing toward a transparent and ephemeral Valhalla, had caused problems from the beginning and was never really satisfactory. Hanslick thought that the "rainbow, over which the gods proceed to Valhalla, was set so low that one could have taken it for a painted bridge in a flower garden."

Reactions

The performance ended at 9:30. The applause lasted twenty minutes. At Wagner's insistence, there were no curtain calls for the artists or the orchestra. Grieg's experience was this: "Though I can tell the audience gets tired of the long monologues, when the curtain falls it is a riot of enthusiasm throughout the auditorium. People stand up to applaud and call for Wagner to appear, even the Kaiser is waiting for him, but the Master is not to be seen. There are differing opinions about this episode—the Wagner-fanatics say it is because he is annoyed with the technical staff for all the little mistakes that crept into the production; the Wagner-enemies say that it is because Wagner, since his Munich days, has become used to taking his calls from the royal box and will not condescend to appear on the stage, something beneath an artist of his calibre."

Hermann Kretzschmar, from the gallery, noted, "When the curtain closed again it was 9:30. For a single act of a normal theatrical performance it was a long time, but yesterday during *Rheingold* one dreamed it away as if it were brief minutes. All had agreed on this even during the dress rehearsal, and it seemed so yesterday to most of those present. We awoke from a silence of a few seconds' duration, and then began a storm of applause, a roar of fiery delight, in which only the name of Wagner could be distinguished, and which was finally called out by all those present. I endured this spirited bacchanale for ten minutes; the Master, awaited, did not appear."

Fricke, who was backstage, recalls, "After the opera was over, the audience called for Wagner, for half an hour—but he did not appear on the stage. He sat in his room backstage, complaining about all the performers, other than Hill and me, who were with him. He was not to be pacified."

Naturally, some liked it and others not. The *Times* of London reported that "it is no opera at all; it is a play, the speeches in which are declaimed rather than sung, to orchestral accompaniment." Eduard Hanslick, the grumpy critic parodied as Beckmesser in *Die Meistersinger,* could only complain (he was at the second cycle of performances). "We sit there, helpless and bored, amid those endless dialogues, thirsting equally for clear speech and intelligible melody."

The orchestra was agreed by everybody to be superb, and the virtuosity of its playing unmatched and unmatchable, especially given the difficulty of Wagner's music. Naumann wrote in the *Neue Zeitung,* "The highest and liveliest praise however is due to the orchestra, who achieved the gigantic tasks set for them by the Master. Not only did one sense no fatigue, not only was everything, from the smallest to the greatest, performed with the same accomplishment and with one and the same love and devotion, but Wagner also has never had such a truly devoted group of artists gathered around him as are included in this Bayreuth orchestra." If there were imperfections in the playing, Grieg saw through them: "The theatre is hot and packed with people and this makes the tone of the orchestra subdued, compared with the rehearsals, and it also affects the pitch of some of the singers. But it is really wonderful."

Despite Wagner's efforts, critics sometimes found it difficult to understand the words, as can be deduced from the praise given to certain singers, but not all, for their clear pronunciation. Naumann was more critical: "If, despite the sunken orchestra, and despite the fact that everything here is done under Wagner's eyes and rehearsed under his own direction, a third of the words are unintelligible to the practiced listener, even if he has studied the text carefully before each performance and even troubled to memorize details of it, there is no stronger proof that the principle of the Master cannot be carried out."

Nowadays we think of "Wagnerian" singers, and discussions of Wagnerian performances are generally about the singers—as well as about other singers at other performances. The reactions to this performance, though, were principally about the nature of the work. This must have pleased Wagner, who wanted the work to be considered as a whole, and who wanted the action, the drama, to take a primary place on stage. Singers who are singled out are most often cited for their acting, for their pronunciation, and for their fine voices. There is not much in the way of show-pieces for singers, so praise for a singer's voice is often a matter of volume. What would become a standard criticism began with the first performance: "The one drawback associated with all this excellence," wrote Joseph Bennett for the *Daily Telegraph*, "was that very few of the artists could be called singer. . . . His artists, moreover, have frequently to make themselves heard through such an orchestra din that singing would avail them little. They must either shout or scream and they do it."

Kretzschmar, however, from the gallery at the dress rehearsal, thought that the orchestra was surprisingly quiet, at least when accompanying singers: "It was an added reflection yesterday [at the rehearsal] after the musical moment subsided, that the orchestra accompanied the singer very softly, yes, softly, as many of those among the few listeners seemed to think. At times from our place in the gallery the motives were barely audible. In soft passages too this orchestra seems to give its utmost, as we formally acknowledge this orchestra to be the most estimable in the world."

"Male singers in Germany as a general thing," wrote Hassard, "sing more or less false, and Herr Wagner's company of gods and heroes offer no exception to the nearly universal rule. But we are ready to pardon occasional lapses of this sort in consideration of the remarkable excellence of their personations, their noble appearance, good voices, and close sympathy with the music."

Stanford was not so dismissive of the men:

> Their ranks contained some great, some passable, and some inferior specimens. Amongst the tenors Vogl [Loge] was easily pre-eminent [Grieg and Hassard agreed], but he was unfortunately heard too seldom. Albert Niemann was a great actor, but his voice was nearly gone; he was but a shadow of his former great self. Unger, the Siegfried, who was popularly supposed to be Wagner's especial choice, was unequal to the part, and did not show the ability, either vocal or histrionic, necessary for it. Of the character parts, Mime and Alberich were supremely well filled. Amongst basses, Betz was admirable [everybody liked Betz]; so was Gura, in a provokingly small part. But many others were rough, though large of voice. The older singers were well trained; the younger not.

Grieg especially liked Vogl as Loge and Schlosser as Mime, and Louise Jaïde's fantastic Erda. For Hassard, Grün as Fricka was charming (for Kretzschmar she sang with *grandezza* and perfect pronunciation), and the Rhine daughters were "almost perfect."

Many of those present felt that they stood at the beginning of a new age in theatrical production, and some felt that Wagner's creation in the theatrical realm would change the way drama was presented. In a sense they were right, as regards darkened theaters, sunken pits, and relative quiet in the hall. But Wagner's production values—his sets, acting, and technological advances—though novel at the time, are often seen nowadays as outmoded period pieces: we preserve the music but not the theatrical parts of the total work of art. "We have seen in astonishment," wrote Hanslick after seeing the second cycle, "the colossal machinery, the gas apparatus, the steam machines above and below the stage at Bayreuth. Wagner could have as little composed the *Ring* before the invention of the electric light as without the harp and bass tuba."

Tchaikovsky, too, seems to have been most impressed with the staging: "Yesterday the performance of *Rheingold* took place. From the scenic point of view it interested me greatly, and I was also much impressed by the truly marvelous staging of the work. Musically, it is inconceivable nonsense, in which here and there occur beautiful, and even captivating moments."

Wagner's staging is specified in every detail, and the orchestral music, the vocal lines, and the action work together to give little room for individual expression on the part of the actor-singers. This was noticed early on: Ernst Lehmann in the *Frankfurter Zeitung* declared, "We have seen there, in everything that is technical in the theatrical art, a significant forward step; it cannot be misunderstood, that for a certain kind of dramatic production the Nibelung trilogy has established a new style. The individuality of this style lies in the fact that every moment is characterized as sharply as possible for each character. The music almost removes from the actor the possibility of giving a false performance.

A caricature of Wagner, from the humor magazine *Der Ulk*.
Aeschylus and Shakespeare pay tribute to Wagner before
a kneeling and adoring crowd.

What in spoken drama the actor must find through profound hard work is in the musical part of a Wagner score already implied in the most graphic fashion."

Paul Lindau poked fun at the lighting effects: "It would be an interesting assignment in arithmetic to count exactly how often in the 'Ring of the Nibelungs' there is sunrise, dusk, and night. Furthermore it would be instructive to establish the number of suns that light the earth on which the Wagnerian poem is played. Now we see red suns, now blue, now yellow. Some of the characters, for example Wotan and Erda, have their own special suns. It flickers around the all-wise woman with a bluish shimmer, but for the one-eyed god it is dark red and attracts his movements."

There were many deficiencies, most of them arising from the inevitable maiden-voyage syndrome. Grieg reports scene changes so slow that the orchestra had to slow down to match the action. Other evenings had their problems, too. Hanslick complained that Brünnhilde, instead of mounting her horse and leaping into the flames, calmly led the horse (who had become a favorite of the cast) off into the wings. He adds: "Hagen, who should throw himself as if crazed into the river, strolled into the wings on the right and turned up a few seconds later in the middle of the Rhine. And finally, the Rhine, which should 'burst its banks in a mighty flood,' wobbled—with its badly daubed and visibly sewn-up waves—like the Red Sea in a provincial production of Rossini's *Moses*." Brockhaus, like many others, was not satisfied with the dragon: "The dragon with a child working its jaws was just as ridiculous as in *Zauberflöte*." The dragon, ordered from London, was made in three pieces, one of which had been sent to Beirut instead of Bayreuth. It arrived just before the opening of *Rheingold*. Fricke thought it was awful, and most of the spectators ultimately agreed.

Brandt was horrified after the premiere; his carefully wrought technical effects, owing to errors during the performance, had called attention to themselves and to him and had distracted the audience from the performance. The next morning, the emperor, on a visit to the theater, said soothing things to him. Fricke reports, "The old Emperor poured balm over Brandt's wounds, because of the errors that had occurred at the scene changes in *Das Rheingold*. The errors had so irritated Brandt that he was almost beside himself, screaming his instructions so loudly [during *Die Walküre*] that the whole audience could hear. (So now what remains of the illusion?)."

At the end of the first cycle, Wagner appeared in front of the audience after thunderous applause. Stanford noted his "attitude of conscious superiority, which contrasted so unfavorably with the kingly modesty of Verdi in a like position." He said (according to Doepler's version), "You have seen what we can do, and it now lies with the future if you want to have an art!" On the next day, in connection with his invitation to a large banquet in the theater restaurant, he made an explanatory addition: "He meant to say with the expression 'ART' a specific 'German Art,' far from foreign influences!" Porges, whose recorded recollections of rehearsals were first published beginning in 1880, gave an opinion of what might be "German" about Wagner's dramas: "It has been Wagner's decisive achievement to liberate us from the witches' brew of modern opera by creating a genuinely German dramatic-musical art. The essential feature of this art—the feature we think of as the German style—is that in articulation and in characterization everything must appear authentic and natural."

Wagner was disappointed, enraged, and encouraged. The audience had behaved as audiences did, but not at first as Wagner wanted. They applauded the set, they applauded good singing, they applauded the work. And they expected curtain calls, and Wagner's appearance. All that had to be straightened out for future evenings: there would be no applause at the revealing of the set; no applause at the ends of acts, no curtain calls.

Wagner also saw mistakes he wanted to correct, and he vowed to fix many things in future seasons. Brandt's staging had not measured up to his expectations; Richter did not get any tempos right. By 1878, when he published his *Retrospective on the Stage Festivals of 1876*, he had calmed down—or put on a public persona—and was much less critical. But he continued to imagine changes and improvements. In his essay "On the term 'music Drama,'" Wagner had said that his works were "acts of music made visible." Evidently the vision in his mind's eye failed to correspond exactly with the reality.

By December it was clear that there was a substantial financial deficit; reports range between 120,000 and 148,000 marks, the whole festival having cost some 1,281,000 marks. Wagner considered, among other things, declaring bankruptcy and emigrating to the United States. Ultimately, of course, Ludwig II paid the debt. Ownership of the theater and the festival passed to Cosima (d. 1930), Siegfried (also d. 1930), and his wife, Winifred. It was taken away in 1945 partly because of her collaboration with Hitler. In 1949 Richard Wagner's grandsons Wieland (d. 1966) and Wolfgang took control; in 1973, ownership passed to the Richard Wagner Foundation.

Wagner, who had hoped to give the *Ring* only at Bayreuth, ultimately released the works for public performances elsewhere. Angelo Neumann produced the *Ring* in Leipzig in 1876 based on the Bayreuth staging; he ultimately bought the sets and costumes from Wagner and toured them for years. The *Rheingold* sets ended up in Prague, where they were used until 1927.

Some of those present may have had a sense of the importance of what they had witnessed, and of the influence that this music, this theater, and this art form would have on the future. After the dress rehearsal of *Rheingold,* Grieg mused, "Returning to my lodging after the rehearsal I tell myself that, in spite of much there is to criticise, the inadequate characterisation of the gods, the ceaseless modulations and wearying chromaticism of the harmonies and the end result of leaving the listener totally exhausted, this music drama is the creation of a true giant in the history of art, comparable in his innovation only to Michelangelo. In music there is nobody to approach Wagner."

Brockhaus took a more personal view: "It is all very fine and doubtless will become finer still but I would not have liked to pay out 100 thalers for the *Ring* when there is so much else I could do with the money."

Page 7 of Wagner's draft score. The opening of the opera is almost
inaudible: a deep E-flat that grows in harmony and rhythm
over a very long span. It was then surely the longest unchanging
harmony ever written, and yet it is fascinating for its swell of
volume, its waves of rhythms.

Documents: *Das Rheingold*

1. FROM WAGNER'S PREFACE TO THE POEM *DER RING DES NIBELUNGEN,* 1862

With me the chief thing is to imagine such a performance as entirely free from the influence of the repertory system in vogue in our permanent theatres. Accordingly, I have in mind one of the smaller German cities, favorably located and adapted to the entertainment of distinguished guests, and particularly a city in which there would be no collision with a larger permanent theatre, and where, consequently, a strictly metropolitan theatrical public with its well-known customs would not present itself. Here a provisionary theatre would be erected, as simple as possible, perhaps only of wood, and with the interior designed only for artistic purposes. I should confer with an experienced and intelligent architect as to a plan for such a house, with amphitheatrical arrangement of the seats, and the decided advantage of an invisible orchestra. Here then, in the early spring months, the leading dramatic singers, chosen from the ensemble of the German opera houses, would be assembled, in order to study the various parts of my stage work, entirely uninterrupted by any other claims upon their artistic abilities.

On the days appointed for the performance—of which I have in mind three in all—the German public would be invited to be present, as these performances, like those of our large music festivals, are to be made accessible, not only to the partial public of any one city, but to all friends of art, far and near.

A complete performance of the dramatic poem in question would take place in midsummer—on a fore-evening *Das Rheingold* and on the three following evenings the chief dramas *Die Walküre, Siegfried* and *Götterdämmerung.*

To complete the impression of such a performance, I should lay great stress upon an invisible orchestra, which it would be possible to effect by the architectural illusion of an amphitheatrical arrangement of the auditorium.

The importance of this will be clear to anyone who attends any of our present operatic performances for the purpose of gaining any genuine impression of the dramatic art work, and finds himself made the involuntary witness of the mechanical movements made by the players and conductor. These should be as carefully concealed as the wires, roped canvas and boards of the stage machinery, the sight of which, as everyone must know, creates a most disturbing impression and one calculated to destroy all illusions.

After having experienced what a pure, etherialized tone the orchestra gains by being heard through an acoustic sounding-board which has the effect of eliminating all the non-musical but inevitable sounds which the instrumentalist is obliged to make in producing the notes; after having realized the advantageous position in which the singer is set before his listeners, by being able to stand, as it were, directly before them—no one could arrive at other than a favorable conclusion as to the effectiveness of my plan for an acoustic-architectural arrangement.

Translated in Robert Hartford, *Bayreuth: The Early Years* (Cambridge: Cambridge University Press, 1980), 20–21.

2. HEINRICH PORGES ON REHEARSALS

Porges, an ardent Wagnerian, was invited by Wagner to document rehearsals of the Ring. *First published in installments, his* Bühnenproben *was not completed in book form until 1896, and it served as an important influence on later performances at Bayreuth and elsewhere. Excerpted here are a few of Porges' general statements.*

It has been Wagner's decisive achievement to liberate us from the witches' brew of modern opera by creating a genuinely German dramatic-musical art. The essential feature of this art—the feature we think of as the German style—is that in articulation and in characterization everything must appear authentic and natural. There must never be any suggestion of false pathos or mannerism; even the most violent outbursts of passion must possess what Schiller so aptly termed a forceful beauty (energischen Schönheit). This heroic element, this character of powerful masculinity, was present in all the many instructions Wagner gave in order to secure a correct and vital performance (p. 4).

Through the performance of the *Ring* the goal was achieved of combining the realistic style of Shakespeare with the idealistic style of antique tragedy; of bringing about an organic union between a highly stylized art, striving for a direct embodiment of the ideal, with an art rooted in fidelity to nature (Naturwahrheit). An ideal naturalness and an ideality made wholly true to nature—this is the direction in which Wagner was endeavouring to guide his performers (pp. 4–5).

There is a particular remark of Wagner's that I must not pass over: when the motive is depicting an actual event it should be delivered in a grand style, slowly and broadly, but when serving as a reminiscence—as for example in Sieglinde's narration—it should be slightly faster and with accents less pointed—as it were, in the throwaway style of an experienced actor delivering an interpolated sentence (p. 12).

A general point of the utmost importance affecting the whole style of music-dramatic art must be considered here. The stage rehearsals of the *Ring* brought home the imperative need to moderate dynamic expression-marks, convert fortissimos into fortes, fortes into mezzo fortes, etc., in order to ensure that the singers' words and inflections make their proper impact. We must never be allowed to forget that we are attending a dramatic performance which seeks to imitate reality; we are not listening to a purely symphonic work. From which it follows that symphonic passages during which words are being sung should never become excessively loud. This was a recurring problem during the rehearsals. Wagner declared that the orchestra should support the singer as the sea does a boat, rocking but never upsetting or swamping—he employed that image over and over again (pp. 12–13).

In his "Survey of Present-Day German Opera" Wagner declared that if the dramatic dialogue, upon the cultivation of which he had staked his whole art, was not immediately comprehensible then his works were bound to be totally unrecognizable. This applies especially to *Das Rheingold,* the portion of the *Ring* furthest removed from old-style opera, of which the chief constituent was, as Wagner put it with characteristic trenchancy, "monologues cast in the form of arias with a succession of soliloquies." His dialogue makes its proper effect only when it is delivered at a tempo essentially the same as that of speech. Not that words must be thrown away without any attention to detail; on the contrary, employing the tempo of natural speech enables the singer to dwell on important words without lapsing into the intolerably mannered, drawn-out phrasing which makes the recitatives in our opera theatres such torture. In any case, in Wagner's works the pace of every syllable is determined by note-values; the performer has only to articulate the rhythmic structure accurately and the expression of the musical speech will be right. If he can also sense—absorb—the harmonic basis, he is on the way to mastering Wagner's new art of speech-melody combining clarity of diction with emotional warmth and vitality (pp. 13–14).

I have already remarked on the pains Wagner took to ensure that those not actually participating in the dialogue should indicate their involvement by characteristic gestures and motions. His underlying principle was that stage action (mimische Aktion) should have the quality of living sculpture. Theoretical considerations apart, there is an important point here that cannot be passed over. The relationship between acting and sculpture should not mislead the performer into making sheer beauty of physical movement his first and foremost aim. That would be utterly self-defeating. A painting or sculpture is an object wrested from the perpetual flux of reality, thus imparting to life a semblance of stillness. It is this that enables the plastic arts beyond all others "to make the passing moment permanent" [Porges is quoting Lessing]. Stage action has a different function: it copies reality (pp. 25–26).

> Heinrich Porges, *Wagner Rehearsing the Ring: An Eyewitness Account of the Stage Rehearsals of the First Bayreuth Festival*, trans. Robert L. Jacobs (Cambridge: Cambridge University Press, 1983).

3. CARL EMIL DOEPLER ON REHEARSAL AND PERFORMANCE

Doepler was the costume designer for the production and was present for the rehearsals. His diary of 1876, now lost, was translated as A Memoir of Bayreuth: 1876— C. E. Doepler, *trans. Peter Cook (London: Staples Printers St. Albans, 1979).*

Regarding also the frequently discussed manner in which Richard Wagner dresses, I have to point out that I have never seen him dressed in an outrageous way. At home he wore a simple short frockcoat with a so-called shawl collar, wide pantaloons and a simple beret, all made out of black velvet and decorated and lined with heavy Atlas. This is all I saw on my frequent visits to "Wahnfried." At the rehearsals he appeared in simple street clothes. I never observed the passion which people thought he had for the colourful, especially pink Atlas. Everything I saw him wear was simple, practical and attractive (p. 29).

Once a week, an evening reception took place at the Villa Wahnfried at which one was obliged to appear. But our high point of the evening, after the heat and work of the day, was on the verandah of the right-hand restaurant in the forecourt of the Festspiel-haus. Wagner and Frau Cosima used to come there as well with their company. Their evening meetings in the theatre restaurant had a character of "holding court" rather than a free gathering of the artists who preferred to sit not in the main room at the Master's table, but instead on the verandah, together with congenial and friendly company, to breathe in God's wonderful evening air and its refreshing coolness (p. 33).

The performances of the three Rhine daughters in the Prelude of "Das Rheingold" were completely admirable. What they had to suffer in the flying and swimming machines was quite unbelievable. Pulled 30 feet high above the stage with enormous speed then down again, turned around and swung about, and all this without their control. To have to sing during these exhausting evolutions was beyond heroism and only the highest degree of enthusiasm for Meister Wagner's great work could justify the death defying sacrifice of these three ladies (p. 39).

During rehearsals for the tetralogy of the "Ring," a provisional bridge had been erected, as requested by the Master, in order to get comfortably from the stage into the auditorium. This bridge, because it was morning in the heights of Valhalla was called by us the Bifroestbrücke [rainbow bridge], and was used frequently by those who had to do with the stage arrangements. Once during an orchestra rehearsal it happened that after the orchestra had just completed playing a brilliant piece of music, the Master stepped onto the bridge and looking into the orchestra pit called out to the musicians "Not badly played Gentlemen! What!" Following this exclamation by the Master the whole orchestra which was composed of exceptional virtuosos, stood up spontaneously and overwhelmed him with enthusiasm and acclamation, showing their agreement with such frenzied excite-ment as I have never witnessed on similar occasions (p. 42).

On the day of the first performance of "Das Rheingold," I alone was not in a mood full of dedication. I was instead in a state of unbelievable excitement, waiting in vain for the hairdresser to the Soloists, who arrived only at the last minute and apologised with the following: he had been obliged to coiffeure first every single lady of the "head-quarters." Fortunately he made good his late arrival through his dexterity. This incident must have arisen from the enthusiasm of the noble ladies and excellencies for this great event of their adored master. They could hardly do without their favourite hair styles when the idea was to serve the master and his great undertaking. Why should they worry what pangs of waiting it caused me—and what was my very understandable confusion to them, not to mention the impatiently waiting performers who would be first on the stage!

Oh these ladies! (p. 48)

4. FROM THE 1876 DIARY OF RICHARD FRICKE

Fricke, the ballet-master, served as a sort of director and stage manager for the Ring. *Citations are from* Wagner in Rehearsal: The Diaries of Richard Fricke, 1875–1876, *trans. George R. Fricke, ed. James Deaville with Evan Baker (Stuyvesant, N.Y.: Pendragon, 1998).*

May 26. Today for the first time I saw the complete scenery for the first scene of *Das Rheingold*. Young Kranich, a pupil of Brandt, got into a bathing suit—I have to admit I was greatly surprised. I still cannot understand, whether or how the female vocalists will have the courage to lie down in this apparatus and—sing. Not that it will be difficult for them to sing in a half upright position, but they will be so frightened that they will not be able to make a sound. The rehearsals for the musicians and machinists are to start Tuesday. I am most curious indeed (pp. 58–59).

May 30. The rehearsal began at 7 o'clock. The first scene, the scene in the Rhine, was set up. It is very original and magnificent. The apparatus worked well, each being operated by three people. The first is the music directors (Seidl for Woglinde, Fischer for Wellgunde, and Mottl for Flosshilde). The second is the person who guides the machine with a sort of steering wheel, and the third sits in the machine and moves the swimmer up or down as required. After about two hours of working out the movements in accordance with my notes, we got as far as Alberich's entrance. Three fairly short and light-weight gymnasts took the place of the three Rhinedaughters (pp. 61–63).

May 31. At 7 o'clock we had the second swimming rehearsal, this time with Hill, from Schwerin, as Alberich. Twice I demonstrated the descent into the depths for him. I told him, "Don't be afraid of Brandt's machines, it is a real thrill to make the plunge. As they say, you are in the lap of Abraham!" Hill is a man about forty-six years old and is easily made nervous, but in all an excellent singer, and a capable actor. He is among the best of the group performing here (p. 63).

June 2. Swimming rehearsal at 7 o'clock. It is beginning to go well, if with effort and sweat. The Master gives out friendly smiles and bad jokes (p. 64).

June 3. I was free until about 3 o'clock when the swimming rehearsal began. Fräulein Lammert and Lehmann sisters Lilli and Marie arrived, greeted in a friendly manner, and examined the swimming apparatus and the gymnasts in it. "No," said Lilli. "Nobody can expect me to do that. I will not do that under any circumstances. I have just arisen from my sick-bed, and I am also continuously dizzy." The other two were quiet. I said, "Fräulein Marie, have courage. Try it just once, and I'll wager the fear will disappear, and a feeling of pleasure in swimming will prevail." They brought the ladder; Brandt and I helped her get in. Amid her "OOH" and "EEE" and screechings and squeaks we strapped her in firmly, and the voyage began, very slowly. She started to lose her terrified expression, began to laugh, and said, it was going very nicely. Now Lilli has agreed, and voilà! in a few minutes she has become the bravest one. Fräulein Lammert now follows, and all three are swimming, amid happy laughter. Wagner now appears, and the whole scene is performed

with no further difficulties. Besides that, the three ladies are singing their parts most beautifully, and they are moving very well. The feeling that took hold of me was indescribable:
my eyes filled with tears because everything was so successful. Everyone except Wagner
had been doubtful, expecting that the ladies would not agree to do it. The scene is so un-
believably beautiful that one can become ecstatic (pp. 64–65).

June 4. At 7:30 in the evening there was a swimming rehearsal. This time the musicians were in the auditorium. It did not take long for the thunderous applause to start.
Today Wagner put a bouquet of flowers in each of the Rhinedaughters' swimming stations.
A bottle of champagne, representing the Rhinegold, was to be placed on top of the cliff,
and Alberich (Hill) was to plunge with it into the depths. Unfortunately, it could not be
fastened there at the top, so I had to give it to him as he arrived at the bottom. Hill no
longer showed any fear, so I have nothing more to do until this line comes: "Ugly, sleek,
slippery slate, how I do slip," and then direct the machinists who slide Alberich up and
down (pp. 64–65).

June 6. The impressions are getting more and more powerful. Yesterday we had
the first blocking rehearsal of the second and third scenes. The metamorphosis from the
depths of the Rhine is a masterpiece: you just have to see it. Every description beggars the
reality. Even so, Wagner had to find fault, and much was changed. The piano rehearsal
began, with Betz (Wotan), Vogl (Loge), Grün (Fricka), Unger (Froh), Kögel (Donner),
Haupt (Freia), Eilers (Fasolt), Reichenberg (Fafner). As a precaution, I had asked my gymnasts, thirty of them, to be on hand early, at 12:30, since this is the first time they have to
appear in these scenes. I explained to them once again the atmosphere and mood of these
scenes, and divided them up into groups. Alberich drives twelve of them before him, whip-
ping them, and the remaining eighteen follow, laden with the Nibelung hoard. They had
been well trained in the body movements, and within a half hour I was satisfied with the
scene. I produced them in the evening, and everyone was astonished. A cheer was given
by all present. Wagner took my head in both hands, and did not seem to want to let go
(pp. 65–66).

June 8. The male and female singers from the second scene of *Das Rheingold*
were ordered to Wagner's for 11 o'clock to try to develop poses, gestures, etc. The same
things happened here as with Unger. They are discouraged, because today he wants it done
this way, tomorrow a different way. It is impossible to firmly establish the various scenes.
He interrupts continuously, he demands outrageous things, which downright confuse these
professionals who after all are not appearing on the stage for the first time. For instance,
he asked that when the two giants appear over the mountain, they should walk in a certain way. He showed them such a strange movement that I broke in, and secretly told him,
"Master, this does not work, it is not natural. I will show you how I have perceived it." I
demonstrated a clumsy walk, in keeping with the motive. "Very good, very good," was
Wagner's response. "My manner of walking was good for nothing." However, at the same
time he still asked Eilers [Fasolt] for some very unnatural gestures which I had to correct.

With all these blocking rehearsals, I am beginning to worry about Wagner's health.
He jumps in among the singers, he stands close to them, showing them how he wants

them to move. His lively temperament makes him forget everything he told them and arranged yesterday, how he wanted the scenes, the poses, the changes in position done. And now, if somebody or other comes up to him and says, "Dear Master, yesterday you asked for it that way," then he immediately responds with strong words: "No, no, this is the way I want it today." Then the next day he will say, "Let it go. Do it the way I told you before." (If that should happen to me, as an actor or singer, ordered around like that by a stage director, I would . . . I don't know what.) In spite of all this I still hope to succeed in straightening out the situation without Wagner realizing it. In the afternoon I went to see Eilers [Fasolt], and taught him the five measures. The two of us perspired freely over this artistic success.

Between 6:00 and 8:30 we rehearsed the second and third scenes of *Das Rheingold*, with orchestra and scenery, but still without props. Again the usual interruptions, the same interference, the same changing of the scene. The situation is enough to drive one to despair. The entrances and exits of the gymnasts are greeted with applause every time, and the whole scene is so straightforward.—The changes of scene, with the help of the steam, are working well. However the movements and disappearance of Alberich through steam and trap doors leave much to be desired. Our good Hill suffers much. Our musicians complain that the steam comes through the wall of the pit, and the harps cannot stay in tune. They also complain of the almost unbearable drafts. Wagner ordered someone to see to it, went along, and then came, back, shouting to the orchestra, "I have composed the opera, now you want me even to close the windows!" (pp. 67–68)

June 9. Wagner commissioned me to drive to town with Frau Cosima to try to borrow from a coppersmith or plumber the props needed for the Nibelung hoard, for to-day's rehearsal. At the shop of Vogel, the plumber, we found the hoard, in the form of forty-four items: oil cans, boxes, funnels, cake pans, buckets, water cans, kettles, etc., and managed to lug these treasures to the Theatre. . . . At 6 o'clock we rehearsed the fourth scene of *Das Rheingold*. This time we (the thirty gymnasts and I) came in with good spirits, with our hard-won Nibelung hoard, and earned new praise and approbation (p. 69).

June 10. Rehearsal at 6 o'clock. The snatching of the *Ring* by Fasolt and Fafner, as well as the death stroke, were acted poorly by Eilers and Reichenberg. I corrected and reblocked it, and—Wagner was delighted (p. 69).

June 11. At 6 o'clock we did the third and fourth scenes of *Das Rheingold* with the orchestra. Again many changes. Betz, Schlosser, Hill, and Vogl went along with them, because Wagner so ordered, but later on they will not bother with them, and will play as they please. Today we found out we have too many Nibelungs—thirty of them. It is too crowded in the small space divided by the rock set. I shall sort out the best of them, and perform the scene with only fifteen gymnasts.

August 14. In the evening, the first performance of *Das Rheingold*. In the changing of the scenery, much went wrong. I can indeed say, mistakes like this were not made during the rehearsals. After the opera was over, the audience called for Wagner, for a half hour —but he did not appear on the stage. He sat in his room backstage, complaining about all the performers, other than Hill and me, who were with him. He was not to be pacified.

On my way home I met Lesimple, who could not assure me enough, how beautiful and powerful the impressions were that were received by the public. I heard this from many sources. Even so, it was just as I thought, we were under the magnifying glass of our critics, who had come from many different countries (pp. 95–96).

August 15. A very hot day! The Emperor with his escort, the Grand Duke of Weimar, the Duke and the hereditary Prince of Anhalt, visited the Theatre in the morning. The old Emperor poured balm over Brandt's wounds, because of the errors that had occurred at the scene changes in *Das Rheingold*. The errors had so irritated Brandt that he was almost beside himself, screaming his instructions so loudly that the whole audience could hear. (So now what remains of the illusion?) He was now very happy, saying, "The Emperor gave me back my self-confidence, with his famous graciousness" (pp. 96–97).

5. FROM COSIMA WAGNER'S DIARY, 1876

July 15. In the evening final rehearsal of *Das Rheingold;* many vexations for R. in the course of it, the rainbow bridge wrong (so far), the steam fails to work, because Herr Brandt, warned by the management committee about the need for economy, could not produce the proper vapors! The Brückner brothers have painted in haste, so there are ineradicable mistakes in the decorations! (p. 915)

July 29. In the evening first *Rheingold* rehearsal in costume, R. very sad afterward, because Herr Brandt himself is in error. The singers very good, particularly Herr Vogl as Loge. After the rehearsal R. and I at home by ourselves, R. deeply worried—The King inquires whether R. is satisfied with the scenery! (p. 917)

August 6. Several arrivals, among others Prince Liechtenstein, cheerful lunch, in the evening dress rehearsal without an audience, the King sends for me as well and tells me I should never have doubted that he would remain loyal to us. The rehearsal goes very well. Great illuminations and cheers for the King (p. 918).

August 13. First performance of *Rheingold,* under a completely unlucky star: Betz loses the ring, runs into the wings twice during the curse, a stagehand raises the backdrop too soon during the first scene change and one sees people standing around in shirt sleeves and the back wall of the theatre, all the singers embarrassed, etc., etc.—Each of us returns home separately, R. at first very upset, but gradually regains his spirits, and the sudden visit of the Emperor of Brazil restores the mood of ebullience. We go to bed in good spirits (pp. 918–19).

Cosima Wagner, *Cosima Wagner's Diaries*, vol. 1: 1869–77, ed. Martin Gregor-Dellin and Dietrich Mack, trans. Geoffrey Skelton (New York: Harcourt Brace Jovanovich, 1977).

6. FROM LILLI LEHMANN'S MEMOIRS

It was on 3 June 1876 that we saw the Rhine-maidens' swimming apparatus for the very first time—this was a sort of cradle stuck on a pole at least twenty feet high and mounted on a little wagon with four wheels. We were to be strapped in this to sing! Now, I had been suffering from attacks of giddiness (due to extended sessions of sitting for my portrait in oils) and for this reason declined to perform in this contraption—until, that is, after much coaxing and pleading, I was put to shame and I climbed up the ladder and allowed myself to be buckled in place. I found myself delighted with the sensation and when Minna Lammert joined me we sang and swam so freely up aloft that it was a pleasure not to be missed. But it was dangerous—for the first scene in *Rheingold* we were pushed about on a high platform that stood on wooden supports which wobbled back and forth. My machine was directed by Anton Seidl and Lammert's by Felix Mottl. As soon as our scene was over we were pushed into the wings and Fricka and Wotan were already well into their duet before anybody gave a thought to releasing us poor creatures. At the very last rehearsals someone had the dreadful idea of fastening a tail to our supporting cradles. This set up a constant quivering motion in the machine which was transmitted back to us. I can hear, even now, the voice of Flosshilde calling out "Mottl, if you don't hold me still, I'll spit on your head!"

During rehearsals Wagner sat on the stage, his legs crossed and the score on his lap. He conducted away to himself while Richter led the orchestra in the pit. They started off together but Wagner became so absorbed in the score that he did not keep up with the orchestra and they went on ahead of him. Then, when he chanced to look up, he perceived for the first time that it was playing something quite different from what he was inwardly hearing. In this respect it is interesting to note his comments on keeping to a strict time beat—something he frequently repeated to all artists who had solo passages—"That is your business, do it as you like."

The singers on the stage saw almost nothing of the conductor. A black sheet was nailed up behind him against the sounding-board, so that Richter in his shirt-sleeves could be made out. He always conducted in his shirt-sleeves (and indeed he usually came up to the theatre for rehearsals sitting in a cart drawn by a pair of oxen). Everything was novel at Bayreuth—there was no prompt box, for example. We Rhine-maidens had no need of one but there were others who seemed to need one just because it was not there. So an army of prompters arose behind every bit of scenery and in every corner of the wings. I myself prompted Siegmund from behind Hunding's fireplace!

Looking back after all these years I recall nothing ever made my heart beat so much as hearing the first sounds of *Rheingold* when the orchestra began to stir in the depths below and I was called upon to make my voice ring out above it—the first tones of the human voice in the magic realm of the *Ring*. For me it was a glorious moment even at the cost of much anxiety and nervous apprehension.

Lilli Lehmann, *Mein Weg* (Leipzig: S. Hirzel, 1913), pp. 292–94, in Hartford, *Bayreuth*, p. 49.

7. ANTON SEIDL'S REMINISCENCES TO COSIMA WAGNER

Seidl was one of the three assistants who operated swimming-machines for the Rhine-maidens. In 1896 he wrote to Cosima Wagner to advise her on staging for the Ring.

The most difficult of all was the Rhine-daughters' scene. Since there must now be new wagons for the Rhine-daughters at Bayreuth, the motions of the machines have surely also changed, and so the notations of my colleagues, even if they are accurate, will not be much help. The general indications of directions, speed or slowness of the motions, the gathering or separation of the machines, the continuous motion of each one independent of the others—all this is written, not under or over the musical notation, but is clear in the music itself. I hope the three gentlemen involved will be able to decipher it and with a little practice bring it about. . . .

The rehearsal of the Rhine-daughters must begin separately from all the others. In those days we began with four-hour rehearsals, and we got only to Alberich's appearance; then to the illumination of the gold; and only in the third rehearsal did we get to the end, and then twice more the same thing, before we could do it fluently. The main thing is that the movements must be *prepared,* quite exact, so that the figure in singing makes no sudden jerky motions calling attention to herself; and that the figure should always be kept moving; and not always bolt upright in the water, but sings one phrase lying forward, another half backwards, again another half sitting. The hands should never make swimming motions, but should be always charming, not posed, easy with natural grace, making slow only almost solemn movements. All that cannot be written, and indeed scarcely demonstrated, only repaired. . . .

Only twice in the scene do all three figures stand still; the first time is at the words "Nur wer der Minne Mach versagt," etc. There the three figures remain motionless, each in her place, but not together, and the singer in the middle in front of the rock, the others to either side but not in a row. At the first orchestral notes of "Wohl sicher sind wir und sorgen-frei" the general movement begins again. The second moment of stillness is at the greeting of the Rhine-gold. The motions had grown slower and stiller during the accompaniment to "Lugt, Schwestern, die Weckerin lacht in den Grund." And the lighting similarly grows slowly brighter. The gold shines in its full brightness here [Seidl gives musical notation indicating a high G] and not already here [the quarter note C preceding]. Since before this all the other lights have been slowly lowered, the gold alone is lit during the playing of the previous seven notes, quickly, almost *accelerando,* and shines out at the dotted quarter-note. Here too, for the coming trio, Heiajaheia, Heiajaheia, [musical notation] thus during these four beats, the Rhine-daughters are beside each other at stage left, still, but with upward motions of the right hand. At "Rheingold! Rheingold!" the Rhine-daughters begin their circling around the rock. This should not be done quickly, but slowly, charmingly, with constant curvings of the body, with their gaze fixed on the gold. Only when they have finished singing do they begin to move faster, so that it seems to be a joyful, jubilant game.

Seidl's letter of May 25, 1896, repr. in Dietrich Mack, *Der Bayreuther Inszenierungsstil* (Munich: Prestel, 1976), pp. 94–95.

8. CLEMENS BROCKHAUS, WAGNER'S NEPHEW, TO HIS WIFE

The interior of the theatre, where I had a very good seat, is very simple. A row of doors leads to the raked amphitheatre. At the back is the Princes' Gallery; the seats there are by no means the best, they are too far away. Above are places for the music students, where they cannot see the orchestra.

I saw Cosima, she has become really ugly and faded. She goes around in white silk with a Mozartzopf. She told me, in a friendly way, she simply had no time to receive me as they were too busy, which I can understand.

A trumpet fanfare announces the arrival of the Emperor and Princes and, at the same time, the start of *Rheingold*. It was pitch black in the theatre and impossible to see one's neighbor.

The curtain went up and the Rhine-maidens began to play. The musical effect was wonderful, with all the magic of Uncle Richard's work, but the most striking thing about the stage apparatus was its shortcomings; I have seen much better in Berlin and Paris. The lighting of the water was so dim the nixies were almost invisible and it was obvious they were in a machine—their swimming movements were just like a roundabout. A few curtains rose and fell at the wrong time and the effect of the transformation from the bottom of the Rhine to the upper ground was lost. The Rhine gold was a feeble glimmer on the rock and had no real glow. The steam curtain came at the wrong time and failed to conceal what was behind it. The dragon with a child working its jaws was just as ridiculous as in *Zauberflöte*.

The impression was one of cost-cutting where money should have been spent. It was effective but, in view of the amount of publicity beforehand, nothing should have been lacking. . . .

To find Uncle Richard was impossible, mainly because the performance yesterday had no interval; I hope it will be possible today at *Walküre*. . . .

In the evening the town was fresh and cool and there were fireworks and illuminations—as beautiful and artistic as I have ever seen in Leipzig. Uncle Richard's house and garden were lit up with little lanterns. . . . It must be very strange for Uncle to see this multitude of people, for thousands are gathered here.

The Emperor has installed himself, with half a dozen Princes too, and this brings a certain pomp to the little town. He is surrounded by admirers but seems to have no real friends. . . .

It is all very fine and doubtless will become finer still but I would not have liked to pay out 100 thalers for the *Ring* when there is so much else I could do with the money.

I am here on my own but know several families; just as well, for to be here quite alone, amongst all these ladies—that would be terribly embarrassing.

The most elegant of ladies are having to force themselves into low pubs and even sit on the doorsteps in the alleyways—and still get nothing. The three Rhine-maidens have just managed to make their midday meal in this fashion, one of them getting sausages, another bread, and the third beer.

Hartford, *Bayreuth: The Early Years*, pp. 85–86.

9. JOSEPH BENNETT ON BAYREUTH

Bennett, dispatched by the London Daily Telegraph, *compiled his dispatches and published them as* Letters from Bayreuth *(London: Novello, Ewer & Co., 1877).*

The theatre, which now stands close to Bayreuth, is not the least noteworthy feature in a remarkable enterprise. It has been described as "a solid structure of red brick and wood, neither beautiful nor ugly, without the slightest attempt at architectural show, but exactly fit for its purpose." So far, it is by no means unique, but the interior arrangements are altogether so as regards the "auditorium," which is intended to accommodate less than 1,500 persons. The peculiarity of this part of the building consists in the fact that there are neither side boxes nor side galleries. Every seat faces the stage, and only those in the end gallery are raised above the level of the floor; the object being, apart from any question of convenience, to secure the invisibility of the orchestra, which Wagner has stationed down in a pit. His theory is that no executive apparatus should come between the spectator and the drama—no gesticulating players upon instruments, no bâton-waving conductor, no orchestra lamps, and no prompter's box. All these are stowed away out of sight, while such parts of the house as command a view of them in their present position are purposely left tenantless. Nothing, therefore, will disturb the scenic illusion of the stage, between which and the audience comes only a screen of orchestral music, rising from its source in the pit, and colouring whatever is seen through it with hues of sensuous beauty (pp. 77–78).

Of all dull towns I imagine Bayreuth, in its normal state, to be the dullest. Moreover, the utter sluggishness of the place has its impression heightened by plentiful signs that, once on a time, there was life here. In the fine old days when Germany grew princes wholesale, Bayreuth had its little court and was a little capital. The potentate whose sway it owned called himself, I believe, a Margrave, and contrived, somehow or other, to keep up a considerable state. He built palaces, whereof two stand in the town, and though used for a variety of purposes, are decaying with a fit air of dignity. The third, some two miles off, serves to perpetuate the memory of its builders, much as the Brighton Pavilion immortalizes our own George the Fourth. But these edifices are by no means the only signs of Bayreuth's dead-and-gone grandeur. The place abounds in fine old houses; its streets are adorned with some very respectable statues—that, among others, of Jean-Paul Richter, who lived and died here—while numerous fountains are continually pouring out streams of clear water. These fountains, by the way, are a distinctive feature of the town which they serve to ornament as well as to bless. Of course they trace their origin to the Margraves, and the question at once arises why it was that the tyrannous old German princes expiated their bad ways by providing so much water. Once on a time they built churches, but the logic of that of course is clear enough, and, unless they saw in the "pure element" a symbol of the "mystical washing away of sin," I cannot account for the fountains. The Bayreuth churches, let me add, are not remarkable, and it is to be feared that the Margraves cared very little about them. On the whole, the town has a stately and dignified look, but is wofully faded. It is a tenth-rate Versailles, crossed with a sleepy provincial borough. Sleepy? I should think so, indeed! Even now, when the place has been galvanized into prodigious activity, one can easily distinguish Bayreuthers from strangers.

The native and his favourite beast of draught, the ox, are well matched, both going dreamily through life at the slowest possible pace, and with a constant disposition to lie down and ruminate. Just now, as I have said, Bayreuth is uncommonly alert, having actually two things on its mind at once—making money in abundance out of the strangers within its gates, and spending a little economically in decoration. The first of these operations Bayreuth will certainly carry out with success, and, as regards the second, a convenient decision has been arrived at to the effect that there is something exhilarating in the appearance of the fir which chances to abound on the neighbouring hills. The result is that Bayreuth has a fir eruption out all over it. Great branches, stuck in the ground to resemble trees, line the pavements—or rather the space where pavements should be—festoons of fir cover the fronts of the houses, and wreaths of the same cheerful material, made more lively by paper flowers, are stuck wherever room can be found for them. Adding to this a crowd of poles, from which in due time—for the Bayreuther is careful of his bunting— flags will fly, and it must be granted that the inhabitants, considering their normal sleepiness, have bestirred themselves to some purpose (pp. 23–35).

The site has been well chosen, some half-a-mile beyond the skirt of the town, and on the top of a gentle eminence which itself is backed by a wooded hill, crowned with a round tower. Rather a pretty way runs thither, the tree-shaded road being flanked by corn-fields and gardens, while the little terrace in front of the building commands an interesting view of the quaint old town and the hills beyond—a view none the less German because the most prominent object in the foreground, next to a lunatic asylum, is a big brewery. Some attempt has been made to lay out the meadow through which the carriage way passes to the theatre as a pleasaunce, but at present the trees are small, the walks ill-kept, and the grass rough. Roughness, indeed, is characteristic of the whole affair, for, to say nothing of the wooden houses flanking the main building, and devoted to refreshment, the theatre itself seems to have been hastily thrown up, and its courses of red brick, left innocent of "pointing." Of architectural beauty the exterior has none whatever. The object was utility, and this gained, nothing beyond was sought. In time to come, perhaps, when funds are plentiful, the artist as well as the builder will have to do with the place, and succeed in making it less of a disappointment than it is now. As with the exterior, so elsewhere. On entering the auditorium, one sees a perfectly plain room, suggesting a college lecture hall on a large scale. It is in the form of a parallelogram, the stage occupying the centre of one of the long sides; the side opposite being devoted to a gallery for distinguished visitors (called the Princes' Gallery), having another for less remarkable people above. The area seats rise tier above tier from the brink of the space occupied by the orchestra to the level of the Princes' Gallery, so that every seat faces the stage, and commands a full view of it. As the seats spread out like a fan from below upwards, it is obvious that there must be a large vacant space along the shorter sides of the parallelogram. The effect of this is, however, broken by a division into bays, separated by Corinthian columns supporting entablatures. Over these entablatures and around the pillars are placed the gas lamps— few in number, because during the performance the house is kept in darkness save for the light reflected from the stage. As the roof is low, and the distance from the stage to the opposite side not great, one is struck on entering with the apparent smallness of the place. In a little while, however, the width of the auditorium asserts itself, and it is possible to believe in the accommodation of some 1,500 people. Regarding the arrangements behind the curtain I cannot speak, but the working of the stage at the rehearsal on Wednesday night was so perfect that reports of admirable ingenuity may be credited without reserve. The rapidity, silence, and smoothness with which the various changes were made contrasted most favourably with the uproar and clumsiness which theatre-goers are so often called upon to notice, while the absence from view of all such executive machinery as orchestra, prompter, and foot-lights made the drama intensely real to the audience, who seemed indeed to be "assisting" at it in a very forcible sense of the term (pp. 28–30).

10. PETER ILYICH TCHAIKOVSKY REPORTS ON THE PERFORMANCE
a. From a Letter to His Brother Modeste, August 14, 1876

Yesterday the performance of Rheingold took place. From the scenic point of view it interested me greatly, and I was also much impressed by the truly marvelous staging of the work. Musically, it is inconceivable nonsense, in which here and there occur beautiful, and even captivating, moments.

Hartford, *Bayreuth: The Early Years*, p. 52.

b. From His Report to the Russky Viedmosty

I made a little excursion through the streets of the town. They swarmed with people of all nationalities, who looked very much preoccupied and as if in search of something. The reason for this anxious search I discovered only too soon, as I myself had to share it. All these restless people, wandering through the town, were seeking to satisfy the pangs of hunger, which even the fullness of artistic enjoyment could not entirely assuage. The little town offers, it is true, sufficient shelter to the strangers, but it is not able to feed all its guests. So it happened on the very day of my arrival, I learnt the meaning of the words "struggle for existence." There are very few hotels in Bayreuth, and the greater part of the visitors find accommodation in private houses. The tables d'hôte prepared in the inns are not sufficient to satisfy all the hungry people; one can only obtain a piece of bread, a glass of beer, with immense difficulty, by dire struggle, or cunning stratagem or iron endurance. Even a modest place at a table, when it has been obtained, is not the end—it is then necessary to wait an eternity before the long desired meal is served. Anarchy reigns at these meals; everyone is calling and shrieking, and the exhausted waiters pay no heed to the rightful claims of an individual. Only by the merest chance does one get a taste of any of the dishes. In the neighborhood of the Theatre is a restaurant which advertises a good dinner at two o'clock. But to get inside it and lay hold of anything in that throng of hungry creatures is a feat worthy of a hero. I have dwelt on this matter at some length with the design of calling the attention of my readers to this prominent feature of the Bayreuth melomania. As a matter of fact, throughout the whole duration of the Festival, food forms the chief interest of the public; the artistic representations take a secondary place. Cutlets, baked potatoes, omelettes—are discussed much more eagerly than Wagner's music.

The performance of the *Rheingold* took place on August 13th at 7 P.M. It lasted without a break two hours and a half. The other three parts will be given with an hour's interval between their Acts—and will last from 4 P.M. to 10 P.M. In consequence of the indisposition of the singer Betz, Siegfried was postponed from Tuesday to Wednesday, so that the first cycle lasted fully five days.

Each of the Acts lasts an hour and a half; then comes an interval, but a very disagreeable one, for the sun is still far from setting and it is difficult to find a place in the shade. The second interval, on the contrary, is the most beautiful part of the day. The sun is already near the horizon; in the air one feels the coolness of the evening, the wooded hills around, and the charming little town in the distance, are lovely (p. 54).

Anyone who believes in the civilising power of Art must take away from Bayreuth a very refreshing impression of this great artistic endeavour which will form a milestone in the history of Art. In the face of this building erected for artistic enjoyment; in the face of the mass of people who have come from all over to a corner of Europe in the name of an unprecedented musico-dramatic Festival; in the face of all this how wretched and ridiculous appear all those prophets who, in their blindness, regard our age as the age of total decay of pure Art. At the same time the Bayreuth Festival is a lesson for those hidden persecutors of Art—those who haughtily believe that progressive people ought to occupy themselves with nothing other than that which is of immediate and utilitarian value. In respect of the welfare of mankind the Bayreuth Festival is of no importance whatsoever. There is, however, an even greater and more eternal meaning—in the sense of a striving towards an artistic ideal. Whether Richard Wagner was right in serving his idea to the extent he has done, whether he neglected the principles of artistic and aesthetic balance and whether Art will now progress from his work as a point of departure or whether the *Ring* will mark a point at which a reaction will set in—who would wish to pronounce on that today? One thing is certain, that something has happened at Bayreuth, something which our grandchildren and great-grandchildren will remember.

If I, as a professional musician, had the feeling of total mental and physical exhaustion after the performance of each of the parts of the *Ring*—how great must be the fatigue of the amateurs! It is true that the latter concern themselves far more with the wonders which take place on the stage than with the orchestra or the singers—but one must assume that Wagner wrote the music for it to be listened to and not to be secondary to the drama. The musician, then, judges the actual music whereas the amateur-dilettante enjoys the scenery and transformations, the dragon and the snakes, the swimming Rhinemaidens and the rest. Since he is, in my opinion, totally incapable of extracting any musical enjoyment out of this sea of sound, he takes his pleasure from the spectacular production. This pleasure he confuses with musical pleasure and he attempts to convince himself and others that he has completely grasped all the beauties of the music of Wagner (p. 55).

I brought away the impression that the *Ring* contains many passages of extraordinary beauty, especially symphonic beauty, which is remarkable, as Wagner has no stated intention of writing an opera in the style of a symphony. I feel a respectful admiration for the immense talents of the composer and his wealth of technique, such as has never been heard before. I will, however, continue the study of the music—the most complicated which has hitherto been composed. Yet if the *Ring* bores one in places, if much of it is incomprehensible and vague, if Wagner's harmonies are at times open to objection as being too complicated and artificial, and his theories false, even if the results of his immense work should eventually fall into oblivion, and the Bayreuth Theatre drop into an eternal slumber, yet the Nibelungenring is an event of the greatest importance to the world, an epoch-making work of art (p. 56).

11. EDVARD GRIEG

From the composer's 1876 reports in the Bergenpost, *in Hartford,* Bayreuth: The Early Years.

[August 7, at the dress rehearsal of *Rheingold:*] As they [the orchestra] gather in the pit it comes to resemble a huge ant-hill of players and instruments. Then the conductor of genius, Hans Richter, comes to take his place. A silence falls on the pit—it is said the King is on his way—and then Wagner's voice roars out from the principal box "Begin!" . . .

Wagner's special ability to describe scenes such as occur in *Rheingold* causes the spectator to be carried away by the effect and to forget the lack of drama in them. Long dialogues such as the gods have cannot be consistently interesting; no matter how much the music sustains them, they still become quite tedious. Again, Wagner writes better for the giants and dwarfs than he does for the gods and goddesses—he does not have the elevated serenity and noble simplicity that the character of Wotan demands.

Returning to my lodging after the rehearsal I tell myself that, in spite of much there is to criticise, the inadequate characterisation of the gods, the ceaseless modulations and wearying chromaticism of the harmonies and the end result of leaving the listener totally exhausted, this music drama is the creation of a true giant in the history of art, comparable in his innovation only to Michelangelo. In music there is nobody to approach Wagner.

That the rehearsal performance itself was outstanding I do not need to assure you. . . . (p. 63)

[August 14:] To be a music critic and journalist in this weather is a tall order. The heat is killing. But, as you will agree, now I have started the job I must proceed to finish it. I will now tell you about the fantastic Festival itself and the occasion of the first public performance of *Rheingold*.

The day is fine and the town all decorated with flags to welcome the German Kaiser who has just turned up; it appears his arrival is to crown the occasion, which we must not forget is the bringing forth of the first real drama festival since the days of the Greek tragedies, or so the Wagner-fanatics would have it. King Ludwig, however, as everyone who knows him feared, has run away from all the tumult; this is odd since he himself invited the Kaiser to Bavaria.

Thank God that the performance is now to begin two hours later at seven o'clock instead of five; the heat in the Festspielhaus at that hour is impossible, it would have been like a Turkish bath.

It is now just four o'clock and people have already started to walk up the hill to the theatre. To judge from their clothes there are people here from all social classes, the gentry in all their grand attire and jewels, young fanatical intellectuals and hundreds of artists and musicians of all kinds, all united by the excitement of the unique occasion.

Everybody is in his place in the theatre. Suddenly a silence. The Kaiser has arrived. In comes one prince of the blood after another and, at the end, the Kaiser who greets his people, in his warm human way, as he passes through to his place in the theatre.

The performance begins. The theatre is hot and packed with people and this makes the tone of the orchestra subdued, compared with the rehearsals, and it also affects the pitch of some of the singers. But it is really wonderful. Of the singers the most impressive are Vogl as Loge and Schlosser as Mime who is actually applauded after his "numbers" and not even Jaïde's fantastic Erda receives such recognition.

Well, I leave all that for the Germans to fight about. Yes, they actually do come to blows—in the local inns, and with beer-mugs for weapons (anybody being hit on the head with a "Töpfchen" is hors-de-combat!).

If Wagner has been annoyed by the imperfect scene-changes and sloppy stage management then he has every right to be, for they all left a lot to be desired. Things like the rainbow on the wrong side of the stage and scene-changing so tardy that the orchestra had to slow down to match up with the action—these are hardly what the Master wanted. Considering the fact that Wagner and his circle have been publicly criticising performances elsewhere (performances generally liked and praised) it must be rather embarrassing for them to have such mistakes at Bayreuth.

Well, I think that, with exceptions such as Valhalla, which looks more like a royal castle than the abode of the gods, these sets, on the whole, were good. Nevertheless, I had expected something more of this *Rheingold* performance—perhaps my trouble was that I had already been to the dress rehearsals of the *Ring; Rheingold* is, of course, a masterpiece, but ought not to be seen immediately following *Götterdämmerung*. It is thus like comparing the Scottish highlands with the Swiss Alps—even big things are diminished when compared with even greater ones (p. 66–67).

August 14: A little town like Bayreuth is in no way prepared for the reception of so many visitors. Not only are there no luxuries: often enough there are not even the necessities. I doubt that the enjoyment of art is furthered by being uncomfortably housed for a week, sleeping badly, eating wretchedly, and after a strenuous five or six hours' performance of opera, being uncertain of securing a modest snack. Even yesterday I saw many who had arrived in the flush of enthusiasm crawling up the hot dusty street to the distant Wagner Theatre in a considerably more sober frame of mind. The participating artists, too, have expressed fully justified reservations. How easily, they say, could many a deficiency, which came to light only at the dress rehearsals (inadequate casting of minor roles) have been corrected in a big city, while here a change is no longer possible. A distinguished member of the orchestra arrived with a cello half-ruined on the journey. In any larger city it could have easily been repaired; Bayreuth, however, has no instrument maker. There is no need to go any further with this chapter . . . I only wish to state my increased conviction that a major artistic undertaking belongs in a major city (p. 73).

Wagner has utilised all the modern advances of applied science. We have seen in astonishment the colossal machinery, the gas apparatus, the steam machines above and below the stage at Bayreuth. Wagner could have as little composed the *Ring* before the invention of the electric light as without the harp and bass tuba. Thus it is that the element of colour in the broadest sense disguises the paltry design in his newest works and usurps for itself an unheard-of self-sufficiency. It is through its sensually fascinating magic that this music, as a direct nervous stimulant, works so powerfully on the audience and on the female audience particularly. The professional musician's part in this highly advanced orchestral technique has rather to do with how it is all accomplished. I underestimate neither the one nor the other; but neither is entitled to violent domination. Neither the conductor's technical gourmet's interest, nor the hashish dream of the ecstatic female, fulfills the nature and benediction of genuine musical composition; both can, and often do, exist independently of the soul of music.

With whatever hopes and fears one may have made the pilgrimage to Bayreuth, we were all united at least in our anticipation of an extraordinary theatrical event. But even this expectation was only partially fulfilled. I have duly acknowledged Wagner's imaginative innovations in the arrangement of his theatre, including, as regards the mechanical side, the scene of the swimming Rhine-maidens in *Rheingold*. From there on there is a gradual descent. That the very first change of scene failed mechanically, that everything went generally awry, is not something to which I can attach much importance. That sort of thing can happen in any theatre, although it would have been better had it not happened in this widely heralded and elaborately prepared "model production" at Bayreuth. There were examples aplenty of incorrect and deficient mounting, and in decisive places. The rainbow, over which the gods proceed to Valhalla, was set so low that one could have taken it for a painted bridge in a flower garden (p. 84).

By far the most successful were the sets by Josef Hoffmann, as well painted as they were original in conception; with faithful execution and more purposeful lighting they could have been even more effective. The painter of the scenery can only account for a half of the total effect; the other half rests with the lighting, which corresponds to the instrumentation of a musical idea. This second half was not fully carried out in Bayreuth, and Hoffmann's ideas appear more melodiously conceived in the photographs than they sounded in the Festival Theatre.

That the vast majority of the Bayreuth pilgrims broke into jubilant applause after each of the four dramas was to be expected; they came for that purpose. The conviction I expressed in my first report, that the durability of Wagner's newest works and their effect on the public will be definitively proved only on other stages, still stands (p. 85).

Cited in Hartford, *Bayreuth: The Early Years.*

13. JOHN R. G. HASSARD FROM HIS REVIEWS IN THE *NEW YORK TRIBUNE*

[At a rehearsal] The proscenium is painted of a somber, dusky-tint; the ceiling is flat, with frescoes of a neutral shade; the benches are plain, with cane seats, and rise with a steep ascent, in rows but slightly curved, the front row being just the length of the proscenium, the rear being nearly twice as long, but all the spectators so placed that they have a clear view of the entire stage. There are no bad seats. At the rear of the benches is the box for the King and other high dignitaries. The auditorium is small, having a capacity of only 1,500, and the width of the proscenium is not remarkable, but the stage itself is of enormous breadth and depth, while a huge loft for the working of the machinery towers above it, and a cellar for the same purpose goes deep below. There are no lights in the auditorium, except a few near the ceiling at the sides and rear, and these are almost entirely extinguished before the curtain is drawn. If one had a libretto, therefore, it would be impossible to follow it during the play. In Wagner's dramas the attention must be concentrated on the stage. Even the orchestra and conductor are out of sight, down in the "mystic gulf" which separates the spectators from the actors. A shelf projecting over the heads of the players hides them and their leader from the house, but they are visible of course to those on the stage.

Twenty minutes after the appointed hour of 7 a sudden hush fell upon our little gathering. Nobody seemed to know whence the signal came, but the word somehow ran around that His Majesty had arrived. We heard cheers from the people outside; a door opened and closed, and we felt that the darkness was more oppressive and mysterious than ever. Then Wagner, behind the scenes, gave a quick shout of command; the orchestra began. I do not intend to anticipate in this letter the full account of the play, which I shall send you after the regular performance. Here I merely set down the first impression produced by a rehearsal, which differed in no essential respect from a public representation except in the absence of spectators. It is enough to say that all my previous ideas of what a Wagner opera might be were set at naught. The most extravagant expectations were more than realized. "Rheingold" is better known than the other parts of the work, but nobody who has not seen it here can form a conception of its unearthly beauties, its stupendous and always increasing effects. It flows on, without pause or division into acts, for nearly two hours and a half, and during all that time we sat spell-bound, our eyes fixed upon the wonderful spectacle, our ears drinking in the strange sounds. It was a hot night, and the theatre is entirely without ventilation; but we forgot the stifling air, and when the curtain fell at last upon the closing scene where the gods cross over the rainbow bridge to their gorgeous castle in the clouds, we seemed to awake from a dream of delight, and wondered at the flight of time. We had entered the theatre by daylight; it was nearly 10 o'clock when, silent and thoughtful, we groped our way out, and then a fresh surprise awaited us. The whole city was illuminated. Rows of lights gleamed along the mile of road which leads from the theatre down to the town. From the hill where we stood Bayreuth was visible in its full extent, bathed in light. The facades of the public buildings were all traced in lines of fire—for illuminations in this part of the world, unlike our own, are always arranged with ingenious architectural effects (pp. 7–9).

[On the scenery at a rehearsal of *Siegfried*] The scenic effects however cannot be adequately described without a much more eloquent pen than mine. There is nothing comparable to them even in our best theatres. The flat picture let down at the back and made to do duty as a house, or a field, or a river, as the case may be, is unknown here. Every scene is built up with the most minute attention to details. There are no wings, but the realistic construction of the scene is continued along the sides and down to the front. There are no flapping borders overhead, but the tree, sky, or roof goes up as high as the eye can reach. The stage is not lighted in the usual way from the wings, borders and foot-lights, but by some contrivance which I do not understand a light seems to be diffused over the whole scene. Sometimes it comes from the back. Moreover, the light is continually changing. Night and day, sunshine and storm, follow each other by nice gradations, and even when all the action takes place by day there are shifting lights and shadows as there are in nature. The cloud effects are beautiful, and Wagner employs them freely. Transparent vapors float over the heavens with incessant motion or hover around the rocky steeps. For this purpose very thin painted gauzes are used. For heavier exhalations an illusion is produced by clouds of steam. A scene is never raised or lowered in sight of the audience; when a change becomes necessary during the progress of an act, clouds settle gradually over the picture, dropping gently from above, while steam rises from a crevice in the stage; and when the atmosphere clears the change has been made. It is by means of steam, reddened by reflected light, and shot here and there with small flames, that the effects of fire are produced, of which I shall have to speak hereafter. All of the illusions are heightened by the utter darkness of the auditorium, and the great distance between the front row of seats and the curtain. The scene-painting is magnificent. Every picture shows the sentiment and hand of an artist in idea and treatment. There is none of the false brilliancy and glaring color of the conventional stage decorator; the painting is not theatrical at all, but it is truthful. The costumes, upon which Wagner has spent great pains and enormous sums of money, are not only brilliant, but they are poetical. Finally, the actors, though differing in degrees of merit, are all imbued with the spirit of the drama and the music. Not one of them thinks of such a thing as singing to the audience, or coming down to the front. Here is indeed a remarkable gathering of distinguished artists, and none of us are likely to see such an assemblage again (pp. 12–13).

[At the premiere of *Rheingold*] It was a victory won in the presence of a most brilliant company of spectators. The long *Fürstenloge,* or the Box of Princes, extending entirely across the theatre at the back of the auditorium, was filled with noble personages, the old Emperor in the middle, grand dukes, duchesses, court officials and titled ladies all about him. Most of the audience were in full evening dress, and the scene reminded me much more of a fashionable metropolitan opera season than of a hot Summer in this remote little Bavarian city. There were tremendous cheers at the entrance of the Emperor, the whole multitude rising to welcome him, and his majesty stood bowing for some time before quiet was restored. At length the trumpet blast was heard which serves here as the signal; the lights were immediately turned down, and the poem of "The Ring of the Nibelungs" began.

The instrumental introduction depicted the restless movement of the deep river. It began away down in the lowest register of the contra bass-tuba, and flowed on, on, on, with the same simple chord of E flat, now rising, now falling, with increasing beauty and variety, till it had changed rather abruptly into the graceful melody of the Rhine-daughters, and the curtain, drawn back to the sides, disclosed one of the most surprising scenes ever set forth in a theatre. We looked into the obscure depths of the Rhine. The stage to its whole height seemed to be filled with water. At the bottom were rugged rocks and dark caverns. Toward the top the waters were a little clearer, and a faint quivering light struggled through them from above. Seen across the dark theatre with the wavy music coming up out of an invisible chasm between us and the river, like a wall of separation between reality and illusion, this far-away picture was like a vision. At first, in the dim and watery light, it was impossible to distinguish one shape from another. Little by little we became aware of graceful forms in flowing blue robes rising and sinking in the upper waters, gliding among the rocks with waving white arms, and calling to one another in a gentle and joyous melody. These were the three Rhine daughters, guardians of the Rhine Gold. Nothing could be more charming than their frolic trio, embellished as it was by such a wealth of instrumental illustration, such remarkable stage mechanism and poetical scenery. Here we saw at the very start the world-wide difference between the orchestra of Wagner with its freedom and eloquence of dramatic expression, and the "accompaniment" which sustains the voices in the old school of opera. Here indeed it may almost be said that individual performers in the band became as truly *dramatis personae* as the actors on the stage. Soon the fluent character of this beautiful water music was disturbed by the introduction of a new theme, and in the increasing light we discerned the figure of Alberich the nibelung groping among the rocks in the bed of the river. He pursued the Rhine daughters with an amorous eagerness, and they swam above him, sinking sometimes almost to his grasp, but always eluding it, and jeering at him with mock tenderness and merry laughter. The Alberich of Karl Hill, and the Rhine daughters personated by Lilli and Marie Lehmann and Minna Lammert, were all admirable in voice and action. To the distant spectator the mechanism by which the motions of swimming and floating were so aptly counterfeited was entirely incomprehensible, and the illusion was perfect. I believe the women rested on saddles supported by iron rods which their long drapery covered. The motion was given from below. In the midst of the sport a bright light began to shine at the summit of the rocks, and suddenly, after a charming orchestral interlude, the glow of the gold broke forth from the point of a steep cliff, the horns giving out at the same moment a motive of great brilliancy and power. The music rapidly became more and more animated as the Rhine daughters greeted the apparition with joyous exclamations. They told Alberich of the wonderful power of this gold, which no one could obtain without renouncing forever the joys of love, and in the course of the dialogue two other motives, both to become important in the development of the drama, were successively introduced. The nibelung pronounced a curse upon love, and with violent effort reached the summit and seized the gold. The light was quenched. We could just see Alberich throw himself headlong from the rock into the deep, while the Rhine daughters with a cry of dismay—a modification of their first cheerful melody, changed into a minor key—sank from sight, and darkness settled over the scene. Here, during the rehearsals, the waters disappeared, almost imperceptibly, as if swallowed up by thick clouds, but to-night a blunder of the machinists marred the effect. The orchestra continued the work of dramatic illusion in a long and beautiful passage, changing gradually to more heroic strains, and as the music changed so the clouds too grew thin, vanished, and left open before us a beautiful morning landscape.

The foreground was a flowery field, supposed to represent a high table-land. A barrier of rock, overlooking the valley of the Rhine, bounded it in the rear, and in the distant background the gates and towers of Walhalla loomed indistinctly through the clouds. Wotan, the chief deity of the Norse mythology, slept on a grassy bank with his spouse Fricka by his side. The splendour of the morning came forth as the orchestra played the magnificent passage which symbolizes the stately castle of the gods, and recurs in the course of the trilogy as one of the principal leading motives. Fricka awoke Wotan from his dreams to look at this stronghold which the giants had built for him while he slept. In a superb dialogue she reminded him that the builders would soon come to claim their promised reward, which was nothing less than the possession of Freia, the goddess of youth, and here we heard one of the most imposing as well as important of all the leading motives in the work, the ponderous descending scale in the bass indicating the law which binds the gods by their plighted word. The proud dignity of the "All-Father," beautifully expressed in the rich bass of Franz Betz, contrasted finely with the agitation of his spouse and the alarm of Freia, who entered hastily a few moments later and prayed for help against her pursuers. Following close upon her delicious melody we heard in the orchestra the measured tramp of the giants, Fafner and Fasolt, and their ungainly figures were seen climbing up from the valley and crossing over the rocks. The rest of this brilliant scene almost baffles description, and certainly to convey by letter any idea of the richness, force, and vividness of the music is quite out of the question. The giants insisted upon the terms of the bargain. The cries of Fricka and Freia, the threats of the brother gods Donner and Froh, the anger of Wotan could not move them. Not daring to break his word, Wotan asked advice of Loge, the god of fire, and as this subtle character was introduced we heard the strains of the fire music so familiar to American audiences in connection with the finale of the "Walküre." Loge, in a melody of the most picturesque beauty, which called out untimely but irresistible applause, declared that there was nothing the gods could offer the giants in exchange for Freia, except the ring forged by Alberich from the stolen treasure of the Rhine, thus formulating, so to speak, one of the chief ideas of the tragedy, which is the conflict between love and the lust of gold. After a magnificent passage, in which the "ring melody" asserted a marked prominence, and each of the divinities in turn asked characteristic questions respecting the power of the gold, the giants agreed to wait until evening for a final answer, taking Freia meanwhile as security.

Dragging after them the distressed goddess, Fafner and Fasolt, great hulking fellows, roughly clad and walking with big staves, climbed down the rocky descent and left the gods in melancholy thought. At once a gray mist settled upon the heights. The light faded. Everything began to wear an appearance of hoary age, for the gods had not tasted that day Freia's life-renewing apples. When they lamented their fading power Loge mocked at them, and at last Wotan agreed to accompany the fire-god to the abode of the dwarfs and take possession of the ring. This was the crime from which flowed all the misfortunes of the divine race and the tragedy of the drama.

As Loge, followed by Wotan, disappeared in a chasm of the rocks, a thick vapor issued from the opening and gradually overspread the whole scene. The vapor changed to dense clouds. The music of the orchestra became more animated; the fire-motive recurred; a deep red glow began to suffuse the clouds, and as they slowly dissolved we heard the hammering of anvils, and then there lay before us the subterranean caverns of the nibelungs, with a long vista of rock, at the extremity of which shone the gleam of forges. We saw Alberich beating his brother Mime, whom he had compelled to forge for him the tarn-helmet, gifted with the power of making the wearer invisible. He tried the helmet, and to the great terror of Mime vanished in a cloud, and then, during an orchestral interlude based upon the anvil melody, Wotan and Loge entered, coming down from above by an opening into the free air. Their scene with Mime was wonderful for its strong definitions of character, and the Mime of Karl Schlosser was enlivened by an amusing grotesqueness, particularly noticeable when in a rude rhythmic melody,

Sorglose Schmiede,
Schufen wir sonst,

with the anvil melody again in the accompaniment, he told Wotan and Loge of his once happy life and his sufferings under Alberich's blows. But if I undertook to describe all the incidents of this visit of the gods to Nebelheim I should soon exhaust your space if not your patience. Alberich was induced by the cunning Loge to exhibit the properties of the tarn-helmet. He disappeared, and in his place there was a hideous crawling creature. He disappeared again, and took the form of a toad. These two contrivances, I may remark, were the only commonplace theatrical devices of the evening. Wotan set his foot upon the toad; Loge grasped it by the head, the helmet came away in his hands and Alberich lay helpless on the ground. The gods bound him, and hurried him to the heights above. Cloud and mist covered the stage once more, as the orchestra, in an interlude so vivid that it might be called a musical panorama, led us back to the assemblage of the divinities. We passed again through the noise of the smithy, and we heard the heavy tread of climbing feet which had ushered in the giants in the second scene. At last we were shown the table land, still covered as before with a dull haze, and Wotan and Loge appeared with their prisoner. For his ransom Alberich caused the dwarfs to bring all the treasures of Nebelheim, and to these the gods forced him to add the helmet and the ring. Thus stripped of all his power he was sent back to the lower world, but before he departed he laid upon the ring the terrible curse:

> Wie durch Fluch er mir gerieth,
> Verflucht sei dieser Ring,

which, as an orchestral motive is to play so important a part in the music of the whole drama. As the giants approached with Freia, the mists broke away; the light of youth appeared again on the faces of the gods; only the towers of Walhalla in the background remained still veiled in the clouds. But Wotan's purpose, while giving the giants the rest of the treasure, was to save the ring for himself, and hence when the payment came to be made he kept it on his finger. Fasolt and Fafner were to have as much gold and silver as, heaped up between their staves, would cover Freia from sight. The whole of Alberich's ransom except the ring was placed upon the pile; even the tarn-helmet was surrendered; still there was a crevice which the ring would just fill. Wotan refused to give it up. The giants in a rage were about to drag Freia away; the scene grew dark again; when from a cleft in the rocks on the right a bluish light appeared, and the figure of Erda, the universal and eternal mother, rose from the earth. She warned Wotan in solemn and mysterious strains of the misfortunes impending over Walhalla, and counseled him to avoid the fatal gold. The god stood for a moment in deep thought, and as he leaned upon his spear we heard the majestic motive which indicates the binding force of Wotan's word. The ring was given up. Joyous strains accompanied the liberation of Freia and the dispersal of the clouds. But Alberich's curse was not long in working its effect. The giants quarreled for the possession of the ring, and Fafner killed Fasolt, put all the treasure into a sack, and took himself off.

Then came a finale, which in picturesque effect and musical beauty surpassed all the great scenes which had gone before it. The gods were at last to take possession of their castle. Donner stood upon the summit of a high rock in the middle of the stage. Swinging his hammer, he collected the mists which still hung about the background, and a black thunder cloud enveloped him. Out of the darkness we heard his voice and the ominous roll of the heavenly artillery, till with a blow of his sledge he dispersed the clouds in a dazzling flash of lightning, and a rainbow stretched from the rock whereon he stood to the stronghold in the sky. A delicious melody succeeded the stormy passage in the orchestra, and the gods, gathering around the rock, prepared to cross to Walhalla by the rainbow bridge. The monologue of Wotan,

Abendlich strahlt
Der Sonne Auge,

before he led the way to the new abode, is one of the most elevated of all Wagner's conceptions, and as it was delivered by Betz, with such richness of illustration and startling harmonic devices in the orchestra, we felt that we had reached the climax of a great poem. The celestial procession ascended and moved slowly on. Suddenly we heard from the depths of the valley below the chorus of the Rhine-daughters bewailing the lost ring, and with this fascinating music resounding in our ears, with the full splendor of the sun revealing for the first time the magnificence of Walhalla, and the refulgent group of the gods advancing toward its shining gates, the curtain fell and the first evening was at an end.

The performance had lasted two hours and a half without intermission of any kind—for the "Rhinegold," unlike the other parts of the work, is not divided into acts—but in spite of the terrible heat of the crowded and unventilated theatre, I am sure that no appreciative person can have found the evening long. The interest rose steadily from the first scene to the last; amazement grew that man should have conceived such wonderful effects, or a single brain have found the means to set before the world in all this clearness and splendor such a subtle and deep-felt poem. We came away not only excited, but bewildered. For there is nothing like this in all music or in all the history of the stage. It was a great surprise to those who have been accustomed to decry Wagner's compositions as abstruse, for they found that it appealed directly to their feelings, and called for no exercise whatever of the reasoning or reflecting powers. The least cultivated spectator could understand and love it. One had only to sit still, look, listen, and enjoy. But nobody can take it all in at one hearing, or at two, or at a dozen. It is a mine that grows richer and richer the more it is explored, and whoever has studied the score for a little while is tempted to drop it in despair of fathoming this wonderful genius. I mention the entire music of Wotan as one of the very greatest dramatic creations in the whole range of the lyric art, and by the music of Wotan I mean not only what is sung, but the equally important and far richer part which is given to the instruments. And for delicacy and sentiment there are few things comparable to the music of Fricka. We shall hear, of course (from those who were not at Bayreuth), the old objection that Wagner's opera contains nothing that can be carried away and whistled as one hurries home to bed, and we shall be asked whether four nights of music without a distinct "tune" can possibly be endurable? I can only point to the enormous success of this experiment as a complete and final answer to the question. In this work, entrancing the senses through a long and uncomfortable evening, the narrower form of rhythmic melody was entirely disregarded. The large, all-pervading melody which took its place reminded us of the beautiful figure in which Wagner once compared his ideal of the opera to the effect produced upon the soul by a beautiful forest in a Summer evening. The wanderer who has just left the town hears in the silence of the wood an endless variety of sweet voices. As they multiply in numbers and increase in mysterious power, they combine to form a great forest of melody which long haunts his imagination. Yet he cannot hum it to himself; to hear it again he must go back to the woods.

I have not said much of the singers, because in a work of this kind it seems to me the height of absurdity to expend much criticism upon the vocalism of a first tenor or a prima donna. It may be said however in brief that a more perfect ensemble could probably not be made in Germany. The central figure of course was the Wotan of Herr Betz; the next in merit and importance was the admirable Loge of Herr Vogl (tenor). Gura and Unger, as Donner and Froh, had comparatively little to do, but will be heard more fully hereafter. The Fricka of Frl. Grün was charming, and the three Rhinedaughters were almost perfect. Male singers in Germany as a general thing sing more or less false, and Herr Wagner's company of gods and heroes offer no exception to the nearly universal rule. But we are ready to pardon occasional lapses of this sort in consideration of the remarkable excellence of their personations, their noble appearance, good voices, and close sympathy with the music (pp. 17–27).

> John R. G. Hassard, *Richard Wagner at Bayreuth: The Ring of the Nibelungs — A Description of the First Performance in August 1876* (*Reprinted from the* New York Tribune) (New York: Francis Hart & Co., 1877).

14. GEORGE FREEMANTLE (?), FROM AN UNSIGNED REVIEW IN THE *MANCHESTER GUARDIAN*, AUGUST 9, 1876

The first grand dress rehearsal took place on Sunday night. Joining the band of profound-looking music lovers, I groped my way to my seat in the gallery. The anxieties of a nervous spectacled gentleman, who was afraid that sufficient support had not been placed beneath the gallery, were hushed at the appearance of Herr Wagner. A curt bow, a few immaterial words in a low monotone, hardly audible from where I sat, a pause, then a rap, and the wonderful waves of undulating music which introduce the prologue to the trilogy, *Das Rheingold,* came floating up from the mysterious depths beneath the stage, without in the least diminishing the volume or dulling the tone. It seemed to flow and follow, growing fuller and grander, like the current of some mighty stream, until the curtain parted and the realistic effect of the scenery was added to the impressive power of the music, and one thought he saw the lonely depth of the Rhine, each crested wave lit with a golden light. Of course there were inevitable hitches and pauses consequent on any rehearsal, yet they were few and far between and everything went most smoothly.

Wagner, as stage director, sat normally in a chair at the side of the stage. He was dressed in light clothes and wore his velvet cap. Suddenly he would shuffle across the stage with his hands beneath his coat tails, gesticulate violently to put more force into the orchestra, or rush up to a singer in the midst of his or her part and say, in a light sharp voice, "No, no no; not so; sing it so," and suiting the action to the direction, would sing the part as it should be, or throw the necessary dramatic fire into the action. All of his directions were given with the aim of producing the greatest naturalness and through this, the most perfect power.

The delighted audience sat in silence, and as they streamed out of the theatre on to the terrace and into the beer-room, in their festal dress, the only word to be heard was "Herrlich" [noble].

Cited in Hartford, *Bayreuth: The Early Years*, p. 96.

15. HEINRICH PORGES ON THE AUDIENCE

With the dress rehearsals, on the sixth through the ninth of the month, the whole events of preparation of the last month have been brought to a close, and now we stand directly before the days of the first performances of the stage festival. Guests are coming here from all the countries of the world to take part in an artistic festival, such as has not happened since the flowering of Athens. For the first time in the modern world has a building been erected and dedicated to dramatic art, in whose construction no other criterion was considered than this: to let the scenic picture come through in its ideal form to the spectator. In order to reach this goal Richard Wagner's orchestra was placed deep and out of sight, and thus inevitably the amphitheatrical arrangement of the auditorium came about. In addition to its central purpose of allowing each spectator a view of the stage, this last arrangement also achieved a second: it had the effect that all those present are merged into an ideal unity, and are able to feel the truth of this unity themselves. If I take up my pen again now before the meaningful moment in which the German people will be shown in tragic artwork a picture of their own innermost life, I do so with that reluctance that seizes us when we stand before the revelation of a long-kept secret. Whoever was present at the last dress rehearsals, which throughout had the character of a performance, probably had the feeling, as I did, though nothing of the kind had happened before, that only a respectful silence was appropriate. How can one who was permitted a glimpse into the depths of all being, then enter the chattering marketplace to talk to another who has not experienced it? It must seem to him like a profanation of the revelation accorded to him. But when he feels that all the power of speech would not suffice to give the right explanation of his experiences to the other, he gives up, and instead he encourages the other with loud voice to take the same path, so as to see with his own eyes. And so I too can do nothing else than to call to all those whose souls are open to the things of the spirit: Abandon all your worldly cares and come, to experience a few unique, consecrated hours, where the veil seems to be removed, which formerly hid from us the true nature of the world; here you can come to understand the deep significance of the poetic words "There are moments in human life when we are nearer than usual to the World Spirit."

What purpose could it serve to extract something in particular from the organic whole of the work which will shortly appear in its full living quality, and in which the poet, crossing the boundaries of sensual existence, brings before us not only the fate of individuals, but that of the world itself, brought to tragedy! The magical means that alone allows him to bring us this rarity is music, and in particular the symphonic music sounding from the hidden deep. . . .

Neue Zeitschrift für Musik, 1876, repr. Susanna Grossmann-Vendrey, *Bayreuth in der* deutschen Presse: Beitrage zur Rezeptionsgeschichte Richard Wagners und seiner Festspiele (Regensburg: Bosse, 1977–1983). Vol. 1: *Die Grundsteinlegung und die ersten Festspiele (1872–1876)*, p. 47.

16. HERMANN KRETZSCHMAR, "BAYREUTHER BRIEFE," *MUSIKALISCHES WOCHENBLATT*, 1876

August 7: The tones sound as though from out of the earth, out of the depths of the forest. Long before the performance begins, time and space are no more. How splendidly then, when the performance actually does begin, the music rings from behind that screen—that is something one must hear for oneself. Every thing is so well balanced, the brass instruments without those shadows of material coarseness, and the woodwinds clearer than ever before. This comes from the arrangement, which affords these last instruments the greatest freedom of playing, while the other two parts of the orchestra must be pleased by the damping that comes from the slanting walls. The solo violin of Herr Professor Wilhelmj sounds grandly and often through this mass, one of the countless delights of the new sounds which the score of "Rheingold" provides. . . .

It was an added reflection yesterday [at the rehearsal] after the musical moment subsided, that the orchestra accompanied the singer very softly, yes, softly, as many of those among the few listeners seemed to think. At times from our place in the gallery the motives were barely audible. In soft passages too this orchestra seems to give its utmost, as we formally acknowledge this orchestra to be the most estimable in the world. Anyone who knows the challenges, and sees the joyful smoothness with which they are dispatched, must be full of admiration. There is for every time and place a fund of enthusiasm and commitment of skill to orchestra-playing, and the dear God makes these relationships improve with time; but here the demands are of such difficulty that I cannot hold back my admiration for the artists of the orchestra, and indeed must award them the first place among the performers. How these three-voiced chromatic scales flow in such a precise ensemble, as though they required no rehearsal! what a quantity of virtuosity and lively quickness of nuance! This is not only the result of study. Since the third of June the whole *Ring* has been rehearsed through three times, first scene by scene, winds and strings alone, piano rehearsals separately, rehearsals for orchestra alone, then in general rehearsals with scenery—in short, so wisely and practically as might be. But such demands on the orchestra would still not have been possible, if each of the participating gentlemen had not brought something extra of interest and participation (p. 444).

August 15: The last three dress rehearsals took place before a full house. His Majesty the King of Bavaria wished this in the interest of the acoustics; but the audience was asked by Wagner himself before the beginning of the "Valkyrie" to withhold any applause. The sound of the softest *piano* was thus audible, all and everything contributed to the conviction that the performances would succeed as well as is only possible when the best forces give their best. Before the beginning of the second act of the "Valkyrie" Wagner said with deep emotion a heartfelt word of thanks to the orchestra for their noble performance. The king expressed his appreciation to several performers during the performance, and thanked all involved as he departed.

After such results, everyone awaited the performances themselves with high anticipation. Its approach was powerfully present. . . .

Yesterday evening precisely at seven o'clock the first festival performance began. The motive with which Donner summons the mist served as the signal for the beginning. Soon thereafter the Emperor appeared, welcomed by a rising cheer from the audience. When the curtain closed again it was 9:30. For a single act of a normal theatrical performance it was a long time, but yesterday during *Rheingold* one dreamed it away as if it were brief minutes. All had agreed on this even during the dress rehearsal, and it seemed so yesterday to most of those present. We awoke from a silence of a few seconds' duration, and then began a storm of applause, a roar of fiery delight, in which only the name of Wagner could be distinguished, and which was finally called out by all those present. I endured this spirited bacchanale for ten minutes; the Master, awaited, did not appear. At first the enchanted audience could hardly bear to leave the house.

Among the performers, first is the indescribably lively performance of Herr Vogl, who was distinguished by a lively applause in the middle of the performance. This at the place where Loge finishes narrating the theft of the ring. Herr Hill also received the same praise, as he cursed the owner of the ring with powerful passion. By the time of the final ovation the audience had grasped the tragic nature of "Rheingold." But these deep feelings were mastered in order to express thanks for the extraordinary grandeur of the performers. Herr Hill performs his Alberich with a superhuman power; one hardly knows where this artist finds the gifts for such exertions, how he softens the tyrannical traits of this passionate tyrant: the tones of soft longing he directs at Woglinde: "Komm doch wieder" ["Come back!"], the heartfelt sorrow when he laments Flosshilde's flight: "Die Dritte so traut" ["The third one so dear"]. Herr Eilers, too, brought much softness to the giant's role of Fasolt, making one think of the sound of the lamented Hans Heiling, whenever he came to speak of womanly bliss and of Freia. One must really hear for oneself what strong reminiscences these gigantic swellings cause one to suffer. The list of stellar roles is far from finished with these citations. There is the beautiful nymph-like song of the three Rhinedaughters (Fräuleins Lilly and Marie Lehmann and Lammert), there is above all the Wotan of Herr Betz to mention, who knows how to represent the unshakeable dignity of the chief of the gods. His task in "Rheingold" deserves to be thought exceptional, for it gives him little opportunity to stir the audience. At only one place all evening, in that elevated religious scene where Erda appears, and the all-wise one approaches with the whispered words "Wer bist du, mahnend Weib" ["Who are you, threatening woman"], was he permitted to abandon his tone of unchangeable calm. There is also the unsurpassable Mime of Herr Schlosser, clear to the last syllable, emphatic in every gesture. The scene where he chatters his description of the power of the Tarnhelm to the serious Loge earned him not applause but a hearty laugh throughout the hall. The Fafner of Herr von Reichenberg also was imposing in its gigantic tone, movement, pace, and posture. Even in the smallest roles lies some character, brought out by the actors. The Donner, received through the resolution of Herr Gura a supplement of individual nobility; Froh was played by Herr Unger, whose best performance was awaited in "Siegfried."

Among the ladies, the role of Fricka fell to Frau Grün, the mother of the gods, who in all Indo-Germanic myth is furnished with the unsympathetic qualities of jealous wives. Frau Grün acts with *grandezza,* and shows through her understandable pronunciation what the Erda of Frau Jaïde lacks, while Fräulein Haupt as Freia was able to send forth with stirring tones the laments of the protector of grace and youth.

If not everything was perfect in the scene-changes, which took place on the open stage: the changing of waves into clouds, mist, and light, back and forth and with suddenness, if technical means and techniques were prominent, this only shows that even with extraordinary equipment the good will and the imaginative fantasy of the spectators are indispensable. Imagination helps surmount such little details; it cannot be dispensed with even in the Wagner theatre even if all goes as it should. Otherwise we poor gallery spectators—do we not need imagination, in order to see the scene from behind the lamp-spheres which block our view of half the stage, or to prevent our being torn away from the magical world that glows below us by the many disturbances caused by the carelessness of other spectators (pp. 463–64)?

17. PAUL LINDAU, "GODS, HEROES, AND WAGNER. A LETTER POST FESTUM."

It would be an interesting assignment in arithmetic to count exactly how often in the "Ring of the Nibelungs" there is sunrise, dusk, and night. Furthermore it would be instructive to establish the number of suns that light the earth on which the Wagnerian poem is played. Now we see red suns, now blue, now yellow. Some of the characters, for example Wotan and Erda, have their own special suns. It flickers around the all-wise woman with a bluish shimmer, but for the one-eyed god it is dark red and attracts his movements.

You see, Wagner needed a very complicated supply of living creatures, lifeless things, and apparitions, in order to bring his work to performance. A normal theatre by its very nature seems not to be capable of satisfying his demands, and the Bayreuth Festspiel-haus should thus give us a sort of foretaste of the theatre of the future. If much did not please, if indeed unpleasant disturbances happened, if the scenic arrangement lagged behind the most moderate demands—all that is already well known. Friend and foe are long since agreed that in this respect the performance was only middling.

> *Die Gartenlaube,* 1876, repr. Grossmann-Vendrey, *Bayreuth in der deutschen Presse,* 1: 63.

18. WILHELM MOHR, "LETTERS OF A BAYREUTH PATRON"
IV. Bayreuth, August 14

The great moment is here. Everyone is flocking since midday over the just-laid broad road to Wotan's new Valhalla, built of wood and brick, as it gleams in reddish light over little

Bayreuth and its lovely valley. Awaiting the Emperor, the crowd spread itself out on the low hill. People sized each other up, greeted thousands of new or old friends who had streamed from all parts of the world to the great work, admired the handsome blond people of the country, and taken a strengthening glass of beer, before setting to work, in the restaurants to the left and right of the theatre. Then came a loud summons from the theatre: the call of the cloud-summoner Donner, sounded by trumpets and inviting entrance. One crowded through the doors and with difficulty squeezed through knees and chair-backs. For a moment the glowing glass globes attached to the Corinthian capitals at the tops of the unequal pilasters and columns continued to shed an uncertain light over the crowd, a group of some 1500 heads waving on the long, slanting rows of seats leading down to the stage. No sooner had many a familiar countenance been revealed, than the lights began to fade. Now the Emperor's arrival was greeted in the half-darkness with a storm of jubilation. Then it was as dark as a cellar in the whole room. It was too dark to read a text-book, the Master wants eye and ear to be entirely occupied with his drama. From the empty space behind the orchestra's balustrade deep under us came a mysterious light and dispersed itself over the simple red curtain which closed the massive proscenium as in any other theatre. From that mystic glowing depth breaks forth now a low E-flat, the lowest that professor Helmholtz—who is present—possesses in his laboratory: the great moment has come. [The author continues with a detailed plot summary but includes some useful descriptions of the set and action.]

Verdi, installed at the Hotel Milano, is the object of general curiosity,

and cannot show himself anywhere without becoming

the center of a respectful demonstration. People remove their hats

when he passes, as for a popular king.

— *Le Matin*

CHAPTER FIVE

Giuseppe Verdi, *Otello*

Milan, February 5, 1887, 8:15 P.M.

*T*here was tremendous excitement in Milan. The premiere of Verdi's *Otello* was a matter of concern to the whole world. There had been such anticipation for Meyerbeer, and for Wagner. But Verdi was an Italian hero, almost a god. He had been beloved for forty years in Italy especially, and *Otello* was a matter of national pride and concern. It made people forget government crises and defeats in Abyssinia. For native speakers of English who feel a certain ownership of Shakespeare it is no easy matter to allow Italian opera singers to bellow abridged versions in a foreign language. The special problems that arise in adapting an existing work for the lyric stage were well known to Verdi, who had done it before, and to his excellent librettist Arrigo Boito, who had the advantage of combining in his person a distinguished writer and an accomplished composer.

Shakespeare was no stranger to Verdi, to Italy, or to non-English speakers in general. Verdi's own *Macbeth* of many years before had whetted his appetite; and his next opera, *Falstaff,* was to be a comic triumph. For *Otello,* Verdi had to contend with the memory, current with many of his listeners, of Rossini's own version of the story (with its own Willow Song).

Giuseppe Verdi had essentially been in retirement from the stage since *Aida.* Although he had revised *Don Carlos* and *Simon Boccanegra,* and although his earlier works continued to hold the stage, patrons of the opera had had to assume that the lyric theater would have to continue without him. Composers who had recently filled the Verdian void included Amilcare Ponchielli, who himself died in 1886 after composing *La Gioconda* (1876), *Lina* (1877), and *Il figliuol prodigo* (1880), Carlo Gomes (*Il Guarany,* 1870; *Salvator Rosa,* 1875), Filippo Marchetti (*Ruy Blas,* 1869; *Don Giovanni d'Austria,* 1880), Catalani (*Elda,* 1880, revised as *Loreley,* 1890; *Edmea,* 1886). The young Giacomo Puccini was as yet known only for his *Le villi* (1884).

But Verdi was not finished; he had been considering, and then working on, *Otello* since 1884, though he had tried to keep it a secret. Before long, though, everybody knew, and every major theater wanted it. Verdi was cautious, but it was announced in early 1886 that it would go to La Scala and its impresarios, the brothers Cesare and Enrico Corti.

Verdi had turned his back on La Scala after a disagreement with the impresario Merelli over *Giovanna d'Arco* in 1845, and although the rift was healed with the revised *La Forza del destino* in 1869, he had written no new opera since the Egyptian *Aida* in 1871. But there were continuing connections between the composer and the opera house. He conducted his Requiem at La Scala on May 25, 1874, and again for a benefit in 1879. His revised *Simon Boccanegra* was performed there on March 24, 1881 (with Victor Maurel and Francesco Tamagno, Verdi's Jago and Otello), and the revised *Don Carlo* in 1884. He had written to his friend Clarina Maffei on March 19, 1878: "You, of all people, advise me to write! Now let's talk about it seriously. For what reason should I write? What would I succeed in doing? What would I gain by it? The results would be quite wretched. I would

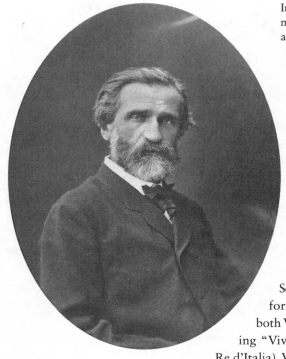

In this photograph Giuseppe Verdi looks much better groomed than he sometimes appears.

have it said to me all over again that I didn't know how to write and that I've become a follower of *Wagner.* Some glory! After a career of forty years to end up as an imitator!" Wagner was indeed an issue in Italy, as everywhere; *Lohengrin* at La Scala in March 1873 had produced much discussion and polemic.

By 1887, Verdi was a national hero. Ever since the audience at La Scala on January 24, 1859, during a performance of *Simon Boccanegra,* hailed both Verdi and the Italian nation by shouting "Viva Verdi" (Verdi = Vittorio Emanuel Re d'Italia), Verdi had been the symbol not only of Italian opera but of Italy itself. Verdi had served in the first Italian parliament, and a statue of him stood in La Scala from 1881.

Verdi had the curious fate of outliving Wagner (who died in February 1883). When Ferruccio Busoni said of *Otello* shortly after its first performance that "*Othello* is perhaps the last work of Italy's greatest living composer, indeed of the only living opera composer," he was skillfully avoiding the comparison with Wagner and choosing to ignore the younger Italian composers, like Giacomo Puccini, who would rush to fill the void left by Verdi's apparent retirement from the stage.

MILAN

Milan in 1887 was, as it is today, a center of commercial and industrial activity. The site is not of geographical interest—the land is flat and central but not attractive. A population of some 300,000 lived mostly within the medieval walls. The tops of the walls served as pleasure gardens (like those of Lucca today), and beyond the walls were a moat and an avenue of trees. The city was even beginning to spread outside its walls.

The city is laid out rather like a spider's web, with the main streets running outward from the Piazza del Duomo to the various gates. The thirteen gates, from the Arco del Sempione to the Porta Romana, included the passage to the magnificent Stazione Centrale (1864) which connected Milan to the rest of the world by railway. There was an excellent

This 1880 tourist map of Milan gives a sense of the city's medieval walls, of the central railway station linking Milan to the rest of the world, and of the proximity of the cathedral, the Galleria (just behind the cathedral), and the Teatro alla Scala (behind the Galleria).

The Lighting of the Gas Lamps Around the Cupola of the Galleria Vittorio Emanuele

From the Illustrated Europe *guidebooks, 1884.*

Early in the day the Gallery shows signs of life. Tourists who disdain to sleep away the entire morning enter and survey the magnificent corridor. Peasant women and servants hurry past, their wooden shoes clattering on the pretty mosaic floor. Priests traverse the Gallery on their way to the early service, for from tower and turret is resounding the musical chime of the church-bells. Waitresses and shop girls appear and set about the work of sweeping out the shops and re-arranging the show windows. The sergeant of police in his close-buttoned coat paces up and down with stately steps, while a band of bersaglieri enter from the Piazza del Duomo, the immense bunch of feathers which adorns their head-gear dancing merrily up and down and keeping time with their hurried strides. By degrees the Gallery begins to fill. Fashionable young gentlemen with plenty of time on their hands stroll by; towards noon the gentlemen of the world of commerce put in an appearance, with the laudable intention of sharpening their appetite for breakfast by a glass of bitters at one of the stalls. About one o'clock the tide of visitors ceases to rise. From two to five the flood increases, but about the latter hour begins once more to ebb. Between five and seven o'clock the Milanese take their principal meal, therefore at this time the Gallery usually presents a deserted appearance. Between seven and eight o'clock the stream again begins to flow and about nine o'clock the building is apt to be somewhat over-crowded. In the twilight there is always a merry company assembled in these halls—children accompanied by their mothers or nursemaids, coming to see the gas lit. The rim of the ledge below the cupola is the centre of attraction for the little eyes. Suddenly a shout of exultation is heard, as the little locomotive starts on its mission of lighting the hundreds of jets along the ledge; in a few moments it has completed its tour and a ring of fire encircles the dome. The noiseless and rapid motion of the little machine has gained it the name of il rat, the mouse, from the young people who watch it with such eager delight.

Almost every evening there is a musical performance in the Café Biffi at the side of the Octagon. The visitors either remain here or walk up and down the gallery alone, in couples or in merry groups. After eleven o'clock the crowd disperses, but at midnight there is a brief renewal of the busy scene; after the theatres are closed a part of the theatre-going public hastens to the Gallery in search of some refreshment before retiring to rest.

horse-drawn tramway and omnibus service, good pavement of streets and sidewalks, adequate gas-lighting of the central streets. Drinking water was not plentiful and not very pure; there was a plan to bring water from the mountains.

At the center of the web is the magnificent Gothic cathedral, and from one side of the Piazza del Duomo runs the splendid glass-roofed Galleria Vittorio Emanuele, full of restaurants, cafés, and shops. Passing through the Galleria takes the visitor to the Piazza della Scala, in which is found the Teatro alla Scala, the site of the premiere of *Otello*.

The artistic élite of Milan gathered often in the salon of Clarina Maffei (Verdi anonymously sent her an elaborate clock in 1884). The group, known as the "scapigliatura," was dedicated to challenging the status quo in the arts and in society, seeking novelty above all, and a fusion of the arts. Bourgeois conformity was to be avoided, and painters, sculptors, and literary and musical figures associated themselves with this informal "Bohemian" movement. The most "scapigliato" (disheveled) of musicians was Arrigo Boito.

Milan had a large theatrical industry. There were at least thirty theatrical agencies; there were scene-shops, tailors, shoemakers, and others who supplied the needs of the theater not only in Milan but around the world. They all worked in the shadow of La Scala. There were many scene-shops that reproduced faithfully the sets from La Scala, adjusted to any size. You could order sets for *Otello* from Milan, and the scene-shops would reproduce those of the premiere, without the original designers having any say in the matter or earning a lira.

There were plenty of theaters in Milan, and indeed other houses giving operas. The Teatro Dal Verme, inaugurated in 1872 with *Gli Ugonotti*, gave the first performances of works by Ponchielli (1872), Puccini (*Le villi*, 1884), and, later, Leoncavallo's *I pagliacci* (1892). But the leading opera house of Italy, and one of the leading houses of the world, even today, was the Teatro alla Scala.

LA SCALA

Of the three hundred or so opera houses in Italy, everyone would agree—with the possible exception of a Neapolitan asked about the San Carlo—that La Scala was the leading house of Italy for the quality of its performances, the high level of its artists, and the richness of its season.

As in most Italian opera houses, the carnival season at La Scala, which usually opened on St. Stephen's Day (December 26) and extended to Lent (or indeed sometimes beyond), was the principal season, during which "heroic" operas were presented, usually accompanied in larger houses by ballets; the ballet was usually performed between the acts of the opera, usually after the second act. (Thus it was no surprise to La Scala's audience that *Otello* too was accompanied by a ballet.) Generally there were two or three operas in a season, which alternated for some forty or fifty performances. Most desirable were operas that were "expressly composed," that is, operas that were given their first performance in this house this season. (In major houses—La Scala, San Carlo, La Fenice—

The eighteenth-century Teatro alla Scala, designed by Giuseppe
Piermarini, occupied the site of the church of Santa Maria della Scala
and housed a singing school, a ballet school, and the headquarters
of the Ricordi publishing firm.

this was almost mandatory.) Next most attractive were "new" operas, works not yet given
in the house in question. Some flexibility was retained by including operas performed in
earlier seasons; this permitted the filling in of gaps in the event that a new opera was not
a success. It was a culture of novelty and thus required a continuous flow of new works.

A secondary season in the spring was customary in most houses. Here were performed the comic "semi-serious" operas, not usually accompanied by ballet. But the major
houses, including La Scala, normally presented serious operas also in their spring seasons.

The 1887 season began on St. Stephen's Day 1886 with *Aida* (with Tamagno, Maurel, Romilda Pantaleoni, Nouvelli, and Navarrini). It also included, in 1887, *Flora mirabilis*,
by the Greek Spiro Samara (not a success), Donizetti's *Lucrezia Borgia*, and, in the spring,
Bizet's *I pescatori di perle*. Other singers that season were Emma Calvé of Opéra-Comique;
tenor Alfonso Garulli; baritone Antonio Magini-Coletti. The ballets were *Rolla* and *Narenta*
(which accompanied the Donizetti). Grand masked balls called *veglioni* were given during
carnival. But the chief event of the season was the premiere of Verdi's *Otello*.

La Scala was inaugurated, though it was not quite finished, on August 3, 1778.

It was built by the architect Giuseppe Piermarini to replace the older Ducal Theatre destroyed by fire in 1776 (which itself had replaced an earlier theater that burned down). Piermarini, architect of the Real Camera, was a pupil of Luigi Vanvitelli and had collaborated with him on the royal palace at Caserta—and had perhaps designed its theater himself. The theater, cramped for space in the city, expanded its footprint by including the site of the church of Santa Maria della Scala, built in 1381. In addition to the theater itself, the building housed a singing school, a dancing school, and the headquarters of the Ricordi publishing firm. The theater was renovated in 1881–84. Near the entrance are the statues of Rossini, Donizetti, Bellini, and Verdi himself (the last two dedicated in 1881).

WHAT TO EXPECT AT THE OPERA

Despite changes in musical style, the Milan audience knew pretty much what to expect of an opera. Standard fare was the four-act serious opera, whose general shape was satisfyingly predictable. The setting was normally a historical time and place outside of Italy. Act 1 presented the essential conflict of the drama and introduced the hero (tenor) or heroine (soprano); it also included the chorus in some capacity, to set the scale of the production. The second act mostly consisted of a series of duet-scenes, in which individual characters interacted with others and intensified and explained the conflict; there was probably no chorus in this act. The third act usually managed to finish with an enormous choral finale, a *pezzo d'insieme,* the most spectacular scene in the opera; and the fourth act, in which the hero or heroine dies, was more intimate and emotional. This well-known pattern was adopted for *Otello,* though with a musical and dramatic force combining Shakespeare's dramatic power, Arrigo Boito's poetic and librettistical skill, and Verdi's surprisingly new musical style.

The traditional musical numbers of Italian opera were still familiar, not only because the works of Rossini, Donizetti, Bellini, and Verdi were regularly performed, but also because newer operas, although they were much influenced by modern trends, still reflected the Italian tradition.

Acts were by definition divided into scenes by the entrances and exits of the principal characters. A scene might be a solo, though by now arias were not much in vogue. Songs inserted into the action, such as Desdemona's Willow Song, have a special position as *canzoni.* But such solos as Jago's Credo, or Desdemona's Ave Maria, were readily recognizable as being in the tradition. Duets had long replaced arias as the principal vehicle for musical numbers. A classic duet began with an alternation between the two characters— a conversation, in recitative or *parlante*—followed by lyrical stanzas from each character in turn but singing together at least briefly; a third section, consisting again of dialogue, leads to a new situation, provoking more lyrical singing (often in a new poetic meter). Remnants of this tradition would be immediately recognizable in *Otello*'s love duet with Desdemona in act 1.

But there was more than Italian opera to be heard in Italy. La Scala repeatedly performed the great French grand operas in these days: Meyerbeer's *Les Huguenots* and

Robert le diable and Halévy's *La Juive*. Massenet was beginning to be heard *(Il re di Lahore, Erodiade)*. The grand opera, like the older Italian works, reminded audiences of the thrill of coloratura, of bravura singing for the sheer delight and beauty of it. Though occasionally a trouser role, or an inserted song, would provide Italian composers with moments for such vocal display, modern operas generally inclined to dramatic singing; virtuoso display was no longer considered an appropriate expression of a main character's emotions. Lyricism, expression, and strength were the qualities to admire.

With the exception of Weber's evergreen *Der Freischütz*, revived at La Scala in 1872 in a translation by Boito, no German opera was heard except for Wagner. And not so much of that, at least at La Scala. Ricordi controlled La Scala, and Wagner was published by the rival firm of Lucca. Although the Ring operas had been heard in several Italian cities, La Scala had presented *Lohengrin* (1873) but would not present more Wagner until after *Otello*.

And yet Wagner was without doubt a force to be recognized. His influence on opera of all kinds was considerable, and Verdi himself, like many other composers, was haunted by the idea that any change he made in his style would be imputed to Wagner's influence. This may have contributed to his long silence. As Italian listeners understood the Wagnerian tradition, it could essentially be reduced to three elements: 1) "continuous melody," by which was understood an unbroken musical flow, without division into numbers and with a consequent reduction in the overtly lyrical forms; 2) a rich and significant orchestration, in which much of the musical interest is to be found in the music of the orchestra; and 3) the use of recurrent musical motives within a work, sometimes associated with characters, emotions, or objects. If all three of these elements are to be found to some extent in *Otello*, they are also found in most other Italian operas of the time, and they show Verdi to be not a Wagnerian but a contemporary composer. We will see that much of the reaction to *Otello* revolved around—or avoided—the question of Wagner's influence.

Shakespeare, and *Othello,* were not unknown to the audience, at least to those who regularly went to the theater or the opera. Rossini's *Otello* was familiar to many, and Shakespeare's tragedy had been published in several Italian translations. It was often acted on the stage, especially by the great Shakespearean Tommaso Salvini (famous for his Othello). Giulio Ricordi reported to Verdi about a performance of *Othello* in December 1886 as acted by the company of Giovanni Emanuel, at which the three stars of Verdi's future opera were also present.

Preparation

Like the trio of singers in *Otello*'s principal roles, there is a trio of people who contributed to the conception and creation of *Otello*. Verdi, of course, but he was reluctant to return to composing operas; without the intervention and collaboration of Ricordi and Boito, *Otello* would never have come into existence.

Giulio Ricordi, the son and heir-apparent of Tito Ricordi of the immensely influential Ricordi music publishers, had made great efforts to bring Verdi back to La Scala and to composition. He carried on a long correspondence with Verdi, did many errands for him, attended rehearsals, generally fixed things up, arranged for the publication of the score and libretto of *Otello*, and was essentially the author of the detailed published mise-en-scène. It was through Ricordi that Verdi dealt with business matters, from replacing a broken piano string at his house at Sant'Agata to granting permissions for further performances of *Otello*. Verdi was, naturally, the prize thoroughbred in Ricordi's stable, but their relationship seems to have been an amiable combination of business and friendship. Verdi was of course in charge. He could set his own terms, and did so in a handwritten memorandum in which he details his requirements to Ricordi:

> *Pro Memoria*
> Assuming I am able to complete what remains to be done for the music of *Otello*, it will be well for the House of Ricordi to establish as of now the conditions above all with the management of La Scala.
> 1. The House of Ricordi shall, with the management, set the rental [of scores and orchestral materials, etc.], of which I shall realize my share, etc., etc.,——
> 2. I will assist in all those rehearsals (which I shall judge necessary); but I do not wish to commit myself in any way to the public, and consequently the poster shall simply say
> *Otello*
> Poetry by Boito
> Music by Verdi
> No one, *absolutely no one,* at the rehearsals, as usual.—I have complete authority to suspend the rehearsals and prevent the performance, even after the dress rehearsal, if
> either the execution
> or the *mise-en-scène*
> or *anything else* in the way the theatre is run should not be to my liking.
> The personnel connected with *Otello* shall answer directly to me ... the *conductor* of the orchestra, of the chorus, the producer, etc., etc.
> The first performance may not take place without my authorization, and should anyone think he can circumvent this condition, the Ricordi Publishers shall pay me a fine of one hundred thousand (100,000) Lire.—
> GV
> [the following two lines are apparently written by Giulio Ricordi]
> —I request normal pitch in the theatres
> —A box for opening night at the disposal of Signora Verdi

The firm of Ricordi had much to gain from *Otello*. Their arrangement, as it had been for so many of Verdi's operas in the past, was that Verdi assigned the rights to Ricordi for a large fixed sum; Ricordi in turn rented scores and parts to theaters with permission to perform the piece. Ricordi received a sizable rental fee, and Verdi took a substantial percentage. In the case of *Otello,* Verdi received 200,000 lire (in four installments), along with 40 percent for rentals and 50 percent for the sale of scores. Thus when the firm of Ricordi published the *disposizione scenica,* and a booklet reprinting reviews of *Otello,* it was in essence selling the opera to other houses.

Boito was a composer (his *Mefistofele* had been hissed in 1868 but later triumphed at La Scala and elsewhere), a poet, and sometime librettist. His libretto for Ponchielli's *La Gioconda* had been signed with his anagram Tobia Gorrio: writing libretti was not the work of a self-respecting poet. Boito, who as a member of the "scapigliati" of Milan had angered Verdi in 1863 with a toast that Verdi had read in the newspaper, had a lot to make up for. But the indefatigable Giulio Ricordi managed gently to bring the two together, to arrange for Boito to work with Verdi on the revisions of *Simon Boccanegra* (as Tobia Gorrio), and to insinuate the idea of an opera on Shakespeare's play. It was a long time in the making. Verdi was diffident; he long refused to say whether he would write, or finish, an opera on *Othello* (originally entitled *Jago*), and he reserved the right to retract the opera at any point.

Boito was willing to turn his hand to libretto writing, even using his own name, for an artist like Verdi. This provided Verdi with an opportunity that few composers had —to develop a libretto that was not the work of a hack. It also involved the composer in an active collaboration in which Boito contributed more than did most of Verdi's earlier, more compliant librettists. Boito's language may have been occasionally obscure or archaic, but it was far superior to that of any librettist of his day. Italian dramatists (in opera and stage plays) preferred to keep the language removed from the everyday, but a libretto in particular was expected to provide the relatively simple situations—love, jealousy, rage, and so forth—that allow the composer to give musical expression to easily understood emotions. Complicated character development and overcomplex plots were not generally useful to a genre in which the music should provide most of the character. One would not perform most libretti as plays.

Verdi prepared his score ("this cursed thirty-two-line music-paper tires my eyes," he wrote to Ricordi), and the firm of Ricordi, charged with producing score, orchestral parts, and vocal score, worked on it as sections arrived from Verdi. It was important to keep the music from being seen. Prying journalists might give early reports, or unscrupulous impresarios might pirate a copy for use in provincial theaters without paying rights. "I am jealously taking care of everything," wrote Ricordi in September, "and I expect to avoid any sort of trickery, either clandestine copies or indelicate journalists—the pages already set up in type are kept under lock and key, and the score, with all the parts being prepared, are locked in the safe every night."

The score was finished on November 1, 1886, as Verdi jubilantly announced to Ricordi and Boito; there would, however, continue to be adjustments and corrections. Meanwhile, many other arrangements needed to be made; the choice of singers, and the designing of sets and costumes.

This 1892 photograph, taken at Casa Ricordi in Milan,
shows Verdi and Arrigo Boito five years after *Otello*, on the
eve of *Falstaff*, their last collaboration.

REHEARSALS

Musical preparations for *Otello* were under the direction of Verdi, though he relied a great deal on the conductor Franco Faccio for the early coaching of singers and the
preparation of the orchestra, as well as on the chorus-master Alfredo Cairati.

Himself a composer of opera (his disastrous *Hamlet* turned him away from composition), Faccio was a lifelong friend of Boito. He became conductor at La Scala in 1871,
giving the Italian premiere of *Aida* there in 1872 and of the revised *Simon Boccanegra* in
1881. He had conducted Verdi at La Scala for years, and he also gave the premieres of operas by Ponchielli, Catalani, and Puccini. He conducted his thousandth performance there
in March 1886. He ended his career at La Scala with the 1889 preparations for *Die Meistersinger* (it was his insistence that the opera had no third act that led to his retirement and

to the recognition of his final illness). Faccio, weakened by syphilis, briefly directed the conservatory at Parma (Verdi arranged this appointment) and died in 1891 in an institution in Monza.

Verdi entrusted Faccio with the coaching of the singers in *Otello,* and with much of the musical detail for the score. Although Verdi supervised rehearsals, his practice was not to conduct but to place himself on the stage during rehearsals and to rely on Faccio for details in the orchestra, making occasional suggestions and corrections.

Everybody wanted to sing in *Otello.* Verdi was very careful in choosing the principal singers, and he was powerful and respected enough that the choices surely were his. It is not certain that he had the ideal singers for two of the major roles, but he certainly knew that his Jago was perfect.

Unlike the roles of Otello and Jago, for which Verdi conceived and required dramatic delivery, Verdi seems to have considered Desdemona a purely lyrical role: "The most perfect Desdemona," he wrote to Ricordi, "will always be the one who sings best." Though Verdi was not at first convinced that Romilda Pantaleoni was right for Desdemona, his rejection of Gemma Bellincioni after hearing Boito's report of her performance in Meyerbeer's *Roberto le diable* convinced him that Pantaleoni should be hired for the La Scala season. She had recently sung, with Tamagno, in an 1884 La Scala production of *Les Huguenots.* She was intimately involved with Faccio, which made things slightly awkward for Verdi and others.

Pantaleoni was not beautiful, and she sang out of tune. And yet her acting, her sensuality, her commitment to her role made her in some circumstances a convincing and moving singer. After rehearsing with Verdi in October, Pantaleoni was convinced that she was perfect, as she wrote to her brother: "He made me work twice a day, morning and evening! and I assure you that with him I have vanquished the enormous beauties of those sweet phrases and at the same time

Romilda Pantaleoni was not beautiful, and she sang out of tune. But she was convincing in the role of Desdemona after a long period of study with Verdi and Franco Faccio. © Archivio Storico Ricordi.

powerful; and I truly believe that with this opera I will achieve the high point of my glory! . . . And how happy he was with me finally, after I had understood him and sang the part just as he wanted, with all of that finesse, those subtle shades of meaning *(sfumature)* and nuances *(accenti)* that he indicated to me!"

Verdi was not so convinced, but he wrote to Faccio about his reactions, which show his deep understanding of the voice, and his delicacy in suggesting to Faccio how to coach his mistress:

> The *canzone del salice* [Willow Song] is causing the composer as well as the artist performing it the greatest problems. She should sing with three voices, like the most sacred Trinity: with one for Desdemona, another one for Barbara (the maid), and a third for the *"salce, salce, salce"* *[willow]*. Signora Pantaleoni's voice becomes cutting at passionate points, and in high notes a little too biting; she gives too much metal, so to speak. If she could get used to singing with a little more head-voice, the *smorzato* [faded away] would come easier to her and her voice would also be more secure and natural.—I have advised her to study this way; and you, with your influence, should give her the same advice. Besides, it isn't always true that her D is such a bad tone, as she says. There is a point where she succeeds the best with it: [here Verdi writes the notation and words for "salce, salce, salce"].
>
> This phrase is repeated three times. The last time she manages it well, the two other times less so.
>
> I told you frankly what I think, and I tell you again that—with her great talent and theatrical instincts, with good will and study—she will succeed very well in the part of Desdemona, even though it is not completely suited to her way of expression and her voice. . . . Mind you, she does many, many things with the greatest ease. . . .
>
> Her tones will go very well if she makes them less biting and all in the *head,* as I have also advised her to sing at many other points. If there is any thing to find fault with, it's the scene of the first act. There, something lighter, airy, and—let's say the word—voluptuous would be called for, as warranted by the situation and the poetry. She sings her *solo* phrases very well, but with too much accentuation and too dramatically.

Not surprisingly, Verdi was a stunningly successful vocal coach, and the results he achieved with Pantaleoni were noticed elsewhere. When she sang *Aida* at La Scala in December (with Tamagno and Maurel), Ricordi was astonished at the improvement she had made since working with Verdi. ("Her singing is easier, more legato, her intonation is no longer as uncertain as before!! . . . . You are a GENIUS!! . . . Maestro!")

Despite Verdi's efforts and her own, we will see that Pantaleoni was not able to overcome all her problems with tuning. Arturo Toscanini, who played in the orchestra, was fined by Faccio for making grimaces at her intonation during rehearsals. Verdi himself, after the production of *Otello,* later objected to her intonation. And her singing was not uniformly praised by those in attendance.

Pantaleoni suffered from the exertions of the twenty-five performances of *Otello* and did not participate in the subsequent tour to Rome and Venice, causing considerable publicity and legal wrangling. Pantaleoni's career did include further performances of *Otello;* she retired from the stage after Faccio's collapse in 1889.

Francesco Tamagno was from the beginning the leading candidate for the role of *Otello.* He had sung the premieres of the revised versions of *Simon Boccanegra* (1881) and *Don Carlo* (1884), Raoul in *Les Huguenots* (1884), and was the leading tenor of the day—or at least the loudest. He was not admired for his rather wooden acting, and his musicality was somewhat stiff. Verdi hesitated about giving this role, which required so much acting skill and musical variety, to Tamagno. In January 1886 he had written to Ricordi: "I'm frightened about the tenor part. For many, many things Tamagno would be wonderful, but in many others no. There are large, long phrases, legato ones that are to be said in a *mezza voce,* an impossible thing for him. What's worse is that the first act would finish coldly, and (what's still worse) the fourth!! There is a short but broad melody, and then some half-voice phrases (after wounding himself), extremely important . . . and we can't do without them. . . . And if I could hear him . . . before deciding?"

Verdi was evidently concerned about Tamagno's ability to act and sing at the crucial ending of *Otello.* As he wrote to Boito, "You do know the end of the opera. I don't think that he could effectively project the short melody '*E tu come sei pallida'* [*And you, how pale you are*], even less '*Un bacio, un bacio ancora'* [*A kiss, yet another kiss*] . . . particularly since between this second kiss and the

The loud but relatively wooden Francesco Tamagno was coached at great length by Verdi, and with *Otello* he became the world's leading tenor.

third, there are 4 measures for the orchestra alone, which must be filled with delicate, moving gestures that I imagined as I was writing the notes. It would be the easiest thing for a real actor to do, but difficult for . . . anyone else."

Tamagno assumed he had the part, but Verdi made it very clear that he had promised nothing. When Tamagno did sing for Verdi, in April, they seemed to work together well, and Tamagno became Otello. But Verdi was concerned with his learning the part, and he wanted Faccio to teach it to him carefully: "I ask you warmly to have Tamagno study his part after he arrives. He is so inexact in the reading of music that I would really like him to study the part with a true musician in order to get him to sing the notes with their true value and in time."

Tamagno needed more than the notes, however. "Even when he has learned the music well," wrote Verdi, "much will have to be said about interpretation and expression. —— I will have to make my observations directly to him, more so than to any of the others." Verdi himself worked with Tamagno in November and later in the January rehearsals. He had very clear ideas of how Otello should sing and was not at all sure that Tamagno's big voice could manage the finesse. As he wrote to Ricordi, "After he has ascertained that Desdemona has been killed [although] innocent, Otello is breathless; he is weary, physically and morally exhausted; he cannot and must not sing any more, except with a *half-muffled, veiled voice* . . . but with a *reliable* one. This is a quality that Tamagno doesn't have. He must always sing with *full voice;* without it his sound becomes ugly, uncertain, off-pitch. . . . This is a very serious matter and gives me much to think about!" Much had to be done with the drama, but Verdi's coaching again worked miracles. A stupendous voice had learned to act—or at least to do what Verdi told him.

With *Otello* Tamagno became the world's leading tenor. Verdi later called him the "5000-lire tenor" on account of his reputed nightly earnings, on a tour of *Otello* to Rome and later at La Scala.

Verdi seemed always to have had Victor Maurel (1848–1923) in mind for Jago, though he declined at first to promise him the role. Maurel was a French baritone who had a substantial career in Italy; he had performed, with Tamagno, in the premiere of the revised *Simon Boccanegra*. Later he was Verdi's first Falstaff, and he created the role of Tonio in *I Pagliacci* (1892). He was a painter, an author of singing treatises, and for a time the director of the Théâtre-Italien in Paris. After his retirement from the stage he taught for many years in New York.

In March, Verdi traveled to Paris, partly to hear Maurel, and by October Maurel had the role. Verdi admired Maurel's pronunciation and acting ability. In November 1886 he wrote to Ricordi: "Maurel, once he has studied the music, will imagine the rest, and with him, too, little or nothing will have to be done." Shortly thereafter he wrote again: "Jago cannot be performed, and isn't possible, without *Maurel's* extremely good enunciation. . . . Always bear Jago's part in mind, however. In this part one must neither *sing* nor (with few exceptions) *raise one's voice.* If I were a singing actor, for example, I would speak it all in a whisper, *mezza voce.*"

Maurel, according to Gino Monaldi, had a voice "not beautiful in timbre, but

This photograph, taken on the occasion of the performance of *Otello*
in Paris, shows Verdi with Victor Maurel in costume as Jago,
rather more flashily dressed than in Milan. Maurel was always
Verdi's choice for Jago, and he made the role his own.

full of color and warmth: a true baritone voice, with a tendency towards darkness, but from which he drew forth pastel colors, even brightness, thanks to certain ingenious modulation which gave his singing an inimitable expression." Maurel was a stupendous success in the role, and later he wrote a book recommending his own views of the staging of *Otello;* his surviving recordings of excerpts as Jago suggest that the ability to vary his voice, and to emphasize speaking, were in accordance with Verdi's wishes.

Verdi did not care very much about the other singers, who have secondary roles in the opera. The choice of these he left to the theater management, which assigned roles to the singers under contract at La Scala. The rest of the cast:

Cassio:	Giovanni Paroli
Roderigo:	Vincenzo Fornari
Lodovico:	Francesco Navarrini
Montàno:	Napoleone Limonta
Emilia:	Ginevra Petrovich
The Herald:	Angelo Lagomarsino

Faccio had worked at length with the singers in December, and many of them had already learned their parts.

Cairati received parts for the chorus on December 15 and had already rehearsed the parts before Verdi's arrival. The chorus, especially augmented at Verdi's request, consisted of 104 singers—64 men and 40 women—and there was a special chorus of children in act 2.

Verdi arrived in Milan on January 4, where he stayed, as usual, at the Albergo Milano, a short walk down the Via Manzoni from the theater. Piano rehearsals with the cast began shortly thereafter. First, though, he worked more with Pantaleoni; this probably involved some changes in the Willow Song. But he was not pleased with her voice, and the fact that she was also singing in *Aida* did not contribute to her focus. Her fatigue was evident: she is said to have returned home with Faccio after grueling rehearsals, slumping into a chair without taking off her coat, and exclaiming, "Oh! if only I could rest a little! When will it end?"

Rehearsals had to be arranged around the schedules of the theater and the singers. Samara's *Flora* opened on January 8, and every day that it was performed would be a day on which Pantaleoni, Maurel, and Tamagno would be free to rehearse with Verdi. After *Flora,* efforts would be made to open the ballet; and on ballet days, too, the principal singers—and the theater—would be free for rehearsals of *Otello.* As Ricordi wrote to Verdi on December 30, "If the *Flora* barely, barely has a fair success, the management will repeat it Saturday and Sunday, the 8th and 9th, thus leaving the artists of *Aida* completely free—and this will allow you to dispose of them as you think best. As soon as the *Flora* has opened the management will make every effort for the ballet; they reckon they will open with this on the 11th; but I think it is impossible. But in any case the ballet will open soon; from that day on you will have the stage, technical personnel, etc., entirely free; and I think this coincides very well with the period in which the musical studies will be completed."

Verdi worked with the singers in the rehearsal room of La Scala, using a piano placed there by Ricordi. Piano rehearsals, designed in the first instance to achieve a satisfactory musical performance, were followed by rehearsals, some of them on stage, in which the staging was prepared.

The staging of an opera was not normally entrusted to a single individual: much had to be negotiated, as in Paris, among composer, singers, set-designer, impresario, and others. In the case of *Otello,* however, it is clear that Verdi was in charge. Though he may not have directed absolutely every movement and arrangement of bodies on the stage, he

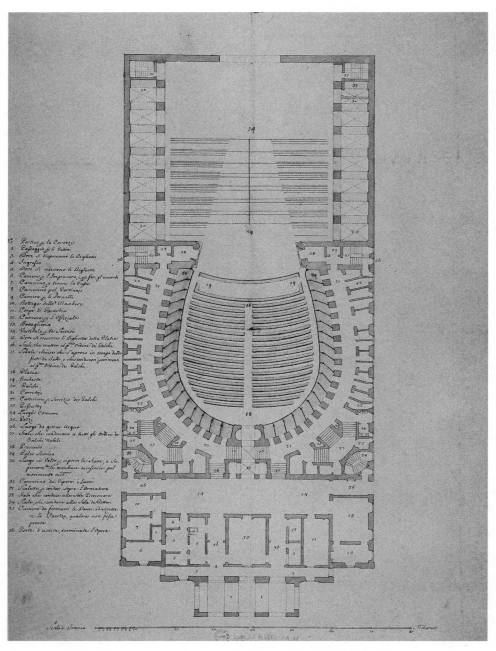

This ground-floor plan of the Teatro alla Scala gives an idea of
the large curve of the horseshoe: from boxes near the front
it is almost easier to see the hall than the stage.

was in a position to suggest, to veto, and to alter, and he took advantage of his brilliant theatrical sense and his decades of experience to see that the action on the stage corresponded closely to the ideas that went along with the music.

Much was under the direct supervision of Verdi, and we are fortunate to have for *Otello* (as we do for other operas of his) a published *disposizione scenica*, a staging manual, assembled by Giulio Ricordi, which incorporates thorough directions as to settings, lighting, and acting, all cued to the music. This detailed book specifically reflects the performance at La Scala and is intended not only to serve as a memory of those performances but to be a specific guide—not to be altered in any way—for those wishing to perform *Otello* in other theaters. Short of a film, a more accurate description could not be imagined. Indeed the disposizione scenica gives more information than a film could because it provides background, describes the emotion that motivates the characters' movements, and explains the character of each of the personages. Movements are aligned to the text or to moments in the music. The text, approved by Boito and Verdi, includes language provided specifically by them. In particular, details of action that are not mentioned in the score are made explicit here, making it clear that text, music, and action are an indivisible whole.

Stories surviving from the rehearsals make clear that Verdi was actively engaged in directing the blocking and the actions of the characters. When Tamagno was ill in January, Verdi stood in for him at rehearsals while Ricordi sang *Otello*'s part (as well as he could). Other rehearsals were held in Tamagno's apartment, particularly of the murder scene, with Tamagno's seven-year-old daughter Margherita standing in as Desdemona. The seventy-three-year-old Verdi is reported showing Tamagno exactly how to stab himself and die, frightening the onlookers, and Tamagno practiced his death-fall over and over to achieve something "à la Salvini" (Tommaso Salvini, the great Italian Othello). Verdi also demonstrated to Pantaleoni what he meant by a "fervent, passionate embrace" during the love duet.

Movement and gesture and acting were essential to Verdi, but whether his movements would look natural or suitable to us today is doubtful. Naturalness in acting is always a relative matter, but the histrionic tradition of the Italian theater suggests that some of the movements and gestures were descended from long tradition on the stage. It is not easy, in any case, to roll down a flight of stairs with a dagger in your chest.

Otello's final scene, as described in the prompt book, gives some idea of the complexity of the acting, and perhaps also of the use of gestures easily understood by the audience:

> Exclaiming 'Oh! Gloria!' he takes a step forwards, raising his eyes and his left arm towards heaven. Then, he adds sombrely, "Otello fu," and lets the scimitar fall. . . . Otello goes slowly towards the bed, climbs the steps, and lovingly contemplates Desdemona's lifeless body. His final farewell to the unhappy woman is said with a very sweet voice, in which love and compassion are united with the most ineffable sadness. . . . In his voice and his gestures, there must be an expression of anguished crying, interrupted by sobs. He remains motionless for a moment, then with abrupt resolution, he comes down the steps, takes a knife from his garments,

and stabs himself, falling to the ground. The other characters make gestures of surprise and go to help Otello, but the tragic and solemn moment so disheartens them, that they stop, immobile, terrified. Otello, dragging himself on hands and knees, returns to the bed, and with repeated efforts manages to end up on the steps, almost on his knees near Desdemona. [He gives the famous three kisses] . . . Otello dies! . . . His body is stretched out near the bed, and rolling down the steps, it remains stiff at the foot of the steps. Emilia, leaning against the prie-dieu, hides her face in her hands. Lodovico puts his hands together sorrowfully. Cassio and Montàno sadly contemplate Otello's corpse. The curtain falls slowly.

The scene is carefully detailed and was certainly rehearsed and acted this way. No wonder Verdi frightened bystanders. There are gestures which here sound stylized: raising eyes and arm to heaven; "gestures of surprise"; face in hands; hands together in sorrow. It is not clear how better to describe these gestures, but it seems clear that gesture is an important part of the acting, and I suspect that many of the gestures are those that anybody used to the stage could have produced at will, and that would have been readily understood. Similar gestures are often required of the chorus and the extras, as in the opening scene, where *Otello*'s ship arrives in a storm: "'Una vela! Una vela!' exclaim those upstage, pointing towards upstage right. Then, they turn towards those under the trellis, whose gestures indicate their concern. . . . Montàno turns to the Chorus shouting, 'È l'alato Leon.' Gestures of surprise from everyone."

Verdi had extremely high standards, and he knew what he wanted. It was difficult to satisfy him, and in the year after *Otello* he wrote to Ricordi, "At La Scala itself not everything was good. . . . Badly conceived sets, badly organized staging . . . the fire of joy . . . The ship, the storm, etc., etc., very, very poor . . . and on and on!—Poor *Otello!* I am sorry that he came into the world."

The first orchestral rehearsal was on January 17, and Faccio had ten days (during which performances of other works also took place) in which to work on the score before the start of rehearsals with cast and action. But his was an extraordinary orchestra, and Faccio was an extraordinary conductor. In 1878, after performing in Paris at the Universal Exposition, Faccio's orchestra of La Scala, led by chief players Giovanni Rampazzini ("violino da braccio"), Antonio Zamperoni (flute), Romeo Orsi (clarinet), Antonio Torriani (bassoon), had formed the Società Orchestrale della Scala for giving concerts of orchestral music. Faccio was the conductor.

In the course of the nineteenth century the orchestra of La Scala, like that of other Italian opera houses, had moved from a system of two directors—a "maestro al cembalo" and an orchestral leader who was normally the first violin—to a single director placed where modern conductors are placed, facing the stage with the orchestra in front of him (not the arrangement in France, where the conductor was near the prompter's box).

Verdi had made a new disposition of the orchestra of La Scala for *Aida,* which

Franco Faccio, a composer and the conductor at La Scala, conducted the Italian premieres of *Aida* and the revised *Simon Boccanegra*. He was a lifelong friend of Boito and was romantically involved with Romilda Pantaleoni. © Archivio Storico Ricordi.

corresponds largely to that still in use. Of particular concern to Verdi in other houses had been the practice of placing the cellos and double-basses here and there throughout the orchestra, and dividing the violas; this was acceptable in earlier music but impractical when these instruments are given important melodic passages. The solo passages for the double-basses at *Otello*'s entrance in act 4, for example, justify the modern seating arrangement.

Some differences between the orchestra of 1887 and that of today are worth noting. Gut strings were the norm for stringed instruments. The double-basses were a mixture of the older three-stringed models and the newer instruments, with four strings. The trombones were piston instruments (which make a considerable difference in such passages as the rising chromatic scale at the beginning of *Otello*), and Verdi preferred a special bass trombone (this is the first of his operas that specifies the instrument) or, at worst, a *cimbasso* (the term was applied to a variety of low brass instruments) to the *serpentone* or *bombardone* so often found in opera houses. Natural horns were still in use in many places, though valve horns were more and more favored by the end of the century. In *Otello* Verdi uses a large orchestra, including three flutes (one of whom also plays piccolo), four bassoons (as at the Paris Opéra), and cornets as well as trumpets.

Twelve special trumpets were made by Mahillon in Brussels, ordered by Ricordi after consulting with Faccio and Orsi (the clarinetist was also an instrument maker) and Verdi (who suggested that some of them be pitched an octave higher to make the high notes easier). These were used for the brilliant on-stage fanfares in act 3.

Verdi insisted on *corista normale*, that is, a pitch of A=435, somewhat below the standard modern pitch of A=440; this had been agreed on by a French commission in 1859 and by an international conference in Vienna in 1885; this pitch was normal at

La Scala, but a higher pitch was found in many other places in Europe. Verdi was a real stickler for this lower pitch—at his insistence, the Italian government adopted it officially in 1887.

Tutti rehearsals began on January 27. By January 30, the whole opera was being rehearsed, and there began to be gossip in the press, which annoyed Verdi. Members of the press were not present, at Verdi's insistence, for the dress rehearsal on February 3. At the last rehearsal the chorus and orchestra presented Verdi with a crown of laurel.

The Performance

La Scala's yellow posters announcing the performance were everywhere, though all the seats had long been sold out. Anticipation in the press was intense. A printed version of Boito's libretto was available for sale, and the music was in the hands of at least some of the critics (Ricordi's advertisement in January announced the availability of the piano-vocal score at the end of the month).

One member of the audience, the American singer Blanche Roosevelt, gave a first-hand account of the situation on the day of the premiere: "On 5 February 1887, the Piazza della Scala was a sight to see, and the cries of 'Viva Verdi! Viva Verdi!' were so deafening that I longed for cotton in my ears. Poor Verdi! had he been there, he would certainly have been torn to pieces. . . . There was death in the eyes of some of those men, waiting like hungry wolves since the night before to be first to crowd into the pit and galleries." By early afternoon the entrance to the gallery, the only unreserved part of the theater, was immensely crowded. Persons attending the opera needed to leave very early for the 8:15 curtain, since the crowd was so dense that carriages could not pass.

Members of the audience entered the theater by one of the three doors under the porch or through one of the two side doors. From a narrow corridor, passages lead to the ground-floor lobby, from which one enters either the auditorium itself or the staircases to upper levels of boxes. The hall measures about 81 by 71½ feet and is about 65 feet high. There is a single enormous chandelier that, since December 26, 1883, has been lit by 344 electric lamps; to these are added, on gala evenings, 258 others, divided into 53 candelabra on the parapets of the boxes. (The Manzoni theater in Milan and the Savoy in London had been electrified even earlier.)

The ceiling had been repainted (for the fifth time) in 1879, with trompe-l'oeil coffers and rosettes rising to the chandelier and exaggerating the shallow curvature of the ceiling. The front curtain was painted (by Giuseppe Bertini and Raffaele Casuedi in 1862) with a scene representing "The Origins of Theatre, or the Atellanian farces."

The five levels of boxes were surmounted by a gallery (the "loggione," where Milan's most vocal and enthusiastic critics made themselves heard). There were 194 boxes in all, with a royal box in the center and four proscenium boxes on each side of the stage. Each could contain as many as ten seats; across a public corridor from each box was its private salon. Many of the boxholders maintained the older gas illumination in their boxes

Although the stage house at the Teatro alla Scala is large,
the audience seems enormous from the stage. Note that the
stage boxes, those between the columns on each side, really are
on the stage. Verdi complained about this, and he admired
the Wagnerian separation of stage and audience.

and salons. Boxes were the property of their owners (though some boxholders made a profit by subletting). The second level of boxes was that of the old aristocracy; the first and third, and the front rows, the *poltrone,* of the orchestra, were the territory of the wealthy bourgeoisie. The normal capacity of the hall, with standing room in the gallery, was about three thousand; but with eight to ten persons in a box, and an overcrowded *loggione,* the audience at the premiere was nearer to four thousand.

At the level of the second row of boxes was the grand *ridotto,* about 81 by 32½ feet, to which patrons retired during intermissions. There they could find souvenirs and refreshments.

The stage of La Scala is suitably deep but cramped at the sides. Two rows of pilasters limit maneuverability in an already restricted space: there is little space for storage or movement of scenery. The house has many traditional features: a deep apron with stage boxes on the side, the orchestra at floor level rather than lowered into a pit. Verdi had complained about the house's layout in 1871:

Take the boxes for spectators away from the proscenium; move the curtain to the front of the apron; . . . make the orchestra invisible. This is not my idea, it is Wagner's: it is very good. It seems impossible that nowadays we tolerate seeing our miserable frock-coats, and white ties, mixed for example with an Egyptian costume, or an Assyrian, Druidic, etc., etc., . . . and to see furthermore the crowd of the orchestra, *which is part of the fictional world,* almost in the middle of the floor, amid the world of those who whistle or applaud. Add to all this the shame of seeing the tops of the harps in the air, the necks of the double basses, and the mechanical gestures [*molinello*] of the conductor.

This was not a typical opera audience, even for La Scala. Everybody of any importance in Milan was present. And there were journalists, musicians, theater directors, intellectuals. It was the moment of Verdi's resurrection, and nobody who could manage to get a ticket would miss it.

Even Blanche Roosevelt was impressed:

From pit to dome, the immense auditorium was one mass of eager faces, sparkling eyes, brilliant toilettes, and splendid jewels. The Italian Court was a rainbow of colours, and Queen Margherita's ladies of honour like a hothouse bouquet of rarest exotics. The first and second tiers of boxes were so packed with Milanese high-bred women, so covered with dazzling jewels and foamy laces, that the house seemed spanned with a river of light, up, up, up to where the last gallery was lost in a dainty cornice of gold. The gleam of diamond tiara and corsage bouquet shot oblong rays on the black-coated background; while the new electric lights, imprisoned in their dead-white globes, shed so unearthly a radiance over the auditorium that we all looked like spectres uprising from some fantastic dead-and-gone rout.

The performance began at a quarter after eight. Unlike most opera evenings, most of the audience was already present. On normal evenings the house was often far from full when the opera began, with the audience arriving gradually in the course of the performance.

Outside the theater some five thousand people waited all evening around the theater, anxious for news.

ACT I

Faccio appeared in the conductor's chair, and there was thunderous applause. The orchestra begins with a storm, and the curtain opens almost as soon as the music begins. The set represents the outside of the castle of the governor of Cyprus. In the background are the castle battlements with a view of the sea. A tavern is in the foreground, downstage right. A storm is raging, with thunder and lightning. On the sea we will see three ships, tossed by the storm, pass from view to the port.

ACT I

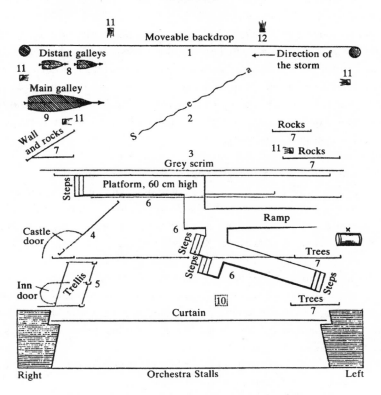

11

Moveable backdrop 12

Distant galleys 1 ←—— Direction of the storm

11
8

Main galley

9 11 a

2

e

S

Wall and rocks 7

3
Grey scrim

Rocks
7

11 Rocks
7

Steps Platform, 60 cm high

6

Ramp

Castle door 4

6

Steps
Steps

6

x

Trees
7

Inn door

Trellis 5

10

Steps

Curtain

Trees
7

Right Orchestra Stalls Left

The set for act 1 of *Otello,* according to Ricordi's *disposizione scenica,* or staging manual. It is redrawn here with labels in English. The disposizione scenica was produced by Giulio Ricordi with direct input from Boito and Verdi. It describes in great detail how the work is to be staged, and it is presumably an accurate record of the original production.

The prompt book gives us a detailed look at the backstage workings of La Scala, and it is worth pausing over. The back of the stage is closed by a backdrop on rollers, which will pass from stage left to right as the storm abates and reveal a gradually clearing sky, in which stars will appear and on which Otello will remark. It is painted with clouds and transparent bolts of lightning (through which flashes of electric light will be directed by a stagehand with a mirror from the electrical apparatus at no. 12 on the floor plan). The electric lighting of the stage includes 98 footlights, 9 overhead rows of lights, 30 *cantinelle* to light the *quinte,* and many reflectors—a total of 1,091 lamps, each of 64 watts. There were sixteen rheostats that could be operated separately or together. In addition there were filters to produce red or blue light.

Verdi himself did not much care for lighting effects except those that emulated natural light: declining sunlight, for example, or the clearing of the sky after the storm in act 1. He did not—as the production books for this and other operas make clear—incline to effects designed to reflect moods.

Visible above the battlements is a transverse cloth painted to represent the sea; this is regularly moved by spiral winches to make waves and is also agitated with hoops by stagehands from below to create large breakers. Three ships (two distant ones, about a meter long, and a nearer one of four or five meters) move across the "sea" behind the cloth, the nearer galley having a complex and realistic motion, side-to-side and front-to-back. Flats representing rocks and part of the castle wall (no. 7) mask the various electrical lights (no. 11) that flash the lightning. In front of the sea hangs a gray transparent scrim, which will be withdrawn as the sky clears later in the act.

In front of all this is a platform (no. 6) representing the battlements, with ramps and steps allowing a great many people to come onstage from the castle and the port. (This same platform, or parts of it, will be used also in acts 2 and 3.) Side flats (4 and 5) continue the castle and include a working door to the castle, and the door to the inn, in front of which a trellis is constructed. On the other side of the stage, flats representing trees close the scene.

The whole storm has to be in motion as the curtain goes up, so it is important that Faccio not begin until a great many stagehands (not to mention cast members) are ready: stagehands are needed to move the ships, the scrim, the sea-cloth, and the sky backdrop; in addition, technicians need to be ready to flash the lightning. The storm is reinforced by an enormous bass drum (a "macchina del tuono," larger than the big bass drum of the Paris Opéra, six feet long and more than four feet in diameter) played by two players and by the use of pedal and timpani stops on the organ.

It is not the only opera of Verdi's that opens with a storm, but it is a good one. Or some thought so: "The scenic decoration is stupendous, perfect. The mechanism of the storm gives a perfect illusion." But Francis Hueffer, writing for the *Times,* was not impressed: "The mise-en-scène, although upon the whole intelligent, was not according to English ideas particularly magnificent. The storm in the first scene was a very tame affair."

The sets had been painted by Carlo Ferrario after submitting sketches for Verdi's approval in October. Ferrario, professor of perspective at the Brera academy, had designed sets at La Scala for years, and we have his designs for *La Traviata* (1859), *Ernani* (1857 or 1861), and *Il Trovatore* (1877). The sets themselves, after approval, were finished and stored away by late December. Ferrario's original designs apparently do not survive, and Verdi insisted on some changes before the opera toured to other cities. Thus Ferrario's sets served as the basis for new sets by Giovanni Zuccarelli for the tour, and Zuccarelli's designs do survive. For the original sets we are limited to the few existing pictures and photographs.

Although La Scala was perfectly capable of elaborate changes of setting and of complicated effects, the sets for *Otello* are relatively simple. There are no set changes within the acts (these were normally accomplished *a vista,* in sight of the audience, and Verdi later rather regretted that he did not divide act 2 into two sets, interior and exterior). There are grand scenes (act 1 includes a storm, the passage of ships, Otello's triumphal arrival,

Giovanni Zuccarelli's design for the setting of act 1 of *Otello*.
The original sets do not survive; Carlo Ferrario's sets served as the
basis for new sets by Zuccarelli for a touring version of *Otello*.
The seawall at the back masks a platform that will be used in later acts.

a grand festival bonfire; act 3, representing the great hall of the castle, includes crowd scenes of full Verdian splendor) and complex settings (act 2 involves a foreground interior through which a garden is seen in which a series of groups present tributes to Desdemona). The first three acts are efficiently arranged to make use of the same practicable platform 26 inches high across the rear of the stage. The last act, in Desdemona's room, is a short set narrowed by the *manteau d'harlequin* enclosed at the sides and with a drop ceiling.

Verdi complained after the fact about the sets: "The sets did not convince me. They may have been so many masterpieces, but they did not serve the action that unfolded in the drama. Too small and short the first scene, and therefore the action clogged up. Too long the scene in the garden. I would change the third [act] and make two [scenes] out of it; a small inner room for the first scenes between Otello, Desdemona, Jago, and Cassio. Then an open change [in sight of the audience] for the rest."

In the opening scene the chorus describes the storm and the naval battle (fanfares and cannons are heard); prays for deliverance; and describes the ship's safe return to port —it is a grand and impressive number. The men's chorus, carefully choreographed on stage, is joined by the women's chorus; they all come together and step toward the footlights during the climactic prayer "Dio, fulgor della bufera." They have been arranged so that at this point they are standing in vocal sections for musical precision.

Alfredo Edel's costume design for Desdemona in act 3 of *Otello*. Edel, who had worked with Verdi on earlier operas, intended his costumes to be historical reproductions of sixteenth-century Venetian dress. © Archivio Storico Ricordi.

Where possible, though, here and elsewhere, the chorus is arranged naturally, and the costumes and acting are individualized: they are not an army or a choral society. The prompt book makes this clear: "The producer must, above all, explain very clearly to the Chorus that they must not appear as an insignificant mass of people, but that each one of them assuredly represents a character and must act as such, moving on his own account, according to his own feelings, preserving with the others only a certain unity of movement in order to ensure the best musical performance. Immobility, at least that not expressly desired in the production book, must be absolutely forbidden."

This quality in the chorus was noticed by at least one critic: "All the choristers have costumes different from each other; all have masterfully been trained, clearly, and they behave in natural and artistic style."

Costumes and props for *Otello* were designed by Alfredo Edel. He had worked with Verdi on *Simon Boccanegra* in 1881 and *Don Carlos* in 1884, so he was perhaps not too chagrined at the many changes Verdi called for, especially his wish to tone down the elegance of Desdemona's costume in act 1 and to make Otello's act 4 costume less exotic. He produced a series of fifty-eight sketches *(figurini)*, costume drawings, which were submitted to Verdi for approval. "If the public should say 'Oh, what a beautiful costume,' we are ruined," said Verdi.

The costumes and sets were intended to be a historical vision of Venetian style of about 1525, and Edel was sent to Venice for the summer to study the styles found in

Venetian painting of the period. (Boito to Verdi: "I've advised our Edel to study the Venetian painters of the last years of the fifteenth and the first quarter of the 16th century. It's our good fortune that the great documents of that period are Carpaccio! and Gentile Bellini! From their paintings will come the clothes of our characters.") The *Corriere della sera* of October 27–28, as part of the run-up to the premiere, carried an article called "Costumes for *Otello*," in which Edel's designs were described:

> Alfredo Edel has finished his important work for the costumes of *Otello*. He has made some seventy sketches which are of a true beauty. "No fantasy," Edel told us, "but the exact reproduction of the truth in each case, from the protagonist's costume down to the last of the props." [Then follows a description of the various costumes.] The great flag of the Venetian Republic—a golden lion on a red field with arabesques, with various images of saints on the sides—the lesser standards, the halberds, the swords, the axes, the knives, the lances, the torches, the Venetian lanterns, all has been designed by Edel in Venice in the public museums, in the Arsenal, or in the galleries of private palaces.

The costumes were executed by the tailoring firm of Vicinelli; the "armorario" Rancati made the armor; Corbella the arms and jewels for the leading parts, including Otello's armor, worn at his first entrance, exactly copied on a Venetian admiral's armor.

Otello, in his armor, followed by his retinue of twenty-nine extras (torches, armorbearers, standard-bearer, guards, sailors carrying trophies, chests, merchandise) arrives at the top of the ramp and delivers his first word: "Esultate!" Tamagno, at the back of the stage with lamps and torches, gives his cry in his ringing tenor, with stupendous effect. The audience shouts and applauds.

What happens next might be unexpected: Otello does not sing an aria. He announces his victory in what at least one critic called a recitative: "The protagonist of the drama at his first appearance has only a recitative, which sometimes is of the declamatory type, and sometimes the melodic. There are a few measures, but full of vigor, and they offer Tamagno a chance to sound some of his best notes."

A chorus of victory ("Vittoria! Sterminio!") masks the preparations on stage for the bonfire and allows Jago and Roderigo to move downstage, where Jago, in an aside, reveals his jealousy and hatred of Otello and promises to help Roderigo win the fair Desdemona. And he delivers his premonitory line: "Se il moro io fossi / vedermi non vorrei attorno un Jago"—not exactly Shakespeare's ("Were I the Moor, I would not be Iago"), but based on Boito's reading of an Italian translation and happily approved by Verdi. As Jago and Roderigo move away to converse in private, the *fuoco di gioia* is lit, and a splendid chorus ensues.

The fire itself was arranged by the *macchinista* of La Scala, Luigi Caprara, who also devised the system of moving the three ships through the stormy sea. A box with a finger's depth of water in the bottom is raised through a trapdoor and disguised by bundles of logs made of metal; in the box are five rods on which brandy-soaked sponges have been impaled; "an intelligent chorister" lights these, while a lighting technician below the stage "should be ready with electric wires, and during the fire he should produce varied lights, which, flickering in the direction of the flames, should increase the flashes of light."

The audience erupts again after the chorus, calling for Verdi. But Verdi is insistent that he will not appear on stage in the middle of an act. So the whole chorus is repeated before the performance can continue. "A repetition is demanded," wrote the critic for *La Lombardia*. "It continues insistently. Verdi is called for, but does not come out. Silence returns. Not allowed the author, they must be satisfied with his music, and the *fuoco di gioia* is repeated. It is sung even better."

At the tavern, stage right, Jago induces Cassio to praise the beautiful Monna Bianca, arousing Roderigo's jealousy (he thinks Cassio is speaking of Desdemona). Jago enlists Roderigo in getting Cassio drunk, and a marvelous *brindisi* ensues, of just the rollicking sort that every good opera should have—except that this one also features the sinister descending chromatic scale of Jago's "beva con me." It was a hit: "Great attention to the Brindisi. The toast is given with great effect by Maurel. The effective phrasing, with its semitone scales of the baritone and the passionate singing of Cassio, provokes new applause. The public cannot stop. Cries and applause interrupt. But silence is restored. There is a phrase of the chorus that laughs at the drunken Cassio. It is strangely produced, performed in an unusual manner. The audience is in tumult and demands a reprise of this piece too. But the wise counsel prevails of those who wish to continue."

Cassio, drunk, begins a fight with Roderigo, but Montàno, who tries to intervene, finds himself in a swordfight with Cassio. This is a complicated piece of staging: the extras have to remove chairs and tables and hanging lanterns, the chorus gathers round, and in a difficult piece of business, Montàno is wounded. The entire swordfight is detailed in the production book, with this note: "This duel must be set up by someone technical and capable, who knows the art of swordsmanship that was used in the fifteenth century. It is a mixture of slashing and thrusting, and, more than from repeated hits, the fight moves along as a result of the swordsmen's rapid moves and appropriate leaps and changes in position."

Confusion is spread by Roderigo at Jago's order, and the alarm bell summons Otello from the castle. He stops the fight, demotes Cassio (who is too drunk to speak), and sends everybody away except for Desdemona, who has been awakened by the noise. (Clearing the stage efficiently and naturally, and keeping perfect silence behind the set for what follows, is emphasized in the prompt book.)

And then follows the stupendously beautiful duet between Otello and Desdemona under a starry night sky. The *Corriera della sera* reported: "Then there is that truly paradisiacal final duet, beginning with the violoncellos divided in four parts, which would be enough by itself to make the fortunes of an opera." The duet follows in large measure the traditional pattern: one character sings, the other character sings; for a moment at least they sing together. Then a new thought provokes new singing, and a final moment of singing together closes the duet.

The pattern is very different from the standard four-part duet form, and the content is wonderful. The characters join together for the lines

E tu m'amavi per le mie sventure
Ed io t'amavo per la tua pietà.

These two lines seem to have struck home with the audience, at least to those who wrote about *Otello,* since the majority of the journalists cite them. They are memorable not only for their music, not only for the fact that they are sung in duet, but also for the fact that, except for large choral numbers, they are the first, and among the only, lines in the libretto that are repeated.

After Otello expresses his worry that such a moment may never come again (and he is right), there follow the wonderful three kisses: "Un bacio . . . un bacio . . . ancor un bacio," whose music nobody ever forgets and which will return in the murder scene and at the terrible end of act 4.

So ends the first act. It has been full of "standard" operatic devices: storm, drinking song, choruses of fear and rejoicing. And it has mostly been large ensemble numbers, setting the scale of the opera. The closing intimate duet makes an effective contrast. And the drama has been set: we have seen Jago's jealousy, dishonesty, and evil; we see how the proud Otello loves the pure Desdemona; and we see how easy it is to take advantage of the lovestruck Cassio. The dramatic machinery has only to be set in motion.

The curtain falls, and ecstatic audience members are on their feet calling for Verdi, who finally appears at the proscenium; there is an enormous shout. Verdi appeared on stage two or three times (reports vary), and there were curtain calls for the singers. The intermission lasted about half an hour.

ACT 2

For the second act the curtain rises on a palace interior whose backdrop, halfway back on the stage, includes large windows through which a garden is seen, with the sea in the distance. A platform at the back (the same as that of act 1) allows access to the stage by a ramp. The garden is brightly lit, the interior slightly less bright. For much of the act Desdemona is in the garden, observed by Otello and Jago.

Jago and Cassio are on stage. Jago persuades Cassio to beg Desdemona to intercede with Otello to pardon him; he sends Cassio out to the garden as she passes on her walk with Emilia, Jago's wife.

And then Jago, alone, delivers his stupendous monologue. His "Credo in un dio crudel," a sardonic and ironic set-piece which surely plays for part of its effect on the religious soliloquies of many Verdian heroines, is sung downstage, near the footlights; the change of effect this has on Jago's appearance amplifies a chief aspect of his character: his chameleonlike ability to change his face and his deportment to suit his needs. He has just been advising and cheering up Cassio—and now, the production books says, "he changes his expression and tone of voice: he is no longer the cheerful and cordial character of a moment earlier. The most loathsome cynicism appears to him." At the end of his "Credo," Jago shrugs, turns his back on the audience, and walks upstage. (He does not utter the now-traditional sardonic laugh.)

The monologue has its effect. Although the production book requires Jago to be "practically immobile during the entire piece, using only a few moderate but effective and clear gestures," the critic for *Le Matin* saw the performance differently. "Maurel sang this long blasphemy with an admirable strident power. It is in fact the only passage in his role where he does not control himself. Everything else he delivers with his arms by his sides, without gesture, without outburst, and his talent is precisely that of producing dramatic emotion by a sort of interior force which purposely does without the assistance of gesture or emphasis of the voice." The blasphemous solo was greeted with loud applause, but, despite requests, the "Credo" was not repeated.

Jago calls Cassio back, points out Desdemona in the garden, and waits to spring his trap on Otello; when Otello appears, Jago is watching the garden closely and saying (to himself, overheard by Otello), "Ciò m'accora" (That grieves me). Their dialogue, in which Otello sees Desdemona smiling at Cassio and interrogates Jago, is full of singers using another voice, quoting music and words: Jago quotes Otello ("Onesto?"), Otello quotes Jago ("Ciò m'accora"), and then quotes Jago quoting Otello ("Che ascondo in cor, signore?"). Jago, pretending to warn Otello against jealousy, instead raises suspicion.

And now comes a lovely tableau in the garden in which children, women, and sailors present gifts to Desdemona in the course of a splendid choral number, accompanied by mandolins and guitars (or, in the libretto, guzla and little harps), along with an oboe (for the sound of the extra who pretends to play bagpipes) and an offstage harmonium (to keep the chorus on pitch, if necessary). A small chorus appears onstage, and a larger one, conducted by the chorus-master, sings in the wings facing away from the hall to achieve the effect of distance.

It is a charming scene, and the music, resembling folk music, is designed to please at first hearing. And it does. One critic wrote, "These [women, children, sailors] sing a very sweet mandolinata which will become popular. The mandolinists are all gentlemen amateurs; among them is even a brother of Giulio Ricordi." However, the placement of such a scene far upstage, heard through the gauze of the palace windows and performed by a somewhat uncertain chorus, weakens the effect: "The pretty mandolinata in the second act lost much of its effect through the players being too far back on the stage" *(Times)*. A Paris journalist noted that "this is where the ballet will come in Paris, which Verdi has promised to write when the opera is given there, that is, very probably next November." The piece was warmly applauded, but the requested repetition did not take place.

The choral scene upstage, which might seem to stop the action, in fact serves as a backdrop for the mimed continuation of the scene between Otello and Jago indoors, and it provides a chilling contrast between the purity and beauty of Desdemona and the growing doubts instilled by Jago. As the prompt book explains: "During this [the chorus] Jago speaks to Otello, who responds with actions that clearly show that he is saying: 'No, it is a groundless fear, mad ravings. It is not possible that such a creature could deceive me.' Jago, prudently, does not insist, and with a look of submission, moves away, returning to his first position on the right, beside the table. . . . This whole counterscene between Otello and Jago should be played in such a way as to use up most of the chorus."

Otello and Jago in act 2 of *Otello*, published in *Il teatro illustrato*,
February 1887. Otello commands Jago to bring him proof
of Desdemona's infidelity or suffer Otello's wrath. Earlier in
the act Desdemona received tributes of songs and flowers
in the garden at the rear.

Now comes what musically is a quartet, a scene in which Desdemona, Otello,
Jago, and Emilia interact in various ways; a combination of static and kinetic strands presented simultaneously. Desdemona comes inside when she notices Otello, and she intercedes for Cassio. Jago meanwhile is outdoors with Emilia, and we hear the last words of
their conversation, when he angrily commands Emilia to obey him. As Desdemona wipes
Otello's angry brow with her handkerchief, he throws it to the ground. Emilia picks it up,
and Jago manages to get it from her in a carefully planned piece of stage business. All this

in the context of a well-wrought quartet. But the effect is not impressive to the audience: "The quartet, which is very beautiful, was not understood" (Filippo Filippi); "The quartet can be, indeed should be, listened to a second time; last night it certainly had little effect" *(Corriere della sera);* "That [the quartet] of *Otello* is short, studied, even obscure, the audience did not understand it" *(La Riforma).*

Otello sends everybody away, but Jago remains upstage; each speaks to himself ("Desdemona false!"; "My poison is working!"). When Jago approaches him, Otello works himself up into a blazing military song of renunciation of his glories. It is magnificent Verdi of the triumphal sort, and everybody recognized it. It is a great moment for Tamagno, whose high notes are his forte, and a good note gets loud applause: once for the high A at "Addio sublimi incanti" and again at the end: "a fervent, inspired ending very well sung by Tamagno and moulded divinely when he says 'Della gloria di *Otello* è questo il fin.' The celebrated tenor filled the house with that desperate B flat which ends the magnificent passage" (Filippo Filippi). And there was tumultuous applause.

There follows a scene between Otello and Jago in which Jago injects further poison. Otello wants proof, and Jago recounts the fictitious dream of Cassio, and in doing so Maurel has to sing with the lovestruck voice of Cassio asleep. "Anyone who has not heard the 'dream' from *Otello,*" writes Gino Monaldi, "cannot have an idea of this marvelous craftsman of the sung word." Jago suggests that if Otello wants proof he has only to ask for Desdemona's handkerchief, which he claims to have seen in Cassio's hand. Otello rages. His oath of vengeance, in which Jago joins (using Otello's words and inflection) brings the act to a stunning if ironic conclusion. (Verdi later rewrote the ending and strengthened the accompaniment—one of the few places where his criticism of the performance led to changes in the music.)

"Ovations," reported *La Lombardia.* "A call for the interpreters. When Verdi appears among the artists, everyone stands to acclaim him. The ladies applaud from their boxes. Verdi is called to the proscenium by continued ovations three more times with the artists. Boito is called for." Other journalists report that Verdi appeared four or five times at the end of the act.

ACT 3

Act 3 is where we expect a big finale, and we get it—but not until the plot advances to an almost intolerable degree. It is an act that was considered "difficult." The scene is in the great hall of the castle. At the rear, a platform (the same as for acts 1 and 2) with a balustrade looks out onto the sea and the side of the castle. Wide steps (they will be needed in the finale) descend into the hall, which is divided into a larger and a smaller room by a series of columns stage right; the downstage column is real, and fixed to the floor.

Otello and Jago are continuing a conversation (interrupted by the announcement of the impending arrival of the Venetian ambassadors). Jago goes to get Cassio, whom he intends to interrogate while Otello watches concealed; meanwhile, Desdemona approaches, and Jago, as he leaves, reminds Otello about "il fazzoletto." Otello returns Desdemona's

A terra!... si, nel livido
Fango percossa io giacio,
Piango, m'agghiaccia il brivido
Dell'anima che muor.

Carlo Ferrario's drawing of a scene from act 3
of *Otello*. This design shows the great hall of the palace after the
grand arrival of the Venetian ambassadors; Desdemona is
forced to her knees by a furiously jealous Otello.

beautiful and lyrical loving greeting with ironical, and then angry, replies, as she again intercedes for Cassio, and Otello demands that she produce the handkerchief. Here Pantaleoni displays her acting skills, for at first she thinks Otello is joking. The production book says, "Here the actress has an opportunity to play a good scene of contrast, but, making obvious this contrast between fear, first, and, later, charming cunning, she should be careful not to exaggerate it." He finally takes again her "ivory hand" and ironically calls her the "vil cortigiana" who is Otello's wife.

Forcing her out, Otello utters a substantial monologue. He is prostrate with emotion, his voice choked, and over a repeated and sinister orchestral motive he sings, or almost speaks, interrupted by sobs, from his chair by the column. Addressing himself to God, he says he could have borne anything (and raises his arm to heaven); he rises, his voice stronger but still parlando, recalling lost happiness. A lyrical moment leads suddenly to violent anger: "Ah. Damnation! First she shall confess, and then die!"

Jago enters, hides Otello ("almost forcibly"—Otello is no longer in charge) on the balcony, and brings in Cassio. After first getting Cassio to pronounce Desdemona's name ("I thought I would find Desdemona here") so that Otello can hear it, Jago then gets Cassio to speak of his love for Bianca (though Otello thinks he is speaking of Desdemona) in a lively scherzo, and induces him to show (Otello has come closer) the beautiful handkerchief he has received from an unknown hand. Jago and Cassio sing of the beauties of the cloth in an elfin scherzo combined with lyrical melody from Cassio that no Mendelssohn or Berlioz could rival; Otello interjects his hidden rage. It is a marvelously woven trio, interrupted by a fanfare of trumpets answered from the castle (this is our first exposure to the new trumpets from Brussels: a stage conductor leads three groups of four trumpets). As the sounds from offstage increase, Otello, on Jago's advice, decides to strangle Desdemona, appoints Jago his captain, and agrees that Desdemona should appear before the ambassadors. Jago's triumph is complete.

Then begins the finale. Verdi and his audiences expected a grand ensemble at this point, and he and Boito had worked hard to provide it. The grand entry of the ambassadors is splendid: guards, standard-bearers, noblemen, counsellors, gentlemen, Knights of the Stocking (whatever they are): a grand assemblage on stage, the chorus shouting "Viva il Leon di San Marco!" (This is where the ballet will be inserted when *Otello* is performed in Paris.) Everybody is present except Cassio. An enormous amount goes on, and it is impossible to detail. Interesting is the combination of public and personal events in the same scene. As Otello reads his orders from the Doge summoning him back to Venice, he interjects insulting asides to Desdemona ("Gentlemen, the Doge"—aside to Desdemona: "How well you pretend to weep"—"recalls me to Venice"). Cassio, named Otello's successor, arrives; Jago is enraged. Otello throws Desdemona to the ground. A sad and desperate scene from her leads to the marvelous *pezzo d'insieme,* in which everybody sings.

This ensemble number, far from being a standard finale, is one of Verdi's great musical creations. Desdemona's voice is heard floating above it all and continuing her lament while the other characters, and the chorus, speak their mind: they are horrified at Otello's treatment of Desdemona. During it all, the plot advances: Jago arranges, with Otello's blessing, the murder of Cassio, convincing Roderigo that he can keep Otello (and his beloved Desdemona) on Cyprus only by eliminating Cassio.

Many of the critics, who had prepared themselves with vocal scores, admired this ensemble, pointing out Verdi's contrapuntal mastery; many noted the presence of ten real parts (one says eleven; actually, there are twelve). "This piece, completely new in conception and execution, will be the marvel of musicians, and the object of study," wrote the *Corriere della sera.* "Verdi has been able to make the various voices on stage sing and express the various passions that move them. He has been able to make the whole orchestra moan with such a careful equilibrium that the ironic part declaimed by Jago becomes quite clear. In this grand piece, in sum, there are so many details that many of them must doubtless have escaped even those ears most familiar with musical complexities."

Otello, having cursed Desdemona, sends everybody away. It is a sort of mad scene, and, overcome by emotion and quoting Jago's words "Cio m'accora," Otello faints. As the offstage chorus hails the Lion of Venice, Jago, with his heel on Otello's head, says, "Ecco il Leone!" The curtain falls to offstage shouts of "Viva Otello!"

It is an act full of action and music, but it does not delight the audience. Critics avoid saying that it does not please, however; the blame is laid on the audience: the act is "not understood." Thus the *Corriere di Roma:* "The third act was not perhaps well enough understood by the audience." And Filippi: "The third act, which is not an easy one to understand immediately, was greatly esteemed and will become enthusiastically accepted once the public comes to understand it." Part of the problem may have been the difficulty of performing such complex ensembles, and critics suggest that there was some uncertainty and even incoherence in the performance.

Nevertheless, there is loud applause. The singers are called to the curtain. Verdi is shouted for and appears three times. "Verdi appears several times at the proscenium to express his thanks," wrote one critic. "He is pale, moved; his face seems to me still to resemble the portrait that Fracassini painted in one of the lunettes over the stage of the Teatro Valle [Rome]. The Maestro, smiling, walks quickly, boldly; the audience seems never to tire of acclaiming him."

ACT 4

The grandeur and spectacle of act 3 turns to the narrow, shallow set of Desdemona's bedroom and an intimate scene between Desdemona and Emilia. This is entirely in the tradition: the fourth act is the one in which the plot has its effect on individuals. Indeed, we know what will happen: we know the story, we see that the plot has decreed Desdemona's death by suffocation. There is only to watch it happen, to see how Verdi brings it to life—and death.

But the quiet English horn solo that begins the act is almost drowned out by an audience that has not yet settled down, and there is insistent loud coughing.

Desdemona too feels the premonition: she asks Emilia to lay out her bridal gown on the bed, and to bury her in it. As Emilia prepares Desdemona's hair for bed, Desdemona sings the song of her childhood servant. This is the Willow Song: it is Shakespeare's Willow Song, and Rossini's, and now Verdi's. No more coughing. The song is haunting, but most of the critics are comparing it with Rossini, and their reports suggest that Verdi has passed the test. Two of many: "The *Romance du Saule* is completely original, Rossini's famous melody is not to be compared with it" *(Le Progrès Artistique);* the Willow Song "will have calmed the anguish of all those who feared the comparison with Rossini: it is difficult to imagine two things more different from each other. . . . Verdi in this has interpreted Shakespeare's wishes in a better fashion, making it a real popular ballad, whose memory comes sadly into the troubled mind of Desdemona" *(Il Caffè-Gazetta Nazionale).* Only a few are able to describe the melody without invoking Rossini: "All the details of such a piece have a beauty which perhaps escapes us at the first hearing" *(La Lombardia).*

Emilia leaves, and Desdemona kneels before the Madonna to say her prayers. A

The cover of *Verdi e l'Otello,* a special number of *L'Illustrazione italiana* issued on the occasion of the premiere. The publication contains much illustrative material, not all of it drawn directly from the production. Verdi was concerned that the costumes not call attention to themselves, insisting that Edel tone down Otello's costume for act 4. However, the costume shown here is that usually shown for the grand third act. Verdi always got his way, and the act 4 costume was probably not this elaborate. © Archivio Storico Ricordi.

solo prayer scene for the heroine is not in Shakespeare, but it not unknown in Italian opera (including Rossini's *Otello*). But coming as it does after Jago's own "Credo" earlier, its purity and its prayer for the hour of death are particularly touching. One spectator wrote, "I heard someone weeping near me during the Ave Maria of Desdemona." And then the audience erupts in applause, demanding Verdi again, but Desdemona has to step out of character and make clear to the audience that the maestro does not come out in the middle of acts. After shouts and continuing applause for Pantaleoni, the Ave Maria is repeated. Desdemona goes to bed.

One of the famous moments in this act is Otello's entrance. It had already been discussed in the newspapers. Verdi composed a thrilling orchestral passage for double-basses (which had given him much trouble in rehearsal, and which still seemed not to go quite right). But this orchestral music is closely allied with the pantomime that, together with the music, displays Otello's highly charged and rapid changes of emotion. The production book makes clear how important this action is, and it is closely coordinated with the music by the use of musical cues in the text:

> . . . precisely on the first note of the solo of the double-basses, the secret door opens rapidly, and Otello appears at the threshold. He takes a small step forwards, then stands still, while he immediately closes the secret door behind him. He holds a scimitar in his right hand.
>
> The actor must memorize the solo of the double-basses well, since all of the action must take place exactly as indicated by the composer on specific beats. Especially at the initial performances, it would be helpful if the same person who has prompted the "Ave Maria" were behind the closed secret door, where, with the score in hand, he could indicate to the actor sotto voce exactly which movements to make. For our part, we will indicate these movements briefly, since it is up to the actor alone, in such a highly dramatic moment, to integrate these movements into an effective scenic action. He should not forget that Desdemona is asleep and must not be awakened by any inopportune noise.
>
> [*Here, as later, there is a musical cue.] He goes quickly towards the table, then stops in front of the lamp, undecided whether to put it out or not. Then he moves to the door, pulls back the tapestry, and locks the door. *Otello turns and looks at Desdemona. *Then, resolutely, he goes to put out the light. He moves forward again and gazes at Desdemona. *Otello is filled with rage. He makes an angry movement, then, deciding quickly, he moves towards the bed with excited steps, stopping suddenly, precisely on the chord marked here.* He goes up the two steps and contemplates Desdemona, who is sleeping, for a long time. A sense of sorrowful tenderness fills him, and, still looking at Desdemona, he moves to the head of the bed. Otello bends down and gives Desdemona a soft kiss, precisely on the note indicated,* then contemplates her once again. Another kiss* as above. *Yet another kiss. The third kiss should be more accentuated. At that point, Desdemona moves with a start.

The double-bass passage seems not to have been perfect; Verdi consulted with the contrabass virtuoso Giovanni Bottesini for fingerings to try to bring the passage into tune. And in 1889 he wrote to Ricordi, "Once more the solo for the double basses has had an indecent performance at La Scala; and I reproach myself for not having thought of a remedy. . . . The task of noting the positions should have been given to the most able bass player and some rehearsals held separately." The four-stringed double-bass had only recently been introduced at La Scala (1882), at Verdi's urging, and perhaps the players had not played passages of this difficulty on the instruments.

Actually, at that point the audience erupts. At perhaps the most passionate moment in the opera the action is stopped by applause, and the whole passage, with Otello's entrance and mimed action, is played again. The *Times* wrote, "The encore nuisance is even more rampant in Italy than among us, and sometimes leads to curious results. When, for example, Othello was compelled to leave his wife's chamber so that the famous recitative in unison for the double-basses preceding his entry might be repeated a second time, the border line between the sublime and the ridiculous was distinctly passed, the more so as that recitative was played indifferently the first and very badly the second time."

The scene of Desdemona's death, carefully staged, was a triumph for the normally wooden Tamagno. Verdi's coaching must have worked. Desdemona is smothered, and Emilia enters to report the death of Roderigo, not of Cassio. Desdemona, with her dying breath, commends herself to Otello and says "muoio innocente . . . Addio." The plot is rapidly untangled by those who have entered: the handkerchief, Jago's treachery. Otello has reached the end of his road. His death scene, with the three kisses recalled from act 1, has been detailed earlier. Tamagno performs it admirably, and his final phrase ("un bacio . . .") gets him a round of applause. Indeed, to the critic of *Corriere della sera,* "the death of the Moor is among Verdi's most beautiful deaths."

Twenty-nine minutes after the beginning of the act, the curtain descends slowly at the end of the opera. The opera ends at 12:10, not quite four hours after it began. Although the music occupies about two hours, the rest of the time was filled by three rather short intermissions and the time it takes for applause, curtain calls, and the repetition of three numbers.

At the end there is thunderous applause. Francis Hueffer reported: "The stalls and the five tiers of boxes (only the Royal box was empty) vied in shouting and waving of handkerchiefs with the noisiest of the gods. The scene, in brief, was one which could be witnessed only in Italy, and, of the Italian cities, in Milan, the musical and the moral capital of the Peninsula, as she is proud to call herself."

Another eyewitness describes the scene:

> New ovations from the audience and Pantaleoni and Tamagno are called to the proscenium. Verdi and his interpreters have to present themselves twice, together with Boito and Maurel. And then twice more Verdi and the others, to which the request for Faccio is added. At this point the enthusiasm becomes a true frenzy. The men, standing, wave their hats. The ladies in their boxes, also standing, wave their handkerchiefs. The same in the orchestra stalls and in the gallery, shouting, gesturing, and calling for Verdi, who presents himself, together with Boito, welcomed with new ovations. Then they wanted him alone, and when he appeared the admiration was unrestrained. It seemed like a sort of general madness.

Verdi and Boito were caught between two fires, for on this side of the proscenium there were the ovations of the audience, and within the applause of the artists and the others. In the midst of this fever of admiration Verdi with the other artists had to cross the stage.

Boito himself was much moved by his curtain call, as he related to Blanche Roosevelt:

When I heard my name I was strangely touched. I had not thought about it. I was up in a box with Signora Verdi when the maestro sent for us. We went to the stage, and when we were called he started, then turned in a half-dazed way for me. He took my hand. No, I shall never forget it. I can never describe to you how he took my hand: his touch—there was something so kind, so paternal, so protecting in it, and the clasp of his fingers so thrilled me that I felt the shock to my heart's core: it was an electric thrill, and yet so delicate I could scarcely realise that our hands had come in contact. Ah! Verdi said more to me in that single hand-clasp than he has said in all our previous intercourse: more than any one ever will say. I shall never forget it!

Verdi was called out many times: reports vary between eight and twenty. Verdi embraced Pantaleoni, Faccio, Maurel—but Tamagno? "Ah, no, dear *Otello:* you will dye my beard!" Instead he embraced Maurel's daughter Margherita.

Then it was time for the ballet.

Reactions

It was a triumph for Verdi, but he was already a national hero. His name had been associated with music, with opera, with politics, with Italy, for so long that it was almost impossible to believe that he was a living human. The critic of *Il Secolo* recognized this: "For now, the whole impression of the audience can be summed up in a shout: Viva Verdi! That shout, thirty years ago, was fortunate in representing, in the sum of its letters, all the national aspirations of our people—last night that shout summed up all its memories of artistic glories, all the aspirations for maintaining intact the ancient and eternal splendor."

But this is an opera, and that means singers. The opera is performed, and the impression of *Otello* is conveyed mostly through the three principal characters.

Pantaleoni, whose role is in a way the least dramatic, was never famous for singing in tune, and her uncertainty and poor intonation were noticed by even the most generous critics. Hueffer reported in the *Times,* "With every wish to treat Madame Pantaleoni's Desdemona with leniency and forbearance, it is impossible not to express surprise that the Italian stage could not have supplied a better dramatic soprano for such an occasion. The lady's uncertain intonation may have been partly the effect of nervousness. It was indeed, noticeable that many things, including the sestet in the third act, went much better at the general rehearsal than in the performance. Certain it is, however, that Signora Pantaleoni

is not above mediocrity; and even respectable mediocrity, placed face to face with a work of genius like *Otello*, must of necessity come to grief." The effusive Roosevelt, a singer herself, was less kind: "Madame Pantaleoni is an excellent person, but as Desdemona she ought to have been suppressed the night before at her dress rehearsal. Her voice is naturally fine and dramatic, but she has no more knowledge of the pure art of singing than I have of the real science of astronomy. She has a vile emission of tone in the medium open notes; the upper notes are clear, but rarely in tune. . . . In appearance Madame Pantaleoni is likewise unfortunate: she is short, slightly cross-eyed, and has a physical plainness, which dwarfed the already insignificant Desdemona. She acted very well in the first and third acts, but not so well in the last."

Others, especially the Italian critics, made allowances for her voice and admired her dramatic ability. The *Corriere di Roma* wrote: "The singing of Pantaleoni, uncertain from unusual fear, warms up. The voice weeps—begs and loves. The Desdemona of Shakespeare's wishes . . . is rendered very well by the extraordinary genius, the artistic intuition, of Pantaleoni." The Milanese critics were especially generous to Pantaleoni. Filippo Filippi, the main critic of Milan, was all admiration: "Signora Pantaleoni was always admirable for her expressive singing, her dramatic temperament and exceedingly appealing artistic gifts." Also admiring was the *Corriere della sera:* "Pantaleoni, fine in the whole opera, was delicious in the last act for the suavity of her singing and acting."

Tamagno's effect seems to be that of a tenor: he sings his best and loudest high notes, and when he sings one of them he gets applause. "Of Signor Tamagno's Othello it is possible to speak in almost equally favourable terms [as of Maurel]," wrote Hueffer.

"He is a *tenore robusto* of the genuine kind, and his voice, although without much charm in the middle register, goes up to B flat with perfect ease. His upper notes, indeed, are magnificent, and it is specially worthy of notice that he is a genuine Italian tenor, and not a mere baritone, with some high notes superadded."

"M. Tamagno possesses an admirable tenor voice," wrote Camille Bellaigue. "He sang certain parts of his role, notably the last act, almost as a great artist, especially at the second performance." The ebullient Roosevelt was less charitable: "When Tamagno sang, I felt as if the Coliseum entire were being hurled in my face. This artist proceeds in blissful ignorance of the fact that there are some people who do not care for so much voice at the expense of even a little art. . . . Nothing can make me believe that Tamagno has ever even intelligently studied his role. However, were Rossini here, he would protect him to his face, and say three things make an artist—voice, voice, voice."

Tamagno's may not have been a great performance, despite its good moments and its ringing high notes; the *Corriere della sera* said of the second performance that Tamagno had taken away the shadow in which the role had remained at the premiere and bravely brought it to the foreground. Evidently he had been a little indisposed, judging from the report at the second performance that he was entirely restored to health. The same paper reported on the first performance that "Tamagno gave out some of those notes that produce shivers of admiration," but there is no mention of acting.

The opera really belongs to the singer of Jago, especially if he is also an actor. And Victor Maurel, Frenchman or not, acted the part to perfection. Hueffer wrote:

> There are virtually three parts in *Otello,* and one of these, that of Iago, was filled by a Frenchman, M. Maurel. That this should have been necessary on so eminently national an occasion as the present is in itself a curious fact. However, M. Maurel is an artist of the first order, and did full justice to the choice. As an actor he realized the character of the plausible villain with a distinctness seldom witnessed, even in the spoken drama. He was honest Iago all over, soft spoken, and looking most innocent when he aimed the most poisonous shafts at the defenceless breast of the Moor. The excellence of M. Maurel's vocalization will be remembered by all who heard him at Covent Garden. In this work he has much to sing, and sings it admirably. Perhaps the finest point was made in a kind of monologue in the pessimistic vein of Schopenhauer, which Signor Boito has somewhat incongruously placed in the mouth of Iago, and which Verdi has set to highly impressive music.

Of act 1 the *Corriere di Roma* wrote, "Maurel is bellissimo—sullen—satanic"; and of act 2, "Maurel is immense. The actor has disappeared." Filippi concurs: "Maurel is a first-rate Jago, as a singer as well as the interpreter of the villainous character; without a beard, as he now is, he cannot be recognized." Bellaigue also agrees: "As for Mr Maurel, he is a perfect Jago. Composed with that keen intelligence and that irreproachable taste, such a role should suffice for the honor of a singer and an actor."

Even Roosevelt had nothing but praise: "Victor Maurel, the incarnation of natural gifts, voice, intelligence, art, and experience. . . . Victor Maurel is the only real artist in the opera, and he is a Frenchman. In voice, acting, appearance, and dress his is the ideal of what an operatic artist should be, and the ideal of what any operatic Jago could be. He sang as even his best friends never dreamed he could sing, and his acting was the consummate work which we always have at his artistic hands."

The other singers were variable: Navarrini as Ludovico has a strong and beautiful voice, and is noticed for it. Paroli, as Cassio, is a fine singer, an intelligent artist, but not strong enough for this cast. Fornari's Roderigo was not strong, though Roosevelt says that he was "not important to help or hinder the work."

A few slips were noticed in ensemble and tuning in choral numbers, but these are inevitable in a first performance, and though they were noticed, they did not hurt the performance. As the *Corriere della sera* reported, "The choral forces, for a first performance of such importance, did well, and will do better in the succeeding evenings."

We have mostly journalists as eyewitnesses to the first performance, but they acknowledge the attentive, knowledgeable, and critical abilities of the audience of La Scala. Hueffer puts it this way: "Such failures of judgment [encores] are more than made up for as regards a Milanese audience by the singular intelligence and receptivity with which that audience places itself *en rapport* with the composer and the singers, taking up every point, and as it were rising and falling with the modulations of the music. Only a nation highly gifted by nature, and trained by centuries of artistic activity, could supply such an instrument for a man of genius to play upon."

Many members of the audience, like the critics, will have brought memories of Verdi's work, and of other Italian opera, with them to *Otello*. Among the things they noticed were the traditional elements already mentioned, but also Verdi's new ability to condense, to avoid repetition, to make each act a continuous event. The opera, they note, is scarcely longer than the libretto itself: there are no repetitions of text to accommodate musical phraseology that are so frequent in other operas. This is like Wagner in a way but entirely different in the lyrical quality that Verdi gives to much of the music. There are not many separate numbers, as in a Meyerbeer opera, working the audience up to applause at the right moment (though applause did happen); and although there are beautiful lyrical passages, and impressive high notes, there is no call for the rapid vocal acrobatics with which the audience was familiar from older operas. And there are not many extended orchestral passages. It is tight, dramatic, even terse. And yet it is no Wagnerian music-drama. As Filippi put it, "While agreeing not to divide the opera into pieces, with fixed forms, with obligatory cadences, with titles like cavatina, aria, duetto, and so on, but to make of each act a single piece, Verdi remains himself, always himself."

The opera is, in a sense, less dazzling than some. It does not have as many singable melodies as some of Verdi's other operas, and it does not have separate numbers calling for applause at the end. Faccio tried valiantly to make this clear, holding his baton in the air to keep the audience from applauding during the acts, but, as we have seen, he did not succeed in restraining them, and three "numbers" had to be repeated. Italian audiences are demonstrative, and Verdi's audience here was exulting in the master's mastery. It is inevitable that observers would describe certain musical "numbers," despite the continuity achieved by Verdi. Certain scenes, choruses, songs, prayers, and so on are certainly set-pieces in some sense. And the dialogue, referred to by some as "declamation" and by others as "recitative," was also noticed. "The recitatives are of a unique beauty," wrote Gramola in *Corriere della sera*, "and I am sure that after several hearings they will not be among the least of the attractions for the audience." By this must also be meant that most attention, or at least reaction, was given to the big musical numbers.

Mentions of continuity, of "true musical drama," are perhaps ways of avoiding saying "Wagner." It is impossible, however, not to think of Wagner. Verdi could not avoid it, and neither could most of those who were there. Here is a selection:

> "Some say that the first act is Wagnerian; but the whole opera is imprinted with Verdi's character" (*La Nazione*, Florence).
>
> "Even now there are some, as there were fifteen years ago, who claim that Verdi has abjured his artistic religion by sacrificing to new gods" *(Gazzetta di Venezia)*.
>
> "The maestro has made great concessions to the so-called Wagnerian ideas, but still retaining the most sublime and genuine Verdian imprint" (*L'Elettrico della Domenica*, Florence).
>
> "To those who want to speak of Wagnerism in the latest work of Verdi, I would reply frankly that it is a gross error. Verdi is Verdi, and he remains that alone" *(Le Progrès Artistique)*.
>
> "We are faced with a veritable *drame lyrique*, conceived in the modern manner, rid of all Italian formula, where nothing is sacrificed to effect, where each character expresses himself musically in a special color which dominates and accompanies his whole role, an original work where Verdi, without borrowing anything from anybody, has only kept his verve, his fire, and his astounding youth" *(Le Matin)*.
>
> "Certainly we no longer find in *Otello* sweet mellifluous melodies without dramatic character; no one dies in waltz tempo; nor does Desdemona before being suffocated, feeling dreadful presentiments, feel the need to do vocalises: those who expected the old cabalettas, the stretto-finales, the easy melodies to remember and whistle at home while going to bed—if indeed there were any such people—were disappointed. . . . It's important to pay attention to the orchestra, because it is not just an enormous guitar for accompanying arias. . . . If all this, or the lack of something else, means having made Wagner, then Verdi has done so in *Otello*—and we should give thanks to the immortal gods!" *(Il Caffè-Gazzetta Nazionale)*

A short notice in the *Messaggero* of Rome reported that the opera was not a

Giulio Ricordi, heir apparent of the enormously influential Ricordi publishing firm, was a sort of godfather to *Otello*.

success: "The new opera has in large point disappointed expectations. The first and the fourth acts pleased; the second was received coldly, and the third was actually judged decadent. . . . The fact that none of the pieces was encored proves that the opera did not much satisfy."

There were twenty-five additional performances of *Otello* in Milan and various further performances in other cities, including a tour to Rome from which Pantaleoni excused herself.

Various tributes were paid to Verdi, who, according to long tradition, felt obliged to remain in Milan for the first three performances. He wanted to get back to his farms in Sant'Agata, and he deeply disliked the tributes and adulation that he constantly received. Nevertheless, he put up with it gallantly.

An enormous luncheon was given by the Ricordis at the Hotel Milano the day after the premiere, for foreign journalists and important persons in the arts and politics; there were impressive speeches by Giulio Ricordi, the mayor, and others (all carefully reported in Ricordi's book of reviews). Verdi was presented with a luxurious album by subscribers, bound in silver and gold; he was made an honorary citizen of Milan; and he received citations and resolutions from everywhere. There were demonstrations in various opera houses of Italy—in Siena, the Carlo in *Ernani* substituted Verdi's name ("Al sommo Verdi") in the line "A Carlomagno sia gloria ed onor"; there were tumultuous cries of "Viva Verdi," and the whole finale was encored in Verdi's honor.

The second performance featured the presentation of a silver crown (with a ribbon that read "A Giuseppe Verdi il suo *Otello*") to Verdi from Tamagno after the first act; Tamagno's daughter made the presentation, and Verdi's embrace charmed the audience.

Everybody talked about *Otello,* and there were special supplements issued by journals. In a parody entitled *Otello Guglielmo della bella Venezia* Otello salutes the creators with his dying words:

Un bacio . . . un bacio . . . un bacio . . .
a Verdi, Boito e Faccio!

Directly after the first performance of *Otello* there was a performance of the ballet *Rolla* of Manzotti and Pontoglio—but in a shortened version. Some members of the orchestra—including Toscanini—who thought the ballet was unnecessary, making the evening too long and insulting Verdi, were fined for their deliberately poor playing. Verdi left the theater after the performance and was surrounded by an enormous throng who detached the horses from his carriage and pulled it themselves to the Hotel Milano. There was such shouting for Verdi that he presented himself on his balcony several times. A choir of amateur mandolinists and guitarists performed a serenade composed especially for the occasion. When Tamagno was summoned to the balcony with Verdi, he summed up the feelings of everybody when he gave a repeat performance of his opening word: "Esultate!"

Documents: *Otello*

1. SELECTIONS FROM CORRESPONDENCE

Extracts from Verdi's copious correspondence are taken from volume 1 of Hans Busch's invaluable Verdi's Otello *and* Simon Boccanegra *(revised version) in Letters and Documents (Oxford: Clarendon, 1988). Busch gives sources for all the original documents on pp. xix–lvii.*

a. Verdi to Giulio Ricordi, January 18, 1886

I'm frightened about the tenor part. For many, many things Tamagno would be wonderful, but in many others no. There are large, long phrases, legato ones that are to be said in a *mezza voce,* an impossible thing for him. What's worse is that the first act would finish coldly, and (what's still worse) the fourth!! There is a short but broad melody, and then some half-voice phrases (after wounding himself), extremely important . . . and we can't do without them. . . . And if I could hear him . . . before deciding? (p. 196)

b. Verdi to Boito, January 21, 1886

The outcome of my long conversation with Corti and Giulio is this: I have not finished the opera and I don't know *whether I will finish it.* If I do, I shall give it [to La Scala], always assuming that the conditions are suitable. No formal commitment, absolutely none. In talking about it I indicated *Maurel, Tamagno, Teodorini.* But afterwards, thinking it over and looking at the score, I realized that Tamagno would be excellent in many places but that he wouldn't succeed in the final duet of the first act, and even less at the end of the opera, so that two acts would end coldly (as I wrote to Giulio). You don't know the first duet, but you do know the end of the opera. I don't think that he could effectively project the short melody *"E tu come sei pallida"* [And you, how pale you are], even less (*"Un bacio, un bacio ancora"* [A kiss, yet another kiss]) . . . particularly since between this second kiss and the third, there are 4 measures for the orchestra alone, which must be filled with delicate, moving gestures that I imagined as I was writing the notes. It would be the easiest thing for a real actor to do, but difficult for . . . anyone else (p. 200).

c. Verdi to Giulio Ricordi, January 22, 1886

I sincerely believe our tenor [Tamagno] could have managed well in the two pieces you sent me. In *Meyerbeer's* there are the B flats at the end which are so good for him. In the other, by Ponchielli, which is more *cantabile* than the first, he also has a few F sharps and G sharps and, at the end, also the final notes that lie well in his voice. . . . It isn't so in *Otello.*—After he has ascertained that Desdemona has been killed [although] innocent, Otello is breathless; he is weary, physically and morally exhausted; he cannot and must not sing any more, except with a *half-muffled, veiled voice* . . . but with a *reliable* one.

This is a quality that Tamagno doesn't have. He must always sing with *full voice;* without it his sound becomes ugly, uncertain, off-pitch. . . . This is a very serious matter and gives me much to think about! I prefer not to give the opera if this point of the score isn't brought out (p. 201).

d. Verdi to Franco Faccio, September 2, 1886

Dear Faccio,

Signora Pantaleoni left just now and gave me hope that she would return towards the middle of October, when her part will be completely copied and even printed. I have entrusted the fourth act to Giulio [Ricordi], in which Desdemona has the largest and most difficult part. The *canzone del salice* [Willow Song] is causing the composer as well as the artist performing it the greatest problems. She should sing with three voices, like the most sacred Trinity: with one for Desdemona, another one for Barbara [the maid], and a third for the *"salce, salce, salce"* [willow]. Signora Pantaleoni's voice becomes cutting at passionate points, and in high notes a little too biting; she gives too much metal, so to speak. If she could get used to singing with a little more head-voice, the *smorzato* [faded away] would come easier to her and her voice would also be more secure and natural.—I have advised her to study this way; and you, with your influence, should give her the same advice. Besides, it isn't always true that her D is such a bad tone, as she says. There is a point where she succeeds the best with it: [here Verdi writes the notation and words for "salce, salce, salce"].

This phrase is repeated three times. The last time she manages it well, the two other times less so.

I told you frankly what I think, and I tell you again that—with her great talent and theatrical instincts, with good will and study—she will succeed very well in the part of Desdemona, even though it is not completely suited to her way of expression and her voice. . . . Mind you, she does many, many things with the greatest ease (pp. 234–35).

e. Giulio Ricordi to Verdi, September 20, 1886

Everybody is working on *Otello;* and to keep you from finding the famous *pretext* . . . with which you threatened me, I tell you that we have fished out a first-rate Rodrigo!! . . . So one of your pretexts is already well destroyed. Now we are fishing for the Signora Emilia, and today I shall hear one with Faccio. We have agreed with Cairati on the chorus; instead of 100, we'll have 104 voices, bringing the women up to 40 instead of 36. I shall also show Cairati the orchestra score so that he may plan for the voices as well as for the children's chorus.—

Edel has been sensible this time!!! . . . That's another Verdi miracle!! . . . He has completed 53 of the 58 costume sketches; and so as not to let him slip away from me, I took him with me to the lake [Como] and locked him up there until he finished everything. So yesterday we had a meeting of three and a half hours with Boito (who is . . . as accurate as a Benedictine monk!!); and since Giacosa was there, too, we thought of inviting him also to the exhibition of the designs; I hope you will have nothing against it—or do you? . . . I am glad to tell you that the costumes were an immense success. Edel has really surpassed himself. We also solved the problem of Desdemona's last costume. Edel completely accepted some observations that Boito and Giacosa made, and today he is working on the required corrections. Only one costume sketch for Otello, one for Emilia, and three for the chorus are still missing; I hope he will be finished in a few days—so that we can submit all the sketches for your approval.

In a few days a part of the reduction of the first act will be ready (pp. 240–41).

f. Verdi to Giulio Ricordi, About October 1, 1886

Pro Memoria

Assuming I am able to complete what remains to be done for the music of *Otello*, it will be well for the House of Ricordi to establish as of now the conditions above all with the management of La Scala.

1. The House of Ricordi shall, with the management, set the rental [of scores and orchestral materials, etc.], of which I shall realize my share, etc., etc.,——

2. I will assist in all those rehearsals (which I shall judge necessary); but I do not wish to commit myself in any way to the public, and consequently the poster shall simply say

Otello

Poetry by Boito

Music by Verdi

No one, *absolutely no one*, at the rehearsals, as usual.—I have complete authority to suspend the rehearsals and prevent the performance, even after the dress rehearsal, if

either the execution

or the *mise-en-scène*

or *anything else* in the way the theatre is run should not be to my liking.

The personnel connected with *Otello* shall answer directly to me . . . the *conductor* of the orchestra, of the chorus, the producer, etc., etc.

The first performance may not take place without my authorization, and should anyone think he can circumvent this condition, the Ricordi Publishers shall pay me a fine of one hundred thousand (100,000) Lire.—

GV

[the following two lines are apparently written by Giulio Ricordi]

—I request normal pitch in the theatres

—A box for opening night at the disposal of Signora Verdi (pp. 241–42).

g. Giulio Ricordi to Verdi, October 8, 1886

Caprara [presumably the head carpenter of La Scala], as I had foreseen, will only be in Milan the day after tomorrow, the 10th, instead of returning on the 2nd. But I have bombarded him with letters and telegrams, and I hope that if not by the 12th, then at least by the 14th the model of the first scene will be ready. I shall telegraph you on the 12th; so I shall see to what point the work has progressed, and you can plan for your journey here so that nothing will be upset that has already been arranged beforehand.

Edel is ready, having finished (unheard-of miracle) all his work—and the scenic designer Ferrario is already putting all the drops into place and is making the first traces. So as soon as you give the order *AVANTI!* everything will move in order and without any trouble (p. 243).

h. Giulio Ricordi to Verdi, October 23, 1886

—News regarding the storm. With the kind co-operation of Prof. Orsi, I believe we shall have a superb storm!!! . . . Having made the necessary comparisons with the dimensions of the thunder [machine] at the *Opéra,* which Muzio sent us, we shall have at La Scala a kind of big drum with these measurements: 1.35 metres wide, 2 metres long. Try to note these measurements and you will see that perhaps not even God Almighty up there disposes of such majestic thunder!!— Now we shall perform some experiments to find out whether a roll by hand or by mechanical means is preferable.

—Backstage trumpets: After talking about them again with Faccio and Orsi, all three of us have reached the same decision, which is: to use 12 trumpets *ad hoc* that would be of the same timbre and sonority; and to solve the problem safely, I have given Orsi a trumpet part, asking him to write to Mahillon in Brussels without telling him, of course, what it is about. Enclosed herewith is Mahillon's reply—marked with blue pencil. He is certainly the foremost builder of instruments in Europe and a distinguished musician in his field. Will you, Maestro, please now decide the matter? In case [you approve] I would order all the 12 trumpets right away (p. 247).

i. Romilda Pantaleoni to Alceo Pantaleoni, October 29 (?), 1886

Last night I returned from Bussetto, where I stayed for twelve days, enjoying the sublime harmony of the great old man! If you could hear the heavenly things—and what strength of artistic fibre! It seems impossible that all this is the work of a man past *seventy!* And how much tenderness and depth there is in the look of the genius! He made me study twice a day, in the morning and the late afternoon! And I assure you that with him I thoroughly examined the immense beauties of those sweet and at the same time powerful melodies; I really believe that with the opera I shall arrive at the height of my glory (p. 251)!

j. Verdi to Boito, October 29, 1886

As you know, Signora Pantaleoni has been here, and she left yesterday. She knows her entire part very well, and I hope she will obtain excellent effects in it. Only in the scene of the first act is something missing. It's not that she doesn't sing her *solo* lines well, but she interprets them with too much accentuation and too dramatically. We'll have other re-hearsals, however, and I'll insist that she manage to find the right accent for the situation and for the poetry (p. 251).

k. Verdi to Franco Faccio, October 29, 1886

As you know, Signora Pantaleoni left yesterday. She knows her entire part very well, and if the *stars,* and the whims of the audience, are not hostile to the opera on that night, one can say that she will obtain effects everywhere. Very good ones in the quartet, and also in the duet and finale of the third act, and in the entire fourth. She need have no stage fright. Her tones will go very well if she makes them less biting and all in the *head,* as I have also advised her to sing at many other points. If there is any thing to find fault with, it's the scene of the first act. There, something lighter, airy, and—let's say the word—voluptuous would be called for, as warranted by the situation and the poetry. She sings her *solo* phrases very well, but with too much accentuation and too dramatically. However, we shall have other rehearsals, and we'll manage to find the right expression.

This is between us, but if you should some time go over the part with her, tell her to sing as much as possible with head-voice.

And now, my dear Faccio, I ask you warmly to have Tamagno study his part after he arrives. He is so inexact in the reading of music that I would really like him to study the part with a true musician in order to get him to sing the notes with their true value and in time. As for the interpretation of the chorus, we'll take care of this when I explain all my intentions concerning the singing, staging, etc., etc. (pp. 251–52).

l. Verdi to Boito, November 1, 1886

Dear Boito,
>   it's finished!
>   Hail to us . . . .
>   (and also to *Him*!!)
>   Addio
>   G. Verdi (p. 253)

m. Verdi to Giulio Ricordi, November 4, 1886

So now, let's seriously take care of the performance, and let's watch out that we don't fall on our faces. Here a serious question arises, more serious than it seems to be at first sight: I mean *the Tamagno question.*

La Pantaleoni knows her part by heart, and when we get to the piano rehearsals I'll have almost nothing to tell her about colours, accents, etc., etc.

Maurel, once he has studied the music, will imagine the rest, and with him, too, little or nothing will have to be done.

Not so with *Tamagno*. Even when he has learned the music well, much will have to be said about interpretation and expression.—— I will have to make my observations directly to him, more so than to any of the others (and to him, the *5,000* Lire tenor!), and these (especially in front of Maurel) could *blesser* his self-respect and his feelings. In this way bad humours, irritations, *insults, quarrels* arise . . . and then *brrrrr* . . . one no longer knows where it's going to end. This is a danger: a danger that must be avoided at all costs (p. 256).

n. Verdi to Giulio Ricordi, November 11, 1886

While I remember it, tell Faccio not to let Tamagno study the very last phrase, *"quella vil cortigiana che è la sposa d'Otello"* [that vile courtesan who is the wife of Otello], of the duet between Otello and Desdemona in the third act. . . . I have done this phrase twenty times and cannot find the right tone . . . and perhaps I won't ever find it . . . but who knows . . . perhaps I'll need Boito's help. . . . We'll see in Milan. I am quite content with the news you give me about Tamagno's study. Tell Faccio he should insist and not get tired of it . . . ; in spite of this study, I shall still have many things to say about the musico-dramatic interpretation, and I really ought to be with him [Tamagno] for 3 or 4 days, but alone, without the company of the other artists! But where? And how? . . .

Jago cannot be performed, and isn't possible, without *Maurel's* extremely good enunciation. . . . Always bear Jago's part in mind, however. In this part one must neither *sing* nor (with few exceptions) *raise one's voice*. If I were a singing actor, for example, I would speak it all in a whisper, *mezza voce* (pp. 261–62).

o. Giulio Ricordi to Verdi, November 12, 1886

Faccio confirms to you that Tamagno is studying daily with great zeal. He reads the first and fourth acts fluently and without errors; and yesterday he started to study the third. —Following your instructions, Faccio is limiting himself to teaching the notes exactly, mathematically—and nothing else (p. 262).

p. Giulio Ricordi to Verdi, January 2, 1887

Faccio has really worked like . . . a martyr; so much so that from yesterday on he has be-gun the rehearsals for *Otello,* with all the other secondary parts, since he is free every day and occupied only at night. Tonight I have a meeting in the costume shop to approve the fabrics, all of which arrived yesterday from Turin; so tomorrow the sewing of costumes will start, since the costume shop has finished the opera and the ballet that must be produced, which is a miracle.

You can imagine with what joy I read the news of your arrival on Tuesday. I shall have the piano (a good one, of course) brought to the rehearsal room; please tell me whether you want a good little upright piano in the drawing room of the Hôtel; I think it will be useful to have it, in case it is needed to try the translation, etc., etc. If this is so please telegraph me so it can be put into place before your arrival, and you will not have the trouble of moving it. Boito is here, always keeping it a secret whether he will go or stay! . . .

The trumpets sent from Brussels work very well (pp. 289–90).

q. Verdi to Giulio Ricordi, March 14, 1887

Yesterday, descending the long staircase of the Hôtel Eden in Nervi with Boito and Du Locle, I said, "Here is the set of the 2nd act of *Otello*!"

The lobby of this hotel is grandiose, and most beautiful. It has three great windows; behind them a garden (still young), beyond the garden the sea.

For *Otello*, therefore: a shallow set, almost down to the curtain, and on the back-drop, many large windows, separated by little Moorish or Venetian columns, etc., etc. Be-yond the large windows, a great park with a great square and a great avenue, and smaller streets crossing it. . . . And plants, plants, plants; the sea, yes or no, as you like. The large glass windows of metallic, very transparent fabric, without fear for the voices! This way the action required by the drama could take place, and the audience would understand, and even hear, that in this moment two events, two actions happen simultaneously: A *feast* for Desdemona, a *conspiracy* between Jago and Otello——

Zuccarelli's set may be as beautiful as you like, but it's still wrong. Give in; I re-peat for the thousandth time that in my opinion there is nothing to be made but a glass wall (pp. 293–94).

2. FILIPPO FILIPPI IN *LA PERSEVERANZA*, FEBRUARY 6, 1887

The première of *Otello* has justified the avid anticipation of those who attended it, as well as the exceptionally high prices charged for the seats. Whoever was there last night can claim to have seen an opera performance unequalled at La Scala or any other theatre in the world.

The theatre was packed. The stalls were filled row upon row. Half a dozen people and sometimes an entire dozen were crammed into the boxes, and in the gallery the audi-ence was squeezed in like sardines.

From the start, the first act delighted with its great musically dramatic beauties, and it surprised the listener with the marvellous transformation of Verdi's genius, which remains always a genius rich in invention to which now has been added a total novelty that cannot be compared to any of the most celebrated operas, including Verdi's own.

While agreeing not to divide the opera into pieces, with fixed forms, with obliga-tory cadences, with titles like cavatina, aria, duetto, and so on, but to make of each act a single piece, Verdi remains himself, always himself.

The ordinary observer might say that he has become Wagnerian. No; he is instead always a composer of unquestionable individuality.

In the first act, the greatest effect is achieved by the stupendous Chorus *Fuoco di gioia,* which had to be repeated, and then the delightful love duet in the end.

In the second act, Jago's stupendous monologue, divinely interpreted by Maurel, was greeted with great applause and requested in vain to be repeated. Most interesting is Otello's first duet with Jago, followed by the Chorus which pleased immensely, especially when the children sing accompanied by the mandolins.

The quartet, which is very beautiful, was not understood, but will be enjoyed when heard again. In the duet between the baritone and the tenor, which ends the act, the finale *a due* gave rise to enthusiastic applause calling for the composer and the performers.

The third act, which is not an easy one to understand immediately, was greatly esteemed and will become enthusiastically accepted once the public comes to understand it. Otello's solo is most beautiful and was well performed. Stupendous also is the following trio for its ingenious interlacement and a most singular originality.

There are no words to describe the beauty of the finale with its novelty of structure and most singular sound effects; altogether, however, all these beautiful things are not easy to comprehend. They also suffered from a somewhat uncertain, incoherent performance.

The fourth act is a wonder from beginning to end, and I think that from a dramatic viewpoint it surpasses the most famous ones [in all opera].

First, there is a characteristic cantilena, "Piangea cantando" [She wept, singing]; then an "Ave Maria," requested to be repeated with sincere enthusiasm.

The awesome duet between husband and wife that follows and ends with the strangling of poor Desdemona, is continuously pulsating with very fast verbal thrusts and replies lasting for about seven pages of the libretto.

The performance in general was truly admirable for its precision, its colours and effects involving a difficult orchestration. The Chorus was very good, as usual.

Only in the knotty finale of the third act was there a bit of uncertainty. Signora Pantaleoni was always admirable for her expansive singing, her dramatic temperament and exceedingly appealing artistic talent.

Also Tamagno was excellent and, in the last acts, an effective actor. Maurel is a first-rate Jago, as a singer as well as the interpreter of the villainous character; without a beard, as he now is, he cannot be recognized. The other parts were also good, especially the bass Navarrini with his phenomenal voice; Jago's wife was a bit weak.

After the last act there was an immense ovation for Verdi.—Filippi

In Busch, *Verdi's* Otello *and* Simon Boccanegra, 2: 680–82.

3. A. GRAMOLA IN *CORRIERE DELLA SERA*

Even though I had prepared for the great event of the first performance by serious thinking about Verdi's *Otello,* the reality was more than anything I expected. And my mind, tossed for four rapid but extraordinary hours between whirlwinds of emotions and contrasts of sweetness, is badly suited, I feel, to write now my strong impressions of the music of Verdi with the serenity that the importance of this artistic festival requires; it is not a rhetorical phrase to say that all of us lucky spectators will preserve an indelible memory of it.

But one must respond to the requirements of journalism, which is the photography of our rushed existence.

And so, without further preamble, here are my impartial, unprejudiced impressions, and an exact report of the impressions of the audience.

In no other opera has Verdi given such attention to detail as in *Otello;* the recitatives are of a unique beauty, and I am sure that after several hearings they will not be among the least of the attractions for the audience. Most notable in this opera is the way in which Verdi underlines, so to speak, the most important words by dramatic expression.

All the instrumental music of the opera, even at the first hearing, seemed to have a rare beauty and balanced taste.

The storm is strangely powerful.

The chorus "Vittoria! Sterminio" had a decisive effect on the audience. The next chorus, "Fuoco di gioia—l'ilare vampa . . ." was cheered and repeated; they wanted Verdi at the proscenium: he was repeatedly called, but he did not appear.

The *brindisi* is easy and gay, and it too was requested again.

The challenge in the same scene has characteristic music, and so without exception does that of the following scenes.

There are delightful choral moments equal to those of the orchestra: the chorus *Fuoco di gioia;* then there is that truly paradisiacal final duet, beginning with the violoncellos divided in four parts, which would be enough by itself to make the fortunes of an opera.

At the end of the first act Verdi acceded to the insistent warm applause of the audience and presented himself gratefully at the proscenium three times.

The second act was very well received. The accompaniment of the chorus to Desdemona is very graceful; that of Jago's *Credo,* a formidable outburst, is interesting. Jago's *Credo* will certainly be one of the pieces listened to very attentively every night.

The quartet can be, indeed should be, listened to a second time; last night it certainly had little effect.

An exquisite orchestral effect is in the great duet of Jago and Otello, when the latter recounts Cassio's dream.

Here we have certainly the Verdi of the new finale of *Boccanegra,* as in the final oath we have the Verdi of *Don Carlo.*

When the curtain fell, the maestro was called to the curtain several times by warm and vigorous applause.

And now we come to the act which the audience, at least for several nights, will call —for reasons that it will think good ones—the most difficult. On the other hand, those who enter into the thought of the maestro even where last night they thought they found superfluity will instead find harmonic beauty. It may be a difficult act, but it is full of beauty.

The attack of the violins and cellos in Otello's solo, prepared by an admirable descending scale in all the strings, is most beautiful. And then the orchestra during the whole trio between Otello, Cassio, and Jago, is a marvel of grace.

When Cassio tells that he found a *vago lino* [a pretty linen] in his own room, there is an accompaniment of pizzicato violins and flute tremolos that is of incomparable gentleness. The novelty of the form and the magnificent instrumentation of this ensemble are truly surprising. The interlace of the voices with the orchestra is new; the chorus murmurs quietly, surprised by Otello's outrage to Desdemona, while she from time to time bursts out with cries of anguish.

Verdi was called daring when in the *Messa di requiem* he wrote a piece in six real parts; here we have no less than ten.

This piece, completely new in conception and execution, will be the marvel of musicians, and the object of study: Verdi has been able to make the various voices on stage sing and express the various passions that move them. He has been able to make the whole orchestra moan with such a careful equilibrium that the ironic part declaimed by Jago becomes quite clear. In this grand piece, in sum, there are so many details that many of them must doubtless have escaped even those ears most familiar with musical complexities.

Giuseppe Giacosa has revealed Verdi's thinking, à propos of this piece, in his splendid article in the *Gazzetta Piemontese*. Verdi, Giacosa says, has noticed that in a conversation there are persons who speak ten words a minute and others who speak a hundred, while time passes for everyone with equal speed; thus he has sought, keeping the same speed, to give us an ensemble in which each person speaks as passion dictates.

And this time, instead of giving us four or five different parts, he has given us ten.

The fourth act received, as everyone expected, a ready, sincere, and unconditional success.

Insistent and highly annoying coughs from the spectators in the orchestra and the boxes almost suffocated the brief prelude. But fortunately the same disturbance was not repeated for the other beautiful pages of music in which Verdi has revealed an insuperable dramatic power.

A strange, anguished lament on the minor sixth, at the words "Salce! Salce! Salce!" The whole accompaniment of the muted strings at Desdemona's prayer is a real inspiration. The audience called insistently for a repetition of the "Ave Maria," and Signora Pantaleoni graciously acceded to their wishes.

Likewise the audience demanded the repetition of the contrabass solo; a new thing, with strange and characteristic effect.

Rapid and terrible was the following duet between Desdemona and Otello.

The following death of the Moor is among Verdi's most beautiful deaths.

The curtain falls while the orchestra repeats the lovely motive that I will call that of the Three Kisses, the only characteristic motive that Verdi repeats in his grandiose work.

He uses it in three very different places, with almost identical notes; he has invented them so well that they take on three colors, three meanings, depending on the dramatic situation, namely: in the final duet of act 1, the first time; and then twice more in the fourth act.

Only a few words today on the performance: the principal artists, Signora Pantaleoni, and Tamagno and Maurel, have given all the care, all the study possible in order to interpret their roles suitably; they were excellent dramatic artists and sang as nowadays few know how and are able. Maurel especially in many places was so effective that he called forth shouts of admiration; Tamagno gave out some of those notes that produce shivers of emotion; and Pantaleoni, fine in the whole opera, was delicious in the last act for the suavity of her singing and acting. Excellent too was Paroli who has a fine voice and in the part of Cassio showed himself to be an intelligent artist.

The orchestra was above all praise; the choral forces, for a first performance of such importance, did well, and will do better in the succeeding evenings.—A. Gramola.

> Reprinted in *Otello. Dramma lirico in quattro atti. Versi di Arrigo Boito. Musica di Giuseppe Verdi. Giudizî della stampa italiana e straniera*, Supplemento straordinario della Gazzetta Musicale di Milano, N. S. (Milan: Ricordi, 1887), 10–13.

4. CAMILLE BELLAIGUE IN *REVUE DES DEUX MONDES,* MARCH 1, 1877

After a long analysis, Bellaigue has only a little to say about the performance itself.

May the interpreters of *Otello* forgive us if we accord them too little place here, and if the creator's genius excels the talent that interprets. Madame Pantaleoni is perhaps not the ideal Desdemona. Mr Tamagno possesses an admirable tenor voice. He sang certain parts of his role, notably the last act, almost as a great artist, especially at the second performance. As for Mr Maurel, he is a perfect Jago. Composed with that keen intelligence and that irreproachable taste, such a role should suffice for the honour of a singer and an actor. An orchestral conductor such as Franco Faccio is enough for the honour of a theatre. With a single gesture, he urges on or holds back an orchestra at his will, charming or terrifying; and the chorus was above all praise.

But one must again return to the master; to the grand old man we must pay our supreme homage following his supreme work. One last time, he has wanted to give a little joy to the world. Someone eloquently said to us the other day that Italy loved Verdi, as Otello loved Desdemona, for the pity that he had for her sorrows. Is it not thus that mankind loves the great artists, the consolers of its wretchedness? May we all be grateful to Verdi for his extended kindness. Never has a more constant glory shed its rays for a longer time upon a human brow. He has known neither shadow nor decline, and his star will go out as upon those blessed horizons that do not know the sadness of twilight and retain until the final hour all the splendour of their sun.—Camille Bellaigue

> Busch, *Verdi's* Otello *and* Simon Boccanegra, 2: 701.

5. FRANCIS HUEFFER IN *THE TIMES* (LONDON), FEBRUARY 7, 1887

At 1 o'clock yesterday afternoon the entrances to the gallery of La Scala, the only unreserved part of the theatre, were crowded by an eager multitude. This morning at 1 o'clock a crowd was shouting and yelling outside the Hotel Milan, compelling Verdi to appear at the window more than once. In other countries such enthusiasm would have been scarcely possible without the excitement of politics and alcohol; here perfect sobriety reigned, and admiration of musical genius was the sole incentive. Neither were the upper classes behind in their demonstrativeness for the glory of Verdi. The stalls and the five tiers of boxes (only the Royal box was empty) vied in shouting and waving of handkerchiefs with the noisiest of the gods. The scene, in brief, was one which could be witnessed only in Italy, and, of all Italian cities, in Milan, the musical and moral capital of the Peninsula, as she is proud to call herself. . . .

The performance commenced at a quarter past 8, and was not over till after midnight, although the actual playing did not occupy much more than two hours. The difference was made up by the usual intervals between the acts, much shorter, by the way, here than in England, and by encores. The encore nuisance is even more rampant in Italy than among us, and sometimes leads to curious results. When, for example, Othello was compelled to leave his wife's chamber so that the famous recitative in unison for the double-basses proceeding his entry might be repeated a second time, the border line between the sublime and the ridiculous was distinctly passed, the more so as that recitative was played indifferently the first and very badly the second time. In another case it amounted almost to cruelty to compel a lady who had sung out of tune once to sing out of tune again. But such failures of judgment are more than made up for as regards a Milanese audience by the singular intelligence and receptivity with which that audience places itself *en rapport* with the composer and the singers, taking up every point, and as it were rising and falling with the modulations of the music. Only a nation highly gifted by nature, and trained by centuries of artistic activity, could supply such an instrument for a man of genius to play upon.

That Verdi is such a man of genius his last work bears ample proof. There is no falling off in melodic power, and there is a marked advance in the purity of aim, and of the means by which that aim is attained. In the matter of orchestration the progress made by the master, even since *Aida,* is specially remarkable. Nothing could be more delicate than the little *pizzicato* passage which accompanies the festive chorus in the first act, and nothing more beautiful in its tonal effect than the treatment of the love-motive, heard first in the duet, and repeated at the end of the opera. In the further course of my remarks it will be my duty to offer some more detailed criticism of Verdi's music, but let me state here first of all that *Otello,* with such faults as it may show, is a great work of art, well worthy of the master who wrote it, and of the land of song which gave him birth.

I wish I could say the same of last night's performance, which unfortunately tended to prove that Italy, although she still possesses a great composer, has no longer singers to do justice to his music. There are virtually three parts in *Otello,* and one of these, that of Iago, was filled by a Frenchman, M. Maurel. That this should have been necessary on so eminently national an occasion as the present is in itself a curious fact. However, M. Maurel is an artist of the first order, and did full justice to the choice. As an actor he realized the character of the plausible villain with a distinctness seldom witnessed, even in the spoken drama. He was honest Iago all over, soft spoken, and looking most innocent when he aimed the most poisonous shafts at the defenceless breast of the Moor. The excellence of M. Maurel's vocalization will be remembered by all who heard him at Covent

Garden. In this work he has much to sing, and sings it admirably. Perhaps the finest point was made in a kind of monologue in the pessimistic vein of Schopenhauer, which Signor Boito has somewhat incongruously placed in the mouth of Iago, and which Verdi has set to highly impressive music.

Of Signor Tamagno's Othello it is possible to speak in almost equally favourable terms. He is a *tenore robusto* of the genuine kind, and his voice, although without much charm in the middle register, goes up to a B flat with perfect ease. His upper notes, indeed, are magnificent, and it is specially worthy of notice that his is a genuine Italian tenor, and not a mere baritone, with some high notes superadded. Among much that was fine in his performance I must single out the lovely melody in A flat minor, which expresses with marvellous force the dejection of Othello after an outburst of passion.

With every wish to treat Madame Pantaleoni's Desdemona with leniency and for-bearance, it is impossible not to express surprise that the Italian stage could not have sup-plied a better dramatic soprano for such an occasion. The lady's uncertain intonation may have been partly the effect of nervousness. It was indeed, noticeable that many things, in-cluding the sestet in the third act, went much better at the general rehearsal than in the performance. Certain it is, however, that Signora Pantaleoni is not above mediocrity; and even respectable mediocrity, placed face to face with a work of genius like *Otello,* must of necessity come to grief.

The *mise-en-scène,* although upon the whole intelligent, was not according to English ideas particularly magnificent. The storm in the first scene was a very tame affair, and the pretty mandolinata in the second act lost much of its effect through the players being too far back on the stage. The most satisfactory features throughout were the perfor-mances of the chorus and the orchestra, the latter most excellent in the strings, although the brass is occasionally too strong, and the woodwind not strong enough. Signor Faccio, who conducted the performance, covered himself with glory, and justly shared in the ovations which called composer, poet, and principal performers before the curtain again and again.

Busch, *Verdi's* Otello *and* Simon Boccanegra, 2: 702–4.

6. *LA LOMBARDIA*

The anonymous reviewer gives an account of the performance, showing almost more interest in the audience than in the opera.

Verdi in *Otello* gives a marvelous example of orchestration. The orchestral part is an extra-ordinary thing. But at the same time in a few places he has found his primary inspiration. If the hurricane of the first act, the quartet of the second and the finale of the third, remind us of the powerful author of *Aida,* the monologue of Jago, the aria of *Otello* and the Ave Maria of Desdemona give us back the inspired and melodic composer of *Rigoletto.*

. . . The invocation has a powerful effect. But silence is imposed. At Otello's entrance, his first phrase brings forth applause. The reprise of the chorus is brief and effective. . . .

The fire-chorus is graceful. Accompanied by arpeggios and pizzicati. The orchestra everywhere elegant. The first cries break out. A repetition is demanded. It continues insistently. Verdi is called for, but he does not come out. Silence returns. Not allowed the author, they must be satisfied with his music, and the *Fuoco di gioia* is repeated.

It is sung even better, and the success is more accentuated.

New applause, but repressed, so as not to interrupt the music.

Great attention to the Brindisi. The toast is given with great effect by Maurel. The effective phrasing, with its semitone scales of the baritone and the passionate singing of Cassio, provokes new applause. The public cannot stop. Cries and applause interrupt. But silence is restored.

There is a phrase that the chorus strangely laughs at the drunken Cassio. It is produced, performed in an unusual manner. The audience is in tumult and demands the reprise of this piece too. But the wise counsel prevails of those who wish to continue.

The love-duet has a little prelude for strings with the principal phrase in the violoncello which is then linked to the tenor's entrance. Lovely the cantabile of Desdemona, lovelier still the second time. We hear the author of Aida in the verses:

Etu m'amavi per le mie sventure
Ed io t'amavo per la tua pietà.

Verdi emphasizes this phrase very delicately.

The curtain falls slowly while the orchestra performs a brief peroration.

There is a delirium of applause. The audience is on its feet demanding Verdi, who finally appears at the proscenium. There is a cry that echoes throughout the theatre. . . .

The prelude that begins the second act is brief, given to the strings. The instrumentation of this piece has the dark powerful vigor of a painting by Rembrandt. The vocal part is all declamation. At the end, a grand ovation for Maurel. New shouts. A bis is demanded, Verdi is wanted.

In the tenor-baritone duet the first phrase is given to the cellos and basses, which with broken phrases develop a lacework of the tenor's motive:

Dunque senza velame.

All this act is declaimed, studied, difficult.

Superb the final phrase with the insistent words on a single note and with the internal chorus.

The audience is unable to restrain its applause, no matter how much silence is called for.

The chorus, accompanied by mandolins, is sung first by women, then children, then basses, with sustained harmonies from the contraltos. It passes with a more developed thought to a full ensemble with the dominant phrase of Desdemona and a mandolin tremolo.

Otello's phrase is a great success: *Addio sublimi incanti* . . . A high A from Tamagno gets an ovation.

The baritone's narration is heard with attention. The descriptive form is singular. The instrumentation fine, especially at the end. Maurel delivers it with rare art. He gets an ovation.

The second part, with the oath and with a unison passage *a due* is grandiose in the orchestration, and has its effect on the audience.

Ovations. A call for the interpreters. When Verdi appears among the artists, everyone stands to acclaim him. The ladies applaud from their boxes.

Verdi is called to the proscenium by continued ovations three more times with the artists. Boito is called for.

The third act, too, has a short prelude, with a marked movement in the brasses.

In the duet between Jago and Desdemona with which the important part of this act begins, there is richness in the orchestration. The vocal part is declaimed.

One of the best moments is the phrase of Desdemona: *Esterrefatto fisso* . . .

The last part is effective, but the orchestral motion is extraordinary, given to a pianissimo in the violins which sustains the first part of Otello's jealousy aria.

Then Verdi moved on to a saddened mood in which there is all the Moor's regret for past good. . . . Then the phrase becomes excited, burning with jealousy. . . . No vulgarity. . . . The first part, by its character, remains the best. But the whole piece is a masterwork.

Then comes an original little terzet. Cassio laughs, Jago deceives, Otello, hidden, listens with fierce jealousy.

Verdi has given a light stamp to this piece. The instrumentation is of the purest elegance.

. . . The preparation for the finale is beautiful. The soprano's phrase, with long notes in the woodwinds, broadens and becomes more accentuated, embroidered by the strings. It is very developed. The tutti begins with a pianissimo with covered voices, but brief.

The suppressed panic is truthfully described. But then follows an explosion of grandly effective sonority.

The act finishes with voices and fanfares from within, with Otello struck down by rage, and an ironic phrase from Jago.

The audience applauds. The performers come to the front. Verdi is called for, and he is again greeted with shouts of admiration.

The prelude to the fourth act begins and continues with interlaces of the winds. It is brief, in a minor key, severe.

Great attention to the Willow Song.

The melodic conceit is repeated two times. The instrumentation, full of sadness, has nevertheless a distinct richness. All the details of such a piece have a beauty which perhaps escapes us at the first hearing.

Then the Ave Maria. The first part is recited on a single note. The second part is an extended and mystical melody accompanied in the orchestra by tender modulations in the strings.

A long ovation. The audience cries again for Verdi, but Pantaleoni makes clear that the maestro will not come out during the act. The repetition of the Prayer is called for, and after new applause for Pantaleoni, it is repeated.

When Otello enters, the contrabasses play the prelude that the newspapers were already talking of before yesterday.

The effect is immense. . . .

It is repeated. This prelude is very brief. At the end there is a movement of six-teenth-notes with a crescendo effect that is imposed on the audience. Then in the orchestra there escapes a movement with high sounds in the strings which effects a surprising antithesis.

The duet that follows is of magisterial dramatic expression. Concise, with a strong idea, but which erupts and disappears.

The whole scene that follows has its most outstanding features in the orchestra, to which the dramatic effect is confided.

Otello's final phrase pleased, and Tamagno got an ovation.

The curtain falls slowly, while the orchestra has long held notes.

Now ovations of the audience, and Pantaleoni and Tamagno are called to the proscenium.

Verdi, among the artists, had to appear twice together with Boito and Maurel.

Then twice more Verdi with the artists, and Faccio also is called for.

At this point the enthusiasm becomes frenzy. Men on their feet wave their hats. The ladies, also standing, wave their handkerchiefs from their boxes. The same in the orchestra, in the balcony, screaming, gesturing, and calling for Verdi, who appears with Boito to renewed applause.

They wanted him alone, and when he appeared the admiration was unrestrained. It was a sort of public madness [Esaltamento].

Verdi and Boito found themselves between two fires, since on this side of the proscenium there was the applause of the audience, and inside the applause of the artists and everyone else.

In the midst of this fever Verdi had to cross the stage with all the artists.

Thus the curtain calls were 3 in the first act, 5 in the second, 3 in the third, and 8 in the fourth.

A total of 19 curtain calls, but which in a sense were wanted by the maestro, since the audience at each piece called for Verdi.

So much for the record.

No need to add that we will discuss, suitably and in detail, the drama, the music, and the performance of *Otello*.

Otello . . . Giudizî della stampa, pp. 6–10.

7. FROM BLANCHE ROOSEVELT'S REMINISCENCES

On 5 February 1887, the Piazza della Scala was a sight to see, and the cries of "Viva Verdi! Viva Verdi!" were so deafening that I longed for cotton in my ears. Poor Verdi! had he been there, he would certainly have been torn to pieces, as a crowd in its enthusiasm rarely distinguishes between glory and assassination. You will ask what I was doing in the streets at such a time; and I will answer: I don't know; I merely obeyed the common impulse—went where the others did: the truth is, I also wanted to watch the Scala bill-board, to see that no change would be made in the announcements. We all stood staring at the old theatre, just as those idiots on the Paris boulevards on a summer night watch the magic-lantern, to read the different advertisements for enterprising firms: and this, you say, in the dead of winter? O, an Italian does not feel the cold on an occasion like this. But to return. In case there had been any change of programme I need not say there would not have been found a person in all Milan courageous enough to have put up the notice. There was death in the eyes of some of those men, waiting like hungry wolves since the night before to be first to crowd into the pit and galleries. Well, at last—after dinner—I didn't dine, I swallowed food—we started to the theatre. The carriage had to be sent off long before we reached the door, the horses could not make their way through the crowd. At best, human beings one by one between a line of police could struggle towards the entrance. I expected my dress would be in rags; however, I managed to get in whole, and once there the sight was indescribable. La Scala has never before held such an audience, and although it was fully an hour before the time to commence, every seat was occupied. . . .

From pit to dome, the immense auditorium was one mass of eager faces, sparkling eyes, brilliant toilettes, and splendid jewels. The Italian Court was a rainbow of colours, and Queen Margherita's ladies of honour like a hothouse bouquet of rarest exotics. The first and second tiers of boxes were so packed with Milanese high-bred women, so covered with dazzling jewels and filmy laces, that the house seemed spanned with a river of light, up, up, up to where the last gallery was lost in a dainty cornice of gold. The gleam of diamond tiara and corsage bouquet shot oblong rays on the black-coated background; while the new electric lights, imprisoned in their dead-white globes, shed so unearthly a radiance over the auditorium that we all looked like spectres uprising from some fantastic dead-and-gone rout. . . .

It is generally supposed that on a first-night Verdi conducts his opera, but the idea is an erroneous one. With very few exceptions, for forty years or more he has not taken his place in the orchestra-leader's chair. On this occasion he would have been too nervous to have attempted such a thing. The present incumbent of the leader's place at La Scala is Franco Faccio, an admirable musician and composer, one who knows his band as a flautist knows his stops, and who for years has directed Verdi's operas under the maestro's own eye and dictation. Faccio's appearance in the conductor's chair, which he has filled so long and so well, was a signal for thunders of applause. The orchestra at once struck up a few glorious chords representing a tempest, which were followed by an instantaneous rise of the curtain.

The scenery, costumes, choruses, and orchestra were nearly perfect; the cast was certainly weak. Victor Maurel is the only real artist in the opera, and he is a Frenchman. In voice, acting, appearance, and dress, he is the ideal of what an operatic artist should be, and the ideal of what any operatic Iago could be. He sang as even his best friends never dreamed he could sing, and his acting was the consummate work which we always have at his artistic hands. He entered at once into the fullest sympathies of the audience, and I could not help then and there contrasting the Iagos we have seen in other countries with the Iagos we always see in Italy. Iago even seems a *persona grata* to the public; the qualities which raise a thrill of horror in the righteous Anglo-Saxon are received by this susceptible nation with placid contentment and relief. His vileness, ruses, and perfidy are accepted for their art, not their nature; his ingenious devices arouse heartfelt plaudits, and let me add that you will never hear a gallery god in Italy express any disapprobation with a successful knave. Had Iago not succeeded there is every reason to believe that *Othello* would be left out of the Italian Shakespearean repertory. On noting his more than prominence in this opera, rendered doubly so by Maurel's sublime creation, I could well understand Boito's and Verdi's inclination to call their work *Iago,* and not *Othello.* Iago is essentially Italian, not in the sense of vice, but of artistic villainy: he reasons from the personal standpoint, and his reasons find a universal echo in the land which gave birth to such a student of human nature as Machiavelli. Othello, you will see, is an inferior creature, and plays an inferior part.

Verdi: Milan and "Othello," repr. in Busch, *Verdi's* Otello *and* Simon Boccanegra, 2: 718–19, 723–24.

8. FROM THE PRODUCTION BOOK OF *OTELLO*

The Disposizione scenica, *published by Ricordi, was written by Giulio Ricordi, with suggestions and alterations from Verdi and Boito. It gives a detailed description of the settings and action of the opera, with the purpose of defining how the work should be performed in other theaters. The text that follows, translated in Busch,* Verdi's Otello *and* Simon Boccanegra, *2: 488–92, describes the setting for the first act, and refers to the diagram on p. 341.*

The directions are intended to be given to the right and left of the stage facing the auditorium. The references to bars and page numbers are taken from the Italian edition of the vocal score.

The producer should, in due time, inform the scenic artists, the stage technicians, the costumer, the prop man, the head of lighting, the director of the extras, etc., of the instructions relating to them which are contained in the present book.

It is *absolutely* necessary that the artists understand the production book completely and conform to it. Likewise, managements should not allow changes of any kind in the costumes: these have been carefully researched and copied from contemporary pictures, and there is no reason why they should be changed according to the whims of this or that artist.

The producer must, above all, explain very clearly to the Chorus that they must not appear as an insignificant mass of people, but that each one of them assuredly represents a character and must act as such, moving on his own account, according to his own feelings, preserving with the others only a certain unity of movement in order to ensure the best musical performance. Immobility, at least that not expressly desired in the production book, must be *absolutely* forbidden.

ACT I
Outside the Castle

1. MOVEABLE BACKDROP, mounted on two revolving drums. It should be about three times the length necessary to close in the back of the stage. At first, when the curtain rises, it represents the night sky, with large, blackish, turbulent clouds. The lightest part of the clouds should be made transparent, and in this same backdrop there should also be two bolts of lightning (made transparent) that extend across the entire sky from top left to bottom right. As will presently be indicated, the backdrop should move from left to right in such a way that the clouds should be seen to disappear slowly until the sky of a splendid night, completely serene and clear, remains in place. In due time, three or four stars, no more, should shine in the sky: one, almost in the centre and halfway up, should be more evident and very bright.

2. CLOTH, represents the stormy sea. The cloth should be moved by various transverse, spiral winches, which should keep the motion going until the end of the act. When the curtain rises, however, the cloth should be vigorously agitated by several stage-hands appropriately placed underneath, lifting wooden hoops upwards (but not too quickly), which should form the high breakers of the waves. Depending on the size of the stage, the cloth should be made so that the sea has the greatest possible depth.

3. GREY SCRIM, closes in the entire stage. Later, it should be moved slowly from left to right.

4. SIDE FLAT, represents one side of the Castle, with an actual door.

5. SIDE FLAT, continues the side of the Castle, with an actual door leading to an inn. In front of this, a trellis, supported at one side by the wall of the Castle and at the other by three thin plaster columns. Underneath the trellis, three wires should be strung, on which various coloured Venetian lanterns should be hung in due time.

6. PLATFORMS, about 60 centimetres high, represent the ramparts of the Castle facing the sea.

7. TREES, ROCKS, WALL, flats and drops which close off the sight lines at the left and mask the Main Galley at the right.

8. DISTANT GALLEYS, should be about 1 metre long and should move across the stage at the back from right to left with a simple motion.

9. MAIN GALLEY, depending on the width of the stage, should be 4 or 5 metres long and should move likewise across the stage from right to left with a double motion: side to side and back to front.

10. TRAPDOOR, used to make the *fuoco di gioia,* as will be discussed later.

11. ELECTRICAL APPARATUS for the flashes of lightning.

12. ELECTRICAL APPARATUS for the thunderbolts.

X. LARGE DRUM, expressly build for the thunder: 2 metres long, a diameter of 1.25 metres.

ILLUMINATION AND ELECTRICAL LIGHTING

Before the orchestra begins, the illumination in the auditorium should be lowered greatly.

On the stage, dark night should be created, making more conspicuous all the effects of the storm. When Jago descends from the platform, only the footlights should be turned up a little. When the *fuoco di gioia* and the lanterns at the inn are lit, the lighting on the entire stage should be generally increased, setting the transverse lights at the back in such a way that, when the clear sky appears, it is appropriately lit.

In large theatres, there should be four electrical apparatuses (11) set in the upper wings; in smaller theatres, two should do. When the curtain rises, they should produce repeated and prolonged flashes of lightning, which should slowly be decreased. When the cloudy sky of the moveable backdrop (1) is almost completely to the right, the flashes at the left should stop, and only those at the right should continue for a while until they stop completely about a minute after the totally clear sky appears.

Behind the moveable backdrop, the electrical apparatus (11) should be regulated for flashes of lightning, as indicated above for the ones in the wings, carrying the effect from one side of the backdrop to the other, where the transparent clouds are found. Apparatus 12, on the other hand, should be one complete lamp with its reflector turned towards the back of the stage. During the storm, it should be turned on no more than three times. At the same moment, a lighting technician with a mirror measuring approximately 40 square centimetres should aim the bright rays reflected in the mirror from top to bottom along the transparent lines of the backdrop which represent the bolts of lightning.

PROPS, ACCESSORIES, ETC., ETC.

Before the curtain rises, the stage manager should set everything and everyone in place as indicated here:

ON THE SET: Jago, Cassio, Roderigo, Montàno: a part of the Men's Chorus.

ON THE RIGHT: Inside the doors to the inn and to the Castle, the rest of the Men's Chorus; inside the door to the Castle, behind the Men's Chorus, a large portion of the Women's Chorus (the rest at the left in the lower wings near the proscenium). Inside the door to the inn, behind the Men's Chorus, the extras and the stage-hands charged with carrying out 3 inn tables, 2 stools, cups, amphoras, etc., etc. Backstage, about 10 or 12 Venetian lanterns should be ready to be lit at an opportune moment and then hung on the trellis of the inn. The same for 4 large lanterns to be carried and held on stage. In the first wing by the proscenium, a large metal plate should be hung and vigorously shaken as indicated in the musical score.

ON THE LEFT: Otello should be near the ramp (6). Behind him, his entire retinue, as will be indicated later. In the wings, 2 trumpets. By the steps near the proscenium,

4 extras with bundles of sticks to light the *fuoco di gioia*.

The Large Drum for the thunder should be placed on the right or on the left, over the stage or on it, depending on the acoustical requirements of the theatre, as should result from various tests. It should be sounded by two players.

The Organ should have the pedal stops ready, as indicated in the score, as well as the timpani stops. On the first notes of the orchestra, the organist should open these stops and maintain the sound without interruption until the end of the storm. In theatres which still do not have an organ, one should use an apparatus constructed of 3 or 4 bass register pipes, used as timpani, which should sound by means of two bellows worked by hand. The stage manager is advised that, in the absence of an organ, this is *absolutely indispensable*.

Three large bells to sound the alarm; the pitches are not important. The electricians in charge of the flashes of lightning must be ready at their respective places; likewise the stage-hands, to put into motion:

a. the two Galleys at the back (8)
b. the Main Galley (9)
c. the grey scrim (3)
d. the sea-cloth (2)
e. the sky-backdrop (1)

The stage manager should be careful, then, that, before giving the starting signal to the orchestra, everything indicated here has been carried out to the letter: the sea-cloth must be agitated before the orchestra begins. All of the scenic action, the machinery, the lighting starts immediately at the first bar of the opera, proceeds quickly, and must be carried out with mathematical precision according to the unfolding of the music, which indicates all of the various phases of the storm.

Conclusion

In surveying these five premieres we have behaved more as investigators than as art lovers. We have tried to find out who was there and how the performance went—what it looked and sounded like. The beauty of the music has been at the center all along, even though it may not have been on the surface. That music, of course, is why we go to the opera, why we write and read about opera.

These are five operas out of many. They are always worth hearing and seeing, and we still listen to them. But there is only one moment when the opera is truly new, and it is those five moments that we have been considering. The operas were made for people in many ways like ourselves, but unlike ourselves, too. They lived in different times, with different expectations; they had heard many operas, but mostly operas of their own times, and in contemporary style. They knew that the composer had written for them and that the singers were singing to them. There were as yet no great traditions for how Iago should sing his Credo, or for how Don Giovanni's serenade should go. It was all new, all contemporary, all cutting-edge art. Whether the opera would be a success or a failure, whether the performance would fall apart, whether indeed the theater would burn down, was not yet known.

If we consider these five operas together we can see characteristics that make us take note of our own relationship to opera and to these particular operas, and of how different in some ways our view is from that of those other audiences.

Each of the operas we have considered was a piece of contemporary music. It was the high point of its season, and audiences in all five cases preferred new music to old. They were generally familiar with the musical style of their own time, with the performers and their voices, and with the dramatic conventions of the day. What they wanted was to see how a new work could fit into an accepted style and still make some artistic contribution. The composers varied in their wish to innovate. Handel, I think, was making an opera as well as he knew how—and he did know how—in a style that the audiences knew perfectly; he was giving them what they wanted. Wagner was giving audiences what he thought they ought to want—and many of them did. Verdi was in a way innovating by summarizing, putting everything he had learned into a compressed lyrical expression.

Not every operagoer nowadays pines for new works. We have a big repertory of classics, and we sometimes prefer pieces we know and love to pieces that we may not like.

Opera seats are expensive, after all, and one hates to waste time and money. Today's musical style is not so predictable that we can be confident of what we will get. We are, perhaps, poorer for our occasional lack of imagination.

For the audiences in this book the opera was unfamiliar, but the singers were well known. Certainly for the established companies in London, Paris, and Prague, the audience had heard all the singers many times. London audiences knew that any opera at the Royal Academy would star Senesino and Cuzzoni; Paris knew Falcon, Nourrit, and Levasseur very well; perhaps at Bayreuth there was a special excitement in hearing well-known singers from several opera companies. For us the situation is usually the reverse: we know the opera very well, and we want to know how this particular cast will "interpret" it.

One thing that becomes clear from these performances is that a great deal of collaboration and flexibility are required in producing a new opera. There are cuts, rewrites, and adjustments up until the last minute. The work of art was far less immutable than it is today. Wagner and Verdi stand out here in the way that they composed their operas and stuck to them, requiring the performers to execute their wishes. This may have had something to do with the Romantic notion of the composer as artist and prophet, but composers who were not Wagner or Verdi mostly found themselves in the usual operatic mayhem before premieres. And even Wagner's orchestra had to slow down for the scene changes.

One doesn't know in advance how long it will take to rehearse an opera, and the difficulties in scheduling singers, sets, stage time, and in working around an ongoing season made the opening dates of many of these operas uncertain. Even Wagner needed to put off one of the first *Ring* performances by a day owing to a singer's indisposition. Such uncertainties would not be possible in today's overscheduled opera houses.

An opera is a play, and the characters act. We are to understand that the world they are in is one we would like to visit. And so the acting must be plausible, or at least inviting. Acting is often described as "natural," but what is natural to one audience may seem stilted and inappropriate to the next generation. Nobody acts natural on a large stage while singing a high note, but what a singer should do seems to reflect the attitudes of the age. Handel's singers were noble rhetoricians, expressing not what the body does but what the heart feels. Their gestures might seem to us overblown, but if we were accustomed to behaving a bit that way ourselves, in a formal and stylized fashion, and if we were adapted to such postures by the clothes we wore and the dances we learned, we might feel very much at home. Who knows how a Norse god behaves? For Wagner, he behaves like a restrained stage actor, using "natural" gestures—natural in nineteenth-century Germany—to express emotion. But he is careful not to let the audience members know that he is singing to them.

Operas are about singing. And there seem to be two things that get discussed above all else in singing: agility and loudness. Handel's singers, and Mozart's and Meyerbeer's, had to execute enormously difficult roulades and flourishes in addition to lyrical melodies. Such ornamentation is not characteristic of Wagner or late Verdi, but it was indispensable until the early nineteenth century. And it is difficult to sing loud and fast at the same time. Handel was always careful to see to it that the orchestra was reduced when the singer did acrobatics, and the same was true of Mozart and Meyerbeer. It is difficult to imagine, though, that a singer did not have to produce an impressive volume of sound even in fast passages in the Paris Opéra. Senesino and his fellow castrati were noted for their trumpetlike voices. Is this a description of volume or of clarity and purity? Nourrit was famous not for his volume but for the beauty of his soft falsetto high notes; his successor, Duprez, seems to have been the artistic ancestor of Tamagno, and of many other tenors, in being famous mostly for his ringing full-voice high notes. That full voice is what is needed for Wagner—along with clear diction—and it is essentially the chief characteristic of today's successful opera singers. Other things being equal, the louder you can sing the more money you can make.

People cared more, and less, about opera in those days than in ours. More because it was the essential entertainment at the pinnacle of the arts and of society, and because the audiences were highly experienced in the style of their own time: they could watch it and listen to it very closely indeed, and make highly discriminating judgments. Less because opera for many people was a regular entertainment, and in a normal season they might hear the same opera many times, listening only to the parts they especially liked and the rest of the time doing the other activities that opera houses offered.

There was certainly more liveliness and more animation, and less ritual, surrounding the opera in these performances than there is nowadays. Even though Wagner wanted his festival to be something of a liturgy, his audience, even his worshippers, behaved like an opera audience: they cheered the singers during the show, and they wanted the singers and the composer to appear at the end. Wagner was furious. Today we dress up in clothes of another era, we sit reverently in silence, we applaud at the end—though we still allow ourselves to stop the show with cheers for a fine aria. We do not, though, often demand and get a repetition of a whole segment of an act.

Much attention was paid in many of these operas to the look of the show: carefully made costumes, sets that reflect the taste of the day even when they intend to reproduce authentic historical settings. Even though we now feel a reverence for the score, we feel free to alter the acting, the gesture, the costumes, the settings. Whether this sort of reinterpretation would have made sense to the composers or the audiences of these operas might be doubted, but we for the moment have decided what is to be retained from the past and what can safely be discarded. Perhaps our view of this matter will change with time. It would be surprising if it did not.

A first-hand view of the realities of a first performance makes us perhaps a bit less reverent even toward the music. If Mozart or Handel were here they would alter the music to fit the singers of this production. We feel less confident about this—at least those of us who are not Mozart—and so we need to fit the singers to the opera.

What is to become of opera? Surely these great works, and others, will continue to hold the stage; surely what seemed to our ancestors the finest achievement in the arts can continue to seem so to us. But will we continue to chew over a shrinking repertory? Will we continue to explore lesser-known operas of the past? Will we ever again have so much excitement about a new opera that reflects the taste and style of our own times?

Recommended Recordings
ROBERT J. DENNIS

The recordings listed below are a sampling from an extensive discography. They were chosen to present the operas in an illuminating variety of performing styles in recordings that offer textual completeness or that reflect specific stages of an opera's performance history. They also showcase the artistry of major singers and conductors with a special affinity for, or association with, these works. Doubtless I have omitted many favored recordings and artists, but these performances should certainly tempt the reader toward the pleasurable pursuit of personal preference.

Giulio Cesare

Dietrich Fischer-Dieskau, Tatiana Troyanos, Franz Crass, Peter Schreier, Julia Hamari; Karl Richter, Munich Bach Orchestra. Deutsche Grammophon 413 897–1 [LP] (1970)

Janet Baker, Valerie Masterson, James Bowman, Della Jones, Sarah Walker; Sir Charles Mackerras, English National Opera. EMI 69760–2 and Chandos CHAN 3019–2 (1984)

Jennifer Larmore, Barbara Schlick, Derek Lee Ragin, Marianna Rørholm, Bernarda Fink; René Jacobs, Concerto Köln. Harmonia Mundi France 901385.87 (1991)

James Bowman, Lynne Dawson, Dominique Visse, Eirian James, Guillemette Laurens; Jean-Claude Malgoire, La Grand Écurie et la Chambre du Roi. Astrée Auvidis E 8558 (1995)

Marjana Mijanović, Magdalena Kožená, Bejun Mehta, Anne Sophie von Otter, Charlotte Hellekant; Marc Minkowski, Les Musiciens du Louvre (Grenoble). Deutsche Grammophon Archiv Produktion B000314–02 (2002)

Giulio Cesare, the most frequently recorded of all Handel's operas, is represented on disc by a number of attractive performances. René Jacobs leads his period-instrument ensemble Concerto Köln in an uncut recording of the original 1724 version, the opera as heard on its first night. In the title role, mezzo-soprano Jennifer Larmore offers smooth, plush vocalism with a mostly clean, accurate account of *fioritura* passages. Soprano Barbara Schlick's slender-voiced Cleopatra misses some of the character's allure, though she projects the words expressively. Countertenor Derek Lee Ragin is a commanding Tolomeo. Jacobs' conducting tends toward extremes of tempo, with some of Cleopatra's and Cornelia's more reflective music rather sentimentalized. As a bonus, the recording also includes an aria for Nireno composed for the work's London revival in 1725, sung by countertenor Dominique Visse.

Jean-Claude Malgoire conducts a livelier performance with La Grande Écurie et la Chambre du Roi, also a period-instrument ensemble, with voices and orchestra recorded with fine clarity and presence. Malgoire's performance incorporates a number of small cuts, mostly involving recitative, as well as some repositioning of music, decisions that sometimes muddle the plot. James Bowman is a splendid Cesare, rhythmically alert and vocally secure, his bright, lustrous countertenor contrasting nicely with the more compact sound of Dominique Visse, also very fine as Tolomeo. Lynne Dawson is perhaps the most appealing of all recorded Cleopatras, her warm, lyrical soprano capturing the character's seductiveness and vulnerability in equal measure.

Perhaps the most satisfying period-instrument recording in terms of dramatic commitment and homogeneity of vocal style is that by Les Musiciens du Louvre under the inspired and energetic leadership of Marc Minkowski. His first-rate orchestra excels in tonal brilliance, dynamic variety, and rhythmic precision; both instrumentalists and singers embellish da capo repetitions creatively and expressively. The opera is given complete but for the omission of a single aria and several shorter passages. Marijana Mijanović and Magdalena Kožená are an arresting pair of protagonists, the former investing Cleopatra with unusual depth. Anne Sophie von Otter vividly brings to life Sesto's inner conflict, while Bejun Mehta as Tolomeo delivers a forceful portrayal with commanding vocal agility. The excitement of the occasion is conveyed in recorded sound of exceptional brilliance and clarity.

Karl Richter's recording, a compelling performance from an earlier generation, also presents Handel's 1724 score without cuts. His Munich Bach Orchestra plays with a rich, full sound, and the cast of mostly German singers address their roles in more conventional operatic style. Baritone Dietrich Fischer-Dieskau represents the best of a once-standard approach to Baroque opera; in his scene before the tomb of Pompeo he remains more moving than any of his successors. Tenor Peter Schreier and mezzo-soprano Julia Hamari sing wonderfully as Sesto and Cornelia, and mezzo-soprano Tatiana Troyanos, though somewhat taxed by Cleopatra's high-lying music, brings her character vividly to life.

Admirers of Handelians Dame Janet Baker and Sir Charles Mackerras will want to explore their English-language recording with the English National Opera. The work is shortened by about an hour, the text being that of John Copley's stage production. He and Mackerras chose to omit ten musical numbers, including one aria each for Cesare, Cleopatra, and Cornelia, and three for Sesto; recitatives are shortened and the final scene of the second act is also jettisoned. In addition to Baker's Cesare, there are fine performances from Valerie Masterson as Cleopatra, James Bowman as Tolomeo, and Sarah Walker as Cornelia.

Don Giovanni

Ina Souez, Luise Helletsgruber, Audrey Mildmay, Koloman von Pataky, John Brownlee, Salvatore Baccaloni; Fritz Busch, Glyndebourne Festival Opera. Naxos 110135–37 (1936)

Lisa della Casa, Suzanna Danco, Hilde Gueden, Anton Dermota, Cesare Siepi, Fernando Corena; Josef Krips, Vienna Philharmonic. London 411 626–2 (1958)

Claire Watson, Christa Ludwig, Mirella Freni, Nicolai Gedda, Nicolai Ghiaurov, Walter Berry; Otto Klemperer, New Philharmonia Orchestra. EMI CDMC 63841 (1966)

Joan Sutherland, Pilar Lorengar, Marilyn Horne, Werner Krenn, Gabriel Bacquier, Donald Gramm; Richard Bonynge, English Chamber Orchestra. London 448 973-2 (1968)

Amanda Halgrimson, Lynne Dawson, Nancy Argenta, John Mark Ainsley, Andreas Schmidt, Gregory Yurisich; Sir Roger Norrington, The London Classical Players. EMI CDCC 54859-2 (1992)

Luba Orgonasova, Charlotte Margiono, Eirian James, Christoph Prégardien, Rodney Gilfry, Ildebrando d'Arcangelo; John Eliot Gardiner, English Baroque Soloists. Deutsche Grammophon Archiv Produktion 445 870-2 (1994)

Complete recordings of *Don Giovanni* span nearly seven decades and include performances for every taste, beginning with the legendary Glyndebourne Festival recording from 1936 conducted by Fritz Busch, featuring Australian baritone John Brownlee in the title role and the still matchless Leporello of Salvatore Baccaloni. Noted for its mercurial ensemble, Busch's performance, like most others, presents the standard performing text, a conflation of Mozart's Prague and Vienna scores, omitting only the Zerlina-Leporello duet.

The beginning of the stereo era coincided with a memorable generation of Mozart singers whose artistry is preserved in several notable recordings. Josef Krips leads the Vienna Philharmonic in a performance of unusual warmth and grace, with the aristocratic Cesare Siepi, whose memorable portrayal of the title role, noted for its epicurian elegance and seductiveness, dominated the world's stages for nearly three decades. He is partnered by the ebullient Fernando Corena as Leporello, who parodies Siepi shamelessly in the cloak-changing scene. This cherishable document of the memorable postwar Vienna Opera Mozart ensemble offers characterful contributions from Lisa della Casa, Hilde Gueden, and Anton Dermota, with an especially engaging Elvira from Suzanne Danco.

The commanding Don of Nicolai Ghiaurov heads an impressive cast on Otto Klemperer's recording with the New Philharmonia Orchestra, a bolder, more granitic approach, notable for its bracing woodwind presence. The work's cosmic elements are ideally suited to Klemperer's temperament; seldom has the confrontation between Don Giovanni and the Commendatore's statue resounded as powerfully as here. Tempos tend toward the leisurely, but orchestra and singers are recorded with exceptional clarity, allowing the listener to savor much detail in both the vocal ensembles and the orchestral writing. A strong cast, including Nicolai Gedda as a patrician Ottavio, all contribute distinguished portrayals.

At the other end of the tonal spectrum is Richard Bonynge's lively performance with the English Chamber Orchestra. This important recording was the first to employ reduced orchestral forces as well as the first to boast imaginative and expressive embellishment of the vocal parts. Bonynge performs a complete conflation of the Prague and Vienna scores, including all the musical numbers Mozart composed for both versions of his opera. French baritone Gabriel Bacquier offers a Don of unusual subtlety and persuasiveness; he plays off the expert Leporello of Donald Gramm with amusing camaraderie. Gramm is perhaps the most musical of all Leporellos, singing with bel canto finesse while contributing a ripe and memorable characterization free of conventional mannerisms. Werner Krenn is an uncommonly elegant Ottavio. Joan Sutherland's imposing Anna is representative of the singer's best work, and she has few rivals in the long arches of "Non mi dir." Pilar Lorengar is an expressive and touching Elvira; her silvery shimmer suits the character's vulnerability ideally, and she is extremely moving in the moments before "Mi tradì." Marilyn Horne eschews the soubrette stereotype, bringing to Zerlina greater spunk and tonal richness than one generally encounters, giving the character an appealing feistiness, particularly in her last-act duet with Leporello. Those listeners seeking a recording that employs modern instruments, with sprightly tempos and a complete text, need look no further than this admirable performance.

There are a number of recordings of *Don Giovanni* on period instruments, notably those of Sir Roger Norrington and John Eliot Gardiner. Norrington's recording is of particular interest in that it presents two complete performances of the opera, the Prague version (the work as given on its first night) and Mozart's revised text for the opera's Vienna premiere. Either version is easily programmable in large blocks of music, but there is no direct access to individual arias or recitatives. In a lengthy and absorbing essay, Norrington discusses the origins and characteristics of Mozart's opera, offering insight into matters of tempo, voice types, and orchestral disposition. Andreas Schmidt's lyical Don Giovanni heads a solid ensemble cast, orchestral textures are lean with strong timpani, and, as in Gardiner's performance, a fortepiano is used to accompany recitatives. Gardiner elicits a somewhat richer, warmer sound from the English Baroque Soloists, and his live recording from the Ludwigsburger Schlossfestspiele boasts a more evenly balanced cast, with particularly fine performances from Luba Orgonasova as Anna and Rodney Gilfry in the title role. Gardiner employs the Vienna version of the opera as his main text, with an appendix of numbers that may be programmed to form Mozart's Prague score. Nicholas McNair's accompanying essay argues persuasively for the revised version of the opera.

Les Huguenots

Joan Sutherland, Martina Arroyo, Huguette Tourangeau, Anastasios Vrenios, Gabriel Bacquier, Dominic Cossa, Nicola Ghiuselev; Richard Bonynge, New Philharmonia Orchestra. London 430 549–2 (1970)

Ghyslaine Raphanel, Françoise Pollet, Danielle Borst, Richard Leech, Boris Martinovic, Gilles Cachemaille, Nicola Ghiuselev; Cyril Diederich, Orchestre philharmonique de Montpellier. Erato 45027–2 (1988)

Despite their popularity among singers and audiences over many decades, Meyerbeer's operas have never been major attractions for the recording industry. *Les Huguenots* has seen but two commercial recordings, both of which serve the work well. Richard Bonynge's groundbreaking effort for Decca in 1970 was the first complete studio recording of a Meyerbeer opera. Among its virtues is a stunning performance by Joan Sutherland as Marguerite de Valois; her appearance in a celebrated production of the opera at La Scala in 1962 was one of her earliest successes, and the role served as her farewell to the operatic stage in 1990 at Australian Opera in Sydney. Her brilliant technical proficiency in the service of lustrous, plangent vocalism reminds us what an extraordinary artist she was. Anastasios Vrenios is an appealing Raoul, light in timbre yet secure in the role's more vigorous demands. Martina Arroyo and Huguette Tourangeau both contribute gratifying portrayals as Valentine and the page Urbain, while Gabriel Bacquir is luxuriously cast in the role of St. Bris. The New Philharmonia Orchestra plays vividly for Bonynge, who prunes the work judiciously, though his cuts in the ensemble finales rob them of full impact. Both recordings include Valentine's romance "Parmi les pleurs," omitted at the opera's premiere, and Bonynge also includes an additional aria for Urbain in the second act, originally composed for contralto Marietta Alboni.

The Erato *Huguenots,* recorded live at a concert performance in Montpellier (the birthplace of Adolphe Nourrit, the first Raoul), presents a cast of French or francophone singers conducted with elegance by Cyril Diederich. One is immediately struck by the grace and stylishness of the orchestral playing, the blend and balance in the orchestral textures, and the emphasis on spectacular historical drama over vocal histrionics and sonic effects. The disparate elements of Scribe's and Meyerbeer's sprawling opus emerge here in more pleasing equilibrium. The well-matched cast exhibits similar virtues. Ghyslaine Raphanel makes an attractive Marguerite, aristocratic and discreet, while Françoise Pollet offers an impassioned Valentine. Danielle Borst is a very attractive Urbain, her singing bright and accurate. Richard Leech meets all of Raoul's hurdles with admirable aplomb, albeit with an occasional Italianate sob; Gilles Cachemaille is an excellent Nevers, and Nicola Ghiuselev's Marcel is more attentive to matters of rhythm and note values here than on the earlier recording. Diederich conducts a fuller score than Bonynge but without the additional bauble composed for Alboni.

Das Rheingold

Hans Hotter, Georgine von Milinkovic, Ludwig Suthaus, Gustav Neidlinger, Jean Madeira; Hans Knappertsbusch, Bayreuth Festival. Melodram GM 1.001 (1956) [Part of complete *Ring* cycle recording]

George London, Kirsten Flagstad, Set Svanholm, Gustav Neidlinger, Jean Madeira; Sir Georg Solti, Vienna Philharmonic. Decca 441101–2 (1958) [Complete *Ring:* Decca 455 555–2]

Dietrich Fischer-Dieskau, Josephine Veasey, Gerhard Stolze, Zoltán Kelemen, Oralia Dominguez; Herbert von Karajan, Berlin Philharmonic. Deutsche Grammophon 457 781–2 (1968) [Complete *Ring:* Deutsche Grammophon 455 780–2]

Theo Adam, Annelies Burmeister, Wolfgang Windgassen, Gustav Neidlinger, Vera Soukupová; Karl Böhm, Bayreuth Festival. Philips 412 475–2 (1967) [Complete *Ring:* Philips 420 325–2]

James Morris, Christa Ludwig, Siegfried Jerusalem, Ekkehard Wlaschiha, Birgitta Svendén; James Levine, Metropolitan Opera. Deutsche Grammophon 427 607–2 (1988) [Complete *Ring:* Deutsche Grammophon 445 354–2]

Sir Georg Solti's pioneering recording of *Der Ring des Nibelungen* remains an excellent introduction to Wagner's massive opus nearly fifty years after the release of *Das Rheingold,* its initial installment. In 1958 Decca made sonic history with its crystalline engineering, the orchestra's multiple harps and anvils emerging with stunning clarity. Time has scarcely dulled the impact of this bright, cleanly focused recording, and for its many admirers this performance is still the yardstick by which all others must be measured. Solti's bracing, muscular approach results in a vivid realization of Wagner's *Konversationsstück,* and his singers contribute many memorable portrayals. George London's commanding Wotan, vocally secure throughout a wide range, heads a cast that also includes Kirsten Flagstad's Fricka, Set Svanholm as Loge, and Gustav Neidlinger's definitive Alberich, a textbook demonstration of consummate vocal artistry allied to unerring theatrical instincts. Eberhard Waechter and Waldemar Kmentt contribute star turns as Donner and Froh.

Herbert von Karajan's performance with the Berlin Philharmonic reveals a more deliberately lyrical approach with no less dramatic impact. The Berlin Philharmonic plays warmly and often with striking delicacy and transparency. Though lacking the tonal weight of most true bass-baritones, Dietrich Fischer-Dieskau as Wotan projects the text vividly, and Josephine Veasey is a sympathetic Fricka. Gerhard Stolze's sharp-edged Loge is a domineering presence, while Oralia Dominguez' soft-grained Erda is very appealing. Matti Talvela and Karl Ridderbusch as Fasolt and Fafner are as commanding and resonant a pair of giants as one is ever likely to hear.

James Levine's recording is distinguished by exceptionally beautiful and accomplished playing from the Metropolitan Opera Orchestra. A clean and spacious acoustic allows for the emergence of much felicitous detail. The strings project a lovely luminous quality, and there is a radiant warmth in quiet passages; even in moments of bracing aural impact there is not a trace of coarseness. Levine projects the work's musical architecture with a sure hand, and events unfold with compelling inevitability. James Morris' firmly sung Wotan is partnered by Christa Ludwig's authoritative Fricka. Siegfried Jerusalem as Loge brings out character without reverting to caricature, and Heinz Zednik contributes a rhythmically incisive Mime. Levine's recording is evenly cast throughout, from a mellifluous group of Rhinedaughters to the imposing giants of Kurt Moll and Jan-Hendrik Rootering.

Das Rheingold has been recorded several times in live performance at the Bayreuth Festspielhaus (always as part of complete *Ring* cycle recordings). Karl Böhm's performance from the 1967 festival, in the last and most renowned of Wieland Wagner's productions, faithfully reproduces Bayreuth's famed acoustic. Voices are very much forward, with an appealing bloom; the orchestra, particularly the brass, is distinctly more recessed than on most studio recordings. This homogeneous blending of orchestral sonorities provides a comfortable cushion of sound over which the singers can easily project words with exceptional clarity. Böhm paces the work with cinematic swiftness; his is not a ruminative approach, and moments of repose as well as catharsis pass quickly. Theo Adam leads a cast notable for its dramatic vitality, in particular Wolfgang Windgassen (Loge), Annelies Burmeister (Fricka), and Gustav Neidlinger (Alberich). Böhm's is a particularly strong ensemble, no doubt due in large measure to Wieland Wagner's taut direction.

Several recordings preserve the magisterial Wotan of Hans Hotter in performance at Bayreuth. In *Das Rheingold* from the 1956 festival he is heard at the top of his form. Hotter's warm, smooth voice, coupled with his extraordinary theatrical skill and personal magnetism, made him one of the great singing actors of his day. His dramatic powers, displayed at their peak in the *Ring,* enabled him to give words their fullest meaning and expressive weight. His scenes with Neidlinger's superb Alberich become a conflict of superior intellects. Other notable cast members include Ludwig Suthaus, a Loge of more substantial vocal weight than most, and Jean Madeira as Erda. Hans Knappertsbusch's expansive pacing allows Hotter full rein in his expressiveness, and the recorded sound is vivid for its time, the voices caught in a flattering ambience.

Otello

Herva Nelli, Ramón Vinay, Giuseppe Valdengo; Arturo Toscanini, NBC Symphony Orchestra. RCA/BMG Classics 60302–2 (1947)

Leonie Rysanek, Jon Vickers, Tito Gobbi; Tullio Serafin, Rome Opera. RCA/BMG Classics 1969–2-RG (1960)

Renata Tebaldi, Mario Del Monaco, Aldo Protti; Herbert von Karajan, Vienna Philharmonic. Decca 411 618–2 (1961)

Mirella Freni, Jon Vickers, Peter Glossop; Herbert von Karajan, Berlin Philharmonic. EMI 69308–2 (1973)

Renata Scotto, Plácido Domingo, Sherrill Milnes; James Levine, National Philharmonic Orchestra. RCA Red Seal RCD2–1951 (1978)

Francesco Tamagno, The complete recordings. Pearl GEMM CD 9027 (*Otello* excerpts, 1903–04)

Victor Maurel, The complete recordings. Opal CD 9846 (*Otello* excerpts, 1903–04)

Arturo Toscanini's 1947 recording of Verdi's *Otello* has long been considered a touchstone performance. The conductor's association with the work goes back to its opening night. On February 5, 1887, Toscanini played cello in the La Scala orchestra; sixty years later the Maestro marked the anniversary with celebrated broadcast performances of the opera in New York. Toscanini obtains protean playing of matchless precision and passionate commitment from the NBC Symphony Orchestra, and the choral work is first rate. Chilean tenor Ramón Vinay, the title role's leading practitioner in the 1940s and early 1950s, heads a strong cast including soprano Herva Nelli as Desdemona, mezzo Nan Merriman as an unusually fine Emilia, and baritone Giuseppe Valdengo, whose Iago plays off the words effectively. Recorded sound in RCA's latest CD transfer is clean and warm.

Vinay's Otello was succeeded on the world's stages by that of Mario Del Monaco, whose thrilling, powerful voice and charismatic personality can be heard on two Decca recordings of the opera, both with Renata Tebaldi and Aldo Protti. The recording featuring the Vienna Philharmonic conducted by Herbert von Karajan captured these artists at the peak of their creative powers. Del Monaco's Otello displays a forceful and volatile personality, and his clarion sound, though lacking in subtlety, has considerable presence. The warmth and generosity of Renata Tebaldi's unique artistry is ideally suited to Desdemona, and her effulgent tone and affecting pathos make for a memorable portrayal. Aldo Protti's Iago downplays outward villainy for something more subtle. The spacious recording captures the performance with exceptional presence and atmosphere.

Jon Vickers also recorded the role twice, once at the beginning of his international career and again toward the end. His later performance with Karajan reflects a greater artistic maturity; he brings to the role a burnished, heroic sound and a dramatic intensity both powerful and subtle. Mirella Freni's delicate, warm Desdemona is an effective foil, while Peter Glossop's Iago is less overtly sinister and consequently more intriguing than most. The Berlin Philharmonic contributes some lovely playing, but the performance is marred by once-common stage cuts in the inner acts, with a particularly damaging excision in the third act finale. For this reason, some listeners may prefer Vickers' first recording with the Rome Opera, featuring Leonie

Rysanek's sympathetic if less than idiomatic Desdemona and Tito Gobbi's Iago, commanding in its virility and malevolence. When released on LP, both this recording, conducted by Tullio Serafin, and Karajan's earlier Decca recording with Del Monaco discussed above originally included the ballet that Verdi composed for the opera's first Paris production in 1894. The ballet music has been removed from both recordings in their CD transfers.

The reigning Otello of the past two decades has been Plácido Domingo. His three recordings of the role reveal continuing artistic growth and vocal refinement, though the first of these, conducted masterfully by James Levine, remains the most consistently satisfying in terms of overall casting. Domingo excels at both the role's lyric and dramatic demands, his beautiful sound in the service of exceptional musicianship and intelligence. He is partnered by frequent stage colleagues Renata Scotto and Sherrill Milnes. Scotto's Desdemona, no wilting violet, displays the passion and conviction that distinguished her performances in the theater, and Milnes brings lyricism to Iago, contributing an especially fine "Sogno" in the second act. The ensemble of singers in supporting roles is particularly strong.

It is rare that an opera composed well over a hundred years ago is represented on recordings by members of its original cast, but such is the case with *Otello*. Baritone Victor Maurel made several recordings of Iago's "Sogno," while Francesco Tamagno recorded Otello's entrance ("Esultate!"), death scene ("Niun mi tema"), and "Ora e per sempre" multiple times. All of these recordings, with piano accompaniment, date from 1903–4; the sound is primitive but the thrill of hearing these artists remains real.

Further Reading

Chapter 1: Handel, *Giulio Cesare*

Biographies of Handel in English include Donald Burrows, *Handel* (New York: Schirmer Books, Maxwell Macmillan, 1994); Christopher Hogwood, *Handel* (London: Thames and Hudson, 1984); Paul Henry Lang, *George Frideric Handel* (New York: W. W. Norton, 1966). The earliest life of Handel is John Mainwaring, *Memoirs of the Life of the Late George Frederic Handel* (London: R. and J. Dodsley, 1760; repr. New York: Da Capo Press, 1980). Another eighteenth-century view of Handel is found in Charles Burney, *An Account of the Musical Performances in Westminster-Abbey* (London, 1785, repr., with introd. by Peter Kivy, New York: Da Capo Press, 1979).

An enormous amount of primary material about Handel and his times is translated into English in Otto Erich Deutsch, *Handel: A Documentary Biography* (New York: W. W. Norton, 1955). Much illustrative material about Handel and his environs is found in Jacob Simon, ed., *Handel: A Celebration of His Life and Times, 1685–1759* (London: National Portrait Gallery, 1985), and in H. C. Robbins Landon, *Handel and His World* (London: Weidenfeld and Nicolson, 1984).

A standard book on Handel's operas is Winton Dean and John Merrill Knapp, *Handel's Operas, 1704–1726* (Oxford: Clarendon, 1987); on *Giulio Cesare*, see pp. 483–526. A thorough study of stagecraft in Handel's operas is Joachim Eisenschmidt, *Die szenische Darstellung der Opern Georg Friedrich Händels auf der londoner Bühne seiner Zeit*, 2 vols. (Wolfenbüttel: Kallmeyer, 1940–41; repr. Laaber, 1987). See also Lowell Lindgren, "The Staging of Handel's Operas in London," in *Handel Tercentenary Collection*, ed. Stanley Sadie and Anthony Hicks (Ann Arbor, Mich.: UMI Research Press, 1987), 93–119.

A facsimile of the original libretto is in Ellen T. Harris, *The Librettos of Handel's Operas: A Collection of Seventy-One Librettos Documenting Handel's Operatic Career*, 13 vols. (New York: Garland, 1989); vol. 4 contains a facsimile of the 1724 libretto, pp. 1–93. For backgrounds on the libretto, see Craig Monson, "Giulio Cesare in Egitto: From Sartorio (1677) to Handel (1724)," *Music and Letters* 66, 313–43. The remarkable Nicola Haym is treated in Lowell Lindgren, "The Accomplishments of the Learned and Ingenious Nicola Francesco Haym (1678–1729)," *Studi musicali* 16 (1987), 247–380.

Very useful information on the institution of the opera is in C. Steven LaRue, *Handel and His Singers: The Creation of the Royal Academy Operas, 1720–1728* (New York: Oxford University Press, 1995). See also Judith Milhous, "Opera Finances in London, 1674–1738," *Journal of the American Musicological Society* 37 (1984), 567–92. Performances in London's theaters are chronicled in Emmett L. Avery, ed., *The London Stage, 1660–1800*, 5 vols. (Carbondale: Southern Illinois University Press, 1960–68).

Chapter 2: Mozart, *Don Giovanni*

General books in English on Mozart include Maynard Solomon, *Mozart: A Life* (New York: HarperCollins, 1995); Andrew Steptoe, *Mozart* (New York: Knopf, 1997); Stanley Sadie, *Mozart* (London: Calder & Boyars, 1965); Alfred Einstein, *Mozart: His Character, His Work*, trans. Arthur Mendel and Nathan Broder (New York: Oxford University Press, 1972); *The Mozart Compendium*, ed. H. C. Robbins Landon (London: Faber and Faber 1974; New York: Schirmer Books, 1990). A handsomely illustrated volume is H. C. Robbins Landon, *Mozart: The Golden Years, 1781–1791* (London: Thames & Hudson, 1989; repr. New York: Schirmer Books, 1989). More illustrative material is in Volkmar Braunbehrens and Karl-Heinz Jürgens, *Mozart: Lebensbilder* (Bergisch Gladbach: Gustav Lübbe, 1990).

A detailed and intimate view of Mozart and his times can be had from reading Mozart's letters: *Letters of Mozart and His Family*, ed. Emily Anderson (New York: Norton, 1989). An enormous amount of primary documentation is translated into English in Otto Erich Deutsch, *Mozart: A Documentary Biography*, ed. Eric Blom, Peter Branscombe, and Jeremy Noble (Stanford: Stanford University Press, 1965).

Mozart's autograph manuscript of *Don Giovanni* has been published in facsimile as *Don Giovanni. Facsimilé du ms autographe, Paris, Bib. nationale, Ms 1548*, ed. Wolfgang Rehm (Paris: Minkoff France Editeur, 1991).

Volumes concentrating on *Don Giovanni* include Julian Rushton, *W. A. Mozart:* Don Giovanni (Cambridge: Cambridge University Press, 1981); Daniel Heartz, *Mozart's Operas*, ed. Thomas Bauman (Berkeley: University of California Press, 1990); Andrew Steptoe, *The Mozart-Da Ponte Operas* (New York: Oxford University Press, 1988). The chapter on *Don Giovanni* in Joseph Kerman, *Opera as Drama*, new and rev. ed. (Berkeley: University of California Press, 1988), is a classic. Detailed attention to stagecraft in this opera is given in Christof Bitter, *Wandlungen in den Inszenierungsformen des Don Giovanni von 1787 bis 1928* (Regensburg: Gustav Bosse, 1961).

Particular details of Mozart's time in Prague are found in Jan Kristek, ed., *Mozart's Don Giovanni in Prague*, trans. Dagmar Steinov (Prague: Theatre Institute, 1987); Paul Nettl, *Mozart in Böhmen* (Prague: Neumann, 1938), a thoroughgoing revision of Rudolph Procháska, *Mozart in Prag* (Prague: Dominicus, 1892). Charles Burney's eighteenth-century views of music in Bohemia are found in his *An Eighteenth-Century Musical Tour in Central Europe and the Netherlands*, ed. Percy A. Scholes (New York: Oxford University Press, 1959).

Lorenzo da Ponte's imaginative and highly readable memoirs are available as *Memoirs of Lorenzo Da Ponte*, ed. Arthur Livingston, trans. Elisabeth Abbott (Philadelphia: Lippincott, 1929; repr. New York: Da Capo Press, 1988).

Chapter 3: Meyerbeer, *Les Huguenots*

There is no adequate biography of Meyerbeer in English. The leading scholar of Meyerbeer, Heinz Becker, has edited Meyerbeer's letters and diaries, and the volume covering *Les Huguenots* is an indispensable source: *Giacomo Meyerbeer. Briefwechsel und Tagebücher,* ed. Heinz Becker (vol. 2, 1826–36, Berlin: Walter de Gruyter, 1970). A selection of the letters is translated in *Giacomo Meyerbeer: A Life in Letters,* ed. Heinz Becker and Gudrun Becker, trans. Mark Violette (Portland, Ore.: Amadeus Press, 1989). The diaries have been translated into English in Robert Ignatius Letellier, ed. and trans., *The Diaries of Giacomo Meyerbeer,* vol. 1: 1791–1839 (Madison, N.J.: Fairleigh Dickinson University Press; London: Associated University Presses, 1999).

Critical writing about the first performances of *Les Huguenots* is summarized in Marie-Hélene Coudroy, *La critique parisienne des "grands opéras" de Meyerbeer,* Studien zur franzö-sischen Oper des 19. Jahrhunderts, 2. (Saarbrücken: Musik-Edition Lucie Galland, 1988). See also Laurie C. Shulman, "Music Criticism of the Paris Opera in the 1830s" (Ph.D. thesis, Cornell University, 1985).

Serious scholarly study of *Les Huguenots* includes Sieghard Döhring, "Die Autographen der vier Hauptopern Meyerbeers: Ein erster Quellenbericht," *Archiv für Musikforschung* 39, 32–63; Michael Walter, *Hugenotten-Studien* (Frankfurt am Main: P. Lang, 1987). Scribe's contribution as librettist is considered in Karin Pendle, *Eugène Scribe and French Opera of the Nineteenth Century* (Ann Arbor, Mich.: UMI Research Press, 1979); see especially "The Technique of Grand Opera and the Transformation of Literary Models: Meyerbeer's *Les Huguenots,*" 465–93.

The original mise-en-scène for *Les Huguenots* is reproducd in facsimile on pp. 133–71 of H. Robert Cohen, *The Original Staging Manuals for Ten Operatic Premieres, 1824–1843,* Musical Life in 19th-Century France, vol. 6 (Stuyvesant, N.Y.: Pendragon, 1998). Staging at the Opéra in these years is studied in detail in Rebecca S. Wilberg, "The Mise en Scene at the Paris Opera—Salle Le Peletier (1821–1873) and the Staging of the First French Grand Opera: Meyerbeer's *Robert le diable*" (Ph.D. thesis, Brigham Young University, 1990). Also useful are Marie Antoinette Allévy, *La mise en scène en France dans la première moitie du dix-neuvième siècle* (Paris: E. Droz, 1938; repr. Geneva: Slatkine Reprints, 1976), and Catherine Join-Diéterle, *Les décors de scène de l'Opéra de Paris à l'Époque romantique* (Paris: Picard, 1988).

Studies of the cultural significance of the Grand Opera include Anselm Gerhard, *The Urbanization of Opera,* trans. Mary Whitall (Chicago: University of Chicago Press, 1998), originally *Die Verstädterung der Oper: Paris und das Musiktheater des 19. Jahrhunderts* (Stuttgart: J. B. Metzler, 1992); Jane Fulcher, *The Nation's Image* (Cambridge: Cambridge University Press, 1987); and William Crosten, *French Grand Opera: An Art and a Business* (New York: King's Crown Press, 1948).

Chapter 4: Wagner, *Das Rheingold*

The literature on Wagner is enormous. A major biography is Carl Friedrich Glasenapp, *Das Leben Richard Wagners,* 6 vols. (Leipzig: Breitkopf und Hartel, 1894–1911), trans. William Ashton Ellis, *Life of Richard Wagner,* 6 vols. (London: K. Paul, Trench, Trubner, 1900–1908).

A major biography in English is Ernest Newman, *The Life of Richard Wagner,* 4 vols. (New York: Knopf, 1933–46; repr. Cambridge: Cambridge University Press, 1976). See also Michael Tanner, *Wagner* (Princeton, N.J.: Princeton University Press, 1996), and John Deathridge and Carl Dahlhaus, *The New Grove Wagner* (New York: W. W. Norton, 1984).

Wagner's voluminous writings have been published in an official edition as *Richard Wagner: Sämtliche Schriften und Dichtungen,* 5th ed. (Leipzig: Breitkopf & Hartel, 1911), trans. William Ashton Ellis as *Richard Wagner's Prose Works,* 10 vols., 1892–99 (New York: Broude, 1966). Much interesting illustrative material is reproduced in Martin Gregor-Dellin, *Richard Wagner: eine Biographie in Bildern* (Munich: R. Piper, 1982).

On the operas of the Ring, and on *Das Rheingold,* see Warren Darcy, *Wagner's Das Rheingold* (Oxford: Clarendon, 1993); Carl Dahlhaus, *Richard Wagner's Music Dramas,* trans. Mary Whittall (Cambridge: Cambridge University Press, 1979), originally *Richard Wagners Musikdramen* (Stuttgart: P. Reclam, 1996). A particular view is given in Robert Donington, *Wagner's "Ring" and Its Symbols: The Music and the Myth* (New York: St. Martin's Press, 1974).

A translation of the German edition of Carl Emil Doepler's diary, now lost, with facsimiles of Doepler's published sketches for the original costumes, is in Peter Cook, *A Memoir of Bayreuth: 1876 — C. E. Doepler* (London: Staples Printers St. Albans, Ltd., 1979).

The diary of Richard Fricke, who oversaw much of the staging, is available in translation, along with facsimiles of a portfolio of photographs of the singers in costume, and of a portfolio of Josef Hoffmann's set designs; see Richard Fricke, *Wagner in Rehearsal: The Diaries of Richard Fricke, 1875–1876,* trans. George R. Fricke, ed. James Deaville with Evan Baker, Franz Liszt Studies Series, 7 (Stuyvesant, N.Y.: Pendragon, 1998).

Heinrich Porges, invited by Wagner to chronicle and record the rehearsals, published his descriptions; an English translation is Heinrich Porges, *Wagner Rehearsing the* Ring: *An Eyewitness Account of the Stage Rehearsals of the First Bayreuth Festival,* trans. Robert L. Jacobs (Cambridge: Cambridge University Press, 1983).

Cosima Wagner's diaries have been translated as *Cosima Wagner's Diaries,* ed. Martin Gregor-Dellin and Dietrich Mack, trans. Geoffrey Skelton, 2 vols. (New York: Harcourt Brace Jovanovich, 1977).

Lilli Lehmann's memoir *Mein Weg* (Leipzig: S. Hirzel, 1913) is translated by Alice Benedict Seligman as *My Path Through Life* (New York: G. P. Putnam's Sons, 1914).

Two volumes giving highly readable accounts of the first Bayreuth festival, with much primary material, are Robert Hartford, ed., *Bayreuth: The Early Years. An Account of the Early Decades of the Wagner Festival as Seen by Celebrated Visitors and Participants* (Cambridge: Cambridge University Press, 1980); and Frederic Spotts, *Bayreuth: A History of the Wagner Festival* (New Haven: Yale University Press, 1994).

A thorough study of the technical aspects of the Festspielhaus is Carl-Friederich Baumann, *Bühnentechnik im Festspielhaus Bayreuth* (Munich: Prestel-Verlag, 1980).

The reactions of the German press to performances at Bayreuth are surveyed in Susanna Grossmann-Vendrey, *Bayreuth in der deutschen Presse: Beitrage zur Rezeptionsgeschichte Richard Wagners und seiner Festspiele* (Regensburg: Bosse, 1977–83), vol. 1: *Die Grundsteinlegung und die ersten Festspiele (1872–1876).*

Chapter 5: Verdi, *Otello*

The standard biography of Verdi is Franco Abbiati, *Giuseppe Verdi*, 4 vols. (Milan: Ricordi, 1959); a brief biography in English is Julian Budden, *Verdi* (London: J. M. Dent, 1985). There is no collected edition of Verdi's voluminous correspondence, but everything connected with the preparation and performance of *Otello* is gathered and translated in Hans Busch, *Verdi's* Otello *and* Simon Boccanegra *(revised version) in Letters and Documents,* 2 vols. (Oxford: Clarendon, 1988), which also contains translations of the production book and critical reviews.

Julian Budden's *The Operas of Verdi,* 3 vols. (1981; New York: Oxford University Press, 1992) includes an extensive study of *Otello.*

James Hepokoski's volume *Giuseppe Verdi: Otello,* Cambridge Opera Handbooks (Cambridge: Cambridge University Press, 1987) is complemented by the same author's volume (in collaboration with Mercedes Viale Ferreira) *Otello di Giuseppe Verdi* (Musica e spettacolo) (Milan: G. Ricordi, 1990), which provides useful essays, a facsimile of the *disposizione scenica,* and many illustrations.

Two pamphlets published in connection with the first performance are hard to find but very valuable: *Otello. Dramma lirico in quattro atti. Versi di Arrigo Boito. Musica di Giuseppe Verdi. Giudizî della stampa italiana e straniera,* Supplemento straordinario della Gazzetta Musicale di Milano, N. S. (Milan: Ricordi, 1887) and *Verdi e l'Otello,* Numero unico pubblicato dalla *Illustrazione italiana* (Milan: Fratelli Treves, 1887).

Blanche Roosevelt's report on the first performance is in *Verdi: Milan and "Othello"* (London: Ward and Downey, 1887).

Notes

Introduction

x Epigraph: Cited in Elizabeth Gibson, *The Royal Academy of Music, 1719–1728: The Institution and Its Directors* (New York: Garland, 1989), 48.

Chapter 1: Handel, *Giulio Cesare*
Boxes

5 César de Saussure on the Dress of the English: César de Saussure, *A Foreign View of England in 1725–1729: The Letters of Monsieur César de Saussure to His Family,* trans. and ed. Madame Van Muyden (London: Caliban, 1995), 70, 126–27.

9 The King's Theatre, 1723–24 Season: Emmett L. Avery, ed., *The London Stage, 1660–1800: A Calendar of Plays, Entertainments & Afterpieces, Together with Casts, Box-receipts and Contemporary Comment. Compiled from the Playbills, Newspapers and Theatrical Diaries of the Period,* 5 vols. (Carbondale: Southern Illinois University Press, 1960–68).

16 John Gay to Jonathan Swift: letter of February 3, 1723, cited in Otto Erich Deutsch, *Handel: A Documentary Biography* (New York: W. W. Norton, 1955), 149.

20 Richard Steele Complains of Stage Seats in the *Spectator*: Donald F. Bond, ed., *The Spectator,* 5 vols. (Oxford: Clarendon, 1965), 1: 65.

29 Joseph Addison Mocks Heroic Costume in the *Spectator*: April 18, 1711, Bond, *Spectator,* 1: 180.

38 Requirements for Librettists: cited in Lowell Lindgren, "The Accomplishments of the Learned and Ingenious Nicola Francesco Haym (1678–1729)," *Studi musicali* 16 (1987), 247–308 at 309; see also pp. 306–7 n. 189.

46 "A full & true Account of the proceedings of the Royal Academy of Music anno 1723": Gibson, *The Royal Academy,* 106.

50 From *Faustina: or the Roman Songstress*: Gibson, *The Royal Academy,* 415–18.

Text

xviii Epigraph: "There are no men or women dancers": Saussure, *A Foreign View of England,* 170.

4 Burney, "The passages in this and the other operas": Charles Burney, *A General History of Music* (1776–1789), 1935 ed., ed. Frank Mercer (New York: Dover, 1957), 2: 722.

4 "A number of them are dirty": Saussure, *A Foreign View of England,* 42.

7 Tony Aston's Medleys: Avery, *The London Stage,* 2: 746.

7 Entertainments of February 20: Avery, *The London Stage,* 2: 751, 761.

8 "The passion for the opera here": Deutsch, *Handel,* 160.

8 "Some say, compar'd to Bononcini": Byrom, *Miscellaneous Poems* (London, 1814), 1: 35, cited in Deutsch, *Handel*, 180.

8 "Proposall for carrying on Operas by a Company of Joynt Stock": Gibson, *The Royal Academy of Music*, 314–16.

10 Heidegger's bet with Chesterfield: Winton Dean, "Handel," in *The New Grove Dictionary of Music and Musicians*, 2nd ed., ed. Stanley Sadie (London: Macmillan, 2001), 11: 313.

10 "always the Confusion, and very commonly, the Ruin": cited in Daniel Nalbach, "Opera Management in Eighteenth-Century London," *Theatre Research* 13 (1973), 75–91 at 76.

11 "He was large in person": Coxe, *Anecdotes of Handel* (1799), cited in Jacob Simon, ed., *Handel: A Celebration of His Life and Times, 1685–1759* (London: National Portrait Gallery, 1985), 34–35.

11 Handel's salary: Deutsch's estimate, quoted in Reinhard Strohm, *Essays on Handel and Italian Opera* (Cambridge: Cambridge University Press, 1985), 105.

12 "never be made second to any other Person": Lindgren, "The Accomplishments," 247–380 at 267.

13 Collaboration with Haym, adaptation of the libretto: see Craig Monson, "*Giulio Cesare in Egitto*, from Sartorio (1677) to Handel (1724)," *Music and Letters* 66 (1985), 313–43.

13 "an intire new Sett of Scenes": Avery, *The London Stage*, 2: 737.

15 "The introduction of eunuchs upon public theatres": William Popple in *The Prompter*, cited in Daniel Nalbach, *The King's Theatre, 1704–1867* (London: Society for Theatre Research, 1972), 59.

15 Gold snuffboxes, a tweezer-case set: *The Prompter*, cited in Nalbach, *The King's Theatre*, 58.

15 Most rehearsals held informally: Lindgren, "The Accomplishments," 268 n. 78.

16 "We hear there have been strange Commotions": Deutsch, *Handel*, 157.

16 at the "too near approach of Senesino": Burney, *A General History*, 2: 729 n.

16 "a spurious Breed": Deutsch, *Handel*, 159.

16 "squabbles": Deutsch, *Handel*, 160.

17 Mount-Edgcumbe described the scene: Richard Edgcumbe, 2nd Earl of Mount-Edgcumbe, *Musical Reminiscences, Containing an Account of the Italian Opera in England, from 1773*, 4th ed. (London: J. Andrews, 1834), 178–79.

17 "a Disturbance happen'd at the opera House": *London Daily Post and General Advertiser*, February 11, 1735, cited in Nalbach, *The King's Theatre*, 66.

18 "Last Night His Majesty": *Daily Journal*, February 21, cited in Avery, *The London Stage*, 2: 761.

18 "For what could their vast columns": John Maurice Evans, ed., *A Critical Edition of "An Apology for the Life of Mr. Colley Cibber, Comedian"* (New York: Garland, 1987), 163–64.

18 "by some of the best Masters": *British Journal*, September 21, 1723, cited in Deutsch, *Handel*, 155.

18 Price of opera tickets: Judith Milhous, "Opera Finances in London, 1674–1738," *Journal of the American Musicological Society* 37 (1984), 567–92 at 584 and passim.

20 "The new Opera Tickets are very high": *London Journal*, March 2, 1723; Deutsch, *Handel*, 150.

20 "And whereas there is a great many Scenes": *Daily Courant*, May 25, 1715, cited in Nalbach, *The King's Theatre*, 35.

20 "The room is small": Winton Dean, "A French Traveller's View of Handel's Operas," *Music & Letters* 55 (1974), 172–78 at 177–78; author's translation.

21 "The orchestra consisted for the greater part of Germans": Deutsch, *Handel*, 754.

21 Initial plan for orchestra: Winton Dean and John Merrill Knapp, *Handel's Operas, 1704–1726* (Oxford: Clarendon, 1987), 303.

21 "above 24 violins": cited in Simon, *Handel: A Celebration*, 145.

22 "The orchestra was composed of twenty-four violins": Dean, "A French Traveller's View," 177; author's translation.

22 "This violinist, who was more than half mad": Burney, *A General History*, 2: 698.

26 "Scenes affect ordinary Minds": Addison, *Spectator*, April 18, 1711, in Bond, *Spectator*, 1: 180.

33 "finest piece of accompanied Recitative": Charles Burney, *An Account of the Musical Performances in Westminster-Abbey* (London, 1785; repr., with introd. by Peter Kivy, New York: Da Capo Press, 1979), 63.

35 "Nicolini sets off the Character": Colley Cibber, citing *The Tatler,* January 3, 1710, in Evans, *A Critical Edition,* 225.

36 "Another mechanical method of making great Men": Addison, *Spectator,* April 18, 1711, in Bond, *Spectator,* 1: 179.

36 "Beyond all criticism": *Mercure de France,* October 1724, pp. 2229–30, cited in Lowell Lindgren, "Parisian Patronage of Performers from the Royal Academy of Musick (1719–28)," *Music and Letters* 58 (1977), 4–28 at 23.

36 "in the pronunciation of recitative": John Hawkins, *A General History of the Science and Practice of Music,* 2 vols. (London: T. Payne and Son, 1776; 2nd ed., London: Novello, 1875; repr. New York: Dover, 1963), 2: 872.

36 "had an effect, when recited on the stage": Burney, *An Account of the Musical Performances,* 61.

36 Quantz on Senesino: Paul Nettl, *Forgotten Musicians* (New York: Philosophical Library, 1951), 292.

36 "We thought it a fat old woman": Winton Dean in *The New Grove,* 23: 79, citing a letter of 1740.

41 "as 'tis said, she far excells Seigniora Duristante": December 29, 1722, cited in Deutsch, *Handel,* 139.

41 Handel threatened to throw Cuzzoni out the window: John Mainwaring, *Memoirs of the Life of the Late George Frederic Handel* (London: R. and J. Dodsley, 1760; repr. New York: Da Capo Press, 1980), 110–11.

41 "But who would have thought the Infection": *The Miscellaneous Works of the Late Dr. Arbuthnot* (Glasgow: Printed for James Carlile, 1751), 1: 214, cited in Nalbach, *The King's Theatre,* 60.

42 "Her style of singing was innocent": Burney, *A General History,* 2: 745; note that an almost identical passage is in Johann Adam Hiller, *Anweisung zum musikalisch-zierlichen Gesange,* trans. Suzanne J. Beicken, *Treatise on Vocal Performance and Ornamentation* (Cambridge: Cambridge University Press, 2001), 46.

42 "It was difficult": Burney, *A General History,* 2: 736–37.

43 "She was short and squat": Burney, *A General History,* 2: 731.

44 "If Cuzzoni's behavior were as good as her singing": Lindgren, "Parisian Patronage," 20.

44 "woman already old": Mr. Lecoq in a letter to Dresden, cited in Deutsch, *Handel,* 160.

44 "person was coarse and masculine": Burney, *A General History,* 2: 719.

44 "an evirato of a huge unwieldy figure": Burney, *A General History,* 2: 719.

44 "and Boschi-like be always in a rage": Winton Dean, "Boschi," in *The New Grove,* 4: 50.

45 "There must be, in every drama": Burney, *A General History,* 2: 745.

45 "Whereas by the frequent calling for the songs again": Burney, *A General History,* 2: 694.

47 "a solo Song out of the Opera of Julius Caesar": Avery, *The London Stage,* 2: 775.

49 "Cleopatra has eight arias": Winton Dean, *Handel and the Opera Seria* (Berkeley: University of California Press, 1969), 68.

49 Reported in the *Mercure de France:* Lindgren, "Parisian Patronage," 23.

49 "I was engaged to dine": Deutsch, *Handel,* 158.

49 "The opera is in full swing": Deutsch, *Handel,* 160.

50 "Three songs out of Julius Caesar": Avery, *The London Stage,* 2: 767.

51 "as done by Sig. Castrucci": Avery, *The London Stage,* 2: 775.

51 "a Piece of the Machinery tumbled down": Deutsch, *Handel,* 305.

Chapter 2: Mozart, *Don Giovanni*
Boxes

68 A Description of Prague: Anton Friedrich Büsching, *A New System of Geography* (London: A. Millar, 1762), 4: 69.

87 Mozart's entry of *Don Giovanni* in his autograph catalogue: facsimile in Rudolf Angermüller and Genviève Geffray, *Mozart auf der Reise nach Prag, Dresden, Leipzig und Berlin* (Bad Honnef: Karl Heinrich Verlag, 1995), 95.

90 The Prague Orchestra Described in 1800: Franz Xaver Niemetschek, in an unsigned article on music in Bohemia, *Allgemeine musikalische Zeitung* 2 (1799–1800), col. 522.

100 From Goethe's Rules for Actors: in Marvin A. Carlson, *Goethe and the Weimar Theatre* (Ithaca, N.Y.: Cornell University Press, 1978), 309–18; see Document 11.

103 Mixed Music in the Ballroom: *Neuesten Sittengemälde von Wien,* 1800, cited in Walter Salmen, ed., *Mozart in der Tanzkultur seiner Zeit* (Innsbruck: Helbling, 1990), 86.

Text

62 Epigraph: "You would have seen all your hopes for opera fulfilled": *Der Briefwechsel zwischen Schiller und Goethe,* ed. Emil Staiger (Frankfurt: Insel Verlag, 1966), 1: 468.

69 "The houses are all of white stone": Charles Burney, *An Eighteenth Century Musical Tour in Central Europe and the Netherlands,* ed. Percy A. Scholes (New York: Oxford University Press, 1959), 132–33.

70 "Whether the general talent for music": Friedrich Ernest Arnold, *Beobachtungen in und über Prag, von einem reisenden Ausländer* (Prague: W. Gerle, 1787), 69; see Document 3.

70 "a beloved singer": Arnold, *Beobachtungen,* 71; see Document 3.

70 "The general inclination for music": Arnold, *Beobachtungen,* 72–73; see Document 3.

72 Lenten drama: this and other productions mentioned here in Volek, "Prague Operatic Traditions and Mozart's Don Giovanni," in Jan Kristek, ed., *Mozart's Don Giovanni in Prague,* trans. Dagmar Steinov (Prague: Theatre Institute, 1987), 24 and passim.

72 "He composes very charmingly": Mozart's letter of August 29, 1781; Emily Anderson, ed., *The Letters of Mozart and His Family,* 4th ed. (New York: W. W. Norton, 1989), no. 422, p. 762.

74 "This impresario offers": Arnold, *Beobachtungen,* 136–38.

74 "It is very encouraging for an Italian singer": Johann Adam Hiller, *Anweisung zum musikalisch-zierlichen Gesange,* trans. Beicken, *Treatise on Vocal Performance and Ornamentation,* 38.

75 Success of *Die Entführung:* Mozart's letter of December 6, 1783, cited in Anderson, *The Letters of Mozart,* no. 500, p. 862.

75 "Now the Bohemians proceeded": Franz Niemetschek, *Life of Mozart* (1798), trans. Helen Mautner (London: Leonard Hyman, 1956), 33.

76 "At once the news of his presence spread in the stalls": Niemetschek, *Life of Mozart,* 36.

76 "Immediately after our arrival": Anderson, *The Letters of Mozart,* no. 544, pp. 903–4.

77 "The opera director Bondini commissioned Mozart": Niemetschek, *Life of Mozart,* 37.

77 "Keep your eye on him": Elliot Forbes, ed., *Thayer's Life of Beethoven* (Princeton: Princeton University Press, 1967), 87.

77 Mozart's address: Anderson, *The Letters of Mozart,* 910 n. 1.

77 Mozart offered Bertati's libretto: Daniel Heartz, *Mozart's Operas,* ed. Thomas Bauman (Berkeley: University of California Press, 1990), 158.

77 Da Ponte's 1819 brochure: Tomislav Volek, Untitled remarks in the round table "'Don Giovanni': Prag 1787—Wien 1788—1987," *Mozart-Jahrbuch* 1987–88, 217–19 at 218, citing John Stone; see Heartz, *Mozart's Operas,* 133 n. 1.

78 Da Ponte paid 50 sequins: Lorenzo Da Ponte, *Memoirs of Lorenzo Da Ponte,* ed. Arthur Livingston, trans. Elisabeth Abbott (Philadelphia: J. B. Lippincott, 1929; repr. New York: Da Capo, 1988), 178.

78 "The three subjects fixed on": Da Ponte, *Memoirs,* 174–76.

81 "Our celebrated Herr Mozart has again arrived": Deutsch, *Mozart,* 299.

82 "The stage personnel here are not as smart": Anderson, *The Letters of Mozart,* letter 550, p. 911; see Document 4.

82 Da Ponte arrives at "Zum Platteis": Deutsch, *Mozart,* 299.

82 Mozart and Da Ponte shout at each other: often reported, e.g., in Paul Nettl, *Mozart in Böhmen* (Prague: Neumann & Comp., 1938), 129.

82 Casanova may have helped Mozart: Deutsch, *Mozart,* 301; Nettl, *Mozart in Böhmen,* 145–48, describes a draft revision by Casanova of the sextet in act 2.

82 "In this connexion I have a good joke": Anderson, *The Letters of Mozart,* letter 550, pp. 911–12; see Document 4.

83 "At half-past six o'clock": Deutsch, *Mozart,* 300; see Document 6.

83 "It was fixed for the 24th": Anderson, *The Letters of Mozart,* letter 550, pp. 911–12; see Document 4.

84 Musical numbers on Prague paper: see Alfred Einstein's preface to *Il dissoluto punito; ossia Il Don Giovanni,* Eulenburg score no. 918 (London, n. d.), XII; see also Tomislav Volek and Jitrenka Pesková, *Mozart's Don Giovanni: An Exhibition to Mark the 2nd Centenary of the World Première of the Opera in Prague, 1787–1987* (Prague: Státní knihovna CSR, 1987), 19.

85 Bassi was unsatisfied: Christof Bitter, *Wandlungen in den Inszenierungsformen des Don Giovanni von 1787 bis 1928* (Regensburg: Gustav Bosse, 1961), 27 and 48 n. 59.

85 Niemetschek reports a conversation: Franz Xaver Niemetschek, *Leben des K. K. Kapellmeisters Wolfgang Gottlieb Mozart, nach Originalquellen beschrieben* (Prague: Herrlische Buchhandlung, 1798; 2nd ed., 1808, repr. Deutscher Verlag für Musik, VEB, 1978), 87–88, trans. in Tomislav Volek, "Prague Operatic Traditions," 77–78.

86 Text of November 30 poster: Deutsch, *Mozart,* 302.

87 Neimetschek reports on crowding: *Allgemeine musikalischer Zeitung* 10 (December 1807), col. 200.

87 "The carriages began to arrive": Meissner, *Rococobildern,* cited in Nettl, *Mozart in Böhmen,* 157.

88 "The new theater will be finished next Easter": *Theatrekalendar auf das Jahr 1783* (Gotha: Karl Wilhelm Ettinger), 274, cited in Véra Ptáčková, "Scenography of *Don Giovanni* in Prague," in Kristek, *Mozart's Don Giovanni in Prague,* 96.

89 "The city of Prague will have to make do with an Italian opera": Arnold, *Beobachtungen,* 131; see Document 3.

89 "At seven in the evening": Štepánek, cited in Nettl, *Mozart in Böhmen,* 139.

90 "Connoisseurs who have seen this opera": Deutsch, *Mozart,* 281.

90 Mozart's letter to Strobach: The letter apparently does not survive but is reported in Niemetschek, *Life of Mozart,* 37.

91 "There was the incomparable orchestra": Niemetschek, *Life of Mozart,* 35.

91 Theater measurements from Bitter, *Wandlungen in den Inszenierungsformen,* 11.

91 "sepulcher with eight flats": Ptáčková, "Scenography of *Don Giovanni,*" 95.

92 "young but highly skilled artist": *Theatrekalendar auf das Schalt-jahr 1784,* Gotha, cited in Ptáčková, "Scenography of *Don Giovanni,*" 97.

92 Bitter prints after Platzer sketches: many of these are reproduced in Ptáčková, "Scenography of *Don Giovanni.*"

93 Bitter's arrangement of scenes: Bittner, *Wandlungen in den Inszenierungsformen,* 34–35.

94 "In the first act Donna Anna and Don Giovanni must not remain in the dark": Alfred Orel, *Goethe als Operndirektor* (Bregenz: Eugen Russ Verlag, 1949), 67.

95 "a bass who has few equals": cited in Bitter, *Wandlungen in den Inszenierungsformen,* 159; Nettl, *Mozart in Böhmen,* 78–79.

95 "man who here, and wherever he has appeared": Deutsch, *Mozart,* 284.

95 "is a complete beginner as an actress": Zdenka Pilková, "Prager Mozartsänger in Dresdner Quellen," *Festschrift Christoph-Helmut Mahling zum 65. Geburtstag,* ed. Axel Beer et al. (Tutzing: Hans Schneider, 1997), 2: 1096; Bitter, *Wandlungen in den Inszenierungsformen,* 13.

96 "Very handsome and very stupid": Meissner, *Rococo Bildern,* 2nd ed., cited in Nettl, *Mozart in Böhmen,* 120.

96 "fiery Italian": cited in Nettl, *Mozart in Böhmen,* 122.

97 "This meritorious singer has been the ornament of society": 1793 *Taschenkalender,* cited in Bitter, *Wandlungen in den Inszenierungsformen,* 14.

97 "Before his voice was lost Bassi was a splendid singer": *Allgemeine musikalischer Zeitung* 2 (April 1800), cols. 538–39.

97 "Herr Bassi is a very able actor": cited in Rudolf Angermüller and Genviève Geffray, *Mozart auf der Reise nach Prag, Dresden, Leipzig und Berlin* (Bad Honnef: Karl Heinrich Verlag, 1995), 96.

97 Lolli information: Dlabacz and Štepánek, cited in Nettl, *Mozart in Böhmen*, 122–23.

98 "A man of perfect taste and great knowledge": Da Ponte, *Memoirs*, 472.

98 "Certainly he deserves his loud applause": cited in Bitter, *Wandlungen in den Inszenierungsformen*, 13; there are operas called *La molinara* by Paisiello and Domenico Fischietti.

98 "This singer left the company a year ago": cited in Angermüller, *Mozart auf der Reise nach Prag*, 98.

98 Micelli was still singing *Don Giovanni* in 1792: Nettl, *Mozart in Böhmen*, 120, citing Dlabacz.

98 "her chief accomplishment is acting in soubrette roles": *Gothaer Taschenkalendar*, 1793, cited in Bitter, *Wandlungen in den Inszenierungsformen*, 13.

98 "as perfectly as a well-made suit of clothes": letter of February 28, 1778, in Anderson, *The Letters of Mozart*, 497.

99 "Bondini sings": from the *Prager Oberpostamtszeitung*, December 19, 1786, printed Nettl, *Mozart in Böhmen*, 74; a complete Italian poem is printed in Nettl, 77–78.

99 "worked formerly as a concert singer in Leipzig": *Berliner Theatre- und Literaturzeitung*, September 21, 1782, cited in Pilková, "Prager Mozartsänger," 1096.

99 Her daughter Marianne performed *Figaro* in Paris: Peter Clive, *Mozart and His Circle: A Biographical Dictionary* (New Haven: Yale University Press, 1993), 26.

99 "every movement made by the hand": Gotthold Ephraim Lessing, *Hamburg Dramaturgy*, trans. Victor Lange (New York: Dover, 1962), 17.

100 Feeling: Lessing, *Hamburg Dramaturgy*, 12.

101 "Everybody sings": Da Ponte, *Memoirs*, 133; an earlier version is cited in Heartz, *Mozart's Operas*, 133–34.

102 On the potential significance of "Viva la liberta!": Volek, "Prague Operatic Traditions," 61–62, 66, 95–96.

103 "At the final rehearsal of the opera": Wilhelm Kuhe, *My Musical Recollections* (London: Richard Bentley and Son, 1896), 9–10; see Document 8.

105 Bitter's suggestion on Bassi's changes: Bitter, *Wandlungen in den Inszenierungsformen*, 27.

105 "The worth of this artist is known": *Allgemeine musikalischer Zeitung* 2 (April 1800), col. 789, cited in Bitter, *Wandlungen in den Inszenierungsformen*, 14.

106 "While Mozart held the first rehearsals": Nettl, *Mozart in Böhmen*, 131, citing Nissen.

107 On the potential significance of the first tune of the stage band: Heartz, *Mozart's Operas*, 170.

107 On the second tune: Volek, Untitled remarks in the round table, 218; Volek, "Prague Operatic Traditions," 73–74; Heartz, *Mozart's Operas*, 169–70.

107 "Nothing is played": Anderson, *The Letters of Mozart*, letter 544, p. 903.

108 "This is all nothing": J. P. Lyser, "Wie wollte Mozart die Tafelszene in 'Don Juan' aufgefasst und gegeben haben," *Wiener allgemeine Musikzeitung* 81 (1845), 322; cited in Bitter, *Wandlungen in den Inszenierungsformen*, 29.

109 "Monday, the 29th, the Italian Opera Company": Deutsch, *Mozart*, 303–4; the same notice appeared in the *Wiener Zeitung*, November 14.

110 "It is now ten years": Niemetschek, *Life of Mozart*, 38, 55.

110 "At the end of that memorable first night": Kuhe, *My Musical Recollections*, 6–8, altered; see Document 8.

110 "My opera 'Don Giovanni' had its first performance": Anderson, *The Letters of Mozart*, no. 551, p. 912; see Document 5.

110 "I would be inconsolable": Niemetschek, unsigned article in *Allgemeine musikalischer Zeitung* 10 (December 1797), col. 189.

110 "It was performed yesterday": Anderson, *Letters of Mozart*, no. 551, pp. 912–13.

111 "Long live Da Ponte!": Da Ponte, *Memoirs*, 179.

111 "The Emperor sent for me": Da Ponte, *Memoirs,* 179.

111 "The opera went on the stage": Da Ponte, *Memoirs,* 179–80.

Chapter 3: Meyerbeer, *Les Huguenots*
Boxes

141 The Theaters of Paris, 1830–31: *Almanach des spectacles pour 1830. Neuvième année* (Paris: Barba, 1830).

161 The Cast as Agreed on by Meyerbeer and Véron: Heinz Becker, ed., *Giacomo Meyerbeer. Briefwechsel und Tagebücher,* vol. 2, 1826–36 (Berlin: Walter de Gruyter, 1970), 664–68.

164 Véron Describes the Contretemps: Louis Désiré Véron, *Mémoires d'un bourgeois de Paris* (Paris, G. de Gonet, [1853]–55), 3: 162ff. Excerpts reprinted as *L'Opera de Paris, 1820–1835* (Paris: Editions M. de Maule, 1987), 115–16.

173 Véron Describes the Effects of Premieres: Véron, *Mémoires,* repr. in *L'Opéra de Paris,* 111.

177 Charles de Forster Describes the Excitement of a Premiere: Charles de Forster [Karol Forster], *Quinze ans à Paris, 1832–1849. Paris et les Parisiens* (Paris: Didot, 1848–49), 1: 211–13.

Text

132 Epigraph: "Is there any thing in the world so perfectly French": Frances Trollope, *Paris and the Parisians in 1835* (New York: Harper & Brothers, 1836), 286.

136 "restrained by no pity for his executants": Henry F. Chorley, *Music and Manners in France and Germany* (London: Longman, Brown, Green, and Longmans, 1844), 1: 190.

139 "It is evident": Trollope, *Paris and the Parisians,* 191.

146 "ruddy, with a pock-marked face": Philarète Chasles, *Mémoires* (Geneva: Slatkine Reprints, 1973), 1: 275.

147 Heinrich Heine describes Véron's attitude: Heinrich Heine, *Über die französische Bühne und andere Schriften zum Theatre,* ed. Christoph Trilse (Berlin: Kunst und Gesellschaft, 1971), 114–15.

149 "Habeneck had the bad habit": Charles de Boigne, *Petits mémoires de l'Opéra* (Paris: Librairie nouvelle, 1857), 298.

151 De Boigne describes Auguste's plans: De Boigne, *Petits mémoires de l'Opéra,* 90–91.

151 "we go to this magnificent theater": Trollope, *Paris and the Parisians,* 287.

152 "lean, yellowish, pale man": Heine, *Über die französische Bühne,* 155–56.

153 "There are, I am very sure, more things": Trollope, *Paris and the Parisians,* 289.

155 "The arrangement and management of the scenery": Trollope, *Paris and the Parisians,* 289.

156 Grillparzer described the Opéra's style of scene-painting: Rebecca S. Wilberg, "The mise en scene at the Paris Opera—Salle Le Peletier (1821–1873) and the staging of the first French grand opera: Meyerbeer's *Robert le diable*" (Ph.D. thesis, Brigham Young University, 1990), 203.

156 "These admirable mechanists": Trollope, *Paris and the Parisians,* 289.

157 "The opera is one of the most admirable creations": F. Stoepel, in *Allgemeine musikalishe Zeitung* (20 June 1836, 269), in Robert Ignatius Letellier, ed. and trans., *The Diaries of Giacomo Meyerbeer,* vol. 1: 1791–1839 (Madison, N.J.: Fairleigh Dickinson University Press; London: Associated University Presses, 1999), 483.

157 "I place him with Franconi's circus people": Robert Schumann, *Gesammelte Schriften über Musik und Musiker,* 4th ed. (Leipzig: Breitkopf & Härtel, 1891), 2: 59. A translation of Schumann's essay is in *Robert Schumann on Music and Musicians,* ed. Konrad Wolff, trans. Paul Rosenfeld (London: Dennis Dobson, 1956), 193–97.

158 "But what is all this in contrast": Schumann, *Gesammelte Schriften,* 2: 62.

158 "On days when his opera is given": Heine, *Über die französische Bühne,* 110–11.

159 "I hosted a dinner for Paganini": Letellier, *The Diaries of Giacomo Meyerbeer,* 1: 413.

159 Meyerbeer delivers the score: Letellier, *The Diaries of Giacomo Meyerbeer*, 1: 461.

159 Véron paid Meyerbeer the 30,000 francs: Becker, *Briefwechsel*, 2: 309 and 669 n.

160 Terms of the contract: Becker, *Briefwechsel*, 2: 664–68, with subsequent alterations on pp. 673–75.

161 "but nobody believes it but Duponchel": Becker, *Briefwechsel*, 2: 503–4.

161 Meyerbeer received 24,000 francs from Schlesinger: Becker, *Briefwechsel*, 2: 679.

162 "pretty, lively trifles": Trollope, *Paris and the Parisians*, 145.

162 "M. Scribe's words are there": A. de Santeul in *L'Époque ou les soirées européennes*, February 1836, cited in Marie-Hélene Coudroy, *La critique parisienne des "grands opéras" de Meyerbeer*. Studien zur französischen Oper des 19. Jahrhunderts (Saarbrücken: Musik-Edition Lucie Galland, 1988), 116.

163 Meyerbeer's additional verses: Becker, *Briefwechsel*, 2: 415.

163 "I wanted to play him all five acts": Becker, *Briefwechsel*, 2: 461.

163 "Everybody knew that the destiny of the opera": Becker, *Briefwechsel*, 2: 472.

163 "Until now there has been no trace": Becker, *Briefwechsel*, 2: 474.

164 Nourrit performed as a tenor Don Giovanni: Rudolph Angermüller, *Mozart's Operas*, trans. Stewart Spencer (New York: Rizzoli, 1988), 169.

165 "The very elegance so highly prized": Chorley, *Music and Manners*, 1: 63.

167 "It can only be said that she has a strong and beautiful voice": Becker, *Briefwechsel*, 2: 222.

167 "She, indeed, was a person to haunt": Chorley, *Music and Manners*, 1: 188.

167 "Ein schlectes hors d'oeuvre": Becker, *Briefwechsel*, 2: 565.

167 "the little Dorus exceeded my expectations": Becker, *Briefwechsel*, 2: 408.

167 Expiration and renewal of Dorus' contract: Louis Quicherat, *Adolphe Nourrit; sa vie, son talent, son caractere, sa correspondance* (Paris: Hachette, 1867), 1: 209, citing *Revue de Paris*, March 1866, p. 55.

168 Suspicion of anti-Semitism in the case of Halévy: Becker, *Briefwechsel*, 2: 459.

168 "Taglioni has returned": Letellier, *The Diaries of Giacomo Meyerbeer*, 1: 465.

169 "Never will we know the true cost": De Boigne, *Petits mémoires*, 12.

169 Véron describes the rehearsal process: Véron, *Mémoires*, repr. in *L'Opéra de Paris*, 181–82.

170 Meyerbeer's complaints: Letellier, *The Diaries of Giacomo Meyerbeer*, 1: 465.

170 Meyerbeer presides at February 11 rehearsal: Letellier, *The Diaries of Giacomo Meyerbeer*, 1: 473.

170 "In the greatest necessity also the following cuts": Becker, *Briefwechsel*, 2: 487.

170 "The one piece which up until now has had the greatest effect": Becker, *Briefwechsel*, 2: 505.

170 On Nourrit's role in the act 4 duet, see the note in Becker, *Briefwechsel*, 2: 676.

170 "new scene of delirious love": Becker, *Briefwechsel*, 2: 414.

170 "Nourrit, who has exerted the greatest possible influence": Becker, *Briefwechsel*, 2: 477.

171 "fatal history with Nourrit": Becker, *Briefwechsel*, 2: 478.

171 "Finally Nourrit's dissatisfaction": Becker, *Briefwechsel*, 2: 484–85.

171 "Nourrit is tormenting me": Becker, *Briefwechsel*, 2: 488–89.

171 "We no longer speak": Becker, *Briefwechsel*, 2: 488–89.

171 "Tired with war": Becker, *Briefwechsel*, 2: 491–92.

171 "Decorations and costumes are so poor": Becker, *Briefwechsel*, 2: 506.

171 "The painters . . . have done the exact opposite": Becker, *Briefwechsel*, 2: 478.

171 Budgets for sets: Catherine Join-Diéterle, *Les décors de scène de l'Opéra de Paris à l'Époque romantique* (Paris: Picard, 1988), 281.

171 "Although I would not claim": Becker, *Briefwechsel*, 2: 473–74.

171 "Duponchel has been named director": Becker, *Briefwechsel*, 2: 476.

172 "I now truly think what I did not want": Becker, *Briefwechsel*, 2: 480.

172 "So I must now offer to the ineptitude of the machinists": Becker, *Briefwechsel*, 2: 501–2.

173 "Our next-to-last rehearsal": Becker, *Briefwechsel*, 2: 508–9.

174 Meyerbeer says *Actéon* has exactly the same plot as act 2 of *Les Huguenots*: Becker, *Briefwechsel*, 2: 484.

174 Late arrival of royal party: Jacques Gabriel Prod'homme, "Die Hugenotten-Première," *Die Musik* 3: 1 (1903–4), 187–200 at 190, citing *Journal des Débats*, March 2.

175 Henry Chorley described the hall: Chorley, *Music and Manners*, 1: 23–25; see Document 11.

176 "When one has the largest theater": Véron, *Mémoires*, repr. in *L'Opéra de Paris*, 135.

179 "The overture began": Grillparzer, April 22, cited in Becker, *Briefwechsel*, 2: 681.

179 "he carried his activity and care into the minutest details": Chorley, *Music and Manners*, 1: 67, quoting *Revue des deux mondes*.

179 "Costume, attitude, by-play": Chorley, *Music and Manners*, 1: 67.

179 "One evening he was distracted": De Boigne, *Petits mémoires*, 147.

180 "will be sung everywhere": Joseph Mainzer in *Le monde dramatique* 2 (1825), 249.

180 "Nourrit delivered it with a ravishing suavity": Quicherat, *Adolphe Nourrit* 1: 201.

180 "One remembers the clarity of his diction": Quicherat, 1: 202.

181 Other reminiscences noted: *Le Charivari*, March 15, cited in Coudroy, *La critique parisienne*, 161.

183 "The fault of the first act is in the book": Grillparzer, April 29, cited in Becker, *Briefwechsel*, 2: 682.

183 Planche in *La Chronique de Paris*, March 6, p. 263.

183 "In the first act, the Orgy": Becker, *Briefwechsel*, 2: 510.

183 "Imagine that you are setting foot": Véron, *Mémoires*, repr. in *L'Opéra de Paris*, 221–22.

184 "what she always is, correct": *La Chronique de Paris*, March 6, p. 262.

184 "This role was the occasion of a complete triumph": *Le Temps*, March 8, cited in Coudroy, *La critique parisienne*, 186.

184 "The second act opens with a grand air": Quicherat, *Adolphe Nourrit*, 1: 202.

185 "By a false calculation of the painters": Becker, *Briefwechsel*, 2: 688.

185 "foot, or we don't know what": *L'Entr'acte*, March 5, 1836, unpaginated.

186 "The second [act], though I had counted on it": Becker, *Briefwechsel*, 2: 510.

186 "In the second [act] some good music": Becker, *Briefwechsel*, 2: 682.

187 "Rataplan" repeated: *Allgemeine musikalische Zeitung*, March 9, 1836, col. 159; see Document 7.

188 "In Paris it [the barque] has a good scenic effect": Becker, *Briefwechsel*, 2: 689.

188 "The third [act], where I was worried": Becker, *Briefwechsel*, 2: 510.

188 Meyerbeer on later performances: letters of March 4 and 6, Becker, *Briefwechsel*, 2: 510–12.

188 "The music of the opera begins with a duet": Becker, *Briefwechsel*, 2: 682.

189 "The third act begins with a very good chorus": Becker, *Briefwechsel*, 2: 682–83.

189 Berlioz fascinated by effects: *Revue et gazette musicale de Paris*, March 6, 1836, cited in Coudroy, *La critique parisienne*, 170.

190 Nourrit acted it with almost no gesture, Falcon with many: *Courrier des Théâtres*, March 2, 1836, p. 2.

190 "Never before has music had so moving a power": *L'Artiste*, undated, 1836, cited in Coudroy, *La critique parisienne*, 148.

191 "The accent of the instrument": cited in Coudroy, *La critique parisienne*, 158.

192 "yesterday's general rehearsal of acts 4 and 5": Becker, *Briefwechsel*, 2: 503.

192 "The fourth act made a great effect": Becker, *Briefwechsel*, 2: 508.

192 "In the fifth [act], the trio—which amounted to little": Becker, *Briefwechsel*, 2: 510.

192 "Nourrit, Levasseur, and Falcon were called for at the end": *Allgemeine musikalische Zeitung*, March 9, 1836, col. 160; see Document 7.

193 "musical encyclopedia," "The author," "Several attentive listenings": *Revue et gazette musicale de Paris*, March 6, 1836, p. 74.

194 "As the public listens to *Les Huguenots*": "J. L." in *Le Ménestrel*, March 6, 1836, unpaginated.

194 "Weber and Beethoven supplied the model": "L. D." in *Le national*, March 15, cited in Coudroy, *La critique parisienne*, 153.

194 "is not remarkable as a work of verve": "J. T." in *La Quotidienne*, March 2, 1836, unpaginated.

194 "the author's name ends in -*er*": Hippolyte Prévost, *Revue du Théâtre*, 172ᵉ livraison, p. 516.

194 "M. Scribe has made every effort": *L'Artiste,* 1836, p. 74.

194 what is the cream of society doing at the Pré aux Clercs: *Journal des débats,* March 7, 1836.

194 "All of Meyerbeer's talent": Joseph Mainzer in *Le monde dramatique* 2 (1835), 249; see Document 4.

194 "Every number is a beautiful and interesting piece": Mainzer in *Le monde dramatique* 2 (1835), 250; see Document 4.

194 "It is not allowed to announce a tableau": Quicherat, *Adolphe Nourrit,* 1: 199.

195 "The first three acts encountered that alternation": cited in Coudroy, *La critique parisienne,* 151.

195 Success of acts 4 and 5, reported in *L'Artiste:* cited in Coudroy, *La critique parisienne,* 149.

195 "The libretto has the failing": Grillparzer, April 22, cited in Becker, *Briefwechsel,* 2: 681–82.

195 "sang more as a careful professional": *La Chronique de Paris,* March 6, p. 263.

195 "either because this role has certain things": *Le Temps,* March 8, cited in Coudroy, *La critique parisienne,* 183.

195 "cold actor": *Le Corsaire,* March 7, cited in Coudroy, *La critique parisienne,* 185.

195 "Levasseur is an excellent performer": Grillparzer, April 28, cited in Becker, *Briefwechsel,* 2: 683.

195 "The crown of all": Grillparzer, April 28, cited in Becker, *Briefwechsel,* 2: 683.

195 "a bit less pretense in her acting equipment": *Courrier des Théâtres,* March 3, p. 4.

195 "I liked Dorus less today": Grillparzer, April 29, cited in Becker, *Briefwechsel,* 2: 683.

195 Correct, vigilant, monotonous: Planche, *La Chronique de Paris,* March 6, p. 262.

196 "A young girl, Maria Flécheux": De Boigne, *Petits mémoires,* 123.

196 "Serda alone is musical": Grillparzer, April 29, cited in Becker, *Briefwechsel,* 2: 683.

196 "The men, who are called dramatic singers": Grillparzer, April 22, cited in Becker, *Briefwechsel,* 2: 682.

196 "If the settings are faultless": De Forster, *Quinze ans à Paris,* 213–25.

197 "The grand choruses placed at the beginning": Joseph Mainzer in *Le monde dramatique* 2 (1825), 250–51.

197 "Poetry has its licenses": cited in Coudroy, *La critique parisienne,* 120; a similar fury exhibited in *La Gazette de France, Feuilleton,* March 3.

197 Five hours of exhilaration: *La Quotidienne,* March 2.

198 "France will be more eager to see than to hear": *La Chronique de Paris,* March 2, p. 252.

198 Meyerbeer writes to Minna after the second performance: Becker, *Briefwechsel,* 2: 510–11.

198 "Do not think, however, despite the huge unanimous applause": Becker, *Briefwechsel,* 2: 511–12.

198 "It is above all at the Opéra": from an article entitled "The plays and the authors in 1836," *Le monde dramatique* 3 (1836), 21–22.

Chapter 4: Wagner, *Das Rheingold*

228 Epigraph: Robert Hartford, ed. *Bayreuth: The Early Years. An Account of the Early Decades of the Wagner Festival as Seen by Celebrated Visitors and Participants* (Cambridge: Cambridge University Press, 1980), 55.

231 Wagner's review of *Les Huguenots:* Richard Wagner, *Sämtliche Schriften und Dichtungen,* 5th ed. (Leipzig: Breitkopf & Hartel, 1911), 12: 22–28.

235 Wagner's initial description of his festival: trans. in Hartford, *Bayreuth: The Early Years,* 20.

236 "But where will such a prince be found?": cited in Hartford, *Bayreuth: The Early Years,* 21.

237 Cost of Garnier's opera house: Frederic Spotts, *Bayreuth: A History of the Wagner Festival* (New Haven: Yale University Press, 1994), 51.

238 "Of all the dull towns": Joseph Bennett, *Letters from Bayreuth: Descriptive and Critical of Wagner's "Der Ring des Nibelungen"* (London: Novello, Ewer & Co., 1877), 23.

239 "It only required seats which were adapted": Charles Villiers Stanford, *Interludes: Records and Reflections* (London: J. Murray, 1922), 139.

240 "a college lecture-hall on a large scale": Bennett, *Letters from Bayreuth*, 29.

241 Hassard describes the lighting effects: John R. G. Hassard, *Richard Wagner at Bayreuth. The Ring of the Nibelungs — A Description of the First Performance in August 1876 (Reprinted from the* New York Tribune) (New York: Francis Hart & Co., 1877), 12–13.

243 "I desired none but tall and imposing figures": Wagner, *Ein Rückblick*, trans. William Ashton Ellis, *Richard Wagner's Prose Works* (1892–1899) (New York: Broude, 1966), 6: 106.

245 "then a yellow-haired Viking": Stanford, *Interludes*, 142.

246 "Hans Richter, who, with his sandy beard": Albert Lavignac, *The Music Dramas of Richard Wagner and His Festival Theatre in Bayreuth*, trans. Esther Singleton (New York: Dodd, Mead, 1902), 4.

246 Richter's unsteady tempos: Heinrich Porges, *Wagner Rehearsing the* Ring. *An Eyewitness Account of the Stage Rehearsals of the First Bayreuth Festival*, trans. Robert L. Jacobs (Cambridge: Cambridge University Press, 1983), vii.

247 Emil Naumann described the sound: Emil Naumann, *Musikdrama oder Oper? Eine Beleuchtung der Bayreuther Bühnenfestspiele* (Berlin: Robert Oppenheim, 1876; reprint of reports in *Neue Zeitung*), 12–13.

247 "The stage rehearsals of the *Ring* brought home the imperative need": Porges, *Wagner Rehearsing*, 12.

248 "Wagner declared that the orchestra should support the singer": Porges, *Wagner Rehearsing*, 13.

248 "Anyone who knows the challenges": Hermann Kretzschmar, *Musikalisches Wochenblatt* 7 (1876), 444.

248 "Allow me today to have a look": Wilhelm Marr, "Bayreuther Festtagebuch," in *Die Gartenlaube* (1876), repr. Susanna Grossmann-Vendrey, *Bayreuth in der deutschen Presse: Beitrage zur Rezeptionsgeschichte Richard Wagners und seiner Festspiele* (Regensburg: Bosse, 1977–83). Vol. 1: *Die Grundsteinlegung und die ersten Festspiele (1872–1876)*, 53.

249 "just what I wanted": Spotts, *Bayreuth*, 61, citing Glasenapp, *Das Leben*, 5: 199.

250 "Suddenly an unusual degree of life": Hartford, *Bayreuth: The Early Years*, 47.

251 "complain of the almost unbearable drafts": Richard Fricke, *Wagner in Rehearsal: The Diaries of Richard Fricke, 1875–1876*, trans. George R. Fricke, ed. James Deaville with Evan Baker, Franz Liszt Studies Series, 7 (Stuyvesant, N.Y.: Pendragon, 1998), 68.

251 "R. very sad afterward": *Cosima Wagner's Diaries*, ed. Martin Gregor-Dellin and Dietrich Mack, trans. Geoffrey Skelton (New York: Harcourt Brace Jovanovich, 1977), 1: 917.

251 "During rehearsals Wagner sat on the stage": Hartford, *Bayreuth: The Early Years*, 49.

251 Doepler reports an event during rehearsals: Peter Cook, *A Memoir of Bayreuth: 1876 — C. E. Doepler* (London: Staples Printers St. Albans, Ltd., 1979).

252 "An army of prompters arose": Hartford, *Bayreuth: The Early Years*, 49.

252 "The singers on the stage saw almost nothing": Hartford, *Bayreuth: The Early Years*, 49.

252 "The piano rehearsals ended with the wholesale dismissal": *Cosima Wagner's Diaries*, 1: 915.

252 "It is absolutely impossible to work with Herr Brandt": Cook, *A Memoir of Bayreuth*, 37.

252 "I am the rager": Cook, *A Memoir of Bayreuth*, 38.

253 "They are discouraged": Fricke, *Wagner in Rehearsal*, 67.

253 "I have no stage director": cited in Fricke, *Wagner in Rehearsal*, 24.

253 Herr Schnappauf: Fricke, *Wagner in Rehearsal*, 71.

254 "Coldly objective," "false pathos": Porges, *Wagner Rehearsing*, 3–4.

254 "Although her movements and gestures": Porges, *Wagner Rehearsing*, 14–15.

254 "Fricka's cries for help": Porges, *Wagner Rehearsing*, 16.

254 "should make a point of accompanying": Porges, *Wagner Rehearsing*, 21.

254 "all the gods must make involuntary movements": Porges, *Wagner Rehearsing*, 22.

254 "Those not actually participating": Porges, *Wagner Rehearsing*, 25.

254 "The actors, though differing in degrees of merit": Hassard, *Richard Wagner at Bayreuth*, 13.

254 "He constantly instructed the singers": Cook, *A Memoir of Bayreuth*, 34.

254 "'Ah,' exclaimed one of the artists": Hassard, *Richard Wagner at Bayreuth*, 14.

255 "latest discoveries of pre-historic times": Cook, *A Memoir of Bayreuth*, 23.

255 "I should like everything to be simpler": *Cosima Wagner's Diaries*, 1: 915.

256 "I saw Cosima": Hartford, *Bayreuth: The Early Years*, 86.

256 "God in Heaven, what could you have achieved": Cook, *A Memoir of Bayreuth*, 43.

256 "There was the free 'union' at Angermanns": Cook, *A Memoir of Bayreuth*, 40.

256 "My lunches at Schierbaum's": Fricke, *Wagner in Rehearsal*, 61.

256 "Mottl delights us in an extremely amusing way": Cook, *A Memoir of Bayreuth*, 38.

256 "Combined with these was a pas de deux": Cook, *A Memoir of Bayreuth*, 39.

256 "I danced with the ballet-master Fricke": Hartford, *Bayreuth: The Early Years*, 50.

257 "There are about one hundred and twenty-five in the orchestra": Hartford, *Bayreuth: The Early Years*, 63.

257 "Bayreuth is uncommonly alert": Bennett, *Letters from Bayreuth*, 25.

258 The *Manchester Guardian* on commercialization: Hartford, *Bayreuth: The Early Years*, 95.

258 "The little town offers, it is true": Hartford, *Bayreuth: The Early Years*, 53.

258 "We are the Nibelungs": Martin Plüddemann, *Die Bühnenfestspiele in Bayreuth, ihre Gegner und ihre Zukunft* (Colberg: C. Jancke, 1877), 17.

258 "The most elegant of ladies": Hartford, *Bayreuth: The Early Years*, 86.

258 "People from all over the world came," "What do you think of Wagner?": Karl Marx, *The Letters of Karl Marx*, selected and ed. Saul Padover (Englewood Cliffs, N.J.: Prentice-Hall, 1979), 310, 312.

259 "I met many people in Bayreuth": Plüddemann, *Die Bühnenfestspiele*, 16–17.

259 "What has Germany to do with my work": Jean Mistler, *A Bayreuth avec Richard Wagner* (N.p.: Libraire Hachette, [1960]), 88; Spotts, *Bayreuth*, 68, citing Glasenapp, *Das Leben*, 5: 286.

259 "Pedro," "Emperor": Spotts, *Bayreuth*, 66.

259 Liszt slept through much of the music: Stanford, *Interludes*, 144.

259 Mrs. Schirmer, Dr. Damrosch: Hassard, *Richard Wagner at Bayreuth*, 5.

259 "To judge from their clothes": Bennett, *Letters from Bayreuth*, 26.

260 "Why, then, is it": Bennett, *Letters from Bayreuth*, 26.

260 "For a distinguished prince": Grossmann-Vendrey, *Bayreuth in der deutschen Presse*, 152–53.

260 "The evil consequences were only too evident": *Ein Rückblick auf die Bühnenfestspiele des Jahres 1876*, trans. Ellis, *Richard Wagner's Prose Works*, 6: 101.

260 Wagner's posted notes to the performers: Carl Friedrich Glasenapp, *Das Leben Richard Wagners* (Leipzig: Breitkopf und Hartel, 1894–1911), trans. William Ashton Ellis as *Life of Richard Wagner* (London: K. Paul, Trench, Trubner, 1900–8), 5: 287.

261 "Every performance is to begin": letter of October 1, 1874, Spotts, *Bayreuth*, 52.

261 "Had it rained hard even once": *Die Gegenwart* 10 (1876), repr. Grossman-Vendrey, *Bayreuth in der deutschen Presse*, 147.

261 "At three o'clock we make our way": Hartford, *Bayreuth: The Early Years*, 54.

262 "The long *Fürstenloge*": Hassard, *Richard Wagner at Bayreuth*, 17.

263 "Now the celebrated prelude to *Rheingold*": Hartford, *Bayreuth: The Early Years*, 63; Grieg is describing the dress rehearsal.

263 "The curtain parted to the sides": Wilhelm Mohr, "Briefe eines baireuther Patronatsherr," in *Kölnischer Zeitung*, 1876, repr. Grossmann-Vendrey, *Bayreuth in der deutschen Presse*, 89–90.

263 "The flat picture let down at the back": Hassard, *Richard Wagner at Bayreuth*, 12–13.

264 "Swimming machine dubious": *Cosima Wagner's Diaries*, 1: 908.

265 "These music directors are the three dancers": Fricke, *Wagner in Rehearsal*, 53–54.

265 "Nobody can expect me to do that": Fricke, *Wagner in Rehearsal*, 64.

265 Lilli Lehmann on the swimming machines: Hartford, *Bayreuth: The Early Years*, 49.

265 "We looked into the obscure depths": Hassard, *Richard Wagner at Bayreuth*, 18–19; see Document 13.

266 "The lighting of the water was so dim": Hartford, *Bayreuth: The Early Years*, 86.

266 Hey on the Rhinemaidens' voices: Julius Hey, *Richard Wagner als Vortragsmeister, 1864–1876, Erinnerungen von Julius Hey,* ed. Hans Hey (Leipzig: Breitkopf & Härtel, 1911), 154–55.

267 On the "Rheingold-Regulator": Carl-Friederich Baumann, *Bühnentechnik im Festspielhaus Bayreuth* (Munich: Prestel-Verlag, 1980), 231.

267 "The movements and disappearance of Alberich": Fricke, *Wagner in Rehearsal,* 68.

267 "certain rough dryness of tone": Porges, *Wagner Rehearsing,* 9.

267 "Herr Hill performs his Alberich": Kretzschmar, "Bayreuther Briefe," *Musikalisches Wochenblatt* 7 (1876): 463; see Document 16.

268 "the individual feeling of the performer must be restrained": Porges, *Wagner Rehearsing,* 11.

268 A stagehand prematurely raised the backdrop: *Cosima Wagner's Diaries,* 1: 918; Fricke, *Wagner in Rehearsal,* 96 n. 279.

268 "It was the first theatre to use steam": Stanford, *Interludes,* 140.

268 "A scene is never raised or lowered": Hassard, *Richard Wagner at Bayreuth,* 13; see Document 13.

268 "The foreground was a flowery field": Hassard, *Richard Wagner at Bayreuth,* 20–21; see Document 13.

268 "When the motive is depicting an actual event": Porges, *Wagner Rehearsing,* 12.

268 "The Wagnerian experts explain": Mohr, "Briefe eines baireuther Patronatsherr," repr. Grossmann-Vendrey, *Bayreuth in der deutschen Presse,* 90.

269 "This Loge is a singular fellow": Mohr, "Briefe eines baireuther Patronatsherr," repr. Grossmann-Vendrey, *Bayreuth in der deutschen Presse,* 91.

269 Applause for Vogl and his melody: Paul Lindau, in the Breslau *Schlesische Presse,* repr. Grossmann-Vendrey, *Bayreuth in der deutschen Presse,* 66.

269 "at once a gray mist settled": Hassard, *Richard Wagner at Bayreuth,* 22; see Document 13.

269 "The gods immediately begin to lose their glowing youthful splendor": Porges, *Wagner Rehearsing,* 26.

269 "A thick vapor issued from the opening": Hassard, *Richard Wagner at Bayreuth,* 22; see Document 13.

271 "Puppet-theater," "commonplace theatrical devices": Hassard, *Richard Wagner at Bayreuth,* 23.

271 Fricke felt that these two transformations (along with the rainbow bridge) were the worst disasters in the *Ring*: Fricke, *Wagner in Rehearsal,* 99.

271 "Cloud and mist covered the stage once more": Hassard, *Richard Wagner at Bayreuth,* 23; see Document 13.

271 Wotan drops the ring: Mistler, *A Bayreuth,* 89; *Cosima Wagner's Diaries,* 1: 918.

271 Fricke assembles the Nibelung's hoard: Richard Fricke, *Wagner in Rehearsal,* 69.

271 "In the foreground Wotan struggling": Porges, *Wagner Rehearsing,* 36.

272 "The scene grew dark again": Hassard, *Richard Wagner at Bayreuth,* 24; see Document 13.

272 "Herr Betz . . . knows how": *Musikalisches Wochenblatt* 7 (1876), 463; see Document 16.

272 "If the excellent Betz from Berlin": Naumann, *Musikdrama oder Oper?* 24.

273 "rainbow, over which the gods proceed to Valhalla": Hartford, *Bayreuth: The Early Years,* 84.

273 "Though I can tell the audience gets tired": Hartford, *Bayreuth: The Early Years,* 67.

274 "When the curtain closed again": *Musikalisches Wochenblatt* 7 (1876), 464; see Document 16.

274 "After the opera was over": Fricke, *Wagner in Rehearsal,* 96.

274 "it is no opera at all": August 19, 1876, cited in Spotts, *Bayreuth,* 72.

274 "The highest and liveliest praise": Naumann, *Musikdrama oder Oper?* 24–25.

274 "The theatre is hot": Hartford, *Bayreuth, The Early Years,* 66.

274 "If, despite the sunken orchestra": Naumann, *Musikdrama oder Oper?* 13.

275 "The one drawback associated with all this excellence": Bennett, *Letters from Bayreuth,* 43, 44.

275 "It was an added reflection yesterday": *Musikalisches Wochenblatt* 7 (1876), 444; see Document 16.

275 "Male singers in Germany as a general thing": Hassard, *Richard Wagner at Bayreuth,* 27.

275 "Their ranks contained some great": Stanford, *Interludes,* 142.

275 *Grandezza,* "almost perfect": Kretzschmar, "Bayreuther Briefe," *Musikalisches Wochenblatt* 7 (1876), 464; see Document 16.

276 "We have seen in astonishment": Hartford, *Bayreuth: The Early Years,* 84.

276 "Yesterday the performance of *Rheingold* took place": Hartford, *Bayreuth: The Early Years,* 52.

276 "We have seen there, in everything that is technical": Grossmann-Vendrey, *Bayreuth in der deutschen Presse,* 131.

277 "It would be an interesting assignment": "Gods, Heroes, and Wagner. A Letter post festum," *Die Gartenlaube,* 1876, repr. Grossmann-Vendrey, *Bayreuth in der deutschen Presse,* 63; see Document 17.

277 Grieg reports slow scene changes: Hartford, *Bayreuth: The Early Years,* 67.

277 "Hagen, who should throw himself as if crazed": Hartford, *Bayreuth: The Early Years,* 85.

277 "The dragon with a child working its jaws": Hartford, *Bayreuth: The Early Years,* 86.

277 "The old Emperor poured balm": Fricke, *Wagner in Rehearsal,* 96.

277 "attitude of conscious superiority": Stanford, *Interludes,* 143.

277 "You have seen what we can do": Cook, *A Memoir of Bayreuth,* 50.

277 "It has been Wagner's decisive achievement": Porges, *Wagner Rehearsing,* 4.

277 "acts of music made visible": Spotts, *Bayreuth,* 75.

278 Cost and deficit: Erich Ebermayer, *Magisches Bayreuth: Legende und Wirklichkeit* (Stuttgart: Steingrüben-Verlag, 1951), 9; Spotts, *Bayreuth,* 8.

278 Bayreuth sets in Prague: Spotts, *Bayreuth,* 78.

278 "Returning to my lodging": Hartford, *Bayreuth: The Early Years,* 63.

278 "It is all very fine": Hartford, *Bayreuth: The Early Years,* 86.

Chapter 5: Verdi, *Otello*
Box

320 Lighting of the Gas Lamps: J. Hardmeyer, *Milan,* from *Illustrated Europe* guidebooks, nos. 15 & 16 (Zürich: Orel Füssli, 1884), 31–32.

Text

314 Epigraph: from *Le Matin,* as reported in *Otello. Dramma lirico in quattro atti. Versi di Arrigo Boito. Musica di Giuseppe Verdi. Giudizî della stampa italiana e straniera.* Supplemento straordinario della Gazzetta Musicale di Milano, *N. S.* (Milan: Ricordi, 1887), hereafter *Giudizi,* 48.

317 "You, of all people": Julian Budden, *The Operas of Verdi, rev. ed.* (New York: Oxford University Press, 1992), 3: 299, citing Alessandro Luzio, *Profili biografici e bozzetti storici* (Milan: L. F. Cogliati, 1927–28), 2: 541–42.

318 "*Othello* is perhaps the last work": Busoni, "Verdi's 'Othello,'" *Neue Zeitschrift für Musik* 54 (1887), 125.

325 Verdi's proposed arrangements with Ricordi: Hans Busch, *Verdi's* Otello *and* Simon Boccanegra *(revised version) in Letters and Documents* (Oxford: Clarendon, 1988), 1: 241–42.

326 Verdi's payments for *Otello:* Busch, *Verdi's* Otello, 1: 213.

326 "this cursed thirty-two-line music-paper": Franca Cella and Pierluigi Petrobelli, eds., *Giuseppe Verdi–Giulio Ricordi: Corrispondenza e immagini 1881–1890* (Milan: Edizioni del Teatro alla Scala, 1982), 49.

326 "I am jealously taking care of everything": Cella and Petrobelli, *Giuseppe Verdi–Giulio Ricordi,* 49.

328 "The most perfect Desdemona": Franco Abbiati, *Giuseppe Verdi* (Milan: Ricordi, 1959), 4: 337, trans. Martin Chusid, "Verdi's Own Words: His Thoughts on Performance, with Special Reference to *Don Carlos, Otello,* and *Falstaff,*" in William Weaver and Martin Chusid, *The Verdi Companion* (New York: W. W. Norton, 1979), 162.

328 "He made me work twice a day": Mario Medici and Marcello Conati, eds., *Carteggio Verdi-Boito* (Parma: Istituto di studi verdiani, 1978), 2: 354.

329 "The *canzone del salice* is causing the composer": letter of September 2, 1886, Busch, *Verdi's Otello*, 1: 234, and of October 29, 1886, 1: 251.

329 "Her singing is easier": Cella and Petrobelli, *Giuseppe Verdi–Giulio Ricordi*, 58.

329 Toscanini fined for misbehavior: Giuseppe Barigazzi, *La Scala racconta* (Milan: Rizzoli, 1994), 252; Harvey Sachs, *Toscanini* (N.p.: Orion, 1978, repr. 1995), 26.

330 "I'm frightened about the tenor part": Abbiati, *Giuseppe Verdi*, 4:173–74, in James A. Hepokoski, *Giuseppe Verdi: Otello*, Cambridge Opera Handbooks (Cambridge: Cambridge University Press, 1987), 97.

330 "You do know the end of the opera": Medici and Conati, *Carteggio Verdi-Boito*, 1: 99, trans. Busch, *Verdi's Otello*, 1: 200.

331 "I ask you warmly to have Tamagno study": Giuseppe Morazzoni and Giulio Maria Ciampelli, *Verdi: letter inedite: le opere verdiani al Teatro alla Scala (1839–1929)* (Milan, 1929), Hepokoski, *Giuseppe Verdi: Otello*, 98.

331 "Even when he has learned the music well": Verdi to Ricordi, November 4, 1886; Busch, *Verdi's Otello*, 1: 256.

331 "After he has ascertained": letter of January 22, 1886, Busch, *Verdi's* Otello, 1: 201.

331 "Maurel, once he has studied the music": Abbiati, *Giuseppe Verdi*, 4: 298, Busch, *Verdi's* Otello, 1: 256.

331 "Jago cannot be performed": Abbiati, *Giuseppe Verdi*, 4: 299, Busch, *Verdi's* Otello, 1: 161–62.

331 "not beautiful in timbre": Gino Monaldi, *Cantanti celebri del secolo XIX* (Rome: Nuova Antologia, [1929]), 252.

333 Numbers of persons in chorus: Cella and Petrobelli, *Giuseppe Verdi–Giulio Ricordi*, 50.

333 Probable changes in Willow Song: see Hepokoski, *Giuseppe Verdi: Otello*, 71–75.

333 "Oh! if only I could rest a little": Raffaello De Rensis, *Franco Faccio e Verdi* (Milan: Fratelli Treves, 1934), 233.

333 "If the *Flora* barely, barely has a fair success": Busch, *Verdi's* Otello, 1: 288.

335 "Fervent, passionate embrace": Ugo Pesci in *Verdi e l'Otello,* Numero unico pubblicato dalla *Illustrazione italiana* (Milan: Fratelli Treves, 1887), pp. 35–38, trans. Richard Stokes as "Rehearsals for Otello" in *Encounters with Verdi,* ed. Marcello Conati (Ithaca, N.Y.: Cornell University Press, 1984), 185.

335 "Exclaiming 'Oh! Gloria!' he takes a step forwards": Busch, *Verdi's* Otello, 2: 625–27.

336 "'Una vela! Una vela!', exclaim those upstage": Busch, *Verdi's* Otello, 2: 493.

336 "At La Scala itself not everything was good": letter of April 29, 1887, Cella and Petrobelli, *Giuseppe Verdi–Giulio Ricordi,* 60; Busch, *Verdi's* Otello, 1: 304.

337 On Verdi and pitch: Cella and Petrobelli, *Giuseppe Verdi–Giulio Ricordi,* 70; Busch *Verdi's* Otello, 2: 770.

338 Press absent at dress rehearsal: *Le Matin,* in *Giudizi,* 53.

338 Laurel crown: *Giudizi,* 64.

338 "On 5 February 1887, the Piazza della Scala": cited in Busch, *Verdi's* Otello, 2: 718.

340 "Take the boxes for spectators away": Verdi to Ricordi, 10 July 1871, in Giuseppe Verdi, *I copialettere di Giuseppe Verdi,* ed. Gaetano Cesari and Alessandro Luzio (Milan: S. Ceretti, 1913), 264–65.

340 "From pit to dome, the immense auditorium": cited in Busch, *Verdi's* Otello, 2: 718.

341 On the stage lighting: Luigi Lorenzo Secchi, *1778–1978, il Teatro alla Scala: architettura, tradizione, società* ([Milan]: Electa, [1977]), 136–37.

342 On the "macchina del tuono": Cella and Petrobelli, *Giuseppe Verdi–Giulio Ricordi,* 51.

342 "The scenic decoration is stupendous, perfect": *Il Capitan Fracasso* (Roma), repr. *Giudizi,* 40.

342 "The mise-en-scène, although upon the whole intelligent": Busch, *Verdi's* Otello, 2: 704.

343 "The sets did not convince me": letter to Giulio Ricordi, January 1, 1889; Busch, *Verdi's* Otello, 1: 350–51.

344 "The producer must, above all, explain": Busch, *Verdi's* Otello, 2: 188.

344 "All the choristers have costumes": *Il Capitan Fracasso* (Roma), repr. *Giudizi*, 40.

344 "If the public should say": Cella and Petrobelli, *Giuseppe Verdi–Giulio Ricordi*, 54.

345 "I've advised our Edel to study": Medici and Conati, *Carteggio Verdi-Boito*, 1: 107.

345 "Alfredo Edel has finished his important work": Medici and Conati, *Carteggio Verdi-Boito*, 2: 354.

345 "The protagonist of the drama at his first appearance": *Il Secolo, Giudizi*, 14.

346 "an intelligent chorister": Busch, *Verdi's Otello*, 2: 503.

346 "A repetition is demanded": *La Lombardia, Giudizi* 7; the repetition is mentioned by several critics.

346 "Great attention to the Brindisi": *La Lombardia, Giudizi* 7.

346 "Then there is that truly paradisiacal final duet": *Giudizi*, 11.

348 "Maurel sang this long blasphemy": *Le Matin, Giudizi*, 50.

348 "These sing a very sweet mandolinata": *Il Capitan Fracasso* (Roma), repr. *Giudizi*, 42.

348 "The pretty mandolinata in the second act": Busch, *Verdi's Otello*, 2: 704.

348 "this is where the ballet will come": *Le Matin, Giudizi*, 50.

350 "The quartet, which is very beautiful": Filippo Filippi, *Giudizi*, 5–6.

350 "The quartet can be, indeed should be": *Giudizi*, 11.

350 "That of *Otello* is short": *Giudizi*, 37.

350 "a fervent, inspired ending": Filippo Filippi, Busch, *Verdi's Otello*, 2: 685.

350 "Anyone who has not heard the 'dream' from *Otello*": Monaldi, *Cantanti*, 252.

350 "Ovations. A call for the interpreters": *Giudizi*, 8.

350 Verdi's appearances at the end of the act: *Giudizi*, 20, 36, 39.

350 "difficult": *Corriere della sera, Giudizi*, 11.

352 Ten real parts: *Giudizi*, 12, 51, 54; eleven parts: *Giudizi* 39.

352 "This piece, completely new in conception": *Giudizi*, 12.

353 "The third act was not perhaps well enough understood": *Giudizi*, 43.

353 "The third act, which is not easy": *Giudizi*, 6.

353 "Verdi appears several times": *Il Capitan Fracasso* (Roma), repr. *Giudizi*, 40.

353 Insistent coughing: *Corriere della sera, Giudizi*, 12.

353 "The *Romance du Saule* is completely original": *Giudizi*, 54.

353 "will have calmed the anguish": *Giudizi*, 28.

353 "All the details of such a piece": *Giudizi*, 9.

354 "I heard someone weeping": *Le Progrès Artistique, Giudizi*, 54.

355 Repetition of Ave Maria: *Giudizi*, 9.

355 "precisely on the first note of the solo": Busch, *Verdi's Otello*, 2: 606–11.

355 "Once more the solo for the double basses": Abbiati, *Giuseppe Verdi*, 4: 366, Chusid, "Verdi's Own Words," 163.

356 "The encore nuisance": Busch, *Verdi's Otello*, 2: 702.

356 "the death of the Moor is among Verdi's most beautiful deaths": *Giudizi*, 13.

356 "The stalls and the five tiers of boxes": Busch, *Verdi's Otello*, 2: 702.

356 "New ovations from the audience": *Giudizi*, 9–10.

357 "When I heard my name": Blanche Roosevelt, *Verdi: Milan and "Othello"* (London: Ward and Downey, 1887), repr. Busch, *Verdi's Otello*, 2: 729.

357 "Ah, no, dear *Otello*": Barigazzi, *La Scala racconta*, 262.

357 "For now, the whole impression of the audience": *Giudizi*, 24.

357 "With every wish to treat Madame Pantaleoni's Desdemona": Busch, *Verdi's Otello*, 2: 703.

358 "Madame Pantaleoni is an excellent person": Busch, *Verdi's Otello*, 2: 724.

358 "The singing of Pantaleoni": *Giudizi*, 33.

358 "Signora Pantaleoni was always admirable": *Giudizi*, 6.

358 "Pantaleoni, fine in the whole opera": *Giudizi*, 13.

358 "Of Signor Tamagno's Othello it is possible": Busch, *Verdi's Otello*, 2: 703.

359 "M. Tamagno possesses an admirable tenor voice": Busch, *Verdi's Otello*, 2: 701.

359 "When Tamagno sang": Busch, *Verdi's* Otello, 2: 722.

359 Tamagno had taken away the shadow: *Giudizi*, 76.

359 Tamagno indisposed at premiere: *Il secolo, Giudizi*, 78.

359 "Tamagno gave out some of those notes": *Giudizi*, 13.

359 "There are virtually three parts": Busch, *Verdi's* Otello, 2: 703.

359 "Maurel is bellissimo": *Giudizi*, 32, 33.

359 "Maurel is Jago numero uno": *Giudizi*, 6.

359 "As for Mr Maurel, he is a perfect Jago": Busch, *Verdi's* Otello, 2: 701.

360 "Victor Maurel, the incarnation of natural gifts": Busch, *Verdi's* Otello, 2: 723.

360 On Navarrini: Filippi, *Giudizi*, 6; *Le progrès artistique, Giudizi*, 55.

360 On Paroli: *Corriere della sera, Giudizi*, 13.

360 On Fornari: *Gazetta di Piemonte, Giudizi*, 44.

360 "not important to help or hinder": Busch, *Verdi's* Otello, 2: 724.

360 "The choral forces, for a first performance": *Giudizi*, 13.

360 "Such failures of judgment": Busch, *Verdi's* Otello, 2: 702.

360 "While agreeing not to divide the opera": *Giudizi*, 5.

360 "The recitatives are of a unique beauty": *Giudizi*, 10–11.

360 "Some say that the first act is Wagnerian": *Giudizi*, 45.

360 "Even now there are some": *Giudizi*, 46.

360 "The maestro has made great concessions": *Giudizi*, 46.

360 "To those who want to speak of Wagnerism": *Giudizi*, 54.

360 "We are faced with a veritable *drame lyrique*": *Giudizi*, 49.

360 "Certainly we no longer find in *Otello*": *Giudizi*, 25.

362 "The new opera has in large point disappointed": *Giudizi*, 58.

362 *Ernani* in Siena: *Giudizi*, 68.

362 Details of second performance: *Giudizi*, 74, 75.

362 *Otello Guglielmo: Verdi, studi e memorie, a cura del Sindacato nazionale fascista musicisti, nel XL anniversario della morte* (Rome: Istituto grafico tiberino, 1941), 231.

363 Toscanini fined for misbehavior: Barigazzi, *La Scala racconta*, 262; Sachs, *Toscanini*, 26.

Index

Page numbers in *italics* refer to illustrations.

Mozart, Leopold, 77
Mozart, Wolfgang Amadeus, 65–66, 76
    conducts/directs *Don Giovanni,* 89, 109,
        111
    conducts *Figaro,* 76, 82–83
    Don Giovanni performed in Paris, 142
    as musician, 91
    as musician/co-director of *Figaro,* 76
    musicians and, 106–107, 121–122
    in Prague, 75–78, 81, 111, 123–124
    recitatives, 124, 182
    rehearsals and, 163
    in Vienna, 75, 111
    Wagner conducts works of, 234
    writings for particular voices, 75, 80, 85,
        95, 98, 104–105, 391
    writings for Prague Orchestra, 90
    See also *Don Giovanni* (Mozart)
muette de Portici, La (Auber), 147, 162, 190,
    219
    plot, 148
    sets and staging, 150, 153
    singers, 164
    special effects, 144, *175*
"Musical Joke" serenade (Mozart), 77
musical theater, 135
Muzio Scevola (Handel, Bononcini and
    Ariosti), 8

National Theatre (Nostitz Theatre), Prague,
    69, 72, 73, 81, *81,* 83, 88–89, *89,* 120,
    122
    sets, 118
    stage, 91, 94, 118
    See also *Don Giovanni* (Mozart)
Naumann, Emil, 247, 272
Navarrini, Francesco, 322, 360, 374
Nazi Party (National Socialist Party), 231
Neumann, Angelo, 263, 278
Neumann, Wilhelm, 239
New Haymarket Theatre, London, 7, 47
Nicolini (Nicolo Grimaldi), 35
Niemann, Albert, 275
Niemetschek, Franz Xaver, 75, 77, 85, 87, 90
    on Baglioni, 98
    on Bassi, 97, 105
    biography of Mozart, 123–124
Nietzsche, Friedrich, 235, 238, 251, 260
Nostitz, Count Franz Anton, 68, 69, 72, 81, 91
Nostitz Theatre. *See* National Theatre (Nostitz
    Theatre), Prague

Nourrit, Adolphe, 160, 179, 390
    acting style and talents, 167, 190
    criticism and reviews, 195, 196, 213, 214,
        217, 219
    curtain calls, 192, 198, 212, 215
    Meyerbeer and, 170–171, 209
    as Raoul in *Les Huguenots,* 163–166,
        165, 166, 173, 183, 188
    revisions to *Les Huguenots* and, 189, 190,
        209
    singing style, 197
    voice quality, 180
Nouvelli, Ottavio, 322

Offenbach, Jacques, 162, 256
Opéra, Paris, 135, 137, 141, *145,* 145–146,
    155–156, *175*
    audience for, 174
    collaborations at, 162
    costumes, 201
    curtains, 153, 155–156, 175–176, 220
    flying and shooting machinery, 155, 171,
        183, 191
    Green Room, *193*
    lighting, 155–156, 177
    Opera Balls, 170, 172
    orchestra and instruments, 337, 342
    premieres at, 177
    seats and seating, 174–175
    sets and scenery, 155, 156, 201
    singing tradition at, 196–197
    spectacle at, 153, 171
    stage and substages, 153–154, *154, 157,*
        174, 201
    stage machinery, 370
    tickets and ticket scalping, 175
    See also *Huguenots, Les* (Meyerbeer)
opera (general discussion)
    accompanied by ballets, 321
    buffa, 65, 74, 80
    German, 142
    heroic, 321
    new, 322
    semi-serious, 322
    serious, 3, 82, 323
opera houses and companies, 91, 390
    German, 234, 283
    investment in, 8–9
    Italian, 321
    roster of singers, 243
    social life surrounding, 3, 146, 175, 391

Illustration Credits

Illustrations are keyed by page number.

Yale University Library, Map Collection: 6, 138
British Museum: 10
Civico Museo Bibliografico Musicale Rossini, Bologna (Photo: Scala/Art Resource, NY): 12, 76
Folger Shakespeare Library: 14
Yale University Library: 19, 35, 152, 154, 157, 193
Yale Center for British Art, Paul Mellon Collection: 23, 33
William Andrews Clark Memorial Library, University of California, Los Angeles: 24
National Portrait Gallery, London: 28, 42, 45
Lewis Walpole Library, Yale University (723.0.11.3): 43
Houghton Library, Harvard University: 48, 89 (Typ 752.92.449 PF)
Royal Collection © 2004, Her Majesty Queen Elizabeth II: 51
Harvard Map Collection: 67, 319
National Gallery, Prague: 69, 81
Osterreichische Nationalbibliothek (FOTO: Bildarchiv, ÖNB Wien): 71, 95, 96
British Library (Zweig MS 63): 84
National Museum, Prague: 92, 106
Bibliothèque nationale de France, Paris: 147, 165, 166, 168, 172, 181, 189, 330
Courtesy of the Yale University Music Library: 158, 175, 318
Richard Wagner Museum, Bayreuth: 234, 237, 240, 242, 246, 249, 252, 255, 257, 262, 264, 266, 267, 270, 272, 273, 276, 279
Museo Teatrale alla Scala, Milan: 327, 332, 339 (Photo: Alinari/Art Resource, NY)
Archivio Storico Ricordi: 328, 337, 344, 354